VENUS AND ADONIS

SHAKESPEARE CRITICISM
VOLUME 16
GARLAND REFERENCE LIBRARY OF THE HUMANITIES
VOLUME 1949

VENUS AND ADONIS
CRITICAL ESSAYS

EDITED BY
PHILIP C. KOLIN

GARLAND PUBLISHING, INC.
NEW YORK AND LONDON
1997

Library of Congress Cataloging-in-Publication Data

Venus and Adonis: critical essays edited by Philip C. Kolin.
     p.   cm. — (Shakespeare criticism ; vol. 16.)
     Includes bibliographical references.
     ISBN 0-8153-2149-X (alk. paper)
     1. Shakespeare, William, 1564–1616. Venus and Adonis. 2. Mythol-
ogy, Classical, in literature. 3. Adonis (Greek deity) in literature. 4. Venus
(Roman deity) in literature. I. Kolin, Philip C. II. Series: Garland reference library of the humanities. Shakespeare criticism ; vol. 16.
PR2845.V46 1997
821'.3—dc21
                                  96–37751
                                   CIP

Cover illustration: Venus and Adonis (PR 2841 1830 copy 1 Sh. Col., plate
facing title page). By permission of the Folger Shakespeare Library.

Printed on acid-free, 250-year-life paper
Manufactured in the United States of America

TO SHARRON
AND
TO MARY

CONTENTS

GENERAL EDITOR'S INTRODUCTION

The continuing goal of the Garland Shakespeare Criticism series is to provide the most influential historical criticism, the most significant contemporary interpretations, and reviews of the most influential productions. Each volume in the series, devoted to a Shakespearean play or poem (e.g., the sonnets, *Venus and Adonis,* the *Rape of Lucrece*), includes the most essential criticism and reviews of Shakespeare's work from the seventeenth century to the present. The series thus provides, through individual volumes, a representative gathering of critical opinion of how a play or poem has been interpreted over the centuries.

A major feature of each volume in the series is the editor's introduction. Each volume editor provides a substantial essay identifying the main critical issues and problems the play (or poem) has raised, charting the critical trends in looking at the work over the centuries, and assessing the critical discourses that have linked the play or poem to various ideological concerns. In addition to examining the critical commentary in light of important historical and theatrical events, each introduction functions as a discursive bibliographic essay that cites and evaluates significant critical works—essays, journal articles, dissertations, books, theatre documents—and gives readers a guide to the research on a particular play or poem.

After the introduction, each volume is organized chronologically, by date of publication of selections, usually into two sections: critical essays and theatre reviews/documents. The first section includes previously published journal articles and book chapters as well as original essays written for the collection. In selecting essays, editors have chosen works that are representative of a given age and critical approach. Striving for accurate historical representation, editors include earlier as well as contemporary criticism. Their goal is to include the widest possible range of critical approaches to the play or poem, demonstrating the multiplicity and complexity of critical response. In most instances, essays have been reprinted in their entirety, not butchered into snippets. The editors have also commissioned original essays (sometimes as many as five to ten) by leading Shakespearean scholars, thus offering the most contemporary, theoretically attentive analyses. Reflecting some recent critical approaches in Shakespearean studies, these new essays approach the play or poem from many perspectives, including feminist, Marxist, new historical, semiotic, mythic, performance/staging, cultural, and/ or a combination of these and other methodologies. Some volumes in the series even include bibliographic analyses that have significant implications for criticism.

The second section of each volume in the series is devoted to the play in performance and, again, is organized chronologically, beginning with some of the earliest and most significant productions and proceeding to the most recent. This section, which ultimately provides a theatre history of the play, should not be regarded as different from or rigidly isolated from the critical essays in the first section. Shakespearean criticism has often been informed by or has significantly influenced productions. Shakespearean criticism over the last twenty years or so has usefully been labeled the "Age of Performance." Readers will find information in this section on major foreign productions of Shakespeare's plays as well as landmark productions in English. Consisting of more than reviews of specific productions, this section also contains a variety of theatre documents, including interpretations written for the particular volume by notable directors whose comments might be titled "The Director's Choice," histories of seminal productions (e.g., Peter Brook's *Titus Andronicus* in 1955), and even interviews with directors and/or actors. Editors have also included photographs from productions around the world to help readers see and further appreciate the way a Shakespearean play has taken shape in the theatre.

Each volume in the Garland Shakespeare Criticism series strives to give readers a balanced, representative collection of the best that has been thought and said about a Shakespearean text. In essence, each volume supplies a careful survey of essential materials in the history of criticism for a Shakespearean text. In offering readers complete, fulfilling, and in some instances very hard to locate materials, volume editors have made conveniently accessible the literary and theatrical criticism of Shakespeare's greatest legacy, his work.

Philip C. Kolin
University of Southern Mississippi

ACKNOWLEDGMENTS

Editing a book like *Venus and Adonis: Critical Essays* is not a solitary venture. Accordingly, I have happily acquired many debts, and I hasten to record what I owe and to whom. First of all, I am grateful to all the journals, presses, and newspapers that gave me permission to reprint reviews, articles, chapters, and sections of chapters. I also thank the various theatre companies for sending me material—programs, photographs, etc.—from their productions of *Venus and Adonis*. A special debt goes to those individuals who have written essays and comments expressly for my volume—João Froes, Richard Halpern, Robert P. Merrix, Patrick M. Murphy, James Schiffer, M.L. Stapleton, Benjamin Stewart, and Georgianna Ziegler.

Several librarians have helped me acquire *Venus and Adonis* criticism—among them are Georgianna Ziegler at the Folger Shakespeare Library and Lisa Brant at the Stratford Shakespearean Festival. I am also grateful to Patrick Murphy for his assistance in helping me gather *Venus and Adonis* materials.

I owe a special thank you to Professors Robert P. Merrix and Patrick M. Murphy for reading earlier drafts of my introduction and for saving me from egregious error. Professor Merrix also read an early draft of my bibliography on *Venus and Adonis,* as did Dr. Georgianna Ziegler. The mistakes that remain are to me as Caliban was to Prospero—a "thing of darkness / I acknowledge [as] mine."

At the University of Southern Mississippi, I have a shopping list of debts to publicize. Karolyn Thompson, the interlibrary loan librarian, and reference librarian Paul McCarver graciously and expeditiously assisted me yet more times. My department chair, Jeanette Harris, has consistently given me release time and encouragement for this project and countless others; Dean Glenn T. Harper established himself once more as my "Patron in the College of Liberal Arts." I owe an enormous debt of gratitude to Dr. Karen

Yarbrough, Vice President for Research and Planning, who most generously assisted me through a research grant that allowed me to pay for permissions, keyboarding, and the sundry other expenses a collection such as *Venus and Adonis: Critical Essays* demands. In fact, Dr. Yarbrough has generously and repeatedly supported my work as general editor of the Garland Shakespeare Criticism Series. Finally, I thank President Aubrey K. Lucas and Vice President for Academic Affairs G. David Huffman for their continuing encouragement and support.

Venus and Adonis: Critical Essays would have never seen the light of day were it not for the thorough and dedicated help of my research assistant Nancy Hill. I am also grateful to David Sedevie, Nancy's predecessor. To Jesse Stevens and Tippy Stevens I owe a giant debt for putting everything on disk and for making countless changes because of revisions and re-revisions. I am grateful to Beverly Ciko and Peggy Bowles for their help. I also express my gratitude to Kathleen Rossman-Pentecost and Marilyn Ford for their careful help in proofreading. To all of these good folks I say, "Thanks, and more thanks."

I am grateful to those souls in the St. Thomas Aquinas Prayer Group in Hattiesburg and to Sister Carmelita Stinn, SFCC, and to Marge and Al Parish, all of whom prayed for this volume and for my sanity as I edited it.

My love goes to my daughter Kristin and to my son Eric, who deserve much praise for patiently bearing with Dad all of the vicissitudes of my work. My love also goes to Theresa, John, and Robin. I also bless my spiritual director, Father G. Eddie Lundin, and Colby Kullman, who has been a faithful friend for thirty years.

Finally, I thank Sharron for her love, encouragement, and Cleopatrian wit and charm.

P.C.K.
1997

Venus (played by Katherine Owens and Sarah Rankin) kisses Adonis (Nathan Hinton) as Mars/Narrator (Bruce DuBose) looks on in the Undermain Theatre production of Venus and Adonis directed by Ted Davey. Courtesy of the Undermain Theatre of Dallas.

I
VENUS AND/OR ADONIS AMONG THE CRITICS

VENUS AND/OR ADONIS AMONG THE CRITICS

Philip C. Kolin

Venus and Adonis merits a special place in the canon as Shakespeare's first published work. Entered into the Stationers' Register on April 18, 1593, *Venus and Adonis* appeared in quarto predating the publication of the plays, though not their production, since *Henry VI, Parts 1, 2, 3, The Comedy of Errors,* and possibly *Titus Andronicus* were all performed before 1593. Happily, *Venus and Adonis* does not present the thorny textual problems of the plays; the poem was scrupulously printed from what must surely have been Shakespeare's own fair copy, or manuscript that the playwright-poet likely corrected and approved. In his 1992 Cambridge edition of the poems, John Roe relevantly asserted: "Because there are no grounds for believing that Shakespeare came back to either poem [*Venus* and *Rape of Lucrece*] with second thoughts . . . little of value can be gained by giving a full collation. There is even an argument for dispensing with collation altogether, apart from listing the substantive errors of Q1 (which number only two)" (75).

Shakespeare's authorship of *Venus and Adonis* has never been in question. His prefatory epistle dedicating the poem to Henry Wriothesley, the Earl of Southampton and Baron of Titchfield, acknowledges the fact. In the spirit and language of high patronage, Shakespeare deprecated his own work—referring to it as "My unpolished lines" and a "weak . . . burden"— yet he assuredly christened *Venus* the "first heir of my invention," dutifully announcing to the literary world his entrance as a poet. Although Ben Jonson caviled that Shakespeare had "small Latin and less Greek," Shakespeare's classical learning shone through *Venus and Adonis.* Through the poem's lush and arresting embellishment, Shakespeare attempted to "'out-Ovid' Ovid" (Baumlin 207), the most influential Latin poet in the Renaissance and the classical writer with whom Shakespeare was often admiringly compared. Significantly, too, Shakespeare chose to start his poetic career writing about

3

the vagaries of love as "Chaucer and Spenser before him did" (Hamilton, *"Venus and Adonis"* 13).

Venus and Adonis was the early flower of Shakespeare's reputation among a wide circle of Elizabethan readers, especially courtiers and students at the inns of court (Gent 722–23). Moreover, "the poem stimulated an extraordinarily rapid surge of excitement and emulation in all literary London" (Duncan-Jones, "Much Ado" 490). Demonstrating its immense popularity, *Venus* went through ten editions between 1593 and 1613 (six of them by 1599), and sixteen editions by 1640. Given the fact that the poem was reprinted so often, it is surprising so few copies survive. As S. Schoenbaum observes: "Multitudes bought *Venus and Adonis*. . . . No other work by Shakespeare achieved so many printings during this period. Readers thumbed it until it fell to pieces; so we may infer from the fact that for most editions only a single copy has survived" (*Compact Documentary Life* 176).

Although overshadowed by the plays, *Venus and Adonis* and *The Rape of Lucrece,* which followed it by one year, are significant scripts in Shakespeare's own creative development, a point fervently stressed by the critics who, starting with Coleridge in *Biographia Literaria,* saw the early signs of Shakespeare's genius in the poem. In 1898, George Wyndham assigned to *Venus* and *The Rape of Lucrece* pride of place in Elizabethan poetry: "They are the first examples of the highest qualities in Elizabethan lyrical verse" (lxxix). In the mid-1940s, Hereward T. Price emphasized that while Shakespeare surely "borrows" from the pastoral tradition, he is "at the same time daringly original. . . . There is probably no other poem in which direct first-hand observation of nature has been used with such brilliant effect to create form" ("Function of Imagery" 289). Continuing the panegyric, J. W. Lever in the 1960s asserted:

> These poems give a striking impression of the energy and range of the early Shakespeare; more so, indeed, than his first experiments on the stage. Written at a time when the theatres were closed on account of . . . plague in the capital, they belong to a phase of rapid maturing and awareness of latent powers. Into them was poured a ferment of intuitions, perceptions, speculations and fancies that had not yet found dramatic expression. ("Shakespeare's Narrative Poems" 116)

Similarly, Nancy Lindheim stressed the importance of *Venus and Adonis* in the creation of Shakespeare's art, particularly as "his earliest poetic or dramatic exploration of love." She argued that the poem is thus a "pivotal work in its author's technical as well as intellectual development" and "tonal complexity"; *Venus and Adonis* "integrates comedy with tragedy, parody with straight representations" (191). Superlatives have flowed from many critics, though not all, over Shakespeare's descriptions of the power and pain of love. As one reviewer of an adaptation of *Venus* noted, "In *Venus and Adonis* Shakespeare combines erotica with brilliant symbolism and parallel evocations all couched in the most graceful, elegant imagery ever written" (Goodwin, "Irene Worth Brings a Love Poem to Life").

According to some famous readers, the poem also reflected a tremendous change in Shakespeare's personal development in love. In *The Portrait of Mr W.H.*, Oscar Wilde identified a specific Elizabethan cohort of Shakespeare's as the young Adonis and the object of the playwright's eye:

> Yes, the "rose-cheeked Adonis" of the Venus poem, the false shepherd of the "Lover's Complaint," the "tender churl," the "beauteous niggard" of the Sonnet was none other but a young actor; and as I read through the various descriptions given of him, I saw that the love that Shakespeare bore him was as the love of a musician for some delicate instrument on which he delights to play, as a sculptor's love for some rare and exquisite material that suggests a new form of plastic beauty, a new mode of plastic expression. (205–06)

Reflecting his own self-indulgence and *fin de siècle* emphasis on sexual pleasures, Wilde continued that "There was, however, more in [Shakespeare's] friendship than the mere delight of a dramatist in one who helps him to achieve his end. This was indeed a subtle element of pleasure, if not of passion, and a noble basis for an artistic comradeship" (207).

Looking closer to Shakespeare's family than Wilde did for a real-life person in *Venus and Adonis,* Stephen Dedalus in Joyce's *Ulysses* offers an even more ingenious explanation. Shakespeare, 28 when he wrote *Venus,* was a man who was commencing his eleventh year of matrimony. Eager to display his learning by puffing himself up in his readers' eyes, Dedalus speculates that Shakespeare was none too happy in that conjugal state: "If others have their will Ann hath a way. By cock, she was to blame. She put the comether on him, sweet and twentysix. The greyeyed goddess who bends over the boy Adonis, stooping to conquer, as prologue to the swelling act, is a boldfaced Stratford wench who tumbles in a cornfield a lover younger than herself" (*Ulysses* [Random House Edition] 191). No less a person than Ann Hathaway, Shakespeare's wife, who was older than he by at least eight years, was the impetus and model for Venus, according to Dedalus' reasoning. However ingenious this approach may be, *Venus and Adonis* is much more than Shakespeare's *bildungsroman*. The poem may not be the key that unlocks Shakespeare's heart.

VENUS AND ADONIS AND THE PLAYS

Since *Venus and Adonis* itself is dramatic, the poem has been compared invariably to Shakespeare's plays, early and late, by critics who find parallels, analogues, and illustrations of intertextuality everywhere. Arguing that the "influence of [Marlowe's] *Hero and Leander* may go beyond the cult of the epyllion," Clifford Leech suggests that these narrative poems "may have constituted a mode of approach that could be, and was carried on in the dramatic form" ("Venus and Her Nun" 250). For Michael Goldman, "Shakespeare's non-dramatic poetry [including *Venus*] reflects his dramatic bent as anything about his life might be expected to" (6). In *Venus,* as in *Lucrece* and the sonnets, Goldman discerns "certain situations and arrangements of material which draw attention to what Shakespeare calls the 'unsounded self,' a condition of being that can be fully explored only in the drama" (10). Accordingly, the first chapter of Goldman's *Shakespeare and the Energies of Drama* is occupied with the poems.

Significantly, then, *Venus and Adonis* seems to have been a governing influence on the plays, thus adding to the poem's immense dramatic significance. *Venus and Adonis* has much in common, therefore, with Shakespeare's early plays, especially *A Midsummer Night's Dream, Romeo and Juliet,* and *Love's Labor's Lost,* all of which were written close to the time Shakespeare prepared *Venus* for the Earl of Southampton. Nancy Lindheim believes that *Venus* came in between these "apprentice comedies" (190–91). Lever usefully generalizes regarding *Venus*' relationship to the comedies:

> The follies of lovers, and the graver follies of those who refuse to love, make up the fabric of Shakespeare's comedies: Titania wasting her raptures upon a mortal; Lysander and Demetrius prating of reason. . . ; Silvius scorning Phebe; Bertram, another would-be hero, refusing Helena. In the comedies, tragic catastrophe is always potential, though happily averted. Tragedy is waiting for Adonis, too, in the inseparable Shakespearean antinomies of beauty and destruction, love and death, creation and chaos. ("Second Chance" 84)

Concentrating on one of the earlier comedies in particular, Price proclaimed that *"A Midsummer Night's Dream* is the most pagan poem in English literature, and in the same class we may put *Venus and Adonis"* ("Function of Imagery" 288).

According to James Schiffer, "Cousins to the aggressive Venus can be found in Nell the kitchen wench in pursuit of Dromio of Syracuse in *The Comedy of Errors*, Helena in pursuit of Demetrius in *A Midsummer Night's Dream*, and that very different Helena who substitutes herself into Bertram's bed in *All's Well That Ends Well*." In his *Shakespeare* (1970), Anthony Burgess links *Venus* with *The Comedy of Errors* in their interest in natural, even "coarse" love. Certainly, too, *Venus*, like *Dream* and many other early Shakespearean plays, is set in a pastoral world of enticements and entrapments, a place Jeanne Addison Roberts calls "The Shakespearean Wild":

> The Wild World in Shakespeare's early works is frequently a forest— mysterious, magical, and ambiguous. Elaborated or suggested forests occur in at least seven of Shakespeare's early works: *Venus and Adonis, Two Gentlemen of Verona, Titus Andronicus, Love's Labor's Lost, A Midsummer Night's Dream, The Merry Wives of Windsor,* and *As You Like It.* (25)

Aptly enough, in all of these works the hazardous landscapes mirror the erotic dangers awaiting the lovers who venture into them.

Several readers have identified common elements between *Venus and Adonis* and *Romeo and Juliet,* four star-crossed lovers to be sure, and *Love's Labor's Lost.* The infamous description of Venus' "sweet bottom grass" (lines 229–40) is for Eugene Cantelupe "worthy of Mercutio" (144), and both Cantelupe and Peter Dow Webster (302) urge strong parallels between Venus and Juliet's bawdy Nurse. Linking *Venus* and *Love's Labor's Lost,* Heather Dubrow finds that "By dramatizing linguistic behavior . . . [Shakespeare] is highlighting the psychological traits that it reflects—an issue that he was, of course, exploring at roughly the same time in *Love's Labor's Lost* and in so many of his later works" (*Captive Victors* 45). And Wayne Rebhorn contends that *Venus*, like *Love's Labor's Lost,* seriously questions, and even mocks, the entire world of courtly love ("Mother Venus" 16–17).

Perhaps an even closer kinship exists between *Titus Andronicus* and *Venus and Adonis* than between the poem and *Love's Labor's Lost,* a connection that goes far beyond what Walter Raleigh observed at the turn of the twentieth century: "His early play of *Titus Andronicus,* which is like the poems, shows how strangely hard-hearted this love of beauty can be, and makes it easier to understand how he was fascinated and dominated, for a time, by Marlowe" (85). Yet the influence of Ovid is even stronger than that of Marlowe on *Titus* and *Venus.* Both *Titus* and *Venus,* Ovidian in origin, contain rape (or attempted rape), transformations, heavily embellished poetry to express the deepest physical and psychic wounds, the curse of doomed love, and the powerlessness of gods and goddesses to protect.

The one later Shakespearean play in which critics most often hear echoes of and/or parallels to *Venus and Adonis* is *Antony and Cleopatra*. The connections between the early poem and the late play are palpable. Cleopatra, the priestess of Isis, provocatively dresses as Venus. Both femmes fatales, Venus and Cleopatra are witty, aggressive, bestriding the world of love like a Colossus. The Queen of Love and the Queen of Egypt radiate immense desire, simultaneously ennobling and destroying. Paradoxically, each undermines her lover's manliness, and then apotheosizes him in a new heaven. Critics have compared the two couples, if only briefly—F.T. Prince (xxxiii); Heather Dubrow (25); and Hereward Price (281). Doebler wryly observes that "an even better parallel to Venus [than Falstaff] is Cleopatra, a glamorous tramp with a capacity for both Chaucerian bawdry and transcendent immortality of fame" ("Many Faces" 38). Schiffer is concerned with "the absence of the phallus" in both *Venus* and *Antony and Cleopatra*. Adrien Bonjour also traces numerous parallels between the couples.

Beyond doubt, though, the most impassioned discussion of the two Shakespearean scripts comes from Lever, whose thesis is that in "Shakespeare's maturity he won through to the concept of tragic drama as a paradoxical triumph. It was thus that the Venus and Adonis myth received its full explication in the late love-tragedy, *Antony and Cleopatra*." According to Lever, "Antony is Adonis allowed . . . to grow up [yet] . . . unlike the chaste, self-regarding boy, he willingly acts Mars to Cleopatra's Venus." And Cleopatra is Venus "In this lost paradise of her wooing of Antony [which] is comical and sensual, immoral and thoroughly reprehensible" ("Second Chance" 87). Ultimately, Lever argues, "Venus and Adonis, fallen and risen as Cleopatra and her Antony, live to triumph in the kingdom of the second chance" (88). The first chapter of Ted Hughes' *Shakespeare and the Goddess of Complete Being* is also relevant to a discussion of *Antony and Cleopatra* and *Venus*. Hughes "trace[s] connections between the Sonnets and *Venus and Adonis*, and between *Venus and Adonis* and *Lucrece*, suggesting how the group of works came to be the foundation of the mythic form of the Tragic Equation as it appears in [Shakespeare's] mature plays" (50).

Other Shakespearean plays also can legitimately claim affinities with *Venus and Adonis*. Streitberger, whose article is reprinted in this volume, examines *Venus and Adonis* in light of the courtesy book tradition informing *The Two Gentlemen of Verona*. Leonard Barkan's *The Gods Made Flesh* discusses *Venus and Adonis* in relation to *The Merchant of Venice* (270–74). William Keach and others have explored boars in *Richard III* (and even later in *Cymbeline*) with reference to *Venus and Adonis* (78). Several critics have identified shared traits between Falstaff and Venus. While seen at first as an unlikely coupling, upon closer inspection the two larger-than-life figures revel in similarities. Dubrow, like many other critics, underscores their "earthiness" (25). Cantelupe puts the case rather well:

> Venus's never flagging efforts to fire the passive youth with either procreative arguments that comprise Shakespeare's first eighteen sonnets or with glowing descriptions of her physical beauty and sexual prowess not only reveal her self-confidence, insatiable appetite, and wit, but also beget sympathy through rollicking, robust humor. Adonis is the inverse of Romeo and Troilus, and Venus the obverse of Juliet's Nurse and Falstaff. (143)

Doebler also claims that "The largely comic Venus at the beginning of the poem is perceived by the distanced reader as appealing one moment and frightening the next, as Falstaff is both a fool and a threat to the state without ever losing our measured admiration and his ability to delight the audience" ("Many Faces" 38). Just as Venus tries to entertain and to persuade Adonis, so Falstaff does with Prince Hal.

Turning to *Measure for Measure,* Christy Desmet believes that "Venus's penchant for amplification and the rhetorical restraints imposed on her speech have parallels in the problem plays." Like Venus, Isabella and Helena from *All's Well* "are both accomplished orators. Both, however, have also been accused of dissimulation" (144). In chastising Adonis for denying "the animal appetites [that] move nature," William Sheidley similarly compares the youth to Angelo in *Measure for Measure* (13). Dubrow concludes that Venus, like Prospero, is an impresario (26).

THE RECEPTION AND REPUTATION OF *VENUS AND ADONIS* UP TO THE TWENTIETH CENTURY

Writing in 1790, Edmond Malone, one of Shakespeare's most illustrious early editors, observed: "The poems of *Venus and Adonis* and *The Rape of Lucrece,* whatever opinion may now be entertained of them, were certainly much admired in Shakespeare's life time" (*Plays and Poems* 186). Tributes from Shakespeare's immediate contemporaries were drenched in admiration. John Weever lauded the "honey-tongued Shakespeare" of whose poems (or "issue") "I swore Apollo got them and none other" (75). The year 1598 saw three key references to *Venus and Adonis*. Frances Meres' *Palladis Tamia,* which helped to verify Shakespeare's authorship of several of the plays, continued Weever's panegyric strain: "As the soul of Euphorbus was thought to live in Pythagoras: so the sweet wittier soul of Ovid lives in mellifluous & honey-tongued Shakespeare; witness his *Venus and Adonis.*" Richard Barnfield proclaimed that Shakespeare's name deserved to be recorded "in fame's immortal book" for his *Venus* (120). The repeated references to the "honey-tongued" Shakespeare cast him as the master Ovidian stylist, the inspired creator of one of love's most troubling epics.

Also in 1598 Gabriel Harvey, the bookish, quirky friend of Edmund Spenser, dichotomized *Venus* and *Lucrece,* insisting on a contrast that trivialized the former and enthroned the later: "The younger sort takes much delight in Shakespeare's *Venus and Adonis* but his *Lucrece* & tragedy of *Hamlet, Prince of Denmark,* have it in them to please the wiser sort" (232). The sage though lugubrious Harvey introduced a way of looking at *Venus* as less worthy (in learning and morality) that would seep into critical discourse on the poem for centuries. Summarizing the reputation the poem had for many of Shakespeare's contemporaries, Katherine Duncan-Jones concludes: "For the Elizabethans . . . Shakespeare's poem was susceptible of numberless applications and adaptations, all associated with erotic play and enchantment" ("Much Ado" 498).

As the seventeenth century progressed, the eroticism increased as the enchantment waned. The reputation of *Venus and Adonis* changed, in general, from that of being an immortal love poem to that of a bawdy tale relished by wastrels and rebuked by moralists. The poem kept company with tapsters, courtesans, and roués. *Venus* became a poem that lived in naughtiness. *The Shakespeare Allusion-Book,* edited by John Munro, contains 61 references to *Venus* from the late 1590s through 1700. As the allusions below testify, *Venus* was widely known and read in Jacobean and Carolingian England. While some of these allusions are flattering, or at least neutral, many more are negative, charting the fall in esteem of Shakespeare's highly embellished poem. References to the poem's immorality in *The Shakespeare Allusion-Book* might be divided conveniently into two groups—those in moral tracts and those in the drama. The following references, all from *The Shakespeare-Allusion Book,* chronicle the fortunes of the poem.

The moralists (and their allies, the satirists) had a field day with *Venus.* A few examples illustrate how pernicious some critics regarded the poem to be. John Davies of Hereford labeled *Venus* "shameless stuff" in his *Scourge of Folly* (1611) and described the plot as "lewd Venus, with eternal lines / To tie Adonis to her love's design." Apostrophizing Shakespeare, Thomas Freeman unhappily noted in a 1614 poem that "Virtues or vice the same to thee all one is." Endorsing Gabriel Harvey's preference, Freeman judged *Lucrece* fit "for a teacher" but he "who list read lust there's *Venus and Adonis,* / True model of a most lascivious lecher" *(Rune, and a Great Cast. The Second Boke).* In 1623, Thomas Robinson had written that *Venus* was a "scurrilous book" read by wags after being enchanted by "bawdy songs" from tarts.

Many warnings about *Venus* were directed to female readers; Richard Halpern's essay, written expressly for this collection, explores the Lacanian dimensions of this audience's reflection in/on the poem. Admonishing the female reader, Richard Brathwait in 1631, for example, denounced *Venus* as unsuitable for young women: "Books treating light subjects, are nurseries of wantonness; they instruct the loose reader to become naught; whereas before, touching naughtiness, he knew naught . . . *Venus and Adonis* are unfitting comforts for a lady's bosom. Remove them timely from you, if they ever had entertainment by you, lest like the snake in the fable, they annoy you." Although R. Henderson attacked "carnal men," he castigated "English and Romish Jezebels and Italian Courtesans" (a litany of familiar seventeenth-century satiric subjects) who "will be frying, boiling, and broiling in their luxurious desires" like that "wanton Venus." More mildly, Thomas Crumble feared in 1635 that the ladies of the day read "amorous pamphlets that best like their eyes" such as *Venus* instead of "prayers of grievous order."

References to *Venus and Adonis* in the drama of the time corroborate the sordid reputation the poem had for moralists. As popular entertainment, theatre clearly mirrored the anxieties of society. In the theatre, *Venus* was almost always associated with debauchery and seduction. In a play written by Cambridge University students in 1599–1602, *The First and Second Part of Parnassus,* allusions to *Venus* characterize it as frivolous, while in the mode of Gabriel Harvey these student-produced dramas honor *Lucrece* as noble. The student Judicio self-assuredly pronounces that Shakespeare's authorship of *Venus* was disappointing: "Could but a graver subject him content, / Without love's foolish lazy languishment." While Meres, Weever, and Barnfield memorialized *Venus* as a poem worthy of the gods, the Cambridge students emphasized its lassitude. Despite his objection, no doubt Judicio and other students savored *Venus* as highly entertaining. In fact, one of the earliest references to Shakespeare in the New World can be found in a commonplace book belonging to Harvard student Elnathan Chauncy, who copied lines from *Venus* (Marder 2, 8). Chauncy's counterparts in England were doubtless no less enthusiastic in their admiration (perhaps clandestine) for *Venus.*

Many other allusions to *Venus* in seventeenth-century drama paint it as taboo. Thomas Heywood's *Fair Maid of the Exchange* (1607) characterizes the poem as a seduction manual. Bowdler, a foolish lothario, swears to his friend: "I'll never read anything but *Venus and Adonis*." Answering him, Cripple admits: "Why that's the very quintessence of love, / If you remember but a version or two / I'll pawn my goods, lands and all 'twill do." *Venus* had become mandatory reading for lustful men trying to conquer a young, vulnerable woman. Jarvis Markham and Lewis Machin in *The Dumb Knight* (1608) observed that the poem was "A book that never an orator's clark in the kingdom but is beholden unto: it is called the maid's philosophy, or *Venus and Adonis*." The same year, in Thomas Middleton's *A Mad World, My Masters,* a jealous husband, Harebrain, righteously prevents his wife from making him a cuckold by censuring her reading materials: "I have conveyed away all her wanton pamphlets, as *Hero and Leander, Venus & Adonis;* O, two luscious marrow-bone pies for a young married wife." *Venus and Adonis* had sordidly descended into being an aphrodisiac, or "marrow-bone," to worry a jealous husband.

Significant for the history of *Venus* criticism, the text had been metamorphosized into a plant or flower—like the anemone into which Adonis was transformed—capable of promoting love. In 1609, *Venus* is mentioned together with some plays for its "salt of wit" in the address prefixed to *Troilus and Cressida,* another appropriately sexual reference, given the fact that *Troilus* (like *Venus*) is one of Shakespeare's greatest exposés of seduction. *Venus'* reputation as a seduction manual continued into the middle of the seventeenth century. In Lewis Sharp's 1640 drama *The Noble Stranger,* Pupillus, another lust-hounded student, and doubtless one of the "younger sort" that Harvey mentions, exclaims: "Oh for the book of *Venus and Adonis,* to court my mistress by; I could die, I could die in the elysium of her arms: no sweets to those of love." Considering the sexual meaning that *die* had in the seventeenth century (to reach a climax), *Venus* was indeed a survival manual, a handy aphrodisiac, for a prowling lad like Pupillus.

Perhaps no part of *Venus and Adonis* better contributed to its reputation to incite lechery than the goddess' description of herself in the toponymic (geographic) terms in lines 229–40. These lines were satirically incorporated into a ballad "The New Married Couple" from the *Roxburgh Ballads* (1675) in which a bawdy wife speaks them to her new husband, Ned. The stanzas were also included in Thomas Durfey's play *The Virtuous Wife, or Good Luck at Last* (1680) in which a lustful squire Sir Lubb and his Boy speak of sexual conquests—in a highly mocking vein.

The reception of *Venus and Adonis* in the eighteenth and nineteenth centuries was not nearly as celebratory as it had been in Shakespeare's lifetime. Most influential eighteenth-century editions of Shakespeare dropped *Venus and Adonis,* displaying that century's lack of attention to the poem and/or its nugatory opinion of it. Katherine Duncan-Jones succinctly summarizes the poem's reputation during the years 1700–1900:

> Somehow or other, as is so often the way with every popular work, during the succeeding centuries interest in the poem collapsed. Its omission from all the great eighteenth-century editions of Shakespeare until Malone's in 1780 contributed to its disappearance from readers' view. Though the Romantics to some extent rediscovered it, the then firmly established notion of Shakespeare as above all a dramatist led to its being seen as a slightly embarrassing cul-de-sac in his *oeuvre.* Coleridge's account in *Biographia Literaria* encouraged readers to see it as essentially preliminary to the plays, and to contemplate it in a distanced and prudish manner. ("Much Ado" 499)

Edmond Malone's response to *Venus* in 1780 may have been typical of many eighteenth-century readers. While Malone readily acknowledged that Shakespeare was following Elizabethan conventions, he still maintained that *Venus* and *Lucrece* offered "wearisome circumlocution" (quoted in *Variorum* 462). No unqualified praise came from this editor as had been forthcoming from Shakespeare's contemporaries.

Focusing on the nineteenth-century response to *Venus and Adonis,* J.W. Lever identified still further reasons for the poem's lack of enthusiastic favor among that century's critics:

> Fair attention had been given to *Venus and Adonis* by nineteenth-century writers, but mainly either as a by-product of dramatic genius or as a quasi-biographical document. Rather vague resemblances had been seen to the works of Titian and Rubens. On moral grounds it was deemed too sensual, yet artistically it was considered too cold. ("The Poems" 19)

We might qualify Lever's assertion by noting, as Roe does, that "Later Romantics such as Keats and Coleridge gave special praise to *Venus and Adonis* for its quickness of wit, imaginative bravura, and liveliness of detail" (3). Unquestionably, Coleridge's comments on *Venus and Adonis,* included in this volume, constitute landmark criticism. According to Rabkin, Coleridge's remarks were among the most significant ever written ("*Venus and Adonis*: Myth"). Coleridge played a valiant part in rebutting charges of immorality leveled against Venus by upholding the essential integrity of the poem. Keats' respect for *Venus* is reflected in his echoing the poem in "Isabella" (Boyar) and *The Fall of Hyperion* (Spiegelman). In a letter to Reynolds, Keats also praised lines 1033–4 in which Venus is compared to a snail (Roe 3). Yet near the time Coleridge and Keats honored *Venus and Adonis,* Ezekiel Sanford, in 1819, spoke, I fear, for the majority of nineteenth-century readers in observing that "So long as we are concerned for the interests of morality, we cannot wish that it may again become popular" (quoted in *Variorum* 467).

Several distinguished writers from the nineteenth century attacked Shakespeare's poem, his skill, and his intent. While Coleridge praised the blending of passion and intellect in *Venus,* William Hazlitt in *Characters of Shakespeare's Plays* (1817) denounced *Venus* and its companion poem *The Rape of Lucrece* for being unengaging, distant, stiff: "It has been the fashion of late to cry up on our author's poems, as equal to his plays: this is the desperate cant of modern criticism. . . . The two poems of *Venus and Adonis* and of Tarquin and Lucrece appear to us like a couple of ice-houses. They are about as hard, as glittering, and as cold." In *Shakespeare* (published in 1909 but written earlier), C.A. Swinburne admired some things about the two poems but concluded that they were unworthy of Shakespeare, whose reputation as a playwright remained unequaled:

> There are touches of inspiration and streaks of beauty in *"Venus and Adonis":* there are fits of power and freaks of poetry in the *"Rape of Lucrece":* but good poems they are not: indeed they are hardly above the level of the imitations which followed the fashion set by them, from the emulous hands of such minor though genuine poets as Lodge and Barksted. (7)

In his *Note-Books* (written around the turn of the century), novelist Samuel Butler also eagerly dismissed *Venus* as unworthy of Shakespeare:

> I have been trying to read *Venus and Adonis* and the *Rape of Lucrece* but cannot get on with them. They teem with fine things, but they are got-up fine things. I do not know whether this is quite what I mean but, come what may, I find the poems bore me. Were I a schoolmaster I should think I was through in three sittings. If, then, the magic of Shakespeare's name, let alone the great beauty of occasional passages, cannot reconcile us (for I find most people of the same mind) to verse, and especially rhymed verse as a medium of sustained expression, what chance has any one else? ("Enfant Terrible" 192)

Perhaps no assessment of *Venus* could be more despondent than Butler's. There is little hope for poetry if Shakespeare himself could fail.

Twentieth-Century Critical Approaches to *Venus and Adonis*

The neglect or, worse yet, the misunderstanding of *Venus and Adonis* continued into the twentieth century. William Keach understates the vexatious nature of *Venus and Adonis* criticism in this century: "The poem . . . has proved especially troubling to modern readers and critics" (52). Such discomfort has extended over 400 years. C.S. Lewis went even farther than Samuel Butler in deploring *Venus and Adonis,* denying the poem any function except to display "disgust":

> Certain horrible interviews with voluminous female relatives in one's early childhood inevitably recur to mind . . . this flushed, panting, perspiring, suffocating, loquacious creature is supposed to be the goddess of love herself, the golden Aphrodite. It will not do. If the poem is not meant to arouse disgust it was very foolishly written. (*English Literature in the Sixteenth Century* 498)

Lewis' observations represent one of the most disappointing responses to *Venus.* Perhaps equally distressing is F.T. Prince's condescending observation that "few English or American readers nowadays will respond to such happily wanton fancies as *Venus and Adonis*" ("Introduction" xxv).

Price identified the long-standing critical habit of not valorizing the poem that extends back to Harvey. "A tendency to deprecate Shakespeare's choice of subject has persisted down to the present day. For shame's sake I shall refrain from giving names or references" (286). Huntington Brown similarly complained: "For one may doubt that any other masterpiece of English poetry has been treated by so many scholars—many of them men of reputation—with the ineptitude and smug condescension that have run like a disease through the critical literature from Edmond Malone's remarks in his edition of 1780 to the present day" (73). As Hyder Rollins, the editor of the magisterial *Variorum Edition,* lamented in 1938: "Scholars and critics seldom mention *Venus* . . . without apologies expressed or implied" (474). An example is W.B.C. Watkins, who asserted in 1950: "All his life Shakespeare indulged in rhetoric from time to time, either for its own sake or to indicate a certain quality of emotion; but the rhetoric in *Venus and Adonis* is disconcerting because it does not seem to be always intentional or under full control. Much of the poem fails where *Hero and Leander* succeeds . . ." (*Shakespeare and Spenser* 6). As the following survey of interpretations of

Venus shows, too many twentieth-century readers have sided with Watkins in labeling the poem a failure.

While *Venus and Adonis* has unquestionably suffered from critical prejudice and myopia, the poem nonetheless has launched a constellation of multivalent readings, some contributing to "mad mischances and much misery" (*Venus,* line 738). William Sheidley commented that "the themes of frustration and incompleteness . . . dominate the poem" (9). The same feelings uneasily accompany twentieth-century readers on their way through the labyrinth of critical pronouncements on what the poem does and does not signify. Many readers agree with Kenneth Muir that "We are driven to conclude that the poem cannot easily be categorized" ("Comedy or Tragedy" 13). Hardly inspiring a reader's confidence, either, Lucy Gent more forbodingly claimed that "The number of published interpretations bears witness to the variety of possible answers [to the poem]; but no one interpretation works for more than one aspect of the poem" (721). Given Gent's admonition, few readers might ever ratify John Klause's benevolent opinion that "*Venus and Adonis* helps to establish the paradox that criticism may sanction charity" ("Can We Forgive Them" 369). The chronological bibliography of *Venus* scholarship and commentary at the end of this volume, pages 407–29, records the intense range of studies on the poem.

Schiffer understandably recognizes that readers have desired "the 'phallocentric' *right* reading" of the poem, but judging from the contrariness of twentieth-century critical views, this desire will never be fulfilled. Any Shakespearean text *a priori* invites faith in and/or the folly of a shifting critical ontological space, and the tectonics of *Venus and Adonis* are no exception. Underneath the multiplicity of interpretations—one is tempted to say penetrations when speaking of *Venus and Adonis*—lie an even more entrenched encampment of confluent contradictions.

Identifying one significant school of critical opinion, John Doebler properly calculated: "The largest single body of opinion on the poem in this century has found Neoplatonism of one sort or another within it." ("Many Faces" 34). Other labels for this critical inquiry include the *moral,* the *allegorical,* and the *thematic.* Readers tutored in this school valorize the poem as a philosophical/theological statement and regard their criticism as unpacking the wisdom the poem offers. One of the most apostolic views of *Venus and Adonis* as a moral document was expressed in E.W. Sievers' *William Shakespeare* (1866): "*Venus and Adonis* . . . is really the foundation of the entire structure of Shakespeare's philosophy of life" (166). According to Lu Emily Pearson, a critic from the 1930s, "the teaching of *Venus and Adonis* is as didactic a piece of work, perhaps, as Shakespeare ever wrote" (285).

For Pearson, Adonis is the embodiment of rational (holy) love and Venus of predatory sensual love, so that "when Adonis is killed beauty is killed, and the world is left in black chaos." T.W. Baldwin also preached that "Adonis is Love and Beauty, and when he dies Chaos is come again." Robert P. Miller takes the high ground, too, when he similarly inveighs against the lust embodied in Venus: "According to Renaissance morality . . . love-making which stresses intercourse for the sake of pleasure only is artificial, a perversion of nature because a misuse of natural functions. This love falls into the old confusion of *utendum* and *fruendum,* use and abuse—a confusion that lies behind much of the persuasive philosophy of the goddess of love throughout *Venus and Adonis*" ("Venus, Adonis, and the Horses" 262). Reversing Harvey's assessment, these critics elevated *Venus* to a sacrosanct text.

Firmly in the camp of the moralists, too, W.R. Streitberger argued that the poem educates a young man in morals and nobility: "Venus presents a moral threat to Adonis despite the fact that he is too young for love" and that her "seduction attempt is potentially destructive" ("Ideal Conduct" 291). In *Not Wisely but Too Well: Shakespeare's Love Tragedies,* Franklin Dickey allegorized the poem for instinctually moral reasons: "As *Aphrodite Pandemos,* she [Venus] is the powerful goddess whose charms continually lure men and animals to reproduce themselves and perpetuate life on earth. For the aspect, she is fair. However, this Venus, this earthly love, despite her proper function, is a violent passion which disturbs men's lives. In keeping with the allegory, lust or desire must be powerful and fair, for lust is enticing" (52).

Plato has been invited into the poem by critics privileging ethical imperatives. Concerned with "moral meaning" in *Venus and Adonis,* Don Cameron Allen sought to distance Shakespeare from Ovid—"Shakespeare's intent and plan is as different from that of Ovid as his Venus"—in order to question the sinful liabilities of Venus and her advocacy of the "love-hunt" ("On *Venus*" 100). Armed with ideas from Plato, medieval poems, and weighty treatises, Allen concluded that "the love-hunt, dangerous and valiant as it may be, does not on the lower venerian level ennoble the soul; hence the classical pedagogues did not recommend it to young men for whom life had a grander course" (105). Of course, Allen wanted readers to believe Adonis should adopt such a higher course. Reading *Venus and Adonis* in light of "the Platonic doctrine that Love is the desire for beauty," Hamilton argued that the "poem treats the mystery of creation and the fall" (*"Venus and Adonis"* 7–8). Even though Hamilton claimed that the poem's message "cannot be simply moral," he analyzed *Venus and Adonis* in moralistic terms. "Traditionally Venus appears in a moral world where her evil temptations must be resisted in order that many may achieve the perfected virtuous life. Shakespeare translates the action of his poem into the prelapsarian state" (14) where Adonis as "unfallen nature" succumbs to Venus' "temptations," and his own unheedful conduct.

Relying on the wisdom of Neoplatonic dichotomies, Rabkin saw in *Venus and Adonis* sensual love opposing a higher spiritual love (*Shakespeare and the Common Understanding* 161). In a very influential article, Heather Asals, too, read the poem "in terms of the Neoplatonic hierarchy of the senses . . . [as] Venus progresses from the lowest desire to touch an ennobled appreciation of what she sees . . . what she begins as lust . . . is fulfilled in love" ("*Venus* . . . Education of a Goddess" 31).

Though these moral/allegorical readings are solidly grounded in historical/philosophical evidence, they have been challenged frequently. Dogmatic (or propositional) readings seem destined to fail in explaining *Venus and Adonis*. Cantelupe rebutted these moralistic readings precisely because they were based on such widespread historical evidence: "Thus the rhetorical burlesque and the comic characters of the legendary lovers travesty Neoplatonic notions of love, which were as current and popular then as Freudian concepts are now" (148). Doebler faulted the fated pair on still other grounds: "The clear limitation of too philosophical an approach is the tendency toward consistent allegory in a poem which resists any one pattern of symbolism. . . . 'Platonic' analyses of literature are often inclined to gather all particulars into transcendent ideals which end up questionable even as philosophy." Venus is both lust and love; Adonis is Love "who loves no one but possibly himself" ("Many Faces" 34). Roe similarly argued that:

> Poetry such as that of *Venus and Adonis* keeps uppermost in mind the relationship between the word and the world. The differences separating Venus and Adonis, differences of temperament, inclination, and disposition, differences in ethical outlook (including each's own internal contradictions), cannot be resolved by the debating parties within the poem nor in the judgment of its readers. Attempting to take a consistent ethical reading of, for example, Venus's sensuality is bound to fail. The play of language in the poem sees to that. (Introduction 5)

Roe is right. The overall effects of the poem supersede any moral categories into which critics try to place *Venus*. More bluntly put, Bullough announced that *Venus* "was anything but a Platonic piece," and Muir even more acrimoniously asserted that since "Shakespeare's plays are singularly free from such Neoplatonic nonsense, why should we superimpose it on *Venus and Adonis*" ("Comedy or Tragedy" 4).

One of the most powerful explanations for the prevalence of moral readings in *Venus and Adonis* comes from Catherine Belsey in a 1995 article, reprinted in this volume. The basis for such a "critical tradition," according to Belsey, lies in promoting the opposition Adonis introduces (lines 799–804) between love and lust, a contradiction not established before in Elizabethan culture. Twentieth-century moral readings have readily valorized love over lust in part because they were "tantalized by the poem's lack of closure" (Belsey 258) and in part because they wanted to "relegate the wayward textuality of the poem" (264). Belsey persuasively identifies the adverse implication of a moral view of *Venus and Adonis*. Agreeing with Roe and Muir, Belsey discovers that a moral approach to the poem "betrays . . . both the complexity of cultural history and the polyphony of Shakespeare's text" (275).

At the other extreme from allegorical/moral interpreters of *Venus and Adonis* are those who support its "daring sensuality" (Muir *Shakespeare*, 51). These readers interrogate and destabilize objections voiced earlier by seventeenth-century moralists, nineteenth-century puritan readers like Ezekiel Sanford, and critics like Pearson and Miller. They go far beyond Coleridge's defense of the poem against moral objection to embrace a lively celebration of sexuality. For Robert Burton, who undoubtedly knew Shakespeare's poem, the very word *Venus* was a term for sexual intercourse in *The Anatomy of Melancholy*. As Muir maintained, Shakespeare wrote about Venus' seduction of Adonis as a way of countering "the effects of Renaissance painting, and of repudiating the denials of the flesh by puritan moralists and Neoplatonic theorists" (*Shakespeare the Professional* 186). In language and tone that Muir would condone, Tita French Baumlin underscores the power of the flesh in the poem:

> Certainly, in terms of the entire poem's erotic language, continually an aspect of the poet's art which readers have often appreciated, there appears an attempt to equal and even exceed Ovid's own mastery of lush, sensuous language. Flesh is a central concern in the poem, particularly its moistness, its texture. . . . ("Birth of the Bard" 199)

Nor do critics in this camp of the flesh try to have it both ways as some nineteenth-century readers did. For example, toward the fin de siècle, when fleshly pleasures were celebrated in poetry and art, Edward Dowden wrote passionately about the physical in *Venus and Adonis* in his *Critical*

Study (1875), but unlike some twentieth-century critics he felt obligated to absolve Shakespeare of lustful intent.

> For a young writer of the Renascence, the subject of Shakespeare's earliest poem was a splendid one,—as voluptuous and unspiritual as that of a classical picture by Titian. It included two figures containing inexhaustible pasture for the fleshly eye, and delicacies and dainties for the sensuous imagination of the Renascence,—Beauty, Lust, and death. In holding the subject before his imagination Shakespeare is perfectly cool and collected. He has made choice of the subject, and he is interested in doing his duty by it in the most thorough way a young poet can, but he remains unimpassioned,—intent wholly upon getting down the right colours and lines upon his canvas. (51)

In his introduction to the narrative poems, Maurice Evans supplies an alternative reason why Shakespeare's age may have had more difficulty with sexuality in *Venus* than Dowden was able to admit.

> The debate about the nature of love and Shakespeare's concern with sexual matters in the poem is typical of the period, which had become less confident about its sexual certainties and very prone to theorize about them. Sex had presented no especial problem to Chaucer, for whom the animal, the human and the spiritual still had their accepted places and roles in a great and all-embracing hierarchy. Much of this had been lost by the end of the sixteenth century, however, and the revival of Platonism in particular had created a new pressure to idealize sexual love and to deplore its animal qualities or at least to make them respectable. (15)

Evans unintentionally explains why the physical and animal can be celebrated by contemporary readers of *Venus and Adonis*. While our society, like Shakespeare's, is prone to theorize about sex, many have shed worry about such things as "sexual certainties" and "idealize[d] sexual love." The sexual revolution of the Flower Children, the long-ranging effects of the *Kinsey Report,* the freedom with which sexual differences are publicized and promoted in the 1980s and 1990s—these lifestyles empower interpretations that do not censure but condone sexuality in the poem. Many readers of *Venus* are a long way from the sentiment expressed in Lever's "sexuality does not pay" ("Second Chance" 81).

One of the most liberating responses to sensual love in *Venus and*

Adonis comes from Muriel Bradbrook: "*Venus and Adonis* is a justification of the natural and instinctive beauty of the animal world against sour moralists and scurrilous invective, a raising of the animal mask to sentient level, the emancipation of the flesh" (70). Some readers might rebuke Bradbrook as a too-jolly pagan, but her response was moderate compared to views of the 1990s.

Greatly expanding Evans' interpretation of how the Renaissance responded to "sexual certainties," Bruce Smith in 1991 advanced a far more radical reading than Bradbrook's. Keeping in the spirit of gender studies of the 1980s and 1990s, Smith argues that "an erotic allure" in the poem (as in other epyllia) for young, innocent boys was "far stronger than that of heroes or heroines whose gender is certain." Consequently, Adonis, like Leander or Hermaphroditus, "inspire[s] in other men, especially older men, a desire to initiate the youths into maleness, to *incorporate* them, physically, into the male power structure" (134), yet how such a homoerotic reading applies to Southampton is not on Smith's agenda. More fully expressed, Smith's views are these:

> In their androgyny, figures like Leander, Adonis, and Hermaphroditus embody, quite literally, the ambiguities of sexual desire in English Renaissance culture and the ambivalences of homosexual desire in particular. They represent not an exclusive sexual taste, but an *inclusive* one. To use the categories of our own day, these poems are bisexual fantasies. The temporary freedom they grant to sexual desire allows it to flow out in all directions, towards all the sexual objects that beckon in the romantic landscape. (136)

No doubt for Smith the time is ripe for a reading of *Venus and Adonis* in light of queer theory. Joseph Pequigney's *Such Is My Love,* which reads the sonnets in this light, makes only occasional and very brief references to *Venus.*

Also re-collecting the sexual fantasies in the poem, though not from the standpoint of homoerotic love, Gordon Williams emphasizes Venus' (the "Vamp") sexual jealousy and Adonis' "sexual awakening" as well as the young hunter's "emotional development associated with the disturbances of puberty" (775).

In his essay written for this collection, Richard Halpern, as we saw, confronts sexuality in *Venus* by studying its impact on Elizabethan female readers, concluding that the poem was "designed to frustrate female desire" and in doing so it is best seen as "a piece of soft core pornography."

Mapping the "erotic ontology of the text," Halpern comes full circle from earlier moralists who castigated erotic displays in the poem. For Halpern these are the sites for an intensive study of the relationship of the erotic and the aesthetic. While interrogating different audiences for the poem, Smith and Halpern offer provocative readings based upon historical evidence that earlier critics viewed myopically or ignored in light of cultural/sexual tensions.

Jonathan Bate's 1993 article "Sexual Perversity in *Venus and Adonis*" also belongs, in a curious way, in the flesh camp of critics. Bate is chiefly concerned with the sexual script in *Venus,* relating it to larger issues while admitting that its "perversity" thwarts fulfillment. Searching for reasons among classical texts about why "coitus is not achieved" in *Venus,* Bate claims that Adonis is not qualified to "participate in an ideal Salmacian/ Hermaphroditic Union" (91). And so "*Venus and Adonis* is a disturbing poem in that perversity takes the place of the unfulfilled Salmacian/Hermaphroditic potential." Here is Bate's reasoning:

> Coitus only occurs in the form of perverted, parodic variations, as Adonis is nuzzled by the boar and Venus cradles the flower—because the partners are not equals. An oppressive power-relation has to exist: after all, this is a goddess dealing with a mortal. Shakespeare has some fun inverting the traditional power structure—Venus's problem is that she can't actually rape Adonis, as Jove rapes Danaë, Neptune Theophane, and Apollo Isse—but in the end the poem shows that a sexual relationship based on coercion is doomed. The inequality is highlighted by the difference in age of the two characters; one function of the allusions to Adonis's mother is to suggest that the sexual dealings of partners of greatly unequal age are bound at some level to replicate the archetypal relationship based on an unequal power-structure, incest between a parent and a child. ("Sexual Perversity" 92)

Besides valorizing *Venus* from either a moral or a sexual perspective, critics have celebrated Shakespeare's poem for its intentional ambivalence. These readers refuse to take sides with Venus or Adonis, preferring instead to de-categorize or defuse the poem as an organic, consistent text. Rebhorn briefly surveys the tenets of this group of critics. Among the ambivalence school Kenneth Muir stands out as chief critic. His opinion of Shakespeare's intentional ambiguity is best expressed in the following comments from his 1964 article "*Venus and Adonis:* Comedy or Tragedy?"

Although an interpretation that seeks to show that Shakespeare was writing a sermon against lust is clearly impossible, it is equally impossible to assume that the poem is a straightforward eulogy of sexual love. Almost everything in the poem appears to be ambivalent. The famous description of Adonis's stallion pursuing the mare can be taken either as an emblem of the naturalness of desire, as Venus herself points out, or as an emblem of uncontrolled desire, or lust, as it frequently was. (9)

Muir argues that such an approach is consistent with Renaissance painting and, on an even deeper level, notes that "The ambivalence of the poem is caused by the poet's own acceptance of the conflicting feelings about love, and partly by the essentially dramatic nature of his imagination" (12). Muir valorizes oppositions to explain the script of *Venus and Adonis*.

David Bevington concurs with Muir's overall assessment, observing that "We must not expect psychological insight or meaningful self-discovery. The conventions of amatory verse do not encourage a serious interest in character. Venus and Adonis are mouthpieces for contrasting attitudes toward love" ("Introduction" 13). Rejecting any "allegory" as a true meaning of the poem, Bevington further claims that its seriousness is as much a part of the poem as the "sexual teasing" and "our own erotic pleasure" (14). The debate between Venus and Adonis, according to the ambivalence school, will never be resolved, nor should it.

The Burdens and Mystery of Readership

Venus and Adonis explores the obligations and power, burdens, and mystery of readership. An indissolvable fascination exists between criticism of *Venus and Adonis* and the idea of readership or, better put, strategies of readership. A theme running through *Venus and Adonis* criticism is what readership entails. Certainly readership is an investment in the text as a fluid economy, and critics have tried to negotiate within that forum. A major article on "the open responsiveness of the earliest readers of *Venus and Adonis*" is Katherine Duncan-Jones' "Much Ado with Red and White." Nona Fienberg also insightfully discusses *Venus'* impact on Elizabethan readers (and contemporary ones as well): "Venus' power extends beyond Adonis to readers of the poem who are challenged to reevaluate a fixed and stable set of standards against her dynamic and shifting self-evaluation" ("Thematics of Value" 21). Fienberg's article is reprinted in this collection.

Antecedent to, yet imbedded in, the idea of readership in *Venus and Adonis* is Shakespeare's act of (re)reading Ovid and Arthur Golding, one of the most frequently consulted Elizabethan translators. This performance is challenging and potentially subversive for many contemporary critics, though it was far less problematical for earlier ones. Editors of *Venus and Adonis* since Malone—including Hyder Rollins, J.C. Maxwell, F.T. Prince, and John Roe—document echoes, catalogue parallels, and chart influences. Rollins and Bullough include Ovidian source material. Just as there is a debate (unrehabilitated for some readers) between Venus and Adonis, for many readers a struggle rages between Ovid and his Renaissance interlocutor Shakespeare. Opinions vary on exactly what Shakespeare saw in and took away or left intact from Ovid. Baldwin conjectured that Shakespeare relied most heavily on Ovid while Muir finds that the poem's overall effect of "mingling . . . wit and seriousness" is unmistakably Ovidian. Dubrow and Keach, however, base their readings on the ways Shakespeare transformed Ovid. Bate as well sees more differences than point-for-point source hunting might unearth. Warning that Ovid "tells the story of *Venus and Adonis* in less than a hundred lines, Shakespeare in more than a thousand," Bate contends that:

> Within Shakespeare's poem there are signals that we must consider the Ovidian source-text to be much broader than the seventy or so lines of direct material. Golding's outward/inward distinction works differently in Shakespeare's reading of Ovid: whilst the moral translator claimed to find meaning "inwardlye" but in fact imposed it from outside the text, the creative imitator interprets his source narrative partly by means of other narratives that lie both outside and inside, around and within, it. Surrounding the text is a distinctly unwholesome context. (*Shakespeare and Ovid* 50)

Bate concludes that Shakespeare's "version [of the story] is very much his own, as Ovid's is his, in that the *Metamorphoses* do not lean particularly on the older versions of Venus and Adonis story . . ." (57). In this respect Bate echoes George Wyndham's observation at the end of the nineteenth century: "Shakespeare's poem is not a classic myth" ("Introduction" lxxxiv). Poet Richard Wilbur similarly stresses that *Venus and Adonis* "differs from Ovidian poetry generally in containing a very high proportion of dialogue . . ."("The Narrative Poems" 1402). Tita French Baumlin further identifies a key difference between Shakespeare's and Ovid's texts in terms of the emerging poet-playwright's development:

> Unlike her Ovidian ancestor, Shakespeare's Venus must learn how to use the language of divine seduction, how to be the goddess she is

reputed to be; this process of apotheosis, of learning and growing into the full-fledged Goddess of Love, mirrors a similar struggle in the inventive process of the new poet. Like Venus, who utilizes and must ultimately reject each of her models' persuasive rhetorics, so must the poet ultimately reject his source materials if he is to fashion his own voice and authority. ("Birth of the Bard" 192)

Like Baumlin, Catherine Belsey separates Shakespeare's Venus from Ovid's: "Shakespeare's Venus . . . unlike Ovid's . . . never succeeds in eliciting the desire of Adonis" (261). Admitting that Shakespeare, like other Renaissance poets, adopted from Ovid "above all the notion of erotic metamorphosis itself," Shakespeare considerably expanded the frame of reference in which love/desire could be represented. "But if Ovid's tale of Venus and Adonis offers absence as the recurring figure of desire, Shakespeare's poem surpasses its sources in audacity as well as length, by setting out to explain the origin of desire in its entirety" (261).

In an essay commissioned for this volume, M.L. Stapleton characterizes Shakespeare as an even more aggressive, less reverent reader of Ovid: "Whether in Latin or in the English translations that were published with great frequency throughout the Renaissance, Shakespeare had access to most of the Ovidian corpus, a poetical body that he cannibalized, reconstituted, and transfused into his own words." As a reader himself, then, Shakespeare was keenly aware of the problems and possibilities of readership as well as the incumbent dangers of an easy *detente*. Once a burgeoning writer is loosed inside a famous author's text, especially such a hallowed script as Ovid's *Metamorphoses*, alterations multiply. No servile redactor was Shakespeare.

Shakespeare was thus caught in a field of anxieties existing between reader and writer in *Venus and Adonis*. In fact, the poem begins with the ontological perplexities of this relationship. As Anthony Burgess put it in his fictionalized life of Shakespeare, *Nothing Like the Sun: A Story of Shakespeare's Love-life* (1964), "Here was WS [William Shakespeare] in naked confrontation with the reader, with, above all, one particular reader" (99). Starting immediately with the prefatory dedication to Southampton, Shakespeare apologetically, yet sophisticatedly, acknowledges the empowerment of readership. Deprecating the "unpolished lines" of the "first heir of my invention," Shakespeare commends *Venus and Adonis* to Southampton's "honorable survey," or reading, and wishes for the earl's "hopeful expectation." Shakespeare chooses the language of patronage cautiously, investing in the act of reading a venerable economy of fame and power. His poem is an "heir," a claimant in a contest for the conveyance of power and property; and in deferentially appealing for Southampton's support, Shakespeare makes the young nobleman's reading a juridical decision in the acknowledgement and transference of power (or, in this case, influence). Southampton's "survey" of the poem is like the earl's appraisal of his baronial estates and rights. Shakespeare thus metaphorizes the act of reading as if it were an economic privilege emanating from the influential nobleman to his subservient though talented admirer/poet/heir. Given that Southampton allowed his name to be used in the dedication, Shakespeare clearly succeeded in his plea for an influential place in the earl's reading.

In *Nothing Like the Sun,* novelist Burgess records conversations between Elizabethan secretary and translator John Florio (who dedicated his own *Worlde of Wardes* to Southampton) and Shakespeare about Southampton's precise "surveying" of *Venus and Adonis.* Florio pointed out to Shakespeare: "I remember your verses about the horse. You will then know my figure and my meaning. If you understand a horse you will understand what I am saying about my lord. He is all fire and air and water. He can hurt and he can be hurt" (101). Continuing, Florio cautioned WS that Southampton was urged to marry by Lord Burghley, his guardian, and that Southampton read/saw himself and his predicament in the poem: "'Oh, already he talks of himself as Adonis. Poets have more power than they think. I think,' said Florio slowly, 'that he ought to marry. Not only for the sake of the house, but for his own sake. There are corruptive forces at court, there are not hands eager to lay themselves on his beauty. I think you, more than any man, might persuade him to think of marriage'" (102–103). Benjamin Stewart, who has performed a one-person *Venus and Adonis* throughout the 1980s and 1990s, interpreted Shakespeare's message to the young earl in unmistakably twentieth-century terms:

> The plague had closed the theaters in London, so he [Shakespeare] was out in the country weathering the storm. And he had a patron, Henry Wriothesley, the Earl of Southampton, to whom the poem was dedicated. It was an artistic way of telling his patron, who was a beautiful young aristocrat, "Please have a child before it's too late. You're getting involved in all these court intrigues, and people get their heads cut off that way. We don't have sperm banks yet." (quoted in Herman, "People Need to Hear a Poem Being Quoted" F1)

The historical connections between Shakespeare and his chief reader, Southampton, have also been explored by G.P.V. Akrigg, A.L. Rowse, and John Roe—though these studies have not progressed much beyond the idea that Shakespeare was a loyal poet soliciting the benevolence of the young earl to prosper in the Elizabethan twin spheres of letters/politics.

In his essay for this volume, Patrick Murphy extends our knowledge of the Southampton–Shakespeare nexus by examining *Venus and Adonis* in the light of cultural materialism as a social practice that comments on Southampton's status as Burghley's ward and his resistance to marry Burghley's granddaughter, Elizabeth Vere. Retrieving social and legal practices surrounding wardship, Murphy believes that *Venus and Adonis* functions as a form of advice literature, counseling Southampton about cultural, personal, and economic prescriptions and prohibitions. Edward de Vere participated in (and apparently believed) rumors that Elizabeth Vere was not his daughter. Foregrounding the details surrounding these rumors and the extant legal options, Murphy outlines Southampton's choices between different orders of prescription and prohibition. Through this "first heir" of his invention, then, Shakespeare provided Southampton with a disguised critique of social pressures and economic practices enabling the earl to avoid complicity with intolerable prescriptions, on one hand, and a destructive revenge against the loss of human distinctions, on the other.

Venus and Adonis has prompted several studies of Renaissance readers besides Shakespeare's primary audience, Southampton. Key questions confronting critics are these: Who precisely was Shakespeare's reading public? What were its attitudes toward the classical myths about the doomed couple of Venus and Adonis? What prejudices and/or tolerances did a Renaissance audience have that contemporary readers may lack? Were Renaissance readers involved (more or less?) in the characters' plight? Did earlier readers feel less anxious because they saw the poem more symbolically/politically than we do? Readers have raised these and other issues with varying degrees of sophistication and success. As we saw from *The Shakespeare Allusion-Book*, late sixteenth- and early seventeenth-century readers were simultaneously enthusiastic about and disrupted by *Venus;* they condemned the poem as dangerous erotica or praised Shakespeare's honey-tongued language.

Studies of Renaissance readers of *Venus* have unearthed a variety of conflicts. Maintaining that "Venus's temptation is not directed against Adonis . . . but against the reader," Hamilton confidently found that "For Shakespeare's first readers the context of the poem would include the spiritual pilgrimage where the pilgrim meets Venus; but of course, she is condemned by the form itself" (*"Venus and Adonis"* 14). Williams describes the meaning Venus had for "the attentive Elizabethan reader" in overtly political terms. Seeing Venus' "outrageous behavior . . . as a reaction against sociosexual tyrannies, contemporaries would have recognized Venus as embodying this new feminism, and qualified their attitudes accordingly" (701). Studying the "nature of romantic love and its analogue of courtly service," Dubrow perceptively suggests a further political link between Venus' flattery of Adonis and Shakespeare's encomium to Southampton. Dubrow concludes that "politics in the narrower sense of the word lies behind the sexual politics of the poem: Venus' assertion of power may well reflect resentment of Elizabeth herself," a view elaborated in Louis Montrose's influential article on Elizabethan mythologies. Peter Erickson also interrogates *Venus* to find "refracted images of Queen Elizabeth": "In *Venus and Adonis* Venus' domination evokes Elizabeth's control, and this undercurrent helps to account for the poem's unstable tonal mixture of defensive jocularity and general alarm" (*Rewriting Shakespeare* 41). Exploring the poem in terms of the politics of class/power, Kenneth Burke earlier wrote: "Venus would stand for the upper class, Adonis the middle class, the boar for the lower classes" (216).

Commenting on still other Elizabethan readers, Maurice Evans paints a different picture of them as sophisticated aesthetes. "The Elizabethans were more flexible readers than we are, able to accept simultaneously, and yet enjoy separately, the levels of allegorical myth and naturalistic narrative" (5–6). Moreover, Evans contends, "A poetry reader of the 1590's would have been quick to recognize the inversion and have found Venus witty and provocative because of it. In contrast to the Petrarchan tradition, Ovid's *Metamorphoses* is full of aggressively passionate women who, like Shakespeare's Venus, do all the wooing" (9). Evans' views are typical of the received opinion about Shakespeare's first readers—they could be more generous than we and applauded eager displays of feminine wit that later generations found suspect or labored, depending on their moral/aesthetic views.

Yet Evans does not sufficiently explain just where and how *Venus* is "provocative." Duncan-Jones' article on Elizabethan reactions ("Much Ado") again is relevant on this point. Halpern's essay, found in this volume, concentrates profitably on the cultural anxieties—the heart of what in society can be most provocative—of Shakespeare's female readers. Forcing contemporary readers to admit that Shakespeare's first audience was not predominately male, Halpern allegorizes Elizabethan female readers to locate their sexual frustrations/anxieties inside the text.

In his introduction to the Cambridge edition, Roe implicates contemporary readers, as Halpern does Renaissance ones, who are surprised at seeing themselves reflected in *Venus*. "Venus's voluptuous appeal is qualified by her disingenuousness; yet that aspect of her too finds an answering chord in the reader who is no longer sexually innocent" (6), which, I daresay, includes most readers in the late twentieth century. Doebler, however, believes that there is a "sudden diverting and distancing of the reader" through Venus' arguments ("Many Faces" 41).

According to Sheidley, Adonis offends male readers because, unlike "the properly ordered male," he does not "accept and realize his phallic potential." As Sheidley emphasizes, "what happens to Adonis is the inevitable result of his *unkindness,* that is, the unnatural role in which he casts himself. It stands in place of the consummation the poem always points toward and causes its readers to desire" ("'Unless It Be a Boar'" 13). Who are these readers? For Sheidley, "The logic of the tragic plot depends upon such great improbability that the disaster which overtakes the boy and the goddess promises quite the opposite for more ordinary men and women like the readers of the poem" (13). So where Halpern identifies frustrated Renaissance female readers in the text, Sheidley locates in *Venus and Adonis* the unfulfilled hopes of all readers rooting for the couple's consummation. Sheidley posits a most perceptive reader (himself!):

> Adonis' last words make up his rigid and single-minded oration against lust. To the reader upon whom the double perspective from which he views the action has enforced ironic detachment, wise empathy, and a compassionate awareness of multiple ramifications and possibilities, such simplicity cannot fail to appear inadequate. Benedick rises to his ultimate happy sanity by climbing a ladder of ironic awareness perceiving first Claudio's folly and finally his own. In *Venus and Adonis* Shakespeare distills a similarly sane and joyful spirit by raising his reader to a viewpoint from which love is revealed not to present (as it seems to Adonis) a dreary choice between lust and chastity but to offer a welcome alternative in the "warme effects" of charity to self-defeating paralysis of pride. (15)

Expressing a contrary view, Bevington wants us to confront "our own erotic pleasures" in *Venus and Adonis* by admitting that "Venus' repeated encounters with Adonis take the form of ingeniously varied positions, ending in coital embrace although without consummation. Adonis' passive role invites the male reader to fantasize himself in Adonis' place, being seduced by the goddess of beauty" ("Introduction" 14–15). Where Halpern sees the female Elizabethan reader frustrated in and by the poem, Bevington finds it more probable that the contemporary male would enjoy being in Adonis' predicament, though, in all likelihood, that *Playboy*-browsing reader would take a different path. Critics like Bevington would have readers be like Puck, "an auditor, an actor, too," in *Venus and Adonis.*

Then there are those commentators like poet-critic Richard Wilbur, who fault Shakespeare for being inconsistent with any reader, abrogating his obligation by employing contradictory imagery for *Venus* and for blending comedy with tragedy:

> Shakespeare's poem breaks its own contract with the reader. By line 551 Venus' eagle has become a vulture, her face "doth reek and smoke," and her "lust" is being denounced by the poet for its shamelessness and its subversion of reason. This passage endorses in advance Adonis' tirade (769 ff.) against "sweating Lust," in which that sweat which first seemed earthily matter-of-fact (25) and later erotically attractive (143–44) becomes wholly distasteful. Is the reader expected, at this point, to make such judgments retroactive, and to see the first part of the poem in a radically altered light? If so, it is too much to ask. One could no more do it than one could reconceive *Macbeth* as comedy. (1402)

As Wilbur's mistrust attests, the relationship between *Venus* and readers of the poem has not always been fulfilling. If the history of criticism on the poem proves anything, it is that the burdens *Venus* places on readers are often reciprocated by the anxieties readers themselves incorporate into the script.

VENUS AND HER INFINITE VARIETY

Like her votary Cleopatra, Venus envelops readers in her infinite variety. In 1953, Rufus Putney comfortably reassured readers that: "The supreme achievement of the poem resides in the characterization of Venus but Shakespeare's success in creating her implies also deft handling of Adonis' role and skillful organization of the narrator" ("Venus *Agonistes*" 58), as if consistency graced the entire poem and every character as well. About twenty years later, S. Clark Hulse, much less confidently, reflected on the centuries-old uneasiness about the goddess: Her presence "is the core of the poem's problem. If one grants that Venus is earthly love, what is the attitude toward earthly love? Is it loathsome, foul lust? Delightful sense? A near-sacred force of natural propagation?" ("Shakespeare's Myth" 97). Venus is both achievement and problem. The combination of these two traits leads to paradox: "She cannot choose but love" yet she is "doomed to the most flagrant incompatibility" (Klause 373).

Since the sixteenth century, Shakespeare's Venus has provoked controversy; she has been remorsefully at strife with herself and with her critics. Among the recurring questions raised about her are: Who is she? What is the precise nature of her love for Adonis? Is her notion of love honorably Platonic or luxuriously sensual, or both? Is she the guiding force of procreation or the dupe of her own unflattering, etiolated attempts at union? What world(s) does she dominate? Does she merit the reader's sympathy or deserve the reader's scorn? The answers to, or attempts to answer, these questions have furrowed critical discourse with vehement contradictions. Venus has been represented as the sublime goddess of love, a denizen of an erotic epyllion, the victim of unmerited hostility, an over-the-hill bully-bawd or, for some, all of the aforementioned. Readers have celebrated her, denounced her, or pitied and excoriated her simultaneously. For James Lake and Kenneth Muir, Venus is a tragic heroine; yet for Robert Miller and David Beauregard, she catapults others into tragedy. For Beauregard, Venus' "desire for the young Adonis can only be taken as unnatural and disorderly" (94). Klause observes that "The indignities that Venus suffers are many and severe" (370). Much of Venus' post–1593 disquietude can be attributed to critical wrangling.

From the start of her Shakespearean existence, Venus has thwarted unequivocal response. By reversing female and male roles, thus transforming Venus from pursued lady into the forceful wooer, Shakespeare destabilized Petrarchan boundaries that embowered Elizabethan lovers. The result has led to a debate about Shakespeare's view of his own creation. According to Cantelupe, the poet is engaged in "parodying not only the myth [of Venus] but also its traditional presentation, literary and pictorial" (148). Yet, contrarily, Sheidley believes that Shakespeare "intends, at least to some extent, to endorse Venus' arguments (but not, of course, her farcical manners). Surely Shakespeare gives her more than adequate space to state her position, as the conclusion of the poem bears her out" (7). Here, then, are two sides of Venus' complex nature.

Venus' credentials as "Goddess of Love" have received scrupulous attention. In an essay prepared for this collection, João Froes explores the many myths out of which Shakespeare's Venus emerged to argue for a classically correct (the critical equivalent of "politically correct"?) goddess. Regarding an Ovidian Venus, Gordon Williams, however, cautions, "Shakespeare is not interested in [an] Ovidian explanation for the tempestuous passion aroused in Venus. Mythic explanations like the mythic powers normally enjoyed by Venus, here yield to a human predicament" ("Coming of Age" 774). As the traditional personification of Love, Venus confidently recounts her victory over Mars, whom she enshackled in a rose chain, to proffer unearthly delights to the young Adonis. Yet some of her Olympian powers have eroded into human dilemmas in Shakespeare's poem. She is powerless to dissuade her would-be paramour from the hunt and she must bow and scrape before the Destinies and Death. For Cousins she is both a goddess and a character in a play ("Venus Reconsidered").

In humanizing her, Shakespeare strengthened her charm as a woman but weakened her Olympian imperiousness. Several critics over the last century have gloated with punitive glee at Venus' diminished pride and mortal-like follies. Other readers, however, have approached her venerably as both goddess and mortal. Roe, for example, prudently stresses: "To some degree Shakespeare follows the practice of classical authors in observing the contradictory behaviour of a deity: a goddess being still a woman and therefore subject to whim might turn petulant when crossed, acting out of character and even contrary to her own interests" (9). Nancy Lindheim expresses the same sentiment: "The identification of Venus and love lies at the heart of Shakespeare's conception of the poem, though this identification is neither allegorical nor doctrinal. Venus is not 'Love' in the abstract way Neoplatonists conceive it, but in the contradictory way it is experienced" (193). Taking her cue from Lacan, Catherine Belsey would censor Venus for committing a crime against holy wedded love.

Admitting Venus' faults is part of appreciating her vitality. Critics like Halpern have tried to rescue her from degradation. When confronted with Venus' shortcomings, some critics rush to her defense. One of the most humane views of the goddess is voiced by Klause:

> We should not conclude, however, that the poet is out to give Venus her comeuppance (what fools these immortals be!), that this proud goddess who so blithely victimizes poor, helpless mortals by making them her slaves will now be placed in thrall herself and deprived of her beloved, so that we her victims can have a good if slightly cruel laugh at her. To mock Venus, the poem suggests, is in some sense to mock ourselves. (371)

Klause concludes that "the denigration of a goddess leads to her identification with a flawed humanity"; to denounce her is to denigrate ourselves. Not all critics agree.

In addition to having her divine powers questioned, Venus has been under intense critical siege for her appearance and her amorous behavior. For some readers her eyes do not drop "silver rain" but ooze rheum; she oppresses the delicate buds of spring with a lust-laden body instead of gliding across them nymph-like. The fact that she is an older, overbearing *amoureuse* who sweats eclipses the beauty of her grey eyes, golden hair, and red cheeks for a goodly number of critics. According to John Doebler, Shakespeare "casts Venus as a frenized older woman driven by comic lust for a very young man barely emerging from boyhood" ("Reluctant Adonis" 484); more respectfully, Gordon Williams holds the same sentiments: Venus' "vulnerability is that of the older woman, desperate to renew her youth in the arms of a young lover" ("Coming of Age" 776).

J.W. Lever summarizes some of the most negative critical reactions to Venus while preserving, in a gentlemanly manner, the identity of her accusers:

> By some she has been portrayed as cruel, a fickle, or a feckless tyrant; others have caught her smiling. Only Shakespeare, it would seem, viewed her as thoroughly absurd, a fat white woman whom nobody loved. Forty years old, fluttery and apprehensive, loquacious and perspiring: such is the impression which the heroine of his first poem has made upon several distinguished scholar-critics. Nor is Venus only ridiculous. She is also the personification of lust that sullies all it touches; mistress of the dark horse from Plato's *Phaedrus;* a figure of evil eminence comparable with Milton's Satan. ("Second Chance" 81)

Yet several pages earlier in his brief survey of Venus scholarship in the same issue of *Shakespeare Survey,* Lever identifies these naysayers. It was Don Cameron Allen who characterized the goddess as "a forty-year-old countess with a taste for Chapel Royal altos." Similarly, C.S. Lewis found her annoying like one of those "effusive female relatives." Lu Emily Pearson denounced Venus as "the destructive agent of sensual love who . . . sullies whatever it touches . . . false and evil." Robert Miller associated her with Plato ("Horses"); and Franklin M. Dickey linked her to Milton's Satan *("Not Wisely").* Perhaps the greatest insult to Venus' female dignity, though, came from Cantelupe, who associated her with the overbearing *femme fatale* of burlesque: she is "this Mae Westian woman, who, like a military strategist, has at last maneuvered the enemy into a vulnerable position" (145). Cantelupe's Venus descends to her nadir—a highly undesirable, even ludicrous, floozy.

Nor are these all Venus' detractors. *Mutatis mutandis,* readers have dredged up other faults to pummel her. For Streitberger, she "presents the temptations—not merely to lust, but to neglect of duty—to succumb to the easy pleasures and endeavors of life, and exhibits in her actions the results of giving in to those temptations" (291). Hamilton mitigates the danger Venus poses even as he castigates her all-too-real threats: "Traditionally Venus appears in a moral world where her evil temptations must be resisted in order that man achieve the perfected virtuous life. Shakespeare translates the actions of his poem into the prelapsarian state" (*"Venus and Adonis"* 15). Unfortunately, though, we are postlapsarian readers and thus, by implication, Venus' victims. For A. Robin Bowers, Venus is doubly alarming, with her kiss and in her complicity with the boar. Her curse "serves as an inverted moral of the story: the irrational is thus perpetuated" (14). In exploring "the darker, more dangerous tendencies in the goddess of love" (*Captive Victors* 36), Dubrow inveighs against Venus' desire for mastery over Adonis and censures the "untrustworthiness of her promises." No wonder Venus flees to Paphos.

Among Venus' most prominent roles is that of the rhetor/orator, and again jarringly conflicting interpretations tell of her talents/entrapments. As Desmet wittily points out, "Although Venus is remembered for her amorous acrobatics, for most of the poem she talks" (138). Coppélia Kahn cites relevant statistics: "Most of the poem's 1200 lines are hers, in the form of direct speech; in contrast, Adonis speaks only eighty-eight lines" ("Self and Eros" 364). Exactly what kind of speaker—honest or deceitful; generous or self-serving—Venus is depends on the critic's aperture into the poem. Earlier critics like Sir Sidney Lee and George Wyndham saw beauty in her language, never thinking of attributing duplicity of motive to the goddess.

On the most positive contemporary front, Nona Fienberg maintains that Venus is in "control of the rhetorical situation" (24), and that she articulates feminist principles an oppressive patriarchy would suppress. For Desmet, Venus is a formidable orator whose status as goddess and whose ethos are impressive though she is eventually "tamed" and "banished" by the narrator. Still, according to Desmet, "As the underpaid lawyer as well as the judge who enforces Love's laws, Venus is an orator, and her weapons are those commonly found in the schoolboy's arsenal; she starts out as a Petrarchan poet but later employs proverb and allegory to persuade her reluctant lover" (138). For Sheidley, Venus speaks movingly in the language of the sonneteers. One of the strongest supporters of Venusian rhetoric is Tita French Baumlin, who contends that the goddess "has progressed from the state of an ineffectual, imitative Petrarchan poet to . . . the sovereign eloquence of a true Olympian" (204). Baumlin elaborates on this metamorphosis:

> This maturation of Venus is most strikingly displayed in the transformation of her rhetoric into the language of divine power. Whereas

her earlier speeches produced none of the intended results, her language now has the power to change the course of human love and to transform Adonis's flowing blood into an anemone. (205)

Far less sympathetic to Venus as rhetor are critics who judge her linguistic feats as a failure. For Hallett Smith, Venus' extended pleas are like "listening to a labored lecture," weighing readers down with arguments "unadapted" to love poetry. Even more serious are charges by other critics who brand Venusian rhetoric as less than noble—a fissure of lures and entrapments. Typical of the suspicion that Venus' rhetoric arouses is A. Robin Bowers' assessment:

> While her first entreaty fails to win the kiss, Venus does not delay in her assault. After this initial expository section, where the reader moves from the hunt of lust to the hunt of the boar, the success of which is symbolized by a kiss, we find an extended section of argument, to be viewed in the context of the traditional *débat* poem, in which Venus first provokes Adonis into taking up the argument on her terms and then wears him down until he finally succumbs. (11)

According to this view, Venus is as much of a juggernaut in the debater's circle as she is on the field where she sweeps Adonis off his courser. Lucy Gent pejoratively dismisses Venus as "the arch-sophist, preaching to Adonis, who is apparently ignorant of everything except hunting" (725). True to her nature, Venus is "governed by paradoxes"; she is a creature of "extravagance, excess, a liking for paradox and antithesis" (723). Studying the goddess's "artifices," Dubrow denounces Venus' "habit of naming and renaming" to exert her domination in the world of sexual politics (37).

Venus is also cast as mother, and as critics point out from studying myth (e.g., Bradbrook; Kahn), one of the goddess' most important titles was *Venus Genetrix,* the propagator of the race. Venus aptly has been compared to such diverse maternal-acting characters as Juliet's wet nurse and the asp-fondling Cleopatra. Precisely what kind of mother she is to Adonis has, of course, been open to question. One of the most sympathetic descriptions of Venus as a caring mother is found in lines 874–76. When, fearing for Adonis' safety once he leaves to hunt the boar, she runs through the brushes harkening after the sound of his horn: "She wildly breaketh from their strict embrace / Like a milch doe, whose swelling dugs do ache, / Hasting to feed her fawn hid in some brake." Venus' tender compassion for Adonis, her unripe son, her wayward boy, is lovingly captured in this simile. Peter Erickson makes use of the milch doe image while discussing Venus' maternal qualities (51–52). But the poem, as other readers have noted, also uncovers the dark, rapacious side of Venus' maternity. She is the "empty eagle" (55) and the swooping vulture devouring all, including Adonis, in her lustful hunt. Like Eugene O'Neill's elms, she displays a "sinister maternity." Generally speaking, then, critics who explore Venus' role as mother have emphasized either the milch doe or vulture side of her nature.

The most maternal part of Venus' anatomy, her "swelling dugs," had been foregrounded and valorized by Renaissance artists. Giorgione's *Sleeping Venus* most readily comes to mind. General studies of Venus in art include Erwin Panofsky's magisterial *Studies in Iconology* and Edgar Wind's *Pagan Mysteries in the Renaissance.* More specific iconographic attention to Shakespeare's Venus is found in Robert Bauer's "Rhetoric and Picture in *Venus and Adonis*"; S. Clark Hulse's "The Iconography of *Venus and Adonis*" (in *Metaphoric Verse* 143–75); and David Rosand's article "*Ut Pictor Poeta*: Meaning in Titian's *Poesie*" discusses Titian's relation to Ovid and Shakespeare's to Titian. Georgianna Ziegler's beautifully illustrated essay, written for this collection, analyzes many of the paintings that accompanied editions of *Venus and Adonis.*

Other redemptive readings of Venus as mother can be found in Lennet Daigle's study of Venus' generative powers in light of medieval commentators on classical myth and Heather Asals' analysis of Venus' evolution from the depths of lust to the highest Neoplatonic sphere of heavenly creation. Similarly, according to Klause, "Venus' maternal instinct, which is present to some extent even in her lust, becomes more (though by no means entirely) altruistic in the second half of the poem" (366). Claiming that when Venus picks the flower, "the terms of [their—Venus and Adonis's] union are no longer sexual; they are infantile" (370), Kahn also ameliorates some of Venus' more dangerous maternal actions: "The devouring mother whose oral demands constituted a threat to Adonis' very identity has now become the nurturant mother on whom he depends as an infant for survival" (370). The closing scene, in which Adonis is transformed into the flower that Venus plucks, has prompted other critics as well to rehabilitate the ambiguity of Venus' role(s) as mother and lover. Desmet, for instance, claims that "Venus seems to exemplify and to exceed feminine stereotypes, for she is simultaneously Adonis's mother and Shakespeare's peer" (143–44).

Explicating the myths behind the poem, Jonathan Bate argues: "Shakespeare's Venus acts out an extraordinary family romance. By imagining her lover as her father, she makes herself into the mother and the flower into the fruit of their union. . . . The fusion of lover and mother in the context of vegetative imagery makes Venus into Myrrha once again. It is as if, having slept with her father, the girl is now sleeping with her son" (*Shakespeare and Ovid* 59). Adonis was incestuously conceived when his mother Myrrha was impregnated by Cinyras, her father. In his psychoanalytical reading, informed by Ovidian mythology as well, Peter Dow Webster offers still another perspective on Venus' maternal role. Pointing out that in Ovid Venus was the "Magna Mother" and that Adonis was her "son-consort," Webster concludes that Shakespeare deplores the crime she committed against Adonis, "the first of many lectures Shakespeare is to give against shameless lust in woman" (299). Painting a picture of Shakespeare as a misogynist, Webster views Venus and the women in the tragedies in unmitigatingly pessimistic terms: ". . . woman is incrementally destructive in her relations with men; she is a thing to be feared . . . and Shakespeare protects himself by refusing to pluck the heart of his own mystery" (302). Also underscoring Shakespeare's misogyny, Leslie Fiedler found that in *Venus* "Shakespeare is driven to embody in Venus—whom he basically distrusts and fears for the nakedness of her lust—his own desire for epicene beauty" ("Some Contexts" 68). Alan Rothenberg also confronted Venus' engulfing maternity in a not-widely-accepted psychoanalytic reading of the poem.

While Venus plays the roles just outlined, she also transcends many or all of them. Several critics have eloquently affirmed Venus' skill as role player. A.C. Hamilton admits that while Shakespeare, like Chaucer and Spenser, paid homage to her as the "Goddess of Love," his specific contribution to the myth of Aphrodite was to "show her intense vitality. In her two postures, reclining in the first part and fleeing in the second, she ranges through all the moods and passions. For the sake of love she is prepared to do and become all things" ("*Venus and Adonis*" 14). Respecting Venus for her multiplicity, and not limiting her to dichotomies, Doebler "propose[s] a response to the shifting rhetoric of the poem that takes into account the several personalities Venus had in both the philosophy and the mythography of the Renaissance" ("Many Faces" 33). Agreeing that Venus should not be restricted to one confining interpretation, Hulse posits three Venuses—comic, lustful, philosophical—and concludes: "Love does not exist in itself as a substance, but is an accident in a substance. Shakespeare's mythic goddess is not so much a person as a diverse group of actions inhabiting a single body" ("Shakespeare's Myth" 98). Appropriately enough, some dramatic adaptations of Shakespeare's poem have put multiple Venuses on stage (see the section "*Venus and Adonis* in Production" below).

Adonis has not received nearly as much attention from the critics as Venus has, yet this "sweet boy"/"wayward boy" is no less a perplexing participant in the equation of Venus and/or Adonis. Dubrow bemoans the critics' fate when confronting Adonis: "If we cannot trust the actions and reactions of Venus, those of Adonis are also problematical. Though he is less fully realized than Venus, his behavior manifests some of the same intriguing ambiguities" (*Captive Victors* 43). Hulse identifies a further problem in responding to Adonis: "Shakespeare's portrayal of Adonis is deceptive only because it is so simple" ("Shakespeare's Myth" 97). The operative word in Hulse's assessment is "deceptive." On the face of things, Adonis' refusal of Venus' love seems relatively straightforward and consistent: he hears her *cri de coeur* as a Circean chant to entrap him in lust during his "unripe years." Yet Adonis' simplicity, for the critics, is no more a given than are Venus' palpable pleasures. Like Venus, Adonis is presented through multiple, conflicting images.

One of the continuing problems in interpreting Adonis is identifying the exact epistomological space in which we as readers can know and respond to him. Scrutinizing Venus' arguments, Muir points out that "as we see everything through Venus' eyes, we cannot help feeling that Adonis is guilty of pride and self-sufficiency" ("Comedy or Tragedy" 7). Assuming that Venus becomes the aperture through which we evaluate Adonis' insight and *in sight*, he clearly is no match for Venusian eloquence, excessive and voluptuous. Gent draws attention to Adonis' implausibility as rhetor in his own cause:

> Adonis is remarkably silent throughout. He has a few words at lines 185–186 and at line 373. At lines 379–384 he is concerned with the practical business of how to retrieve his horse. At line 409 she [Venus] prods him into saying more. He uses ploce prettily at line 412, but relies heavily in defending himself in traditional proverbs. . . . The Euphusistic elements of Adonis's style are out of date for the 1590's. (726)

Desmet similarly stresses Adonis' verbal weaknesses: "On the level of language . . . Adonis is alienated, having no voice of his own and no choice but to adopt Venus' style or stay silent. The text is too old, the orator too green" (141). Thus when judged through Venusian eyes, Adonis is intentionally silenced in the goddess' self-validating script. Apropos of the young man's silence, a French adaptation of the poem in 1984 omitted Adonis altogether.

Foreclosing Adonis were two Venuses, one to enact and one to decipher events (Ghrenassia 132).

Viewing the young huntsman *solus,* without Venusian bias, could be a critical impossibility, since we may never be able to escape Venus' charm, coercion, or our desire for her correction. Still, even when they attempt to listen to Adonis' arguments, critics often seek validation in either/or categories. Accordingly, Adonis either falls into a solipsistic trap or he diminishes the sincerity of Venus' passion to the point of fetishizing the poem. As they have with Venus, contemporary critics have generally polarized Adonis' presence, denouncing his arrogant self-fashioning or assigning him to the moral high ground. Other critics contend that the young huntsman offers a mediating ambivalence.

Perennial questions asked about Adonis include: Who is he and what does he represent? Webster claimed that "the youth is Shakespeare himself" (29), though few have endorsed this view. Readers since the sixteenth century have coupled Adonis with Henry Wriothesley, Shakespeare's patron. G.P.V. Akrigg claimed that in Adonis Shakespeare presented a highly complimentary portrait of Southampton to counter John Clapham's poem *Narcissus,* which criticized the young nobleman for self-love and for his refusal to wed the bride of his guardian's choice (*Shakespeare and the Earl of Southampton* 33–34, 195–96). While a key passage of *Venus and Adonis* does link Adonis with Narcissus (lines 157–62), it does not seal Southampton's fate as Adonis, although, as we saw, such identification became the basis for Anthony Burgess' fictional dialogue between John Florio and WS. One might even recruit, I suspect, A.C. Hamilton's point of view that the Ovidian epigraph belongs to Adonis for his impeccable moral stand to support an Adonis/Narcissus/Southampton triangle/union. Yet according to Halpern, Venus, not Adonis, is Narcissus, and no one to date has claimed that the young nobleman is Venus in drag.

In light of Patrick Murphy's semiotic study of the complexities of such representations, earlier equations between Adonis and Southampton appear simplified or incomplete. Murphy's essay may be the new locus for historicizing the poem and thus challenge Roe's observation that "arguments concerning the biographical aspects of *Venus and Adonis* are limited in the information and insights they afford . . ." (Introduction 15).

Just as he had done with Venus, Shakespeare amplified and deepened the character of Adonis from what he found in Ovid's *Metamorphoses.* It is misleading to conclude simply that he "popularized" Ovid, as Douglas Bush and Clifford Leech maintained. Closer to the truth is that "The picture he presents of Adonis is more complex than that of Ovid's thoughtless young blood who indulges the goddess's passion but then recklessly goes off and gets himself killed hunting the boar" (Roe, Introduction 14–15). Recognizing that Shakespeare fled from tradition to create his own version of the story/character, Allen believed that Shakespeare "alters Adonis from the soft hunter of hares, who meets death when he turns to the harder hunt, to a youth whose whole intent is on hunting of the boar. . . . As for Adonis— since all Adonises must die—this one, the invention of Shakespeare, gets off with a cleaner biography than any" (106). Many more differences between Ovid's short narrative and Shakespeare's poem are important; studies by Bate, Dubrow, Baumlin, and Belsey perceptively comment on Shakespeare's un-Ovidian Adonis.

Behind and beyond the vicissitudes of biographical speculation and Ovidian models lie the thickets of critical pronouncements about what Adonis represents. Again, as with Venus, conflict of opinion rules. For the critics who shower the adulation of allegory on him Adonis is the sun and the "fairest flower of the field." Many readers have enrolled Adonis in the annals of hagiography. As we saw, Lu Emily Pearson and T.W. Baldwin beatified him as "reason in love," the guardian of unsullied "Beauty." Studying the poem in terms of pathetic fallacy, J. Wilkes Berry likewise claimed that "Shakespeare has mirrored the failure of Venus's sanguine plans for winning Adonis in the day's moving from dawn through sunset to black night" (72). For Venus as well as for Berry, "Adonis represents light and beauty" (76) and his death is "quenched light" (75). Price, too, concluded that he is the "symbol" of beauty and the "darling of nature" (296). For Hamilton, Adonis "represents the perfection of nature in its unfallen state" (*The Early Shakespeare* 155).

For several critics, Adonis' stalwart defenses against Venus' animal passions and his victorious escape from her earn him reverence. Adonis' argument, as expressed in *A Midsummer Night's Dream,* is "Things growing are not ripe until their season" (2.2.123). Accordingly, Miller avowed that Adonis "is exhibiting not modern priggishness but sound Renaissance morality when he somewhat coldly chides Venus" at lines 787–92 ("Venus, Adonis, and the Horses" 263). An even more sobering view was later voiced by Hamilton: "Adonis is more rigorous than the compromising Church Fathers" ("*Venus and Adonis*" 3). Reading the poem in light of religious politics, Hughes allegorized the temptations Adonis must overcome: "The new Christ, Adonis, seems to be rejecting the Catholic Church, personified in the poem by the Great Love Goddess as a whore. This is how Shakespeare seems to have updated and retheologized the archaic myth" (*Shakespeare and the Goddess of Complete Being* 57).

Humanizing Adonis, Streitberger exclaims that he is a fine young man who, with Shakespeare's help, will grow into moral maturity, a point seconded by Jonathan Hart. In Gordon Williams' view, Adonis is also demythicized: he "is treated naturalistically: no legendary youth but an ordinary boy" entering the rites of puberty (773). And even though he laments that Venus "wears [Adonis] down until he finally succumbs" (11), A. Robin Bowers honors the youth for pursuing a chaste love.

Over the years, then, Adonis has garnered much sympathy for his status as victim, the target of Venus' rapacious lust. Interestingly enough, a contemporary expression (1994) of alarm at a predatory Venus is contained in Dr. Joseph Wortis' editorial in *Biological Psychiatry*, included in this volume, associating a victimized Adonis with male workers battling reverse sexual harassment on the job.

Yet Adonis does not smell like a sweet anemone for all critics. He has detractors, a number that has grown considerably in the last twenty to thirty years. Earlier critics, to be sure, were not always comfortable with Adonis' smugness and cold stiffness (e.g., Hazlitt), but the young hunter who disdains love and conceitedly shuns the warmth of the sun on his face has angered contemporary critics for much more serious faults. Relating Adonis to similar-acting young men in the plays, Michael Goldman observes: "Adonis is an early instance of a familiar Shakespearean type—the closed off or cautious man who is not ready to hazard enough of himself for the woman who loves him" (*Shakespeare and the Energies of Drama* 17). Labeling Adonis a prig, Muir denounces the young man's hubris disguised as moral necessity: Adonis "preserves his virginity more because of his self-centeredness than because of his virtue, and Venus arouses our pity as any woman will whose passion is not reciprocated" ("Comedy or Tragedy" 12).

Adonis' twin faults of self-centeredness and disdain of mutuality also figure prominently in other critics' assessments. Rabkin isolates in Adonis a "self contradiction injurious to love," and, as we have seen, Kahn diagnoses Adonis' weakness as acute narcissism which impels him to defend "his inner self against" Venus and to renounce "the physical act of love." Adonis denies the very "existence" of love. As Kahn appropriately notes: "In Adonis, Shakespeare depicts a narcissistic character who regards eros—sexual encounter—as the most serious threat to his self. But the real threat is internal and comes from that very urge to defend against eros" (360). Conceding the ambiguity in the role Adonis plays, Dubrow rebukes the "callowness" in his dialogue and the "distrust" engendered by his "rationales" (43–44). Agreeing with Kahn, Dubrow claims: "Recognizing that Adonis does not fully understand his own behavior, we begin to suspect subterranean motives that he cannot or will not face, such as the narcissism of which Venus accuses him" (44). Klause similarly finds sins abounding in both Adonis and Venus:

> On the other hand, the insensitivity and self absorption of Adonis . . . are enough to lend some credence to Venus's complaint that he is another Narcissus (lines 157–62). Although like Hero and Leander, he lacks the gift of a mature conscience, his faults, however venial, are made to appear morally unattractive. There is certainly, then, in both Venus and Adonis enough that might be absolved, if absolution is to be given. (365)

Concentrating on the idea of "synthesis" in *Venus and Adonis,* Sheidley and Robert P. Merrix (in his essay written for this volume) chastise the disdainful Adonis for his pride. According to Sheidley, "Adonis's . . . definition of love leads him to search for a purity attainable only in death" (32); and for Merrix, "Adonis' refusal to reciprocate the various social and sexual roles embodied in Venus . . . leads to the grotesque images of unfulfilled sexuality" ("The Sexual Conflict"). Merrix humorously remarks: "In desire he is a youthful Tamburlaine 'always moving as the restless spheres.' Unfortunately, in execution, he resembles Don Quixote's Sancho Panza." While critics like Miller, Streitberger, and Asals honored Adonis for his steadfast rejection of Venus' advances, Halpern uncovers in Adonis' unwillingness a physical impairment that correlates with an artistic failure: "The strategic absence of Adonis' erection locates the ontological lack of structuring in the literary art work and particularly the erotic art work. The point is that literary imagination, without some sort of physical intervention, lacks the means to satisfy erotic desire."

Undoubtedly, though, Adonis' most aggressive detractor is J.D. Jahn, whose 1970 article amasses more evidence and specifies more charges against Adonis than any other interpretation of the poem. Simply put, Jahn's thesis is: "For Adonis is guilty not only of self-centeredness, but of a seductive coquetry as well. The poem is by no means a simple presentation of eroticism versus chastity; it reveals, rather, two kinds of human culpability in the realm of courtship" ("Lamb of Lust" 12). Conscious of his own "sexual arousal," Adonis plays the coquette with Venus, enticing yet slaying his wooer with his eyes. Denying him protection as "the sacrificial lamb of a lustful goddess" (13), Jahn contends that Adonis' "passivity . . . constitutes only a token show of resistance" (14) and that his alleged moral arguments are based on "little more than a fortuitous turn of phrase" and afterthoughts. Ultimately, for Jahn, Adonis is "unresponsive to the passion he stirs in others and is, therefore, as morally reprehensible as Venus, if not more so" (16). In addition to Adonis' feigned morality, the jennet episode for Jahn damns the young huntsman: "The male coquette, like the jennet, ought to come through with his implied promise, otherwise he adds cruelty to his sins" (22). Jahn concludes that Adonis must be convicted for being "the cruelest" (16). Historically, Jahn's essay comes full circle from the criticism of the 1930s and 1940s that viewed the boy as blameless. Jahn's essay was ripe for the decade in which it was written: the 1970s were a time of culpability and accountability (e.g., the Vietnam War; Watergate) for those who cloaked themselves in moral respectability.

Within Jahn's reading lies the desire to explain in some rational fashion Adonis' own complicity in his death. While most critics do not subscribe to Jahn's interpretation, several still have implicated Adonis in his own destruction. As A. Robin Bowers points out: "The failure of Adonis to survive the boar hunt at the end of the poem is seen by Shakespeare to be the proper result of his failure to resist the temptations of Venus in the course of the poem. Toward the end of the poem, Adonis thinks he can return to undertake the hard trials of the boar hunt, but his efforts are doomed to fail" (9). Linking the boar's kiss to Venus', Bowers contends that Adonis falls victim to "unchaste love." So much for an unsullied youth. Asals similarly finds that Adonis is punished for not accepting the Platonic love extended by Venus, a twist of fate in the culture of interpretation. Venus is now the lofty, noble one. Gordon Williams adroitly turns such readings upside down to stress the unparochial nature of the poem:

> Herein lies the crux. Frequently critics looking for consistent meaning in the poem have seen Adonis's death as a species of punishment. On some interpretations the punishment is for a lapse into sensuality. But this ignores the difficulty that there seems to be no such lapse. Hence a neat modification is to see him punished for failing to love. What is to be argued here is that Adonis's death, far from being a punishment, is a consummation devoutly to be wished. ("Coming of Age" 770)

However guilty or guileless Adonis may be, the questions of how and why he rejects Venus are central to interpretations of the poem. As we saw, while some critics bestow a moral guerdon on Adonis to honor his implacable chastity, later readers have been more inclined to fault the priggish hunter. Hamilton shrewdly called attention to previous explanations while at the same time anticipating future ones: Adonis' "dilemma is simply that he is Adonis: If he yields to Venus, he will not grow to himself, but be plucked. If he does not yield, he will be plucked by the enemies of Beauty: by mortality and time, and by the imperfections of Nature which result from jealousy, disease, Death. His greatest enemy is himself" ("*Venus and Adonis*" 13). Castigating Adonis for his narcissism, Kahn and Dubrow squarely lay the blame on the selfishly-guarded young man who wards off Venus as a threat to "his own body" (Kahn); he is branded a hypocrite as well since, as Dubrow (88–90) and Leech (263) note, his "own perspiration belies his attempts to escape the flesh" (Dubrow 89). A self-loving Adonis for Merrix avoids "the reciprocal experience, an involvement diametrically opposed to what Adonis desires. He, therefore, rejects the goddess for an entirely different composite—the Boar" ("Sexual Conflict").

For some readers Adonis' refusal of the goddess originates in his sexual dysfunctionality. It is easy to outline the reasons why Adonis is censured. Sheidley marks his behavior as inadequate while Schiffer, more bluntly, observes that he is a "boy who cannot give satisfaction" in a poem presenting "the comedy of the absent phallus." Bate, as we saw, locates Adonis' sexual reticence in his mythological heritage. Adonis resists Venus for fear of incest; he does not want to "re-enact . . . his mother's incestuous affair" ("Sexual Perversity" 84). Still another sexual explanation is offered by Rebhorn: Adonis does not want to risk "losing his male autonomy" (9); he strives to keep his manhood. According to these critics, then, Adonis has an absent, mythologically-sheathed, or unready penis. In a feminist reading of the poem, Fienberg does not question Adonis' manhood, but she does deplore his misogyny, conveyed through an uncompromising patriarchal (phallic) superiority ("Thematics of Value").

Still other interpreters have avoided grave, moral, or even problematic implications in Adonis' behavior as Venus' reluctant suitor. Rufus Putney, for example, judged the episode of Adonis' remonstrances against an aggressive Venus as a superb example of "sophisticated comedy," liberating Venus from heavy moral judgment and portraying a coy Adonis who purposely "goes against the grain of weighty Petrarchan verse" ("Venus *Agonistes*"). Leech, too, found that a demurring Adonis dismissing a passionate Venus is intentionally funny: "In the region where human and nonhuman animals are at one, [Shakespeare] found the predicament of both Venus and Adonis comic: in the situation presented they make far too much verbal fuss" ("Venus and Her Nun" 263). Honorable, tragic, priggish, comic—Adonis has been labeled many things by the critics seeking hegemony over Shakespeare's huntsman.

Although he is "unseen" and relegated to relatively few lines (614–42; 900–903; 1105–1116), the boar is a major player in the drama of *Venus and Adonis*. According to Merrix, "The boar in Shakespeare's *Venus and Adonis* has long been the *bête noire* for critics, both the most puzzling object in the poem and the most controversial. It has been interpreted realistically, allegorically and mythically" ("*Beste Noire*" 117). For Lever, "The boar that slays Adonis is no common beast like the many wild animals against which he had been warned in Ovid's story. Unique in its blind ferocity, it is presented as the antitype of destruction, unmotivated, brutishly unaware of the death it carries" ("Shakespeare's Narrative Poems" 120). As Williams cautions, though, "we are thus given ample warning against taking the boar too simply" ("Coming of Age" 774). Indissolubly tied to Venus and Adonis, the boar is "the third character in the[ir] unusual triangular situation" (Hatto 361). The boar with bristled hair has raised perplexing questions for readers: What does he represent? What is his background, his pedigree for puzzlement? What is his relationship to Venus and to Adonis? Is he the projection or antithesis of Venus and/or Adonis? That is, does he symbolize Venus for Adonis or is he a more complete version of Adonis or Venus? Over the centuries numerous solutions have been proposed for these and other questions about the boar. Studies concentrating heavily on the boar by Merrix, Hatto, and Sheidley and, more recently, theoretically-inspired readings by Schiffer and Williams are required reading.

Earlier scholarship investigated primarily the traditional functions of boars in myth, literature, and folklore. A typical discussion of the boar in myth is in Joseph Campbell's *Masks of God: Creative Mythology* (123–28). Bate carefully summarizes the thrust of such mythic readings:

> In both Ovid and Shakespeare the story ends with the death of Adonis, described as a pattern which will be repeated perpetually. This sense of inevitable future repetition is what gives the story its mythic, archetypal quality. One tradition of interpretation thus comes to read the story as a vegetation myth: Abraham Fraunce, in a mythography published the year before *Venus and Adonis,* interpreted Adonis as the sun, Venus as the upper hemisphere of the earth, and the boar as winter. (*Shakespeare and Ovid* 58)

With convincing astrological detail, Butler and Fowler (whose work is reprinted in this volume) incorporate these and other mythic resonances into their numerological reading of the poem, surveying "the various explanations as to why the boar should symbolize winter" (131). Arguing that the "poem's solstitial state is interrupted to become the equinox," Butler and Fowler claim the beast is "lust's winter": "the boar has intervened, the equinoctial point is passed, and winter has begun" (132). Critics who object to a reading of *Venus* as a "vegetation myth" point out that "Ovid and Shakespeare do not take their interpretations in this direction; they are not interested in external nature so much as the nature of sexual desire" (Bate 58; Schiffer also makes this point). Source studies (e.g., Baldwin, Bullough) explore the function of the boar in Ovid and Theocritus, comparing and contrasting Shakespeare's presentation of the animal with mythological antecedents. In Ovid the boar is dismissed in a few lines as a ferocious beast "whose crooked teeth are lightning flashes" (*The Metamorphoses,* trans. by Horace Gregory).

But Shakespeare's knowledge of the boar was not confined to classical models. For many readers (e.g., Lee, Price, Rowse) the Calydonian boar was translocated to Shakespeare's English countryside, although Muir contends Shakespeare's description of the beast is "derived from Golding and Brooke . . . and based not merely on observation" ("Comedy or Tragedy" 10). A.T. Hatto's 1946 article masterfully portrays Shakespeare as the "heir and literary executor to the great poets of the Middle Ages" (Thomas of Britain, Gottfried, Boccaccio, Chaucer) in capturing the immense significance of the boar, "a symbol of general validity" (358). Essentially, Hatto argues, boars of the Middle Ages were "a symbol of overbearing masculinity in love and war, with unmistakable and long-standing associations of nobility" (355). Although boars in Shakespeare *(Venus, Richard III, Cymbeline)* were "foul usurpers in their several ways" (360), Hatto maintains that they possessed an "irresistible triumphant hold on the overheated imagination of a defeated and jealous rival" (355) and that in *"Venus and Adonis* the Boar still largely retains his nobility" (359).

Merrix, too, convincingly traces the boar's presence in medieval romances and concludes that the beast symbolizes a "death in life" (*"Beste Noir"* 125), thus leading Adonis into a mysterious and foreboding territory. The boar ties into Adonis' "ego-centricism, a compulsive need for apotheosis; the beast thus represents a force that can be sinful, horrific, excessively chaste or excessively erotic. It is a need to experience life *in extremis,* indeed, to go beyond life to a death that at least for Adonis erotically annihilates experience itself" (127). Also comfortable with polarities, Don Cameron Allen compares the boar hunt with the hunt for love, finding that the former is the "hard hunt" or death while the latter is the "soft hunt." Allen, therefore, disagrees that there is any vestige of nobility in the boar, though he does refer to the beast as "a worthy adversary."

Critics like Hatto and Merrix helpfully relate the boar to other creatures in Shakespeare; "poets of the past knew their wild animals" (Hatto 358). The boar, though, seems to be more treacherous than the lion in *As You Like It*, the bear in *The Winter's Tale*, or the tiger in *Othello*. The boar as a symbol of treacherous sexuality appears in Richard III. *A Midsummer Night's Dream* (2.3), *Cymbeline* (4.2), and *Timon of Athens* (5.1). In *As You Like It*, the young Ganymede/Rosalind is forced to carry a "boar-spear" (1.3.17) for protection against the sexually aggressive beast.

Exactly what the boar represents has energized critical commentary, producing widely divergent interpretations as readers fetishized the beast. Reading the poem allegorically, critics indict the boar as the personification of lust. Hamilton announced that "The Boar signifies concupiscence or (spiritual) Death which results from concupiscence" (*"Venus and Adonis"* 7), adding that "the Boar oppresses all these forces which seek to pluck the flower of Beauty. Accordingly, it functions as a poetic symbol through which Shakespeare explores the mystery of evil" (13). Evans also underscores the boar's symbolic function:

> On the moral level, the boar carried the traditional associations of virility and lust: the image of Venus riding on a boar was a familiar medieval emblem, and in the *Faerie Queene* Lust himself has "Huge great teeth, like to a tusked boar." The death of Adonis was commonly taken as an allegory of lust's destructive power; and Shakespeare's introduction of an overly lustful Venus into the myth of the death-dealing boar invites the reader to expect the conventional moral. ("Introduction" 12–13)

Yet Evans deconstructs this very line of reasoning, arguing: "But the expectation is disappointed: whatever Adonis may be punished for, it is certainly not lust" (13), a point Schiffer reiterates.

Also allegorizing the boar, Cantelupe maintains that the beast represents gluttony, rage, and fury. As we saw, the boar symbolizes death for Allen, and also for Muir. In Price's allegorical/moralistic analysis, Shakespeare's "overwhelmingly predominant" theme is located in the conflict between Adonis and the boar as "the destruction of something exquisite by what is outrageously vile"; consequently, the boar represents "the complete irrationality of evil" (277). For Lever, Adonis through death is "redeemed from time associated with the boar" ("Second Chance" 86), a creature that is a "mindless nemesis at the core of life" (84).

Many critics situate the encounter between Adonis and the boar on a sexual playing field. Most notably, Williams argues that "The boar means not only death and lust, but the dialectal relationship of these things." The boar's murder of Adonis, therefore, must be seen as "several ravishments" (775), a "consummation devoutly to be wished" (770). According to Smith, the boar described with a mingling of seminal foam and blood rapes the maiden Adonis, "a killing represented as a kiss," the common Elizabethan euphemism for copulation. Williams continues: "This collocation of sex and death is appropriate. . . . It permits us to retain the notion of Adonis being killed by the boar while superimposing a view of a violent sexual awakening" (775). Adonis' spear cannot penetrate the boar's hide, but the boar's "tushes" rip into the young man's groin.

Readers have further explained the boar's function(s) from a psychoanalytical perspective. Webster believed that "the boar obviously as totem animal is the primal father who seeks the life but becomes in time satisfied with the circumcision of the son, a symbolic pars pro toto. Here is the archetypal, primal father with whom Shakespeare is to be so much concerned . . ." (300). In her much more influential article, reprinted in this collection, Coppélia Kahn maintained that the boar is a vital participant in Adonis' narcissistic destruction. "The boar . . . embodies all that is inimical to life, beauty, and love. Adonis scornfully rejects the easier, more overtly pleasurable and normal course for the fatal one" (369). While Sheidley also observes that the boar is "the destructive agent whose entrance into the poem will resolve the frustrating stalemate between Venus and Adonis," he claims that Shakespeare "drew the boar closely into the thematic architecture of the poem, not only by the associative power of contiguity, but also by making him the locus of the missing phallic impulse" (10). For Sheidley, the boar possesses what Adonis lacks; "the dislocation of phallic potency predicates the frustration of Venus and brings about the destruction of Adonis. Properly placed, in Adonis, if that were possible, it might have rendered all well" (11).

Venus herself has been identified with the boar, usually more to her discredit than to his. Several critics argue that the boar is a projection of Venus' own amorous furor directed at Adonis. Her lovemaking for some readers is as aggressive, dangerous, and fatal as the boar's charge at Adonis' loins. Critics in the 1940s usually approached the association of the love goddess and prickly boar matter-of-factly, even pejoratively. Price, for example, equated the two as killers. Yet protesting Price's damning equation, Huntington Brown came to Venus' defense: "If it had been her suggestion that Adonis should hunt the boar—supposing her the vengeful woman scorned—the boar would indeed illustrate her character; but, as we know, the whole burden of a hundred lines of her best eloquence is the plea that he shun the boar and chase the timid hare instead" (79). More moderately, Sheidley justified the presence of porcine traits in the goddess:

> Sexual love is not composed entirely of soft sweetness and warmth, but involves an untender element, an element even, as with human nature itself, of the bestial. Venus, Love herself, becomes through Shakespeare's imagery partly a gluttonous vulture of a bird of prey, fit mate for a suitably boarlike lover, but in Adonis's eyes an enemy that would constrain, defile, and devour him. (12)

In 1973, Asals recognized that Venus and the boar were joined in their predatory, amorous rites, yet the goddess was ultimately "distinguished" from the boar. While the boar was blind to beauty and "restricted to the level of lust," Venus represented Love as a type of Death. "By opposing herself to the boar, by contrasting her ability to see with the sightedness of the boar, she purges from herself the nature of the boar" ("Venus . . . Education" 46). According to Schiffer as well, readers should distinguish the boar from Venus on other grounds: however much of the beast's temperament they find in her, "the boar is Venus's masculine rival, perhaps, but not her double."

Venus' view of the boar has also sparked controversy. Several critics point to her lament over Adonis' death as an unequivocal sign of the goddess' contempt for this "foul, grim, and urchin-snouted boar" who "digs sepulchres." David Beauregard, however, detects a forgiving note in the goddess' lament: "Instead of retaliating against the boar, she imagines that it has acted out of ignorance. . . . Consequently, Venus' anger at the boar is lessened and irrationally directed at future lovers" (93). Venus' most controversial remarks about the boar are found in lines 1117–18, her description of his fatal kiss: "Had I been tooth'd like him, I must confess, / With kissing him I should have killed him first." While some readers detect in these lines Venus' admission that she and the boar act in concord, Keach judiciously rebuts such claims:

> One must hesitate in interpreting the boar's deadly kiss as the ironic literal fulfillment of the destructiveness of Venus's lust. What the reader gets is Venus's view of Adonis's death. . . . Has Venus imposed her sexually-oriented vision of experience upon a more general force of unthinking evil and destruction? Perhaps she has, but the traditional symbolism of the boar lends support to her vision. (*Elizabethan Erotic Narratives* 80–81)

Adonis' view of the boar also links the beast to Venus for readers. According to Kahn, for example, Adonis "projects his anxiety about being devoured by Venus onto the boar, and attempts to destroy the boar so that Venus will not destroy him. . . . He takes the boar as his object because, like her, it is blindly destructive in an oral way and thus most dangerous and most real to him" (368–69). As they have with Venus and her Adonis, critics have repeatedly projected their sexual expectations on the boar.

The Narrator and His (Dis)guises

The overall function and influence of the narrator are crucial to readership. What the narrator selects to tell or show, what he leaves unsaid or unshown, or what he himself might have experienced in the telling and showing (or not doing so) are among the problematic elements affecting a reader's reception of *Venus and Adonis*. For a good many centuries readers unthinkingly assumed that Shakespeare was the narrator of *Venus and Adonis*. Certainly Coleridge identified Shakespeare as the narrator and, accordingly, viewed *Venus* as a personal effort, thus setting the critical pace for a long time. Yet when critics invented formalism and a corresponding language for narrative practice, Shakespeare as the narrator went out of favor. In his place, though, came polysemous narrators in their various (dis)guises.

Depending on a critic's point of view, the reader is asked to endorse, indemnify, disregard, or repudiate the narrator. Reactions to the narrator vary widely from granting him great powers to suspecting his motives to undermining his attempts to dismissing him as naive. Whatever opinion of the narrator a critic holds, there lurks the persistent issue of whether a reader should become an active, even willing accomplice in interpreting the action or must succumb as simple auditor/witness to the narrator's point(s) of view. The narrator's powers and sincerity are, therefore, essential issues for critical interrogation and perhaps necessary to (re)solving any reader dilemma. Ultimately for recent critics, the crucial issue the narrator raises for readers involves accepting or rejecting the indeterminacy of many of his views.

According to Rebhorn, the narrator benignly controls our response to *Venus and Adonis*: "The narrator deliberately shapes the reader's responses to emphasize the ambiguity, and the status of *Venus and Adonis* as a tragi-comedy. . . ." After Adonis decides to hunt the boar, "the narrator begins to shift his and the reader's sympathies markedly toward Venus" even though before she was presented as "predatory and suffocating." In exhorting Adonis to hunt safer game, "the narrator, by means of a series of effective images, underscores the pathos of her inability to save the life of the infant she loves" (7). For Rebhorn, then, the narrator is a reliable source of information because he records what happens honestly. Klause similarly advocates the narrator's effectiveness in reclaiming sympathy for Venus and Adonis. Insisting that the narrator is "not an indifferent spectator" (365), Klause finds that he "rarely comes to the fore to demand sympathy for Venus and Adonis; but his reticence often has the effect of allowing the sufferings of his characters to plead for them" (367).

Keach, on the other hand, denies the narrator an enlightened purpose or even an identity: "All the narrator's exclamations and apostrophes are directed towards the event or situation he is describing. Shakespeare's narrator has no persona. . . . It is partly the neutrality and transparency of Shakespeare's narrator that give the style of *Venus and Adonis* its special effectiveness . . ." (72). Protesting the narrator's neutrality, Desmet, for example, insists that "For the first half of the poem he competes with her directly, undermining Venus's arguments to Adonis by parodying them" (138). And while "Venus and the narrator are engaged in a battle of wits" (140), the goddess is at the end "subjected to the narrator in this view, who exiles her to Paphos to play the lamenting lover" (144). The narrator, according to this reading, has fallen considerably from Rebhorn's benevolent view of him.

Expressing yet another view of the narrator, Evans judges him as narcissistic as Adonis, whose vain protestations he relates:

> The narrator draws attention both to the scene and to the skill of his own verbal picture; he comments with kindly detachment on the characters—"poor fool," "good queen"—and he presents his whole account of them as a narrative artifact in conceited language which continually directs attention to the art of the story-teller. . . . The reader, in consequence, is kept at a distance from the action, made to observe rather than to participate. ("Introduction" 10–11)

According to Evans, then, readers are disempowered because the narrator disengages them from feeling, distancing events from their emotional investment.

Bevington refuses to judge the narrator as being for or against the couple, collectively or as individuals. Emphasizing the purposeful ambivalence of the poem and its characters, Bevington claims: "Like Ovid's usual persona, the speaker . . . is both intrigued and amused by love, compelled to heed its power and yet aware of its absurdities. The result is a characteristic Ovidian blend of irony and pathos" ("Introduction" 14).

For Huntington Brown, to cite still another critical view, the narrator is least effectual in influencing the reader's reactions. Characterizing the narrator as a quixotic dilettante lacking the skill to make value judgments, Brown sees him as

> an ideal chorus. At his side we receive through him as conductor the current of enchantment that the ancient myth discharges into every fibre of his being. He leads us on a swift chase, as if barely able to keep pace with his own story . . . nowhere does he undertake to summarize a theme or point out a moral, or that the comments he makes from time to time that express or imply moral judgment of either Venus or Adonis (as distinguished from judgments made by these persons) are impulsive, more like reflexes than considered opinions? So far from expressing a judicious point of view, they show him . . . wholly absorbed in the passing moment. He gives no indication of having decided what to make of the whole. (*"Venus and Adonis"* 83)

The narrator's being is inextricably caught up with the key issue of who has the authority to speak in the poem. As the critical discourse on the narrative voice demonstrates, such authority is not readily apparent or easily recovered.

VENUS AND ADONIS AS PLAY

Inevitably, *Venus and Adonis* has been compared to the plays, but not without punctilious debate over the poem's own status as drama. Earlier critics generally regarded *Venus and Adonis* as soberly static; J.S. Hart, for example, claimed: "The poem is not marked by stirring action, but by a series of minutely finished pictures" (129). Referring to *Venus and Adonis* and *The Rape of Lucrece* as "a couple of ice-houses," William Hazlitt unfavorably compared Shakespeare's undramatic poems to the plays: "In a word, we do not like Shakespeare's poems, because we like his plays: the one, in all their excellencies, are just the reverse of the other" (214). In 1934, George Rylands concluded that "there is no drama and no characterization" in *Venus and Adonis*. More recently, Lever insisted: "But the poem is, in fact, not a comedy or a tragedy. It is not a drama. It is occupied with narrating a myth, and characteristically the aim is to maintain a certain detachment or 'distancing' of sympathetic response" ("Second Chance" 81), yet Lever identified numerous, salient parallels between the plays and *Venus*.

Yet, beyond doubt, *Venus and Adonis* has much to recommend it as drama. The poem offers a classic struggle (several, in fact) between Venus and Adonis, Venus and Mars, Venus and herself, Venus and the Narrator,

Venus and the boar, Venus and the reader, Adonis and the boar, etc. As Coleridge recognized, Shakespeare's *Venus and Adonis* "seem[s] at once the characters themselves, and the whole representation of those characters by the most consummate actors. You seem to be told nothing, but to see and hear every thing" (*Biographia Literaria* I:14). The characters are as memorable as any in the canon—Venus, the goddess of love; Adonis, the putative cynosure of beauty; the rose-chained Mars; the sepulcher-digging boar; and the Narrator in his various poses. Each of these *dramatis personae* is embroiled in an unfolding plot, with a classical *hamartia, peripeteia,* and *anagnorisis.* According to James Lake, *Venus and Adonis* is in fact a model Aristotelian tragedy containing all these strategic elements ("Shakespeare's Venus"). Several years before Lake, Rufus Putney cogently maintained: "It requires only a little more attention than readers accord the poem to see that Shakespeare conceived it like a play in a series of dramatic episodes, which may conveniently if not accurately be compared to acts." Putney then divided the lines of the poem as if it were a play. "The first forty-two lines . . . perform the expository functions of the first act . . . Venus's courtship makes up the bulk of the narrative and provides the equivalent to acts two and three . . . her soliloquies . . . may be equated with the fourth act; her discovery of Adonis's body and final lament, with the fifth" ("Comedy" 58). One of the poem's earliest readers, William Reynolds in the seventeenth century even saw *Venus and Adonis* as "a kind of stage-play dealing with his own life" (Duncan-Jones 489).

Many critics have tried to identify the exact kind of drama *Venus and Adonis* represents. In his Arden edition of the *Poems,* F.T. Prince claimed for *Venus* what he found in the comedies: "There is an indulgent mood of Shakespeare's comedies, with their delight in human energies and emotions, their keen savour of everyday life mixed with abundant poetry, and their undertones of deep seriousness" (xxxii). Similarly, Hamilton observed: "Venus presides as the goddess of the romantic comedies, and her love for Adonis makes her the archetype of the romantic heroines who yearn to submit to their lovers" (*The Early Shakespeare* 145). Cantelupe labeled the poem "a tragicomedy of love" (151); and speaking of Venus' conquest of Mars, he added: "Shakespeare renders the scene as a magnificent Medieval pageant" (143).

Whether the poem is comic, tragic, epic, bawdy, romantic, or a blend of "comedy and pathos" (Rebhorn 8), critics have searched for satisfying explanations for its overall dramatic effect. A. Robin Bowers maintained that "*Venus and Adonis* is completely consistent with Shakespeare's dramatic works, where tragedies manifest the devastating triumphs of the senses and the flesh, while the comedies demonstrate the successful bridling of the sensual appetites for the preservation of life and society; and they are in keeping with the dramatic milieu from Robert Wilson to Lyly . . ."(18). Muir inquired, in his article of the same title, if *Venus and Adonis* is "Comedy or Tragedy?" while Doebler avoided the strict limitations of such a dichotomy, asserting instead that "*Venus and Adonis* is a constantly shifting drama of the mind" ("Many Faces" 37).

VENUS AND ADONIS IN PRODUCTION

However it might be classified as drama, ample practical evidence exists that *Venus and Adonis* is eminently stageworthy. The poem has been adapted successfully, if not frequently, for the stage and for opera. The myth that captivated Shakespeare also won the hearts of other dramatists and composers. A brief survey shows how popular these adaptations have been.

Throughout the seventeenth and eighteenth centuries adaptations of *Venus and Adonis* were frequent. In 1656, Samuel Holland wrote a play entitled *Venus and Adonis* included in his *Wit and Fancy in a Maze.* Sometime between December 1680 and August 1687, John Blow's masque of *Venus and Adonis,* a vocal score with piano accompaniment, was performed in London. In 1715, Colley Cibber's *Venus and Adonis, a Masque: As It Is Presented at Theatre-Royal* was published in London and printed for B. Lintott. A notorious Shakespearean adapter and actor, Colley Cibber is best remembered for Pope's savage attack on him in Book II of *The Dunciad.* Yet the songs and the symphonies for Cibber's masque of *Venus and Adonis* were artfully done by Dr. John Christopher Pepusch (1667–1752), a highly respected composer who also printed his scores separately the year following the publication of Cibber's script. And around 1790 composer Michele Mortellari (1750?–1807) gathered and published twelve pieces of music selected from J. Giannini's drama *Venus and Adonis.*

Two nineteenth-century adaptations deserve notice as well. James Robinson Planche and Charles Dance wrote the libretto for a highly diverse one-act musical version of the myth of Venus and Adonis entitled *The Paphian Bower, or Venus and Adonis: A Classical, Mythological, Astronomical, and Tragicomical Burlesque Burletta in One Act.* Published in London in the 1850s, Planche and Dance's opus would, it appears, content any critic who had Polonius' penchant for classification. Certainly the title of this burletta anticipated many twentieth-century critical approaches to Shakespeare's poem. In 1864, Sir Francis Cowley Burnard published an intriguingly entitled musical review, with libretto and airs to be sung—*Venus and Adonis, or The Two Rivals and the Small Boar: Being a Full, True, and*

Particular Account, Adapted to the Requirements of the Present Age, of an Ancient Mythological Piece of Scandal. Presenting Venus and Adonis as rivals and diminishing the size of the boar doubtless qualified tradition, but labeling the story *"A Mythological Piece of Scandal"* was very much in keeping with the naughty reputation the story had acquired down through the centuries.

All these adaptations—masques, plays, burlettas—were, like Shakespeare's poem, responding to classical sources. But even more important for a study of *Venus and Adonis,* several dramatic and operatic versions of the famed myth were taken, or adapted, directly from Shakespeare's poem, which established its own mythology in performance. I now turn to these Shakespearean adaptations, which date primarily from the 1980s and 1990s.

Irene Worth, one of "classical theatre's foremost actresses" (*"Venus . . .* July 12") gave a spirited one-woman reading of *Venus and Adonis* (only two performances, alas) on July 12 and 20, 1983, at the Stratford Shakespeare Festival in Ontario. Desmond Heeley designed the sets, Steven Hawkins arranged the lighting, and Patricia Henderson oversaw stage management. Delivered as part of the Festival's "Letters of Love and Affection" Series, Worth's 35–minute performance was given in the 500–seat Third Stage, "with only a solitary rug covering the wood floor" showing that "the Bard's words coupled with Worth's expert expression of them are more than enough decoration for any stage" (Gallagher). According to Lynda Weston, "The intimacy of the Third Stage setting does more to successfully match the inherent intimacy of most of the letters [series] than did the Avon Theatre" ("Intimate Third Stage"). Worth was elegantly clad in a golden gown, suggesting Venus' radiance.

Some reviewers found the performance captivating (Gallagher); "a virtuoso performance" (Goodwin). Admitting that *Venus and Adonis* was a difficult choice, Goodwin stressed that "without changing the picture, Worth manages to present them as two very human characters in spite of their God-like status". Gallagher exclaimed that Shakespeare's "word pictures came again to vivid life in the emotion-arousing reading".

Yet Worth's rendition was judged as abbreviated as the script from which she based her reading. Weston found that the performance "brought a stunned silence from the audience and then the question 'Is that it,'" referring to Worth's heavily truncated text of the poem. Echoing the image of Venus as eagle, Weston concluded that "Miss Worth swooped and dived her way through the poem ending on a particularly melodramatic note and gesture."

In June 1984, a production of Shakespeare's *Venus and Adonis* was done at the La Rochelle Festival, a French premiere. Michel le Doeuff translated Shakespeare's poem into French for director Luis Menasé. Attendant problems for translator and director were, first off, Shakespeare's language and, second, the violence of feminine desire, problematized in Venus' long erotic monologues to convince Adonis to love. "Faithful to the source of the *Venus and Adonis* myth, Menasé returned to the Near Eastern inspiration for the poem." Thus Adonis became "a Phoenician deity, and the drama was played in Arabia" (Ghrenassia 131), an appropriate setting for Shakespeare's exotic romance. In this production Adonis does not appear on stage; the "luminous object of desire is hidden from our sight" (Ghrenassia 132), perhaps encoding a Lacanian influence—the *objet a,* as Catherine Belsey reminds us—for director, cast, and audience as well. Menasé instead created two Venuses (Nicole Bourlier-Derlon and Dido Likoudis), one to live out the passion Adonis shuns and the other to narrate it. These two Venuses represented the pagan deity and the vulnerable woman wounded in love. "Feminine desire thus found both erotic refinement and cruel disappointment" (Ghrenassia 132). Menasé's *Venus and Adonis* was played on a bare stage containing only two trunks, or "magical chests." Situating Shakespeare's poem on the soil of the original myth, one of the most famous Elizabethan poems became a Gallic descant on erotic, fatal love.

In the mid- to late 1980s, Bardy Thomas valiantly promoted productions of *Venus and Adonis* in London. She directed and adapted the poem twice for the stage. The first was a private performance as a studio exercise at the National Theatre on March 21, 1986. Thomas then directed the adapted poem at the Almeida Theatre in the winter of 1988. The producing company, Art Depot, claimed that Thomas' adaptation was "a Shakespearean world premiere" (Wardle), a truthful enough statement given the fact that even though Benjamin Stewart (see below) had performed the poem several years earlier in California, his was a solo production, while Thomas employed seven actors to stage her 1988 *Venus.* She won praise for "leaving the structure and language [of *Venus*] fairly intact" (Caplan), if not for her overall interpretation.

To highlight the dramatic elements of Shakespeare's poem, Thomas created not one but three Venuses, and substituted "a Warwickshire pastoral for an Ovidian fable" (Wardle). In the 1988 production, Julia Ford, Catherine Russell, and Julia Swift played the tripartite goddess; Jerome Flynn was the solitary Adonis. The three Venuses, costumed like rustic thrashing maids and "conspicuously in heat," assaulted a sullen Adonis in "a Mummerset orchard" (Hilley). As Caplan observed, "They have a wonderful romp when the women pin him down and get on top, but that's about as far as it goes." Flynn doubled as the young hunter and as Adonis' steed with, ironically enough, "precisely the brute sensuality the lady Mummersetians crave" (Hilley). But this Adonis was not moved, which led Wardle to protest that "any stud would quail." However daring and innovative Thomas' *Venus* was, the critics disapproved of her adaptation on the grounds that it was little more than "fumbled gymnastics" or rustic clowning. Ultimately, the reviewers resisted dramatization of the poem, insisting, as Caplan did, that "No amount of running up or down or panting will make this a play—the form remains obdurately poetic."

From January 15 through February 4, 1990, Anthony Naylor directed his adaptation of Shakespeare's poem at the Cubiculo Theatre in New York.

In the summer (July) of 1991, Ted Davey directed an abbreviated (about 850 lines) adaptation of *Venus and Adonis* for Dallas' Undermain Theatre, a spirited production sponsored by the Shakespeare Festival of Dallas. In his witty review for *The Dallas Times Herald,* Porter Anderson exclaimed, "Oh, yes, Oh, literature, Oh, who would have thought it was Shakespeare getting way down with his bad self . . .", suggesting the mood of the production.

Davey was keenly aware of the problems of transforming Shakespeare's long, lusty poem into a "stage piece" for a contemporary (1990s) audience. The real problem the Undermain faced, Davey claimed, was "how to interpret grand passion to a group of couch potatoes," while avoiding charges of presenting just a "'filthy play' from the perspective of our time" (quoted in Anderson). Davey encouragingly believed that the poem-become-drama offered "themes of voyeurism, narcissism, nobility, naivete, the death of innocence, virginity"—all of which his Dallas audience could understand. There is no doubt Davey succeeded in contemporizing *Venus and Adonis.* As Julie Dam's review, included in this volume, picturesquely put it, "This *Venus and Adonis* is part epic tragedy, part bawdy comedy, and part Obsession commercial."

As Bardy Thomas had done five years earlier, Davey gave his audience three Venuses—"deeply feeling Earth Venus . . . Water Venus oozing with sexuality; and . . . playful and vibrant Fire Venus" (Dam)—one more than at the La Rochelle Festival. The three Venuses were Katherine Owens, Sarah Rankin, and Erin Ryan. For Adonis, director Davey chose Black actor Nathan Hinton. As interpreted by Hinton, the Undermain's Adonis was more a "victim of emotional harrassment" (Dam), predating by only a few years Dr. Wortis' editorial. Davey innovatively blended and thus transformed the Narrator into Mars (played by Bruce DuBose), adding a new speaking character to the script. Davey, like Bardy Thomas, had faith in the dramatic flexibility of Shakespeare's poem. I am grateful to the Undermain Theatre for the photos from their production of *Venus and Adonis* that appear in this collection.

In October of 1992, a dramatic adaptation of Shakespeare's poem opened at Glasgow's Citizens Theatre along with a production of Tennessee Williams' *Sweet Bird of Youth,* "the closest modern equivalent" in spirit about the misfortunes of a fallen "movie star, a screen goddess" (Kingston 33). Matthew Radford played Chance Wayne and Adonis while Stobban Stanley, who took the part of Venus, was "power-dressed and jetting in from Olympus." Critic Kingston observed "Salted, with almost rough-house comic routine . . . the production uses masks and silhouettes to suggest a nightmare beast of a death . . ." (33).

In 1993, Opera Omaha produced "The World Premiere" of Hugh Weisgall's *The Gardens of Adonis,* the libretto for which, done by John Olon Schrymgeous, was "adapted gently" from Shakespeare's *Venus and Adonis* and Andre Obey's play (Blumenfeld 156). Keith Warner, who was responsible for the staging, gave audiences a vividly contemporary Venus whose "gardens [were] surrounded by her swimming pool" in a "neoclassic pastorale amusingly updated with Art Deco trimmings and peppered with anachronisms" (Blumenfeld 156). Weisgall's chamber opera included a prologue and two acts, yet *Gardens of Adonis* "differs radically in style and substance from its ultimate model 'Venus and Adonis'" (Blumenfeld 165). New characters are included: Adonis' hunting partner Martial, Death dressed as a foreign princess. Moreover, Weisgall and Olon "elaborated their version with a secondary action involving an ancient dame and a rickety old gardener, who are amusingly set aflame by a dart from Cupid's box" (Blumenfeld 165). Reviewer Jeffrey C. Smith observed: "All was well sung— Melanie Helton (Venus)—was a standout. John Garison (Adonis) was convincingly boyish, Eric McCluskey (Martial) the perfect pal, Jayne West (Zoe) in *high* heels and *short* skirt, musical and funny, and Kristine Jepsen (Death) ominous" (25).

From February 14 to 18, 1994, Nick Philippou directed Carmelle McAree, Ona McCracken, and Susan Swanton in the Actors Touring Company production, with the Hairy Marys at Jacksons Lane, Highgate, London. A stirring production, Philippou's *Venus* was heightened by a haunting original score by Pinkie McClure.

No other actor has performed *Venus and Adonis* more than Benjamin Stewart, who confesses that "It's my mission to do it." Although Stewart admired Irene Worth's performance, he disagreed with offering an audience an abbreviated version of Shakespeare's poem. He adapted and performed the poem in 1984 at the Mark Taper Forum's Literary Caberet in Los Angeles; in 1988 at the Gem Theatre in Garden Grove for the Grove Shakespeare Festival in Orange County, California; and in June 1995 at the Waltman Theatre at Chapman University for Shakespeare Orange County. Stewart's *Venus and Adonis,* essentially uncut, mesmerized audiences for an hour and a half. Stewart describes his achievement playing the one-performer show in a lively essay commissioned for this collection, "Strange Bedfellows— Venus, Adonis, and Me." Playing all parts—Venus, Adonis, the Narrator—Stewart told one reporter, however, "I do not try to become Venus or Adonis . . . I try to become the poem" (Hodgins, "All"). Still, Stewart maintains: "I think the poem is a man's piece. It has a masculine sensibility about it that crosses over to the feminine and not the other way around" (Koehler, *Los Angeles Times,* 1988). Stewart is said to look more like "a puckish version of Charles Laughton, with jowls that made him seem a cherub rather than a bulldog" (Herman, "People Need").

Over the years, reviewers have applauded Stewart's performances. At his 1995 *Venus and Adonis* for Shakespeare Orange County, the *Los Angeles Times* reviewer enthusiastically noted: "Stewart is such a charismatic performer and his solo presentation so captivating that he easily passes for both the sexually aroused Venus in all her lasciviousness and the virginally disdainful Adonis in all his pristine chastity" (Herman "Charisma").

Venus in production sheds light on the entire critical response to the poem by taking us full circle. Poetic readings of *Venus* turn dramatic for many critics, while dramatic performances turn back to the work's poetic stubbornness. Either way it is (per)formed in the critical eye, *Venus and Adonis* defies easy categorization, as Kenneth Muir wisely observed in the 1960s. Let him have the last word.

WORKS CITED

Akrigg, G.P.V. *Shakespeare and the Earl of Southhampton.* Cambridge: Harvard UP, 1968.

Allen, Don Cameron. "On *Venus and Adonis.*" *Elizabethan and Jacobean Studies Presented to Frank Percy Wilson.* Oxford: Clarendon P, 1959. 100–11.

Anderson, Porter. "Revising Your Will." *Dallas Times Herald,* July 7 1991: G1, G6.

Asals, Heather. "*Venus and Adonis:* The Education of a Goddess." *Studies in English Literature, 1500–1900* 13 (Winter 1973): 31–51.

Baldwin, T.W. *On the Literary Genetics of Shakespeare's Poems and Sonnets.* Urbana: U of Illinois P, 1950. 1–93.

Barkan, Leonard. *The Gods Made Flesh: Metamorphosis and the Pursuit of Paganism.* New Haven and London: Yale UP, 1986.

Barnfield, Richard. "A Remembrance of Some English Poets." *Poems: 1594–1598.* Ed. Edward Arber. London: The English Scholar's Library, 1882. 119–20.

Bate, Jonathan. "Sexual Perversity in *Venus and Adonis.*" *Yearbook of English Studies* 23 (1993): 80–92.

————. *Shakespeare and Ovid.* Oxford: Clarendon P, 1993. 48–67.

Bauer, Robert J. "Rhetoric and Picture in *Venus and Adonis*." *Explorations in Renaissance Culture* 1 (1974): 41–56.

Baumlin, Tita French. "The Birth of the Bard: *Venus and Adonis* and Poetic Apotheosis." *Papers on Language and Literature* 26 (Spring 1990): 191–211.

Beauregard, David N. "*Venus and Adonis*: Shakespeare's Representation of the Passions." *Shakespeare Studies* 8 (1975): 83–98.

Belsey, Catherine. "Love as Trompe-l'oeil: Taxonomies of Desire in *Venus and Adonis*." *Shakespeare Quarterly* 46 (Fall 1995): 257–76; rpt. in *Venus and Adonis: Critical Essays.* Ed. Philip C. Kolin. New York: Garland, 1997. 261–85.

Berry, J. Wilkes. "Loss of Adonis and Light in *Venus and Adonis*." *Discourse* 12 (1969): 72–76.

Bevington, David. "Introduction" to *Venus and Adonis: Poems.* Toronto: Bantam, 1988.

Blumenfeld, Harold. "Hugo Weisgall's 66th Birthday and the *New Garden of Adonis*." *Perspectives of New Music* 16 (1978): 156–66.

Bonjour, Adrien. "From Shakespeare's Venus to Cleopatra's Cupids." *Shakespeare Survey* 15 (1962): 73–80.

Bowers, A. Robin. "'Hard Amours' and 'Delicate Amours' in Shakespeare's *Venus and Adonis*." *Shakespeare Studies* 12 (1979): 1–23.

Bowers, R.H. "Anagnorisis, or the Shock of Recognition, in Shakespeare's *Venus and Adonis*." *Renaissance Papers 1962* (1962): 3–8.

Boyar, Billy T. "Keats's 'Isabella': Shakespeare's *Venus and Adonis* and the Venus-Adonis Myth." *Keats and Shelley Journal* 21–22 (1972–73): 160–69.

Bradbrook, Muriel C. "Beasts and Gods: *Greene's Groatsworth of Witte* and the Social Purpose of *Venus and Adonis*." *Shakespeare Survey* 15 (1962): 62–72.

Brown, Huntington. "*Venus and Adonis*: The Action, the Narrator, and the Critics." *Michigan Academician* 2 (Fall 1969): 73–87.

Bullough, Geoffrey. *Narrative and Dramatic Sources of Shakespeare.* Vol. 1, *Early Comedies, Poems, "Romeo and Juliet."* London: Routledge and Kegan Paul, 1957. 161–78.

Burgess, Anthony. *Nothing Like the Sun: A Story of Shakespeare's Love-life.* New York: Norton, 1964.

————. *Shakespeare.* New York: Knopf, 1970.

Burke, Kenneth. *A Rhetoric of Motives.* Berkeley and Los Angeles: U of California P, 1969.

Burton, Robert. *The Anatomy of Melancholy.* Ed. Floyd Dell and Paul Jordan-Smith. New York: Tudor Publishing Company, 1955.

Bush, Douglas. *Mythology and the Renaissance Tradition in English Poetry.* Minneapolis: U of Minnesota P, 1932; rev. ed. New York: Norton, 1963. 137–48; rpt. in *Venus and Adonis: Critical Essays.* Ed. Philip C. Kolin. New York: Garland, 1997. 91–102.

Butler, Christopher, and Alaster Fowler. "Time-Beguiling Sport: Number Symbolism in Shakespeare's *Venus and Adonis*." *Shakespeare 1554–1964: A Collection of Modern Essays by Various Hands.* Ed. Edward A Bloom. Providence: Brown UP, 1964. 124–33; rpt. in *Venus and Adonis: Critical Essays.* Ed. Philip C. Kolin. New York: Garland, 1997. 157–69.

Butler, Samuel. "The 'Enfant Terrible' of Literature." *The Note-Books of Samuel Butler.* Vol. 20 of *The Works of Samuel Butler.* London, 1926; rpt. New York: AMS, 1968.

Campbell, Joseph. *Masks of God: Creative Mythology.* New York: Penguin, 1976.

Cantelupe, Eugene B. "An Iconographical Interpretation of *Venus and Adonis*, Shakespeare's Ovidian Comedy." *Shakespeare Quarterly* 14 (Spring 1963): 141–51.

Caplan, Betty. "Almeida: *Venus* and *Lucrece*." *The Guardian,* Jan. 29 1988: 21; rpt.

in *Venus and Adonis: Critical Essays.* Ed. Philip C. Kolin. New York: Garland, 1997. 289.

Coleridge, Samuel Taylor. *Biographia Literaria.* London, 1817.

Cousins, A.D. "Venus Reconsidered: The Goddess of Love in *Venus and Adonis.*" *Studia Neophilologica* 66 (1994): 197–207.

Daigle, Lennet. "*Venus and Adonis:* Some Traditional Contexts." *Shakespeare Studies* 13 (1980): 31–46.

Dam, Julie. "Undermain's 'Venus' Shines Brightly." *The Dallas Morning News,* July 5 1991: 4C; rpt. in *Venus and Adonis: Critical Essays.* Ed. Philip C. Kolin. New York: Garland, 1997. 291–93.

Desmet, Christy. *Reading Shakespeare's Characters: Rhetoric, Ethics, and Identity.* Amherst: U of Massachusetts P, 1992.

Dickey, Franklin M. *"Not Wisely but Too Well": Shakespeare's Love Tragedies.* San Marino, CA: Huntington Library, 1957.

Doebler, John. "The Many Faces of Love: Shakespeare's *Venus and Adonis.*" *Shakespeare Studies* 16 (1983): 33–43.

Dowden, Edward. *Shakespere: A Critical Study of His Mind and Art.* London: Henry S. King, 1875.

Dubrow, Heather. *Captive Victors: Shakespeare's Narrative Poems and Sonnets.* Ithaca: Cornell UP, 1987.

Duncan-Jones, Katherine. "Much Ado with Red and White: The Earliest Readers of Shakespeare's *Venus and Adonis.*" *Review of English Studies* 44 (Nov. 1993): 479–501.

———. "*Venus* and *Lucrece.*" *Times Literary Supplement,* May 11 1988: 136.

Dundas, Judith. "Shakespeare's Imagery: Emblem and the Imitation of Nature." *Shakespeare Studies* 16 (1983): 45–56.

———. "Wat the Hare, or Shakesperean Decorum." *Shakespeare Studies* 19 (1987): 1–15.

Erickson, Peter. "Refracted Images of Queen Elizabeth in *Venus and Adonis* and *The Rape of Lucrece.*" *Rewriting Shakespeare, Rewriting Ourselves.* Berkeley: U of California P, 1991. 31–56.

Evans, Maurice. "Introduction: *Venus and Adonis.*" *William Shakespeare: The Narrative Poems.* New York: Penguin, 1989.

Fiedler, Leslie. "Some Contexts of Shakespeare's Sonnets." *The Riddles of Shakespeare's Sonnets.* New York: Basic Books, 1962. 67–73.

Fienberg, Nona. "Thematics of Value in *Venus and Adonis.*" *Criticism* 31 (Winter 1989): 21–32; rpt. in *Venus and Adonis: Critical Essays.* Ed. Philip C. Kolin. New York: Garland, 1997. 247–58.

Froes, João. "Shakespeare's Venus and the Venus of Classical Mythology." *Venus and Adonis: Critical Essays.* Ed. Philip C. Kolin. New York: Garland, 1997. 301–47.

Gallagher, Noel. "Worth's Recitation Captivating but Too Brief." *Free Paper Press* [London, Ontario], July 13, 1983.

Gent, Lucy. "*Venus and Adonis:* The Triumph of Rhetoric." *Modern Language Review* 69 (October 1974): 721–29.

Ghrenassia, Patrick. "Review of Luis Menasé's *Venus and Adonis.*" *Cahiers élizabethains* 26 (Oct. 1984): 131–32.

Goldman, Michael. *Shakespeare and the Energies of Drama.* Princeton: Princeton UP, 1972.

Goodwin, Carol. "Irene Worth Brings a Love Poem to Life." *Kitchener Waterloo (Ontario) Record,* July 13, 1983.

Griffin, Robert J. "'These Contraries Such Unity Do Hold': Patterned Imagery in Shakespeare's Narrative Poems." *Studies in English Literature, 1500–1900* 4 (1964): 43–55.

Halpern, Richard. "'Pining Their Maws': Female Readers and the Erotic Ontology of the Text in Shakespeare's *Venus and Adonis.*" *Venus and Adonis: Critical Es-*

says. Ed. Philip C. Kolin. New York: Garland, 1997. 377–88.

Hamilton, A.C. *The Early Shakespeare*. San Marino, CA: Huntington, 1967.

——. *"Venus and Adonis." Studies in English Literature, 1500–1900* 1 (1961): 1–15; rpt. in *Venus and Adonis: Critical Essays*. Ed. Philip C. Kolin. New York: Garland, 1997. 141–156.

Hardin, Craig. *An Interpretation of Shakespeare*. New York: Dryden P, 1948.

Hart, John S. "Shakespeare's Minor Poems." *Sartain's Union Magazine* 6 (Feb. 1850): 129–32; rpt. in *Venus and Adonis: Critical Essays*. Ed. Philip C. Kolin. New York: Garland, 1997. 77–78.

Hart, Jonathan. "'Till forging nature be condemned of treason': Representational Strife in *Venus and Adonis*." *Cahiers élisabethains: Études sur la Pre-Renaissance et la Renaissance anglaises* 36 (Oct. 1989): 37–47.

Harvey, Gabriel. *Gabriel Harvey's Marginalia*. Ed.G.C. Moore Smith. London: Shakespeare Head P, 1913. 225–34.

Hatto, A.T. *"Venus and Adonis*—and the Boar." *Modern Language Review* 41 (Oct. 1946): 353–61.

Hazlitt, William. *The Round Table. Characters of Shakespear's Plays*. London, 1817; rpt. New York: Dent, 1960.

Herman, Jan. "Charisma Carries *Venus*." *Los Angeles Times*, June 19, 1995: F4.

——. "Heavenly Embodiment of Shakespeare's *Venus*." *Los Angeles Times*, June 19, 1995: F3, F11.

——. "People Need to Hear a Poem Being Emoted. Q/A with Benjamin Stewart." *Los Angeles Times*, "Orange County Calendar," June 16, 1995: F1, F27.

Hilley, James. "On the New Productions." *The Listener*, Feb. 4, 1988.

Hodgins, Paul. "All the Poem's a Stage for Stewart." *Orange County Register*, "Show," June 16, 1995: 68.

——. "Venus Wiles, Adonis Resists and Audience Delights." *Orange County Register*, "Stage," June 19, 1995.

Hughes, Ted. *Shakespeare and the Goddess of Complete Being*. New York: Farrar Straus Giroux, 1992.

Hulse, S. Clark. *Metaphoric Verse: The Elizabethan Minor Epic*. Princeton: Princeton UP, 1981.

——. "Shakespeare's Myth of *Venus and Adonis*." *PMLA* 93 (Jan. 1978): 95–105; rpt. in *Venus and Adonis: Critical Essays*. Ed. Philip C. Kolin. New York: Garland, 1997. 203–22.

Jahn, J.D. "The Lamb of Lust: The Role of Adonis in Shakespeare's *Venus and Adonis*." *Shakespeare Studies* 6 (1970): 11–25.

Joyce, James. *Ulysses*. Paris, 1922; rpt. New York: Modern Library, 1979.

Kahn, Coppélia. "Self and Eros in *Venus and Adonis*." *Centennial Review* 4 (1976): 351–71; rpt. in *Venus and Adonis: Critical Essays*. Ed. Philip C. Kolin. New York: Garland, 1997. 181–202.

Keach, William C. *Elizabethan Erotic Narratives: Irony and Pathos in the Ovidian Poetry of Shakespeare, Marlowe, and Their Contemporaries*. New Brunswick, NJ: Rutgers UP, 1977.

Kingston, Jeremy. "Bird and Bard Have Timely Messages." *London Times*, Oct. 12 1992: 33.

Klause, John. *"Venus and Adonis:* Can We Forgive Them?" *Studies in Philology* 85 (Summer 1988): 353–77.

Kolin, Philip C. "A Chronological Bibliography of Scholarship and Commentary on *Venus and Adonis*, Including Editions and Reviews of Performances." *Venus and Adonis: Critical Essays*. Ed. Philip C. Kolin. New York: Garland, 1997. 407–29.

Lake, James H. "Shakespeare's Venus: An Experiment in Tragedy." *Shakespeare Quarterly* 25 (Summer 1974): 351–55.

Lee, Sidney, ed. "Introduction." *Shakespeare's Venus and Adonis. Being a Reproduc-*

tion in Facsimile of the First Edition, 1593. Oxford: Clarendon, 1905; rpt. in Venus and Adonis: Critical Essays. Ed. Philip C. Kolin. New York: Garland, 1997. 89–90.

Leech, Clifford. "Venus and Her Nun: Portraits of Women in Love by Shakespeare and Marlowe." Studies in English Literature, 1500–1900 5 (Spring 1965): 247–68.

Lever, J.W. "Shakespeare's Narrative Poems." A New Companion to Shakespeare Studies. Ed. Kenneth Muir and S. Schoenbaum. Cambridge: Cambridge UP, 1971. 116–124.

———. "Twentieth-Century Studies in Shakespeare's Songs, Sonnets, and Poems." Shakespeare Survey 15 (1962): 19–22.

———. "Venus and the Second Chance." Shakespeare Survey 15 (1962): 81–88.

Lewis, C.S. English Literature in the Sixteenth Century, Excluding Drama. Oxford: Oxford UP, 1954.

Lindheim, Nancy. "The Shakespearean Venus and Adonis." Shakespeare Quarterly 37 (Summer 1986): 190–203.

Malone, Edmond. Plays and Poems. London, 1790; rpt. New York: AMS, 1970.

Marder, Louis. "Shakespeare in America until 1776." Shakespeare Newsletter 26 (Feb. 1976): 2, 8.

Maxwell, J.C. "Introduction." The Poems: By William Shakespeare. Cambridge: Cambridge UP, 1966.

Merrix, Robert P. "The 'Beste Noir': The Medieval Role of the Boar in Venus and Adonis." The Upstart Crow 11 (1991): 117–30.

———. "'Lo, in This Hollow Cradle Take Thy Rest': Sexual Conflict and Resolution in Venus and Adonis." Venus and Adonis: Critical Essays. Ed. Philip C. Kolin. New York: Garland, 1997. 341–58.

Miller, Robert P. "Venus, Adonis and the Horses." ELH: Journal of English Literary History 19 (Dec. 1952): 249–64.

Montrose, Louis. "'Shaping Fantasies': Figurations of Gender and Power in Elizabethan Culture." Representations 1 (Spring 1983): 61–94.

Muir, Kenneth. Shakespeare the Professional and Related Studies. London: Heinemann, 1973.

———. "Venus and Adonis: Comedy or Tragedy?" Shakespearean Essays. Vol. 2 of Tennessee Studies in Literature. Ed. Alwin Thaler and Norman Sanders. Knoxville: U of Tennessee P, 1964. 1–13.

Munro, John, ed. The Shakespeare Allusion-Book: A Collection of Allusions to Shakespeare from 1591 to 1700. New York, 1909; rpt. London: Oxford UP, 1932.

Murphy, Patrick. "Wriothesley's Resistance: Wardship Practices and Ovidian Narratives in Shakespeare's Venus and Adonis." Venus and Adonis: Critical Essays. Ed. Philip C. Kolin. New York: Garland, 1997. 323–40.

Ovid. The Metamorphoses. Trans. Horace Gregory. New York: Viking, 1960.

Panofsky, Erwin. Studies in Iconology. New York: Harper, 1962.

Pearson, Lu Emily. Elizabethan Love Conventions. Berkeley: U of California P, 1933.

Pequigney, Joseph. Such Is My Love: A Study of Shakespeare's Sonnets. Chicago and London: U of Chicago P, 1985.

Price, Hereward T. "Function of Imagery in Venus and Adonis." Papers of the Michigan Academy of Science, Arts, and Letters 31 (1945): 275–97; rpt. in Venus and Adonis: Critical Essays. Ed. Philip C. Kolin. New York: Garland, 1997. 107–22.

Prince, F.T. "Introduction." The Arden Edition of the Works of William Shakespeare: The Poems. 3rd. ed. London: Methuen, 1960. xi–xxxiii.

Putney, Rufus. "Venus Agonistes." University of Colorado Studies, Series in Language and Literature, No. 4 (1953): 52–66; rpt. in Venus and Adonis: Critical Essays. Ed. Philip C. Kolin. New York: Garland, 1997. 123–40.

Rabkin, Norman. "Venus and Adonis and the Myth of Love." Pacific Coast Studies *in Shakespeare*. Ed. Waldo F. McNeir and Thelma N. Greenfield. Eugene: U of Oregon P, 1966; rpt. in *Shakespeare and the Common Understanding*. New York: Free Press, 1967.

Raleigh, Walter. *Shakespeare*. London: Macmillan, 1907.

Rebhorn, Wayne A. "Mother Venus: Temptation in Shakespeare's *Venus and Adonis*." *Shakespeare Studies* 11 (1978): 1–19.

Roberts, Jeanne Addison. *The Shakespearean Wild: Geography, Genus, and Gender*. Lincoln: U of Nebraska P, 1991.

Roe, John, ed. "Introduction: *Venus and Adonis*." *The Poems: Venus and Adonis, The Rape of Lucrece, The Phoenix and the Turtle, The Passionate Pilgrim, A Lover's Complaint*. Cambridge: Cambridge UP, 1992. 3–21.

Rollins, Hyder Edward, ed. *A New Variorum Edition of Shakespeare: The Poems*. Philadelphia: J.B. Lippincott, 1938.

Rosand, David. "*Ut Pictor Poeta*: Meaning in Titian's *Poesie*." *New Literary History* 3 (1971–1972): 527–46.

Rothenberg, Alan Baer. "The Oral Rape Fantasy and Rejection of Mother in the Imagery of Shakespeare's *Venus and Adonis*." *Psychoanalytic Quarterly* 40 (1971): 447–68.

Rowse, A.L. *Shakespeare's Southampton: Patron of Virginia*. New York: Harper, 1965.

Rylands, George. "Shakespeare the Poet." *A Companion to Shakespeare Studies*. Ed. Harley Granville-Barker and G.B. Harrison. Cambridge: Cambridge UP, 1934. 103–09.

Schiffer, James. "Shakespeare's *Venus and Adonis*: A Lacanian Tragicomedy of Desire." *Venus and Adonis: Critical Essays*. Ed. Philip C. Kolin. New York: Garland, 1997. 359–76.

Schoenbaum, S. *Shakespeare: A Compact Documentary Life*. New York: Oxford, 1977.

Sheidley, William E. "'Unless It Be a Boar': Love and Wisdom in Shakespeare's *Venus and Adonis*." *Modern Language Quarterly* 35 (March 1974): 3–15.

Sievers, E.W. *Shakespeare*. Gotha: Besser, 1866.

Smith, Bruce R. *Homosexual Desire in Shakespeare's England: A Cultural Poetics*. Chicago: U of Chicago P, 1991.

Smith, Hallett. "Introduction to *Venus and Adonis*." *The Riverside Shakespeare*. Ed. G. Blakemore Evans. Boston: Houghton Mifflin, 1974. 1703–04.

Smith, Jeffrey. Review of *The Gardens of Adonis*. *Opera Canada* 34 (Spring 1993): 25.

Spiegelman, Willard. "Another Shakespearean Echo in Keats." *AN&Q* 17 (1978): 3–4.

Stapleton, M.L. "Venus as *Praeceptor*: The *Ars Amatoria* in *Venus and Adonis*." *Venus and Adonis: Critical Essays*. Ed. Philip C. Kolin, New York: Garland, 1997. 309–21.

Stewart, Benjamin. "Strange Bedfellows—Venus, Adonis, and Me." *Venus and Adonis: Critical Essays*. Ed. Philip C. Kolin. New York: Garland, 1997. 295–297.

Streitberger, W.R. "Ideal Conduct in *Venus and Adonis*." *Shakespeare Quarterly* 26 (Summer 1975): 285–91; rpt. in *Venus and Adonis: Critical Essays*. Ed. Philip C. Kolin. New York: Garland, 1997. 171–79.

Swinburne, Algernon Charles. *Shakespeare*. Oxford: Oxford UP, 1909.

"*Venus and Adonis*, July 12, July 20." Stratford Shakespeare Festival Program. Stratford, Ontario, 1984.

Watkins, W.B.C. *Shakespeare and Spenser*. Princeton: Princeton UP, 1950.

Wardle, Irving. "Adonis Reduced to Pastoral Gang-bang." *London Times*, Jan. 29, 1988: 20G.

Webster, Peter Dow. "A Critical Fantasy or Fugue." *American Imago* 6 (1949): 297–309.

Weever, John. "Ad Gulielmum Shakespeare." *Epigrammes in the Oldest Cut and Newest Fashion*. Ed. R.B. McKerrow, 1911. Rpt. London: Shakespeare Head P, 1922. 75.

Weston, Lynda. "Intimate Third Stage Matches Intimate Letters." *Stratford Beacon Herald* [Ontario], July 11, 1983.

Wilbur, Richard. "The Narrative Poems." *The Pelican Shakespeare.* Ed. Alfred Harbage. Baltimore: Penguin, 1969.

Wilde, Oscar. "The Portrait of Mr W.H." London, 1889; rpt. in *The Riddle of Shakespeare's Sonnets: The Text of the Sonnets with Interpretive Essays by Edward Hubler [and others] and Including the Full Text of Oscar Wilde's "The Portrait of Mr W. H."* New York: Basic Books, 1962. 163–256.

Williams, Gordon. "The Coming of Age of Shakespeare's Adonis." *Modern Language Review* 78 (Oct. 1983): 769–76.

Wind, Edgar. *Pagan Mysteries in the Renaissance.* London: Faber and Faber, 1958.

Wortis, Joseph, M.D. "*Venus and Adonis:* An Early Account of Sexual Harassment." *Biological Psychiatry* 35 (March 1994): 293–4; rpt. in *Venus and Adonis: Critical Essays.* Ed. Philip C. Kolin. New York: Garland, 1997. 259–60.

Wyndham, George. *The Poems of Shakespeare.* London: Methuen, 1898; rpt. in *Venus and Adonis: Critical Essays.* Ed. Philip C. Kolin. New York: Garland, 1997. 79–88.

Ziegler, Georgianna. "Picturing Venus and Adonis: Shakespeare and the Artists." *Venus and Adonis: Critical Essays.* Ed. Philip C. Kolin. New York: Garland, 1997. 389–403.

11

VENUS AND ADONIS AND THE CRITICS

SHAKSPEARE'S *VENUS AND ADONIS*

Samuel Taylor Coleridge

In this investigation I could not . . . do better, than keep before me the earliest work of the greatest genius, that perhaps human nature has yet produced, our *myriad-minded* Shakspear. I mean the "Venus and Adonis," and
the "Lucrece;" works which give at once strong promises of the strength,
and yet obvious proofs of the immaturity, of his genius. From these I ab-
stracted the following marks, as characteristics of original poetic genius in
general.

　　In the "Venus and Adonis," the first and most obvious excellence is
the perfect sweetness of the versification; its adaptation to the subject; and
the power displayed in varying the march of the words without passing into
a loftier and more majestic rhythm, than was demanded by the thoughts,
or permitted by the propriety of preserving a sense of melody predominant.
The delight in richness and sweetness of sound, even to a faulty excess, if it
be evidently original, and not the result of an easily imitable mechanism, I
regard as a highly favorable promise in the compositions of a young man.
"The man that hath not music in his soul" can indeed never be a genuine
poet. Imagery (even taken from nature, much more when transplanted from
books, as travels, voyages, and works of natural history) affecting incidents;
just thoughts; interesting personal or domestic feelings; and with these the
art of their combination or intertexture in the form of a poem; may all by
incessant effort be acquired as a trade, by a man of talents and much reading, who, as I once before observed, has mistaken an intense desire of poetic reputation for a natural poetic genius; the love of the arbitrary end for
a possession of the peculiar means. But the sense of musical delight, with
the power of producing it, is a gift of imagination; and this together with
the power of reducing multitude into unity of effect, and modifying a series

---

Reprinted from *Biographia Literaria* (1817): II, pp. 13–22.

of thoughts by some one predominant thought or feeling, may be cultivated and improved, but can never be learnt. It is in these that "Poeta nascitur non fit."

A second promise of genius is the choice of subjects very remote from the private interests and circumstances of the writer himself. At least I have found, that where the subject is taken immediately from the author's personal sensations and experiences, the excellence of a particular poem is but an equivocal mark, and often a fallacious pledge, of genuine poetic power. We may perhaps remember the tale of the statuary, who had acquired considerable reputation for the legs of his goddesses, though the rest of the statue accorded but indifferently with ideal beauty; till his wife elated by her husband's praises, modestly acknowledged, that she herself had been his constant model. In the "Venus and Adonis," this proof of poetic power exists even to excess. It is throughout as if a superior spirit more intuitive, more intimately conscious, even than the characters themselves, not only of every outward look and act, but of the flux and reflux of the mind in all its subtlest thoughts and feelings, were placing the whole before our view; himself meanwhile unparticipating in the passions, and actuated only by that pleasurable excitement, which had resulted from the energetic fervor of his own spirit in so vividly exhibiting, what it had so accurately and profoundly contemplated. I think, I should have conjectured from these poems, that even then the great instinct, which impelled the poet to the drama, was secretly working in him, prompting him by a series and never broken chain of imagery, always vivid and because unbroken, often minute; by the highest effort of the picturesque in words, of which words are capable, higher perhaps than was ever realized by any other poet, even Dante not excepted; to provide a substitute for that visual language, that constant intervention and running comment by tone, look and gesture, which in his dramatic works he was entitled to expect from the players. His "Venus and Adonis" seem at once the characters themselves, and the whole representation of those characters by the most consummate actors. You seem to be *told* nothing, but to see and hear every thing. Hence it is, that from the perpetual activity of attention required on the part of the reader; from the rapid flow, the quick change, and the playful nature of the thoughts and images; and above all from the alienation, and, if I may hazard such an expression, the utter *aloofness* of the poet's own feelings, from those of which he is at once the painter and the analyst; that though the very subject cannot but detract from the pleasure of a delicate mind, yet never was poem less dangerous on a moral account. Instead of doing as Ariosto, and as, still more offensively, Wieland has done, instead of degrading and deforming passion into appetite, the trials of love into the struggles of concupiscence; Shakspeare has here represented the animal impulse itself, so as to preclude all sympathy with it, by dissipating the reader's notice among the thousand outward images, and now beautiful, now fanciful circumstances, which form it dresses and its scenery; or by diverting our attention from the main subject by those frequent witty or profound reflections, which the poet's ever active mind has deduced from, or connected with, the imagery and the incidents. The reader is forced into too much action to sympathize with the merely passive of our nature. As little can a mind thus roused and awakened be brooded on by mean and indistinct emotion, as the low, lazy mist can creep upon the surface of a lake, while a strong gale is driving it onward in waves and billows.

It has been before observed, that images however beautiful, though faithfully copied from nature, and as accurately represented in words, do not of themselves characterize the poet. They become proofs of original genius only as far as they are modified by a predominant passion; or by associated thoughts or images awakened by that passion; or when they have the effect of reducing multitude to unity, or succession to an instant; or lastly, when a human and intellectual life is transferred to them from the poet's own spirit. . . . It is by this, that [Shakespeare] . . . still gives a dignity and a passion to the objects which he presents. Unaided by any previous excitement, they burst upon us at once in life and in power. . . .

As of higher worth, so doubtless still more characteristic of poetic genius does the imagery become, when it moulds and colors itself to the circumstances, passion, or character, present and foremost in the mind. . . .

Scarcely less sure, or if a less valuable, not less indispensable mark . . . will the imagery supply, when, with more than the power of the painter, the poet gives us the liveliest image of succession with the feeling of simultaneousness!

> With this he breaketh from the sweet embrace
> Of those fair aims [*sic*], that held him to her heart,
> And homeward through the dark lawns runs apace:
> *Look how a bright star shooteth from the sky!*
> *So glides he through the night from Venus' eye.*

The last character I shall mention, which would prove indeed but little, except as taken conjointly with the former; yet without which the former could scarce exist in a high degree, and (even if this were possible) would give promises only of transitory flashes and a meteoric power; is DEPTH, and ENERGY OF THOUGHT. No man was ever yet a great poet, without being at the same time a profound philosopher. For poetry is the blossom and the fragrancy of all human knowledge, human thoughts, human passions, emotions, language. In Shakspeare's *poems,* the creative power, and the intellectual energy wrestle as in a war embrace. Each in its excess of strength seems to threaten the extinction of the other. At length, in the DRAMA they were reconciled, and fought each with its shield before the breast of the other. Or like two rapid streams, that at their first meeting within narrow and rocky banks mutually strive to repel each other, and intermix reluctantly and in tumult; but soon finding a wider channel and more yielding shores blend, and dilate, and flow on in one current and with one voice. The "Venus and Adonis" did not perhaps allow the display of the deeper passions. But the story of Lucretia seems to favor, and even demand their intensest workings. And yet we find in *Shakspeare's* management of the tale neither pathos, nor any other *dramatic* quality. There is the same minute and faithful imagery as in the former poem, in the same vivid colours, inspirited by the same impetuous vigour of thought, and diverging and contracting with the same activity of the assimilative and of the modifying faculties; and with a yet larger display, a yet wider range of knowledge and reflection; and lastly, with the same perfect dominion, often *domination,* over the whole world of language. What then shall we say? even this; that Shakspeare, no mere child of nature; no automaton of genius; no passive vehicle of inspiration possessed by the spirit, not possessing it; first studied patiently, meditated deeply, understood minutely, till knowledge become habitual and intuitive wedded itself to his habitual feelings, and at length gave birth to that stupendous power, by which he stands alone, with no equal or second in his own class; to that power, which seated him on one of the two glory-smitten summits of the poetic mountain, with Milton as his compeer not rival. While the former darts himself forth, and passes into all the forms of human character and passion, the one Proteus of the fire and the flood; the other attracts all forms and things to himself, into the unity of his own IDEAL. All things and modes of action shape themselves anew in the being of MILTON; while SHAKSPEARE becomes all things, yet for ever remaining himself.

SHAKSPEARE'S POEMS

Y.J.

The blaze of glory which encircles the dramatic writings of Shakspeare, has eclipsed his earlier poems, and few have ever read them through; yet they are not without great merit, and some of them are remarkable in that the traces of passages in his more celebrated works may be met with among them. . . . [*Venus* and *Lucrece* are Shakspeare's] first productions, and had he not written for the theatre, would have given him no inconsiderable reputation among the writers of his day, though they have been naturally thrown into shade by the dazzling lustre of his dramatic productions.

Johnson says that the dawn of *Paradise Lost* is to be found in Comus, and it is also certain that Shakspeare's knowledge of the human mind, and his wonderful skill in delineating the workings of passion, are to be clearly discovered in his *Venus and Adonis*. . . . Its whole cast is in unison with the taste of the time, and was suggested to its author, as some think, by the third book of the *Fairy Queen*. He calls it himself "the first heir of his invention." The subject forbade any delineation of manners; but the spell by which this poet above all others, commanded the mysterious emotions of the heart to come before him embodied in language, was never more potent than in the description of the love of Venus for her favourite.

This composition is agreeable to the coarseness of manners in the time of Elizabeth, being deficient in that delicacy which has happily been introduced by modern refinement. It is rather for the purpose of directing attention to the links which connect incipient genius with maturity—the character of primitive attempts with more finished excellencies—to shew how the poet's genius may be traced from its juvenility to manhood, and to display, besides his surprising knowledge of our common nature, the great power of description of the author in his first productions, that I would draw the

Reprinted from *New Monthly Magazine*, May 1823.

attention of the reader to this poem. It is not a proper book to be in all hands, and of late years has not been much read; nor can it be so in future, because it is out of keeping with our times, and is on a subject which the most pure pen could scarcely be expected to delineate and escape the censure of conveying indelicate impressions. It is to be perused by the discriminating and curious in literature, rather than by those who seek amusement only. . . .

The love of the goddess, her fruitless efforts to move the obdurate heart of the youth, her actions, her address to him, her solicitations, her ungovernable passion, have never been exceeded in truth and force of description by any poet. There is every where in the picture easy and beautiful drawing. In colouring, the artist knew every rainbow hue in nature, and dispensed all with the prodigality and confidence of a master. It satiates the eye with richness, but it is not overwrought; and, in contemplating it, one is more than ever disposed to wonder by what means the painter could have acquired such a knowledge of the subject and its details, unless he felt himself all which he represents others as feeling, and depicted every separate emotion as it arose in his own bosom. There is great inequality in the poem: some parts are written with carelessness, and are unvaried and formal; others are exquisitely beautiful. It is a work of genius not touched by a hand of critical skill and learning, but left with its sharpness of mould and defects of casting about it, noble in outline, and graceful in proportion.

Some of the descriptive passages are of rare elegance, as that where Venus recommends herself to Adonis, and describes the ethereal nature of love [lines 145, 156]. . . . Is there any thing surpassing the picture of the horse of Adonis to be met with in the English language? The character, temper, and description of the animal, are wonderfully vigorous and spirited. To my feeling there is no pen, ancient or modern, that has more happily drawn that noble animal, except Job, whom the Poet doubtless had in his eye. . . .

The *Rape of Lucrece* is by no means equal in merit to *Venus and Adonis;* yet there are some fine passages here and there, particularly in Lucretia's lamentation. . . .

I must not be *lengthy,* though I have hardly skimmed the poems, and thereby done them injustice; yet what I have said may induce some discriminating readers to take them down from a dusty shelf and peruse them. They will find themselves repaid for their trouble—they will find much weighty bullion and pure gold, in its rough state, perhaps, but not less rich on that account.

VENUS AND ADONIS

G.G. *Gervinus*

Everything betrays that *[Venus* and *Lucrece] . . .* were written in the first passion of youth.

How in matter and treatment they are interwoven with the youthful circumstances and moods of the poet . . . strikes us at once. . . . In the first part [of *Venus and Adonis*] the poet has endowed the wooer with all the charms of persuasion, beauty, and passionate vehemence, with all the arts of flattery, entreaty, reproach, tears, and violence; and he appears in doing so as a Croesus in poetic ideas, thoughts, and images, a master and victor in the matter of love, a giant in passion and sensual power. From this point of view, the whole piece is one brilliant error, such as young poets so readily commit: immoderate sensual fervour mistaken for poetry. Yet in the opinion of the time this poem alone placed Shakespeare in the rank of admired poets. The very point, we mention, gave the poem at once its winning power. What at that time had been read in similar mythological poems by English and Italian writers of the nature and effects of love, was an elaborate ideal work in a polished form, more brilliant in words, than profound in truth of feeling. But here indeed Love is a "spirit, all compact of fire," a real paroxysm and passion, which surpasses the artificial bombastic manner of representation. Thus by its truth to nature, the poem had a realistic effect beyond any similar mythological and allegorical pictures. . . .

With whatever glowing colours Shakespeare has painted the image of this passion, his delight in the subject of his picture has never betrayed him into exclusive sensuality. He knows, that he sketched, not the image of human love in which mind and soul have their ennobling share, but the image of a purely sensual desire, which merely animal, like "an empty eagle,"

Reprinted from *Shakespeare's Commentaries*, 1849. Trans. F.E. Burnett. London, 1863. I: pp. 51–55.

feeds on its prey. In the passage, where he depicts the wooing of Adonis' horse which had broken loose from its rein, his intention is evident to compare the animal passion in the episode with that of the goddess, not in opposition but in juxtaposition. Rebukingly Adonis tells the loving goddess, that she should not call that love, which even he, the poet, names careless lust, "beating reason back, forgetting shame's pure blush, and honour's wrack." This purer thought, which more than once occurs in the poem, is yet, it must be admitted, half concealed by the grace of the style, and by the poet's lingering on sensual descriptions.

Shakespeare's Minor Poems

VENUS AND ADONIS

J.S. Hart

In the main incidents and in the leading idea [of Venus], there is nothing original. All the creative power is in the filling up. Here the poet distances all competitors ancient or modern. The various scenes are painted with a distinctness—a sort of visibility—not surpassed even by Spenser, while there is throughout a compactness and force of expression of which Spenser was entirely incapable. The actors stand out to the mind's eye with all the distinctness of a group of statuary.

One peculiarity, first observed I believe by Coleridge, is worthy of note. The poem is not marked by stirring action, but by a series of minutely finished pictures. In other words, it is descriptive, not dramatic. Yet the character of these descriptions is precisely that which would indicate the possession of the dramatic power. Drama is action. That the action may be consistent and suitable, the dramatist while composing must have the actors and the scene of action most vividly and palpably before his own mind. He must be present to every scene and every soul, as really as though he were at the moment actually on the stage, surrounded by the characters whom he has summoned into existence. He must therefore have the power of conception in the highest degree. The fact to be noted is, that this power is equally shown in the *Venus and Adonis*. In other words, a poem essentially and characteristically undramatic evinces at the same time the possession of high dramatic power. The pictures given to the reader in the poem are such as must be ever present to the mind's eye of the poet while writing a drama. Shakespeare's descriptions in his *Venus and Adonis* raise in our minds just such scenes as I suppose always existed in his own mind while putting language into the mouth of his dramatic characters. . . .

No one, I think, can read it without being struck with the ease and

Reprinted from *Sartain's Magazine* (Feb. 1850), pp. 129–32.

sweetness of the versification, the splendour and polish of the diction, the concentrated energy of expression in some places and the extraordinary command of language throughout—in short, with a high state of finish in the style and a thorough mastery of the art of composition, which we rarely expect to find except in the practised writer. . . .

THE POEMS OF SHAKESPEARE

George Wyndham

[*Venus and Adonis* reveals] Shakespeare's loving familiarity with Ovid whose effects he fuses: taking the reluctance of Adonis from *Hermaphroditus* [in the *Metamorphoses*]; the description of the boar from Meleager's encounter . . . and other features from the short version of *Venus and Adonis* which Ovid weaves on to the terrible and beautiful story of Myrrha. In all Shakespeare's work of this period the same fusion of Ovid's stories and images is obvious. Tarquin and Myrrha are both delayed, but, not daunted, by lugubrious forebodings in the dark; and *Titus Andronicus*, played for the first time in the year which saw the publication of *Venus and Adonis*, is full of debts and allusions to Ovid. Ovid, with his power of telling a story and of eloquent discourse, his shining images, his cadences coloured with assonance and weighted with alliteration; Chaucer, with his sweet liquidity of diction, his dialogues and soliloquies—these are the 'only true begetters' of the lyric Shakespeare. In these matters we must allow poets to have their own way: merely noting that Ovid, in whom critics see chiefly a brilliant man of the world, has been a mine of delight for all poets who rejoice in the magic of sound, from the dawn of the Middle Ages down to our own incomparable Milton. His effects of alliteration . . . his gleaming metaphors . . . are the very counterpart of Shakespeare's manner in the Poems and the Play which he founded in part on his early love of the *Metamorphoses*.

But in *Titus Andronicus* and in *Venus and Adonis* there are effects of the open air which hail, not from Ovid but, from Arden:

> The birds chant melody on every bush;
> The snake lies rolled in the cheerful sun;

Reprinted from "Introduction" to *The Poems of Shakespeare, Edited with an Introduction and Notes* by George Wyndham (London: Methuen, 1898), pp. xxix–xciii. Reprinted with the permission of Reed Books, London.

> The green leaves quiver with the cooling wind,
> And make a chequer'd shadow on the ground.
> > (*Titus Andronicus,* II.iii.12–15)

Thus the Play (ii. 3), and thus the Poem:

> Even as the wind is hush'd before it raineth . . .
> Like many clouds consulting for foul weather.
> > (ll. 458, 972)

Indeed in the Poem, round and over the sharp portrayal of every word and gesture of the two who speak and move, you have brakes and trees, horses and hounds, and the silent transformations of day and night from the first dawn till eve, and through darkness to the second dawn so immediately impressed, that, pausing at any of the cxcix stanzas, you could almost name the hour. The same express observation of the day's changes may be observed in *Romeo and Juliet.* It is a note which has often been echoed by men who never look out of their windows, and critics, as narrowly immured, have denounced it for an affectation. Yet a month under canvas, or, better still, without a tent, will convince any one that to speak of the stars and the moon is as natural as to look at your watch or an almanack. In the *Venus* even the weather changes. The Poem opens soon after sunrise with the ceasing of a shower:

> Even as the sun with purple colour'd face,
> Had ta'en his last leave of the weeping morn.

But by the 89th Stanza, after a burning noon, the clouds close in over the sunset. 'Look,' says Adonis:

> The world's comforter with weary gate
> His day's hot task hath ended in the west,
> The owl (night's herald) Shrieks, 'tis very late,
> The sheep are gone to fold, birds to their nest,
> And coal-black clouds, that shadow heaven's light,
> Do summon us to part and bid good-night.
> > (ll. 529–34)

The next dawn is cloudless after the night's rain:

> Lo here the gentle lark, weary of rest,

From his moist cabinet mounts up on high,
And wakes the morning, from whose silver breast
The sun ariseth in his majesty;
Who doth the world so gloriously behold,
That cedar tops and hills seem burnisht gold.

(ll. 853–58)

Beneath these atmospheric effects everything is clearly seen and sharply delineated:

The studded bridle on a ragged bough
Nimbly she fastens.   (ll. 37–8)

The illustrations from nature:

As the dive-dapper peering through a wave
Who being lookt on, ducks as quickly in . . .
As the snail whose tender horns being hit
Shrinks backward in his shelly cave with pain
(ll.86–7, 1033–34)

are so vivid as to snatch your attention from the story; and when you read
that 'lust' feeding on 'fresh beauty,'

Starves and soon bereaves
As caterpillars do the tender leaves,   (ll. 797–98)

the realism of the illustration does violence to its aptness. It is said that such
multiplicity of detail and ornament is out of place in a classic myth. But
Shakespeare's Poem is not a classic myth. Mr. Swinburne contrasts it
unfavourably with Chapman's *Hero and Leander* (in his "Essay on the Poetical and Dramatic Works of George Chapman"), in which he finds 'a small
shrine of Parian sculpture amid the rank splendour of a tropical jungle.' Certainly that is the last image which any one could apply to *Venus and Adonis*. Its wealth of realistic detail reminds you rather of the West Porch at
Amiens. But alongside of this realism, and again as in Mediaeval Art, there
are wilful and half-humorous perversions of nature. When Shakespeare in
praise of Adonis' beauty says that

To see his face, the lion walked along

> Behind some hedge, because he would not fear him,
>> (ll. 1093–94)

or that

> When he beheld his shadow in the brook,
> The fishes spread on it their golden gills,
>> (ll. 1099–1100)

you feel that you are still in the age which painted St. Jerome's lion and St. Francis preaching to the birds. But you feel that you are half way into another. The poem is not Greek, but neither is it Mediaeval: it belongs to the debatable dawntime which we call the Renaissance. There is much in it of highly charged colour and of curious insistence on strange beauties of detail; yet, dyed and daedal as it is out of all kinship with classical repose, neither its intricacy nor its tinting ever suggests the Aladdin's Cave evoked by Mr. Swinburne's Oriental epithets: rather do they suggest a landscape at sunrise. There, too, the lesser features of trees and bushes and knolls are steeped in the foreground with crimson light, or are set on fire with gold at the horizon; there, too, they leap into momentary significance with prolonged and fantastic shadows; yet overhead, the atmosphere is, not oppressive but, eager and pure and a part of an immense serenity. And so it is in the Poem, for which, if you abandon Mr. Swinburne's illustration, and seek another from painting, you may find a more fitting counterpart in the Florentine treatment of classic myths: in Botticelli's *Venus,* with veritable gold on the goddess's hair and on the boles of the pine trees, or in Piero di Cosima's *Cephalus and Procris,* with its living animals at gaze before a tragedy that tells much of Beauty and nothing of Pain. Shakespeare's Poem is of love, not death; but he handles his theme with just the same regard for Beauty, with just the same disregard for all that disfigures Beauty. He portrays an amorous encounter through its every gesture; yet unless in some dozen lines where he glances aside, like any Mediaeval, at a gaiety not yet divorced from love, his appeal to beauty persists from first to last; and nowhere is there an appeal to lust. The laughter and sorrow of the Poem belong wholly to the faery world of vision and romance, where there is no sickness, whether of sentiment or of sense. And both are rendered by images, clean-cut as in antique gems, brilliantly enamelled as in mediaeval chalices, numerous and interwoven as in Moorish arabesques; so that their incision, colour, and rapidity of development, apart even from the intricate melodies of the verbal medium in which they live, tax the faculty of artistic appreciation to a point at which it begins to participate in the asceticism of artistic creation. 'As little can a mind thus roused and awakened be brooded on by mean and indistinct emotion, as the low, lazy mist can creep upon the surface of a lake while a strong gale is driving it onward in waves and billows';—thus does Coleridge resist the application to shift the venue of criticism on this Poem from the court of Beauty to the court of Morals [see excerpt above, 1817], and upon that subject little more need be said. How wilful it is to discuss the moral bearing of an invitation couched by an imaginary Goddess in such imaginative terms as these:

> Bid me discourse, I will inchant thine eare,
> Or like a Fairie, trip upon the greene,
> Or like a Nymph, with long disheveled heare,
> Daunce on the sands, and yet no footing seene!
> (ll. 145–48)

As well essay to launch an ironclad on 'the foam of perilous seas in fairy-lands forlorn' (John Keats, "Ode to a Nightingale").

When Venus says, 'Bid me discourse, I will inchant thine eare,' she instances yet another peculiar excellence of Shakespeare's lyrical art, which shows in this Poem, is redoubled in *Lucrece,* and in the Sonnets yields the most perfect examples of human speech:

> Touch by my lips with those fair lips of thine,
> Though mine be not so fair, yet are they red . . .
>
> Art thou ashamed to kiss? Then wink again,
> And I will wink, so shall the day seem night . . .
> (ll. 115–16, 121–22)

These are the fair words of her soliciting, and Adonis' reply is of the same silvery quality:

> If love have lent you twenty thousand tongues,
> And every tongue more meaning than your own,
> Bewitching like the wanton mermaid's songs,
> Yet from mine ear the tempting tune is blown . . . .
> (ll. 775–78)

You catch a note prelusive to the pleading altercation of the Sonnets. It is the discourse in *Venus and Adonis* and *Lucrece* which renders them discursive. And indeed they are long poems, on whose first reading Poe's advice, never to begin at the same place, may wisely be followed. You do well, for instance, to begin at Stanza CXXXVI (ll. 811–16) in order to enjoy the narrative of Venus' vain pursuit; with your senses unwearied by the length and sweetness of her argument. The passage hence to the end is in the true romantic tradition: Stanzas CXL and CXLI (ll. 835–46) is the child of Chaucer. The truth of such art consists in magnifying selected details until their gigantic shapes, edged with a shadowy iridescence, fill the whole field of observation. Certain gestures of the body, certain moods of the mind, are made to tell with the weight of trifles during awe-stricken pauses of delay. Venus, when she is baffled by 'the merciless and pitchy night,' halts

> amazed as one that unaware
> Hath dropt a precious jewel in the flood,
> Or stonisht as night wanderers often are,
> Their light blown out in some mistrustfull wood.
> (ll. 821, 823–26)

She starts like 'one that spies an adder'; 'the timorous yelping of the hounds appals her senses'; and she stands 'in a trembling extasy' (ll. 878, 881–82, 895).

Besides romantic narrative and sweetly modulated discourse, there are two rhetorical tirades by Venus—when she 'exclaimes on death':

> Grim grinning ghost, earth's-worme, what dost
>   thou meane
> To stifle beautie and to steale his breath, etc.:
> (ll. 930, 933–34)

and when she heaps her anathemas on love:

> It shall be fickle, false and full of fraud,
> Bud, and be blasted in a breathing while;
> The bottome poyson, and the top ore-strawed
> With sweets, that shall the truest sight beguile,
> The strongest bodie shall it make most weake,
> Strike the voice dumbe, and teach the foole to speake:
> (ll. 1141–46)

and in both, as also in Adonis' contrast of love and lust:

> Love comforteth, like sunshine after raine,
> But lust's effect is tempest after sunne,
> Love's gentle spring doth always fresh remaine,
> Lust's winter comes ere summer halfe be donne;
> Love surfets not, lust like a glutton dies:
> Love is all truth, lust full of forged lies:
>
> (ll. 799–804)

You have rhetoric, packed with antithesis, and rapped out on alliterated syllables for which the only equivalent in English is found, but more fully, in the great speech delivered by Lucrece. The seed of these tirades, as of the dialogues and the gentle soliloquies, seems derived from Chaucer's *Troilus and Criseyde;* and in his *Knight's Tale . . .* there is also a fore-shadowing of their effective alliteration, used—and this is the point—not as an ornament of verse, but as an instrument of accent . . . .[This use of alliteration by Shakespeare] does not consist in collecting the greatest number of words with the same initial, but in letting the accent fall, as it does naturally in all impassioned speech, upon syllables of cognate sound. Since in English verse the accent is, and by Shakespeare's contemporaries was understood to be, 'the chief lord and grave Governour of Numbers' (Samuel Daniel in his *Defense of Ryme*), this aid to its emphasis is no less legitimate, and is hardly less important, than is that of rhyme to metre in French verse: we inherit it from the Saxon, as we inherit rhyme from the Norman; both are essential elements in the poetry built up by Chaucer out of the ruins of two languages. But Shakespeare is the supreme master of its employment: in these impassioned tirades he wields it with a naked strength that was never approached, in the Sonnets with a veiled and varied subtilty that defies analysis. There are hints here and there in the *Venus* of this gathering subtilty:

> These blew-vein'd violets whereon we leane
> Never can blab, nor know not what we meane . . .
> Even as a dying coale revives with winde . . .
> More white and red than doves and roses are.
>
> (ll. 125–26, 338, 10)

But apart from the use of cognate sounds, which makes for emphasis without marring melody, in many a line there also lives that more recondite sweetness, which plants so much of Shakespeare's verse in the memory for no assignable cause:

> Scorning his churlish drum and ensigne red . . . .
> Dumbly she passions, frantikely she doteth . . . .
> Showed like two silver doves that sit a billing . . . .
> Leading him prisoner in a red-rose chaine . . . .
> Were beautie under twentie locks kept fast,
> Yet love breaks through and picks them all at last . . . .
> O learne to love, the lesson is but plaine
> And once made perfect never lost again.
>
> (ll. 107, 1059, 366, 110, 575–76, 407–08)

Herein a cadence of obvious simplicity gives birth to an inexplicable charm.

I have spoken of Shakespeare's images, blowing fresh from the memory of his boyhood, so vivid that at times they are violent, and at others wrought and laboured until they become conceits. You have 'No fisher but the ungrown fry forbears' (l. 526), with its frank reminiscence of a sportsman's scruple; or, as an obvious illustration, 'Look how a bird lies tangled in a net' (l. 67); or, in a flash of intimate recollection:

> Like shrill-tongu'd tapsters answering everie call,
> Soothing the humours of fantastique wits:
>
> (ll. 849–50)

the last, an early sketch of the 'Francis' scene in *Henry IV.* (*1 Henry IV*, Act II, Scene iv), which, in quaint juxtaposition with 'cedar tops and hills' of burnisht gold' [l. 858], seems instinct with memories of John Shakespeare and his friends, who dared not go to church. But, again, you have conceits:

> But her (eyes), which through the crystal tears
>   gave light,
> Shone like the Moone in water seen by night;
>
> (ll. 491–92)

'A lilie prison'd in a gaile of snow' (l. 362); and 'Wishing her cheeks were gardens full of flowers So they were dew'd with such distilling showers' (ll. 65–6). But, diving deeper than diction, alliteration, and rhythm: deeper than the decoration of blazoned colours and the labyrinthine interweaving of images, now budding as it were from nature, and now beaten as by an artificer out of some precious metal: you discover beneath this general interpretation of Phenomenal Beauty, a gospel of Ideal Beauty, a confession of faith in Beauty as in principle of life. And note—for the coincidence is vital—that these, the esoteric themes of *Venus and Adonis,* are the essential themes of the Sonnets. In Stanza XXII:

> Fair flowers that are not gathered in their prime
> Rot and consume themselves in little time:
>> (ll. 131–32)

and in Stanzas XXVII, XXVIII, XXIX (ll. 157–74), you have the whole argument of Sonnets I–XIX. In stanza CLXXX:

> Alas poore world, what treasure hast thou lost,
> What face remains alive that's worth the viewing?
> Whose tongue is musick now? What canst thou
>> boast,
> Of things long since, or any thing insuing?
> The flowers are sweet, their colours fresh, and trim,
> But true sweet beautie liv'd, and di'de with him:
>> (ll. 1075–80)

you have that metaphysical gauging of the mystical importance of some one incarnation of Beauty viewed from imaginary standpoints in time, which was afterwards to be elaborated in Sonnets XIV, XIX, LIX, LXVII, LXVIII, CIV, CVI. And in Stanza CLXX:

> For he being dead, with him is beautie slaine,
> And beautie dead, blacke Chaos comes again:
>> (ll. 1019–20)

you have the succinct *credo* in that incarnation of an Ideal Beauty, of which all other lovely semblances are but 'shadows' and 'counterfeits,' which was to find a fuller declaration in Sonnets XXXI and LIII, and CVIII.

But in Shakespeare's Poems the beauty and curiosity of the ceremonial ever obscure the worship of the god; and, perhaps, in the last stanza but one, addressed to the flower born in place of the dead Adonis and let drop into the bosom of the Goddess of Love, you have the most typical expression of those merits and defects which are alike loved and condoned by the slaves of their invincible sweetness:

Here was thy father's bed, here in my brest,
Thou are the next of blood, and 'tis thy right,
So in this hollow cradle take thy rest,
My throbbing hart shall rock thee day and night;
There shall not be one minute in an houre
Wherein I will not kiss my sweet love's floure.

(ll. 1183–88)

Here are conceits and a strained illustration from the profession of law; but here, with these, are lovely imagery and perfect diction and, flowing through every line, a rhythm that rises and falls softly, until, after a hurry of ripples, it expends itself in the three last retarding words.

Introduction to Shakespeare's
Venus and Adonis

Sidney Lee

Shakespeare's poem of *Venus and Adonis* has a peculiar fascination alike for the poet's biographer, critic, and bibliographer. It is sufficient to mention three points of interest. Firstly, the volume, alone in the great roll of Shakespeare's works, includes a precise personal statement from the dramatist's own pen respecting its composition. Secondly, it supplies a singularly illuminating clue to the relations subsisting between Shakespeare's early work and the poetic efforts alike of his contemporary fellow countrymen and of the poets of the Italian Renaissance. Thirdly, it was the earliest of his writings to find its way to the printing press, and, although the early editions were extraordinarily numerous, exceptionally few early copies survive. Neither the intrinsic nor the extrinsic character of the volume is to be exactly matched in variety of interest in the whole range of Shakespearean literature.

No more valuable fragment of autobiography exists than the dedicatory letter bearing the poet's signature, which is prefixed to the original edition of *Venus and Adonis*. It is addressed to 'The Right Honourable Henry Wriothesley, Earl of Southampton and Baron of Titchfield'. Only one other of Shakespeare's works, *The Rape of Lucrece,* was similarly distinguished by a prefatory epistle from the poet's pen, and that was addressed to the same patron. But the inscription before the *Venus and Adonis,* which is somewhat fuller and yet at the same time somewhat simpler in expression than its successor, differs from it, too, in supplying impressions of the country-side—impressions which lost something of their concrete distinctness and filled a narrower space in his thought in adult years, amid the multifarious distractions of the town.

Reprinted from Sidney Lee, "Introduction" to *Shakespeare's Venus and Adonis: Being a Reproduction in Facsimile of the First Edition, 1593* (Oxford: Clarendon, 1905), pp. 1–4.

The subject, too, savours of the conditions of youth—of what Shakespeare called in his *Sonnets* (LXX.9) 'the ambush of young days'. Shakespeare chose to occupy his budding fancy with a somewhat voluptuous story—an unsubstantial dream of passion—which was first revealed to him in one of his classical schoolbooks, and had already exercised the energies of famous versifiers of his own epoch in England and on the continent of Europe. As in the case of most youthful essays in poetry, the choice of so well-worn a topic as Venus and Adonis shows Shakespeare to have embarked at the outset of his poetic career in a consciously imitative effort, even if the potency of his individuality stamped the finished product with its own hallmark. Ovid in his *Metamorphoses* had emulated the example of Theocritus and Bion, the pastoral poets of Greece, in narrating the Greek fable of Venus and Adonis. Ovid's poem filled a generous space in the curriculum of every Elizabethan school, and at all periods of his career Shakespeare gave signs of affectionate familiarity with its contents.

But Ovid was only one of the literary companions of Shakespeare's youth, and the Latin poet dealt with this tale of Venus and Adonis in bare outline. In spite of his deep obligation to the great Roman, Shakespeare did not confine his early poetic studies to him. There are ample signs that he filled out Ovid's brief and somewhat colourless narrative on lines suggested by elder English contemporaries, Spenser and Marlowe, Lodge and Greene. In finally manipulating the theme there cannot be much doubt, too, that Shakespeare worked up some vitalizing conceptions which were derived from the Italian poets. Long before he wrote, foreign writers had elaborated the simple classic myth in narrative verse which closely anticipated his own in shape and sentiment.

Most of the varied influences which moulded Shakespeare's poetic genius, indeed, find a first reflection in *Venus and Adonis*. In it, recent impressions of the country life of Warwickshire seem to be fused, not merely with schoolboy devotion to Ovid and youthful enthusiasm for the new birth of English poetry, but with genuine appreciation of the taste and feeling which the Renaissance had generated in all cultivated minds of Western Europe. On foundations offered by the novels of Italy and France—some of the most characteristic fruit of Renaissance literature—Shakespeare at the height of his powers reared many of his best-known plays. The same elements of literary sustenance, the same force of literary sympathy, which fed the stream of Shakespeare's genius in its maturity, seem, in the eye of the careful student, to course in embryo through *Venus and Adonis*, 'the first heir' of his invention.

VENUS AND ADONIS
AND MYTHOLOGY

Douglas Bush

Venus and Adonis was entered in April, 1593, and published shortly afterward. There is no need of considering the old theory that the poem had been written years before, since there is no evidence in favor of such a speculation and very much evidence against it. The obvious facts are that the mythological poem was beginning to be fashionable and that the young playwright, in a theatrical off-season, decided to try the new recipe.

There is no reason to think that Shakespeare borrowed from any Italian source. The citations of Sir Sidney Lee and others only help to show, what is important enough in itself, that certain motives and methods of treatment were common property among Renaissance poets. It is hardly necessary to ransack continental authors to find a source for the sunny atmosphere of *Venus and Adonis,* or for such a conceit as the boar's wanting merely to kiss the youth, which was a commonplace of sixteenth-century verse.[1] Shakespeare's appropriation, if direct, of Ronsard's lines,

> Les Muses lierent un iour
> De chaisnes de roses, Amour[2]

does stimulate one to look further, especially in Ronsard's version of the story of Adonis. This is quite different in conception from Shakespeare's, but there is, as Sir Sidney Lee observed, a similarity in tone and temper, though perhaps no more than natural coincidence.[3]

The chief items in Shakespeare's debt to Ovidian material are set forth in every edition of the poems and may be briefly summarized.[4] From the

---

tenth book of the *Metamorphoses* he takes the central figures and something of the general background; from the eighth book the description of the boar, which reveals verbal echoes of Golding.[5] Since the Adonis of Ovid and common tradition is not a reluctant lover, it has generally and reasonably been assumed that Shakespeare partly modeled his characters on the wanton and dominating Salmacis and the shy young Hermaphroditus, as these appear in Ovid's fourth book.[6] The somewhat similar story of Narcissus and Echo may also have been in the poet's mind; but more will be said of Adonis a little later. This outline gives an exaggerated notion of the actual amount of matter taken over from Ovid, for, in proportion to the length of Shakespeare's poem, it is really slight.

A few not insignificant details of probable Ovidian coloring may be added. When we read

> Look, how a bright star shooteth from the sky,
> So glides he in the night from Venus' eye,

we may be justifiably content to praise a vivid original image. But we may also remember these lines from Golding's second book:

> But Phaeton (fire yet blasing stil among his
>   yellow haire)
> Shot headlong downe, and glid along the Region of
>   the Ayre
> Like to [a] Starre in winter nightes (the wether
>   cleare and fayre),

or this,

> There glyding from the sky a starre streyght downe too ground was
> sent.[7]

There may be a similar mingling of common observation and bookish or pictorial reminiscence in the description of Venus running:

> And as she runs, the bushes in the way
> Some catch her by the neck, some kiss her face,
> Some twine about her thigh to make her stay . . .

There is a hint of this in Ovid's first book, in the words of Apollo to the fleeing Daphne, and more than a hint in the picture offered to Christopher Sly:

> Or Daphne roaming through a thorny wood,
> Scratching her legs that one shall swear she bleeds;
> And at that sight shall sad Apollo weep,
> So workmanly the blood and tears are drawn.[8]

The most attractive passage of any length in *Venus and Adonis* is the account of the hunted hare, a very English vignette in this conventional Arcadia. Reading it we may say, with Bagehot, that we know Shakespeare had been after a hare. But recollections of Warwickshire seem to be mixed with recollections of Ovid. Poor Wat in desperation

> sometime sorteth with a herd of deer;
> Danger deviseth shifts; wit waits on fear.

Ovid, describing the pursuit of Daphne by Apollo, has an elaborate simile of a hare and hound, which ends with a typical Ovidian line, *Sic deus et virgo est, hic spe celer, illa timore.*[9] Shakespeare's phrase is an evident attempt to rival in English the antithetical brevity of the Latin.[10]

This particular example suggests the importance of Ovid as one source of a conspicuous element in the style of *Venus and Adonis,* that is, the antithetical pattern of lines and phrases. Here are some of the more obvious instances in the first fifty lines:

> Hunting he lov'd, but love he laugh'd to scorn.

> Saith that the world hath ending with thy life.

> But rather famish them amid their plenty.

> Ten kisses short as one, one long as twenty.

> He red for shame, but frosty in desire.

> Backward she push'd him, as she would be thrust,
> And govern'd him in strength, though not in lust.

It is hardly too much to say that the whole fabric of the poem is woven of antitheses, as if Shakespeare had fallen in love with one of Ovid's tricks and worked it to death. The central antithesis of subject, between the warm goddess and the cold youth, is reflected in line after line that breaks more or less clearly into two parts containing opposed ideas. The use of the antithetical formula is marked enough in narrative and descriptive passages; it is, as one would expect, still more persistent in the speeches. One must allow of course for the Petrarchan and euphuistic delight in logical and verbal antitheses, but eager first-hand imitation of Ovid evidently counted a good deal. When one compares *Venus and Adonis* with the work of Lodge and Spenser it is plain that, while Shakespeare exploits Italianate conventions, his taut style is different in texture from the smooth velvet of Italianate verse.[11]

To say that *Venus and Adonis* reveals hardly a trace of direct foreign influence is not of course to say that apart from Ovidian elements it is an original poem. Even in the plays Shakespeare was seldom an innovator; his way was to accept the current fashion and excel in it. His first narrative poem, naturally, is almost wholly conventional, an exhaustive collection of traditional motives and devices, though he appropriates them, and plies his nimble wit in embroidering them, with as much zest as if they were his own jerks of invention. Shakespeare breathed the same air as other men, and his scent for popular formulas was unusually keen and prophetic. The luxuriant Italianate manner had been naturalized in England, and no immediate foreign contacts were necessary. Not only was every poetical device at hand, there was also Elizabethan fiction. If in Shakespeare's poems action bears to rhetoric much the same proportion as bread to sack in Falstaff's bill, we may remember the technique of Pettie, Lyly, and Greene in their prose tales.

Shakespeare's representation of a chaste youth solicited by an amorous woman had precedents not only in Ovid but in the pastoral traditions derived partly from Ovid. The vain pursuit of a woman by a man or of a man by a woman was, as we have seen in connection with Lodge, the stock situation of the Italian pastoral. The conventions had now become familiar in English, and *Venus and Adonis,* like the other mythological poems, makes use of them (though it stands somewhat apart on account of its more direct imitation of Ovidian style). There must be an obstacle somewhere in such stories of love; if Adonis were as willing as Barkis, and Venus equally laconic, what would become of the poem? As for Shakespeare's choice of the more piquant of the two standard situations, it offered some obvious advantages. Since it appears virtually certain that he had read *Hero and Leander,* he might have felt as Rosetti did about *The Raven*—that, as Poe had said all that could be said on one aspect of the theme, *The Blessed Damozel* would take the other side.

Anyone who knew Leander's plea could hardly avoid the conviction that the subject must be freshened by reversal of the parts.

For the particular conception of a reluctant Adonis there were suggestions at hand also. There is a faint hint of initial coyness in the Adonis of Spenser:

> Then with what sleights and sweet allurements she
> Entyst the Boy, as well that art she knew,
> And wooed him her Paramoure to be.

Further, Spenser's picture of Venus watching Adonis bathe suggests a mild combination of the story with that of Salmacis and Hermaphroditus.[12] Less vague are two songs of Greene's quoted by all the editors, which show that the notion of a chaste Adonis was current; they appear in *Perimedes the Blacke-smithe* (1588) and *Never Too Late* (1590). Marlowe's allusions to Venus and "proud Adonis" is sufficiently different from Shakespeare's conception to suggest independent use of a non-classical variant. Thus Shakespeare had only to look about him to find hints for a cold Adonis.[13]

Shakespeare was obviously indebted to Lodge's languidly pretty *Glaucus and Scilla,* both in the central theme and in details, such as the popular sixain stanza and the likewise popular "echo" device. Lodge's purple patch on Venus and Adonis, which was quoted above, is enough to indicate not only the degree to which Shakespeare caught the Italianate style, but the extent of his rhetorical originality and vigor. In all points, form as well as detail, Shakespeare greatly bettered his instruction.[14]

Shakespeare doubtless knew at least two treatments of Adonis in Spenser; a few lines from one passage have already been quoted. Spenser's symbolic adaptation of the myth in the sixth canto of the third book is quite remote from Shakespeare's, for Shakespeare's attitude toward his material is simply that of a Renaissance Ovid; his Venus and Adonis are symbolic only in the sense that they and everything connected with them are manifestations of physical beauty. The pictorial warmth and richness of Spenser's work in general must have affected Shakespeare, as such qualities affected most poets of the day, but *Venus and Adonis* has a distinct hardness and precision of line which is not Spenserian. Whatever Italian Shakespeare picked up, he does not, even at his most florid, write like Spenser and others to whom the soft fluidity of Italian verse was both more familiar and more congenial.[15]

The influence of Marlowe the dramatist upon Shakespeare was so strong that it affected the structure, characterization, and style of some of the earlier plays. The influence of *Hero and Leander* upon *Venus and Ado-*

nis, however, is both obvious and superficial. Some apparent resemblances are only characteristics of the mythological genre. What seem to be demonstrable borrowings, though numerous, are mainly incidental and external, and Shakespeare, for good or ill, subdues them to his own style and mode of treatment. Many passages in the Marlowesque plays one might assign to Marlowe; there are few bits of *Venus and Adonis* that could be mistaken for quotations from *Hero and Leander.*

Conceits of course everyone delighted in, but Shakespeare's, especially those of the myth-making sort, sometimes resemble Marlowe's. Mythological allusions were also common property, and Shakespeare, like his fellows, took them indifferently from Ovid and from modern sources.[16] Since Shakespeare's plays are full of mythological allusions,[17] and since these were a conventional element in the mythological poem as established by Lodge and Marlowe, it may be observed that such allusions in *Venus and Adonis* are relatively scanty and unadorned. If in this respect Shakespeare departed from the convention he was evidently following Lodge and Marlowe—and Ovid—when he scattered aphorisms and epigrams through an erotic poem. The amorous arguments of Venus recall Leander's and those of the *Sonnets,* where the theme of procreation is decidedly more pertinent than in the mouth of the undomestic goddess.[18]

The differences between Marlowe and Shakespeare are no less obvious, and more important, than the resemblances. Hero and Leander, despite Marlowe's inconsistencies of characterization and excess of decoration, win our sympathy; there is warmth and something of natural passion. Shakespeare, dealing with an unattractive pair who are more remote from humanity, fiddles on the strings of sensuality without feeling or awakening any such sympathy, without even being robustly sensual. Marlowe has too many merely pretty lines, but generally he is strong, masculine, swift; Shakespeare is much more content with prettiness, and the poem, though far from languid, is sickled o'er with effeminacy. Many lines in *Hero and Leander* glow with a beauty that might be called haunting if the word were not overworn; the reader of *Venus and Adonis* is chiefly impressed by the astonishing skill of phrase and rhythm—

Which bred more beauty in his angry eyes.

Leading him prisoner in a red-rose chain.

Full gently now she takes him by the hand,
A lily prison'd in a gaol of snow.

But when one thinks of "Love's not Time's fool," not to mention the plays, one is made aware of the fatal lack of emotion. Finally it is noteworthy, in a poem which is a tissue of bookish conventions, that Shakespeare's best bits of imagery are fresh pictures of nature. Marlowe's images are almost wholly a fusion of art, literature, and imagination.

Incongruity of costume we have already observed as a normal element of mythological poems as well as other types of Renaissance writing, and Shakespeare of course does not depart from the mode. When Venus approaches Adonis and "heaveth up his hat," and at other times, we have a suspicion that we are witnessing an Arcadian encounter between a scantily clad Maid of Honor and, say, the Earl of Southampton in a rare moment of satiety.[19] Indeed if one considers the opportunities offered by Shakespeare's subject, and the popularity of voluptuous anatomical catalogues, in which even the sober Sidney and the philosophic Spenser and Chapman indulged, Shakespeare's neglect of "the nude" is somewhat remarkable. This is another respect in which Shakespeare is closer to Ovid—the Ovid of the *Metamorphoses,* that is—than to the Italianate fashion.[20]

The Shakespeare of the mature plays is greatest perhaps in his power over words; he uses language as if it were his own creation and he alone understood its infinite capacities. In the poems there are few traces of such concentration and suggestion; the words mean what they say, and this is not much. Only a few times in *Venus and Adonis* is there a slight break in the flat, two-dimensional surface, when the poet works in a natural image from his own observation, the dive-dapper, the snail, the gentle lark, the dew-bedabbled hare, and such fresh glimpses of something real, welcome as they are, heighten the total effect of artifice. In them, however, we do have a faint promise of the real Shakespeare, the poet who can see and feel and communicate what he sees and feels. On the other hand the auctioneer's description of the horse, which, since Hazlitt, has so often been put beside the passage on the hounds in the *Midsummer Night's Dream,* shows the difference between the minute, self-defeating realism of the tyro and the swift, suggestive strokes of the master. The horse embodies all the good points prescribed in Elizabethan treatises on the animal, and remains a catalogue; we see, hear, touch, and smell the hounds.

The living things described in the poem are not all creatures of the English countryside. We know that the man who wrote of the lark ascending, or of "poor Wat," had been in the fields as well as in his study. We know that the same man fully shared the taste of his age when we read this:

To see his face the lion walk'd along
Behind some hedge, because he would not fear him;
To recreate himself when he hath sung,
The tiger would be tame and gently hear him;
  If he had spoke, the wolf would leave his prey,
  And never fright the silly lamb that day.

When he beheld his shadow in the brook,
The fishes spread on it their golden gills. . . .

Even if such a string of fancies be half humorous—and Venus' lamentation is not especially merry—it reminds us that Shakespeare not only laughed at euphuism but practiced it with some relish. The poem everywhere shows that its author lavished artistic labor upon it, in a sense put himself into it, yet perhaps nothing proves more clearly what a circumscribed self it was than the fact that the creator of this polite lion behind an English hedge was shortly to create another kind of polite lion for Snug the joiner. But every age, our own included, has its stylistic tricks which lose their charm for posterity.

    The Elizabethans generally anticipated Wilde in believing that nothing succeeds like excess, and if we dislike their rhetorical extravagance it is after all no great price to pay for their unique virtues. Their exuberant excesses, were the natural overflow of tremendous energy in an era of uncertain taste and an intoxicated delight in words. In the plays Shakespeare never entirely outgrew his love of rhetoric, though his critical powers ripened with his other faculties and enabled him to satirize flamboyance. In *Venus and Adonis* he seems quite satisfied and happy in seriously exploiting the popular conceits, decoration, rhetorical wooing, rhetorical declamation. In the speeches of Venus we have the arguments of an Ovidian lover combined with the strained fancies of a sonneteer, moral aphorisms, and, even from Adonis when he finds his tongue, some of the paradoxes on the nature of love so dear to Elizabethan writers,[21] all worked out with an inexhaustible ingenuity that compels a kind of admiration. The poem is indeed a bible for lovers. To quote one allusion out of many, a character in a play of 1640 longs for "the book of *Venus and Adonis* to court my mistress by."[22] And when speaking of rhetoric one must notice Venus' apostrophe to Death, which is thoroughly of the Renaissance and also thoroughly medieval.[23]

    F.T. Prince, the latest editor of Shakespeare's poems, finds *Venus and Adonis* "a complete artistic success, despite some flaws or weaker passages," and sees its "imaginative unity" in its view of elemental and human passions as a feast for the mind and the spirit: as sometimes moving, and sometimes amusing, but always offering an absorbing living spectacle. This is the indulgent mood of Shakespeare's comedies, with their delight in human energies and emotion, their keen savour of everyday life mixed with abundant poetry, and their undertones of deeper seriousness.

He also sees a unique fusion of "romance and humour" and "sympathetic irony" in the presentation of Venus.[24] Professor Prince, as both a poet and a scholar, is the best kind of judge, but one may be unable to go along with such a favorable view. Also, Professor Prince makes no reference to numerous critics of recent years who have reinterpreted the poem in various ways that go well beyond Coleridge. For example, Adonis represents the destruction of beauty by evil, or an incapacity to respond to the ideal of Platonic love and beauty, or a rational and ethical rejection of lust (Venus having the several corresponding roles, earthy or transcendental); and the poem as a whole is a tragic parable of the fall of man or a farcical comedy or several things between. The fact that Elizabethan readers were apparently unaware of all these themes does not of course prove that they are not there. Yet the multiplying of such contradictory interpretations may suggest, if not that the vagaries of current symbolical criticism are limitless, at least that Shakespeare's intention, whatever it was, does not come through very clearly. If *Venus and Adonis* were plainly nothing more than a two-dimensional tapestry, all would be well, in a limited way. But for a sensual orgy it is too intellectual and serious, for a metaphysical fable it is too Ovidian. We observed partly similar discords in *Hero and Leander,* but in *Venus and Adonis* they are more central. The poem seems to waver between cool rhetorical contrivance and impassioned engagement, although the author seems to feel himself in complete and assured control of his direction and tone.

NOTES

1. The conceit had lately appeared in English in the *Sixe Idillia* of 1588. It occurs also in a French translation by Saint-Gelais (*Oeuvres,* Paris, 1873, I, 127) and in Latin in *Adonis Theocriti, ex Gallico Sangellasii* (Gruter, *Delitiae C. Poetarum Gallorum,* Part II, Sec. 1, p. 470); and in Minturno's *De Adoni ab apro interempto* (Gruter, *Delitiae CC. Italorum Poetarum,* II, 924).

2. These lines had already been cited and turned into English by that indefatigable borrower, Thomas Watson (*Poems,* ed. Arber, Sonnet lxxxiii, p. 119):

The Muses not long since intrapping Loue
In chaines of roases linked all araye.

Shakespeare's much finer phrase, "Leading him prisoner in a red-rose chain" (l. 110), admirably suggests the tone of a mass of amatory and mythological verse of the Renaissance. For Ronsard's poem see *Oeuvres*, ed. Marty-Laveaux, II, 360; and Lee, *French Renaissance in England*, p. 221.

3. *Oeuvres*, IV, 26 ff. Passages illustrating the similarity are collected in my note in *PQ*, VI, 300; one is quoted below, note 8. Lee's parallels with other French poets seem quite fanciful.

4. The fullest accounts of sources and themes are in H.E. Rollins and T.W. Baldwin.

5. This useful boar also contributed, apparently, to Spenser's dragon (L. Rick, *Ovid's Metamorphoses*, p. 58), though Whitney Wells showed the dragon's kinship with medieval monsters (MLN, XLI, 1926, 143 ff.).

6. On the resemblances between Adonis and Hermaphroditus see Pooler's edition of the poems, pp. xxxi–xxxii.

7. Golding, ed. Rouse, p. 49, ll. 404–06; p. 294, l. 978; *V. and A.*, ll. 815–16.

8. *Taming of the Shrew*, Induction, ii.59 ff. Cf. Ronsard's poem on Adonis (Oeuvres, IV, 34):

> Furieuse d'esprit, criant à haute vois,
> Ie veux escheuellée errer parmy les bois,
> Pieds nuds, estomac nud: ie veux que ma poitrine
> Se laisse esgrafiner à toute dure espine,
> Ie veux que les chardons me deschirent la peau.

Of course the idea is in Bion.

9. *Metam.* i.539; cf. Golding (p. 34, ll. 659–60):

> So farde Apollo and the Mayde: hope made Apollo swift,
> And feare did make the Mayden fleete devising how to shift.

10. With *V. and A.*, ll. 681 ff. and 703 ff., compare Golding's lines about the hound of Cephalus (pp. 156–57, ll. 1014–17):

> And like a wilie Foxe he runnes not forth directly out,
> Nor makes a windlasse over all the champion fieldes about,
> But doubling and indenting still avoydes his enmies lips.

See also Pooler's notes on the Shakespearian lines.

11. This poem, like the plays, shows that Shakespeare was familiar with both Ovid's Latin and Golding's English. See Rollins, Baldwin, and Bullough.

12. *F.Q.*, III.i.35–36.

13. Adlington's *Golden Asse* (ed. Seccombe, 1913, p. 48) has the phrase "as the proude yonge man Adonis who was torne by a Bore"; the epithet does not seem to be the common one for Adonis. There is a hint of a chaste Adonis in Servius on *Ecl.* x.18 (ed. Thilo and Hagen, III.i, pp. 121–22). It will be remembered that the Venus of Lyly's *Sapho and Phao* (1584) is decidedly aggressive.

For later combinations of Venus and Adonis with Salmacis and Hermaphroditus (*Taming of the Shrew*, Induction, ii.52–55; *Passionate Pilgrim*), it is enough to refer to some discussions in editions of Shakespeare's poems, such as those of Pooler (pp. xxx–xxxi), Carleton Brown (pp. xxi ff.), Feuillerat (pp. 185–86); and Chambers, *William Shakespeare*, I, 547–48.

14. Pooler, pp. xvi–xvii, gives the chief parallels between Shakespeare and Lodge.

15. Spenser's *Astrophel* was published in 1595, though probably written some years earlier. The passage on Adonis (ll. 151 ff.) is somewhat akin to Shakespeare, but still closer to Lodge and continental imitations of Bion.

Another luxuriant handling of the story appears in Fraunce's *Third part of the Countesse of Pembrokes Ivychurch* (1592). Since the book is rare I may quote some lines:

> Sometimes downe by a well with Adonis sweetly she
> sitteth,
> And on Adonis face in well-spring louely she looketh,
> And then Adonis lipps with her owne lipps kindely she
> kisseth,
> Rolling tongue, moyst mouth with her owne mouth all to be
> sucking,
> Mouth and tong and lipps, with Ioues drinck Nectar
> abounding.
> Sometimes, louely records for Adonis sake, she
> reciteth;
> How Lænder dyde, as he swamme to the bewtiful Hero,
> How great Alcides was brought from a club to a distaffe
> . . . .
> Sometimes unto the shade of a braunched beech she
> repaireth,
> Where sweete bubling brook with streames of siluer
> aboundeth,
> And faire-feathred birde on tree-top cherefuly
> chirpeth;
> There her voyce, which makes eu'n Ioue himselfe to be
> ioying,
> Unto the waters fall, and birds chirpe ioyfuly tuning.

Venus is here presented as the wooer. In particular one may compare the fourth and fifth lines of the quotation with *V. and A.*, ll. 541 ff., and l. 572. "Such nectar from his lips she had not suck'd"—which, to be sure, is not beyond Shakespeare's unaided imagination. One may note, with the same reservation, Shakespeare's "Ten kisses short as one, one long as twenty" (l. 22), and Fraunce's

> Thinking euery howre to be two, and two to be twenty,
> Til she beheld her boy . . .

16. For instance, though Shakespeare knew Ovid so well, he was content to take over, perhaps from Marlowe, the non-Ovidian drowning of Narcissus.

17. In addition to the older discussions of mythology in the plays there are the brief but suggestive remarks of George H.W. Rylands in his *Words and Poetry* (1928), pp. 87 ff, 135 ff.

18. Parallels between *Hero and Leander* and Shakespeare are recorded in various editions, e.g., Pooler (pp. xxii ff.).

For echoes of Ovid in Shakespeare's poems (and *Sonnets*), see T.W. Baldwin.

19. In his first *Elizabethan Journal* (London, 1928, pp. xii, 236) Mr. G.B. Harrison gives a reproduction of a tapestry that depicts Venus and Adonis in the dress of the period, and remarks: "This, rather than the more fleshly kind of painting, was the Elizabethan conception of Venus. The connection between tapestry pictures and such narrative poems as *Venus and Adonis* and *Hero and Leander* is close."

20. There are to be sure such lines as 233 ff., which are sensual enough, but their indirectness is far from the set description.

21. For these paradoxes see lines 649 ff., 793 ff., 1137 ff. Since almost every Elizabethan indulged in at least one such series it is needless to give references. Miss Jeffery comments on the habit (*John Lyly*, pp. 82, 123).

22. Pupillus in Lewis Sharpe's *The Nobler Stranger*.

23. Cf. the address to Death in the *Philomena*.

24. *The Poems* (Arden Edition, 1960), pp. xxv–xxxii.

Shakespeare's Philosophy of Love

Lu Emily Pearson

Shakespeare had to solve the problem of harmonizing physical and rational love, and like a true Petrarchan, he approached this analysis through a study of the soul of woman. But in order to follow him as he worked his way toward a solution, we shall have to leave the sonnets for a time and consider his early poems and plays about love. In *Venus and Adonis,* he used the sonnet theme of the contest between sensual love and reasonable love, elaborating the whole struggle with all the gorgeous descriptions one might expect from his Renaissance age. He showed Venus, trying all the sweet snares of the flesh, in her effort to win the youth, but Adonis, who loved hunting and the manly sports of wholesome living, "laughed love to scorn" (l. 4). He "blush'd and pouted in a dull disdain" when Venus took him by the arm (l. 33), and when he saw her hot desire, he was "red for shame," and called her "immodest." Unable to withdraw himself from her kisses, he lay panting, "forc'd to content, but never to obey!" (l. 61). When she continued to entreat him for just one kiss, he was sullen "'Twixt crimson shame and anger ashy-pale" (l. 76), but in order to free himself he promised a kiss, only to turn away his lips as she advanced to claim it. Hereupon, Venus began to plead that "Beauty within itself should not be wasted" (l. 130), and "Things growing to themselves are growth's abuse" (l. 167), and "beauty breedeth beauty" (l. 168). But still Adonis looked on her with a "heavy, dark, disliking eye" till in desperation, Venus taunted him with "Art thou a woman's son, and canst not feel What 'tis to love?" (ll. 201–202). She declared hotly that he was no man, but his only answer was to struggle to free himself from her clasp. At this point Shakespeare introduced the natural love of the libertine. "A breeding jennet, lusty, young, and proud," burst from a

---

Reprinted from *Elizabethan Love Conventions* (Berkeley: U of California P, 1933), pp. 283–85, with permission.

thicket (l. 260), and Adonis' charger broke loose from where he was tied, to follow his love. Adonis, angry, asked Venus to leave him, for now his only thought was how to "get his palfrey from the mare," to which she but advised him "To take advantage of presented joy" (l. 405), and he in dark anger replied:

> My love to love is love but to disgrace it;
> For I have heard it is a life in death,
> That laughs and weeps, and all but with a breath.
> (ll. 412–414)

Unable to send sensual love from him, Adonis finally said plainly:

> Remove your siege from my unyielding heart;
> To love's alarms it will not ope the gate:
> (ll. 422–424)

As a last resort, Venus tried her most appealing charm; she fainted, all lovely as beautiful death before the youth's glance of fierce disdain. And when he revived her, and she renewed her entreaties to love, he answered:

> I hate not love, but your device in love
> That lends embracements unto every stranger
> You do it for increase: O strange excuse!
> When reason is the bawd to lust's abuse.
> (ll. 789–792)

All the pent-up anger of reason in love then burst forth against lust:

> Call it not love, for Love to heaven is fled,
> Since sweating Lust on earth usurp'd his name;
> Under whose simple semblance he hath fed
> Upon fresh beauty, blotting it with blame;
>   Which the hot tyrant stains and soon bereaves,
>   As caterpillars do the tender leaves.(ll. 793–798)

And like a cooling shower in the heat of summer, came the following words:

> Love comforteth like sunshine after rain,
> But Lust's effect is tempest after sun;

Love's gentle spring doth always fresh remain,
Lust's winter comes ere summer half be done.
　　Love surfeits not, Lust like a glutton dies;
　　Love is all truth, Lust full of forged lies.

(ll. 799–804)

So Venus is shown as the destructive agent of sensual love; Adonis, as reason in love. The one sullies whatever it touches; the other honors and makes it beautiful. The one is false and evil; the other is all truth, all good. Reason in love, truth, beauty—these are the weapons with which lust must be met, or the ideals of man must go down in defeat before the appetites. Thus it is that when Adonis is killed, beauty is killed, and the world is left in black chaos, for beauty, the soul of matter, unites all parts of creation with the great God of beauty. This is the teaching of *Venus and Adonis*, as didactic a piece of work, perhaps, as Shakespeare ever wrote.

FUNCTION OF IMAGERY IN *VENUS AND ADONIS*

Hereward T. Price

It has now become a commonplace procedure to interpret a poet by an examination of his imagery. Since Miss Spurgeon[1] blazed the trail, scholars have poured out innumerable books and articles on imagery in Shakespeare. They have collected, numbered, filed, sorted, and pigeonholed Shakespeare's images on every conceivable system. Their work has established beyond a reasonable doubt the principle that Shakespeare so subtly interlaced the images in a particular work that by supporting, reinforcing, and echoing one another they help to build up, together with other aids, a logical and coherent "form."

In *Venus and Adonis* Shakespeare has devised for himself a new technique of imagery. The microcosm, the little world inside man, is carried out into the macrocosm, the great world of Nature at large.[2] By strictly adhering to a special sort of figure Shakespeare has made his poem appear so "objective" or so "external" that most scholars and critics ignore its power of projecting in a chosen form the inner life of man, the only reality for which Shakespeare ever cared.

Nobody has worked this out for *Venus and Adonis* in detail. Coleridge, of course, in a memorable passage, has celebrated the power that Shakespeare displayed in the images of *Venus and Adonis*.[3] J.S. Hart has put Shakespeare's technique into a sentence: "The poem is not marked by stirring action, but by a series of minutely finished pictures."[4] In this paper my purpose is to go beyond Coleridge and Hart in an endeavor to show how a common center of reference links all these images together and so gives them meaning. It is unnecessary to point out that meaning cannot be separated from form. I stress meaning, however, because, so far as I am aware, nobody has given adequate thought to the meaning of *Venus and Adonis* and,

Reprinted from *Papers of the Michigan Academy of Science, Arts, and Letters* 31 (1945), 271–7 and 285–92. Copyright © University of Michigan Press.

as a consequence, the poem has been hugely underrated.

Let us then, at the risk of repeating what has been said too often, make clear what Shakespeare was doing. He was not a Sophocles or a Boccaccio telling a tale that holds us by the faultless development of the action. He has, indeed, a story that gives the poem a beginning, a middle, and an end. But on a superficial view at any rate, his work seems to be flooded by an ocean of superfluous images. The truth is that Shakespeare makes the plot of *Venus and Adonis* as simple as possible in order to enable the reader to follow the intricate imagery more easily. It is important, therefore, to show that Shakespeare's images are interrelated by a general similarity of subject and that they all bear reference to the same central idea. They are full of the open air and the life of man and beast and plant in wild nature, and they are all steeped in the same implication with regard to the nature they symbolize. *Mutatis mutandis,* the technique is not unlike that of T.S. Eliot's *Waste Land.* As in all his works, Shakespeare creates a world existing by its own laws and so powerfully alive that it makes on us the impression of being as real as the world in which we move. It is not a pleasant place. The business both of the scholar and of the critic is to discover what happens in that world to make it a thing of such horror.

I propose to proceed by the historical method and to see the poem in connection with its age. The young Aristotelians of my acquaintance depreciate such methods. They assert that a poem must be considered as a thing apart and that the critic must never explain one work of art by another. A poem, they say, must stand on its own legs; the poet made it the way it is, and we must take it or leave it, just as he gave it to us. But I do not see why we should refuse the aid of history. It is important to point out that there is some resemblance between the work of Shakespeare and of Dürer. In an engraving by Dürer we have a multitude of details, all reinforcing one another, all pointing in the same direction, but they are so numerous that they have prevented critics from seeing what the picture is about. As a consequence, we have had to wait until the present generation for an adequate interpretation of his "Melancolia." Now it is curious that *Venus and Adonis* and *Lucrece* are in the same case as the "Melancolia." I am not accusing Shakespeare of being Dürer, but it is important to note that the art of these two men rises from the same sources. They are both the offspring of the Gothic, and the principle of their technique is to convey a great idea not through economy and the clear line, but through a multiplicity of significant detail. A student of the Renaissance who has soaked himself in Dürer and recognized how superb is his achievement will find himself at home in *Venus and Adonis.*

But there is a more intimate aspect of the historical method. It is a sober fact that *Venus and Adonis* does not stand alone in Shakespeare's work. On the contrary, it is more or less contemporary not only with the historical plays like *Henry VI, Richard III,* and *Richard II,* but also with *Romeo and Juliet* and with *Lucrece.* In these works we find the same theme, intermittent in some, overwhelmingly predominant in others—the theme, namely, of the destruction of something exquisite by what is outrageously vile. Man and the cosmic process are at irreconcilable war; the ends of man are denied by the world he lives in. The good life is at the mercy of a blind destructive force. All these works are tragedies, and the fundamental theme of Shakespeare's tragedy is the existence of evil. Πόθεν τὸ κακόν; Whence evil? All these works are concerned with the same problem of why evil should be free to destroy the good. Shakespeare can no more answer the question than any other poet, but in posing it he shows that negative capability of which Keats speaks. What is not clear to him, what he does not know, he excludes; he gives only that aspect of the problem which he sees, without trying to bring in the whole of truth. In these works he is fascinated by the complete irrationality of evil. It is the situation he treats most superbly in *Othello.* New York critics of the recent performance of that play were inclined to blame Shakespeare for the irrationality of the action. The whole thing appeared to them meaningless, and they appeared to think that this lack of meaning was Shakespeare's fault. They suggested or implied that a more intelligent dramatist would have arranged a catastrophe subtle enough to satisfy the intellect of the New York press. Now *Othello* and *Romeo and Juliet* and *Lucrece* and *Venus and Adonis* are all about the same thing—that is to say, the destruction of something good by a force that is not only vile but also so blind that it does not even know what it is destroying.

* * *

We now come to the real subject of the paper, to *Venus and Adonis.* The poem has had its ups and downs. At first a best seller, it ran to sixteen editions in Shakespeare's lifetime, but from 1655 to 1866 not a single separate edition was published. The general attitude of critics is indicated by the note in Gabriel Harvey's *Marginalia:* "The younger sort takes much delight in Shakespeare's Venus and Adonis: but his Lucrece, and his tragedie of Hamlet, have in them to please the wiser sort." A tendency to deprecate Shakespeare's choice of subject has persisted down to the present day. For shame's sake I shall refrain from giving names or references. But one critic speaks of the poem's being "saved from degradation" by airiness and grace. Another rejects it for its sensualism and speaks of its "occasional and tardy morality" but praises its "outdoor poetry." As a rule, the criticism of *Venus and Adonis* reminds us of Tennyson in a black Victorian mood ranting about "art with poisonous honey stolen from France" and the "troughs of Zolaism." Few critics see that Shakespeare is both fascinated and appalled by the evil he is describing; fewer still have penetrated his savage irony.

Scholars and critics have all earned the same reproach. They see the poem as a fortuitous concourse of atoms that have nothing to do with one another. Surely nobody ought to have set pen to paper until he had brought the "sensualism," the "morality," and the "outdoor poetry" into line. Even when critics are not offended by the subject matter, there is no disposition to treat the poem seriously. Coleridge, as one might expect, has dug deepest. He is the only critic who has even attempted to understand the poem properly or whose judgment of it approaches the truth. I propose to show that *Venus and Adonis* is much greater than Coleridge knew or, at any rate, implied. It is a serious attempt to grapple with a problem that gave Shakespeare for the greater part of his career no rest—the problem, that is, of evil.

Philologists who have a way of saying all that can be said about a poem and who yet miss the point have wreaked their wicked will on *Venus and Adonis*. They have pointed out that Shakespeare did not invent the motif of the coy Adonis, that the stanza he uses was not new in narrative, that the poem is permeated with the sweetness of mellifluous Ovid, that Shakespeare in an effort to make poetry do the work of painting blazoned the tale in splendid colors, that for the rest he proceeds by means of an old and almost threadbare technique, employing the debate, elaborate dialogue, long speeches and apostrophes, amplification, and God's plenty of proverbs, wise saws, and gnomic sayings. In his narrative technique Shakespeare is a disciple of Chaucer, starting where Chaucer left off. Scholars add that Shakespeare's use of images observed directly from nature proves that he wrote *Venus and Adonis* in the countryside of Stratford-on-Avon, apparently before he lost contact with nature in the town. It has never occurred to them to ask about the function of such natural imagery in this poem, and until that question has been answered, nothing else matters.

It is important to notice that Shakespeare's scale of images comes to him from Bion's elegy on Adonis. Venus mourns Adonis, whom a boar has slain by a wound in the thigh. She rushes to the body of Adonis, through brake and brier, her clothes torn, and the sharp thorns covering her body with blood. All nature mourns for Adonis, the mountains, the oaks, the rivers, and the flowers. From the ground where he dies two flowers spring up, the rose from his blood, and the anemone from the tears of Venus. Apart from the details of the story, Shakespeare may have learnt from Bion's skill in contrasting color; purple and black robes, blood on snow-white skin, bright eyes and rosy lips fading to pallor, the purple pall on the corpse of Adonis, the two contrasting flowers. But, most significant of all, Bion's elegy is not *about* Venus and Adonis. With a Greek delicacy and subtlety that an English pen finds it hard to convey, it is *about* a process of nature. One might almost say that the spirit of Bion had passed into Shakespeare. At any rate, whether by accident or design, *Venus and Adonis* resembles no poem so closely as it does the elegy of Bion.

One might digress for a moment to say that Shakespeare differed from other Renaissance poets in not imitating the ancients. He drank in the beauty of their poetry, but he observed them as a free man; he did not become their slave. The figures that Shakespeare borrows from classical myth are not in the least like those a Greek or a Latin poet would use. However, without smelling of the lamp they capture the full beauty of the original. They are often as fresh and lively as if stamped out new for the first time. Shakespeare is the most pagan of the English poets, and in nothing is he so pagan as in his power to present nature at work on man. Being quite untrammeled by conventional religion, he contemplates nature with a freedom of spirit such as we find only in the ancients. *A Midsummer Night's Dream* is the most pagan poem in English literature, and in the same class we may put *Venus and Adonis.*

Shakespeare read up his story in other classical sources besides Bion. He complicated Bion's simple tale by many inventions. From the thirty-first idyl of Theocritus he brought in the motif of the boar killing Adonis by misadventure, without intention. "I him beheld for love . . . Which made me forward shove His thigh . . . Thinking to kiss, alas."[5] Moreover, Shakespeare obviously knows Ovid's story of Adonis, and he interweaves with it motifs from the fables of the coy Salmacis. Shakespeare takes his boar from Ovid, but he makes significant additions, such as that the boar strikes whatever is in his way, his snout digs sepulchers, and the brambles and bushes are afraid of him.

The red and white flower into which *Shakespeare* transforms Adonis has a long history. We have seen that in Bion two flowers spring up from the blood of Adonis, a red one and an anemone. Ovid transforms Adonis into a red flower, and in another story tells how Narcissus was transformed into a white and yellow flower. In the Renaissance Ronsard follows Bion closely in his elegy on Adonis. Spenser, in his *Astrophel,* a pastoral elegy on the death of Sidney, tells how his love flung herself upon his dead body, and died of a broken heart. The gods in pity transformed them into a flower "both red and blue." It is certain that the Elizabethans read a meaning into the incident of the flower. George Sandys says:

> The Boy, *with whom Loue seemd'd to dy,* [italics added]
> Bleeds in the fresh Anemony.[6]

And later on:

> The louely Adonis is fained to haue been changed into Anemony, a beautifull but no permanent flower: *to expresse* the fraile condition and short continuance of Beautie.[7]

I may add that the Elizabethan botanists associated Adonis with the anemone. Thus Lyte:

> *Flos Adonis* should seeme to be none other, than a kind of Anemone. . . . Anemone is also called in shoppes likewise of some Flos Adonis.[8]

We also know that the anemone was a purple and white flower. Parkinson describes many varieties:

> There is also another [anemone] of the same Violet purple colour with the former, but a little paler, tending more to rednesse, whose flowers have many white lines and stripes through the leaues . . . [another] the colour of Carnation silke . . . with a whitish circle about the bottome of the leaues . . . [another] a faire whitish red, which we call, The Blush Anemone.[9]

Thus Shakespeare's red and white flower comes to him through Bion, Ovid, Spenser, and perhaps Ronsard. Sandys sees in this flower a symbol of the frailty of Beauty, of the boy with whom Love seemed to die. It gives one a thrill of pleasure to know that Shakespeare's symbolism was based not only upon tradition but also upon observed fact; the *flos Adonis* was an anemone, and some forms of anemone were "purple . . . checkred with white" (l. 1168).

However, the truth about *Venus and Adonis* is that, while Shakespeare borrows much from established convention, he is at the same time daringly original. In the main the poem is constructed with two series of images, finely articulated and often interlacing, namely, the images from nature, especially from wild animals, on the one hand; on the other, the images of red and white, dark and light. There is little about these images that is bookish, most of them being observed straight from the object. There is probably no other poem in which direct first-hand observation of nature has been used with such brilliant effect to create form. It is important to note how closely nature links *Venus and Adonis* with the *Midsummer Night's Dream* and *Romeo and Juliet*. In these three works nature is shown with subtle and profound significance, not as a backdrop to action but itself as a force, active in human life. The important matter, then, is to consider what sort of force this nature is shown to be.

The other set of symbols, the contrast between red and white, runs through the whole poem. In the use of this image Shakespeare shows as much originality and perhaps even more subtlety than in the images from nature. The technique of intertwining two or more series of images is the same as in *Lucrece* . . . where the main image is taken from war, while a subsidiary image, that of contrasting red and white, is also used.

Let us consider the nature symbol first. In *Venus and Adonis* nature is first of all a symbol at large. The story is about a boar hunt in a forest; the whole action occurs in the open air, and it might be said that the story is really about this nature in which men live, and move, and have their being. To repeat, nature interpenetrates the story so intimately that one cannot say that nature is the background or scene of events; rather, she is part of the action. Her colors are those of the characters:

> Even as the sunne with purple-coulourd face,
> Had tane his last leaue of the weeping morne,
> Rose-cheekt Adonis hied him to the chace. . . .
>
> (ll. 1–3)

When we say that the poem is about nature, then it is about nature in the widest possible sense. Shakespeare is not giving us a mere study of Stratford woods and fields. The subject is boldly announced in the opening of the poem:

> Nature that made thee *with her selfe at strife,* [italics added]
> Saith that the world hath ending with thy life.
>
> (ll. 11–12)

The poem is about "nature with herself at strife." In these words Shakespeare states the subject of all tragedy, the problem of the dissonances that destroy the harmony in the moral order of the world. Using nature in this sense as the subject of the poem, Shakespeare proceeds to set forth his meaning by a closely related chain of figures drawn entirely from nature in the sense of the world exterior to man. At the same time the system of natural imagery mirrors both the workings of whatever power rules the world and the moral qualities of human beings.

As the story takes place entirely in the open, so the poem vibrates with the movement of the air. Shakespeare fills it with the changes of nature as day passes into night and night again into day or as they are shown in the phenomena of the weather.[10] As one example for many:

> Loue comforteth like sun-shine after raine,
> But lusts effect is tempest after sunne,
> Loues gentle spring doth always fresh remaine,
> Lusts winter comes, ere sommer halfe be donne.
>
> (ll. 799–802)

This image is not simply something that occurred to Shakespeare and that he thought worth putting into his poem. He invents it with cold deliberation, illustrating the division of man's nature into good and bad by a figure showing that nature at large is split in the same way. By strictly limiting his choice of figures to such as accord with his central theme, Shakespeare achieves that unity of impression at which all poets aim, Classical or Romantic.

Since Homer elaborate descriptions of sunrise and sunset have been traditional in epic poetry. In days when there were neither clocks nor watches, time was observed from the progress of the sun or the stars. Shakespeare, following the ancient tradition, marks the passage of events by two descriptions of sunrise (ll. 1–2, 853–858) and one of sunset (ll. 529–534). In this way he kills two birds with one stone; he plays the game according to the rules, while at the same time making his poem as purely natural as possible. His first sunrise, with which the poem opens, is a red one and thus indicates the disaster to come. The coming of the second day is celebrated at ll. 853–858. Venus immediately salutes the sun:

> Oh thou cleare god, and patron of all light . . .
> There liues a sonne that suckt an earthly mother,
> May lend thee light, as thou doest lend to other.
>
> (ll. 860–864)

Adonis, like Juliet, is identified with light. The coming of night (529–534) is heralded by that fatal bellman the owl. Night is one of the most frequent figures in Shakespeare to symbolize Death. Nor is it mere prettiness that makes Shakespeare conclude his picture of nightfall with the line: "Coleblack clouds, that shadow heauens light" (l. 533). In these passages Shakespeare hints at the division of nature—this time into night and day, death and life, into darkness that swallows up light.

The persons of the poem are placed then in this setting of a world divided against itself. But what about these persons? For them Shakespeare invents a finely linked chain of animal images. Venus and Adonis are the huntress and the hunted. There is one set of figures for Adonis and a much larger and more important group for Venus. The figures invented for Adonis stress, of course, his sensitive delicacy.

> Vpon this promise did he raise his chin,
> Like a diuedopper peering through a waue,
> Who being lookt on, ducks as quickly in.
>
> (ll. 85–88)

His mood is described:

> Like a wild bird being tam'd with too much handling,
> Or as the fleet-foot Roe that's tyr'd with chasing.
>
> (ll. 560–561)

Shakespeare foreshadows his fate in the long figure of the hare, lust's victim, relentlessly pursued to be enjoyed, only to its destruction (ll. 679–708). Shakespeare did not invent these figures merely because he still happened to be living in the country. They are part of an intricate scheme in which the cruelties practiced in nature symbolize the fate of something too bright and exquisite to live.

Venus is described in a series of figures that represent the various sides of her nature. Her irrepressible desire to possess and to destroy is represented in three figures; she is the eagle (ll. 55–60), the horse (ll. 259–318), the boar (ll. 614–642, 1105–1118). The figures gradually rise in intensity. The eagle's fierce desire is remorseless as it tears its prey to pieces. It is a figure of lust and cruelty joined in destruction, but as Shakespeare is for the present only foreshadowing the climax, he keeps it short. Then comes the figure of the horse, its uncontrollable animal passion a convincing picture of the power of lust in Venus, lust that has taken the bit between its teeth.

> The yron bit he crusheth tweene his teeth,
> Controlling what he was controlled with.
>
> (ll. 269–270)

Then the boar, that kills blindly, not seeing or knowing what it destroys, Venus in her most horrible symbol.

But the boar loves while he blindly slays, and Venus also has her moments of tenderness.

> She wildly breaketh from their [bushes'] strict imbrace,
> Like a milch Doe, whose swelling dugs do ake,
> Hasting to feed her fawne, hid in some brake.
>
> (ll. 874–876)

Only the man to whom has been vouchsafed the luck of seeing the milch doe in the forest can realize the wonder of this figure. I have enjoyed it once when a milch doe loped by me with an indescribable grace and bent over a fence to lick its young, a tiny stag calf, and, when I approached, lightly footed away with the same entrancing beauty. This is the most glorious sight that the forest has to show. It would not be easy to imagine any other figure from animal life that should depict so aptly the Queen of Love in her distress for Adonis.

The primary importance of these images is that they are not chosen at random, the idle harvest of a luxurious mind remembering happy hours. Zola is said to have observed that the artist when he begins to write must be as cold as ice. In order, then, to build up his great symbol of life in nature, Shakespeare, in Zola's spirit, puts together these figures with cunning deliberation. The images cohere and form a logical unit. Carefully planned, they lend on from one to another in a rising scale of intensity, with the result that in no other Elizabethan poem is the intellectual interest sustained at such a high level.

When we come to the second series of symbols, the conflict of red and white which is resolved in the flower that springs from the corpse of Adonis, it is difficult at first for the modern reader to find his way. We cannot nowadays recapture the Elizabethan delight in the symbolism of colors and flowers. But taking probability as our guide, we can say that we shall probably go wrong if we are insensitive to the manifold suggestions of meaning that are implied by the use of colors and flowers in poetry. The difference between Shakespeare and the other Elizabethan poets of the nineties is that his flowers and colors are firmly integrated into a scheme of symbols, so firmly that they are, like his animal pictures, fitted into a tight, logical structure.

. . . The colors red and white thread *Lucrece* and how aptly Shakespeare uses them to convey certain meanings. "The war of red and white" is one of those figures that Elizabethan poets wore thin. Shakespeare makes fun of it in *The Taming of the Shrew* (IV.v.30), but in *3 Henry VI* (II.v.97–101) he uses it to symbolize the tragic mess of the Wars of the Roses. No doubt the bitter memory of these disastrous wars heightened any reference to the "war of red and white." In the same way the union of red and white was seen as a symbol of reconciliation such as was effected by the union of Lancaster and York in the house of Tudor.

Thus Drayton:

> That red, or white,
> Or mixed, the sense delight,
> Beholding,
> In her complexion:
> All which perfection,
> Such harmony infolding,

> That divided,
> Ere it was decided
> Which most pure,
> Began the grievous War
> Of York and Lancaster,
> That did many years endure.[11]

And Daniel's *Vision of the Twelve Goddesses:*[12]

> Next all in party-coloured Robes appeares,
> In white and crimson, gracefull Concord drest
> With knots of Vnion, and in hand she beares
> The happy ioyned Roses of our rest.

The conflict between red and white runs through the poem. It is suggested in the opening lines when the sun "with purple-colourd face" takes his leave of the "weeping morne," and the suggestion is carried to its height in the second stanza:

> More white, and red, than doues, or roses are:
> Nature that made thee with her selfe at strife,

Saith that the world hath ending with thy life.

(ll. 10–12)

At line 21 Venus tells him her kisses will make his lips "red, and pale, with fresh varietie," alternating "sacietie" and "famishing." At line 36 Adonis is "red for shame, but frostie in desier." Frosty-cold, but hoarfrost is white. At line 50 "red for shame" becomes "the maiden burning of his cheekes." At line 76 you have:

Twixt crimson shame, and anger ashie pale,
Being red she loues him best, and being white,
Her best is betterd with a more delight.

(ll. 76–78)

In these cases red and white are in conflict; they are the symbols of passions fighting one another. This mingled red and white is the fatal livery of the boar that kills while meaning to be kind;

Whose frothie mouth bepainted all with red,
Like milk, & blood, being mingled both togither.

(ll. 901–092)

In Venus herself red wars with white:

O what a sight it was wistly to view,
How she came stealing to the wayward boy,
To note the fighting conflict of her hew,
How white and red, ech other did destroy:
But now her cheeke was pale, and by and by
It flasht forth fire, as lightning from the skie.

(ll. 343–348)

The two colors cannot exist together; they are always in conflict. They are mutually contradictory, and they symbolize the conflict and the contradictions that are the subject of the poem. But the two colors are not only at war with one another; each is at war with itself. Red is the color of disaster as in the opening stanza or in ll. 451–456, where the red of Adonis's lips is likened to a red morn. But it is also the symbol of vigor, richness, and warmth of life; it is the color of the life-giving blood. Again, red is the symbol of shame in Adonis but of passion in Venus. It is the same with white; anger makes Adonis pale, while fear does the same for Venus. Shakespeare even invents a stanza to show white at war with white:

> Full gently now she takes him by the hand,
> A lillie prisond in a gaile of snow,
> Or Ivorie in an allablaster band,
> So white a friend, ingirts so white a fo.
>
> (ll. 361–364)

But after Adonis dies, the red and white are reconciled:

> By this the boy that by her side laie kild,
> Was melted like a vapour from her sight,
> And in his blood that on the ground laie spild,
> A purple floure sproong vp, checkred with white,
>> Resembling well his pale cheekes, and the blood,
>> Which in round drops, vpon their whitenesse stood.
>
> She bowes her head, the new-sprong floure to smel,
> Comparing it to her Adonis breath. . . .
>
> (ll. 1165–1172)

> She [Venus] crop's the stalke, and in the breach appeares,
> Green-dropping sap, which she compares to teares.
>
> (ll. 1175–1176)

The flower is to wither in her bosom. Adonis was twice butchered, once in blindness by the boar, and the second time in equal blindness but no less effectively by Venus. I know of no irony in literature so savage as this.

Shakespeare reinforces his tragic imagery by emphatic statement. The curse that Venus pronounces on love cannot be dismissed as mere rhetoric. It reinforces the well-known lines in the *Midsummer Night's Dream,* which I have already quoted. It states in so many words the meaning of *Romeo and Juliet* and of *Lucrece.* One must admit that the curse is expressed in conventional terms, but that should not blind us to the bitter passion by which it is inspired. It bears every mark of utter sincerity. The pessimism of the poem is emphasized by two lines that only one scholar has noticed:

> For he being dead, with him is beautie slaine,

And beautie dead, blacke Chaos comes againe.

(ll. 1019–1020)

"When Adonis is killed, beauty is killed, and the world is left in black chaos, for beauty, the soul of matter unites all parts of creation with the great God of beauty. This is the teaching of *Venus and Adonis,* as didactic a piece of work, perhaps, as Shakespeare ever wrote."[13]

To this I might add that in reading Elizabethan poetry we are apt to forget that beauty refers in the first place not to what gives a sensual pleasure but to the principle, Platonic idea or Christian plan, of which the thing seen is but a reflection or a symbol. Adonis is so often described in the poem as "beauty" that there can be no doubt that Shakespeare sees him as a symbol.

> Thrice fairer than my selfe . . .
> The fields chiefe flower, sweet aboue compare,
> Staine to all Nimphs, more louely than a man,
> More white, and red, than doues, or roses are:
> > Nature that made thee with her selfe at strife,
> > Saith that the world hath ending with thy life.

(ll. 7–12)

"The fields chiefe flower"—almost the words with which Capulet describes the daughter he believes to be dead:

> Death lies upon her like an untimely frost
> Upon the sweetest flower of all the field.

(IV.iv.28–29)

"Nature that made thee. . . ." There is the problem of the poem. In *Romeo and Juliet* Shakespeare stresses the perfection of his hero and heroine as children of nature, and yet there is some power in nature to destroy them. Adonis is the darling of nature.

> To see his face the Lion walkt along,
> Behind some hedge, because he would nor fear [i.e., terrify] him
> To recreate himself when he hath song,
> The Tygre would be tame, and gently heare him. . .

(ll. 1093–1096)

When he died:

No floure was nigh, no grasse, hearb, leaf, or weed,
but stole his blood, and seemd with him to bleed.

(ll. 1055–1056)

Shakespeare states the problem, but he offers no answer. He is content for the time being with presenting it. *Venus and Adonis* displays the dualism of all Shakespeare's work up to *Coriolanus*. No saint ever adored spiritual beauty with Shakespeare's passion, but his bitter pessimism about whatever power may rule the world makes it unlikely that the Church will ever canonize him. However, after *Coriolanus* in his last plays Shakespeare finds his answer, and he becomes, to use a phrase coined for Spinoza, "a God-intoxicated man."

Now you will probably say this paper is off its subject. The object of criticism is to show whether the work under consideration communicates the joy appropriate to poetry. That is just my point. I make the immodest claim that I am the only man of our days to say in print that he has really received from *Venus and Adonis* the joy that Shakespeare intended to communicate. The cause of my enjoyment is simple. I have found the poem full of meaning. It links the images and interrelates all the various parts of the poem in such a way that by meaning alone does *Venus and Adonis* achieve form. The meaning gives to the poem its magnitude, its importance, and its value. Now I will not imitate the vices of the modern school by limiting poetry to just one kind or variety and assert that no poetry has value unless it has meaning or that all poetry must be like *Venus and Adonis*. I cannot tell how many different sorts of poetry are to be found. There may be plenty of good poems that lack meaning. All I say is that Shakespeare has based this one poem at least on a profound conception, held with passionate intensity and conviction, expressed in finely imagined symbols that are combined with subtlety and delicate art into a form of such beauty that it thrills the reader with an immense joy.

NOTES

1. Spurgeon, Caroline E., *Shakespeare's Imagery, and What It Tells Us*. New York: The Macmillan Co., 1936.
2. See Donz C. Allen, "Shakespeare and the Doctrine of Cosmic Identities," *Shakespeare Association Bulletin*, 14 (1939): 182–189.
3. See *Biographia Literaria* (1817), II: 15–17.
4. *Sartain's Union Magazine of Literature and Art*, 6 (1850): 129. The sentence is quoted by Hyder E. Rollins, ed., *A New Variorum Edition of Shakespeare: The Poems* (1938), p. 488.
5. *Six Idillia . . . Chosen out of Theocritus*, 1588, in *An English Garner, Some Longer Elizabethan Poems*, ed. A.H. Bullen, 1903, 146.
6. Translation of *Ovid* (1632), "Vrania to the Queene."
7. *Ibid.*, 367.
8. Translation of *Dodoens A Nievve Herball* (1578), pp. 188, 423.
9. *Paradisi in Sole Paradisus Terrestris* (1629). Methuen's reprint (London,

1904), p. 206.

10. See ll. 65–66, 71–72, 183–184, 353–354, 451–462, 747–750.

11. Odes viii.

12. Published 1623. Reprinted and edited by Ernest Law. London: B. Quaritch, 1880.

13. Pearson, L.E., *Elizabethan Love Conventions* (1933), p. 285.

VENUS AGONISTES

Rufus Putney

Even a hasty glance at the comments on *Venus and Adonis* reprinted in the *Variorum* edition of Shakespeare's *Poems* suggests that reading the poem has often proved a dull or a disturbing experience. The failure of readers to see the poem as Shakespeare created it is the most probable explanation for this distress. In this case we have the rare good fortune of receiving some help from Shakespeare himself. A real clue to his spirit and intentions while writing *Venus and Adonis* is provided by Rosaline's description of Berowne in *Love's Labour's Lost*, a play probably written at the same time as the poem and similarly calculated to impress what Shakespeare took to be the literary *avant garde* of the day. Readers need to be better acquainted with the concept advanced here of a lyric comedy, ravishing by its eloquence and humorous through its combination of wit and fancy.

> Berowne they call him; but a merrier man,
> Within the limit of becoming mirth,
> I never spent an hour's talk withal.
> His eye begets occasion for his wit;
> For every object that the one doth catch
> The other turns to a mirth-moving jest,
> Which his fair tongue, conceit's expositor,
> Delivers in such apt and gracious words,
> That aged ears play truant at his tales,
> And younger hearings are quite ravished;
> So sweet and voluble is his discourse.
>
> (II.1.66–76)

Reprinted from *University of Colorado Studies: Series in Language and Literature Series 1* (1953), pp. 52–66, with permission of the University Press of Colorado.

"Sweet" and "voluble" are adjectives that all will agree describe Shakespeare's discourse in *Venus and Adonis*. To show that the poem also contains enough mirth to have been written by the merry man Berowne is the purpose of this essay.

Coleridge's commentary remains the most illuminating discussion of the poem. He is the only critic, so far as I know, who, viewing the two narratives as a dramatist's sally into an alien genre, emphasizes their profoundly dramatic nature.[1] But most scholars and critics, after a perfunctory reading of Coleridge, have preferred to let Hazlitt and Swinburne mislead them. Now, unhampered by that ethical solemnity that forced Coleridge to add that the poem deals with a subject that "cannot but detract from the pleasure of a delicate mind," we may be struck by the comic nature of the spectacle Shakespeare presents. And once the reader sets out in quest of comedy, the poem that has usually seemed a mellifluously told, richly decorated, erotic story, long-winded, cold, and dull, is completely metamorphosed. All that has been branded lascivious, tedious, or inept is transformed into stuff for laughter. The narrative, instead of appearing an amorphous mass, assumes form, and Shakespeare's vivacity, invigorating every part of the work, reflects the writer's joy in his mastery and power. His control over his verse is almost if not quite complete as he adapts it to narrative, dialogue, description, to farce, comedy, lyric humor, and pure lyricism. In his images are blended Elizabethan literary conventions, rural observations, and the sights, sounds, and smells of the taverns, shops, courts, and streets of London to create the ridiculous, the grotesque, and the charming. Dialogue outweighs description or narration, and the dramatic power of the poem is further enhanced by the diversities of the characters' emotions as well as by vivid pictorial images and intimations of action. Above all, the reader finds himself unexpectedly confronted in Venus with Shakespeare's first great comic character.

In asserting the humourous nature of the poem, one finds it difficult to be sure from precisely what critics one is differing. The enthusiasm or disapproval of Elizabethan and Jacobean readers has been recorded, but in so equivocal a manner that the interpretation of their allusions is more difficult than reading the poem. The work of other contemporary poets yields, however, a kind of circumstantial evidence. Since that was presented with some completeness in a former study,[2] I shall here repeat only enough to support my view that Shakespeare, like his predecessors and imitators in the light, pseudo-Ovidian legend, intended to write a sensuous, sophisticated farce. He changed the story as Ovid narrated it, and his alterations are essentially comic. Venus and Adonis, in the Latin version, unite in reciprocal passion, but Shakespeare's wretched goddess cannot with all her divinity, wit, and beauty awaken desire in a youth whose sweating palm was "precedent of pith and livelihood". Not only was the poem popular with readers; it also set the wits of other poets working, and their bawdy rather than lascivious imitations can be illustrated while disposing of the most common source of error in interpretation. Adonis urges his youth as the reason for rebuffing Venus, and many a critic has sentimentalized over this Elizabethan Joseph. Such lucubrations reveal more ethical nicety than literary acumen, for Shakespeare, one must confess, placed less value on male chastity than the biblical author. In Sonnet XLI he excused the "pretty wrongs" his friend had committed with the Dark Lady, saying:

> Gentle thou art, and therefore to be won,
> Beauteous thou art, therefore to be assail'd;
> And when a woman woos, what woman's son
> Will sourly leave her till she have prevail'd?

The same amoral tolerance was displayed by many contemporaries. The ghost of Narcissus in Thomas Edwards' clever perversion of that legend invokes Adonis' spirit to bear witness that no good comes of too strict chastity.[3] Most of the other imitators adopted like attitudes. A complete survey of them would require inordinate space since to regain fully the contemporary perspective one has only to read the four sonnets in *The Passionate Pilgrim* that toy with Shakespeare's story. In all of them, the following for example, Venus is made ludicrous and Adonis a fool:

> Scarce had the sun dried up the dewy morn,
> And scarce the herd gone to the hedge for shade,
> When Cytherea, all in love forlorn,
> A longing tarriance for Adonis made
> Under an osier growing by a brook,
> A brook where Adon us'd to cool his spleen:
> Hot was the day; she hotter that did look
> For his approach, that often there had been.
> Anon he comes, and throws his mantle by,
> And stood stark naked on the brook's green brim:
> The sun look'd on the world with glorious eye,
> Yet not so wistly as this queen on him:
> > He spying her, bounc'd in, whereas he stood:
> > 'O Jove,' quoth she, 'why was not I a flood!'

This and its companion sonnets represent in miniature the longer narratives of the species. Here in narrow compass are displayed the principal features of the genre: conceits, hyperbole, myth-making, *double-entendre,* wit, and the perception of the comedy inherent in the situation and the characters.

Before proceeding to the narrative and the actors, we may with profit observe the similarity between Berowne's conversational style and Shakepeare's method. Rosaline said of him,

> His eye begets occasion for his wit;
> For every object that the one doth catch
> The other turns to a mirth-moving jest.

Such jests crowd the poem as they do the play. The modern reader may not be prepared at the outset to laugh at the parody in Venus' first greeting to Adonis, where she seeks to gain his immediate acquiescence with the flattery and promises of the male seducer. But when desperate passion compels the goddess to shift from words to action, the result is a kind of farce to which the Elizabethans were always responsive. Even if no pun was intended in the lines

> Being so enrag'd, desire doth lend her force
> Courageously to pluck him from his horse,
>
> (ll. 29–30)

the absurd picture that follows of Venus with the flushed, indignant Adonis tucked under one arm, his horse's reins over the other, hastening to the bank that is their destined battle-ground should acquaint us with Shakespeare's mirth:

> Over one arm the lusty courser's rein,
> Under her other was the blushing boy,
> Who blush'd and pouted in a dull disdain
> With leaden appetite, unapt to toy;
> She red and hot as coals of glowing fire,
> He red for shame, but frosty in desire.
>
> (ll. 31–36)

Nor could it ever have been easy to write or read solemnly a poem in which falling is so common an activity. At the start, impatience overcoming Venus' tenderness,

> Backward she push'd him, as she would be thrust,
>
> (l. 41)

and, as he falls, she falls beside him. Venus, at line 463, faints and falls. Presently they kiss, and,

> Their lips together glu'd, fall to the earth.
>
> (l. 546)

Finally, at line 594, they tumble most comically,

> He on her belly falls, she on her back.

If we may judge from the conversation of Rosaline and her friends, those cheerful girls would not have thought this exceeded "the limits of becoming mirth."

Shakespeare's eye lit constantly upon objects which his pen, in this case "conceit's expositor," could turn into humor. Many instances of his incongruous imagery will appear in this essay. For the present, a few other examples will be cited by way of introduction. Venus is compared to a starving eagle (l. 55), to a glutton (l. 548), and to a vulture (l. 551). Inflamed by kissing Adonis, she is daintily described:

> Her face doth reek and smoke, her blood doth boil.
>
> (l. 555)

To illuminate her plight when she is briefly denied the solace of speech, Shakespeare employed the following clever but graceless similes:

> An oven that is stopp'd, or river stay'd
> Burneth more hotly, swelleth more with rage;
> So of concealed sorrow may be said:
> Free vent of words love's fire doth assuage,
>   But when the heart's attorney once is mute,
>   The client breaks as desperate of his suit.
>
> (ll. 331–336)

Her disappointment when she cannot accomplish her desire is likened to birds deceived by painted grapes. As she grapples him to her bosom and blurts our her fears should he go boar-hunting, Venus vividly suggests the discomfort of his posture as well as her own distress:

> My boding heart pants, beats, and takes no rest,
> But like an earthquake shakes thee on my breast.
>
> (ll. 647–648)

To these comparisons one might add such witty epigrams as the observation, "O how quick is love," where at least one pun is surely intended, and the Mercutio-like comment,

> Love is a spirit all compact of fire,
> Not gross to sink, but light and will aspire,
>
> (ll. 149–150)

or another pun that makes a joke, since an immortal goddess cannot actually die, of the slight confidence Venus placed in Diana's vow of chastity:

> So do thy lips
> Make modest Dian cloudy and forlorn,
> Lest she should steal a kiss and die forsworn.
>
> (ll. 724–726)

In these and many other places, Shakespeare's jocose tone fumigates the eroticism and belies the critical conviction that he had any serious intention beyond writing a delightful poem.

For the purposes of literary debate, the "argument from the sensitive ear" has often proved an effective and sometimes a valid form of the *argumentum ad hominem*. It is no less dear to the New Critics than it was to George Saintsbury, though they are too genteel to snort down the opposition with his charming ferocity. This argument is indispensable to the analysis of Shakespeare's purpose in *Venus and Adonis* for two reasons. First, the tone and texture of the verse provide the most reliable evidence of the author's intention in a case like this where historical scholarship has postulated an ideology of sober sensuousness to give plausibility to a serious interpretation of the narrative, and, second, it has long been received, though Coleridge would not have assented, that the verse of *Venus and Adonis* is a cloying amalgam of saccharine conceit and honeyed melody. Although enough has already been quoted to dispel this opinion, it is desirable before proceeding to insist that the verse itself is comic. Since I have just cited examples of the realistic and grotesque, the variety of the poem requires illustrations more imaginative and fanciful. The following stanza is one of three in which her desperate passion makes Venus assert that Adonis has charms powerful to enchant her through any one of the five senses:

> Say that the sense of feeling were bereft me,
> And that I could not see, nor hear, nor touch,
> And nothing but the very smell were left me,
> Yet would my love to thee be still as much;
>> For from the stillitory of thy face excelling
>> Comes breath perfum'd that breedeth love by smelling.
>>> (ll. 439–444)

So banal are the first four lines of this stanza, exhibiting even such impoverished rhyming as "bereft me" with "left me," that one must explain their flatness as the result either of ineptitude or of dramatic propriety. Inadequate as lyric verse, these lines neatly convey the folly Venus' passion induces. Similarly, the extravagant handling in the couplet of the convention that the lover's sweet-smelling breath enamours can be the product only of appalling tastelessness or of deliberate burlesque. Perhaps, Shakespeare's comments on his mistress' breath in Sonnet CXXX should not be brought into this argument, but the facile, charmless sound of the couplet,

> For from the stillitory of thy face excelling
> Comes breath perfumed that breedeth love by smelling,

as well as the grotesque conceit it contains, indicates burlesque when contrasted with a passage which treats the same convention with genuine, though humorous, loveliness:

> Forc'd to content, but never to obey,
> Panting he lies, and breatheth in her face;
> She feedeth on the steam, as on a prey,
> And calls it heavenly moisture, air of grace;
>> Wishing her cheeks were gardens full of flowers,
>> So they were dew'd with such distilling showers.
>>> (ll. 61–66)

The lyrical rapture of Venus' hyperboles makes this stanza as ravishing as it is amusing. Comic verse of this eloquence is rare, but this example is by no means unique in a poem where the versification constantly matches the writer's intentions.

The supreme achievement of the poem resides in the characterization of Venus, but Shakespeare's success in creating her implies also deft handling of Adonis' rôle and skillful organization of the narrative. A simple, severe structure supports the weight of decoration. Venus' vain attempts throughout one day to fire Adonis' love and his death the following morning, by which the problem is resolved, comprise the plot. It requires only a little more attention than readers usually accord the poem to see that Shakespeare conceived it like a play, as a series of dramatic episodes, which may conveniently if not accurately be compared to acts. The first forty-two lines, eighteen of them in dialogue, perform the expository functions of the first act. They set the scene, introduce the characters, and stretch them out side on the grassy bank. Venus' courtship makes up the bulk of the narrative and provides the equivalent to acts two and three. Her wooing is interrupted first at line 258, when Adonis escapes from her arms only to be stranded by his stallion's pursuit of the mare. Venus renews her suit and holds him fast until, at line 816, he wrenches himself loose and runs from her into the darkness. To maintain the analogy to conventional dramatic structure, Venus' soliloquies, in which during the remainder of the night and early next morning she bewails her unrequited passion and apostrophizes Death, may be equated with the fourth act; her discovery of Adonis' body and final lament, with the fifth. Stated baldly these divisions seem somewhat arbitrary and obscure too much the diversities of tone within each section, but there is reasonable basis for them, and they emphasize the real simplicity of the structure.

The obvious farce inherent in the representation of the Goddess of Love's failing to arouse passion in a mortal youth is transmuted and heightened by the beauty of the characters and the lyrical humor of the dialogue. Both Venus and Adonis are comic types, the frustrated, voracious woman and the shy, diffident male, but neither the situation nor the characters are developed in precisely the fashion to which we have been accustomed by popular playwrights and novelists. Although the violence of Venus' passion makes her ludicrous, she is beautiful and attractive rather than grotesque or sinister. She provokes both sympathy and laughter. Adonis' naïveté is comic, his priggishness repellent, yet he is far from seeming preposterous.

In developing his characters Shakespeare used the method he employed in the theatre. Having indicated their essential qualities, he hurried them into the dramatic action and set them talking. A pair of lines in the first stanza suffices for Adonis:

Rose-cheek'd Adonis hies him to the chase,
Hunting he lov'd, but love he laugh'd to scorn.

Slightly more scope is needed to introduce Venus since she has the stellar rôle and will do most of the speaking. The fifth stanza not only completes the preliminary sketch of the impatient goddess, but also illustrates the lyrical humor, the mixture of wit and charm, diffused throughout the story:

With this she seizeth on his sweating palm,
The precedent of pith and livelihood,
And trembling in her passion calls it balm,
Earth's sovereign salve to do a goddess good:
Being so enrag'd desire doth lend her force
Courageously to pluck him from his horse.

Adonis is distinctly secondary to Venus and only occasionally appealing. He is rendered comic by the obtuse view he takes of the passion he has inspired in the goddess, but even more by his petulance and self-pity. He writhes and squirms in Venus' arms and, when he finds words, reprehends her:

'Fie, fie,' he says, 'you crush me; let me go;
You have no reason to withold me so.'
(ll. 611–612)

'Give me my hand,' he saith, 'why dost thou feel it?'
(l. 374)

You hurt my hand with wringing; let us part.
(l. 421)

'For shame,' he cries, 'let go, and let me go;
My day's delight is past, my horse is gone,
And 'tis your fault I am bereft him so;
I pray you hence, and leave me here alone.'
(ll. 379–382)

He complains, though only scholars believe him, that he is too young for Venus. Finally, he refuses even to listen to her:

Lest the deceiving harmony should run
Into the quiet closure of my breast;
And then my little heart were quite undone,
In his bedchamber to be barred of rest.
No, lady, no; my heart longs not to groan,
But soundly sleeps while now it sleeps alone.
(ll. 781–786)

The plaintive tone of the verse even more than the fantastic metaphor reduces Adonis to unheroic and unallegoric absurdity.

The comic nuances in Shakespeare's treatment of such delicately predatory heroines as Juliet, Viola, and Desdemona suggest his robust mode of presenting Venus. The rôle of wooer, the exorbitance of her passion, and her perplexity when refused render humorous the long harrangues in which she flatters, reasons, rants, shames, chides, pleads, and weeps. Her manner is alternately argumentative, abusive, lyrical, persuasive, and witty, and the tone of the comedy ranges from playfulness to absolute farce.

Since Shakespeare's method of characterizing his frustrated and, presently, perspiring goddess is the same he used with such figures as Falstaff and Juliet's Nurse, it can be studied best by tracing it progressively. With unflagging gusto he invented the amorous dialectic in which, with infinite diversity and verve, Venus pursues her courtship from the first encounter until Adonis' flight. When early in the story he ducks to elude her kiss, the occasion is presented for her first long appeal:

'O pity!' gan she cry, 'flint-hearted boy:
'Tis but a kiss I beg; why art thou coy?'
(ll. 95–96)

Adonis' disinterest inspires the recital of her conquest of Mars, but her narration of that triumph brings fears lest Adonis pride himself on excelling the god and consequently scorn her. Reprobation of pride, calculated to forestall that disaster, soon gives way to pleading in a stanza of characteristic excellence for its combination of insatiate desire, illogical disputation, and pictorial suggestion:

Touch but my lips with those fair lips of thine,—
Though mine be not so fair, yet are they red,—
The kiss shall be thine own as well as mine:
What seest thou in the ground? hold up thy head:

> Look in mine eyeballs, there thy beauty lies;
> Then why not lips on lips, since eyes in eyes?
> (ll. 115–120)

The sharp, peremptory tone of the fourth line—so similar to the hints to actors in the plays—creates a vivid picture and provides here the dramatic variety that Venus' speeches constantly display.

Praise of her own pulchritude comprises much of Venus' early assault. The unsparingly elaborate description of the heroine's beauty, which became a convention of the Ovidian narrative poem, had appeared in the *Arcadia* and elsewhere before Thomas Lodge incorporated an "anatomical catalogue" in the little verse tale that graces his *History of Forbonius and Prisceria* and another in *Scylla's Metamorphosis*. Marlowe in *Hero and Leander* gorgeously surpassed all rivals. In keeping the lush inventory of the lady's charms, Shakespeare made it part of his comic characterization of Venus by transferring the description from the poet or the lover to the goddess herself. He further enhanced its dramatic quality by providing an internal motivation, by breaking into it with Adonis' preposterous complaint that he is suffering from sunburn, by altering Venus' moods during her long speech, and by varying the tone of her self-description from the lyrical to the ridiculous.

Venus' perception of Adonis' youth and beauty provides the motive. She must prove herself a suitable mate for him. Hence she begins:

> Were I hard favour'd, foul, or wrinkled-old,
> Ill-nurtur'd, crook'd, churlish, harsh in voice,
> O'erworn, despised, rheumatic, and cold,
> Thick-sighted, barren, lean, and lacking juice
> > Then mightst thou pause, for then I were not for thee;
> > But having no defects, why dost abhor me?
>
> Thou canst not see one wrinkle in my brow;
> Mine eyes are grey and bright and quick in turning:
> My beauty as the spring doth yearly grow:
> My flesh is soft and plump, my marrow burning;
> > My smooth moist hand, were it with thy hand felt,
> > Would in thy palm dissolve, or seem to melt.
> > (ll. 133–144)

After two more intoxicating stanzas have produced no sensible effect, she explores the possibility that self-love is the cause of his indifference and warns him of Narcissus' fate. Then for twelve lines she showers him with the arguments used in the early sonnets to promote reproduction, until, finally out of breath, she is silenced long enough for a brief bit of description and rejoinder:

> By this the love-sick queen began to sweat,
> For where they lay the shadow had forsook them,
> And Titan tired in the midday heat,
> With burning eye did hotly overlook them,
>   Wishing Adonis had his team to guide,
>   So he were like him and by Venus' side.
>
> And now Adonis with a lazy spright,
> And with a heavy, dark, disliking eye,
> His louring brows o'erwhelming his fair sight,
> Like misty vapours when they blot the sky,
>   Souring his cheeks cries, 'Fie! no more of love:
>   The sun doth burn my face; I must remove.'
>   (ll. 175–186)

Venus' first answer to this rebuff is the mild, sad chiding of

> 'Ay me,' quoth Venus, 'young and so unkind!
> What bare excuses mak'st thou to be gone!'
>   (ll. 187–188)

But presently the sense of injury arouses her indignation, and she scornfully upbraids him:

> Art thou a woman's son, and canst not feel
> What 'tis to love? how want of love tormenteth?
>   (ll. 201–202)
>
> What am I that thou shouldst contemn me thus?
> Or what great danger dwells upon my suit?
> What were thy lips the worse for one poor kiss?
>   (ll. 205–207)
>
> Fie! lifeless picture, cold and senseless stone,
> Well-painted idol, image dull and dead,

Statue contenting but the eye alone,
Thing like a man, but of no woman bred:
　　Thou art no man, though of a man's complexion,
　　For men will kiss even by their own direction.

　　　　　　　　　　　　　　　　　　　　(ll. 211–216)

When Adonis can be neither allured nor shamed into gratifying her, frustration leads her into such absurdities that the concupisence of Lodge and Marlowe evaporates:

'Fondling,' she saith, 'since I have hemm'd thee here
Within the circuit of this ivory pale,
I'll be a park, and thou shalt be my deer;
Feed where thou wilt, on mountain or in dale:
　　Grace on my lips, and if those hills be dry,
　　Stray lower where the pleasant fountains lie.'[4]

Adonis smiles, albeit in disdain, at these conceits, well worthy of Berowne, and in a moment makes his escape from the goddess' arms.

　　After the entr'acte of the stallion and the jennet, introduced as an object lesson in proper masculine conduct, Venus recaptures Adonis, whom she then manages to control for four hundred and ninety lines. This second stage of her wooing is interlarded with more digressions, notably the description of the boar and the hunting of poor Wat, but there is no slackening in Shakespeare's invention of comic dialogue. Prominent in this section are Venus' assertion that, were their positions reversed, she would suffer even bodily harm to please him, her plea that he learn appropriate behavior from his stallion, and the three stanzas in which she analyzes his charms that enchant each of the five senses. When he again rebuffs her, she farcically faints. His rough and humourous efforts to restore her culminate in a kiss. The enthusiasm with which Venus responds to the last remedy is funny in itself and leads to two witty stanzas, in which, using imagery derived from commercial law, she begs for prolonged treatment:

Pure lips, sweet seals in my soft lips imprinted,
What bargains may I make still to be sealing?
To sell myself I can be well contented,
So thou wilt buy, and pay, and use good dealing;
　　Which purchase if thou make, for fear of slips
　　Set thy seal manual on my wax red lips.

> A thousand kisses buys my heart from me;
> And pay them at thy leisure, one by one.
> What is ten hundred touches unto thee?
> Are they not quickly told and quickly gone?
>   Say for non-payment that the debt should double,
>   Is twenty hundred kisses such a trouble?
>   (ll. 511–522)

Can we doubt that "younger hearings were quite ravished" by such sweet and voluble discourse?

Gently and more hopefully now Adonis begs her to let him go and promises a kiss in payment. The interlude has no other purpose than to make the transition to new complications:

> Her arms do lend his neck a sweet embrace;
> Incorporate then they seem: face grows to face.
>   (ll. 539–540)

Kiss follows kiss until Venus out of pity resolves to let him go, but in a superbly dramatic stanza begs an assignation on the morrow:

> 'Sweet boy,' says she, 'this night I'll waste in sorrow,
> For my sick heart commands mine eyes to watch.
> Tell me, love's master, shall we meet tomorrow?
> Say, shall we? shall we? wilt thou make the match?'
>   He tells her no; tomorrow he intends
>   To hunt the boar with certain of his friends.
>   (ll. 583–588)

Overcome with terror she falls and drags him down on top of her. After she has warned him against the frightful boar and urged him to hunt the timorous hare instead, two stanzas of grotesque dialogue ensue:

> Lie quietly and hear a little more;
> Nay, do not struggle, for thou shalt not rise:
> To make thee hate the hunting of the boar,
> Unlike myself thou hear'st me moralize,
> Applying this to that, and so to so;
> For love can comment upon every woe.

'Where did I leave?' 'No matter where,' quoth he;
'Leave me, and then the story aptly ends:
The night is spent.' 'Why what of that,' quoth she.
'I am,' quoth he, 'expected of my friends;
    And now 'tis dark, and going I shall fall.'
    'In night,' quoth she, 'desire sees best of all.'
                                            (ll. 709–720)

Her pleading continues in fanciful conceits and wild hyperboles until Adonis interrupts, refuses to listen longer to her, and scolds her with his famous comparison of love and lust. This is the most serious passage in the poem, and we may assume that Shakespeare agreed now as later with much that Adonis says. Nonetheless, it should be noted that in the lines describing Adonis' flight,

With this he breaketh from the sweet embrace
Of those fair arms which bound him to her breast,
                                            (ll. 811–812)

Shakespeare still espoused the cause of Venus. It is scarcely effective preaching that leaves the preacher openly infatuated with the temptress.

Shakespeare relied upon Venus' character not only to make the wooing comic, but also to cancel the pathos at the end of the story. After his escape into the darkness, Adonis reappears only as a corpse. The major problem was to suggest Venus' emotions without allowing the reader to feel her pain. Shakespeare accomplished this by making her speeches burlesques of conventional Elizabethan complaints. The elegiac tastes of the late sixteenth century ran to such extravagance that parody was not easy; yet differences are apparent between Venus' exclamations against Death and, for example, Lucrece's apostrophes to Night and Opportunity. Shakespeare, furthermore, gave his readers indications of his intentions. Deserted by Adonis, Venus is overwhelmed with grief:

And now she beats her heart, whereat it groans,
That all the neighbour caves, as seeming troubled,
Make verbal repetition of her moans:
Passion on passion deeply is redoubled:
'Ay me!' she cries, and twenty times, 'Woe, woe!'
And twenty echoes twenty times cry so.
                                            (ll. 829–834)

That Shakespeare intended his readers to be amused by the caves that echo Venus' plaints —and have aroused critics'—is clinched by the stanza that rounds out the conceit:

> For who hath she to spend the night withal,
> But idle sounds resembling parasites;
> Like shrill-tongu'd tapsters answering every call,
> Soothing the humour of fantastic wits?
> She says, 'Tis so;' they answer all, 'Tis so;'
> And would say after her if she said, 'No.'
>
> (ll. 847–852)

We have no justification for assuming Shakespeare even in 1593 a poet so maladroit that he would try to heighten Venus' pathos by means of this magnificent simile with its realistic detail of drunken gallants and obsequious tapsters. The imagery here completes the burlesque of the romantic convention.

Dawn finds Venus first cursing then flattering Death as she alternately fears Adonis dead and hopes he is alive. Even though there is nothing shockingly outlandish in her apostrophes, Shakespeare paused, lines 985–990, to remark that these vacillations which love inspires render the lover ridiculous. Suddenly she comes upon Adonis' body. Of the first conceit in the stanza that opens her lament over his corpse, one can say, at least, that it has no parallel elsewhere in Shakespeare's works and that its extravagance is such that genuine emotion is inhibited. Venus has stared so long at Adonis' body before she speaks that her sight is blurred and she sees double:

> 'My tongue cannot express my grief for one,
> And yet,' quoth she, 'behold two Adonis dead!'
>
> (ll. 1069–1070)

The quality of the conceit may well be questioned, but it enabled Shakespeare to surmount the most difficult point in the story without even inadvertent pathos.

There can be no question of the skill with which he brought the story to its conclusion. The pathetic fallacy, responsible for so much sixteenth century bathos, becomes in Venus' final lament a diverting parody of mourners, zoological, inanimate, and disembodied. With Adonis dead, no one need wear bonnet or veil, for the sun scorns and the wind hisses humanity. But when he was alive, all nature loved and wooed him:

To see his face the lion walked along
Behind some hedge because he would not fear him.
To recreate himself when he hath sung,
The tiger would be tame and gently hear him.
(ll. 1093–1096)

The considerate lion and the music-loving tiger only begin the list. Fish vied to sport in the shadow he cast in their brooks, and the birds fed him berries. As in Bion, the boar sought only to kiss him, and multigenarian Venus, in words that anticipate Falstaff's cry, "They hate us youth," reflects:

Had I been tooth'd like him, I must confess,
With kissing him I should have killed him first;
But he is dead, and never did he bless
My youth with his; the more I am accurst.
(ll. 1117–1120)

With goddess-like egoism she prophesies that love, since it has brought woe to her, shall be bitter to men for evermore. Adonis is metamorphosed into a flower, and the poem ends in the perfection of the last stanza with Venus, all passion temporarily spent in grief, departing for her shrine at Paphos, there to mourn.

Shakespeare, it must be clear, deliberately and deftly avoided the pathos the legend contained. Instead, he maintained the comedy from first to last on a variety of levels. He achieved his diverse effects primarily through his brilliant and dramatic characterization of the suffering goddess. Venus, though she is enchantingly persuasive to readers more susceptible than Adonis, we not only love but laugh at. We see her amorous, tender, violent, lustful, distraught, perplexed, in joy, tears, and frustration. Although she lacks Cleopatra's infinite variety and many of her mature and subtle allurements, Venus is nonetheless the earliest intimation of Shakespeare's power to create his great, tragic wanton queen. Meanwhile, Venus is in her own right a fine and satisfying comic character.

NOTES

1. Coleridge's remarks on the poem in *Biographia Literaria* are well-known, but the following passage deserves more thoughtful consideration than most critics of *Venus and Adonis* seem to have given it: "I think, I should have conjectured from these poems, that even then the great instinct, which impelled the poet to the drama, was secretly working in him, prompting him by a series and never broken chain of imagery, always vivid and, because unbroken, often minute; by the highest effort of the picturesque in words of which words are capable, higher perhaps than was ever

realized by any other poet, even Dante not excepted; to provide a substitute for that visual language, that constant intervention and running comment by tone, look and gesture, which in his dramatic works he was entitled to expect from the players. His 'Venus and Adonis' seem at once the characters themselves, and the whole representation of those characters by the most consummate actors. You seem to be told nothing, but to see and hear everything" (*Biographia Literaria,* ed. Shawcross, 2 vols., Oxford, 1907, II, 15). Louis R. Zocca's discussion of the poem, written in the spirit of Coleridge's criticism, is remarkable for the warm praise he accords *Venus and Adonis* (*Elizabethan Narrative Poetry,* New Brunswick, New Jersey, 1950, pp. 248 ff.).

2. Rufus Putney, "*Venus and Adonis:* Amour with Humor," *PQ,* XX (1941), 533–548. It was the purpose of that study to show that the pseudo-Ovidian narratives of such poets as Lodge, Marlowe, Barnfield, Thomas Edwards, Dunstan Gale, Marston, Barkstead, and Francis Beaumont, if he wrote *Salmacis and Hermaphroditus,* contains humorous elements that render them deliberately comic in whole or in part. I sought to show that there was such a group of comic narrative poems, to which Shakespeare could have contributed *Venus and Adonis,* because one is then justified in interpreting that poem as a comedy. Further support could be derived from the treatment of mythological figures in such plays as Peele's *Arraignment of Paris,* where the gods and goddesses are represented with a lively humor, and Lyly's *Sapho and Phao* and *Galatea.* Indeed, the reader of the narrative poems can ill afford to forget what he has learned from the drama about Elizabethan tastes in comedy. In 1941, I was unaware that Miss Bradbrook (*The School of Night,* Cambridge, 1936, p. 122) had found *Hero and Leander* "written in a mood of exultant comedy." Latterly, Douglas Bush (*English Literature in the Earlier Seventeenth Century,* Oxford, 1945, p. 120) has revised his opinion regarding *Salmacis and Hermaphroditus,* in which he now believes the author "added an unusual degree of humour to the luxuriant Ovidian tradition." In his recent book (*Shakespeare and Spenser,* Princeton, 1950) W.B.C. Watkins continually alludes to *Venus and Adonis* as serio-comic.

3. Thomas Edwards, *Cephalus and Procris, Narcissus,* ed. Buckley, Roxburghe Club, London, 1882, p. 44.

4. That the *double-entendres* in this and the following stanza seemed funny to the Elizabethans is demonstrated by the outrageous imitation of them by T. H. in *Oenone and Paris,* published in 1594. Oenone says to Paris,

> Be Phaoes Boatman, I will be thy barke;
> Bathe in this fountaine here a while to sporte thee,
> Thy milke-white skinne, the pebbles shall not marke,
> Twixt them and thee Ile lye me, least they hurt thee;
> Oh be my sternesman, I will be thy barge,
> Its not thy weight that can me overcharge.

(*Oenone and Paris,* ed. J.Q. Adams, Washington, D.C., 1943, p. 28).

VENUS AND ADONIS

A.C. Hamilton

After having been greatly in vogue in its own day, and establishing a tradition of erotic mythological poetry, *Venus and Adonis* was neglected by the later centuries until, in Coleridge's judgment, the poem "gave ample proof of [Shakespeare's] possession of a most profound, energetic, and philosophical mind."[1] This judgment has not been accepted and today, as Hyder Rollins noted in 1938, "scholars and critics seldom mention *Venus* . . . without apologies expressed or implied."[2] One apology is to find that the poem is written against lust. According to L. E. Pearson's neat account,

> Venus is shown as the destructive agent of sensual love; Adonis, as reason in love. The one sullies whatever it touches; the other honors and makes it beautiful. The one is false and evil; the other is all truth, all good. Reason in love, truth, beauty—these are the weapons with which lust must be met, or the ideals of man must go down in defeat before the appetites. Thus it is that when Adonis is killed, beauty is killed, and the world is left in black chaos, for beauty, the soul of matter, unites all parts of creation with the great God of beauty. This is the teaching of *Venus and Adonis,* as didactic a piece of work, perhaps, as Shakespeare ever wrote.[3]

In T.W. Baldwin's judgment, two Platonic ideas—namely, Beauty and Love keep the world from returning to Chaos, and Love enjoys Beauty through the eyes—shape the poem into a Platonic argument: "Adonis is Love and Beauty, and when he dies Chaos is come again. Consequently, Venus argues for procreation that Love–Beauty–Adonis may not die."[4] R.P. Miller offers

Reprinted, with permission, from *Studies in English Literature, 1500-1900,* 1, 1 (Winter 1961), pp. 1–15.

a heavily moral reading by analysing two episodes, one where Adonis' horse breaks away to follow the jennet after which Venus counsels Adonis to follow desire too, and the other where Venus tells Adonis how Mars courted her. To the first episode he applies the iconographical interpretation of the horse as the lower appetites of the flesh uncontrolled by reason; and in this light, Venus' praise of the horse as an example for Adonis to follow becomes darkly ominous: "Venus is depicted exuberantly praising fallen and unregenerate man as the ideal lover, to be emulated by Adonis; and it is evident that her school lesson is intended to teach him the 'wisdom' by which Adam fell."[5] For the second episode he notes that Venus fails to tell Adonis the whole story of her affair with Mars, of how they were later caught together by Vulcan. In Ovid the gods laughed; but the Renaissance allegorical commentators whom Mr. Miller quotes were not even amused. To them the myth was a moral lesson against man yielding to lust, with the rider that adultery is sure to be found out. In the light of this moral reading of a part of the myth of Venus and Mars which Shakespeare does not tell, Mr. Miller interprets the whole poem as "a mythological reenactment of man's fall to sin."[6]

Modern judgment, without apology, is given by C. S. Lewis:

> As we read on we become more and more doubtful how the work ought to be taken. Is it a poem by a young moralist, a poem against lust? There is a speech given to Adonis (769 et seq.) which might lend some colour to the idea. But the story does not point the moral at all well, and Shakespeare's Venus is a very ill-conceived temptress. . . . If, on the other hand, the poem is meant to be anything other than a "cooling card," it fails egregiously. Words and images which, for any other purpose, ought to have been avoided keep on coming in and almost determine the dominant mood of the reader— "satiety," "sweating," "leaden appetite," "gorge," "stuff'd," "glutton," "gluttonlike." . . . And this flushed, panting, perspiring, suffocating, loquacious creature is supposed to be the goddess of love herself, the golden Aphrodite. It will not do. If the poem is not meant to arouse disgust it was very foolishly written: if it is, then disgust (that barbarian mercenary) is not, either aesthetically or morally, the feeling on which a poet should rely in a moral poem.[7]

But there are several ways in which we can learn something of how the poem is to be taken. Mr. Lewis' "It will not do," was not echoed by Shakespeare's contemporaries, and their praise and imitation offer us an insight, unique among his works, into how he was read and understood by his age. Secondly, there is the treatment of the myth of Venus and Adonis by contemporary poets, and by the allegorical commentators, which may suggest how Shakespeare would read the myth, and how he would expect his audience to read his treatment. At the very least, the first may show us what the poem is not, and the second may suggest what it could be. I shall consider later what, in my judgment, the poem is.

If Shakespeare really wrote his poem against lust, all his contempo raries were deceived. Barnfield, who is entirely representative of their judgment, writes:

> And *Shakespeare* thou, whose hony-flowing Vaine,
> (Pleasing the World) thy Praises doth containe,
> Whose *Venus,* and whose *Lucrece* (sweet, and chaste)
> Thy Name in fames immortall Booke haue plac't.[8]

They may have been deceived, of course, and there is no evidence from their allusions that they read the poem as carefully as the modern apologists have done. Yet the numerous imitators from T.H. in *Oenone and Paris* (1594) to Phineas Fletcher in *Brittain's Ida* (1628), who clearly did read the poem carefully, all reinforce the praise of the "sweet," "wittie," and "honey-tongued" Shakespeare. "Who loues not *Adons* loue?" Judicio asks in *The Return from Parnassus,* and since everyone did, adds a judgment which became more vocal, that the poem was written *for* lust:

> His sweeter verse contaynes hart robbing lines,
> Could but a grauer subject him content,
> Without loues foolish lazy languishment.[9]

Of course, imitators rarely clarify a tradition, being content to feed upon crumbs from the banquet, which for the erotic tradition is Venus' banquet. Chapman is the exception, and he illuminates Shakespeare's poem by adapting it to his own purposes. In *The Shadow of Night* (1595) he urges his Muse to sing of Cynthia's glory, but warns:

> Presume not then ye flesh confounded soules,
> That cannot beare the full Castalian bowles,
> Which seuer mounting spirits from the sences,
> To looke in this deepe fount for thy pretenses. (D1ʳ)

These lines, with their apparent reference to the motto of *Venus and Adonis,* rebuke Shakespeare, so it has been argued, for his eroticism. Yet Chapman does not deny the senses their pleasure, for only through their contentment is the spirit free to mount. Accordingly, his *Ovids Banquet of Sense* (1595) derives from the banquet of the senses which Venus seeks in Adonis, but adds:

> The sence is giuen vs to excite the minde,
> And that can neuer be by sence exited
> But first the sence must her contentment [find],
> We therefore must procure the sence delighted,
> That so the soule may vse her facultie. (D1ʳ)

Love satisfies sensual desires; lust does not. It follows that when he writes in "A Coronet for his Mistresse Philosophie" to "Mvses that sing loues sensuall Emperie," he helps define the kind of poem that Shakespeare writes. When man is inspired by proper self-love, sensual love is not an end in itself, for he may proceed from the banquet of the senses to the banquet of the mind. Since Shakespeare's poem shows only that first stage when the banquet of the senses is denied, Chapman pleads with him (and his followers) to go beyond love's sensual empery and sing of his mistress Philosophy. Whatever the poem is, its contemporary reputation and the tradition it established show that it is not a poem against lust.

But does the poem itself reveal that it is written against lust in its picture of the "loue-sicke Queene" who so violently rapes Adonis to the limit of her power, and especially in his lecture against her conduct:

> I hate not loue, but your deuise in loue,
> That lends imbracements vnto euery stranger,
>> You do it for increase, o straunge excuse!
>> When reason is the bawd to lusts abuse.
>
> Call it not loue, for loue to heauen is fled,
> Since sweating lust on earth vsurpt his name,
> Vnder whose simple semblance he hath fed,
> Vpon fresh beautie, blotting it with blame;
>> Which the hot tyrant staines, & soone bereaues:
>> As Caterpillers to the tender leaues.
>
> Loue comforteth like sun-shine after raine,
> But lusts effect is tempest after sunne,

Loues gentle spring doth alwayes fresh remaine,
Lusts winter comes, ere sommer halfe be donne:
  Loue surfets not, lust like a glutton dies:
  Loue is all truth, lust full of forged lies.

                            (ll. 789–804)

Certainly his argument is powerful enough to prevent our saying that the poem is *for* lust. Mr. Miller comments on these lines that Adonis rightly names Venus' passion as mere lust which seeks pleasure and not love which seeks procreation, and finds support for his distinction in the Church Fathers.[10] But, in fact, Adonis is more rigorous than the compromising Church Fathers: their reason, too, is the bawd to lust's abuse when they allow sexual union for procreation. Adonis' rejection of love is absolute. In the opening lines we are told "hunting he lou'd, but loue he laught to scorne," as later he maintains:

I know not loue (quoth he) nor will not know it,
Vnlesse it be a Boare, and then I chase it,
Tis much to borrow, and I will not owe it,
My loue to loue, is loue, but to disgrace it.

                            (ll. 409–412)

The distinction which he draws between love and lust *is* valid, but only after his death. In the poem that destroying power which feeds on beauty, which is the tempest after the sun, the destroying winter, the surfeiting glutton, and the forged truth is not Venus but the Boar. As Adonis breaks away "from the sweet embrace, / Of those faire armes" ("sweet" and "fair" mocking his disdain), one line surrounds the whole distinction he has made with the strongest irony. Breaking away, he "leaues loue vpon her backe, deeply distrest" (l. 814). He has claimed that "loue to heauen is fled, / Since sweating lust on earth vsurpt his name"; but Love has not fled, for she is with him now. Only with his death, as Venus prophesies, will discord, dissension, and hatred—that is, lust—usurp the name of love. And only after his death does Love, that is, Venus, flee to heaven.

    Contemporary treatments of the myth of Venus and Adonis suggest what the poem could be. In the *Countess of Pembroke's Iuychurch* (1592), Abraham Fraunce translates certain Ovidian myths and adds philosophical explications, for he believed, in common with his age, that poetry is radically allegorical:

Poeticall songs are Galeries set forth with varietie of pictures, to hold every mans eyes, Gardens stored with flowers of sundry sauours, to delite euery mans sence, orchyards furnished with all kindes of fruite, to please euery mans mouth. He that is but of a meane conceit, hath a pleasant and plausible narration, concerning the famous exploites of renowned *Heroes,* set forth in most sweete and delightsome verse, to feede his rurall humor. They, whose capacitie is such, as that they can reach somewhat further then the external discourse and history, shall finde a morall sence included therein, extolling vertue, condemning vice, euery way profitable for the institution of a practicall and common wealth man. The rest, that are better borne and of a more noble spirit, shall meete with hidden mysteries of naturall, astrologicall, or diuine and metaphysicall philosophie, to entertaine their heauenly speculation. (4ʳ)

He translates Ovid's story of Venus and Adonis in highly erotic terms, and appends, without any sense of incongruity, a highly philosophical explication:

> By *Adonis,* is meant the sunne, by *Venus,* the vpper hemisphere of the earth (as by *Proserpina* the lower); by the boare, winter: by the death of *Adonis,* the absence of the sunne for the sixe wintrie moneths; all which time, the earth lamenteth: *Adonis* is wounded in those parts, which are the instruments of propagation: for, in winter the son seemeth impotent, and the earth barren: neither that being able to get, nor this to beare either fruite or flowres: and therefore *Venus* sits, lamentably hanging downe her head, leaning on her left hand, her garments all ouer her face.

To this traditional interpretation, he adds the moral: "*Adonis* was turnd to a fading flowre; bewty decayeth, and lust leaueth the lustfull, if they leaue not it. . . . *Adonis* was borne of *Myrrha; Myrrhe* prouoketh lust: *Adonis* was kilde by a boare, that is, he was spent and weakened by old age: *Venus* lamenteth, lust decayeth" (45ᵛ). The potentialities of the Venus-Adonis myth, as Shakespeare inherited it, were enormous: possibly, a naive literalism; perhaps, but not likely with this myth, a moral significance; and most likely, what Fraunce calls the "hidden mysteries of naturall . . . philosophie."

If Shakespeare needed to be taught how poetry can realize those potentialities, he could have turned to Spenser, and probably did.[11] Since Adonis resists Venus' love, the first part of his poem centers upon the theme of temptation, as does *The Faerie Queene,* Book II. Acrasia, like Venus, meets a very reluctant Adonis in Guyon, who resists all the seductive persuasions of her garden, what Venus calls her park. In the opening episode of Book III, the walls of Castle Joyeous are decorated by a tapestry which portrays Venus' love for Adonis in all its stages. Her passionate love is manifest in the Lady of delight who loves Britomart, taking her for a man, but on coming to her bed, finds a very reluctant Adonis. Later in Canto VI, Spenser exploits the myth for its philosophical significance: Venus is the great mother of all creation, *Venus Genetrix,* Adonis who has been preserved from the Boar is "the Fathcr of all formes." and their love in the Garden of Adonis sustains all creation. Spenser's allegory in Book III moves in the area defined by these two versions of the myth, displaying its full poetic potentiality. Shakespeare's poem is somewhere between.

What is so surprising, and the mark of his poetic genius, is his simple, yet profound, change in the myth. Adonis does not yield to Venus. Although he is forced to submit passively to her, she must let him go, and at the end laments that "neuer did he blesse / My youth with his, the more am I accurst" (1119–1120). In the traditional version, his yielding to Venus brings his death by the Boar. In *Perimedes the Blacke-Smith* (1588), Greene tells the story of Venus and Adonis, and adds the moral:

> The *Syren Venus* nourist in hir lap
> Faire *Adon,* swearing whiles he was a youth
> He might be wanton: Note his after-hap
> The guerdon that such lawlesse lust ensueth,
>   So long he followed flattering *Venus* lore,
>   Till seely Lad, he perisht by a bore. (H1ᵛ)

The Boar signifies concupiscence or (spiritual) Death which results from concupiscence. By his change, Shakespeare frees the myth from that heavy weight of moral meaning, freeing it for the kind of poetic meaning which he wished to supply. Whatever that meaning is, it cannot be simply "moral." Since Adonis does not yield to Venus, the poem's center becomes a mystery. Why was he slain by the Boar? What does the Boar signify? Why does Adonis resist? What is the nature of Venus' love for him? These questions may now be explored in a poetic context, freed from the traditional associations which affirm, and give the poem its reason for existing.

That Shakespeare shared Fraunce's belief that poetry treats the "hidden mysteries of naturall . . . philosophie" is suggested by his choice of the Venus-Adonis myth, and also by the Ovidian motto so daringly placed on the title-page of his poem: "let the crowd admire what is common, for me

golden Phoebus ministers full cups from the Muses' well." Upon that level,
beyond the moral, where readers "entertaine their heauenly speculation,"
his poem treats the mystery of creation and the fall. While Venus is traditionally identified with Beauty, and her son Cupid with Love, Shakespeare
identifies Venus with Love. Adonis is identified with Beauty: "true sweet
beautie liu'd, and di'de with him" (l. 1080). He represents the perfection of
Nature in its unfallen state, for to frame her "best worke," as Venus tells
him, Nature stole divine moulds from heaven. His beauty is seen as the sustaining power of creation, the sun, in the opening lines where "the sunne
with purple-colour'd face" is aptly compared to the "rose-cheekt Adonis,"
and later in Venus' praise of him as the greater sun (ll. 859–864). His death
means an end to the world: "Nature that made thee with her selfe at strife,
/ Saith that the world hath ending with thy life" (ll. 11–12). He "must not
die," she pleads with Jove,

> Till mutuall overthrow of mortall kind.
> For he being dead, with him is beautie slaine,
> And beautie dead, blacke Chaos comes againe.
>   (ll. 1018–1020)

But his power to sustain creation must be sustained, in turn, by Venus, for
only Love seeks to preserve Beauty. She counsels him against the enemies of
Beauty who are her enemies: mortality, time, Nature's imperfection, those
perversions of love in the self-loving, the love-lacking, and the love-deny-
ing, Death, and the Boar. "That his beautie may the better thriue" (l. 1011),
she will even flatter Death. By his own "will" (l. 639), however, he chooses
to leave her for the Boar. And when he dies, Beauty dies, Love leaves the
world with her place usurped by "lust," Nature lies ruined, creation reverts
to original chaos, and there is the "mutuall ouerthrow of mortall kind."

This philosophical level of the poem shown in Adonis' death becomes
the framework within which is shown Venus' love. With Shakespeare's
change in the myth, the poem's center shifts from Adonis to Venus. Unlike
all other poems of temptation in which the one tempted is the subject—
Ulysses with Circe, Aeneas with Dido, Troilus with Criseyde, Guyon with
Acrasia, or the Lady with Comus—Shakespeare's temptress is the subject
through whom we see all the action. First we see her erotic courtship of
Adonis, and then her grief on finding him dead. The first part of the poem
reaches its erotic climax when Adonis tells Venus that he intends to hunt
the boar, and in her anguish she pulls him to the ground. At the beginning
he was mounted on his horse: now he is mounted on her; but when he re-

mains "liuelesse" she is frustrated in her desire. The mention of the boar, her violence, and frustration coincide to link the first part with the second where the action is climaxed in the Boar's violent kiss and her final frustration on finding his lifeless body. Tone changes between these two parts. The bawdy, even comic,[12] account of Venus' actions which we see through the witty and dispassionate eye of the poet gives place to a plaintive, even tragic, lament. The change is seen in Venus herself: before Adonis leaves, she is aggressive, domineering, and lustful; afterwards, she becomes humble, submissive, and pathetic. She appeals to her divinity when she is with Adonis; without him, she sees herself as a woman suffering in love. For when he leaves her, like the earth without the sun, all her strength goes: she is left amazed, astonished, her senses appalled and her spirit confounded, lost in a labyrinth of emotions. Over two hundred lines anatomize her "variable passions" (l. 967) until, seeing him dead, she leaves the world in anger, anguish, and despair. Her agony confirms all that Adonis had feared once love had disturbed the quiet heart, and fulfills her own prophecy of how love will bring dissension and grief. Further, all that she had feared once Adonis had refused her for the boar is confirmed through his death. Her violence is now justified by his death, as her suffering now separates her love from the pure lust seen in Tarquin after his rape of Lucrece, or in the withdrawn, self-possessed, and silent Acrasia. Through the pattern set up between the two parts, the poem explores the nature of Venus' love, of Adonis' refusal, and the significance of the Boar.

The basis for Shakespeare's treatment of Venus' love for Adonis is the Platonic doctrine that love is the desire for beauty. For this reason he identifies Venus with Love, and Adonis with Beauty. That doctrine, however, is treated with a sophisticated play of wit through her "deuise in loue" (l. 789). According to Platonic doctrine, Love turns from the enjoyment of the sight and hearing of the beloved to the love of Beauty itself which is not found in the outward show of things. The "Platonist" Spenser asks:

> Hath white and red in it such wondrous powre,
> That it can pierce through th'eyes vnto the hart,
> And therein stirre such rage and restlesse stowre,
> As nought but death can stint his dolours smart?[13]

Yet just this outward show of Adonis' beauty, and specifically the white and red of his cheeks and lips, arouses Venus' passion.[14] She does not distinguish between outer and inner beauty: with ears alone she would love "that inward beautie and inuisible" (l. 434), with eyes alone each part of her would love his outward parts, with touch alone she would be in love, the smell from his face would breed love, but with taste as "nourse, and feeder of the other foure" (l. 446) she seeks to banquet all the senses. Again according to Platonic doctrine, the climax of courtship comes with the kiss which joins the souls of reasonable lovers. In Castiglione's *Courtier,* Bembo says:

> a kisse may be said to be rather a cooplinge together of the soule, then of the bodye, bicause it hath suche force in her, that it draweth her vnto it, and (as it were) seperateth her from the bodye. For this do all chast louers couett a kisse, as the cooplinge of soules together. . . . *Salomon* saith in his heauenly boke of *Balattes, Oh that he would kiss me with a kisse of his mouth,* to expresse the desire he had, that hys soule might be rauished through heauenly loue to the behouldinge of heauenly beauty in such maner, that cooplyng her self inwardly with it, she might forsake the body.[15]

The poem's witty play upon this doctrine is shown through the action turning upon a kiss. At the beginning when Venus plucks Adonis from his horse to "sit, where neuer serpent hisses, / And being set, Ile smother thee with kisses," hissing herself like a serpent, she begs a kiss. He promises, but refuses. Later his kisses revive her from her swoon. Finally when he leaves, his kiss arouses all her violence:

> Her armes do lend his necke a sweet imbrace,
> Incorporate then they seeme, face growes to face . . .
> Now quicke desire hath caught the yeelding pray,
> And gluttonlike she feeds, yet neuer filleth . . .
> And hauing felt the sweetnesse of the spoile,
> With blind fold furie she begins to forrage,
> Her face doth reeke, & smoke, her blood doth boile,
> And carelesse lust stirs vp a desperat courage.
>
> (539–556)

The description given her seems almost designed to answer Bembo's description of the conduct of reasonable lovers. Yet the second part of the poem does not allow us to contrast her conduct with theirs. In the world of the poem her kiss is contrasted to the Boar's kiss which brings Adonis' death.

In his morally "innocent" state as one who "knows[s] not loue . . . nor will not know it," Adonis sees Venus as lust. But Shakespeare does not,

and neither may readers of the poem. Venus' dilemma is precisely that she
is Love:

> Looke how he can, she cannot chuse but loue . . .
> Being Iudge in loue, she cannot right her cause.
> Poore Queene of loue, in thine own law forlorne . . .
> She's loue; she loues, and yet she is not lou'd . . .
>   (ll. 79, 220, 251, 610)

The law of which she is judge is illustrated in the jennet episode: Adonis' horse
being all that a horse should be, responds to the breeding jennet as a horse
should. The example is used by Venus to urge Adonis to "learne to loue":

> Who sees his true-loue in her naked bed,
> Teaching the sheets a whiter hew then white,
> But when his glutton eye so full hath fed,
> His other agents ayme at like delight? . . .
> Let me excuse thy courser gentle boy,
> And learne of him I heartily beseech thee,
> To take aduantage on presented joy.
>   (ll. 397–405)

Her law is that all creatures must love in return when they are truly loved.[16]
After Adonis' death she inverts that law: love becomes discordant, suspicious,
deceiving, and perverse; and "they that loue best, their loues shall not enjoy" (l. 1164). Though she strives to present herself as his "true-loue," he
chooses to remain "vnkind" (l. 187), that is, unnatural and outside the law
which she invokes. In her dilemma, she asks: "why doest abhor me?"

> Thou canst not see one wrinckle in my brow,
> Mine eyes are grey, and bright, & quicke in turning:
> My beautie as the spring doth yearelie grow,
> My flesh is soft, and plumpe, my marrow burning,
>   My smooth moist hand, were it with thy hand felt,
>   Would in thy palme dissolue, or seeme to melt.
>   (ll. 139–144)

Just here where we may wish to see her simply as Lust, she continues:

> Bid me discourse, I will inchaunt thine eare,
> Or like a Fairie, trip vpon the greene,

> Or like a Nimph, with long disheueled heare,
> Daunce on the sands, and yet no footing seene.
>   Loue is a spirit all compact of fire,
>   Not grosse to sinke, but light, and will aspire.
>   (ll. 145–150)

Moreover, she offers us visible proof that she is Love in the flowers which support her without bending and in the doves which draw her through the sky. This juxtaposition of flesh and spirit is too deliberate, too much part of the poem's wit to be cancelled out by any reduction of Venus to a moral description as lust opposed to love. The union in Venus of the "marrow burning" and the "spirit all compact of fire" is essential to the poem's argument.

The "marrow burning" is the reason which Adonis finally offers for rejecting Venus. Earlier he had equivocated: he hated love yet didn't know it, he didn't hate love but only Venus' device in love. As we have noted earlier, even his lecture against Venus as lust is undercut by its context. He could be seen as Aristotle's truly temperate man, one lacking all desire, if only he were supported by reason. He cannot be seen as the merely innocent boy too young to love, for Venus, who should know, says that he is old enough to be tasted. Again, that first stage belongs to love, as we see in Longus' romance where Daphnis who does not know love is brought to the same erotic position as Venus brings Adonis, only Nature teaches him the way. The poem's Ovidian motto is really Adonis': let the base crowd admire what is vulgar, that is, follow *Venere vulgare,* and being Adonis he may claim the ministrations of the golden-haired Apollo. Yet Shakespeare strips him of all the defence that arms heroes similarly tempted: Guyon is sustained by moral virtue assisted by grace, the Lady in Comus by "the Sun-clad power of Chastity," Aeneas by his sacred mission, Ulysses by the need to return to his own home and wife. All other heroes have a way to follow which ends in triumph: Adonis prefers to hunt the Boar which brings his death. He alone resists temptation, only to die. He has one desire, as Venus tells us at the end: "to grow vnto himselfe was his desire" (l. 1180). Her metaphor is revealing, for Adonis is described throughout the poem as the flower that wishes to grow and not be plucked. In the beginning Venus calls him "the fields chiefe flower" and plucks him from his horse. To make him yield, she argues that "faire flowers that are not gathred in their prime, / Rot, and consume them selues in litle time" (ll. 131–2), to which he replies:

> Who plucks the bud before one leafe put forth?
>   (l. 416)

The mellow plum doth fall, the greene sticks fast,
Or being early pluckt, is sower to tast.

(ll. 527–8)

He rejects lust because it feeds on beauty "as Caterpillers do the tender
leaues" (l. 798). "Thou pluckst a flower" (l. 946), Venus accuses Death; then
with his death we see the "solemne sympathie" (l. 1057) of all the flowers
that seem to bleed with him. At the end he is changed into a flower which
Venus plucks. In his conception of Adonis, Shakespeare reverts to that primitive figure in Bion's *Lament,* one who is the god of Nature.

His dilemma is simply that he is Adonis. If he yields to Venus, he will
not grow to himself, but be plucked. If he does not yield, he will be plucked
by the enemies of Beauty: by mortality and time, by the imperfections in
Nature which result from Cynthia's jealousy, disease, Death. His greatest
enemy is himself:

What is thy bodie but a swallowing graue,
Seeming to burie that posteritie.
Which by the rights of time thou needs must haue,
If thou destroy them not in darke obscuritie?
If so the world will hold thee in disdaine,
Sith in thy pride, so faire a hope is slaine.

(ll. 757–762)

All these enemies of Beauty are seen ultimately in the ugly Boar. Though
Venus warns Adonis, "Beautie hath naught to do with such foule friends, /
Come not within his danger by thy will" (ll. 638–9), he chooses to follow
his own will. Yet we cannot name the Boar for what it is, unless we say that
it is the violence of Love's desire not to let Adonis grow to himself (as she
says: "had I bin tooth'd like him I must confesse, / With kissing him I should
haue kild him first" (ll. 1117–8), and love's jealousy which first projects the
image of Adonis slain by the boar, and Cynthia's shame which causes her
to corrupt the works of Nature and hide her light that Adonis might fall (in
accord with the tradition that Diana sent the boar that killed Adonis), and
death, and Adonis himself. In short, the Boar expresses all those forces which
seek to pluck the flower of Beauty. Accordingly, it functions as a poetic symbol through which Shakespeare explores the mystery of evil.

Against this background that yields Adonis' death, the poem projects
the immortal goddess of love. It was inevitable that Shakespeare's first work,
one in which he announced himself as a poet, should be dedicated to Ve-

nus. For the major poets in the English tradition, Spenser and Chaucer, were poets of love. Both poets display Venus chiefly as a statue to be adored, while Shakespeare's contribution is to show her intense vitality. In her two postures, reclining in the first part and fleeing in the second, she ranges through all moods and passions. For the sake of love she is prepared to do and become all things: at times she is the bustling mother caring for that petulant boy who weeps when the wind blows his hat off, or the coy disdainful woman with Mars, or the predatory female. Her roles are nicely catalogued by Helena in *All's Well,* who is herself an aggressive Venus wooing a reluctant Adonis in Bertram:

> A mother, and a mistress, and a friend,
> A phoenix, captain, and an enemy,
> A guide, a goddess, and a sovereign,
> A counsellor, a traitress, and a dear.
> (I.i.163–166)

Which aspect of her dominates in our total impression becomes a deeply personal question, and indeed that may be Shakespeare's point in centering the myth upon her. Certainly our response to her must remain ambivalent.

The erotic element in the poem is designed to turn the poem towards us: for Venus' temptation is not directed against Adonis—he is no more capable of responding than a flower—but against the reader. How may we answer her frank question:

> What am I that thou shouldst contemne me thus?
> Or what great danger, dwels vpon my sute?
> (ll. 205–206)

A simple moral response becomes as irrelevant as it is to Chaucer's Wife of Bath. (Her rambling in her tale to Adonis, "where did I leaue?" [l. 715] seems directly reminiscent of the Wife's "but now, sire, lat me se, what I shal seyn?") How are we to respond to the girlish tone of "say, shall we, shall we, wilt thou make the match?" (l. 586), or to the poet's tone in telling Adonis' refusal: "the poore foole praies her that he may depart" (l. 578), and Venus' frustration:

> But all in vaine, good Queene, it will not bee,
> She hath assai'd as much as may be prou'd,
> Her pleading hath deseru'd a greater fee.
> (ll. 607–9)

For Shakespeare's first readers the context of the poem would include the spiritual pilgrimage where the pilgrim meets Venus; but, of course, she is condemned by the form itself. In De Guileville's *Pilgrimage of the Life of Man,* translated by Lydgate, the pilgrim meets Venus riding on a swine (or boar). She disguises herself, so she reveals, because she is so ugly. She has him bound, fastened to the swine, beaten, and robbed. But the pilgrim may escape, as Grace Dieu has already told him, by flight. In Nicholas Breton's *Pilgrimage to Paradise* (1592), the pilgrim may escape Venus' temptations and keep on the right way by holding his hand before his face. Or in another form, amatory yet still moral, Gower's *Confessio Amantis,* the lover may separate himself from Venus because he is in the time of winter— here Gower is closer to the Venus-Adonis myth than is Shakespeare— and she leaves the earth. For Adonis, however, there is no escape, except to death. Traditionally Venus appears in a moral world where her evil temptations must be resisted in order that man may achieve the perfected virtuous life. Shakespeare translates the action of his poem into the prelapsarian state.

The poem moves from Venus' temptations, to her grief, to her prophecy of what love will become now that she is "accurst": that is, from her role as goddess, to a woman, and ends with her seen suspended as a planet ruling the world:

> Thus weary of the world, away she hies,
> And yokes her siluer doues, by whose swift aide,
> Their mistresse mounted through the emptie skies,
> In her light chariot, quickly is conuaide,
>> Holding their course to Paphos, where their queen,
>> Meanes to immure her selfe, and not be seen.
>> (ll. 1189–94)

When she prophesies that hereafter love will "bud, and be blasted, in a breathing while" (l. 1142), she defines the state of mutability—as in Spenser's Garden of Adonis—which succeeds that state where Love strove to enjoy and propagate the divine Beauty seen in Adonis. That this vision of Venus was indeed the "first heire" of the poet's "inuention" is shown in the plays that follow. Venus becomes the presiding goddess of the comedies, and her love for Adonis is their archetype. Adonis' death and her flight prepare for the world of the tragedies. Perhaps Shakespeare was, after all, tempting himself.

NOTES

1. Coleridge, *Lectures and Notes on Shakespere*, ed. T. Ashe (London, 1883), p. 223.

2. In his *Var. Ed.* of Shakespeare's *Poems* (Philadelphia, 1938) p. 474. Line references to *Venus and Adonis* are to this edition. It contains most of the references which I cite below on the vogue of the poem.

3. *Elizabethan Love Conventions* (Berkeley, 1933), p. 285.

4. *On the Literary Genetics of Shakspere's Poems & Sonnets* (Urbana, 1950), 73.

5. "Venus, Adonis, and the Horses," *ELH*, 19 (1952), p. 263.

6. "The Myth of Mars' Hot Minion in *Venus and Adonis*," *ELH* 26 (1959), p. 475.

7. *English Literature in the Sixteenth Century* (Oxford, 1954), pp. 498–499.

8. *Poems: In Diuers Humors* (London, 1598), sig. E2ᵛ.

9. *The Three Parnassus Plays* (1598-1601), ed. J. B. Leishman (London, 1949), p. 244.

10. "Venus, Adonis, and the Horses," p. 261.

11. See *Var. Ed.*, pp. 390-400.

12. See R. Putney, "Venus *Agonistes*," *Colorado Studies in Language and Literature*, 4 (1953), where he argues that the comic tone extends throughout the whole poem.

13. *Hymne in Honour of Beautie*, pp. 71–74, in *Minor Poems*, ed. de Selincourt (Oxford, 1910).

14. See H.T. Price's study of the imagery of the poem in "The Function of Imagery in *Venus and Adonis*, *Papers of the Michigan Academy of Science, Arts, and Letters*, 31 (1945), pp. 175–297.

15. Hoby's trans. (1561).

16. Venus offers two persuasions to appeal to Adonis' twofold nature. She tells the story of how the god Mars submitted his will to her. Mr. Miller, in the article cited previously, sees a moral significance, but the context determines rather the philosophical, as in Chaucer's *Complaint of Mars* and the proem to *The Faerie Queene*, where Venus represents friendship or harmony that subdues Mars's strife. Edgar Wind, *Pagan Mysteries in the Renaissance* (New Haven, 1958) shows this reading in Pico and Plutarch, and illustrated in many Renaissance idylls. Sandys, in his *Ovid's Metamorphoses . . . Mythologized* (Oxford, 1632) treats the astrological sense of the Venus-Mars myth to show that the fable "was invented to expresse the sympathy that is necessary in nature. . . . *Mars* likewise signifies strife, and Venus friendship; which, as the ancients held, were the parents of all things." In a concluding line he adds that "morally adulteries are taxed by this fable" (p. 157). Venus' coy disdain and Mars' submission is later acted out in the courtship of the horses. Venus argues that the beasts teach Adonis to follow his own will. Later he does so, though not as she intended, by choosing to hunt the boar. (Her moralizing shows that the horse symbolizes *will*, rather than the *passions*. That Adonis should fall through his own will, rather than the passions, is theologically exact.)

TIME-BEGUILING SPORT

NUMBER SYMBOLISM IN SHAKESPEARE'S *VENUS AND ADONIS*

Christopher Butler and Alastair Fowler

Professor A. Kent Hieatt, in his study of Spenser's *Epithalamion*,[1] demonstrates a complex number symbolism controlling the structure of the poem. He shows for instance that the poem's twenty-four stanzas are divided, by a change in the refrain, into two groups which bear the same proportions as the hours of daylight and darkness on the longest day of the year, that of Spenser's wedding. The line total is also shown to be significant, since the "long lines" add up to 359, a representation of the "imperfect" apparent daily movement of the sun (one degree short of a full 360–degree revolution). The short final stanza or envoi of six lines brings the total to 365, a representation of the days in the year. Towards the end of his argument (p. 77), Hieatt wonders whether there may not be other Renaissance poems which are governed by a similar numerological decorum. And in fact research in progress[2] is beginning to show that such poems are quite numerous.

It is, however, startling to find among them a poem by Shakespeare. Numerological patterns are not perhaps so contrary to expectation in the works of a Benlowes, a Spenser, or even a Milton; but the current conception of Shakespeare does not encourage us to look for esoteric structures in his poetry. And yet, doesn't his Ovidian epigraph hint at the possibility of a meaning denied to the common reader?

> Vilia miretur vulgus: mihi flavus Apollo
> Pocula Castalia plena ministret aqua.
>
> (*Amores* I.xv)

Reprinted, with permission, from *Shakespeare 1564–1964: A Collection of Modern Essays by Various Hands,* edited by Edward A. Bloom (Providence: Brown UP, 1964), pp. 115–33 and 217–18.

(Let the vulgar throng admire worthless things;
but to me may the golden-haired Apollo supply
cups filled at the Castalian stream.)

The curious frequency of the poem's mentions of specific numbers, and of indications of time, incline us to attempt to draw its "thousand honeyed secrets" from a numerological pattern, and in particular a temporal one.[3]

The myth of Venus and Adonis was commonly understood in the Renaissance as having a temporal or seasonal import. Sometimes Adonis was thought to symbolize the sun, sometimes seed; but almost always interpretation of the myth was concerned with its contrast of summer fulfillment and winter deprivation, and with the transition from one to the other at the equinox. The separation of Adonis from Venus, and his departure to the underworld, was interpreted as the entry of the sun into the lower or nocturnal hemisphere. This was conceived as occurring not with the beginning of the winter season proper, but at the precise moment of the autumnal equinox. That is to say, the cosmological interpretation of the myth posited a bisection of the year. George Sandys' commentary on the tenth book of Ovid's *Metamorphoses* provides a convenient popular statement of these ideas:

> Now *Adonis* was no other then the Sun, adored/under that name by the *Phoenicians;* as *Venus* by the name of *Astarte:* for the Naturalists call the upper Hemisphere of the Earth, in which we inhabit, *Venus;* as the lower *Proserpina:* Therefore they made the Goddesse to weepe, when the Sun retired from her to the sixe winter signes of the Zodiacke; shortning the daies, and depriving the earth of her delight and beauty: which againe he restores by his approach into *Aries. Adonis* is said to be slaine by a Bore, because that beast is the Image of the Winter; savage, horrid, delighting in mire, and feeding on ackornes, a fruit which is proper to that season. So the Winter wounds, as it were, the Sunne to death, by deminishing his heate and lustre; whose losse is lamented by *Venus,* or the widdowed Earth, then covered with a vaile of clowds; Springs gushing from thence, the teares of her eies, in greater abundance; the fields presenting a sad aspect, as being deprived of their ornament. But when the Sun returnes to the Æquator, *Venus* recovers her alacrity; the trees invested with leaves, and the earth with her flowrie mantle: wherefore the ancients did dedicate the month of Aprill unto *Venus.*[4]

Shakespeare's *Venus and Adonis* is based upon a similar reading of the myth, to which it gives numerological expression by its adjustment to an exact set of numbers drawn from astronomy. The explicit action of the poem, the attempted seduction of Adonis by Venus, has behind it an implicit time scale. This is no mere static decorum, for the form of the poem participates in its thematic development, and displays a tragic movement from the solstitial to the equinoctial stages of the myth.

The traditional connection of the mythological Venus and Adonis with cosmic movements justifies us in exploring the symbolic value of the astronomical events narrated in the poem. In particular, its insistent identification of Adonis with the sun—he is Venus' "earthly sun" (l. 198) and when he leaves her she loses "the fair discovery of her way" (l. 828)—prompts us to trace the reported movements of the sun in relation to the plot. The simplest calculation of this order that can be performed is to determine the length of day and night in terms of lines of the poem. This is made easy for us, since Shakespeare has carefully noted the occurrence of midday and sunset on the first day of the poem's action, and of sunrise on the second day. We are not given, however, any account of the first sunrise—an omission which, as we shall see later, is not without significance—since the sun must have risen before the poems begins:

> Even as the sun with purple-colour'd face
> Had ta'en his last leave of the weeping morn,
> Rose-cheek'd Adonis hied him to the chase.[5]
>
> (ll. 1–3)

This means that, in order to arrive at the metrical duration of the first day, we have to double the number of lines from noon to sunset.[6] The relevant places in the poem are:

> And Titan, tired in the mid-day heat,
> With burning eye did hotly overlook them . . .
>
> (ll. 177–78)

> Look the world's comforter with weary gait
> His day's hot task hath ended in the west . . .
>
> (ll. 529–30)

and, finally, sunrise on the second day of the poem:

> The sun ariseth in his majesty.   (l. 856)

Thus the first day occupies 706 lines, that is, 353 (ll. 178–530 inclusive) multiplied by two; and the subsequent night, 326 lines. The number of lines for a full day and night of twenty-four natural hours would therefore be 1032. Hence, dividing by twenty-four, we determine the measure for one hour: a modulus which turns out to be exactly forty-three.[7] Working from this modulus, we arrive at the durations in hours and minutes of the first day and night with which Shakespeare is concerned. These are: approximately sixteen hours, twenty-five minutes for day; and seven hours, thirty-five minutes for night.

Of course, this operation can be performed with *any* number larger than twenty-four; and any two parts of such a number, when divided by the appropriate modulus, will add to twenty-four. But, in this present case, the given numbers have a significance independent of the mathematical calculation. They are, as we shall see, known astronomical values: a fact that obliges us to regard them as intentional. It is notable (and consistent with the seasonal version of the Venus and Adonis myth) that the proportions of the poem's first day and night are commensurable with those of a solstitial, midsummer's day, in a northern temperate latitude.[8]

At the solstice, the difference between the periods of day and night, and therefore of the lengths of the temporal hours (that is, the hours arrived at by dividing each of these periods separately by twelve)[9] is extremely noticeable. The apparent amplitude of the temporal diurnal hours, at the summer solstice, and the corresponding brevity of the temporal nocturnal hour, are twice adverted to in the poem. When Venus promises Adonis that

> A summer's day will seem an hour but short,
> Being wasted in such time-beguiling sport,
>
> (ll. 23–24)

the rhetorical amplification depends on the comparatively great length of a summer's day, and the "hours" of such a day. Venus' kisses will make a long day seem "an hour: but short." On the other hand, during the solstitial night, the temporal hours have the opposite appearance. When Venus, separated from Adonis, sings her "heavy anthem"—

> Her song was tedious, and outwore the night,
> For lovers' hours are long, though seeming short
> (ll. 841–42)

—why are the hours described as "seeming short"? Only because the temporal nocturnal hours do in fact seem short in summer.[10]

The objection might conceivably be raised, at this point, that our argument is somewhat dependent upon its internal consistency. But the number 1032 as a measure of the full day occurs again—and in a line series completely independent of that discussed above. For the proportion of the poem representing Adonis' life consists of 1032 lines;[11] so that in one sense we can say that Adonis is alive during twenty-four hours. In view of the mythological identification of Adonis with the sun, this correspondence is easily understandable: the numerological trajectory of the actual sun is equivalent to that of the symbolic sun Adonis. Perception of this pattern increases the poignancy of Venus' outcry:

> "Wonder of time," quoth she, "this is my spite,
> That thou being dead, the day should yet be light."
>
> (ll. 1133–34)

These lines, which have no doubt been previously construed as mere hyperbole, are now seen to have been intended with a precise connotational meaning.

It remains to consider the given numbers 353 and 326 (denoting the semi-diurnal and nocturnal periods) which determined the length of the twenty-four-hour day as 1032 lines.[12] These figures 353 and 326 are curiously "one short" of the lengths of the lunar synodic and sidereal years respectively.[13] Nor are these the only instances in the poem of numerological counts that fall short. The portion representing midday to sunset is fifty-nine stanzas, one short, that is, of the sixty minutes of an hour. Wasted in time-beguiling sport, a summer's day seems literally "an hour but short," even though it is in fact the longest possible day.[14] These failures to complete an expected measure are obviously to be related to the turning point of the poem's plot. For the latter is also a failure to reach fulfillment: Venus, unable to seduce Adonis, finds that even when she is in "the very lists of love" she has "to clip Elizium and to lack her joy."

Further, one can establish parallels in the action and structure of the poem which develop this effect of falling short. It is particularly marked in the case of the kisses, chronicled throughout the poem with odd persistence, and more than once connected explicitly with the passing of time:

> Ten kisses short as one, one long as twenty.
> A summer's day will seem an hour but short . . .
>
> (ll. 22–23)

There shall not be one minute in an hour
Wherein I will not kiss my sweet love's flower.
                                                    (ll. 1187–88)

We notice that in stanzas 8, 9, and 10, we have a first series of kisses, all
of them given by Venus to Adonis. In stanza 8 she "stops his lips, / And
kissing speaks"; in stanza 9 she "murders with a kiss"; and in stanza 10
she achieves no fewer than three kisses—"she kiss'd his brow, his cheek,
his chin." This series of five kisses, moreover, is doubled; for "where she
ends, she doth anew begin." Thus, up to the end of the first ten stanzas,
Venus bestows in all ten kisses. We might expect, as did Venus, that the
series of kisses would be answered by Adonis; but in the event he is reluctant to "pay this comptless debt" (l. 84), and "when her lips were ready
for his pay, / He winks and turns his lips another way" (ll. 89–90). This
sequence of events in stanzas 8, 9, and 10 finds an exact antithesis in the
similar sequence of events in stanzas 80, 90, and 100—stanzas whose numbers are multiples of the previous ones. Here, at the climax of the poem's
action, Adonis is at last kissing Venus. In stanza 80 "He kisses her, and
she by her good will / Will never rise, so he will kiss her still," and in stanza
90 "the honey fee of parting tender'd is." But in stanza 100, where we
should expect the fulfillment and completion of the series, it does not come.
Instead, Venus is refused:

Now is she in the very lists of love,
Her champion mounted for the hot encounter.
All is imaginary she doth prove;
He will not manage her, although he mount her:
That worse than Tantalus' is her annoy,
To clip Elizium and to lack her joy.
                                                    (ll. 595–600)

Thus, in the very center of the poem (conventionally a significant place, in
numerical composition),[15] we find the same falling short as in the astronomical calculations. It seems only reasonable to suppose that the numerological structure of the poem is intended to provide an unequivocal comment
on the symbolic meaning of the human events.[16]

A further numerological complex associated with the number of kisses
bestowed in the poem is announced by Venus' early prediction of their duration. This prediction seems very strange in its context, unless it can be given
some esoteric meaning:

And yet not cloy thy lips with loath'd satiety,
But rather famish them amid their plenty,
Making them red, and pale, with fresh variety:
Ten kisses short as one, one long as twenty.
A summer's day will seem an hour but short,
Being wasted in such time-beguiling sport.

(ll. 19–24)

The line "ten kisses short as one, one long as twenty" makes sense, if taken quite literally and regarded as expressing a ratio of line-durations. The *ten* kisses given by Venus to Adonis up to the end of the first ten stanzas occupy the same space in the poem as the *one* kiss given by Adonis to Venus in stanza 90, which has taken ten stanzas to elicit. There is thus a literal enactment of the phrase "ten kisses short as one." (Similarly, Venus' first kiss to Adonis is in stanza 8, and Adonis' first kiss to Venus is in stanza 80: again a ratio of ten to one.)

The series of Venus' kisses which is completed in ten stanzas can also be considered as being completed in sixty lines. This points to the sixty minutes of an hour, a measure which is alluded to in Venus' later vow: "There shall not be one minute in an hour / Wherein I will not kiss my sweet love's flower." We notice that on a modulus of one line per minute, the whole poem falls just one stanza short of twenty hours. (Like the "copious stories" of all lovers, stanza 141, it is "never done.") The same number twenty is also mentioned verbally with an astonishing frequency:[17] yet it is at first difficult to assign to it any precise numerological significance. Sometimes it occurs in situations with an emotive connotation of grief:

"Ay me," she cries, and twenty times, "Woe, woe,"
And twenty echoes twenty times cry so.

(ll. 833–34)

This is in agreement with the symbolic value attached to the number by the numerologist Pietro Bongo, who says: "Numquam Vicenarium numerum adhibet, nisi ad res tristes, luctuosas, acerbas. . . ."[18] The character of the other numbers in the poem, however, leads us to expect the number twenty to have a temporal import.

That this is in fact so becomes clear as soon as we grasp the occasion of the poem. The clue to this is given by the dedication. For Southampton was exactly twenty years old in the year of the poem's first appearance, 1593. The conclusion seems inescapable that the number symbolism of *Venus and Adonis* is so adjusted as to refer to the age of Shakespeare's patron. Casting Southampton in the role of Adonis suggests many tantalizing questions with regard to the poem's content that are beyond the scope of the present paper. Certain results relevant to our present approach, however, are immediately obtained. For example, it becomes more intelligible why the poem should contain so many references to Adonis' age; why he should appeal to Venus, "Measure my strangeness with my unripe years" (l. 524), and why, in Venus' hyperbole, she should exclaim, "the world hath ending with thy life." Moreover, not only are all the references to the number twenty more meaningful—

> Were beauty under twenty locks kept fast,
> Yet love breaks through, and picks them all at last
> (ll. 575–76)

—but also the length of the poem is itself explained. For the "complete" length of the poem is 1200 lines (that is, 20 x 60): a representation of twenty hours. Thus the very form of the poem sets forth the theme of time's brevity. A whole summer is compressed into a single day, and that long day into "an hour but short." Southampton's twenty summers seem but twenty hours.

The notion of a twenty-year period enables us to explain a number not previously dealt with, the total number of kisses bestowed throughout the poem. Such prominence is given to the kisses that they should have some symbolic force more exact than that arrived at above. In view of the planetary roles of the human characters, we should expect their kisses to refer to conjunctions of the planets Venus and Sol. And indeed we notice that the closeness of the human Venus and Adonis as they kiss is repeatedly stressed: "Incorporate then they seem, face grows to face"; "their lips together glued." Moreover, the most elaborately described kiss, that begun in stanza 90, occurs at sunset, one of the two occasions when Venus and the sun may appear in the sky together. Now it was well known in the Renaissance that the motion of the planet Venus appears as an oscillation from one side of the sun to the other; the complete period of the oscillation being about 1.6 years or 584 days. In elongation east of the sun Venus is seen as the evening star, while towards western elongation it is visible in the morning. (This fact, that the planet is sometimes a morning, and sometimes an evening, star seems covertly alluded to in the exclamation of Shakespeare's Venus:

> "O where am I?" quoth she, "in earth or heaven?
> Or in the ocean drench'd, or in the fire?

What hour is this, or morn, or weary even?
Do I delight to die, or life desire?"

(ll. 493–96)

Between the elongations of Venus there lie the superior and inferior conjunctions with the sun; of which conjunctions the inferior, when Venus is two and a half times more brilliant than at the superior, is much the more noticeable. The interval between the inferior conjunctions is such that in the twenty years of Southampton's lifetime, represented in the poem, a total of twelve occurred. This total is in accord with the number of kisses exchanged between Venus and Adonis throughout the poem.

The *dénouement* of the myth of Venus and Adonis, as cosmologically interpreted, is the tragic destruction of Adonis by the boar of winter. We notice that at the corresponding point in the poem, when Venus discovers "the foul boar's conquest on her fair delight" (l. 1030), this event is immediately connected with the alternation of light and dark. The goddess's light-giving eyes "Like stars asham'd of day, themselves withdrew . . . / Into the deep dark cabins of her head" (ll. 1032–38) and were commanded by her troubled brain to "consort with ugly night" (l. 1041). Moreover, since the boar kills Adonis with a kiss, it may be regarded as supplanting Venus as his lover: the sun has been removed from proximity with Venus in the upper hemisphere to a dark vicinity with the boar in the lower. Various authorities advance various explanations as to why the boar should symbolize winter. Some give the trivial reason that the animal is at his best in that season; others, more obscurely, say that the beast's bristliness resembles the condition of nature in winter; while, according to a tradition that is given its fullest expression by Valeriano, the explanation is made to rest in the boar's love of darkness. Its downward-directed eyes, we are told, betray a hate and fear of light; and justify a further, moral allegorization of the polysemous animal, as lust. This last development of the myth is reflected in Adonis' unwittingly accurate prophecy:

But lust's effect is tempest after sun,
Love's gentle spring doth always fresh remain,
Lust's winter comes ere summer half be done.

(ll. 800–802)

In the normal seasonal order of things Adonis should be parted from Venus at the equinox. We should therefore expect some formal representation of an equinoctial state in the latter part of the poem. This in fact proves to be the case. For the metrical durations of the night and the second day of the poem (stanzas 89 to 144, and 144 to the end) turn out to be equal, as are the durations of day and night at the equinox. Thus the poem's structure dramatically telescopes the movement from the solstitial to the equinoctial situation. The statement "lust's winter comes, ere summer half be done" is mimed very precisely, since the poem's solstitial state is interrupted to become the equinox. Indeed, the first, midsummer day is incomplete. For, as we have seen, its sunrise is not included within the poem's frame. If that twenty-four-hour period at the solstice were completed, no doubt summer *would* half be done; but before this can happen—"ere summer half be done"—the boar has intervened, the equinoctial point is passed, and winter has begun. It is natural to ask what the duration is, of this first, unfulfilled day. The answer adds yet another strand to the poem's complex texture of temporal symbolism. For Venus hails the sun on the second morning ("Oh thou clear god, and patron of all light") at line 860—just twenty hours from the beginning of the poem, on our forty-three-lines-per-hour modulus. Thus the midsummer hours of the first day briefly recapitulate the twenty years of Southampton's lifetime.

So far we have demonstrated certain numerical patterns occurring in the formal structure, which provide a counterpoint to the themes of the poem. There is also, however, a series of substantive numbers, occurring in the text itself. Most prominent among these are the large numbers referred to in a variety of contexts. The hyperboles that introduce the number twenty ("twenty hundred kisses"; "twenty thousand tongues") point to some relationship with the vigesimal patterns considered above: the formal representations of twenty-year and twenty-hour periods. In the last paragraph, we saw that the first, solstitial day was only twenty hours long. Now the large numbers mentioned in the text within this same portion of the poem—that is, before sunrise on the second day—are as follows:

A thousand honey secrets shalt thou know.	1000
(l. 16)	
No dog shall rouse thee, though a thousand bark.	1000
(l. 240)	
. . . a thousand ways he seeks	1000
To mend the hurt . . .	
(ll. 477–78)	
A thousand kisses buys my heart from me.	1000
(l. 517)	
What is ten hundred touches unto thee?	1000
(l. 519)	

Is twenty hundred kisses such a trouble?	2000
(l. 522)	
He cranks and crosses with a thousand doubles.	1000
(l. 682)	
If love have lent you twenty thousand tongues . . .	20,000
(l. 775)	
"Aye me," she cries, and twenty times, "Woe, woe,"	
And twenty echoes twenty times cry so.[20]	800
(ll. 833–34)	

By addition, we find that if the total of these figures is regarded as a temporal measure, it confirms the pattern already established on a formal basis. For the summation of the substantive series is 28,800, the number of minutes in twenty days. Here again the "little time" of Southampton's twenty summers is epitomized in a numerical metaphor.

If the foregoing analysis is correct, or if even a fraction of it is correct, we must assume that interpretation of *Venus and Adonis* has scarcely begun. Any overall reading of the poem must now take as its starting point the number symbolism we have attempted to reconstruct. For the numerological form points to astronomical and mythological spheres of reference, in terms of which alone the poem's intended meaning may be understood. In spite of Shakespeare's undeniably ironic handling of conventional Ovidian situations, the deceptively simple human events adumbrate their philosophical and cosmological counterparts more fully and seriously than has yet been suspected. He seems to manifest, in this poem at least, the same preoccupation with the processes of time which is observable in certain of his contemporaries. *Epithalamion* might almost have been written in emulation of *Venus and Adonis* in an attempt to "overgo" Shakespeare in the field of subtle temporal numerology.

Notes

1. *Short Time's Endless Monument* (New York, 1960).
2. E.g., Gunnar Qvarnström, "Dikten och den nya vetenskapen. Det astronautiska motivet," *Acta Reg. Soc. Humaniorum Litterarum Lundensis*, LX (Lund, 1961), reviewed by Maren-Sofie Röstvig in *Seventeenth-Century News*, XIX (1961). Qvarnström discusses the numerology of Benlowes' *Theophila* and of Milton's *Paradise Lost*. See also Miss Röstvig's "The Hidden Sense," *Norwegian Studies in English*, IX (1963), 1–112, and a study of *The Faerie Queene* by one of the present authors (Alastair Fowler, *Spenser and the Numbers of Time*, London, 1964).
3. The epigraph occurs in a context which might even be interpreted as presenting the idea of poetry as "short time's endless monument"; for, in the course of a discussion of the enduring quality of art, Ovid mentions the astronomical poet Aratus:

"With the sun and moon Aratus will ever exist."

4. *Ovid's Metamorphoses. Englished Mythologiz'd and Represented in Figures by G[eorge]. S[andys].* (Oxford, 1632), pp. 366–67. Cf. Valeriano, *Hieroglyphica*, IX, xx–xxiii (Frankfurt, 1613), p. 106; and Macrobius, *Saturnalia*, I, xxi, 1–4, ed. Eyssenhardt (Leipzig, 1868), pp. 117–18.

5. For convenience, the text here followed is that of F. T. Prince's Arden edition (London, 1960). The 1593 text differs in no particular material to our purpose.

6. This operation of basing calculations upon the time from noon to sunset can be paralleled in contemporary astronomical writing. See, for example, Giov.-Battista Riccioli, *Almagestum novum*, I, xxvii (Bologna, 1651, Vol. I, pp. 33–34): "De Invenienda quantitate Semidiurna, et Seminocturna; cognitis Altitudine Poli, et gradu Eclipticæ, in quo Sol versatur."

7. Significantly, the modulus is an integer; a fact which much facilitates the reader's calculations. Other figures would have produced complicated fractions. The probability of such an integer's occurring is one in twenty-four.

8. That is, somewhat north of the seventh of the zones or climes of earth for which Sacrobosco gives the solstitial durations of day and night. See *The "Sphere" of Sacrobosco and Its Commentators*, ed. Lynn Thorndike (Chicago, 1949), p. 140.

9. Riccioli gives a convenient account of measurement by temporal hour in *Almagestum novum*, I, xxviii, "De diversis Dierum Naturalium Initiis, unde Horarum quasi species quatuor; et de mutua illarum Conversione" (Vol. I, pp. 34–35).

10. According to the modulus given, a temporal nocturnal hour would be little more than half a natural hour.

11. Adonis is discovered dead in stanza 172.

12. I.e., ll. 178–530, and ll. 531–856, inclusive.

13. The lunar sidereal year is twelve times the sidereal period, that is, the time taken by the moon to return to the same apparent position with respect to the zodiac; while the lunar synodic year is twelve times the synodic period of lunation, that is, the time from new moon to new moon.

14. Also, the total stanza count for the summer's day of the poem, which is also incomplete, is eighty-nine, one short of the ninety degrees of the (summer) quarter of the sun's revolution through the zodiac.

15. Cf., for example, Christ's mounting his chariot at the exact center of *Paradise Lost*, by line-count: a matter discussed at some length by Qvarnström.

16. One might note also that at stanzas 50 and 150, the midpoints of the two halves of the poem, its symmetrical balance about stanza 100 is most emphatically struck. In stanza 50 comes the only direct description of Adonis' courser; it concludes with the lines "Look what a horse should have he did not lack, / Save a proud rider on so proud a back," which find an echo in "He will not manage her, although he mount her," in the central stanza. In stanza 150 comes the first appearance of the horse's antitype: "And with that word she spied the hunted boar." These two stanzas epitomize the contrast between summer and winter, on which the poem is based; the generative power of the horse emblemizes summer; the destructiveness of the boar, winter. Verbal links between stanzas 100 and 150 should also be observed: with "All is imaginary she doth prove" cf. "cheering up her senses all dismay'd, / She tells them 'tis a causeless fantasy."

17. "Ten kisses short as one, one long as twenty" (l. 22); "Is twenty hundred kisses such a trouble?" (l. 522); "Were beauty under twenty locks kept fast, / Yet love breaks through, and picks them all at last" (ll. 575–76); "If love have lent you twenty thousand tongues" (l. 775); "Ay me,' she cries, and twenty times, 'Woe, woe,' / And twenty echoes twenty times cry so" (ll. 833–34).

18. *Petri Bungi Bergomatis numerorum mysteria* (Paris, 1618), p. 424, where many instances are given from Homer, and a few from Genesis (e.g., that "Jacob servit annis viginti"). A briefer but similar account of the number appeared earlier in the same author's *Mysticae numerorum significationis liber* (Bergamo, 1585), pt. II, p. 46.

19. This stanza appears to mingle the Petrarchan rhetoric of love with allusion to an astronomical state of affairs. Mythologically, Phoebus was accustomed "to steepe / His fierie face in billowes of the west" (*Faerie Queene* I.xi.31) at close of day; so that Venus, in close proximity to the setting or rising sun, would be simultaneously in Sol's "fire" and in the drenching ocean.

Adonis' presence after sunset is probably to be accounted for in terms of the *crepusculum*: that is, the interval between the setting of the sun ("His day's hot task hath ended in the west," l. 530) and the departure of its light ("Confounded in the dark she lay, / Having lost the fair discovery of her way," ll. 827–28).

20. Twenty times "Woe, woe" would come to forty utterances of the word "woe." But each of these is echoed twenty times; so that a total of 800 sounds is arrived at.

Ideal Conduct in Venus and Adonis

W.R. Streitberger

Although the sonnets in *The Passionate Pilgrim* (IV, VI, IX, XI) represent, as T.W. Baldwin observed, "a kind of first handling of the Venus and Adonis story, out of which the poem of *Venus and Adonis* grew,"[1] Don Cameron Allen has pointed out that the narrative poem takes an entirely different position. The substitution of the courser and jennet episode for the legend of Atalanta and Hippomenes indicates that Shakespeare's plan is as different from Ovid's "as his Venus—a forty-year-old countess with a taste for Chapel Royal altos—is. . . ." Professor Allen notes that the imagery associated with Venus, the "emptie eagle" given to "vulture" thoughts, points to her as the hunter, and that the imagery associated with Adonis, the bird "tangled" in Venus' "net," the deer in Venus' "parke," points to him as her prey. He goes on to connect the hare imagery with Venus, noting that she was often represented accompanied by a hare as the symbol of generative love, and traces the notion of love as a hunt from its classical origins to Shakespeare's Orsino who could "hunt the hart." Equating Venus' attempt to persuade Adonis to hunt the hare with her attempt to seduce him, Professor Allen establishes that Adonis, in refusing to be won by her arguments, rejects the love hunt and embraces the fierce animal hunt. Thus, the poem can be partially explained in terms of a timeless hunt: "Venus, the amorous Amazon . . . hunts with her strong passions; the hunted Adonis lives to hunt the boar; and the boar is death, the eternal hunter."[2]

While helping to resolve many of the troubling aspects of the poem, the interpretation has specific limitations. First, Venus attempts to persuade Adonis to hunt, not only the hare, but also the fox and the deer, and Professor Allen attaches no more than a general significance to the hunting of these animals. Further, no explanation of Venus' extreme reaction to Ado-

---

Reprinted, with permission, from *Shakespeare Quarterly* 26 (1975), pp. 285–91.

nis' death is provided. Finally, the significance of Adonis' youth and the fact that he is too young for love is not explained. Obviously, if Adonis is too young to be tempted by love, identifying the encouragement to hunt easy animals solely with the love hunt does not entirely clarify the situation. There is a great deal more to the poem than Adonis' rejection of Venus—too much, as Allen admits, to be reconciled under the theme of the timeless hunt alone. Shakespeare has synthesized his material from at least three sources, and the poem contains several seemingly disparate episodes. Unless we are willing to give the poem up as defective, the key to a unified interpretation must lie in a theme which satisfactorily relates all of its elements.

A consideration of the two major episodes—the seduction attempt and the hunt—and the background for them indicates that, while in general the action moves in terms of a timeless hunt, on a more specific level the concern in the poem is centered on conduct which leads to a moral, healthy, and heroic life. Adonis acts as the adolescent in training who concerns himself with proper preparation which will lead him to the ideal of noble manhood. Venus presents the temptations—not merely to lust, but to neglect of duty—to succumb to the easy pleasures and endeavors of life, and exhibits in her actions the results of giving in to those temptations. The major opposition in the poem develops between an ideal of conduct and action and the approximation of that ideal which leads to an unheroic existence. Success in pursuing proper training for manhood opens the way not only for a heroic life but also for a moral and healthy one.

Critics in the past have tended to assume that, as a serious work, the poem is defective.[3] More recent reviewers have attempted to circumvent the charge of defectiveness by suggestions that the poem is humorous or that Shakespeare is satirizing various conventions.[4] To deny that the poem is humorous or satirical is not to deny that there are elements of humor or satire in it. Indeed, Professor Allen observes that under the fabric of the epyllion "one hears the faint murmur of an inverted pastourelle, [and] of a mythological satire."[5]

The problems that critics have faced in connection with this poem are similar in certain respects to those encountered in *The Two Gentlemen of Verona*. Both works come fairly close together in Shakespeare's early period; both works have long been considered defective; and both, at times, have been defended against the charges of defectiveness by suggestions that Shakespeare intended to satirize the conventions he employed. "When *The Two Gentlemen of Verona* is performed nowadays the surrender of Sylvia is cut. . . . We leave it out because that special convention which Shakespeare was trying to satirize no longer exists and therefore we do not understand the passage."[6] It has also been argued that in *Venus and Adonis* Shakespeare changed Ovid's legend for essentially comic purposes and that "It is far better to possess a flawless trifle than a superannuated failure."[7] But these arguments do not take sufficient account of the backgrounds against which the works are set.

Shakespeare appears to have taken the conventions that he had to work with in his early period rather seriously and attempted to deal with them in terms of the problems they presented to the age. The evidence that critics have amassed concerning the male friendship convention, for example, indicates that Shakespeare worked out a perfectly orthodox solution for *The Two Gentlemen of Verona*. L.J. Mills has demonstrated that the concern in Sonnets 40, 41, 42, 133, and 144 is the resolution of that tension between love and friendship.[8] R.M. Sargent has pointed out that tension between love and friendship developed through the clash of the medieval courtly ethic, which placed women at the center of the male/female relationship, and the classical idea of friendship as it was revived during the Renaissance.[9] The resolution of this tension, suggested by Sir Thomas Elyot and adapted by Lyly before Shakespeare, was that constancy in friendship held as the cornerstone of a personal morality was a necessary prerequisite for true love between the sexes.[10] From this perspective, the tension between clear moral duty dictated by the friendship convention and irresponsible passion centers in the character of Proteus in *The Two Gentlemen of Verona*. Once one is aware of the background it becomes clear that the play, far from being a satire, is a perfectly orthodox handling of the theme (whether or not it is good theater is another question). Similarly, in *Venus and Adonis* a tension centers in Adonis that we are unable to appreciate without an understanding of the background against which the poem is set.

The framework of the poem is certainly the erotic, mythological narrative in the vein of Lodge's *Scylla's Metamorphoses*. Using ornate imagery and the erotic tone of the genre, Shakespeare, as indicated by the dedication, is making a bid for acceptance into the sophisticated literary world. The audience here could be counted on to be receptive to a range of sophisticated allusions, and the prefatory couplet should suggest that we be careful in taking the poem too lightly:

> Vilia miretur vulgus: mihi flavus Apollo
> Pocula Castalia plena ministret aqua.[11]

Shakespeare drew on three sources from Ovid's *Metamorphoses* for the poem. In the story of Venus and Adonis (*Met.* X, 585–651; 826–63),[12] Ovid describes Venus' love for Adonis. She pleads with him to give up the hunt of the boar and the lion and relates the story of Atalanta and Hippomenes, who were changed into lions for defiling the garden of Cybele with their lovemaking. After Venus leaves him, Adonis is fatally wounded while hunting the boar. Adonis in this story exhibits none of the reluctance of Shakespeare's protagonist. For this dimension Shakespeare drew on two other Ovidian sources. He takes Venus' forwardness, Adonis' blush (ll. 49–50; 76–78), the debate over the kiss (ll. 84–89; 115–28), the embrace (ll. 52–72; 225–30), and Adonis' reluctance (ll. 379; 710) from the story of Salmacis and Hermaphroditus (*Met.* IV, 347–481).[13] The third source is the story of Echo and Narcissus (*Met.* III, 427–542; 635–42), from which Shakespeare draws the accusation of self-love which Venus uses as an argument in her attempt to seduce Adonis (ll. 157–62). In addition there are suggestions throughout of other sources in the Ovidian corpus.[14]

If Shakespeare was merely looking for erotic material he could certainly have gotten enough from the Venus and Adonis story. The fact that he chose two other sources from Ovid for a reluctant Adonis indicates that he was working toward other ends. It does not follow, however, that those ends were necessarily humorous. The story of Echo and Narcissus might provide humor enough, and the question of why Shakespeare chose the story of Venus and Adonis arises. Other than providing a structure for the poem, the story provides the warning of Venus against the hunting of fierce animals and, an element overlooked by commentators, Adonis' insistence that he not be swayed from his purpose: ". . . manhood by admonishment restreyned could not bee" (*Met.* X, 832).[15] A consideration of the courser and jennet episode, the virtues considered important in a young nobleman, and Venus' attempt to persuade Adonis to hunt the fox, deer, and rabbit will show that there is a real dramatic situation in the poem and that Venus is, in fact, tempting Adonis.

R.P. Miller takes the courser and jennet episode in the poem to be an early ironic treatment of the romantic courtship theme.[16] Perhaps there is the dimension of irony here, but more obviously and more importantly in light of Professor Allen's suggestions and the Ovidian source it is a double-edged *exemplum*. Venus points to the situation as an allegory, proof that lust is natural, and attempts to entice Adonis. As Miller notes, she praises the courser's rebellion in crushing the bit with his teeth, "Controlling what he was controlled with" (l. 270). At this point, however, the narrator helps us with the interpretation of the line. He observes that the horse is a noble creature, but lacks "a proud rider on so proud a back" (l. 300). Professor Allen has perceptively drawn the parallel between this horse and Plato's passionate horse in the *Phaedrus,* but concludes that Venus' lesson is blunted by

Shakespeare's description of the mare as a "breeding jennet."[17]

This description of the horse in Plato, however, is part of his description of the soul, composed of the passionate and docile horses and the charioteer.[18] Shakespeare's sophisticated readers could hardly have missed seeing the reverse of Venus' allegory—the bit and rider as morality and reason abandoned for passion. Even if his readers did not get the point from reading Plato, they could have gotten it in a more complete form in Sir Thomas Elyot's *The Book Named the Governor*. If Shakespeare was familiar enough with *The Governor* to use it as a source for *The Two Gentlemen of Verona*, it seems reasonable to suppose that he was familiar enough with the rest of the work to use it as a background for *Venus and Adonis*, especially since the two works come so close together in Shakespeare's early period.

In Book III of *The Governor*, Elyot provides a discussion of the virtues that must be fostered in a young nobleman in order to produce the necessary constancy and stability which will make him a fit governor. He notes that in the training of youth "it ought to be well considered that the cement wherewith the stones be laid be firm and well binding. . . . Semblably, that man which in childhood is brought up in sundry virtues . . . be not induced to be alway [sic] constant and stable, so that he move not for any affection, grief or displeasure, all his virtues will shortly decay."[19] In Book I, Elyot sets out in detail the kind of cement the stones of the nobleman's personality ought to be laid with in order that he not swerve from his duty. He points out that in infancy only virtuous women should attend the child and that no wanton words should be spoken in front of him. He counters the charge that an infant does not know good from evil by asserting that "in the brains and hearts of children, which be members spiritual, whiles they be tender and the little slips of reason begin in them to burgeon, there may hap by evil custom some pestiferous dew of vice to pierce the said members and infect and corrupt the soft and tender buds."[20] The basic principle of Elyot's notion of virtue, Platonic in origin, is that virtue exists as a potential in the soul, but that it must be nourished and practiced so that, finally, virtuous action will follow from a knowledge of the right.[21] From the foregoing account it is clear that despite the fact that Adonis is too young for love—"Measure my strangeness with my unripe years" (l. 524)—he is still in moral danger. Indeed, Elyot points out that the chief enemy of virtue throughout man's life is lust: "nothing so sharply assaileth a man's mind as doth carnal affection, called (by the followers thereof) love."[22] Adonis is old enough to recognize Venus as a threat, and responds to her procreation argument in terms suggestive of Elyot: "Call it not love, for Love to heaven is fled, / Since sweating Lust on earth usurp'd his name" (ll. 793–94).

Throughout the debate Adonis acts as an ideal Renaissance school-boy who has learned his lesson well. Indeed, he is in the second of the seven ages of man, noted by Jaques in *As You Like It* (II.vii.143–66). He rejects Venus' procreation argument in terms reminiscent of the grammar school debate. T.W. Baldwin observes that Erasmus recommends the subject as good for the development of rhetorical technique, and that it was quite common for schoolboys to debate the pros and cons of procreation via marriage.[23] In the *Sonnets* Shakespeare took seriously the idea of gaining immortality through procreation, but that project belongs to men in the third stage of development, not the second to which Adonis belongs.[24] He has learned his lessons well and reproves Venus with an effective grammar school counter:

> What have you urg'd that I cannot reprove?
> The path is smooth that leadeth on to danger.
> I hate not love, but your device in love,
> That lends embracements unto every stranger.
> You do it for increase: O strange excuse,
> When reason is the bawd to lust's abuse!
> (ll. 787–92)

Adonis, although in moral danger according to Elyot's theory, is too young to be actually tempted to incontinence in pleasure. The temptation that Venus presents is to neglect of duty. She attempts to persuade him to give up the hunt of the boar for the rabbit, the fox, and the deer. Elyot maintains that hunting in the manner of the ancients is a "laudable exercise." He gives the chief animals that the ancients hunted as the lion, leopard, wild swine, and bear, and claims that "therein is the very imitation of the battle, for not only it doth show the courage and strength as well of the horse as of him that rideth . . . but also it increaseth in them both agility and quickness, also sleight and policy."[25] After praising several famous classical hunters, Elyot goes on to clarify why it is that Adonis must reject Venus' invitation to hunt these timid animals. Elyot states that "I dispraise not the hunting of the fox with running hounds, but it is not to be compared to the other hunting in commodity of exercise. . . . Hunting of the hare with greyhounds is a right good solace for men that be studious, of them to whom nature hath not given personage or courage apt for the wars. And also for gentle-women. . . . Killing of deer with bows or greyhounds serveth well for the pot. . . . But it containeth therein no commendable solace or exercise, in comparison to the other forms of hunting."[26]

Quite clearly Venus attempts to persuade Adonis to reject everything that a young noble must train for. But Adonis is a good student and a firm and constant young man on his way not only to a noble life but to a healthy one. Adam in *As You Like It,* despite his almost fourscore years, claims that

> . . . in my youth I never did apply
> Hot and rebellious liquors in my blood,
> Nor did not with unbashful forehead woo
> The means of weakness and debility;
> Therefore my age is as a lusty winter.

(II.iii.48–52)

Of course, Adam does not refer to a nobleman's training, he is merely a servant; but if proper training and discipline in youth leads to a healthy life for a servant it will accomplish at least the same for a nobleman.

Venus' reaction to Adonis' death graphically exemplifies the inconstant and unstable behavior that is generated by succumbing to passion and the easy pleasures of life. In contrast to Elyot's contention that a nobleman must be constant in the face of "affection, grief, or displeasure," Venus shifts from groundless jubilant hope to excessive grief and despair. Of course, it is a woman's grief and this must be taken into account. But Elyot's suggestion that the easy hunt of the hare is fit sport for a gentlewoman or for men who do not have courage apt for war paves the way for a comparison of the youth who neglects his training to Venus. She vividly portrays the passions to which Adonis would be subject in the event that he responded to her arguments and neglected his training and purpose.

I conclude, then, that the courser and jennet episode is a double-edged *exemplum,* that Venus presents a moral threat to Adonis despite the fact that he is too young for love, that her attempt to persuade him from the noble to the easy hunt would destroy his virtues and make him an unfit gentleman, and that the striking similarities between Elyot's and Shakespeare's treatments of the material point to the fact that the seduction attempt is of real dramatic interest and is not merely an example of Shakespeare playing with literary conventions. Venus' temptations to neglect of duty are not merely part of an *argumentum* which sets her and Adonis off as representatives of particular qualities. Tension between clear duty and the temptation to neglect it centers in Adonis and is, like the tension in Proteus of *Two Gentlemen,* unrecognizable without an awareness of the background against which the work is set.

Professor Allen speculates that Shakespeare was fascinated "as young men often are, by innocent and unmerited death in youth."[27] Perhaps he was;

Adonis in rejecting Venus embraces constancy to duty, the only choice proper to a young nobleman. It seems relevant here to recall that the poem is dedicated by a struggling young artist, who claims in that dedication to embrace his own form of constancy to duty, to a promising young nobleman who, it is hoped, will answer "the world's hopeful expectations." And I suspect that the irony and poignancy of the death of a promising youth in the pursuit of duty would have been appealing to both men at this point in their careers. Shakespeare has succeeded admirably with this poem. For, while he manages to retain the erotic tone of the genre, he presents on another level an essentially moral struggle, one which his sophisticated readers were not likely to miss.

NOTES

1. T.W. Baldwin, *On the Literary Genetics of Shakespeare's Poems and Sonnets.* (Urbana: Univ. of Illinois Press, 1950), p. 44.

2. D.C. Allen, "On *Venus and Adonis.*" In *Elizabethan and Jacobean Studies in Honour of F.P. Wilson,* ed. H. Davis and H. Gardner (Oxford: Oxford Univ. Press, 1959), pp. 100–105.

3. Hazlitt's assessment is that the poems "appear to us like a couple of ice-houses. They are about as hard, as glittering, and as cold. The author seems all the time to be thinking of his verses, and not of his subject—not of what his characters would feel, but of what he shall say; and as it must happen in all such cases, he always puts into their mouths those things which they would be the last to think of, and which it shews the greatest ingenuity in him to find out. . . . The images, which are often striking, are generally applied to things which they are the least like: so that they do not blend with the poem, but seem stuck upon it." *Collected Works,* ed. A.R. Waller and A. Glover (London: J.M. Dent, 1902), I, 358–59. See also Hyder Rollins, *New Variorum, Poems,* pp. 390–405; 447–523.

4. R. Putney, "*Venus and Adonis:* Amour with Humour," *PQ,* 20 (1941), 533–48, suggests that Shakespeare omits the description of the death of Adonis and focuses on Venus' reactions for humorous purposes: "She merely finds the body. Thus a scene potentially painful is avoided. Then Venus' grief spurs her to such heights of absurdity that we are first incredulous, then amused." R.P. Miller, "*Venus and Adonis* and the Horses," *ELH,* 19 (1952), 249–64, takes the courser and jennet episode as an ironic treatment of the romantic courtship theme.

5. Allen, p. 101.

6. H.T. Price, "Shakespeare as a Critic," *PQ,* 20 (1941), 390–99.

7. Putney, p. 548.

8. L.J. Mills, *One Soul in Bodies Twain* (Bloomington: Indiana Univ. Press, 1937), pp. 239–43.

9. Cicero claimed that "friendship is nothing else than an accord in all things, human and divine, conjoined with mutual goodwill and affection, and I am inclined to think that, with the exception of wisdom, no better thing has been given to man by the immortal gods." *De Amicitia,* trans. W. Falconer (London: William Heinemann, 1923), pp. 130–31. See R.M. Sargent, "Sir Thomas Elyot and the Integrity of *The Two Gentlemen of Verona,*" *PMLA,* 65 (1950), 1166.

10. This is suggested in his story of Titus and Gisuppus from *The Governor.* L.J. Mills, p. 407, points out that there are many similarities between this story and *TGV* (see also Bullough, I, 203–17). Lyly adopted this resolution in two of his works.

In *Endymion,* Eumenedes, having been counseled by Geron at the sacred fountain, elects the friendship of Endymion over his love for Semele. All works out for the best and he is reunited with Semele. There is little doubt that Shakespeare knew this play; he uses the subplot for his own subplot in *LLL.* Lyly's *Euphues: The Anatomy of Wit* deals with a variation of the theme. Euphues learns about the convention the hard way. He entices Philautus' love away only to be betrayed by her for another.

    11.   All quotations from Shakespeare are from *The Complete Plays and Poems of William Shakespeare,* ed. W.A. Neilson and C.J. Hill (Cambridge, Mass.: Houghton Mifflin, 1942).

    12.   The line references are to Golding's translation. See Geoffrey Bullough, *Narrative and Dramatic Sources of Shakespeare* (London: Routledge and Kegan Paul, 1957), I, 166–76, for the text and Latin line equivalents.

    13.   Allen, pp. 106–7, suggests that Adonis is a remaking of Hippolytus.

    14.   See Bullough, I, 161–5.

    15.   Bullough, I, 168.

    16.   Miller, op. cit. in footnote 4.

    17.   Allen, p. 108.

    18.   "Now when the charioteer sees the vision of his Love and his whole soul is warmed throughout by the sight and he is filled with the itchings and prickings of desire, the obedient horse, giving in then as always to the bridle of shame, restrains himself from springing on the loved one; but the other horse pays no attention to the driver's goad or whip, but struggles with uncontrolled leaps, and doing violence to his master and teammate, forces them to approach the beautiful and speak of carnal love" (*Phaedrus,* 254a).

    19.   Sir Thomas Elyot, *The Book Named the Governor,* ed. S.E. Lehmberg (London: J.M. Dent, 1963), pp. 205–6.

    20.   Elyot, p. 16.

    21.   John M. Major, *Sir Thomas Elyot and Renaissance Humanism* (Lincoln: Univ. of Nebraska Press, 1964), pp. 241–69.

    22.   Elyot, p. 204.

    23.   T.W. Baldwin, op. cit., 183–86; and *Small Latin and Less Greek* (Urbana: Univ. of Illinois Press, 1944), II, pp. 339–40.

    24.   Professor Allen observes that "hunting became first the proper preparation for knighthood and, later, for the forming of a gentleman" (p. 105). He goes on to point out the King Alfred was famous as a skilled hunter at twelve years of age. It seems then that Adonis should be taken at his word when he insists that he is too young for love and it should be clear that he belongs to the second, not the third, age of man.

    25.   Elyot, p. 66.

    26.   Elyot, p. 68. See also Allen, p. 105.

    27.   Allen, p. 111.

SELF AND EROS IN *VENUS AND ADONIS*

Coppélia Kahn

Shakespeare's contemporary Gabriel Harvey dismissed *Venus and Adonis* as a poem which would delight only "the younger sort." His judgment reflected the moral decorum of Renaissance taste: physical love was a concern proper to hot-blooded youth, and usually matter for comedy. "The wiser sort," Harvey declared, would interest themselves in tragedies like *Lucrece* or *Hamlet,* in dilemmas more profound than how to answer an invitation to erotic pleasure on a summer's day.[1]

Modern critics have taken the poem more seriously, and have explained the central conflict and the narrative action as illustrating a philosophical or moral theme. T.W. Baldwin finds the poem a Platonic argument in which Love and Beauty, the forces that sustain creation, are menaced by chaos. Kenneth Muir sees it as an Ovidian refutation of Neo-Platonic and Puritan arguments against the flesh. Robert P. Miller calls the poem "a mythological re-enactment of man's fall to sin." Exploring the metaphor of the hunt, Don Cameron Allen argues that through it Shakespeare presents a moral lesson against yielding to passion. Hereward T. Price holds that the imagery embodies the tragic paradox of "Nature with herself at strife," mirroring "the problem of the dissonances that destroy harmony in the moral order of the world." A.C. Hamilton reads it as "an allegory of the myth of creation and the fall," and Norman Rabkin, as a myth of the genesis of love in terms of the neo-Platonic opposition between sensual and spiritual love.[2]

In contrast to this prevailing critical tendency, I propose a radically psychological reading of the poem. I see it as a dramatization of narcissism—self-love in the form of withdrawal from others into the self. This theme was richly explored in Shakespeare's source, Ovid's *Metamorphoses.* Brilliantly

Reprinted from *The Centennial Review* 20, 4 (Fall 1976), pp. 351–71, with permission.

improvising on several Ovidian tales, Shakespeare portrays the paradox of the narcissist, whose attempt to protect himself against the threat of love actually results in his self-destruction. The conflict between Venus and Adonis is essentially a conflict between eros and death fought within the narcissistic self. The boyish Adonis, whom Venus, the very incarnation of desirable femininity, presents with an enviable chance to prove his manhood, sternly rejects that opportunity, meets death in the boar hunt, and metamorphosed into a flower, ends up as a child again, sheltered in Venus' bosom. A similar conflict is strongly implied in the first seventeen of Shakespeare's sonnets, possibly written about the same time as *Venus and Adonis*. There the speaker urges the beautiful youth contracted to his own bright eyes to love and procreate, as Venus urges Adonis, and warns him that in his refusal to love he will become "the tomb / Of his self-love."[3]

In the *Metamorphoses,* in the sonnets, and in *Venus and Adonis,* narcissism is specifically a crisis of identity which occurs in youth. Ovid's Narcissus and his Shakespearean successors are male adolescents, poised between youth and manhood, forced to confront the emerging imperative of mature sexuality, but reluctant to answer it and define themselves as men by making love to women. In a way, *Venus and Adonis* portrays a *rite de passage* in reverse. As an archetypal event in youth, the *rite de passage* marks "the complete symbolic separation of the male adolescents from the world of their youth, especially from their close attachment to their mothers."[4] At the same time, this separation marks the youth's new sexual and social identity as a man, whose future love-choices will be women not his mother. The Adonis of Shakespeare's poem is caught between the poles of intimacy and isolation: intimacy with Venus, which constitutes entry into manhood, and the emotional isolation of narcissism, which constitutes a denial of growth, change, and the natural fact of mortality which underlies them. But Adonis' self-absorption and claims of autonomy actually mask an intense need for dependency, a wish to escape the risk and conflict involved in having a separate identity, a wish symbolically fulfilled in his metamorphosis into the flower which Venus treats as her child.

Shakespeare's characterization of Venus and Adonis, and the coherence of the narrative, can best be understood in terms of this dilemma. The following interpretation will center on four major questions suggested by the poem. Why does Adonis refuse to love Venus? Why does he choose the boar instead, and what does the boar signify? What does his metamorphosis mean? In answering these questions, I will stress Shakespeare's use of Ovid and the way in which Ovidian myth can be a means of expressing the unconscious needs and conflicts of narcissism.

Before I proceed, I want to distinguish between the context in which I use this concept and other contexts for it. In Shakespeare's day, the story of Narcissus was allegorized in accordance with medieval tradition, the fate of its hero illustrating the folly of trusting in riches, beauty, and the things of this world.[5] The common meaning of the term today arises from the idea that Narcissus loved his own beauty; in most dictionaries, narcissism is defined as self-love, excessive admiration of oneself or interest in all that pertains to oneself.[6]

As a psychoanalytic concept, however, narcissism has subtler and more inclusive reference to the effect of self-love on one's relations with others. Freud first used in it 1910, in discussions of homosexuality, characterizing it as the choice of love objects modelled on the self rather than on the mother.[7] Later he differentiated between this sense of the word and "primary narcissism," normal in infancy and early childhood, when satisfactions experienced in the body itself are the object of libido.[8] Since Freud, an extensive and complicated controversy over the concept has arisen, involving the serious theoretical questions of when and how the ego is formed and the role that object relations play in its formation.

Whatever the theory of its etiology, however, a paradox lies at the center of narcissism: the one who seems to love himself does not really have a self and thus is not really capable of loving himself or others. The narcissist lacks a coherent, stable, realistic image of himself as distinct from others:

> he has not become a securely independent person—not created a core of himself—and unless he becomes an independent person he cannot himself in turn love. . . . Such separation as the narcissist achieves will remain uncertain and he will always be more than willing to put it off.[9]

His apparent preference for himself over others, his superior attitude or claims of autonomy, are actually defensive attempts to keep this inner deficiency secret, even from his conscious self. They enable him to withdraw into himself, to avoid the risk of opening up to others in the challenge, conflict, and frustration of normal intimacy. In such relationships as he does pursue, the narcissist seeks total, unquestioning reassurance and acceptance, and finds ordinary demands from others threatening. I refer to "the narcissist" only for convenience, for narcissism is a component of many neurotic illnesses, as well as a trait of many healthy people.[10] Not only in the character of Adonis, but as a narrative and poetic whole, *Venus and Adonis* reveals its nature.

I. ADONIS

It has long been known that Shakespeare took the narrative outline of his poem from Ovid's tale of Venus and Adonis. But his fidelity to the Ovidian concept of eros as an imperative, an inescapable force which creates and destroys, hurts and delights, has not been adequately recognized. Nor has the significance of his alterations to the source material been noted. He actually created the character of Adonis and the conflict between him and Venus not from the tale of Venus and Adonis, but from the stories of Narcissus and of Salmacis and Hermaphroditus, which are dominated by the figure of the youth who refuses to love a woman and suffers for it.[11] Shakespeare worked in fruitful harmony with Ovid, taking from him the theme of self in conflict with eros which gives his poem a firm psychological coherence.

The story of Deucalion and Pyrrha in Book I of the *Metamorphoses* is a symbolic statement of Ovid's conception of eros. Sole survivors of the first iniquitous race of men, which Jove destroyed in the flood, this innocent and worshipful couple are advised by the oracle of Themis, goddess of Justice,

> Go hille your heads, and let your garments slake,
> And both of you your Graundames bones behind your
>   shoulders cast.[12]
>
> (I. 451–452)

Horrified at this commandment to desecrate the sacred worship of their ancestors, at last they realize that the earth is their mother, that the stones of earth are her bones. When they do as Themis commands, the stones become the men and women of a new human race. The story insists that our primary obligation is to the Great Mother; the goddess of justice hands down only one law, the law of generation, which is conditional on an act of destruction. Born of mothers who must die, nourished by the fruitful earth, we all in turn must love, procreate, and die. It is the only norm Ovid recognizes, and in Shakespeare's poem, it is Venus' most compelling argument for love: "Thou wast begot, to get it is thy duty" (l. 168).

Eros regulates nature, but, paradoxically, eros creates anarchy. Anyone, god or mortal, may be struck with desire for anyone else, and whatever the cost, even to an innocent victim, that desire must be satisfied. One group of stories emphasizes the inexorable character of sexual passion by treating incest and homosexuality at length. Though Ovid often affects, usually through the persona of a narrator, a decorous horror of such perversions, he no doubt does so only to amuse an audience which he assumes to be as sophisticated and unshockable as himself. We share the author's know-ing smile rather than the narrator's pious judgment. Ovid as author regards men and women as creatures of nature, and to him nothing in nature is un-natural. Thus he relates with a sympathy born of tolerance the story of Byblis, who loved her brother Caunus and in her crazed passion was turned into a fountain; of Iphis, a girl raised as a boy who loved the bride chosen for her and, in answer to her prayers, was changed into a man; of Adonis' mother Myrrha who, horrified at her own passion, slept with her father and was changed to an ever-weeping tree. No moral scheme governs the dénouements of these stories: a capricious fate either gratifies or denies, le-gitimates or punishes the forbidden wishes.

Though eros is the only constant that Ovid recognizes, he is too much of a realist to believe that it reigns unchallenged. As the stories I have touched on make clear, conflict is inherent in love. The illicit lovers deplore their unnatural desires, but cannot help loving. Lust struggles with love, perver-sion with normal affection. Similarly, Shakespeare announces "Nature with herself at strife" as a theme in the second stanza of the poem. The idea of a conflict in which neither side is right, in the sense of being more reasonable, more natural, or morally more justifiable, is as basic as Shakespeare's poem as it is to Ovid's. The beauteous war of red and white repeatedly reminds us of this conflict. If in nature roses and lilies have equal claims, do not de-sire and rejection, blushes and pallor, Venus and Adonis? Because eros it-self is potentially destructive as well as creative, the human reaction to it is necessarily ambivalent, compounded of joy and fear, loathing and desire.

Yet in Adonis' rejection of Venus there is something more than natu-ral. He does not merely shun her as a particular woman, for she is a god-dess and represents love itself, no matter how realistically Shakespeare por-trays her. Rather, in repudiating her he repudiates love itself. His reasoned arguments are less convincing than his emotional stance: a cold and harsh withdrawal from the very idea of sexual union. Impervious to her erotic appeal, he meets all her pleas with withering scorn and sweeping negation. Shakespeare might have depicted Adonis as experiencing a common ado-lescent conflict between newly felt desire and a fear of sexual inadequacy due to inexperience. But though Adonis claims he is too young to love, what he conveys in deeds as well as in words is that he will not love. What lies behind this adamant refusal?

In Ovid's tale of Venus and Adonis, Adonis is characterized merely as a handsome youth. He is Venus' lover, and no point is made of his atti-tude toward her. He merely ignores her fond warning against the boar hunt; there is no conflict between them about it.[13] In Shakespeare's poem, that conflict is the main issue, and in a striking reversal of roles which parallels that in the stories of Narcissus and of Hermaphroditus, the hero is courted by the heroine, and strenuously rejects her advances.

Though Shakespeare directly compares Adonis to Narcissus only once (ll. 1616–1620), Ovid's conception of the cold, withdrawn, beautiful youth and his self-destructive resistance to love permeates the poem. The frequent comparison of Adonis to a flower, for instance, is more than a merely conventional compliment because it refers unconventionally to a man, and thus recalls Narcissus, who was changed into a flower. Insofar as Adonis' beauty is fresh, delicate, and richly hued, the flower metaphor daintily suggests his physical qualities. It furnishes arguments for Venus' urgency ("For flowers that are not gathered in their prime / Rot, and consume themselves in little time," ll. 131–132), but also for Adonis' stubbornness ("Who plucks the bud before one leaf put forth?" l. 416). Poignantly, it hints at early mortality for the youth but also foreshadows his transformation to a flower after death.

Most significantly, the flower image comments on Adonis' attitude toward himself and others. Flowers grow and die heedless of human existence; they blush unseen on the desert air, sublimely indifferent to admiration or its absence. Capable of inspiring the tenderest feelings, they themselves feel nothing. Such flower-like self-regard and self-sufficiency typifies a number of Ovidian heroes and heroines: Daphne, Syrinx, the nameless heroines of the tales of Jove in Arcady and of the raven; Arethusa, and most notably, Hermaphroditus and Narcissus. All are young and surpassingly beautiful; all flee sexual encounter, perceiving it as an ultimate danger, and find their escape in metamorphosis.

In some stories, the youth's transformation into a natural object represents the power of art to sublimate sexuality: Daphne becomes the laurel, symbol of poetic achievement; Syrinx, the reed through which Pan pipes his songs. But in other stories, the children of earth who begged to be relieved of their bodies as a way of escaping from sex ironically become images for the imprisonment of human consciousness in mere physicality. Whether or not they themselves feel alien to their new non-human forms, Ovid makes us feel their transformations as a pathetic loss of human identity. For instance, the daughter of Coroneus flees Neptune's embraces only to be turned into a raven:

> Then called I out on God and man. But (as it did appeare)
> There was no man so neare at hand that could my crying heare.
> A Virgin Goddesse pitied me bicause I was a mayde:
> And at the utter plunge and pinche did send me present ayde.

I cast mine armes to heaven, mine armes waxt light with fethers
    black,
I went to cast in hast my garments from my back,
And all was fethers. In my skinne the rooted fethers stack.
I was about with violent hand to strike my naked breast,
But nether had I hand nor breast that naked more did reast.
I ran, but of my feete as erst remained not the print,
Me thought I glided on the ground, Anon with sodaine dint,
I rose and hovered in the Ayre. And from that instant time
Did wait on Pallas faithfully without offence or crime.
But what availes all this to me. . . .

                (II. 728–741)

The flower-children who unconditionally refuse love are trying to assert their
separateness from eros, an impossibility in the Ovidian world. They flee the
personal imperatives of their own natures, only to end up immured in the
terrifyingly impersonal natural world. Though they retain their minds, without their bodies, they no longer have human identities, and are cut off forever from love and community.

    These Ovidian stories provided Shakespeare with a broad sense of the
role of the body and sexuality in the formation of identity. More specifically,
he found the major elements of Adonis' character in Ovid's account of Narcissus, which begins,

For when yeares three times five and one he fully lyved had,
So that he seemde to stande betweene the state of man and Lad,
The hearts of divers trim young men his beautie gan to move,
And many a Ladie fresh and faire was taken in his love.
But in that grace of Natures gift such passing pride did raigne,
That to be toucht of man or Mayde he wholy did disdaine.

                (III. 437–442)

Rarely does Ovid give the precise age of his characters. Here and in the story
of Hermaphroditus he notes that the hero is an adolescent, implying a connection between his age and his rejection of love. Significantly, Narcissus is
"betweene the state of man and Lad"; since he is already sexually attractive to others, he can define himself as a man if he wishes to. But he would
like to remain a boy forever, and repels attempts at sexual intimacy so strenuously that "no one can touch him," hinting at a fear that sexual contact
might damage him physically, as it damages Hermaphroditus, who loses his

masculinity as a result of Salmacis' embrace.[14]

Ovid stresses Narcissus' self-protective autonomy through a contrast with Echo, an image of the person wholly dependent on others for the creation and maintenance of a self. Incapable of speaking first, but also unable to remain silent when others talk, she parrots their words but cannot say anything of her own. When Narcissus fails to respond to her ardent wooing, she literally wastes away, becoming only a voice. His stout resistance to bodily contact with her emphasizes his precious dedication to his own body as an object:

> Upon these wordes she left the Wood, and forth she yeedeth streit,
> To coll the lovely necke for which she longed had so much.
> He runnes his way, and will not be imbraced of no such.
> And sayth: I first will die ere thou shall take of me thy pleasure.
>
> (III. 484–487)

Shakespeare's Adonis reveals a similar attitude toward his body in the famous "divedapper" passage when he offers his lips to Venus, then "winks" and turns away. Venus, of course, is the counterpart of Echo, and though she easily manages to do more than get her arms around Adonis, he stalwartly maintains his emotional distance from her: "Still is he sullen, still he lours and frets," despite her tenderest embraces.

Narcissus' rejection of Echo stands for his rejection of all proffered love, and Ovid portrays his death as resulting directly from this rejection. One of his despairing suitors prays that the youth may actually fall in love with himself so that he too will suffer unrequited love, and Nemesis, goddess of vengeance, answers the prayer. Even though Narcissus realizes that his self-love is destroying him, he is helpless to stop it. Burning with love of his own body, he prays to escape from it in order to possess it; but death brings only the ironic retribution of transformation into the object he most resembled in life, a flower.

Shakespeare, following Ovid's tale of Narcissus, centers his poem on a conflict between the ardent pursuing female and the retreating, rejecting male. In both heroes, the preference for the self is revealed only by pressure to give the self to another. While the exceptional beauty of both heroes leads others to love them, that is not why they love themselves. Their primary need is to defend against sexual involvement in order to protect the fragile inner self. This defense is ironically self-destructive, as Narcissus' death (in Ovid's version, he wastes away gradually, literally consumed by love of himself) and Adonis' in the boar hunt, as I shall show, make clear. Shakespeare suggests that Adonis' fate will resemble Narcissus', because he is similarly unable to nourish and develop the self by intimacy. In the striking phrase,

> Narcissus so himself himself forsook,
> And died to kiss his shadow in the brook.

(ll. 161-162)

the repetition of "himself" imitates Narcissus' intense need to fasten on himself as an object to the exclusion of others. To forsake oneself means to lose consciousness of oneself in relation to others and to external reality, as in the expression "to forget oneself"; in the context of the legend, it means to die, symbolizing the utter annihilation of self. When Venus reproaches Adonis with failing a duty to reproduce his kind, she calls his body "A swallowing grave" which buries his posterity, and phrases the idea much as in the earlier passage, commenting "So in thyself thyself art made away" (l. 763). The second "thyself" means both Adonis' potential offspring and his sense of himself, which he makes away or destroys by rejecting Venus. In Adonis, Shakespeare depicts a narcissistic character who regards eros sexual encounter—as the most serious threat to his self. But the real threat is internal, and comes from that very urge to defend against eros.

II. Venus

Adonis would be threatened by any kind of intimacy, because it might force him to reveal his secret—that he has no core, nothing to offer from within, only an enormous need to be reassured. It is precisely Venus' kind of love, however, which mirrors this inner need which Adonis would keep hidden.

First, both by virtue of traditional associations invoked in the poem and through Shakespeare's characterization of her, Venus is something of a mother figure. When she bases her arguments for love on procreation as the law of nature, she is *Venus genetrix,* and she presides over a lush natural ambiance which suggests omnipresent fecundity, especially in the coupling of the horses and the rabbit hunt. Her oft-repeated plea for a kiss is an invitation to physical fusion which suggests a parallel with the infant's relation to the mother at the breast, before he has begun to differentiate between self and others—precisely the stage at which Adonis exists psychologically. In this sense, Venus offers the only kind of relationship with another that Adonis is capable of—one in which he is totally dependent on a nurturing figure who offers him unending oral gratification.

But the kiss is also an act of sexual intimacy, so that to kiss willingly would in a crucial way define Adonis as a man. And Venus is the queen of love, the supreme object of desire for any man, whose manliness is defined by his desire for a woman; thus Venus asks,

Art thou a woman's son and canst not feel
What 'tis to love, how want of love tormenteth?
(ll. 201–202)

Furthermore, at certain moments she embodies lust as a blind impersonal
force in the Ovidian sense, desire for the opposite sex which overwhelms
man or woman and momentarily obliterates self-consciousness. It is this
aspect of her that mirrors the narcissist's basic fear: that he who has such
a slender sense of self will lose it all if he allows himself to be loved.

All these aspects of Venus—mother, woman, eros itself—are depicted
in oral imagery, the imagery of kissing or eating. At the crises of her passion,
the two kinds of imagery merge, in the kiss that devours its object. Thus Venus bears a highly ambivalent quality; union with her would both confer manly
identity and obliterate the self. The kiss she pleads for evokes conflicting reactions from the reader, in effect putting us in Adonis' place. The oral contact she seeks bears, despite her good intentions and the naturalness of her
desire, an aggressive and even murderous quality. As she begins, trying to be
gently seductive, she unwittingly conveys an insatiable eagerness:

Here come and sit, where never serpent hisses.
And being set, I'll smother thee with kisses.
And yet not cloy thy lips with loathed satiety,
But rather famish them amid their plenty. . . .
(ll. 16–19)

After she "plucks" Adonis from his horse and pushes him to the ground,
she "stops his lips" with kisses to keep him from speaking, and when he
protests, "What follows more, she murders with a kiss" (ll. 42–54).

That kiss is described through the comparison of Venus to an eagle
devouring its prey, a simile which both repels and awes the reader:

Even as an empty eagle, sharp by fast,
Tires with her beak on feathers, flesh, and bone,
Shaking her wings, devouring all in haste,
Till either gorge be stuffed or prey be gone:
Even so she kiss'd his brow, his cheek, his chin,
And where she ends she doth anew begin.
(ll. 55–60)

This all-consuming, never-ending kiss becomes rapaciously impersonal. Yet the stanza also suggests an Ovidian perspective on it as a natural urge. We learn in the first line that the eagle is "empty" and "sharp by fast"; therefore, her ferocious appetite gains a certain legitimacy. In the next stanza, when the panting Adonis breathes in Venus' face,

> She feedeth on the steam as on a prey,
> And calls it heavenly moisture, air of grace. . . .
>> (ll. 63–64)

The imagery of preying is softened and prettied into a joke: Venus may act like a hungry eagle, but she is forced to content herself with conceits. Finally, in a third stanza, Adonis is no longer being devoured; he is merely "a bird . . . tangled in a net," captured in Venus' loving embrace.

Shakespeare orchestrates this dominant oral motif in various keys. In the following lines, for example, Venus' devouring qualities are balanced by the erotic appeal of her coy preoccupation with "lips":

> Touch but my lips with those fair lips of thine—
> Though mine be not so fair, yet are they red—
> The kiss shall be thine own as well as mine.
> What see'st thou in the ground? Hold up thy head,
> Look in mine eyeballs, there thy beauty lies:
> Then why not lips on lips, since eyes on eyes?
>> (ll. 115–120)

The description of the kiss begins as a "touch" in the first line, and the fusion it involves is pictured as a gain to Adonis in the third line ("The kiss shall be thine own. . ."). But by the fifth line, Adonis, his image reflected in Venus' eyes, has become part of her, and the last line suggests a blurring of boundaries, an anonymous merging of "eyes" and "lips" which echoes the narcissistic fear of losing the self. In the famous passage in which Venus compares her body to a park (ll. 229–240), inviting Adonis to "Feed where thou wilt," her devouring aspect gives way to her nurturing side. Yet later, when Adonis offers her a goodnight kiss (only in order to make his escape), her voracious drive returns, again in the imagery of an animal devouring its food:

> Now quick desire hath caught the yielding prey,
> And glutton-like she feeds, yet never filleth.
> Her lips are conquerors, his lips obey,
> Paying what ransom the insulter willeth;

Whose vulture thought doth pitch the price so high
That she will draw his lips' rich treasure dry.

And having felt the sweetness of the spoil,
With blindfold fury she begins to forage;
Her face doth reek and smoke, her blood doth boil,
And careless lust stirs up a desperate courage,
Planting oblivion, beating raenson back,
Forgetting shame's pure blush and honor's wrack.

(ll. 547–558)

In contrast to the earlier eagle image, these lines convey a cruel lust for conquest, rather than hunger. In the first stanza, gluttony has replaced fast; the
eagle is now a vulture, and the kiss a kind of rape in which eros seems heartless fury rather than pleasure. These stanzas, in fact, use imagery strikingly
similar to that describing Tarquin when he is about to rape Lucrece; in both
situations, lust becomes a tyranny of force, likened both to the animal world
and the battlefield.[15] In the first stanza, Venus' lips are "conquerors," and
the kisses she takes, "ransom" and then (in the first line of the second stanza)
"spoil." The dehumanization of Venus is stressed more strongly than that
of Adonis, for the reeking, smoking and boiling of the third line make her a
personification of the turmoil and destruction of battle itself.

This frightening depersonalization strongly recalls Ovid's tale of
Hermaphroditus, in which the amorous woman destroys the sexual and thus
the human identities of herself and her reluctant lover. Venus' style of wooing is, in general, inspired by that of Salmacis, who first offers herself to
Hermaphroditus boldly, but in carefully controlled rhetoric. Later, her desire inflamed by the sight of his naked body, she cries in the language of conquest, "*Vicimus, et meus est*" ("I win, and he is mine"), as she struggles to
clasp him to her. When he resists, she struggles the harder, and her embraces
are compared to a snake coiling itself around the eagle which has caught it,
to ivy twining itself around tree trunks, and to an octopus' tentacles grasping its prey on every side. When she prays that she and Hermaphroditus may
never be separated, the prayer is granted with ironic literalness:

The members of them mingled were and fastened both together,
They were not any longer two: but (as it were) a toy
Of double shape. Ye could not say it was a perfect boy,
Not perfect wench; it seemed both and none of both to beene.

(IV. 367–370)

Had Hermaphroditus yielded to her, the actual intimacy would have been less injurious than the metamorphosis he suffers. Like Narcissus and Adonis, he is in effect punished for his resistance by being robbed of his individuality and in his case, of his manhood. While Salmacis obtains the eternal union she desires, he suffers a loss and becomes "but halfe a man." The defense brings worse results than the fear threatens; the attempt to protect the self ends in the loss of self.

We know Venus as a character only through the demands she makes on Adonis; the overwhelming impression we have of her is of a mouth, pressing insistently on or toward him.[16] Most of the poem's 1200 lines are hers, in the form of direct speech; in contrast, Adonis speaks only eighty-eight lines. Venus pours forth a flood of words at Adonis and at us. This volubility contributes to the comic situation, of course; the queen of love can only assuage "love's fire" through words, and her oral aggressiveness is humorously at variance with the conventional female role of silent auditor receiving poetic tribute from a male poet-speaker. Adonis' passive silence also becomes a joke when, after speaking only two curt sentences in the first 400 lines, he opens up with three stanzas of high-pressured argument against love. Venus remarks in mock surprise, "What, canst thou talk?" (l. 427), and then, true to form, launches into another amorous sermon. The more stubbornly a silent Adonis "winks, and turns his lips another way," the thirstier Venus grows for a taste of those lips. For each character, a fundamental need is at stake. The struggle of the open heart against the closed heart is imaged in an oral war.

III. The Boar and the Flower

The needs which impel Adonis to reject Venus are now clear, I hope, and we are ready to ask why he should choose to hunt the boar *instead* of loving her. I propose two kinds of explanation for his strange choice: a general one, in which hunting serves as a defense against eros; a specific one, in which the boar, though it is inimical to all Venus stands for, serves as a projection of Adonis' fears of her.

If Shakespeare had intended hunting to be understood as an acceptable alternative to Venus and a viable mode of releasing Adonis' closed self, he might have presented it as an activity suitable to young men of good birth, valuable in teaching skills and forming character, pleasant in the male camaraderie it affords.[17] He might have sketched a scene of hairbreadth 'scapes and heroic challenge in the hunt. But the hunt appears only in terms of its object, the boar—a powerful creature wholly and blindly destructive. We see it only through Venus' jealous and fearful eye; significantly, we are given no other view. Adonis himself makes no arguments for hunting *per se;* in opposition to Venus, he holds only that he is too young to love, without saying why boar hunting is a better pursuit for one of his age.

In fact, hunting serves Adonis' deepest unconscious need, which is to keep eros out of his life. He acts as though hunting *is* his life; the action begins when Venus accosts him even as he "hies him to the chase," and their encounter consists of her resourceful (but ultimately futile) attempts to stop him from mounting his horse to resume that chase. In his first major speech, Adonis states his opposition to love in a strangely turned phrase which puts the boar in the place of the love object:

> "I know not love," quoth he, "nor will not know it,
> Unless it is a boar, and then I chase it.
> 'Tis much to borrow, and I will not owe it;
> My love to love is love but to disgrace it,
> For I have heard, it is a life in death,
> That laughs and weeps, and all but with a breath."
>   (ll. 409–414)

The alliterated double negatives of the first line, "not," "nor," and "not," stress the intensity of his aversion. After its first use, the word "love" is suppressed into the unaccented pronoun "it" and the contraction "'tis" in lines one through three, minimizing its importance. In the fourth line it is the repetition of "love" which serves a similar purpose— to mock it; here Adonis comes close to saying that he hates love. In the last two lines, he seems to ridicule love as it appears in Petrarchan poetry, making its paradoxes and oxymorons sound absurd. But the phrase "life in death" alludes ironically to the boar hunt as well, since it is quite easily a fatal sport, and one to which he devotes his life.

Adonis' use of the word "know" in the first line provides a clue to the nature of his defense against love. In this context, knowing suggests carnal knowledge, and the verb hints at a criticism of the youth on his own grounds. How can he reject something of which he "knows" nothing? Later he plays on "know" again in the sense of carnal knowledge: "Before I know myself seek not to know me" (l. 525), he warns Venus, and again unintentionally raises the question of how he can know what his self is by isolating it from experiences which help to form it. The playful suggestion in the second line that he would rather "know" or love the boar seems a kind of risqué joke at first, a glance at sodomy. But it carries the serious undertone that he is deeply alienated from his own kind, determined not to love even at the expense of being perverse. The boar, as Elizabethans knew, is an ugly creature, and the effect of identifying it with love is to make love not only repulsive but impossible; he could never love a boar. All the poetic devices employed in this stanza combine to reveal Adonis' unconscious intention; to make love nonexistent by denying its existence for him. Clearly, he is using denial as a defense against love.

His conscious objection to love elsewhere is that he is too young for it. He compares himself to an unfinished garment, a leafless bud, an unbroken colt, an undersized fish, and a green plum, with an air of narcissistic pride in his very insufficiency (ll. 415–420, 526–528). By arguing that he is too young, he uses defenselessness as a defense, and dares Venus to be so heartless as to hurt him.

In a similar sense, it is not hunting which Adonis uses as a defense, but his very self, precarious and incomplete though it is. This is revealed in the imagery of the following stanzas, which is so strongly oriented toward outer threat and resistance from an inner stronghold:

> If love have lent you twenty thousand tongues,
> And every tongue more moving than your own,
> Bewitching like the wanton mermaid's songs,
> Yet from my heart the tempting tune is blown;
>   For know, my heart stands armed in mine ear,
>   And will not let a false sound enter there;
> Lest the deceiving harmony should run
> Into the quiet closure of my breast,
> And then my little heart were quite undone,
> In his bedchamber to be barr'd of rest.
>   No, lady, no; my heart longs not to groan,
>   But soundly sleeps, while now it sleeps alone.
>   (ll. 775–786)

Adonis begins by hyperbolically evoking Venus' amorous rhetoric ("Twenty thousand tongues") as an oral threat against which his heart "stands armed," oddly perched outside the body, in the ear. But then in the second stanza, the heart turns out to be not only protector and defender but also the thing being protected which ordinarily swells inside, in a "quiet closure" like the womb. The contradictions in this metaphor are psychological truths. If "heart" is the inmost self, and the capacity for loving, it is Adonis' inmost self which keeps him from loving, in order to protect him from a threatening seductive female (the "wanton mermaid" in the first stanza) who, like the sirens singing to

Ulysses, deceptively lures him not to love but to death. The conception of the heart as a static realm of pure rest, dwelling in the solitude and quiet of a bedchamber, is rather preciously emphasized in the repetition of "my" before heart and breast in both stanzas. That his heart is *his* matters to Adonis, and so long as it is his he can remain in a regressive, unchanging state of utter calm.

Edward Hubler's remarks on "the closed heart" of the young man in the sonnets are highly appropriate to Adonis. Commenting on Sonnet 94, he says,

> The closed heart may be poor, but it is at ease. Those men are most content who, though they inspire affection in others, have no need of it themselves. . . . They are the owners of themselves, whereas throughout Shakespeare's works self-possession in the sense of living without regard for others is intolerable.[18]

Shakespeare's great heroes are men who finally appreciate the supreme value of love and human bonds, no matter how blindly they may have denied it before: Lear, Othello, Macbeth. His great villains are solitary individualists who hate love: Iago, Edmund, Richard III. In *Venus and Adonis* Shakespeare is saying the life apart from eros is death.

Turning now to the specific way in which the boar reflects Adonis' fear of Venus, though from the first stanza hunting is opposed to love, curiously it is Venus who describes the boar at some length, who actually sees it, and who supplies our only vision of the boar killing Adonis. Even more curiously, Shakespeare suggests through imagery associated with these two opposed figures a similarity in their meanings for Adonis. The hero's insistence on an absolute boundary between hunting and love actually masks the way in which, by chasing the boar, he acts out his deeper feelings toward Venus.

What Venus stresses most in her account of the boar is, not surprisingly, his destructiveness; in particular, his tusks. Those are his mortal weapons, and make him, like Venus, the personification of an oral threat:

> Oh be advis'd, thou know'st not what it is,
> With javelin's point a churlish swine to gore,
>   Whose tushes never sheath'd he whetteth still,
>   Like a mortal butcher, bent to kill.
>
>   (ll. 615–618)

The phrase "bent to kill" refers to the placement of his tusks, pointing downward, and his natural habit of foraging by "rooting the mead" with his snout to earth. Driven by instinct, he seeks food and unintentionally "digs sepul-chres," "killing whate'er is in his way." Just as Venus at the height of her desire turns into an eagle or a vulture blindly seeking the natural needs she is denied, and thus seems to murder what she would enjoy, so does the boar. Both are capable of a purely natural, unreflective, and impersonal kind of aggression. The boar personifies the aspect of Venus most threatening to Adonis: her seemingly unsatiable desire. The more he resists her, the more her ardor increases, and causes him to resist her all the more. In a supremely revealing speech delivered as she gazes at the dead Adonis, the fondly grieving goddess imagines that the boar was as taken with his beauty as she was. The boar becomes the very image of Venus:

> If he did see his face, why then I know
> He thought to kiss him, and hath kill'd him so. . . .
>
> (ll. 1109–1110)

> Had I been tooth'd like him, I must confess,
> With kissing him I should have kill'd him first.
>
> (ll. 1117–1118)

Then why does Adonis prefer the boar to Venus, when both bear a fatal quality for him? We can look at the hunt as Adonis' attempt to regain mas-tery over the inner danger of losing his sense of self by mastering an exter-nal representative of that danger. In short, he projects his anxiety about be-ing devoured by Venus onto the boar, and attempts to destroy the boar so that Venus will not destroy him. The danger emanating from the boar hunt is physical, and that emanating from Venus is emotional, but insofar as Ado-nis is narcissistically oriented toward his own body, the physical act of love carries a threat, pointedly suggested in the goddess-vision of the boar emas-culating Adonis (ll. 1115–1116).[19] Thus the hunt allows Adonis to "experi-ment" with an inner danger through confronting an outer danger.[20]

But in a deeper sense, projecting Venus into the boar allows him to establish a rudimentary, provisional kind of "negative identity," a total iden-tification with what he is least supposed to be.[21] Venus argues that a lover "follows the law of nature" (l. 171) and feels desire like every man or woman bred (ll. 214–216); it would be only normal, she makes us feel, for the youth to love her. The boar, on the other hand, embodies all that is inimical to life, beauty, and love. Adonis scornfully rejects the easier, more overtly pleasur-able and normal course for the fatal one. He takes the boar as his object because, like her, it is blindly destructive in an oral way and thus most dangerous and most real to him. Yet it also provides a way of defending his inner self against her; it gives him a substitute self as a hunter, as one who loves a boar instead of a woman. His readiness to face danger or death in the manly boar hunt conceals his inability to be more than a boy—"not-quite-somebody"—in the love hunt. He would rather pursue death in seeking the boar, than risk the annihilation of self which loving Venus threatens.

In Venus' rage and grief at being cheated by death of her prize, she utters a long prophecy that is part curse. In predicting that "Sorrow in love hereafter shall attend," she expresses the Ovidian view of eros as a capricious, arbitrary force which levels mankind. All must love, but none shall find perfect satisfaction:

> It shall be sparing, and too full of riot,
> Teaching decrepit age to tread the measures;
> The staring ruffian shall it keep in quiet,
> Pluck down the rich, enrich the poor with treasures;
> It shall be raging mad, and silly mild,
> Make the young old, the old become a child.
>
> (ll. 1147–1152)

Her own aborted love affair is the model for this vision of a world turned upside down by love: the woman aggressively wooing the passive boy, the goddess of love herself denied love. In five stanzas of encyclopedic example, she equates eros with conflict and frustration: "They that love best, their loves shall not enjoy" (l. 1164).

This picture of perpetual struggle then gives rise to Adonis' metamorphosis, the symbolic resolution of his struggle against eros. His transformation to a purple (from Lat. *purpureus,* a variety of red) and white flower represents the ending of the war of white and red mentioned so often.[22] Adonis' pale coldness opposed Venus' fiery ardor; in death, his red blood stained the perfect whiteness of his skin. Now, as a flower, he can "grow unto himself" as he wanted to in life, and Venus can possess him totally and forever as she could not before. But in order to do so, she must pick the flower—that is, she must kill him.

Thus in one sense, the ending recapitulates the fear of eros which dominated Adonis in life. When Venus picks the flower and puts it in her bosom, sexual fusion is equated with death, and envisioned as her total possession of him, obliterating his identity. But the terms of union are no longer sexual: they are infantile. Venus calls Adonis the father of this flower, and puts the baby in the father's place, at the breast:

Here was thy father's bed, here in my breast;
Thou are the next of blood, and 'tis my right.
Lo in this hollow cradle take thy rest;
My throbbing heart shall rock thee day and night:
  There shall not be one minute in an hour
  Wherein I will not kiss my sweet love's flower.
                  (ll. 1183–1188)

The devouring mother whose oral demands constituted a threat to Adonis' very identity has now become the nurturant mother on whom he depends as an infant for survival. Several previous mentions of Adonis as an infant and Venus as a mother have hinted at this relationship. Taunting him for his coldness, Venus asks "Art thou a woman's son. . . ." (l. 201) and later describes him as "a son that sucked an earthly mother" (l. 863). When she searches anxiously for him in the hunt, she is compared to "a milch doe, whose swelling dugs do ache, / Hasting to feed her fawn" (ll. 874–875). In the stanza quoted above, the fierce oral qualities of Venus' desire are transmuted to an omnipotent maternal tenderness which nevertheless carries disturbing overtones of Adonis' anxieties about sexual fusion: "it is as good / To wither in my breast as in his blood," says Venus to the flower. Here Shakespeare suggests that this resolution of Adonis' dilemma is but another kind of death, parallel to the murder of the self through narcissistic withdrawal. Venus' apostrophe to the flower concludes with the image which dominates the poem, a kiss—the kind of perpetual oral gratification she sought in the poem. No longer able to deny her, Adonis is now but a gratifying object, lacking mind and will.

The metamorphosis, however, can just as fittingly be seen as the fulfillment of his deepest narcissistic wish: to regress to the state in which he had no separate identity—nothing to fight for and nothing to lose. Paradoxically, though in this state he is wholly dependent on Venus, he also dominates her totally; he is always with her and she kisses him every minute. The metamorphosis is undeniably tender and moving: it appeals to a desire present to some degree in all of us. But it also implies the desperation underlying the narcissist's dominance. Adonis has finally allowed Venus to get close to him, on the only terms he can tolerate: her total subservience to his need for constant reassurance.

Thus the poem's ending is as ambivalent as any narcissist could wish. Venus loses her lover to the boar, but wins symbolic possession of him as a flower. Adonis successfully fights off Venus' sexual demands, but surrenders to her all-embracing love after death. In his total passivity, he dominates

Venus, but she also dominates him. *Venus and Adonis* has long been seen as a young man's poem for relatively superficial reasons: its erotic subject matter and sensuous playfulness. But Shakespeare deserves more credit than he has been given for his understanding of youth's deeper conflicts, of the ways in which eros shapes the growing self.

NOTES

1. Quoted in *The Poems*, by William Shakespeare, ed. Hyder C. Rollins, A New Variorum Edition, Philadelphia: J.B. Lippincott and Co., 1938, p. 455.

2. See T.W. Baldwin, *On the Literary Genetics of Shakespeare's Poems and Sonnets*, Urbana, Ill.: University of Illinois Press, 1950; Kenneth Muir, "*Venus and Adonis*: Comedy or Tragedy?," in *Shakespeare the Professional and Related Studies*, Totowa, N.J.: Rowan and Littlefield, 1973; Robert P. Miller, "Venus, Adonis, and the Horses," *ELH*, XIX (1952), 250–264; in a later article, "The Myth of Mars' Hot Minion in *Venus and Adonis*," *ELH*, XXVI (1959). Miller sees the poem in less moralistic terms, closer to mine; Don Cameron Allen, "On *Venus and Adonis*," in *Elizabethan and Jacobean Studies presented to F.P. Wilson*, Oxford: Clarendon Press, 1959, pp. 100–111. Hereward T. Price, "The Function of Imagery in *Venus and Adonis*," *Papers of the Michigan Academy of Sciences, Arts and Letters* XXXI (1945), 275–297; A.C. Hamilton, "*Venus and Adonis*," SEL 1500-1900, I (1961), 1–15; Norman Rabkin, *Shakespeare and the Common Understanding*, New York: The Free Press, 1967, pp. 150–162. The essays by Hamilton and Rabkin are sensitive to the problematical aspects of the poem and avoid the over-schematized approach of the other critics. The best of the few interpretations which do not take a moral or philosophical approach are: Rufus Putney, "Amour with Humour," *PQ*, xx (1941), 533–554; J.W. Lever, "Venus and the Second Chance," *Shakespeare Survey*, XV (1962), 1–8; and most recently, William Sheidley, "'Unless it be a boar': Love and Wisdom in Shakespeare's *Venus and Adonis*," *MLQ*, XXXV, no. 1 (March, 1974), 3–15.

3. This and all subsequent quotations from *Venus and Adonis* are taken from the Arden Shakespeare paperback edition of *The Poems*, ed. F.T. Price, London: Methuen & Co., 1969.

4. S.N. Eisenstaedt, "Archetypal Patterns of Youth," in *The Challenge of Youth*, ed. Erik H. Erikson, Garden City, N.Y.: Doubleday Anchor Books, 1965, p. 33.

5. Douglas Bush, *Mythology and the Renaissance Tradition in English Poetry*, new rev. ed., New York: W.W. Norton and Co., 1963, pp. 47–8.

6. See the *American Heritage Dictionary of the English Language*, *Webster's New World Dictionary of the American Language*, and the *Oxford English Dictionary*.

7. Sigmund Freud, *Three Essays on the Theory of Sexuality*, Standard Edition, VII, 145n; *Leonardo da Vinci and a Memory of His Childhood*, Standard Edition, XI, 50.

8. Sigmund Freud, "On Narcissism: An Introduction," *Standard Edition*, XIV, 73–107.

9. Grace Stuart, *Narcissism: A Psychological Study of Self-Love*, London: George Allen Unwin, 1956, p. 45. This book provides a lucid and searching account of narcissism in myth and post-Freudian psychoanalytic thought.

10. I am also indebted to Karl Abenheimer, "On Narcissism," *British Journal of Medical Psychology*, XX (1944), 322–329; Philip Slater, *The Glory of Hera: Greek Mythology and the Greek Family*, Boston: Beacon Press, 1968; and to Miriam Miller, for the understanding of narcissism on which my interpretation of *Venus and Adonis* is based.

11. T.W. Baldwin, *On the Literary Genetics of Shakespeare's Poems and Son-*

nets (cited in note 2, above), has systematically presented evidence for Shakespeare's borrowings from Ovid. His conclusions are the opposite of mine, however, for he argues that Shakespeare was mainly interested in portraying Venus as female wooer, and only used in the Narcissus story to heighten that motif. Douglas Bush, *Mythology and the Renaissance Tradition* (cited in note 5), pp. 138–140, briefly outlines Shakespeare's use of Ovid. He notes that Venus as wooer and Adonis as reluctant lover are modelled on Salmacis and Hermaphroditus, and that "The somewhat similar story of Narcissus and Echo may also have been in the poet's mind" (l. 139), but takes the idea no farther. No critic, so far as I know, has assessed the influence of Ovid's conception of eros, or of the Narcissus story, on the poem.

12. This and all subsequent quotations from Ovid's *Metamorphoses* (except one, to be given in Latin) will be given in Golding's translation; Shakespeare probably made use of both his translation and the original Latin version. I have used *Shakespeare's Ovid, Being Arthur Golding's Translation of the Metamorphoses*, ed. W.H.D. Rouse, Carbondale, Ill: Southern Illinois University Press, 1961, and Ovid, *Metamorphoses*, with an English translation by Frank Justus Miller, 2 vols., London: William Heinemann, Ltd.; Cambridge, Mass: Harvard University Press, 1936.

13. See *Metamorphoses*, Book X, 585–863 (Golding's translation).

14. Philip Slater, *The Glory of Hera: Greek Mythology and the Greek Family*, Boston: Beacon Press, 1968, notes:

> For individuals in whom narcissistic anxieties are severe, the sexual act shatters the body image of both male and female. The boundary between Me and Not-Me crumbles, since the female is penetrated and part of the male disappears inside of another. In addition, psychological boundaries are obliterated through orgasm. The ego dissolves inundated with impulse, and this may be experienced as a kind of death—as complete submersion of unconsciousness. (101)

15. See *Lucrece*, ll. 421–427, 554–560, in the Arden edition cited in note 3, above.

16. The words, "kiss," "kiss'd," "kisses," and "kissing" are used more often in *Venus and Adonis* than any other Shakespearean work. *The Harvard Concordance to Shakespeare*, by Martin Spevack, Cambridge, Mass.: Harvard University Press, 1973, lists 32 instances of them, compared with the next highest number of 20, in *Troilus and Cressida*.

17. See Don Cameron Allen, "On *Venus and Adonis*," cited in note 2, for a discussion of the traditional distinction between the soft hunt of love and the hard hunt, "the honest training of those who would be heroes."

18. Edward Hubler, *The Sense of Shakespeare's Sonnets*, Princeton: Princeton University Press, 1952, p. 103.

19. The irony of his death parallels the irony of narcissism suggested throughout the poem. Adonis flees Venus to avoid becoming a man at the cost of losing all manhood, just as the narcissist withdraws into the self at the cost of killing it. The emasculation of Adonis recalls that of Hermaphroditus; see note 14, above.

20. Though no social setting for the hunt is realized in the poem (as I have noted), Adonis mentions twice that he hunts with "friends." Shakespeare thus hints at the existence of what Erik Erikson calls "an adolescent pre-society" which provides "a sanctioned moratorium and lent support for experimentation with inner and outer dangers (including those emanating from the adult world)." Erik Erikson, "The Problem of Ego Identity," in *Identity and the Life Cycle: Selected Papers by Erik H. Erikson, Psychological Issues* I, no. 1 (1959), 102.

21. Erikson, "The Problem of Ego Identity," 131.

22. Hereward T. Price (cited in note 2) notes that in Ovid Adonis is turned

into a red flower, while in Bion's elegy for Adonis, two separate flowers, red and white, spring up after Adonis' death. Shakespeare seems to have conflated these two sources in making the single flower both red and white, intending a unification of opposites for which the Tudor rose gave him ample precedent.

Shakespeare's Myth of Venus and Adonis

S. Clark Hulse

Shakespeare alters the myth of Venus and Adonis so casually that the importance of his change is not at first apparent. Instead of being Love's lover, as in ancient literary sources,[1] Adonis leaves her flat on her back and runs off to hunt with the boys. This interpretation had appeared before in the Renaissance, in Titian and in Marlowe, and Shakespeare's treatment may owe something to them, to the stories of Narcissus and of Salmacis and Hermaphroditus, or to the poet's obscure relationship with the Earl of Southampton.[2] Whatever its origin, though, the change threatens to make hash of the poem. Advancing on Adonis in the first lines, Venus seems to become a sweaty, muscular rapist. In the middle, as Adonis resists her, the sweet couple fall into a philosophic bicker over whether Venus or Diana is the author of death. At the end, Venus bursts into a passionate lament over the dead Adonis, which is admirable poetry but is utterly inconsistent with her earlier characterization as a comic seducer and immoral lecher. And why is Adonis killed for what he didn't do or, worse yet, why didn't he do it? The modern reader, as J.W. Lever sums it up, usually takes the poem as "a very funny story which somehow forgets the joke; or as a highly cautionary tale which, in showing the dangers of caution, does not point the moral at all well."[3]

A famous poet has remarked that it is hard to applaud *Venus and Adonis* unless one knows the rules of the game.[4] A basic rule of myth, which differentiates it from other stories, is that it has some force, or appeal to the imagination, that overcomes seeming contradictions and improbabilities. It creates chimeras—serpent, goat, and lion held together by unnatural force. Shakespeare draws far more than we have realized on the highly sophisti-

Reprinted by permission of the Modern Language Association of America from "Shakespeare's Myth of Venus and Adonis," *PMLA* 93 (1978), pp. 95–105.

cated tradition of allegorical poetry and painting, so that the various aspects of his Venus portray alternately the comic and serious qualities of physical love, while the death of Adonis suggests the internal contradiction of earthly beauty, whose splendor comes at the price of transience.[5] Yet the poem adds up to no homily on love. In the strife between Venus and Adonis, Shakespeare holds his conflicting attitudes toward earthly love in an esthetic balance through a form that, in the same iconographic tradition, is both narrative and pictorial. This form in itself seems to be one solution to that characteristic Shakespearean ambivalence, the living "in uncertainties, Mysteries, doubts," which, as a systematic way of thinking, resembles primitive myth.

I. MYTH AND MEANING

An acceptable general theory of myth is hard to come by. With the passing of the once easy rule of the *Golden Bough,* the territory has been reduced to chaos amid the strife of ritualists, psychologists, and structuralists.[6] One might try to reconcile them around the idea of mediation. For Frazer, Cassirer, and the ritualists, myth intervenes between the sacred and the profane; for Freud and Campbell, between the unconscious and the conscious; for Jung, between the individual and the collective; for Lévi-Strauss, between the polarities and contradictions of a social system.[7] But even if one could overcome the vast differences in methodology involved, such a compromise definition can finally be no more than an analogue to esthetic form and can only account for some rudimentary unity that Shakespeare's poem would share with any work based on the same myth. To account for Shakespeare's variations on the story, myth criticism must be joined to literary history, to see how the myth developed in the Renaissance, especially in the mythographic tradition that largely shaped Shakespeare's material.

Most significant for Shakespeare's poem was the development of the attribute system as a way of representing mythic characters in allegorical poetry and painting.[8] A description of a god or goddess in, say, Vincenzo Cartari's *Le imagini de i dei de gli antichi* (1556; 1st illus. ed., 1571) will show a unitary figure—suitable for a painting, emblem, or medallion—decorated and embellished with various attributes, each the relic of a story about the deity and the symbol of an abstract quality. Venus, for instance, is described with a rose, which recalls how she cut her foot as she ran to the dying Adonis and represents the painful side of love.[9]

The technique is, of course, not restricted to pagan subjects. The archangel Raphael, for instance, is regularly depicted with a youth carrying a fish, recalling the tale of Tobias and signifying Raphael's role as the "affable archangel" who aids and protects men.[10] Tobias is his attribute, as the rose is Venus', or the caduceus is Mercury's. Mythography, then, is not just a content but a *process* of representation, a continual infolding and unfolding of pictorial and narrative forms. It mediates between two modes of conception, between discursive and nondiscursive thinking: the material of the visual world is made into narrative, narrative into argument, and argument into vision.

That Shakespeare uses mythography as a formal constituent of his poetry is amply illustrated by the figure of Adonis. Arthur Golding, Shakespeare's favorite translator of Ovid, wrote in his Dedicatory Epistle to the Earl of Leicester that Book X of the *Metamorphoses* "chiefly doth containe one kind of argument, Reprooving most prodigious lusts."[11] The same argument springs to the lips of Adonis when he rejects Venus. Yet she has a word or two of answer; and anyway, Adonis' refusal means that the pair will enact no lusts worthy of reproof, so Shakespeare's own position must go beyond Golding's simpleminded moral. Golding's source, the Regius-Micyllus Ovid, indeed offers more varied allegory. Historically, the myth recalls ancient religious festivals in Assyria.[12] Physically interpreted, Adonis represents the crops of the earth, as Micyllus learned from scholia in Theocritus, No. 3 (Micyllus, p. 243; cf. Giraldi, p. 397, and Conti, p. 162a). Or, in Boccaccio's version, Adonis is the sun and Venus the earth; their love brings forth lush flowers, leaves, and ripe fruit. But winter is like the boar that slays the beautiful Adonis, for then the sun seems banished from our world, Venus mourns, the earth lies barren.[13]

The most common interpretation, though, is suggested by Ovid himself. When Adonis is changed to a flower at the end of his tale, he writes:

> . . . brevis est tamen usus in illo [flore];
> namque male haerentem et nimia levitate caducum
> excutiunt idem, qui praestant nomina, venti.[14]

> . . . But short-lived is their flower;
> for the winds from which it takes its name shake off the flower
> so delicately clinging and doomed too easily to fall.

This sense of transience acquires almost proverbial weight as it is repeated by mythographers. Boccaccio writes:

> But as to the fact that Adonis is transformed into a flower: by that invention I think is shown to us the brevity of beauty, which in the

morning is richly colored, but at a late hour, drooping and pale, grows feeble; and so mankind in the morn, that is, in the time of youth, is blooming and splendid; but in the eve, that is, in the time of old age, we grow pale, and we fall into the shadows of death.[15]

What this philosophical interpretation has in common with the physical is the importance given to flowers. In one case, Adonis is *like* a flower; in the other, he *causes* flowers. Both statements describe the action of Shakespeare's poem. Its opening lines link Adonis to the purple sun:

> Even as the sun with purple colour'd face
> Had ta'en his last leave of the weeping morn,
> Rose-cheek'd Adonis hied him to the chase.[16]

At the end, his purple blood begets a flower:

> And in his blood that on the ground lay spill'd,
> A purple flower sprung up, checker'd with white,
> Resembling well his pale cheeks and the blood
> Which in round drops upon their whiteness stood.
>
> (ll. 1167–70)

Throughout, he is linked to flowers, explicitly as a metaphor for his beauty:

> "Thrice fairer than myself," thus she began,
> "The field's chief flower, sweet above compare;
> Stain to all nymphs, more lovely than a man,
> More white and red than doves or roses are."
>
> (ll. 7–10)

The realization that Adonis is Beauty, which fadeth like the flower, explains his peculiar, unmotivated death. Beauty fades, flowers wither, no matter what. His death does not show a doom that awaits lechery, since he will have none, and Venus (who he does think is a lecher) has sought to protect him. Certainly it does not prove that sex is very nice; it proves simply that beauty fades. In short, the sequence of the narrative is not finally a causal or argumentative sequence; rather, it is an unfolding of Adonis' attributes, a making explicit of what is implicit in line 8—"the field's chief flower." Shakespeare can say he *is* a flower, while a painter would show him *with* a flower; the narrative repeats this attribute by showing him *becoming* a flower.

Narratively, he must die to become that flower, and what the flower means is that he must die.

If Shakespeare's portrayal of Adonis is deceptive only because it is so simple, the portrait of Venus is a genuine problem. That Venus is Love is axiomatic; that she is earthly love is quickly apparent.[17] Adonis calls her Lust; she herself claims to be fruitful and generative; and her hand is moist, the proper characteristic of a passionate lover. George Wyndham, the first modern critic of the poem, likened her to Botticelli's Venus, rising from the foam.[18] But, if she is born of the sea, it is in Abraham Fraunce's sense:

> She is borne of the sea, lovers are inconstant, like the troubled waves of the sea: Hereof was she also called *Aphrodite,* of the froath of the sea, being like to *Sperma.*[19]

Shakespeare's description of her is a metaphoric catalog of the characteristics of physical love. When he wishes to show that love is light, that is, merry and delightful, he says that Venus does not weigh much:

> "Witness this primrose bank whereon I lie:
> These forceless flowers like sturdy trees support me.
> ⋅
> Is love so light, sweet boy, and may it be
> That thou should think it heavy unto thee?"
>
> (ll. 151–56)

The pun is outrageous, and the figure contorted, for its literal and metaphoric senses have reversed positions. As Cartari prescribes, the principal characteristics of the god are those that signify the god's nature and effects (p. 16). We are used to the physical being the literal, but literally Venus is delightful, and so she is figured as if she were light in weight. But, curiously, this reversal changes the impact of the image; instead of seeing a sylph supported on flowers, we see tree trunks, holding aloft an awesome bulk. This is the core of the poem's problem. If one grants that Venus is earthly love, what is the attitude toward earthly love? Is it loathsome, foul lust? Delightful sense? A near-sacred force of natural propagation?

The most casual glance at the sonnets would remind us that Shakespeare is perfectly capable of portraying love in all three ways. *Venus and Adonis* opens in travesty, as if love were something that reduces humans to the grotesque and foolish:

> Over one arm the lusty courser's rein,
> Under her other was the tender boy.
>
> (ll. 31–32)

> Backward she push'd him, as she would be thrust,
> And govern'd him in strength, though not in lust.
>
> (ll. 41–42)

> Were I hard-favour'd, foul, or wrinkled old,
> Ill-nurtur'd, crooked, churlish, harsh in voice,
> O'erworn, despised, rheumatic and cold,
> Thick-sighted, barren, lean, and lacking juice,
>   Then mightst thou pause, for then I were not for thee.
>
> (ll. 133–37)

> He wrings her nose, he strikes her on the cheeks,
> He bends her fingers, holds her pulses hard.
>
> (ll. 475–76)

> She sinketh down, still hanging by his neck;
> He on her belly falls, she on her back.
>
> (ll. 593–94)

If the moments of direct physical contact are ludicrous, the passages of enticement reveal the sensuality that led Francis Meres to call Shakespeare "Mellifluous & hony-tongued":

> Bid me discourse, I will enchant thine ear,
> Or like a fairy trip upon the green,
> Or like a nymph, with long dishevell'd hair,
> Dance on the sands, and yet no footing seen.
>
> (ll. 145–48)

> Sweet bottom grass and high delightful plain,
> Round rising hillocks, brakes obscure and rough,
> To shelter thee from tempest and from rain:
> Then be my deer, since I am such a park.
>
> (ll. 236–39)

These two moods have won the poem its reputation for comic sensuousness. But there is another tone, like to that of Sonnet 129—"The expense of spirit in a waste of shame"—in which love is presented as a violent force of destruction:

> Even as an empty eagle, sharp by fast,
> Tires with her beak on feathers, flesh and bone,
> Shaking her wings, devouring all in haste,
> Till either gorge be stuff'd or prey be gone:
>   Even so she kiss'd his brow, his cheek, his chin.
>   (ll. 55–59)

> And having felt the sweetness of the spoil,
> With blindfold fury she begins to forage;
> Her face doth reek and smoke, her blood doth boil,
> And careless lust stirs up a desperate courage,
>   Planting oblivion, beating reason back,
>   Forgetting shame's pure blush and honour's wrack.
>   (ll. 553–58)

We have, in effect, not one but three Venuses—comic, sensual, and violent—all embodying earthly love but differently depicted to reveal different aspects. Venus is the empty eagle, the randy jennet, the tender snail, the anguished milch doe, and the timid hare. Even the boar is finally her animal. Traditionally, the boar represents jealousy, because Mars took its shape to eliminate his rival.[20] In Shakespeare's version, Mars has been mastered by Venus, who is herself the jealous one, that is, possessive of Adonis. When first the boar is mentioned, she quakes with fear of loss:

> For where love reigns, disturbing jealousy
> Doth call himself affection's sentinel;
> . . . .
> Distemp'ring gentle love in his desire,
> As air and water do abate the fire.
>   (ll. 649–54)

So, when the boar appears, he possesses Adonis with a firm embrace that Venus can only envy:

> And nuzzling in his flank, the loving swine

Sheath'd unaware the tusk in his soft groin.
Had I been tooth'd like him, I must confess,
With kissing him I should have kill'd him first."[21]

(ll. 1115–18)

Venus is a series of images, even of puns, like the strange animal-headed figures who inhabit the pages of Cartari. Contradictory elements require contradictory figures. Cartari depicts Venus five different ways, and once, rather
like Shakespeare, groups three different Venuses in the same frame (Cartari,
p. 549).

Too much can be made of the "character" of Shakespeare's Venus.
She is no Lady Macbeth or Prince Hamlet. The idea of character requires a
personality continuous over a period of time. But not the allegorical figure,
as Dante explained in *La vita nuova*: one "could be puzzled at my speaking
of Love as if it were a thing in itself, as if it were not only an intellectual
substance, but also a bodily substance. This is patently false for Love does
not exist in itself as a substance but is an accident in a substance."[22]
Shakespeare's mythic goddess is not so much a person as a diverse group of
actions inhabiting a single body.

II. Visual Syntax

If the characters of Venus and Adonis show the kinship in this instance between poetry and the visual arts, they may also remind us of Lessing's warning about the fundamental difference between the arts. Painting, he says,
employs figures and colors in space and imitates bodies; poetry articulates
sounds in time and imitates actions.[23] The mythographic depiction of
Shakespeare's characters gives them a self-contained unity, a perfect balance
of action and physique within each figure. But that very completeness *within*
the figures transforms the traditional relationship *between* them: Adonis no
longer needs an affair with Venus to define himself. Shakespeare goes further still, making Adonis not just indifferent to Venus but downright disdainful of her. This novel arrangement, we may recall, was devised by Titian,
in whose painting we may find mythographic structures that break down
Lessing's dichotomy between iconic and discursive forms and offer a model
for Shakespeare's handling of the affair.

Titian's *Venus and Adonis* is built around conflict—Adonis pulls
away, Venus restrains him. Dogs and boar spear are his attributes; an over-
turned urn is hers. In the background is an inert, winged figure, his bow
and quiver hanging from a nearby tree. Panofsky identifies him as a sleeping Cupid, symbolic of cool passions (*Titian*, p. 151). Ovid and others,

though, tell us of the resemblance of Adonis to Cupid; they look so much alike that, unless one had wings and the other his quiver, we could not tell them apart.[24] This figure, equipped with both wings and quiver, lies in the same position as the dying Adonis in illustrated Ovids of the Renaissance, so the dead shepherd may here be fused with the sleeping boy, reminding us of the conclusion of the tale.[25] The allegorical significance of the physical conflict is clear enough: *eros* versus *heros*. But the painting offers no solution to the conflict—its unity is strictly esthetic, achieved through synthetic perspective, a masterful use of color, and a balance of horizontals and verticals accented by the single diagonal of the intertwined figures.

Titian's painting, then, can work as a narrative, much as narratives can work as pictures. He can imply narrative through the depiction of attributes; through gesture, which is itself interrupted action; and through the device of continuous representation, in which the several scenes of a painting depict successive events. He can also use space as an equivalent to logical extension, so that the visual relationship of his figures expresses their conceptual relationship. As each figure is allegorized to become an abstraction, so space is allegorized to become a visual syntax.[26] The introduction of temporal and allegorical sequence, though, threatens to fragment the visual realm of imitation. Pictorial success then depends upon the artist's ability to control the tension between visual and rhetorical schemes through the unifying forces of three-dimensional perspective and two-dimensional symmetry, in order to create a "speaking picture," in which the ocular unity of the scene brings a sense of completeness to the story and argument.

In attaining its narrative unity, Shakespeare's poem, like Titian's painting, seems to operate through a reconciliation of tension, in which visual images hold together the machinery of an incomplete argumentative sequence. Shakespeare's fundamental alteration of the myth, we may recall, was to make Venus and Adonis antagonists instead of lovers. Precisely what this does is to place them physically in a tableau of conflict and to transform this conflict of action into a conflict of ideas, enacted in a formal debate. Why does beauty wither? Venus argues that Diana, goddess of chastity and narcissism, is to blame and that love is the force that preserves:

> And therefore hath [Diana] brib'd the destinies
> To cross the curious workmanship of nature,
> To mingle beauty with infirmities

And pure perfection with impure defeature,
  Making it subject to the tyranny
  Of mad mischances and much misery.

  (ll. 733–38)

Adonis will have none of it. Venus he sees unequivocally as lust—not Venus Genetrix, but Venus Vulgaris. Passion itself, then, is the force of death:

Call it not love, for love to heaven is fled,
Since sweating lust on earth usurp'd his name;
Under whose simple semblance he hath fed
Upon fresh beauty, blotting it with blame;
  Which the hot tyrant stains and soon bereaves,
  As caterpillars do the tender leaves.

  (ll. 793–98)

The debate between Venus and Adonis persistently resolves into the more traditional debate between Venus and Diana, which, in as immediate a source as Book III of the *Faerie Queene*, represents warring attitudes toward sexual love. Both goddesses are, in their way, hunters, though of different prey. Ovid tells how Venus,

  per silvas dumosaque saxa vagatur
fine genu vestem ritu succinta Dianae
hortaturque canes tutaeque animalia praedae,
aut pronos lepores aut celsum in cornua cervum
aut agitat dammas.

  (*Metamorphoses* X.535–39)

  over mountain ridges, through the woods, over rocky places set with thorns, she ranges with her garments girt up to her knees after the manner of Diana. She also cheers on the hounds and pursues those creatures which are safe to hunt, such as the headlong hares, or the stag with high-branching horns, or the timid doe.

Ovid lightly parodies the passage in Vergil's *Aeneid* where Venus in the guise of Diana helps Aeneas in his epic quest.[27] The choice between the "hard hunt" for the boar and the "soft hunt" for Wat the hare becomes a choice between the heroic and erotic lives, as Titian knew.[28]

Venus tells us how in erotic mastery she subdued the virile Mars:

> Thus he that overrul'd I oversway'd,
> Leading him prisoner in a red rose chain:
> Strong-temper'd steel his stronger strength obey'd,
> Yet was he servile to my coy disdain.
>
> (ll. 109–12)

If Mars here is robbed of heroism, one may recall that to the Neoplatonists the love of Mars and Venus was an allegory of a transcendent concordance of Virtue and Pleasure.[29] Shakespeare too crosses his debate structure with images suggesting a reconciliation between eros and heroism. Adonis' horse is an epic steed, fit for the fields of praise; yet he is also a descendant of Plato's dark horse, the emblem of license.[30] The horse simultaneously breaks his servile bondage and unbridles his lust:

> The iron bit he crusheth 'tween his teeth,
> Controlling what he was controlled with.
>
> (ll. 269–70)

Adonis too has been in bondage to Venus:

> Look how a bird lies tangled in a net,
> So fasten'd in her arms Adonis lies.
>
> (ll. 67–68)

Although Venus conquered Mars, Adonis has conquered her, and has a chance to reenact his horse's epic deed:

> Now is she in the very lists of love,
> Her champion mounted for the hot encounter.
> All is imaginary she doth prove;
> He will not manage her, although he mount her.
>
> (ll. 595–98)

The moment of union slips away, love's freedom and bondage still at strife.

The debate structure of the poem permeates not only individual symbols but the syntax of the verse as well, so that images are yoked in warring pairs. At the opening of the poem, red and white appear as a smooth parallel: Adonis' cheek is "more white and red than doves or roses are" (l.

10). It is a familiar Petrarchist trope for the complexion of the beloved, embodying that blend of opposites which define beauty and linking this master-mistress with the birds and flowers sacred to Venus.

As Adonis demurs, the conceit is inverted to show his unreadiness for love: "He red for shame, but frosty in desire" (l. 36). Syntactically the colors are now in opposition, yet metaphorically they again express parallel sentiments—shame and disdain, both aspects of *pudor*. When the figure is transferred to Venus, its tension is heightened, reflecting a clash of emotions:

> . . . the fighting conflict of her hue,
> How white and red each other did destroy!
> But now her cheek was pale, and by and by
> It flash'd forth fire, as lightning from the sky.
>
> (ll. 345–48)

The figure then goes underground, only to make two startling reappearances, one at the first sight of the boar:

> Whose frothy mouth bepainted all with red,
> Like milk and blood being mingled both together.
>
> (ll. 901–02)

Syntactically the colors are in harmony, but, because of its position in the narrative, the conceit is a torturous mockery, death in the garments of love. Then the corpse of Adonis is transformed:

> A purple flower sprung up, checker'd with white,
> Resembling well his pale cheeks and the blood
> Which in round drops upon their whiteness stood.
>
> (ll. 1168–70)

In the dozens of versions of this myth in classical and Renaissance verse and prose, nowhere else is the flower both red and white. Some say Adonis is turned to a rose, some say to an anemone, and some record that the flower formerly was white but now is stained red with the shepherd's blood. Shakespeare's insistence is clear, recalling the antithesis one last time, restored nearly to its original form but applied now to an object that is the negation of the original—a summation of the struggle among Venus, Adonis, and the boar.

The war of red flame and pale frost is echoed by the more elementary strife of fire and water. Ovid, at the opening of the *Metamorphoses,* tells how an unknown god bound in harmony the warring elements.[31] Natali Conti, meditating on a passage in Euripides, discovers that Harmony is "the offspring of the elements of all things; and that force which is born from the motion of celestial bodies, whether we call it divine or natural, acting so that the elements themselves are led into this mixture, or rather leading them, that force is called Venus."[32] Shakespeare's Venus strives to harmonize the elements, as they appear in various guises: in climatic terms, they are wind, sun, earth, and rain; in emotional terms, sighs, desires, disdain, and tears. As Aphrodite, foam-born, she is already hot and moist (Giraldi, p. 372):

> My flesh is soft and plump, my marrow burning.
> My smooth moist hand, were it with thy hand felt,
> Would in thy palm dissolve, or seem to melt.
>
> (ll. 142–44)

While love is, as she tells us, all fire (l. 149), the excess of burning passion will "set the heart on fire" (l. 388) and must be cooled with tears. The hot and dry of fire oppose the cold and moist of water, so that between the two elements there can be either chaotic strife or creative union. In the balance of these elements, as Adonis points out, lies the distinction between sweet love and sour lust:

> Love comforteth like sunshine after rain,
> But lust's effect is tempest after sun;
> Love's gentle spring doth always fresh remain,
> Lust's winter comes ere summer half be done.
>
> (ll. 799–802)

The union of Mars and Venus is precisely the harmonious blending of heat and moisture (Sabinus, p. 143). Venus seeks such a union with Adonis, but he is cold and dry, with his eyes and passions fixed on earth (ll. 118, 340), and he can only intermittently supply either heat or moisture:

> Panting he lies and breatheth on her face.
> She feedeth on the steam as on a prey,
> And calls it heavenly moisture.
>
> (ll. 62–64)

He sees her coming, and begins to glow,

Even as a dying coal revives with wind.

(ll. 337–38)

Adonis spoke sound doctrine concerning the elements but refuses the act of temperance of which Shakespeare wrote in his Anacreontic sonnets (nos. 153–54): to cool his torch in her fountain. The strife of elements with which Venus is left makes her subject to a chaos within, the very tempest that Adonis predicted. Her grief at his loss is an earthquake of wind struggling with earth (ll. 1046–47), and she threatens finally to consume herself in a reaction of air, earth, fire, and water that seems like a reverse alchemy:

My sighs are blown away, my salt tears gone;
Mine eyes are turn'd to fire, my heart to lead.
Heavy heart's lead melt at mine eyes' red
fire!
So shall I die by drops of hot desire.

(ll. 1071–74)

The struggle to harmonize the elements, as Pico believed, was the struggle for the *discordia concordans* that sustains love and beauty.[33] The inability of Venus to overcome that strife foreshadows the tragic ending of the poem. The debate structure, operating in individual lines and images as well as in the central action of the poem, becomes a syntactic principle that prepares us for a resolution, in which the unity of the poem would reside in the simultaneous closure of plot and argument. The ending of the poem, indeed, is cast as an etiology, appropriate for the conclusion of a rationalized myth:

For he being dead, with him is beauty slain,
And beauty dead, black Chaos comes again.

(ll. 1019–20)

Since thou art dead, lo here I prophesy,
Sorrow on love hereafter shall attend:
It shall be waited on with jealousy,
Find sweet beginning, but unsavoury end.

(ll. 1135–38)

Precisely at the point where we expect logical conclusion, though, the syntax of plot and argument breaks down, for the etiology is false. Black Chaos is already loose in the world in Cynthia's jealousy, in the bristling boar, and in Venus' own passions, which from their sweet beginning were full of gluttony, jealousy, wrath, and anguish. Shakespeare has stretched the sinews of prolepsis, for the action of the poem is as much a result as a cause of its conclusion. As if that were not enough, Shakespeare adds a second conclusion, which demonstrates the opposite point about love. From the blood of Adonis springs a flower, which Venus plucks; so Venus remains faithful to Adonis, and the two are, finally, fruitful:

> Here was thy father's bed, here in my breast;
> Thou art the next of blood, and 'tis thy right.
> Lo in this hollow cradle take thy rest;
> My throbbing heart shall rock thee day and night:
> There shall not be one minute in an hour
> Wherein I will not kiss my sweet love's flower.
> (ll. 1183–88)

The debate between Venus and Adonis is never resolved. A series of metaphors mediates between them, each of which generates the same antithesis. Love is life and death, harmony and chaos, bliss and agony, beauty and horror—the paradoxes teeter out of sight on the even feet of oxymoron:

> Ne'er settled equally, but high or low,
> That all love's pleasure shall not match his woe.
> (ll. 1139–40)

The tension of paradox, though, is constantly released by the shifting structures of the poem: by its proleptic narrative, by its double ending. The terms of the debate slide from one set of images to another, joined at innumerable points. The conflict moves from syllogisms to proverbs, to goddesses, to horses and rabbits, to colors and elements. With each set of terms, an abstract dualism is momentarily balanced in a sensible image, generating a kind of "insight," or brief resolution, for, as E.H. Gombrich observes, "the sense of sight provides an analogue to the non-discursive mode of apprehension which must travel from multiplicity to unity."[34] In that pattern of tension and release, of the recurrent dualism momentarily resolved in an image, lies the experience of cohesion that gives unity to the poem.

III. Shakespearean Paradox

Shakespeare's literary myth comes surprisingly close to the function that Lévi-Strauss suggested for primary myth: to bridge the gap between conflicting values through "a series of mediating devices, each of which generates the next one by a process of opposition and correlation. . . . The kind of logic in mythical thought is as rigorous as that of modern science . . . the difference lies, not in the quality of the intellectual process, but in the nature of the things to which it is applied" (pp. 226, 230). Just as primary myth may be an alternative form of logical reasoning indulged in by whole societies, Shakespeare's manner of paradox making has the characteristics of a persistent personal syntax. Indeed, if we once again think of myth as a conceptual form rather than as a content, we might call it Shakespeare's personal myth, a way of perceiving and reconciling the paradoxes of experience.

Venus and Adonis has been compared to the sonnets, the early comedies, even the tragedies. In its handling of paradox, it most closely resembles the mature comedies, or even a problem comedy. What makes a problem comedy problematic is the realization that the tension between opposed values is a permanent condition of life.[35] In Measure for Measure, Angelo and Escalus enter into a formal debate between Justice and Mercy in Act II, but the conflict disappears in the final sentencing of all the characters to marriage. High comedy conceals similar difficulties, for its argument, as Northrop Frye tells us, is individual fulfillment and social harmony—admirable values both, but perhaps less easily reconciled than Frye's formula would admit.[36] As You Like It is obviously a play working toward both values, and its ending brings them into a theatrical balance through the simple technique of a double ending. First Hymen, the embodiment of social harmony, links each couple; then Jaques, the soul of humorous individualism, repeats Hymen's action and nearly his very words, giving to each the fulfillment of his ambition.

Two insightful critics of Shakespeare, Norman Rabkin and Stephen Booth, have examined this obsessive paradox making. In Hamlet, Rabkin finds, "Shakespeare tends to structure his imitations in terms of a pair of polar opposites," between which we must, but cannot, choose (p. 12). Examining the sonnets, Booth finds the reverse—that one set of opposites is incommensurate with another—that syntactic paradox leads us one way, imagistic paradox another, prosodic a third, and with no release of the tension created.[37] Venus and Adonis offers us, I think, something between the two models: by shifting, in the manner described by Booth, from one set of terms—one whole structure—to another, a release from paradox is achieved. The style of Venus and Adonis might best be epitomized in the metaphors of red and white: a constant shifting of the significance of the images and of the syntactic structures linking them, which are held together as a series simply by the repetition of the image itself.

As Rabkin observes, though, the reconciliation "cannot be reduced to prose paraphrase or statements of theme because the kind of 'statement' a given play makes cannot respectably be made in the logical language of prose" (p. 12). For a work like *Venus and Adonis,* where the serial form of narrative encourages the serial form of logical discourse, the achievement of a purely esthetic resolution is particularly fine. It is done by shifting out of the dialogue of argument into a discourse of images —iconography—thus opening the possibility of an iconic resolution of the same sort that Shakespeare habitually achieved on the stage through the visual image of coupling. Paradox, then, is too neat a word; it suggests a final, balanced position, the *seeming* opposition overcome. Shakespearean paradox, in *Venus and Adonis* at least, is a problem, not of seeing or seeming, but of being. Erotic experience can be described only by combining two ways of thinking, the discursive and the iconic, and shuttling from one to the other when the variety of that experience can be described in no other words and the unity recalled in no other way.

NOTES

1. Orphic Hymns, No. 56; Theocritus, Nos. 1, 3, 15; Bion, "Epitaphium Adonidis"; Ovid, *Metamorphoses* X; also Cicero, *De Natura Deorum* III.59; Servius, commentary on Vergil's *Aeneid* VII.761; Hyginus, *Fabulae,* Nos. 164, 271; Fulgentius, *Mythologia,* Bk. III.

2. Titian's painting of 1554, delivered to Philip II in England, widely reproduced in etchings, and now in the Prado, is suggested as a source by Erwin Panofsky, *Problems in Titian, Mostly Iconographic* (New York: New York Univ. Press, 1969), pp. 150–54. For a sharp rebuttal to Panofsky, see Harold E. Wethey, *The Paintings of Titian,* III (London: Phaidon, 1975), 188–89. Southampton's role is discussed by A.L. Rowse, in *Shakespeare's Southampton: Patron of Virginia* (New York: Harper, 1965), pp. 74–81, and, more judiciously, by G.P.V. Akrigg, *Shakespeare and the Earl of Southampton* (Cambridge: Harvard Univ. Press, 1968), pp. 33–34, 195–98. Other classical and Renaissance sources are examined in the *New Variorum Edition* by Hyder Rollins (Philadelphia: Lippincott, 1938), pp. 390–400; Douglas Bush, *Mythology and the Renaissance Tradition in English Poetry* (1932; rev. ed., New York: Norton, 1963), pp. 137–45; T.W. Baldwin, *On the Literary Genetics of Shakespeare's Poems and Sonnets* (Urbana: Univ. of Illinois Press, 1950), pp. 2–48; and Geoffrey Bullough, *Narrative and Dramatic Sources of Shakespeare,* I (New York: Columbia Univ. Press, 1957), 161–65.

3. "Venus and the Second Chance," *Shakespeare Survey,* 15 (1962), 81–88. See also Lever's review of modern criticism in the same volume (pp. 19–22). Among recent discussions, Heather Asals' "*Venus and Adonis:* The Education of a Goddess," *Studies in English Literature,* 13 (1973), 31–51, argues that Venus progresses from lust to love through a Neoplatonic ladder of the senses, even though the banquet of sense (ll. 433–50) moves in the reverse order. Christopher Butler and Alastair Fowler, "Time-Beguiling Sport: Number Symbolism in Shakespeare's *Venus and Adonis,*" in *Shakespeare 1564–1964,* ed. Edward A. Bloom (Providence: Brown Univ. Press, 1964) pp. 124–33, offer a provocative numerological reading. Paula Johnson, *Form and Transformation in Music and Poetry of the English Renaissance* (New Haven: Yale Univ. Press, 1972), pp. 143–52, describes a climactic progression akin to a musical

crescendo or to the rhythm of sexual experience. A "radically psychological" reading of the poem is advanced by Coppélia Kahn, "Self and Eros in *Venus and Adonis*," *Centennial Review*, 20 (1976), 351–71.

4. Richard Wilbur, Introduction to the Narrative Poems, *The Pelican Shakespeare*, ed. Alfred Harbage (Baltimore: Penguin, 1969, p. 1401).

5. Steps in this direction have been taken by Lever and by A.C. Hamilton, *The Early Shakespeare* (San Marino: Huntington Library, 1967), who attempt to deal seriously with Venus and Adonis as mythic rather than dramatic characters; and by Eugene B. Cantelupe, "An Iconographical Interpretation of *Venus and Adonis*, Shakespeare's Ovidian Comedy," *Shakespeare Quarterly*, 14 (1963), 141–51. Closest to my own conclusion is Norman Rabkin's in *Shakespeare and the Common Understanding* (New York: Free Press, 1967), pp. 150–62 (see below, Sec. III). Appearing after this article was completed, William Keach's *Elizabethan Erotic Narratives* (New Brunswick: Rutgers Univ. Press, 1977), argues that Shakespeare's ambivalence is characteristically Ovidian.

6. The schools of modern mythography are surveyed in *Myth: A Symposium*, ed. Thomas A. Sebeok (Bloomington: Indiana Univ. Press, 1958). Lévi-Strauss' structuralism is tested against older views of Greek myth by G.S. Kirk, *Myth: Its Meaning and Functions in Ancient and Other Cultures* (Cambridge: Cambridge Univ. Press, 1970).

7. Ernst Cassirer, *Language and Myth*, trans. Susanne K. Langer (New York: Dover, 1953), pp. 17–41; Jane E. Harrison, *Themis: A Study of the Social Origins of Greek Religion* (Cambridge: Cambridge Univ. Press, 1912), pp. 327–31; Claude Lévi-Strauss, *Structural Anthropology*, trans. Claire Jacobson and Brooke G. Schoepf (New York: Basic Books, 1963), pp. 213–23. Frazer's flirtations with the Cambridge ritualists are examined by Robert Ackerman, "Frazer on Myth and Ritual," *Journal of the History of Ideas*, 36 (1975), 115–34.

8. The development of allegory is examined in detail by Jean Pépin, *Mythe et allégorie: Les Origines greques et les contestations judéo-chrétiennes* (Paris: Aubier, 1958); it is surveyed by Ernst R. Curtius, *European Literature and the Latin Middle Ages*, trans. Willard Trask (Princeton: Princeton Univ. Press, 1973), pp. 203–13; Don Cameron Allen, *Mysteriously Meant: The Rediscovery of Pagan Symbolism and Allegorical Interpretation in the Renaissance* (Baltimore: Johns Hopkins Univ. Press, 1970); Jean Seznec, *The Survival of the Pagan Gods*, trans. Barbara F. Sessions (New York: Pantheon, 1953); C.S. Lewis, *The Allegory of Love* (Oxford: Clarendon, 1936), pp. 44–111; and Michael Murrin, *The Veil of Allegory* (Chicago: Univ. of Chicago Press, 1969), pp. 21–53.

9. Vincenzo Cartari, *Le imagini de i dei de gli antichi* (Venice, 1571), pp. 536–37. The etiology originates with Bion's "Epitaphium Adonidis" and is repeated in Jacobus Micyllus' commentary on Ovid (Basel, 1543), p. 243, and in Natali Conti, *Mythologia* (Venice, 1568), p. 230a. Its allegorical significance is expounded by Fulgentius, *Mythologia* (Paris, 1578), p. 136a, quoted by Giovanni Boccaccio, *Genealogie Deorum Gentilium*, Bk. III, Ch. xxiii, ed. Vincenzo Romano (Bari: Laterza, 1951), I, 152.

10. E.H. Gombrich, "Tobias and the Angel," in his *Symbolic Images: Studies in the Art of the Renaissance* (London: Phaidon, 1972), pp. 26–30.

11. *The XV. Bookes of P. Ovidius Naso, Entituled Metamorphosis* (London, 1593), sig. A4ʳ. This is a common understanding of the myth, shared by Georgius Sabinus in his commentary on Ovid (Cambridge, 1584), p. 419; by an early commentary on Bion (Bruges, 1565), p. 38; by Abraham Fraunce, *The Third Part of the Countesse of Pembrokes Yvychurch* (London, 1592), p. 45b; and by Claude Mignault in his commentary on the *Emblemata* of Andrea Alciati (Antwerp, 1577), p. 288.

12. Micyllus, p. 243; probably based on Lucian. A much fuller account, based on Pausanius, is given in Bartholomew Merula's commentary on the *De Arte Amandi*, ed. Micyllus (Basel, 1549), p. 379. Theocritus, No. 15, describes an Alexandrian fes-

tival, cited in Lilio Gregorio Giraldi, *De Deis Gentium* (Basel, 1560) p. 397. Cf. Conti, p. 161b; Cartari, p. 553.

13. *Genealogie*, Bk. II, Ch. liii, ed. Romano, I, 102. Boccaccio's source is Macrobius, *Saturnalia*, and derives ultimately from the Orphic "Hymn to Adonis." Cf. Conti, p. 162a; Cartari, pp. 553–54; Fraunce, p. 45b and Sabinus, p. 418, who attributes the allegory to Giovanni Pontano.

14. *Metamorphoses* X.737–39, Loeb ed., trans. Frank Justus Miller (London: Heinemann, 1916), II, 116–17.

15. "Quod autem sit Adon transformatus in florem ob id fictum puto, ut nostri decoris brevitas ostendatur, mane quidem purpureus est, sero languens pallensque marcidus efficitur, sic et nostra humanitas mane, id est iuventutis tempore, florens et splendida est, sero autem, id est senectutis evo, pallemus et in tenebras mortis ruimus" (*Genealogie*, Bk. II, Ch. liii, ed. Romano, (I, 103). Andrea dell' Anguillara smuggles this interpretation into his Latin translation of Ovid (Venice, 1578), p. 186b. Cf. Regius-Micyllus, p. 243; Sabinus, p. 418; Fraunce, p. 45b. The garden of Adonis as a proverbial example of transience is cited in Erasmus' *Adagia*.

16. Lines 1–3, in *Poems*, ed. F.T. Prince, New Arden ed. (London: Methuen, 1960). All subsequent citations are to this edition.

17. The iconography of Venus is examined by Erwin Panofsky, *Studies in Iconology* (1939; rpt. New York: Harper, 1962), pp. 129–230; Edgar Wind, *Pagan Mysteries in the Renaissance*, rev. ed. (New York: Norton, 1968), pp. 81–151; and E.H. Gombrich "Botticelli's Mythologies," in *Symbolic Images*, pp. 39–78.

18. George Wyndham, ed., *The Poems of Shakespeare* (New York: Crowell, 1898), pp. lxxxv–lxxxvi.

19. Fraunce, p. 45a. The etymology derives from Hesiod, *Theogony*, ll. 188–204, allegorized by Fulgentius, *Mythologia*, p. 135b.

20. Micyllus (p. 243) attributes the anecdote to a Greek source; Giraldi (p. 397) traces it to Eusebius and Augustine; Conti (pp. 121b, 230a) wrongly derives it from *Metamorphoses* X; cf. Cartari, (p. 537), and Ronsard's "Adonis," in *The Pastoral Elegy*, ed. T.P. Harrison (Austin: Univ. of Texas Press, 1939), pp. 161–65. A.T. Hatto, "'Venus and Adonis'—and the Boar," *Modern Language Review*, 41 (1946), 353–61, examines the boar as a symbol of jealousy, but ultra-masculine and opposed to Venus.

21. The conceit of the boar's kissing Adonis derives from the pseudo-Theocritan "Death of Adonis," accepted as Theocritus, No. 30, in the Renaissance; see Bush, pp. 54, 137, and Baldwin, p. 42. It was translated anonymously into English in *Sixe Idillia* (1588, rpt. London: Duckworth, 1922); cited by Giraldi, p. 374 and imitated by Ronsard and by Minturno, "De Adoni ab Apro Interempto," in *Epigrammata et Elegiae*, pp. 7a–8b, bound with *Poemata* (Venice 1564).

22. "Persona . . . dubitare potrebbe di ciò, che io dico d'Amore come se fosse una cosa per sè, e non solamente sustanzia intelligente, ma sì come fosse sustanzia corporale: la quale cosa, secondo la veritade, è falsa; chè Amore non è per sè sì come sustanzia, ma è uno accidente in sustanzia" (*La vita nuova* xxv.1, ed. Michele Barbi [Milan, Hoepli, 1907], p. 67). The English version is from *Dante's Vita Nuova*, trans. Mark Musa, rev. ed. (Bloomington: Indiana Univ. Press, 1973), p. 54.

23. J.G.E. Lessing, *Laocoon*, trans. Sir Robert Phillimore (London: Macmillan, 1874), p. 149. The very real difficulties in comparisons between art and literature are demonstrated by René Wellek, "The Parallelism between Literature and the Arts," in *English Institute Annual*, 1941 (New York: Columbia Univ. Press, 1942), and by Svetlana and Paul Alpers, "*Ut Pictura Noesis*? Criticism in Literary Studies and Art History," *New Literary History*, 3 (1972), 437–58.

24. "Qualia namque / corpora nudorum tabula pinguntur Amorum, / talis erat, sed, ne faciat discrimina cultus, / aut huic adde leves, aut illi deme pharetras?" (*Metamorphoses* X.515–18).

25. Titian's Adonis-Cupid may also be compared with the figure of the dead

Adonis in two paintings of the *Death of Adonis,* one by Sebastiano del Piombo and one by Baldassare Peruzzi, reproduced in S.J. Freedberg's *Painting of the High Renaissance in Rome and Florence,* 2 vols. (1961; rpt. New York: Harper, 1972), pls. 200 and 481.

26. The rhetorical development of Renaissance painting is examined by Rensselaer W. Lee, *Ut Pictura Poesis: The Humanistic Theory of Painting* (1940; rpt. New York: Norton, 1967); John R. Spencer, "*Ut Rhetorica Pictura*: A Study in Quattrocento Theory of Painting," *Journal of the Warburg and Courtauld Institutes,* 20 (1957), 26–44; Michael Baxandall, *Giotto and the Orators* (Oxford: Clarendon, 1971); and, especially pertinent here, David Rosand, "*Ut Pictor Poeta*: Meaning in Titian's *Poesie,*" *New Literary History,* 3 (1972), 527–46.

27. *Aeneid* I.320. The passage became a Neoplatonist allegory of the chaste Venus; see Wind, pp. 73–77, 85–88.

28. Regius (p. 239) suggests that Adonis goes to the hunt in pursuit of glory, while Sabinus (p. 418) concludes that Adonis' death shows that such weaklings should leave the sport to real men. Don Cameron Allen's study of the hunts, "On *Venus and Adonis,*" in *Elizabethan and Jacobean Studies Presented to F. P. Wilson* (Oxford: Clarendon, 1959), pp. 100–11, has recently been amplified by W.R. Streitberger, "Ideal Conduct in *Venus and Adonis,*" *Shakespeare Quarterly,* 26 (1975), 285–91.

29. Hesiod, *Theogony,* ll. 934–37, and Plutarch, *De Iside et Osiride,* Sec. 48, record that Harmony is the daughter of Venus and Mars. See Panofsky, *Iconography,* pp. 163–64, and *Titian,* p. 127; Wind, pp. 85–89; and Gombrich, "Botticelli's Mythologies," pp. 66–69.

30. Lever objects that Plato's dark horse is vicious and misshapen, no fit ancestor for Shakespeare's stallion (p. 83). However, Achilles Bocchi, *Symbolicae Quaestiones* (Bologna, 1555), No. 115, depicts a bridled beast in good point as an emblem of contained lust, as does Titian in the sculptural frieze in the *Sacred and Profane Love.* Harington sees Renaldo's charger Bayardo as a symbol of lust in *Orlando furioso,* Canto ii. See Guy de Tervarent, *Attributs et symboles dans l'art profane: 1450–1600,* II (Geneva: Droz, 1959), 418, and Panofsky, *Titian,* p. 118.

31. *Metamorphoses* I.16–68. Cf. Platon, *Timaeus,* 32c; Macrobius, *Expositio in Somnium Scipionis* VI.24–33.

32. "At gravissimus & suavissimus scriptor Euripides multo etiam clarius demonstravit rerum omnium procreationem ex elementorum esse symmetria; atque vim illam sive divinam quem nascitur e motu coelestium corporum, sive naturalem vocemus, quae facit ut in hanc commistionem elementa ipsa deducantur, vel potius deducit, Venerem appellavit" (Conti, p. 125a).

33. *A Platonick Discourse upon Love . . . in Explication of a Sonnet by Hieronimo Benivieni,* Bk. II, Ch. V, trans. Thomas Stanley (1651; rpt. Boston: Merrymount, 1914), p. 26.

34. "*Icones Symbolicae*: Philosophies of Symbolism and Their Bearing on Art," in *Symbolic Images,* p. 170.

35. A.P. Rossiter, *Angel with Horns and Other Shakespeare Lectures,* ed. Graham Storey (New York: Theatre Arts, 1961), pp. 116–17.

36. "The Argument of Comedy," in *English Institute Essays,* 1948, ed. D.A. Robertson (New York: Columbia Univ. Press, 1949), pp. 60–61.

37. An *Essay on Shakespeare's Sonnets* (New Haven: Yale Univ. Press, 1969), esp. pp. 59–60, 104–07.

"Upon Misprision Growing"

Venus and Adonis

Heather Dubrow

Readers have long acknowledged certain similarities between Venus and some of Shakespeare's dramatic characters: she shares, we are told, the earthiness of Falstaff, the sensuality of Cleopatra, and the determination of comedic heroines like Rosalind.[1] Yet we have been slow to admit that the sophisticated techniques through which she is characterized represent yet another link between Venus and her counterparts in the plays. And we have been equally slow to admit the many regards in which her behavior mimes that of actual people.

I do not mean that Shakespeare's portrait of Venus is mimetic in every sense of that term. Few women could literally tuck a young man, however slim and "hairless" (487) he might be, under their arms, fewer yet react to the death of their beloved by flying into the air. And the characterization of Venus does lack one type of complexity that we encounter even in Shakespeare's earliest plays, as well as in *The Rape of Lucrece*: the poem does not explore the relationship between a temperament and a social milieu. Moreover, we never wholly forget her symbolic significance: she is not only a lover acting in very human ways but also the abstract force of Love itself. Indeed, for all of Venus' follies the figure of Venus Genetrix evidently lies behind her. Yet facts like these need not, of course, preclude a portrait that is mimetic in broader senses of the word—a portrait that mirrors the ways actual people think, feel, and talk—any more than the allegorical significance with which Cordelia or Britomart are weighted precludes their being representational as well.[2]

Venus plucks Adonis from his horse at the beginning of the poem just

Reprinted from Heather Dubrow, *Captive Victors: Shakespeare's Narrative Poems and Sonnets*. Copyright © 1987 by Cornell University. Used by permission of the publisher, Cornell University Press.

as, symmetrically, she plucks the flower that represents him at the end (in the world of *Venus and Adonis,* as in the *Metamorphoses,* one may be literally as well as symbolically carried away by love). It is evident, then, that Venus connects loving Adonis with controlling him, mastering him; indeed, so deep is the connection as to make us suspect that even had he been less reluctant her impulse would have been to assert sovereignty by grasping and entrapping him. Yet her concern for mastery is more pervasive than it might at first appear: that concern shapes how she perceives many situations and how she reacts within them.

The goddess of love, like that other impresario Prospero, is prone to describe events, especially those involving love, in terms of mastery. She narrates her relationship with Mars in those terms:

> Yet hath he been my captive and my slave,
>
> (l. 101)

> Thus he that overrul'd I oversway'd,
> Leading him prisoner in a red rose chain:
> Strong-temper'd steel his stronger strength obey'd,
> Yet was he servile to my coy disdain.
> Oh be not proud, nor brag not of thy might,
> For mast'ring her that foil'd the god of fight!
>
> (ll. 109–114)

That extraordinary line "Leading him prisoner in a red rose chain" (l. 110) draws attention to the moral ambiguities we so often find in her behavior: on the one hand, a chain of roses charms us more than it troubles us, and yet even in this image Venus is stressing her own power and control (notice, for instance, that she chooses the verb "leading" rather than "making"). Similarly, Adonis is called "love's master" (l. 585). When she sings of the effects of love, she describes "How love makes young men thrall, and old men dote" (l. 837). (It is suggestive, too, that the subject of this ditty is the power of women over men even though the most recent events in Venus' own past have illustrated how love makes *women* thrall and makes them dote.)[3] Even when she is soliciting agreement from Adonis, the verb she chooses suggests domination: "But if thou needs wilt hunt, be rul'd by me" (l. 673). And it is telling that this same phrase, "be ruled by me," is used by other Shakespearean characters enamored by power, notably the Bastard in *King John* (II.i.377).[4] In other words, in a few instances Venus' preoccupation with power is manifest in her desire to submit to that of Adonis; but more often she is concerned to assert her own power.

The troubling undertones in the passages we have been examining lead us to reflect on how Venus' character has been shaped, and misshaped, by her tendency to see love not as "mutual render" (Sonnet 125.12) but rather as an aggressive struggle for domination. And since her vocabulary of mastery and captivity is drawn from the stock language of love poetry, our reflections on her aggressiveness generate literary questions as well. On one level, it is merely amusing to encounter a putative goddess who sounds like an Elizabethan sonneteer, much as we enjoy Leander's predilection for the tones of a university orator. But on another level the frequent echoes of Elizabethan poesy are disturbing: we again think about the underlying assumptions of that literary system (or, more precisely, systems) and in so doing wonder in particular whether it breeds in its speakers, fictional or otherwise, the tendency to conjoin and confound the sexual and the aggressive that we find in Venus. That tendency provides, as we shall see, a more intimate link between *Venus and Adonis* and *The Rape of Lucrece* than we generally acknowledge.[5] In both a central character connects passion and power; in both the conventions of love poetry express—and, more disturbingly, perhaps encourage—that connection.

Many of Venus' habits, whether they are linguistic gestures or psychological patterns, are a way of achieving and asserting domination. Writing in a genre that traces metamorphoses of all kinds, Shakespeare characteristically focuses on the transformations his heroine performs through her words: much as she appropriates Adonis, so she appropriates language itself. And much as her assertions of power over Adonis often generate subtle reminders of his power over her, so her attempts to impress language into her service often lead us to recognize that she is herself imprisoned by it, once again a captive victor.

It is suggestive, to begin with, that she talks as much as she does: of the 1,194 lines in the poem, 537 are spoken by the goddess of love. The only analogues to this garrulity that we can find in other epyllia are passages anchored in the complaint tradition, such as the laments intoned by Lodge's Glaucus and Heywood's Oenone. But Venus is not delivering a complaint: she is cajoling, insisting, insinuating. Her talkativeness, like that of the Wife of Bath, reflects her desire to impose her presence, to dominate the conversation just as she dominates in so many other ways.

Assuming Adam's function, this postlapsarian Eve repeatedly names—or, more to the point, renames—the objects around her:[6]

> With this she seizeth on his sweating palm,
> The precedent of pith and livelihood,

And trembling in her passion, *calls it* balm,
Earth's sovereign salve to do a goddess good:
(ll. 25–28; italics added)

Panting he lies and breatheth in her face.
She feedeth on the steam as on a prey,
And *calls it* heavenly moisture, air of grace.
(ll. 62–64; italics added)

To name something is to assert one's power over it—as Hal recognizes when
he festoons Falstaff with epithets and as Petruchio acknowledges when, in
one of his most subtle but most effective gestures of domination, he insists
that his future wife be called not Katherine but Kate. Another function of
Venus' naming, however, is to attempt to change the nature of sweat and
breath. The earthiest of heroines, she is transforming both into something
more ethereal, a habit in her to which I will return shortly. The ambiguity
of "calls it" emphasizes the same issue we encountered in the deer park stanzas: does she believe in the transformation she is effecting, or is it merely
another way of flattering Adonis? The fact that we cannot know for certain
reflects, I would suggest, a telling confusion in Venus herself: she, no less
than Richard II, is prone to become carried away by her own words.

In the second passage I quoted, the dramatist who wrote *Venus and
Adonis* plays two voices against each other in one of the ways nondramatic
poetry permits: he establishes a dialogic tension between the speaker's "as
on a prey" (l. 63) and the goddess' "And calls it heavenly moisture" (l. 64).
That speaker's honest appraisal of the situation contrasts with her self-serving
one. It is suggestive, too, that the more honest and more objective of the ob-
servers relies on a simile, "*as* on a prey": rather than transforming the steam
into something else, he is respecting and retaining its individuality, its identity. In a sense, then, Venus substitutes a metonymic approach for the
speaker's metaphoric one: unlike him, she attempts to change the identity
of the breath as totally as Petruchio tries to change his Kate.

Venus' predilection for renaming the world typically assumes one
form in particular: she tries to transform the material into the spiritual. The
poem in which she appears insistently bodies forth the details of the natural world: people sweat and lust, aggressive eagles demonstrate that nature
is indeed red in tooth and claw, and divedappers and rabbits remind us that
it includes gentleness and frailty as well. Against this complex vision of the
physical world is played Venus' distortion of it.[7] We have already observed
the ways she uses language in an attempt to effect transformations, turning

steamy breath into "heavenly moisture" (l. 64). And she attempts to reshape her own image along similar lines. This earthy goddess unpersuasively insists on the spirituality of love and on her own virtual lack of corporeality:

> Love is a spirit all compact of fire,
> Not gross to sink, but light, and will aspire.
>
> Witness this primrose bank whereon I lie:
> These forceless flowers like sturdy trees support me.
> Two strengthless doves will draw me through the sky
> From morn till night, even where I list to sport me.
>
> (ll. 149–154)

Attuned to this habit in her, we find its analogue in her repeated descriptions of the earth as Adonis' lover:

> And therefore would he put his bonnet on,
> Under whose brim the gaudy sun would peep:
> The wind would blow it off, and being gone,
> Play with his locks; then would Adonis weep.
>
> (ll. 1087–1090)

And she interprets the boar's attack as a kiss: "If he did see his face, why then I know / He thought to kiss him, and hath kill'd him so" (ll. 1109–1110). While in these instances she is not spiritualizing the natural world, she is performing a comparable travesty by idealizing it and by attributing her own emotions to it.

Such travesties serve as a commentary not only on Venus' artifices but also on Shakespeare's art. For many of her conceits exemplify one of his most familiar tools of trade, the pathetic fallacy. By placing it in Venus' mouth rather than that of a narrator, the poet leads us to evaluate that rhetorical technique more critically than we would otherwise do (in fact, in the lines from the poem in Theocritus' *Sixe Idillia* that may have influenced Shakespeare, the speaker, not Venus, attributes an amatory motive to the boar).[8] We recognize, in other words, that the pathetic fallacy may reflect the pathetic self-centeredness of its proponent. Shakespeare is dramatizing a rhetorical pattern by associating it with a psychological one, a habit we shall observe repeatedly in his major poems. And in so doing he is also problematizing a literary convention that is uncritically adduced in many other epyllia—an approach to genre that we will also meet many times in

The Rape of Lucrece and the sonnets.

Another way in which Venus uses language to create a fictitious and factitious world is by telling stories—her habit of naming and renaming writ large. Like the improvisator figure whom Stephen Greenblatt has anatomized for us,[9] she turns the facts about her relationship with Mars into a scenario more attractive to herself—and more amenable to her aim, persuading Adonis to succeed the god of war in her bed. Thus she defines the relationship in terms of mastery—but then, as if realizing that this may not be the best strategy for wooing Adonis, she ends on a suggestion that the roles have been reversed, that he has mastered her: "Oh be not proud, nor brag not of thy might, / For mast'ring her that foil'd the god of fight!" (ll. 113–114). Most revealing, however, is her omission of the humiliating conclusion of her liaison with Mars: they were both mastered, both caught in a net.[10] And by alluding to that type of trap in a different context only forty lines earlier ("Look how a bird lies tangled in a net" [l. 67]), Shakespeare subtly reminds us of the very fact Venus is attempting to conceal: the net result, as it were, of her involvement with Mars. Later, too, the goddess of love is characterized as a storyteller: her song is compared to the "copious stories" (l. 845) of all lovers, she whispers "a heavy tale" (l. 1125) to the dead Adonis, and, of course, she recounts the story of Wat.

But if Venus is a narrative poet, she is also a lyric one: her delivery of an elegy on Adonis is the appropriate culmination of her recurrent tendency to adopt the conventions of Elizabethan art, especially the traditions of love poetry. As many readers have observed, she repeatedly deploys hyperbole, the figure that Puttenham terms the "loud lyar":[11] "More white and red than doves or roses are" (l. 10), "A thousand kisses buys my heart from me" (l. 517), and so on.[12] And her courtship of that "lifeless picture, cold and senseless stone" (l. 211) evidently parallels the situation of the Petrarchan lover—with the important difference, of course, that the sex roles are reversed. We may suspect that the exaggerations of her language not only reflect but also encourage the unhealthy emotiveness of her own character—yet another reminder that rhetoric can be as dangerous for its speaker as its victim. Moreover, we never forget how self-serving her poesy is: Adonis' accusation that her speeches are "full of *forged* lies" (l. 804; italics added) underscores the link between the artistic and fraudulent connotations of that adjective.

Venus' aim, like that of other love poets, is less *educere* or *delectare* than *permovere,* and much of her language is directed toward persuading Adonis by flattering him. Because her initial words in the poem are devoted to such flattery, just as *The Rape of Lucrece* opens on Collatine's tributes to his wife, the reader's attention is immediately focused on the problems of praise:

> "Thrice fairer than myself," thus she began,
> "The field's chief flower, sweet above compare;
> Stain to all nymphs, more lovely than a man,
> More white and red than doves or roses are."
>
> (ll. 7–10)

The first of Venus' many attempts to seduce Adonis, this passage reminds us how much of her behavior is in fact self-centered and self-serving. That self-centeredness is especially evident in her line, "Thrice fairer than myself" (l. 7): she is really lauding her own beauty even while seemingly concentrating on his, presenting herself as the measure of all loveliness. In another sense, too, the passage, like Venus' other compliments, reverses the hierarchies that it ostensibly establishes and in so doing fulfills a function opposite from the one it apparently assumes. If on the most overt level her paeans are a tribute to the power of Adonis—he is beautiful enough to evoke such glowing tributes—on another level they are, as we have observed, an attempt to assert power over him. In short, Venus is preoccupied with mastery even when delivering lines that are seemingly self-effacing.

Nor is it an accident that, though the passage labels Adonis "sweet above compare" (l. 8), it in fact incorporates no fewer than three explicit comparatives: "Thrice fairer than myself" (l. 7), "more lovely than a man" (l. 9), and "More white and red than doves or roses are" (l. 10). Furthermore, behind the epithet "The field's chief flower" (l. 8) lie comparisons with other flowers that have been found wanting in contrast to Adonis, just as "Stain to all nymphs" (l. 9) establishes his superiority over those maidens. Venus' preoccupation with mastery, we come to realize, encourages her to cast relationships in terms of competition. We find allusions to competition, too, in some of the conventional imagery of the poem, such as, "To note the fighting conflict of her hue, / How white and red each other did destroy!" (ll. 345–346). And of course two actions in the physical world—the hunt for the boar, and Wat's attempts to escape—involve the competition between hunter and hunted. Venus' predilections, then, are mirrored in the world she inhabits. And they also find echoes in the competitive behavior of the characters in Shakespeare's other major poems.

We observed earlier that some of her tributes to Adonis unpersuasively claim to be self-effacing. Other compliments she delivers, however, are not even nominally self-effacing: she blatantly flatters herself as well as Adonis.

In Fletcher's *Venus and Anchises,* for example, the goddess of love is praised by the narrator, whereas in Shakespeare's poem Venus describes her own beauty: "My eyes are grey and bright and quick in turning" (l. 140), and so on. Though such tributes may well be objectively true, they make us uneasy. The oddity of complimenting oneself alerts us to the general problems involved in compliments, and we have more reason to distrust Venus' rhetoric than that of Fletcher's speaker. Hence the passage from *Venus and Adonis,* unlike the blazons in *Venus and Anchises* and other epyllia, again draws our attention to the moral dangers of flattery.

Given how characteristic a mode flattery is for Venus, we should not be surprised that she not only opens on it but also returns to it in a moment of crisis: fearing for Adonis' well-being, she attempts to insure his future by flattering death:

> And that his beauty may the better thrive,
> With death she humbly doth insinuate;
>   Tells him of trophies, statues, tombs, and stories
>   His victories, his triumphs and his glories.
> (ll. 1011–1014)

The jingly feminine rhyme in the final two lines reflects the mechanical quality of her compliments.

If Venus' compliments to Adonis function centripetally, directing our attention to the nuances of her own psyche, so too do they move centrifugally, highlighting the broader social ramifications of her epideictic mode. A number of scholars have recently demonstrated that Elizabethans were keenly aware of the parallel between courtiership and courtship.[13] Shakespeare activates that awareness by comparing his heroine to a "bold-fac'd suitor" as early as line 6 of the poem, and a subsequent allusion to a "suit" (l. 336) reinforces the parallel. One effect of these references is to underscore Venus' ambiguous and tenuous grasp on power. In the first quotation, "suitor" (l. 6) evidently suggests the efforts of the powerless to ingratiate themselves with the powerful, while "bold-fac'd" is the earliest of many indications in the poem that the goddess of love cannot or will not acknowledge that in certain regards she is indeed powerless. But the lines also serve to comment on the nature of romantic love and its analogue of courtly service: coming to see Venus' flattery as courtly in several senses of the term, we are reminded that the compliments delivered by courtiers are as self-serving as those delivered by lovers. In both instances flattery functions as an implicit bargain—"I will give you praise in return for your favors"—a function very different from the nobler one of inspiring virtue assigned to it by classical rhetoricians.[14]

We encounter lines that introduce these issues, notably Venus' initial tributes to Adonis, very shortly after we read the author's own sally into courtiership, his dedication to Southampton. Perhaps the necessity of praising a patron encouraged the young Shakespeare to think further about the issues raised by flattery. But if biographical experiences lie behind his interest in those issues, so too do literary ones; he repeatedly, perhaps even obsessively, explores flattery in his plays. In particular, in the personages of that triad Bushy, Bagot, and Green we find the clearest embodiment of a dramatic convention and political problem that runs throughout the other history plays as well: kings are susceptible to the compliments of bad advisers, prone to be infected by "the monarch's plague, this flattery" (Sonnet 114.2).

We are now in a position to address a question that has long troubled readers of the poem: why did its author make Venus the aggressor? Though that decision may have been influenced by pictorial or literary treatments of the story (scholars have enumerated parallels ranging from Titian's *Venus and Adonis* to Abraham Fraunce's *Amintas Dale* to putative hints of a reluctant Adonis in Ovid himself),[15] the mere presence of such models cannot, as some have asserted, explain Shakespeare's reinterpretation of the goddess of love. After all, also accessible to him were a far greater number of versions in which the two lovers retain traditional sex roles.

Certain answers lie instead in the same impulse that, as we will see, led other epyllion writers to create aggressive women: the aim of commenting on the chaste heroines of Elizabethan love poetry. And politics in the narrower sense of the word lies behind the sexual politics of the poem: Venus' assertions of power may well reflect resentment of Elizabeth herself.[16] The sexually forward women in sixteenth-century epyllia reverse the customary roles of man and woman, much as a female monarch reverses those same roles. Hence in this epyllion, as in many others, ambivalence about an unsuccessfully manipulative heroine encodes ambivalence about a brilliantly manipulative queen.

Yet in this instance—as in many other recent scholarly discussions of the interplay between social history and literature—the vocabulary of encoding is potentially misleading: it can imply that all meanings save the covert political one are mere decoys. The political resonances that I am attributing to *Venus and Adonis* and other epyllia are no doubt present, but they do not subsume the more obvious significances of the poem. In this case, while Shakespeare's preoccupation with powerful women may initially have been sparked by the Britomart on England's throne, it is also likely that he had a deep and sustained interest in such temperaments for other reasons as well. In Venus we encounter a preliminary study of a character type that, as his later works testify, intrigued him: the heroine who, refusing to be daunted by literal or metaphoric shipwrecks, energetically attempts to take control of her destiny. But the obvious contrasts between the realization of that figure in Rosalind or Portia and in Venus herself indicate yet another facet of Shakespeare's interest in this plot. Accustomed to her power, evaluating experience in terms of it, Venus is confronted by her own powerlessness, engendered first by the unwilling Adonis and then by the willful boar. She reacts by desperately adducing the strategies that have helped her to assert and maintain her power before, such as renaming the objects around her and flattering his opponents. Shakespeare's concern with the powerlessness of the erstwhile powerful, a preoccupation embodied in the phrase, "She's love, she loves, and yet she is not lov'd" (l. 610), recurs in the other nondramatic poems as well and, of course, in many of the plays, testifying to his attraction to this situation.

Venus' most characteristic speech mannerism is one that critics have neglected, her reliance on conditionals:

> If thou wilt deign this favour, for thy meed
> A thousand honey secrets shalt thou know.
> > (ll. 15–16)
> If thou wilt chide, thy lips shall never open.
> > (l. 48)
> If they burn too, I'll quench them with my tears.
> > (l. 192)
> But if thou needs wilt hunt, be rul'd by me.
> > (l. 673)

In addition to this list—and one could extend it—Venus formulates many sentences that are implicit conditionals. "Is thine own heart to thine face affected? . . . Then woo thyself" (ll. 157, 159), for example, can be transformed into "If thine own heart is to thine own face affected, then woo thyself." "Give me one kiss, I'll give it thee again" (l. 209) implies the conditional formulation, "If you give me one kiss. . . ."

Venus' conditional mode is the syntactical manifestation of habits of mind that emerge in many other ways as well: her propensity for establishing bargains and her closely related tendency to see one action as a payment for another. As "Give me one kiss, I'll give it thee again" (l. 209) would suggest, she uses kisses as counters in her bargains. Similarly, when she tries to arrange another meeting with Adonis, she selects a phrase that has connotations of bargaining: "wilt thou make the match" (l. 586). And she bargains even with death, in effect proffering the boar as a target for his rage.

The tendency we are observing, like so many of Venus' other predilections, is not wholly negative. In a sense, in fact, Venus' conditionals assume the function of the etiological myths that Shakespeare, unlike other practitioners of his genre, virtually omits: they symbolize a world of order, of rules—a world that is played against the irrational sphere of the boar, who respects no rules at all. Hence Venus' ability to shape sentences into conditionals—and the ability to promulgate rules, to predict patterns that it implies—breaks down when she fears Adonis' death: "If he be dead,—O no, it cannot be" (l. 937).

In practice, however, this speech mannerism generally manifests the darker, more dangerous tendencies in the goddess of love. First of all, it again signals the issue of power: when her conditionals involve a threat ("If thou wilt chide, thy lips shall never open" [l. 48]), they are evidently an attempt to dominate, to manipulate. This aspect of bargaining becomes explicit in an allusion to ransom that figures in the most negative description of Venus that we find in the whole poem:

> Now quick desire hath caught the yielding prey,
> And glutton-like she feeds, yet never filleth.
> Her lips are conquerors, his lips obey,
> Paying what ransom the insulter willeth.
>
> (ll. 547–550)

And if Venus' conditionals in theory attest to at least a modicum of trust and communication between her and her listener, in fact they more often manifest the dissolution of both social and linguistic norms. For example, "If thou wilt deign this favour, for thy meed / A thousand honey secrets shalt thou know" (ll. 15–16) not only implies that Adonis has the choice of doing the favor or not but also stresses his authority and autonomy through the strikingly courtly, humble formula, "If thou wilt deign." But in truth he has no choice at all: without even giving him a chance to reply, Venus drags "the tender boy" (l. 32) from his horse.

Other conditionals rank as infelicitous speech acts in the sense Austin and Searle have defined: they violate one of the essential conditions for promising. In Searle's schema, one of the preparatory rules for promising is: "Pr is to be uttered only if the Hearer H would prefer S's doing A to his not doing A and S believes H would prefer S's doing A to his not doing A."[17]

Often, however, Venus promises something that Adonis does not want at all. Thus in "Here come and sit, where never serpent hisses, / And being set, I'll smother thee with kisses" (ll. 17–18), her promise to kiss him must in fact seem more of a threat to her listener.[18] Nor would he necessarily welcome the promise she bestows on him later: "If they burn too, I'll quench them with my tears" (l. 192).

The violation of the normal rules for promising reflects the instability of a world in which generic and other stylistic rules break down as rapidly and as unpredictably as social ones. We may recall 2 *Henry IV*, where Prince John's violated pledge to the rebels is merely the most overt manifestation of a society in which Diogenes would grow cold and weary roaming the streets. But Venus' untrustworthy promises also serve to reflect her characteristic self-centeredness: unable to admit that Adonis is radically different from herself, she cannot recognize that he will not appreciate the sexual favors she promises him. The same type of self-centeredness is reflected in the rhetorical questions on which she so often relies: "Then why not lips on lips, since eyes in eyes?" (l. 120) and "Is thine own heart to thine own face affected?" (l. 157). Sentences like this imply that their answer is obvious—but Adonis would not in fact give the answer that Venus wants.

The self-centeredness of Venus' linguistic mannerisms is mirrored throughout the poem. We have already observed that her first words measure her beloved against her own beauty: "Thrice fairer than myself" (l. 7). As many readers have noticed, her repeated conceits about the earth and the boar kissing Adonis also represent a kind of self-centeredness: here, as in her conditionals and her rhetorical questions, she is refusing to acknowledge the Other, metonymically making the world over in her own image. And, as petulant and vengeful as an Ovidian god, after Adonis' death she prophesies that all lovers will suffer as she has done: "It shall be fickle, false and full of fraud" (l. 1141). The echoes with which she is surrounded the night before Adonis dies are an externalization, a bodying forth, of her tendency to live in a house of mirrors.

Venus' deceptive rhetoric exemplifies one of the broadest—and deepest—issues in the poem: failures of speech and of language itself. *Venus and Adonis* is concerned with faulty or failed communication, as well as faulty or failed perception; the one isolates us from the people around us, the other from the world we inhabit. The significance of communication in the poem is reflected in the fact that here, as in Shakespeare's other major poems and, indeed, in the *Metamorphoses*, the inability to speak repeatedly symbolizes other losses, other griefs; Adonis' initial silence aptly represents his loss of power, and even Venus herself is temporarily rendered speechless, first by impatience and then by grief.

One reason communication is problematical, Venus' behavior reminds us, is that language can serve multiple and often contradictory ends. In particular, its expressive and its persuasive aims may be at odds; in describing her love for Adonis the goddess of love in fact weakens her case, repelling rather that persuading him. And the poem plays on the paradox that Adonis' demurrals actually render him more, not less, attractive, much as Elizabeth Bennet finds that her most serious protests are merely interpreted as the coquetry of an elegant female. The failure of words to say what the speaker intends is one more breakdown in expectations and one more collapse of social codes in a poem that depicts so many of these failures. But if verbal signs cannot always be trusted to communicate as intended, neither can their gestural equivalent. The gestures of the horses, their tailwaving, stamping, and biting, effectively prevent a nascent breach between them. Yet in the human semiotic system gestures can be misleading in much the same way as words: though the red and white hues of Adonis' face in fact express his shame and grief, Venus finds them attractive.

Sexual gestures, too, can be an antithesis to communication rather than an extension of it:

> And kissing speaks, with lustful language broken,
> "If thou wilt chide, thy lips shall never open."
>
> (ll. 47–48)

> He saith she is immodest, blames her miss;
> What follows more, she murders with a kiss.
>
> (ll. 53–54)

On one level, of course, we should not take all this too seriously: Venus is again indulging in playful sexual games, and one would have to be as "unmoved, cold, and to temptation slow" as Adonis himself wholly to disapprove. The word "murders" (l. 54), however, reminds us that serious issues are at stake. The way kissing interrupts language in these instances is a microcosm of the way sexuality bars genuine communication between Venus and Adonis throughout the poem.

But much as Venus' aggressiveness does not preclude tenderness, so the violence that she inflicts on language does not preclude her using it with more respect and to more respectable ends.[19] Venus approaches rhetoric much as she approaches people: overwhelmingly, disturbingly, and yet with a type of vitality and verve that qualify the negative judgments we are tempted to make. As we saw, the deer park episode reflects not only her intention of manipulating Adonis but also the delighted and delightful fluency of her imagination. It is, however, the Wat incident that best exemplifies the positive uses to which she can put language. Though the iconographic association between Venus and hares may explain some of her interest in the unfortunate Wat,[20] in her precisely realized, sympathetic observations we find the very ability to transcend her own interests, look beyond her own mirrors, that she elsewhere lacks:

> By this, poor Wat, far off upon a hill,
> Stands on his hinder-legs with list'ning ear,
> To hearken if his foes pursue him still.
> Anon their loud alarums he doth hear.
>
> (ll. 697–700)

It is the process of storytelling, elsewhere used for self-serving ends, that here allows both Venus and her listeners to empathize with Wat. In fact, so involved are we with her descriptions that even after repeated readings we are startled when we are reminded of the framing story of Venus and Adonis by the line: "Lie quietly, and hear a little more" (l. 709).

The acuity of Shakespeare's portrayal of Venus is manifest not only in the broader psychological patterns we have been sketching but also in more isolated reactions. As one editor has noted, the multiple images of Adonis that she sees are a recognizable symptom of hysteria;[21] since the incident reminds us also that she has never seen him clearly, it functions symbolically as well as psychologically. At one point she is so involved in her own world that she forgets what she is saying ("'Where did I leave?' 'No matter where,' quoth he" [l. 715]), a moment that may well remind us of our own responses to stress. Also acute are Venus' rapid transitions from depression to anger. Grieving at Adonis' death, she vents her spleen by mocking the rest of the world:

> Bonnet nor veil henceforth no creature wear:
> Nor sun nor wind will ever strive to kiss you.
> Having no fair to lose, you need not fear.
>
> (ll. 1081–1083)

A little later her sorrow is transformed into the anger of her prophecy: "The bottom poison, and the top o'erstraw'd / With sweets that shall the truest sight beguile" (ll. 1143–1144).

If Venus' opening words aptly introduce her, her concluding ones are
equally characteristic. So revealing is the final passage in the poem, in fact,
that it demands to be cited in full:

> She bows her head, the new-sprung flower to smell,
> Comparing it to her Adonis' breath,
> And says within her bosom it shall dwell,
> Since he himself is reft from her by death.
> > She crops the stalk, and in the breach appears
> > Green-dropping sap, which she compares to tears.
>
> "Poor flower," quoth she, "this was thy father's guise,—
> Sweet issue of a more sweet-smelling sire,—
> For every little grief to wet his eyes;
> To grow unto himself was his desire,
> > And so 'tis thine; but know, it is as good
> > To wither in my breast as in his blood.
>
> "Here was thy father's bed, here in my breast;
> Thou art the next of blood, and 'tis thy right
> Lo in this hollow cradle take thy rest;
> My throbbing heart shall rock thee day and night:
> > There shall not be one minute in an hour
> > Wherein I will not kiss my sweet love's flower."
>
> Thus weary of the world, away she hies,
> And yokes her silver doves, by whose swift aid
> Their mistress mounted through the empty skies,
> In her light chariot quickly is convey'd,
> > Holding their course to Paphos, where their queen
> > Means to immure herself and not be seen.
> > > (ll. 1171–1194)

The repetition of "compare" in the first stanza I quoted draws our
attention to the fact that Venus, like Richard II, is responding to grief by
assuming the role of poet. Unlike that monarch, however, she also reacts with
violence, plucking the flower much as she had plucked Adonis. In the next
stanza, she develops the conceit that the flower is Adonis' son, an image that
evidently reflects her maternality. But that maternality involves little genuine concern for the flower and less yet for the truth. When, for example, she

claims that it is the flower's "right" (l. 1184) to wither in her breast, she is making the same mistake that marked and marred her promises to that fair flower Adonis: she implies that the blossom is grateful to have the right, that it would wish to wither in her breast. In another way, too, she is twisting facts: if her breast was Adonis' "bed" (l. 1183), he allowed it to be so only very briefly and unwillingly. But if our reactions up to this point have been negative, the assertion "There shall not be one minute in an hour / Wherein I will not kiss my sweet love's flower" (ll. 1187–1188) confounds our responses by increasing our pity for her. On the one hand, we have learned by now to distrust Venus' promises, and the hyperbolic vocabulary of this one makes it seem especially unreliable. Yet in this case we also feel that the extravagance of her language reflects the depth of her emotion, and we sympathize with her in her grief.

It is instructive to read through the ending of *Venus and Adonis* twice, once pretending that its penultimate stanza in fact terminates the poem and the second time including the actual ending. The difference is striking. First of all, had Shakespeare ended on "Wherein I will not kiss my sweet love's flower" (l. 1188), our final reactions to Venus would have been involvement and sympathy, though a sympathy laced with distrust of her hyperboles. The actual conclusion, however, distances us from her and in so doing enforces more negative moral judgments, a seesawing between sympathy and judgment that characterizes the whole poem. Moreover, by including the final stanza the poet reinforces certain points about Venus' temperament that have emerged throughout the poem. She is enacting her ability to avoid realities she does not wish to face; having escaped into an airy world of words earlier, now she is quite literally escaping into the air. And if her desire to "immure herself" (1194) once again testifies to her genuine sorrow, the preceding phrase in the line, "means to," surprises us by its ambiguity. It can, of course, merely function as a neutral announcement of her intentions—but as we read about her flying away we reflect that the intentions of this, as it were, highly volatile character are not always to be trusted. We may even suspect that her immuring herself is the last of many vows she does not keep, conditions she does not meet.

But these doubts necessarily cannot be confirmed: the poem is over. Hence our responses to the ending are uncertainty and even dismay, reactions all the more intense because they conflict with the aesthetic finality we associate with closure; the text no less than Venus is breaking a promise.[22] Venus' statements and actions represent an unreliable form of closure, an assertion of finality that jars against the irresolution introduced by "means to" (l. 1194). We react rather as we do at the end of *Measure for Measure*, where the sense of finality that the comedic conclusion offers conflicts with our expectations about how Isabella would really respond to the proposal. In short, then, Shakespeare is conjoining an aesthetic and a psychological problem here, as he so often does elsewhere in the poem: he is examining the issue of closure by associating that literary question with his heroine's sensibility.

Venus' inability to effect a satisfactory conclusion to her experiences is in fact foreshadowed a few stanzas earlier in one of the most revealing changes Shakespeare makes in his sources. In both Ovid and Golding, Venus wills the flower into being and in so doing creates an apt symbol for her grief as well as an apt ending for the story. Here, however, the blossom merely springs up unaided:

> By this the boy that by her side lay kill'd
> Was melted like a vapour from her sight,
> And in his blood that on the ground lay spill'd,
> A purple flower sprung up, checker'd with white.
> (ll. 1165–1168)

If we cannot trust the actions and reactions of Venus, those of Adonis are also problematical. Though he is less fully realized than Venus, his behavior manifests some of the same intriguing ambiguities.[23] In other epyllia, the few ambiguous moments we encounter typically reflect simple hypocrisy—Hero says *"Come thither"* (l. 358) because she is more interested in sex than she cares to admit—while in the case of both of Shakespeare's title characters such moments reveal more complex ethical and psychological problems. Adonis' youthfulness is a case in point. Emphasized by Shakespeare's repeated references to him as a boy (for example, ll. 32, 95, 344), his immaturity represents a striking deviation from the sources. Though Golding once calls his Adonis a "tender youth" (l. 634), elsewhere he indicates that he has reached manhood, and Ovid explicitly states that he was "iam iuvenis, iam vir" ("now a youth, now man," *Metamorphoses* X.523).[24] On the one hand, the youthfulness of Shakespeare's Adonis breeds sympathy for him, encouraging us to cast him as a victim of a scheming older woman and, in particular, providing at least a partial explanation for his reluctance. On the other hand, however, his chronological age also reflects his emotional immaturity, the callowness manifest in such dialogue as his comically petulant excuse, "Fie, no more of love! / The sun doth burn my face, I must remove" (ll. 185–186).

But we cannot rest satisfied that his youthfulness justifies his rejec-

tion of Venus; like the goddess of love herself, we are confused by his behavior. For one thing, that rejection is explained too frequently and too con-
tradictorily: here, as with the plethora of motives that Iago announces, the
very abundance of rationales leads us to distrust all of them—and to distrust the character who is so profusely offering them. In the opening stanza,
the narrator clearly announces that "love he laugh'd to scorn" (l. 4), while
later in the poem Adonis himself as firmly asserts, "I hate not love, but your
device in love / That lends embracements unto every stranger" (ll. 789–790).
Similarly, he declares that he hates love because "it is a life in death" (l. 413)
but only a few lines later implies that it is not the nature of love but rather
his own youthfulness that impels him to scorn it (ll. 415–420). Recognizing
that Adonis does not fully understand his own behavior, we begin to suspect subterranean motives that he cannot or will not face, such as the narcissism of which Venus accuses him. The poem nowhere confirms those suspicions—Venus, herself narcissistic, is not the most reliable of judges on this
issue, as on so many others—but they remain a troubling undertone as we
read.

Evaluating Adonis' ethical position is as complicated as assessing the
reasons he assumes it. There is no question but that his coy, petulant tone
leads us to distrust his moral stance.[25] At times asyndeton contributes to the
impression of abruptness and churlishness:

> You hurt my hand with wringing, let us part,
> And leave this idle theme, this bootless chat;
> . . . .
> Dismiss your vows, your feigned tears, your flatt'ry,
> For where a heart is hard they make no batt'ry.
> (ll. 421–422, 425–426)

Like the academicians in *Love's Labour's Lost,* he sounds a little too smug
and self-righteous when he dismisses love's "batt'ry" (l. 426).

The smugness finds its rhetorical equivalent in the aphorisms that
characterize his speech:

> The colt that's back'd and burden'd being young,
> Loseth his pride, and never waxeth strong.
> (ll. 419–420)

> Love comforteth like sunshine after rain,
> But lust's effect is tempest after sun;

Love's gentle spring doth always fresh remain,
Lust's winter comes ere summer half be done.

(ll. 799–802)

As we read these lines, we sense a tension between their neatness, the sense of intellectual and poetic stasis that they convey, and the rapidly moving, unpredictable world we encounter elsewhere in the poem.[26] As we will see, the couplets in Shakespeare's sonnets function in much the same way. The fact that Adonis' sentiments were Elizabethan truisms does not prove that Shakespeare was endorsing them, as some readers have assumed; rather, the author of the poem is holding these conventional "forms" up for our scrutiny, a scrutiny that would become all the more charged for a reader who had accepted and even repeated such aphoristic sentiments unthinkingly. Nor, however, should we assume that Shakespeare is merely mocking the conventional wisdom of his culture. Venus, surely a "tempest" (l. 800) as well as a temptress, exemplifies many of the points Adonis is making. And however suspicious his neat truisms may make us, they clearly provide him with an important bulwark against her attacks.

Where other epyllia typically assign aphorisms to an undramatized, vaguely defined narrative voice, Shakespeare places them in the mouth of one of his principal characters. Similarly, the hyperbolic language in which the narrators in other epyllia revel is here primarily associated with Venus. By dramatizing linguistic behavior in this way, he is highlighting the psychological traits that it reflects—an issue that he was, of course, exploring at roughly the same time in *Love's Labour's Lost* and in so many of his later works.[27] Both in the plays and in *Venus and Adonis* itself, one effect of this dramatization is to encourage us to question patterns of speech and thought that we might otherwise too readily accept; similarly, it is precisely because they are spoken by a Jaques or a Polonius that we reconsider our attitudes to the moral truisms those characters convey.

However antithetical the ethical positions of Shakespeare's two title characters may be, Adonis adopts some of the linguistic patterns we also found in Venus, demonstrating that here, as in *The Rape of Lucrece* and the *Sonnets,* the lovers share deeper affinities than they themselves would care to admit. Adonis too is very concerned with naming and misnaming: "Call it not love, for love to heaven is fled, / Since sweating lust on earth usurp'd his name" (ll. 793–794). Our first impression may be that he, unlike the huntress who pursues him, is assigning names correctly. But in him as well as her the process is self-serving in its aims, deceptive in its effects. Though lust is Venus' primary motive, it is by no means her only one and by no means an adequate label for her behavior: tender maternal love is commingled with her lust, as certain images testify ("Like a milch doe, whose swelling dugs do ache, / Hasting to feed her fawn, hid in some brake" [ll. 875–876]). And Adonis too makes and breaks promises, though not as frequently as Venus:

> So offers he to give what she did crave,
> But when her lips were ready for his pay,
> He winks, and turns his lips another way.
>
> (ll. 88–90)

> Now let me say good night, and so say you;
> If you will say so, you shall have a kiss.
>
> (ll. 535–536)

It is by subtly but significantly recasting his sources that Shakespeare develops another facet of Adonis: he is figured as entrapped, enclosed—sometimes by Venus but sometimes by his own chastity. When recounting the story of Salmacis and Hermaphroditus, Ovid writes, "in liquidis translucet aquis, ut eburnea si quis / signa tegat claro vel candida lilia vitro" (IV.354–355). Golding renders this as, "As if a man an Ivorie Image or a Lillie white / Should overlay or close with glasse" (IV.438–439).[28] But in Shakespeare's hands the image becomes:

> Full gently now she takes him by the hand,
> A lily prison'd in a gaol of snow,
> Or ivory in an alabaster band.
>
> (ll. 361–363)

The charged word "prison'd" (l. 362) serves to develop the imagery of entrapment that runs throughout the poem (compare the deer park stanzas with which we began: "Since I have hemm'd thee here / Within the circuit . . . Within this limit" [ll. 229–230, 235]).[29] Later in the poem, however, Adonis speaks of a very different type of enclosure:

> Lest the deceiving harmony should run
> Into the quiet closure of my breast,
> And then my little heart were quite undone,
> In his bedchamber to be barr'd of rest.
>
> (ll. 781–784)

Here the protective custody of the breast displaces imprisonment. While Shakespeare does not recur to these figures or the implicit relationship between them elsewhere in *Venus and Adonis,* it is telling that they were present in his imagination this early in his career. They surface in the other nondramatic poems (as well as in several plays), and there they assume a more central role.

However we interpret Adonis' behavior, it is difficult to consider the boar a fitting punishment for it.[30] Those readers who have argued that the natural world is punishing him for his rejection of naturalistic love neglect the fact that the poem is ambivalent about that rejection. In any event, the punishment does not seem to fit the crime, even if we concentrate on its symbolic ramifications. Its inappropriateness is, I would suggest, the very point: Shakespeare is stressing the randomness, the injustice of fate. There is at times no providence in the fall of a sparrow. That randomness renders Venus' and Adonis' efforts to order experience, whether by renaming it or forcing it into the mold of aphoristic or conditional utterances, all the more understandable—but also all the more foolish.

Though they are alike in that "blessed rage for order," Venus and Adonis evidently differ from each other in their approach to morality. In anatomizing that difference, Shakespeare once again couples the formal and the psychological. Adonis not only subscribes to the conventional pieties, he repeatedly expresses them in a series of sententiae that would make even *A Mirror for Magistrates* look like an exemplar of amoral naturalism by comparison. What results is a poem in which one character bodies forth an amoral delight in sexuality, while the other both symbolizes and expresses a rejection of it in the name of higher philosophical verities. Hence *Venus and Adonis*—and Venus and Adonis themselves—dramatically enact a tension in the generic potentials of Ovidian mythological poetry. Venus stands for the amoral eroticism so common in the mythological narratives of Ovid himself, while Adonis represents the pieties of *Ovide moralisé.* The tension between Venus and Adonis is in effect also a tension between two possible ways of imitating and adapting Ovid, two potential metamorphoses of the *Metamorphoses*: the amoral, Italianate narrative and the pious commentary on human follies. Rosalie Colie has shown us how often Shakespeare's plays envision literary problems in terms of human psychology;[31] the same is no less true of his Ovidian narrative. By thus relating the literary to the psychological in *Venus and Adonis,* he deepens the resonances of his characters—we become aware that they represent distinctive responses to literary dilemmas as well as nonliterary ones—and also enlivens and dramatizes the questions raised by his genre. To be sure, other sixteenth-century Ovidian epyllia are packed with sententiae, but their truisms are normally assigned to the narrator, not one of the personages. Since these narrators are not fully realized characters, the conflict between the two approaches to Ovid is not enacted dramatically as it is in Shakespeare's poem. Shakespeare is, in other words, interpreting his genre and its mode very differently from the way his contemporaries do.

NOTES

1. For such parallels see, e.g., Adrien Bonjour, "From Shakespeare's Venus to Cleopatra's Cupids," *Shakespeare Survey,* 15 (1962), 73–80; Robert Grudin, *Mighty Opposites: Shakespeare and Renaissance Contrariety* (Berkeley: U of California P, 1979), pp. 171, 207; Prince, "Introduction," p. xxxii.

2. For an opposing view, see Clark Hulse, *Metamorphic Verse: The Elizabethan Minor Epic* (Princeton: Princeton UP, 1981), p. 155. Also compare Lennet J. Daigle, "Venus and Adonis: Some Traditional Contexts," *Shakespeare Studies,* 13 (1980), 31–46, on the combination of realistic and allegorical elements in her character. James J. Yoch ("The Eye of Venus: Shakespeare's Erotic Landscape," *SEL,* 20 [1980], 59–71) discusses characterization in terms of Venus' approach to the landscape.

3. William Keach notes in a different context that Shakespeare realizes that the wooer is really more dependent than the person being wooed (*Elizabethan Erotic Narratives: Irony and Pathos in the Ovidian Poetry of Shakespeare, Marlowe, and Their Contemporaries.* [New Brunswick: Rutgers UP, 1977], p. 59).

4. All citations from Shakespeare's plays are to William Shakespeare, *The Complete Works,* ed. Alfred Harbage (Baltimore: Penguin, 1969).

5. Though his psychoanalytic reading of the poem is on the whole unconvincing, Alan B. Rothenberg offers the interesting observation that *Venus and Adonis, The Rape of Lucrece,* and *The Taming of the Shrew* all involve types of rape ("The 'Speaking Beast': A Theory of Shakespearean Creativity," *Psychocultural Review,* 3 [1979], 239).

6. On naming in the plays, see, e.g., Joseph A. Porter, *The Drama of Speech Acts: Shakespeare's Lancastrian Tetralogy* (Berkeley: U of California P, 1979), esp. pp. 12–19.

7. Lucy Gent also observes this habit in Venus but interprets it differently, concentrating particularly on the use of hyperbole ("Venus and Adonis: The Triumph of Rhetoric." *MLR,* 69 [1974], 721–29).

8. Theocritus, *Sixe Idillia* (London, 1588), "The XXXI Idillion," 27–31.

9. Stephen Jay Greenblatt, *Renaissance Self-fashioning from More to Shakespeare* (Chicago: U of Chicago P, 1980), pp. 227–228.

10. Compare Robert P. Miller, "The Myth of 'Mars' Hot Minion in *Venus and Adonis.*" *ELH,* 26 (1959), 470–481.

11. George Puttenham, *The Arte of English Poesie,* ed. Gladys Doidge Willcock and Alice Walker (1936; rpt. Cambridge: Cambridge UP, 1970), p. 191.

12. Though Venus' rhetoric has been neglected by most readers, a few have commented sensitively on it from perspectives different from my own. See Gent; Richard A. Lanham, *The Motives of Eloquence: Literary Rhetoric in the Renaissance.* New Haven: Yale UP, 1976), pp. 82–94. The latter analysis, though useful, is limited by its exclusive emphasis on the negative aspects of her rhetoric.

13. See esp. Arthur Marotti, "'Love Is Not Love': Elizabethan Sonnet Sequences and the Social Order," *ELH,* 49 (1982), 396–428; Leonard Tennenhouse, "Sir Walter Raleigh and the Literature of Clientage," in *Patronage in the Renaissance,* ed. Guy Fitch Lytle and Stephen Orgel (Princeton: Princeton UP, 1981).

14. On attitudes to epideictic oratory, see O.B. Hardison, Jr., *The Enduring*

Monument: A Study of the Idea of Praise in Renaissance Literary Theory and Practice (Chapel Hill: U. of North Carolina P, 1962), chap. 2.

15. On these precedents, see Bush, *Mythology and the Renaissance Tradition*, p. 143; Keach, pp. 53–56.

16. The ways Elizabeth I affected literature have, of course, been exhaustively studied, both by traditional literary critics and by proponents of the "new historicism." On the tensions generated by the presence of a powerful female monarch, see esp. Louis Adrian Montrose, "'Shaping Fantasies': Figurations of Gender and Power in Elizabethan Culture," *Representations*, I (1983), 61–94.

17. John R. Searle, *Speech Acts: An Essay in the Philosophy of Language* (Cambridge: Cambridge UP, 1969), p. 63.

18. Jerome Schneewind argues that we must distinguish offers and promises ("A Note on Promising," *Philosophical Studies*, 17 [1966], 33–35); in the case of a promise, he contends, the promiser must have good reason to think the promisee wishes the act to be done. Even if one accepts this delimitation of the speech act of promising, however, my general argument about Venus remains valid: rather than suggesting that her infelicitous speech act reflects her self-centeredness, one could maintain that her inability to recognize that Adonis does not want what she promises, her unwillingness to distinguish offer from promise, itself demonstrates self-centeredness.

19. Compare Coppélia Kahn's point that Venus' sexuality itself is both healthy and destructive ("Self and Eros in *Venus and Adonis*," *Centennial Review*, 20 [1976], pp. 360–364). An abbreviated version of the article appears in *Man's Estate: Masculine Identity in Shakespeare* (Berkeley: U of California P, 1981), with the relevant section on pp. 33–34.

20. On the iconographical connections between Venus and the hare, see, e.g., Don Cameron Allen, "On *Venus and Adonis*," in *Elizabethan and Jacobean Studies Presented to Frank Percy Wilson* (Oxford: Clarendon, 1959), pp. 109–110.

21. Prince, p. 57.

22. For an overview of poetic closure, see Barbara Herrnstein Smith, *Poetic Closure: A Study of How Poems End* (Chicago: U of Chicago P, 1968).

23. Most studies of Adonis interpret him allegorically rather than psychologically. For a psychological reading different from my own but not incompatible with it, see Kahn, "Self and Eros in *Venus and Adonis*"; this article focuses on his narcissism.

24. All citations from Ovid are to *Metamorphoses*, trans. Frank Justus Miller, 2nd ed., 2 vols. (Cambridge, Mass. and London: Harvard UP and Heinemann, 1966).

25. On this and other faults in Adonis, cf. J.D. Jahn, "The Lamb of Lust: The Role of Adonis in Shakespeare's *Venus and Adonis*," *Shakespeare Studies*, 6 (1970): 11–25. Norman Rabkin suggests that the imagery associating him with animals, as well as his own perspiration, belie his attempts to escape the flesh (*Shakespeare and the Common Understanding* [New York and London: Free Press and Collier Macmillan, 1967], p. 161). For an earlier version of this chapter, see "*Venus and Adonis* and the Myth of Love," in *Pacific Coast Studies in Shakespeare*. ed. Waldo F. McNeir and Thelma N. Greenfield (Eugene, OR: U of Oregon P, 1966). These and other arguments about Adonis' faults call into question G.P.V. Akrigg's assertion that Shakespeare's epyllion compliments Southampton by implicitly rebutting the portrait of him in John Clapham's *Narcissus* (*Shakespeare and the Earl of Southampton* [Cambridge, Mass.: Harvard UP, 1968], pp. 33–34, 195–196). Other possible connections between *Narcissus* and *Venus and Adonis*, however, deserve more attention than they have received.

26. Lanham (pp. 82–94) argues that he is being criticized for his aphoristic rhetoric; Franklin M. Dickey, in contrast, maintains that he speaks "rather nobly" (*Not Wisely but Too Well: Shakespeare's Love Tragedies* [San Marino: Huntington Library, 1957] p. 50). This chapter suggests that the truth lies somewhere in between.

27. On attitudes to language in *Love's Labour's Lost*, see esp. William C.

Carroll, *The Great Feast of Language in "Love's Labour's Lost"* (Princeton: Princeton UP, 1976).

28. All citations from Golding are to *Shakespeare's Ovid, Being Arthur Golding's Translation of the Metamorphoses*, ed. W.H.D. Rouse (Carbondale, Ill.: Southern Illinois UP, 1961).

29. For a different but not incompatible reading of the image, see M.C. Bradbrook, *Shakespeare and Elizabethan Poetry: A Study of His Earlier Work in Relation to the Poetry of the Time*, (London: Chatto and Windus, 1951), p. 64.

30. The significance of the boar has been discussed by many readers. The thesis of Don Cameron Allen's "On *Venus and Adonis*" is that Shakespeare is contrasting the soft hunt of love with the hard hunt for the boar; A.C. Hamilton interprets that destructive beast as the forces that threaten beauty ("*Venus and Adonis,*" *SEL*, 1 [1961], 13).

31. *Shakespeare's Living Art*, esp. chap. 2.

THEMATICS OF VALUE
IN *VENUS AND ADONIS*

Nona Fienberg

When Venus finds Adonis able to resist her love, she wonders of course what his nature is, "Art thou a woman's son and canst not feel / What 'tis to love?" (ll. 201–02).[1] But her energies and the interest of the poem engage the question of her nature. We seem to know so much more about Venus than about Adonis. As Coppélia Kahn points out, however, what we know about Venus is severely limited; "We know Venus as a character only through the demands she makes on Adonis; the overwhelming impression we have of her is of a mouth, pressing insistently on or toward him."[2] Since Venus' representation in all its mutability and variety so dominates the poem that she threatens to consume it quite, that representation of a woman rewards further investigation. What is this creature whom Shakespeare found to offer to the Earl of Southampton as "the first heire of my invention"? What is the representation of the female limned in the "unpolished lines" through which Shakespeare first presented his published self? Venus' power extends beyond Adonis to readers of the poem who are challenged to reevaluate a fixed and stable set of standards against her dynamic and shifting self-evaluation.

Venus' mutability and diversity contrast with Adonis' fixity and absoluteness. Her productivity contrasts with his fearful solipsism. In her confrontation of Adonis' value system with her own more dynamic sense of multiplicity, she provides a way to reevaluate patriarchy. Because the question of value and evaluation is central to my argument, I want to provide a theoretical framework for the issues. My theoretical beliefs are articulated by Barbara Herrnstein Smith's powerful assertion, "All value is radically contingent, being neither an inherent property of objects nor an arbitrary pro-

Reprinted from *Criticism* 31, 1 (1989), pp. 21–32. Copyright Wayne State University Press.

jection of subjects, but, rather, the product of the dynamics of an economic system. . . . Like its price in the marketplace, the value of an entity to an individual subject is *also* the product of the dynamics of an economic system, specifically the personal economy constituted by the subject's needs, interests, and resources—biological, psychological, material, and experiential."[3] Smith's argument frees readers from bondage either to the value system of the Renaissance world in which Shakespeare writes or to the contemporary world in which we fix the worth of texts. Instead, Smith's argument invites a new kind of cultural investigation of the contingencies in diverse local conditions of evaluation. An examination of the thematics of value can be particularly powerful for the study of the representation of females in historical texts. Without a sense both of the distance of historical texts and of the values we use texts to produce, we may be bound by oppressive absolutism.

As Smith notes, and as Venus enacts, the marketplace of value is continuously shifting, changing, dynamic, not fixed, absolute, or subject to predictable natural law. Such relativism proves liberating, since it frees women's representation from biological and social determinism. Instead of responding with alarm to Venus' range of self-representation, to her power and dynamism, we are enabled to identify her mutability, her risk-taking, and her appropriation of a system of rhetorical display with the changing cultural conditions of the early 1590s in England.[4] Venus becomes, then, a part of the cultural work of her own time and of ours.

In one stanza she addresses the economic, sexual, and epistemological range of the reevaluation of the patriarchy which she invites her audience to engage in:

> What am I that thou shouldst contemn me this?
> Or what great danger dwells upon my suit?
> What were thy lips the worse for one poor kill?
> Speak, fair, but speak fair words, or else be mute.
> Give me one kiss, I'll give it thee again,
> And one for int'rest, if thou wilt have twain.
>
> (ll. 205–10)

In her first question, "What am I that thou shouldst contemn me this?", she poses the question of knowledge of selfhood that engages her and her readers throughout her poem. The next question offers an alternative formulation of the epistemological issue by introducing the possibility that she poses a danger to those she entices. For Adonis, the dangers are multiple and various. They range from the sexual, through the epistemological, and finally to the economic. In her final lines Venus poses the social and economic dimension of this dynamic interplay of the forces of reevaluation. She offers Adonis a good bargain, as a self-confident, somewhat prodigal entrepreneur, "Give me one kiss, I'll give it thee again, / And one for int'rest, if thou wilt have twain." While Adonis remains an unresponsive audience through Venus' powerful display, Venus succeeds in winning assent to her subversion of an oppressive dominant group.

At times, the Venus of Shakespeare's poem represents the misogynist phenomenon Neil Hertz exposes in "Medusa's Head: Male Hysteria under Political Pressure."[5] Hertz argues that under political pressure male hysteria creates representations of female sexuality and power which carry all the male fears: "The dangers to be avoided here are indeterminately political, sexual and epistemological. Enslavement, seduction, the loss of manhood and the unfixing of determinate ideas of what things mean are held up as equivalent threats" (Hertz 47). Hertz illustrates his argument using verbal and visual representations of women's parts in particular moments of French Revolutionary activity. In Hertz' view, the primary fears posed by the vision of Medusa's head are fears of castration. Powerful women in the particular moment of danger, flux, and change he chooses, then, pose a threat to male potency, a threat to patriarchy, and to an authority structure. But, as Joel Fineman points out, the issues might be seen as less particular, more perennial, indeed, a commonplace. He notes "the self-conscious way that Astrophil, at the beginning of Sidney's sonnet sequence, looks into his heart to write, and finds there pre-engraved or stelled upon it the image or *imago* of the Stella whom he loves" (Hertz 57). In freeing the Medusa's head argument from the particular historical circumstances of the French Revolution, Fineman suggests that the fascination with and terror of female difference impells, for example, Sidney, in late Elizabethan England, when the patriarchal court circle expressed its profound anxiety about the question of succession. This anxiety moved Sidney to write his ill-received Letter to Elizabeth in 1582, and increased in the 1590s, as Queen Elizabeth aged without a dynastic heir.[6]

The dynamic interaction of political and sexual exigencies is especially pertinent, then, to the patriarchal anxiety and poetic productivity of the Elizabethan 1590s. In this age of primogeniture, the female's power is socially and historically tied to her ability to produce a child. If uncertainty prevails regarding the reproduction of children, of goods, and of systems of value of all kinds, then the representation of women will bear the fears of society. In Venus, male fears of the female combine with wonder at her strength. A feminist reading, however, notes that in Venus Shakespeare portrays a woman engaged in the reevaluation demanded by a marketplace world. Her conflict is with the naive Adonis, himself a relic of the time before the commercial and humanist revolutions, when value was a given, not a measure of achieved and mutable standing.

Written in late 1592, when the theaters were closed because of the plague, *Venus and Adonis* marks Shakespeare's entry into the world of publication. As such, he presents the poem to the Earl of Southampton as his first claim to authorship, in a sense, his first assumption of the power to create life. Shakespeare calls the poem his "first heire," the claimant to his goods, or, in this context, his value. Despite the patriarchal family, in Shakespeare's social and economic world, such value rested in the biological power of the mother, for through her reproductive power came the name, the goods, and the value of the child.[7] If the woman's sexuality is not contained, then the social world loses knowledge of who and what it is. When Shakespeare leaves for the first time the world of the theater to enter into the different literary realm of publishing poetry, he portrays in Venus a multiple, a various selfhood, which cannot be predicted or controlled. Through the dynamic interplay of economic, sexual, and epistemological dangers, Shakespeare's Venus links "what is politically dangerous to feelings of sexual horror and fascination" (Hertz 32). While it is revealing to expose this part of Venus' representation, it is important to note that Venus controls the rhetorical medium. When your name is Venus, the stakes are high in the game of love. She is willing to risk her name in winning over an unresponsive audience. The bargains she offers are asymmetrical, like the risks involved in the modern commercial world, and like the risks Shakespeare takes in presenting the "first heire of my invention" to the "Right Honorable Henrie Wriothesley, Earle of Southampton, and Baron of Titchfield." The asymmetry between the poet's name and his prospective patron's names measures the social distance between them, and thus the danger inherent in the gift of the poem. Similarly, Venus' willingness to take great risks involves danger, but also creativity. She uses the very rhetorical tools of the patriarchy to subvert its fixed values.

Venus' rhetorical displays have irritated some readers, like Hallett Smith, who complains, "instead of realizing evoked physical beauty we are listening to a lecture."[8] The rhetorical foundation of value in Elizabethan England is, however, particularly pertinent to her representation. In *Ambition and Privilege: The Social Tropes of Elizabethan Courtesy Theory,*[9] Frank Whigham analyzes the central trope of the court world of the period. That trope, *paradiastole,* governs evaluation, and involves the ability to turn praise to blame and reverse as needed, thus bringing to this opposition the "potential for awareness of relativized multiplicity." Its importance lies in "positing a matrix in which praise and blame, flattery and slander, interpenetrate absolutely." The trope becomes central to an analysis of thematics of value in the first work Shakespeare published for a member of the court world. Moreover, the rhetorical foundation of value serves a central role for Venus' particular persuasive strategies. Her rhetorical versatility frees her to determine her own nature as a female.

The power struggle between Venus and Adonis is imagined as that between courtier and courted: "O what a war of looks was then between them! / Her eyes petitioners to his eyes suing" (ll. 355–57). We measure her success with the immediate audience she addresses by such small gains as might flatter a favor-seeker. Even his objections to her forwardness become material for her rhetorical play. Adonis protests, "Give me my hand, . . . why dost thou feel it?" And Venus responds with an asymmetrical offer, "'Give me my heart, 'saith she, 'and thou shall have it'" (ll. 373–74). In this exchange, Venus seizes the advantage he gives her by meeting his words one by one, an echo, but with the difference of a heart replacing a hand. Here, for the only time in the poem, Adonis addresses Venus with the familiar "thou." While she retains the "thou" in her speeches to him, he immediately corrects himself to call her the most distant "you": "And 'tis your fault I am bereft him so" (l. 381). Through that shift he fixes on her status as "other."

While Adonis remains tied to a single sense of selfhood, characterized by epistemological, social, and sexual fears, Venus engages in play, exchange, and risk. Their first debate might be seen as a rhetorical display on the subject of love. Adonis' speech of blame exposes his fear of economic risk-taking: "'Tis much to borrow, and I will not owe it" (l. 411). Like a parsimonious peasant, he is out-shone by the liberal Venus. Economic fear is homologous to the sexual fear he reveals, "If springing things be any jot diminish'd, / They wither in their prime, prove nothing worth" (ll. 417–18). While the immediate context refers to botanical "things," Adonis also fears phallic exhaustion and impotence. His phallocentric sense of himself leads him to associate ejaculation with annihilation: springing things that wither in their prime prove worth nothing. In contrast to Adonis' single-minded desire, "For all my mind, my thought, my busy care, / Is how to get my palfrey from the mare" (ll. 383–84), Venus' desire is unlimited, multiple, "The sea hath bounds, but deep desire hath none" (389).[10] Not annihilation and impotence, but expansion and power characterize Venus.

She subverts Adonis' absolutism through playful comic "supposes." In each of her supposes, Venus, whose imagination is not limited by a single focus, tests the value of one of the senses to love. She toys with various contingencies to discover different ways of measuring love:

> Had I no eyes but ears, my ears would love
> That inward beauty and invisible,
> Or were I deaf, thy outward part would move
> Each part in me that were but sensible;
> Though neither eyes nor ears to hear nor see,
> Yet should I be in love by touching thee.
>
> (ll. 433–38)

Venus' rhetorical versatility creates a number of erotic pleasures despite Adonis' limitations. For example, she brings the subjunctive supposes into action in her comic pretense of a dead faint at Adonis' harsh look, "For on the grass she lies as she were slain, / Till his breath breatheth life in her again" (ll. 473–74). Later, she translates Adonis' simple offer of an exchange of salutations into a more complex transaction:

> "Now let me say 'Good night,' and so say you;
> If you will say so, you shall have a kiss."
> "Good night," quoth she, and ere he says "Adieu,"
> The honey fee of parting tend'red is;
> Her arms do lend his neck a sweet embrace;
> Incorporate then they seem, face grows to face.
>
> (ll. 535–40)

Venus does not settle for the meager reward he proposes. Instead, she takes the initiative, plays the entrepreneur, lends the capital she deals in, and creates a new "corporate" entity.

So often in *Venus and Adonis* does Venus employ the language of the marketplace as language of seduction, that she seems to have come to earth to learn to speak commercial jargon. In the marketplace, where the values of goods, like the value of words, were, as Bacon would soon articulate, unpredictable, uncertainty pervades communication between humans. Such uncertainty informs the humorous language of love with which she presents Adonis the economics of sexuality:

> Pure lips, sweet seals in my soft lips imprinted,
> What bargains may I make, still to be sealing?
> To sell myself I can be well contented,

So thou wilt buy, and pay, and use good dealing,
Which purchase if thou make, for fear of slips,
Set thy seal manual on my wax-red lips.

A thousand kisses buys my heart from me,
And pay them at thy leisure, one by one.
What is ten hundred touches unto thee?
Are they not quickly told, and quickly gone?
Say for non-payment that the debt should double,
Is twenty hundred kisses such a trouble?

(ll. 511–22)

We are, here, in a commercial world gone haywire. If she sounds like a prodigal spender, expecting a return in prodigality from her partner in exchange, she soon hears her language countered by the language of the natural world. The system Adonis operates in obeys natural, orderly, predictable laws:

The mellow plum doth fall, the green sticks fast,
Or being early pluck'd, is sour to taste.

(ll. 527–28)

Like a country boy come to late sixteenth-century London, he holds on to his old ways of measuring time, growth, maturity, and value. But his simple world of just price, natural time, and seasonal development is being replaced. Not only does the economic language indicate such change, but the physical description of the narrative voice suggests Venus' overturning of conventional values. She responds to the transition from a late-Medieval feudal order to a pre-capitalist society by adjusting her personal economy to a new set of contingencies.

Venus' rhetoric adjusts the flexibility of language to her changing personal economy. The complex mixture of sexual and political language in these stanzas suggests her subversion of patriarchy through parody. The comic hyperbole undermines the chivalric old order being mocked:

Now quick desire hath caught the yielding prey,
And glutton-like she feeds, yet never filleth;
Her lips are conquerors, his lips obey,
Paying what ransom the insulter willeth;
Whose vulture thought doth pitch the price so high
That she will draw his lips' rich treasure dry.

And having felt the sweetness of the spoil,
With blindfold fury she begins to forage;
Her face doth reek and smoke, her blood doth boil,
And careless lust stirs up a desperate courage,
Planting oblivion, beating reason back,
Forgetting shame's pure blush and honor's wrack.

(ll. 547–58)

It is easy, at first, to judge Venus' aggression harshly. This is the devouring mouth Kahn has spoken of. And the threat extends to the political realm, as her lips are conquerors, demanding ransom, sucking his treasure dry. She is like an invader in the sovereign realm of his body. Moreover, she is so full of the signs of her physical selfhood, "Her face doth reek and smoke, her blood doth boil," that those abstractions which once determined fixed, controlled behavior, "reason," "shame," and "honor," are now subverted. Even those very words like "reason" soon placed in Adonis' mouth come to seem diminished. Adonis' few speeches are in relatively child-like language, "Fie, fie," he says, "you crush me, let me go, / You have no reason to withhold me so" (ll. 611–12). In this context, his infantile objections contrast with her impressive claims:

But all in vain, good queen, it will not be;
She hath assay'd as much as may be prov'd.
Her pleading hath deserv'd a greater fee;
She's Love, she loves, and yet she is not lov'd.

(ll. 607–10)

The value of "reason" slips, while Venus' mutable, flexible sense of self meets the contingencies of a newly commercial world. Moreover, her use of parody aligns her with the humanist effort to attain power through language, rather than force.

The question of danger has been implicit throughout the poem, but once the prospect of the boar is introduced, the theme of danger becomes explicit. Venus first associated herself with danger in the passage we began with, "Or what great danger dwells upon my suit?" (l. 206). When Adonis reveals his plan to hunt the boar with his friends, Venus pleads with him, "Come not within his danger by thy will." Here, the phrase "within his danger" places her plea and Adonis' choice of dangers in a social and economic context. The OED tells us that danger can involve the power of a lord or master, involving jurisdiction, dominion, and the power to dispose of or to hurt or harm, specifically at times in his debt or under obligation to him. Venus, therefore, speaks to Adonis in the old feudal terms he favors, presenting the boar as a competing claimant to the dominance of Adonis. She would dominate him and keep him "within her danger," through physical, economic, and epistemological claims. But Adonis prefers the hunt of the boar to the hunt of love. Death is simpler than the reevaluation she offers.

But for Venus, the possibility of Adonis' death provokes a confusion that tests even her variable and flexible sense of self. In her range of emotions as she first fears, then curses, then hopes, and again laments, Venus is presented as maternal, infantile, and again maternal. The changes she undergoes suggest the flexibility of her nature. When she hears the cry of the hounds, a sign of Adonis' presence, she races, "Like a milch doe, whose swelling dugs do ache, / Hasting to feed her fawn hid in some brake" (ll. 875–76). Here, her nurturing maternal love is so physically drawn that the maternal and the sexual are powerfully intermingled. We remember the association of liquidity and female sexuality from her earlier offer to Adonis:

> I'll be a park, and thou shalt be my deer:
> Feed where thou wilt, on mountain, or in dale;
> Graze on my lips, and if those hills be dry,
> Stray lower, where the pleasant fountains lie.
>
> (ll. 231–34)

Soon after her fears of the hunt are realized, it is not the soothing flow of milk that conveys her love, but the flow of tears, when she is sure Adonis has died. Even then, the shout of a huntsman overcomes her tears, and she responds, "A nurse's song ne'er pleas'd her babe so well" (l. 974). But when we read this line we pause and make mental adjustments, for we expect her now to be the nurse, and Adonis the babe. Instead, she is the babe pleased by a nurse's song. The change is a quick and surprising one, from mother to child, but one that undermines any fixed and inflexible sense of selfhood. When she finally takes the broken flower into her bosom, she again plays the nurse, "Lo in this hollow cradle take thy rest, / My throbbing heart shall rock thee day and night" (ll. 1185–86). But she has not finished either as nurturing mother, or as sexual partner, or as child. The "wide wound the boar had trench'd / In his soft flank" (ll. 1052–53) is figuratively reopened when she decapitates the purple flower. The fear of the castrating female is transferred to the imagery of a metamorphosed flower.

In this dissolving of the usual distinctions between maternal and infantile roles, between generation and castration, Venus prepares us for her range of responses to Adonis' death. But we must again add the political to the dimensions of her representation. As she tucks the flower in her bosom, she says:

> Here was thy father's bed, here in my breast;
> Thou art the next of blood, and 'tis thy right.
> Lo in this hollow cradle take thy rest,
> My throbbing heart shall rock thee day and night.
>
> (ll. 1182–86)

She speaks as the mother to an infant, or as the nurse to a baby. But she also alludes to the rights of inheritance and succession according to primogeniture. In the late Elizabethan world, to speak of the issue of succession was to risk physical and emotional danger. For Venus to speak of the purple flower as "next of blood" is for her to broach the political dimension of generativity. This queen, however, retreats as soon as she has engaged the dispute, when she mounts to Paphos, where she "means to immure herself, and not be seen" (l. 1194). In this final act of walling herself up not to be seen, Venus retreats from the marketplace realm which the poem has impinged upon. But she has not internalized the values of her silly dead Adonis; instead, she leaves her legacy of reevaluation in the thematics of value we produce through the poem.

Thus, although Venus becomes silent, after all that eloquence, her prophecy enters into the marketplace of poetry. She prophesies that in love all fixed, stable values shall be made unpredictable and uncertain. Communication between humans will be as inadequate and incomplete as was communication between herself and her beloved. All measures of an orderly society will become contingencies, subject to psychological, biological, economic needs. All lovers will confront the problematics of desire that she has met; but not all will face these circumstances with the flexible personal economy Venus can bring to them:

> Since thou art dead, lo here I prophesy,
> Sorrow on love hereafter shall attend;
> It shall be waited on with Jealousy,
> Find sweet beginning, but unsavory end;
> Ne'er settled equally, but high or low,
> That all love's pleasure shall not match his woe.
>
> (ll. 1135–40)

The asymmetrical bargains which we have seen Venus offer in love to her unresponsive audience become the very conditions of love itself. But when we read her words, we need not see love as a terror, any more than her presence is a terror. Venus articulates the conditions of love willingly undertaken by most humans. Whether willing or not, humans are impelled by the desires she articulates.

A feminist reading of *Venus and Adonis* reveals an analogy between the bargains Venus continuously reenacts in operating on earth, and the dynamic renegotiating we do in creating our understanding of her. Such bargains may, in turn, be analogous to the strategies Shakespeare, already a man of the theater, would employ as he both "immures" that multiple, shifting, subversive theatrical talent between the fixed covers of a published poem, and risks exposing his poetry to the commodification of the court marketplace. Then Venus represents the politically, sexually, and epistemologically subversive realm of the theater invading the realm of published poetry. But she also suggests a liberating reevaluation of the patriarchal world she both plays in and subverts, as she demonstrates the usefulness of the thematics of value to expose the limitations of absolutist perspectives.

NOTES

1. William Shakespeare, *The Riverside Shakespeare*, edited by G. Blakemore Evans (Boston: Houghton Mifflin, 1974). All line references to this edition of *Venus and Adonis* will be provided in parentheses following the quotation.

2. Coppélia Kahn, *Man's Estate: Masculine Identity in Shakespeare* (Berkeley: Univ. of California Press, 1981). Kahn provided a generous critical response to an early version of this paper presented at the 1986 Shakespeare Association of America meeting.

3. Barbara Herrnstein Smith, "Contingencies of Value," in *Critical Inquiry*, 10 (1983), 1–35.

4. For an admirable reading of the poem and an able review of the critical debate over the moral perspective "readers" are to take on the poem, see Clark Hulse, *Metamorphic Verse: The Elizabethan Minor Epic* (Princeton: Princeton Univ. Press, 1981), pp. 147–148. In n.7, Hulse refers to "the new orthodoxy of an ambivalent *Venus and Adonis*," and argues that "such pluralism is perfectly consonant with an informed understanding of Renaissance poetics." The present paper intends to advance such a reading.

5. Neil Hertz, "Medusa's Head: Male Hysteria under Political Pressure," *Representations*, 4 (1983), 27–54, and Gallagher, Fineman, Hertz, "More about 'Medusa's Head,'" 55–71.

6. In a series of articles, Louis Adrian Montrose has been analyzing the uses of power by Queen Elizabeth. See, for example, "'Eliza, Queene of Shepheardes,' and the Pastoral of Power," *ELR*, 10 (1980), 153–82.

For an important collection of essays using a historical materialist approach to Shakespeare, see Jonathan Dollimore and Alan Sinfield, eds., *Political Shakespeare: New Essays in Cultural Materialism* (Manchester: Manchester Univ. Press, 1985). In particular, see Kathleen McLuskie, "The Patriarchal Bard; Feminist Criticism and Shakespeare: *King Lear* and *Measure for Measure*," pp. 88–108.

7. Lawrence Stone, "The Rise of the Nuclear Family in Early Modern England: The Patriarchal Stage," in Charles E. Rosenberg, ed., *The Family in History* (Phila-

delphia: Univ. of Pennsylvania Press, 1975).

8. *The Riverside Shakespeare,* p. 1704.

9. Frank Whigham, *Ambition and Privilege: The Social Tropes of Elizabethan Courtesy Theory* (Berkeley: Univ. of California Press, 1984). The discussion of *paradiastole* begins on p. 40. This book illuminates the context for the poem. Whigham's approach also provides an opportunity for feminist criticism, since he declares in note 36 to p. 22, "my concern in this book is with courtesy for *men* at court. I have chosen to bracket for the moment issues regarding courtesy and women, whose situations were distinctly different, both in life and in the literature, owing to complex interactions of social and gender codes. I hope to treat these matters elsewhere." This essay begins, I hope, to treat such matters.

10. In her helpful comments on an early version of this paper, Heather Dubrow cites John Donne's "The Apparition": "he, whose thou art then, being try'd before, / Will, if thou stirre, or pinch to wake him, thinke / Thou call'st for more, / And in false sleepe will from thee shrinke."

VENUS AND ADONIS: AN EARLY ACCOUNT OF SEXUAL HARASSMENT

Joseph Wortis, M.D.

Venus and Adonis, Shakespeare's first published poem, based on Ovid, appeared in 1593, and depicts the sexual pursuit of the young hunter Adonis by Venus, the goddess of love. It is made clear at the outset that handsome Adonis has no interest in sex ("love he laughed to scorn"), but it is made equally clear that Venus has designs, "and like a bold suitor 'gins to woo him." She butters him up with all kinds of inane flatteries, and then tells the boy she'd like to smother him with kisses. With insatiable lust she tries to knock him from his horse—which embarrasses him enormously without enhancing his interest. She makes a brave attempt to trumpet all her assets to the youth ("Thou canst not see one wrinkle in my brow"), to no avail. Adonis says, in effect, "Go 'way, it's getting hot." She, in turn, taunts him as a lifeless wimp who ought to propagate. He declares her urgency will get her nowhere, and makes him like her worse and worse. He finally packs her off, and leaves for the hunt (which ends up tragically, but that is another story).

We have here an early account of sexual harassment, presented as part of the give and take of love's vicissitudes, but with no hint that this kind of aggressive pursuit is improper or immoral. Since we do not know Adonis' exact age (Shakespeare's Juliet was only 13) we cannot tell if Venus risked statutory rape. Adonis, the callow youth, was no match for Venus, who was mature, confident, competent, and (as classically depicted) pretty hefty. Moreover, she had the authority of a goddess.

Similar, but less athletic, sexual harassment, more typically directed at women,[1] goes on constantly everywhere and is a result of unequal power regardless of the setting. It may reflect inequality in authority, physical

Reprinted by permission of Elsevier Science, Inc., from *Biological Psychiatry* 5 (1994), pp. 293–94. Copyright © 1994 by the Society of Biological Psychiatry.

strength, gender dominance, income, social position, ethnic status, or age. The boss who dates his secretary is taking advantage of his position, even if the secretary enjoys the experience and benefits from it. The same applies to intimate doctor-patient relationships. Though distinctions can be made between duress, persuasion, and temptation, there are twilight areas. The victim may be the seducer: it is often hard to know. In spite of all the emphasis on romantic love, most marriages in the world have little to do with romance, and the equivalent of rape may occur within a marriage. The practices are ancient, but feminine protest has served to publicize and redirect attention to the problem.

Because of the privacy of the events, legal recourse is difficult and expensive; many charges are not substantiated. A verdict of guilty can secure some redress, but it might be more effective if the courts encouraged class action. It is proper to seek justice, but the cases adjudicated in the courts are only samplings of a wider problem. The hypocritical morality and social fervor that suffuse the area obscure the basic issues. Self-serving behavior at the expense of others is not taboo in our society. Overlording power tends to corrupt: when power sits at the apex, and filters down through an hierarchical structure, there will always be abuses in sex behavior and in other spheres. Each kind of abuse has its own particular history and needs its special defenders. The isolated complainant is vulnerable to retaliation. When it concerns sex, the organized defense by some women's groups (or by trade unions) has had some good results, but the real remedy lies in more general empowerment of the people below, whose day may dawn in the unforeseeable future.

As an afterthought, and in fairness, it should be acknowledged that Zeus, unlike Venus, engaged in innumerable amours and capricious adventures, bore illegitimate children, and made of a mockery of his supposed exemplary marriage to Hera.

NOTES

1. Charney, D.A., Russell, R. C. (1994): An overview of sexual harassment. *Am. J. Psychiatry* 151:10–17.

LOVE AS TROMPE-L'OEIL

TAXONOMIES OF DESIRE IN VENUS AND ADONIS

Catherine Belsey

I

The painter Zeuxis excelled in the art of trompe-l'oeil, a mode of painting that is capable of deceiving the eye by its simulation of nature. Zeuxis portrayed grapes with such success that birds flew toward his picture. His younger rival, Parrhasius, however, challenged Zeuxis to a competition to decide which painter's work was more true to life. Parrhasius won—by depicting a curtain so convincing that Zeuxis begged him to draw it and reveal the picture behind.[1] Jacques Lacan, in his seminar "Of the Gaze as *Objet Petu a,*" makes a distinction between the two pictures: only the curtain that Parrhasius painted is a true trompe-l'oeil, because its effect depends on what is missing, the absence of a secret concealed behind the paint. For Lacan it is not deception alone that defines the trompe-l'oeil: on the contrary, its determining characteristic is the promise of a presence that it fails to deliver. Trompe-l'oeil tantalizes.

At a critical moment in Shakespeare's *Venus and Adonis,* when the goddess has succeeded in maneuvering her reluctant suitor into a promising physical position, but without the consequence she seeks, the text compares Adonis to the painting by Zeuxis:

> Even so poor birds deceiv'd with painted grapes
> Do surfeit by the eye and pine the maw:
> Even so she languisheth in her mishaps,
> As those poor birds that helpless berries saw.
> The warm effects which she in him finds missing
> She seeks to kindle with continual kissing.
>
> (ll. 601–6)[2]

Reprinted by permission of *Shakespeare Quarterly* and Catherine Belsey from *Shakespeare Quarterly* 46 (Fall 1995), pp. 257–76.

But in Shakespeare's poem the grapes also represent a trompe-l'oeil in accordance with Lacan's definition. Deceptively promising oral gratification, the enticing picture of the grapes yields no pleasure for the stomach. In the same way, despite her best efforts, Venus finds that the provocative outward image of Adonis conceals nothing to her purpose: his beauty evokes a longing, which remains unsatisfied, for his desire—or for its phallic signifier.

In painting, deceit gives pleasure. "What is it," Lacan asks, "that attracts and satisfies us in *trompe-l'oeil?* When is it that it captures our attention and delights us?" He proposes that the trompe-l'oeil pleases by presenting the appearance of a three-dimensional object which we go on to recognize as exactly that: no more than an appearance, painted in two dimensions. In order to enjoy the trompe-l'oeil, we have to be convinced by it in the first instance and then to shift our gaze so that, seeing the object resolve itself into lines on a canvas, we are no longer convinced; we have to be deceived—and then to acknowledge our own deception. The gap between these two moments is the place, Lacan affirms, of the *objet a,* the lost object in the inextricable real, the cause of desire.[3] That which delights in art—the civilizing, sublimated product of the drive—is experienced in psychosexual life as a lack, the $-\phi$ (minus *phi*), a source of indestructible longing.

The type of the desiring subject according to classical myth was Tantalus in the underworld, unable to reach the fruit that would allay his insatiable thirst. Shakespeare's Venus outdoes Tantalus in frustration, however, when she holds Adonis in her arms but can elicit no response. "That worse than Tantalus' is her annoy, / To clip Elizium and to lack her joy" (ll. 599–600). The desire of Adonis is not subject to her control: love cannot be commanded. The third dimension she wants is missing, and the absence she encounters serves only to intensify her longing.

In the event, nothing very much happens in this narrative of desire. Tantal-ized as she is, Venus cajoles and entreats. Adonis resists, rejects, and finally escapes her; he is killed by the boar, and Venus laments. The poem, exceptionally popular in its own period,[4] prompts in the reader a desire for action that it fails to gratify. Meanwhile, the critical tradition in its turn, tantalized by the poem's lack of closure, has sought to make something happen, at least at the thematic level, by locating a moral center that would furnish the work with a final meaning, a conclusion, a definitive statement. It is possible, however, to read the text itself as a kind of trompe-l'oeil, moving undecidably between modes of address and sustaining the desire of the reader in the process. I propose that it is precisely in its lack of closure that Shakespeare's poem may be read as marking a specific moment in the cultural history of love. A literary trompe-l'oeil, a text of and about desire, *Venus and Adonis* promises a definitive account of love but at the same time withholds the finality that such a promise might lead us to expect. Instead, it tantalizes and, in so doing, throws into relief the difference between its historical moment and our own.

II

Venus and Adonis is a poetic record of the originating moment of desire. In Shakespeare's narrative poem the goddess of love, traditional object of all men's admiration, unexpectedly appears as a desiring subject, herself at the mercy of an intractable passion. Led by experience to expect the devotion of others and accustomed to master, imprison, and enslave her lovers (ll. 101–12), Venus is here reduced to the role of suitor (l. 6), overpowered by another's beauty and subject in her turn to indifference and disdain. The protagonist of the story thus comes to represent what the text identifies as a personification of desire itself, which is by definition unsatisfied: "She's love, she loves, and yet she is not lov'd" (l. 610). Lost, ironically, in the emotion she herself traditionally promotes, a subjection that "makes young men thrall, and old men dote" (l. 837), the queen of love has now become love's helpless victim, in her "own law forlorn" (l. 251). The goddess of love stoops—and fails to conquer.

Because she cannot command the desire of Adonis, or even protect his life, Venus finally delivers, over his mutilated body, a curse on the emotion that subjects her, condemning love itself to perpetual dissatisfaction and despair:

> Since thou art dead, lo here I prophesy,
> Sorrow on love hereafter shall attend:
> It shall be waited on with jealousy,
> Find sweet beginning, but unsavoury end;
> Ne'er settled equally, but high or low,
> That all love's pleasure shall not match his woe.
>
> (ll. 1135–40)

Though Venus has been unable to prevail upon her unwilling lover, she has authority, nevertheless, as the personification of love, to define the condition she both represents and shares. The goddess's words thus summarize her own story and at the same time "explain" proleptically the tragic endings of those romances that constituted the classic love stories of Shakespeare's period: Troilus and Cressida, Pyramus and Thisbe, Dido and

Aeneas. As a result of Love's distress, suffering and loss have become the destiny of lovers.

All myth can be read as explanatory, a record of how things came to be the way they are: a sexual relation between the sky and the earth generates life; the story of the Fall explains the presence of evil in the world. *Venus and Adonis* is also a myth of origins. In this respect it is, of course, true to its source. Ovid's *Metamorphoses* records the origins of things and accounts in the process for their present character.[5] The long narrative poem begins with the creation of the world, Jupiter's disappointment in the human beings he has made, and the consequent flood, from which only Deucalion and Pyrrha are saved. Under divine instruction, the couple throw stones over their shoulders and thereby generate a new race of human beings. The "stoniness" of their origins explains the hardy nature of the Romans as well as their capacity for work.[6] More specific in its reference, the story of Daphne, which follows that of Deucalion and Pyrrha, accounts for the sacred character of the laurel. There was a time when Apollo was happy to wreathe his forehead with the leaves of any tree, but when Daphne eludes him, he feels a special warmth for the laurel she becomes and declares that from now on it will be the source of garlands for him and, ironically, for Roman generals returning in triumph.[7] Later in Book 1, Argus asks how the reed pipe came to be invented, and Mercury responds by telling him the story of Pan and Syrinx.[8] An assembly of classical narratives, the *Metamorphoses* retains the mythic character of much of the material it so elegantly rewrites.

The stories from this familiar grammar-school text[9] which were most widely reproduced, elaborated, and imitated in the Renaissance concern the quest for a prohibited sexual pleasure either frustrated or compensated by metamorphosis: Daphne and Syrinx saved from rape in the nick of time; Narcissus unable to satisfy the erotic impulse his own image arouses and transformed into a flower. If desire is a quest for presence, for the full (imaginary, impossible) presence of the beloved to the lover, and to the degree that its perpetuation is an effect of presence deferred, these Ovidian narratives surely constitute perfect fables of desire. Daphne in flight, still out of reach, represents an emblem of the condition that subsists on the basis that possession eludes it; Daphne immobilized, meanwhile, putting down roots, fixed, remains the figure of unfulfilled desire, precisely because she is no longer Daphne. What Apollo now holds is not the nymph he wanted, though he loves the laurel and takes it for his tree.

In the case of Ovid's Venus and Adonis, presence is doubly deferred, gratification doubly displaced. The mythic story is explanatory, an account of the origin of the annual Adonia. This festival, the rite of Adonis, appears to have taken place in spring or summer all over the Mediterranean region.[10] It seems that on the first day of the Adonia, the reciprocal love of Venus and Adonis was celebrated, with ripe fruit and sweet cakes, in the presence of their images as lovers, while on the second, the body of the hero was ritually consigned to the waves with bitter lamentation.[11] Love and death were thus brought into close conjunction, the intensity of desire affirmed by the emphasis on its transience.

Ovid's version of the story begins with the passing of time and the swift succession of the years; it ends with the short-lived anemone.[12] The flower that springs from the blood of Adonis is explicitly identified as a reminder of Venus's grief, her longing for the lost presence; but by insisting on its ephemeral character, the text presents the flower itself as the emblem of yet another absence. Venus promises that the metamorphosis she brings about will constitute an everlasting memorial, but it is at once made clear that this is to be no more than an annually recurring image, and an image that is in turn especially fleeting, since the winds for which it is named so easily destroy it. In this way Ovid's lyrical narrative progressively withdraws the compensating presence it promises. The flower—beautiful, fragile, mutable, and all that remains of a youth who became an object of desire for the goddess of love—thus appears in its elusiveness the quintessential signifier of desire itself. Nor is it named: even the identity of the windflower is deferred for the reader, the unspecified answer to a kind of riddle constructed by the text.[13]

Shakespeare's Venus, however, unlike Ovid's we are to assume, never succeeds in eliciting the desire of Adonis. All she gets is the flower; but in Shakespeare's poem she does possess it, indeed, cradles it in her breast next to her throbbing heart, and kisses it (ll. 1173, 1185–86, and 1188). And yet its destiny there, she recognizes, is to wither, and in Shakespeare's version there is no mention even of its annual reappearance. What the Renaissance in general and this text in particular adopt from Ovid is above all the notion of erotic metamorphosis itself: the object the lover finally possesses is not the object of desire but something else, a substitute, a stand-in. At the moment when the desiring subject takes possession of the object, something slips away, eludes the lover's grasp, and is lost.

But if Ovid's tale of Venus and Adonis offers absence as the recurring figure of desire, Shakespeare's poem surpasses its source, in audacity as well as length, by setting out to explain the origin of desire in its entirety. Love, we are invited to understand, was once reciprocal, which is to say that its conquest was absolute: Mars, stern god of war, became Venus's prisoner and learned to be a lover (ll. 97–114). But Venus's new love is unrequited: now the goddess is "Sick-thoughted" and Adonis "sullen" (ll. 5 and 75). When Adonis's insistence on hunting the boar brings his death and her irretrievable loss, Venus decrees that henceforth love will always be anarchic in character:

> It shall suspect where is no cause of fear,
> It shall not fear where it should most mistrust;
> It shall be merciful, and too severe,
> And most deceiving when it seems most just;
>> Perverse it shall be, where it shows most toward;
>> Put fear to valour, courage to the coward.
>>> (ll. 1153–58)

Her words are necessarily authoritative. As the personification of love, Venus does no more here than proclaim her own nature. Shakespeare's myth of origins is also a definition of love.

III

A definition, however, ought surely to be definitive, a characteristic account of a representative state of affairs. And yet this narrative is hardly a typical love story. By conventional standards the gender roles of the central figures are disconcertingly reversed; meanwhile, the genre of the narrative, now lyrical, now bordering on farce, seems oddly unresolved. As a result, love itself appears at one moment grossly material and at another delicately insubstantial, no more than airy nothing. Is there, then, a definition here or only a bravura display of a range of skills on the part of a young and ambitious poet, in a text as anarchic as the emotion its central figure both demonstrates and defines?

First, gender. There can be little doubt that Elizabethan heroines, whether tragic or comic, whether Juliet or Rosalind, are permitted to be more outspoken in love than their Victorian counterparts. Even so, the voluble and unremitting pursuit of a coy young man by a relentless goddess wildly exceeds romantic convention. As is commonly noted, it is "Rose-cheek'd Adonis" (l. 3), with his white hands (ll. 362–64) and his voice like a mermaid's (l. 429), who blushes and pouts (l. 33), while Venus pulls him off his horse and tucks him under her arm (ll. 30–32). The "tender boy" (l. 32) is inert, like a bird in a net (l. 67), but Venus resembles an eagle (l. 55). And in case the reader should forget how these things are traditionally done, the poem gives us horses that behave in a much more predictable manner.

Adonis's coursers neighing and bounding imperiously at the sight of the jennet (l. 265) and majestically asserting control (l. 270). The text makes witty capital out of the scandal it creates when Venus draws explicit attention to the role reversal. Adonis is, she tells him, "'more lovely than a man'" (l. 9); if only, she sighs, things were the other way round: "'Would thou wert as I am, and I a man'" (l. 369).[14]

But palpably she is not, and the result is a good deal of slightly salacious comedy at the level of the poem's action, or rather lack of action: "Backward she push'd him, as she would be thrust, / And govern'd him in strength, though not in lust" (ll. 41–42). Venus pins Adonis to the ground as she kisses him goodnight, "And glutton-like she feeds, yet never filleth" (l. 548). The exhausted Adonis eventually ceases to struggle. "While she takes all she can, not all she listeth [i.e., wants]" (l. 564). A good joke is evidently worth repeating. Even when their physical positions are reversed, the text explains, the case of Venus remains hopeless:

> Now is she in the very lists of love,
> Her champion mounted for the hot encounter.
> All is imaginary she doth prove;
> He will not manage her, although he mount her.
>
> (ll. 595–98)

At the same time, however, *Venus and Adonis* is lyrical about the passion it also presents as absurd and, at Adonis's death, is unaffectedly elegiac in its lament for perfection destroyed:

> Alas, poor world, what treasure hast thou lost!
> What face remains alive that's worth the viewing?
> What tongue is music now? what canst thou boast
> Of things long since, or any thing ensuing?
>   The flowers are sweet, their colours fresh and trim
>   But true sweet beauty liv'd and died with him.
>
> (ll. 1075–80)

Throughout the text one mode of address displaces another with remarkable agility. For earlier generations of critics the resulting question of genre represented the central critical problem of the poem. Was it primarily comic, or mainly tragic, or possibly satirical?[15] Or was it simply so confused in its rapid shifts from high camp to low mimetic that it was impossible to make any real sense of it at all?[16] Despite stylistic and thematic debts to the

Metamorphoses, the text is no mere imitation of Ovid's disengaged and economical narrative; neither is it a generic copy of any existing Elizabethan text, regardless of parallels with Lodge's *Glaucus and Scilla.* In terms of poetic decorum, this tragical-comical-pastoral (-mythical) love story defies the literary classifications of its period.

Where, then, in all this indeterminacy, is any consistent definition of love to be found? Is passion no more than the crude appetite of an overheated, "love-sick queen" (or quean [l. 175])? Or is it, conversely, the effect of a delicate appeal to the finest senses?

> Bid me discourse, I will enchant thine ear.
> Or like a fairy trip upon the green,
> Or like a nymph, with long dishevell'd hair
> Dance on the sands, and yet no footing seen.
> Love is a spirit all compact of fire,
> Not gross to sink, but light, and will aspire.
>
> (ll. 145–50)

What exactly is the significance of the personification of love as a goddess who leaves no imprint on the sand, makes no dent in a bank of primroses, and has no impact on her beloved either? Is her reiterated lightness (ll. 151–52, 155, and 1192) an indication of lyric grace or vacuous triviality? What is the character of the desire that finds its inaugural moment in this myth of origins?

IV

At one place the poem makes what appears to be a categorical statement, and the text seems, indeed, definitive. Adonis is speaking. He insists that Venus' desire is not love at all but rather its promiscuous, irrational, destructive simulacrum, lust (ll. 789–98). The goddess has misrepresented the true nature of her desire: "'Call it not love, for love to heaven is fled, / since sweating lust on earth usurp'd his name'" (ll. 793–94). And Adonis undertakes to disentangle the two, specifying each as the antithesis of the other:

> Love comforteth like sunshine after rain,
> But lust's effect is tempest after sun;
> Love's gentle spring doth always fresh remain,
> Lust's winter comes ere summer half be done;
> Love surfeits not, lust like a glutton dies;
> Love is all truth, lust full of forged lies.
>
> (ll. 799–804)

A grateful critical tradition, eager to regulate the wayward textuality of the poem by locating within it a clear thematic statement, the expression of an *author*itative design, has tended to reproduce Adonis' values as the key to the moral truth of the text.

The tradition goes back at least to Coleridge, who was relaxed about the identification of Venus with lust, arguing that although the poem was about concupiscence, it was not morally dangerous because Shakespeare had directed the reader's attention beyond "the animal impulse itself" to the images and circumstances in which it is presented.[17] A century later, however, Lu Emily Pearson emphasized how much was at stake in the antithesis Adonis had affirmed:

> Venus is shown as the destructive agent of sensual love; Adonis, as reason in love. The one sullies whatever it touches; the other honors and makes it beautiful. The one is false and evil; the other is all truth, all good. Reason in love, truth, beauty—these are the weapons with which lust must be met, or the ideals of man must go down in defeat before the appetites.[18]

Pearson's moral vehemence sounds archaic now, but what surprises is the degree to which Adonis's condemnation of Venus and lust has survived the sexual revolution of the 1960s. Heather Dubrow is much kinder than Pearson, but the term *lust* reappears in her account, however softened by the attribution to Venus of motherliness: "Though lust is Venus' primary motive, it is by no means her only one and by no means an adequate label for her behavior; tender maternal love is commingled with her lust. . . ."[19] Male critics, meanwhile, are relentless: according to one writer who echoes the view of his fellows, Shakespeare "casts Venus as a frenzied older woman driven by comic lust for a very young man barely emerging from boyhood."[20] And although the poem has nothing to say about her age except that her beauty is perfect and annually renewed (ll. 133–34), the goddess's supposed decline has nonetheless proved explanatory for some male readers: "Her vulnerability is that of the older woman, desperate to renew her youth in the arms of a young lover."[21] Even a critic who allows that Venus represents "the drastically imperfect amalgam of lust and caring that is likely to be found in all lovers" finds it necessary to point out that "the suffocating, devouring lust of Venus is too 'vicious' (in both the antique and the modern senses) to escape censure."[22] In this way criticism provides itself with a definitive signified, a univocal thematic "message" beyond the undecidabilities of the text, beyond, that is to say, the heterogeneity of its mode of address.[23]

This critical reiteration of the taxonomy of desire that Adonis so confidently delivers is problematic, however, because it inevitably attributes the central affirmation of the poem to a hero who is, as the text repeatedly reminds us and the plot of the story insists, so young that he knows nothing of love (ll. 127–28, 409, and 806). It is, of course, not inconceivable that Adonis could be speaking with preternatural wisdom: Helena in *A Midsummer Night's Dream* speaks of love with an insight that her role in the story might not lead us to expect (1.1.232–39).[24] But if Helena speaks "out of character" here, her observations are confirmed, in the absence of a controlling narrative voice, by the events of the play. The narrative voice in *Venus and Adonis,* however, does not reproduce the neat antitheses the hero enunciates. On the contrary, while Adonis urges Venus to call it not love but lust, the text names desire both love and lust with apparent indifference:

> The studded bridle on a ragged bough
> Nimbly she fastens—O how quick is *love!*—
> The steed is stalled up, and even now
> To tie the rider she begins to prove:
>> Backward she push'd him, as she would be thrust,
>> And govern'd him in strength, though not in *lust.*
>>> (ll. 37–42 [emphasis added])

Meanwhile, the steed in question leaps, neighs, and bounds (l. 265) in response to a jennet identified as his "love" throughout (ll. 287, 307, and 317). The animal's condition is variously "love" and "desire" (ll. 311 and 276). As for Venus, "desire doth lend her force" (l. 29); her language is "lustful" (l. 47); still, "she cannot chose but love" (l. 79). In her case "careless lust stirs up a desperate courage," but "love," too, lacks moral scruples and picks locks to get at beauty (ll. 556 and 576). Venus, of course, calls it love, but the text calls *her* "love" the moment Adonis has completed his disquisition:

> With this, he breaketh from the sweet embrace
> Of those fair arms which bound him to her breast,
> And homeward through the dark laund runs apace;
> Leaves love upon her back deeply distress'd.
>> (ll. 811–14)

It is not obvious that one set of terms is used ironically: indeed, irony is precisely the quality that the polyphony of the text renders elusive. The poem seems to invest with a certain indeterminacy the terms Adonis so categorically distinguishes.

In this respect the narrative voice is characteristic of its historical moment. In the early modern period *love* and *lust* are not consistently used as antitheses: on the contrary, both terms are synonyms for desire, each innocent or reprobate according to the context, and occurring interchangeably without apparent irony. The emergence of a radical distinction between the two—a process inadvertently encouraged, as it turns out, by the voice of Adonis—marks a moment in the cultural history of desire which, as modern criticism unwittingly reveals, has proved formative for our own cultural norms and values.

In the mid-sixteenth century William Baldwin published *A treatise of Morall Phylosophie,* a collection of precepts derived from a range of classical authorities, each duly named in the margins of the page. The work was exceptionally popular: twenty-four editions appeared between 1547 and about 1640. The earliest editions allow a certain overlap between the categories of love and lust: indeed, in 1550 the chapter heading "Of the worlde, the loue, and pleasures therof" appears in "The Table" as "Of the worlde, the lustes, and pleasures therof."[25] While this might be no more than a printer's error, we should note that Baldwin places "Loue, luste, and lecherye" together in a single short chapter.[26] The love in question is mainly *caritas,* which has no sexual connotations, except that in one instance he defines "Repentaunce" as "the ende of fylthy loue," where the adjective has the effect of aligning love with the sin of lechery. At the same time, "Luste is a lordlye and disobedient thynge," whereas, "Dishonor, shame, euell ende and damnacion, wayte upon lecherie, and all other like vyces."[27] The implication seems to be that lust is a powerful impulse but in itself morally neutral, so that, like the will, it needs to be brought under control in the interests of virtue, while lechery is by definition wicked.

Later editions of the *Treatise* are modified by the intervention of Thomas Paulfreyman, who repeatedly edited and enlarged Baldwin's text. By 1564 *love* has been removed from the chapter heading and from the table of contents. But if this simplifies the position in respect of love, lust remains as equivocal as before. Appropriately qualified, it evidently belongs with lechery, as in "Flie lecherous lusts" or "fired to the filthy luste of lecherie."[28] On the other hand, in a different context it might equally well be morally neutral: "Enforce thy self to refraine thine euill lustes and folow the good: For the good mortifieth and destroieth the euill."[29] Evidently at this moment *lust* is not necessarily to be condemned out of hand.

In 1594, a year or more after the publication of *Venus and Adonis,*

Thomas Bowes issued an English translation of Pierre de la Primaudaye's *Academie Francoise*. There is in Bowes' translation some uncertainty about the moral implications of lust: "I will begin then with the affection of loue, which is a motion whereby the heart lusteth *[appete]* after that which is good. . . ."[30] Almost immediately, however, a tentative moral distinction begins to appear. The will is drawn to what is good and desires to embrace it, "and this loue is called *Cupiditie, Lusting*, or *Coueting [cupidité, ou concupiscence, ou convoitise].*" But this love is not "true love," which is the love of the good for itself and not for the sake of possession.[31] Here lust is evidently not to be endorsed since it is proprietary, but at the same time, it has no specifically sexual connotations; as in Baldwin, it is possible to lust after the good.

In the longer term, however, a change was taking place. During the course of the sixteenth century, *lust* was to lose its innocence, or at least its potential innocence, since a reprobate meaning was always available. Understood in the Middle Ages as delight, pleasure, desire, or sinful passion, according to context, by the mid-seventeenth century the term had acquired a primary sexual and strongly pejorative meaning. Coverdale's version of Numbers 14:8, "Yf the Lorde haue lust vnto us," was evidently acceptable in 1535; but in the Authorized Version of 1611, the phrase appeared as "If the Lord delight in us."[32] In 1533 the translator of the popular *Enchiridion* of Erasmus thought it appropriate to render *libido* as "bodyly luste," "the luste of the body," "lechery," "fylthy lust," or "unclenly lustes."[33] *Lust* alone was evidently considered not specific enough:[34] a qualifier of some sort was necessary to do justice to a condition in which human beings, God's handiwork, are reduced to "fylthy swyne / to gotes / to dogges / and of all brute beestes / unto ye most brute," and which, in Erasmus's humanist analysis, wastes time, destroys health, hastens old age, and (perhaps worst of all) obliterates the use of reason.[35] Just over 150 years later, a new translation of the *Enchiridion* was published as *A Manual for a Christian Soldier*. Here the qualifying words and phrases have disappeared, and *libido* is translated simply as "lust." Without in any way softening the value judgments inscribed in Erasmus's text, the version of 1687 leaves it to "lust" alone to do the work of defining a condition that reduces human beings to the level of beasts.[36] (Twentieth-century translators also tend to render *libido* as "lust.")[37]

This handful of examples, most of them taken from repositories of popular morality, merely amplifies what the *OED* already indicates: in the course of the early modern period, with whatever advances and reversals, *lust* gradually became exclusively sexual and specifically reprobate. But the dictionary, which defines individual words in isolation, on the assumption that they are "full" of their own meanings, does not record the network of differences which constitutes a taxonomy. The shifting meaning of *lust* depends, at least in part, on the emergent difference between *lust* and *love*. Predictably, therefore, in this period of change the connotations of *love* are no less problematic. The name of a condition that may be divine, purely social, romantic, or exclusively sexual, but which is in all these cases intense, leads to semantic indeterminacies and gives rise to anxieties in the process. Sir Thomas More, for example, was deeply critical of William Tyndale because Tyndale translated the biblical "charity" as "love." The problem, from More's Christian humanist point of view, is that *love* carries the wrong connotations unless it is appropriately qualified by an adjective that distinguishes between the divine and the sexual, since sexual love is not, of course, highly valued.[38] Tyndale, however, to More's disgust, consistently repudiates the adjective:

> If he called charitie sometyme by the bare name of loue: I wold not stick therat. But now wheras charite signifieth in english mens eares, not euery common loue, but a good vertuous & wel ordred loue, he ... wyl studiously flee fro ye name of good loue, & alway speke of loue, & alway leaue out good.[39]

The problem, as More identifies it, is that Tyndale's practice is motivated by the Lutheran project of elevating faith at the expense of charity. Because their theology makes salvation a question of faith and not good works, the Reformers deliberately conflate charity with the merely erotic love that exists between a man and his paramour:

> and therfore he chaungeth ye name of holy vertuous affeccion, into ye bare name of loue comen to the vertuous loue that man beareth to god, and to the lewde loue that is betwene flecke & his make.[40]

While poetry and romance idealize love, humanist morality holds it in contempt. Erasmus has no greater patience than does his friend More with sexual love *(amor)*, and he includes it under the heading of *libido* in the *Enchiridion*. Love is just as absurd and just as reductive as all erotic desire:

> Set before thyne eyen howe ungoodly it is / howe altogyder a mad thing to loue / to waxe pale / to be made leane / to wepe / to flatter / and shamfully to submyt thy selfe unto a stynkyng harlot most fylthy and rotten / to gape & synge all nyght at her chambre wyndowe / to

be made to the lure & be obedyent at a becke / nor dare do any thing except she nod or wagge her heed / to suffre a folysshe woman to reigne ouer the / to chyde the: to lay unkyndnesse one agaynst ye other to fall out / to be made at one agayne / to gyue thy selfe wyllynge unto a queene / that she myght mocke / k[n]ocke / mangle and spolye the. Where is I beseche the amonge all these thynges the name of a man? Where is thy berde? Where is that noble mynde created unto moste beautyfull and noble?[41]

In view of our own taxonomies, it is tempting to speculate on the meaning of *love* in this instance. The emotions described are romantic, even Petrarchan. "Harlot," however, is not appropriate in the context of romantic love; nor, of course, is violence, which evokes the fabliau genre rather than romance. But the point, presumably, is that Erasmus does not distinguish among them: all passion is degrading.

The humiliating harlot reappears in the first part of *The French academie;* evidently she had entered into the European popular consciousness, along with the corresponding value judgment on love. "True" love, by contrast, is not sexual:

> For we see some men so bewitched with a harlot, that if neede bee, and shee command it, they will hazard their honour and credit, and oftentimes make themselues an example to a whole countrey vpon an open scaffold. And then they labour to couer their folly with this goodly name of *Loue,* which is better tearmed [of] *Euripides* by the name of *Fury* and madnesse in men. For true and good loue, which is the fountaine of friendship, is alwaies grounded vpon vertue, and tendeth to that end: but this slipperie and loose loue, is a desire founded vpon . . . the opinion of a *Good,* which indeede is a most pernitious euill.[42]

It is not clear that the moralists commonly recognize a radical difference between love and lust, or even between love and lechery. As late as 1616, Thomas Gainsford's commonplace book *The Rich Cabinet* demonstrates that there was still some uncertainty about whether these two categories were antithetical or synonymous. Gainsford at first sets up a contrast between the two, but this gradually gives way to similarity. His observations are divided under topics and are listed alphabetically. "Love" therefore comes immediately after "Lechery." If this is simply a trick of the alphabet, Gainsford nonetheless exploits its effect by setting up love initially as the contrary of lechery. While lechery reduces human beings to the level of beasts and generally performs much as love does in Erasmus, love in Gainsford at first uplifts and ennobles. But the simple opposition does not hold for long. Gradually there is a reversion to type, as it emerges that love is irrational, frivolous, a form of madness, like a monster, and then "libidinous and luxurious like a Goat."[43] Eventually all the old commonplaces are reaffirmed, and any clear distinction between love and lechery can no longer be detected: "Love doth trouble wit, hinder Art, hurt nature, disgrace reason, lose time, spoile substance, crosse wisedome, serue folly, weaken strength, submit to beautie, and abase honour."[44] Meanwhile, it is worth noting, lechery is a kind of love and a form of lust, the differences once again specified only by the appropriate adjectives: "Lechery is in plaine tearmes extreame lust, vnlawfull loue, brutish desires, beastlie wantonnesse, and the itch or scab of old concupiscence."[45]

VI

Evidently, the terms *love* and *lust* were changing in relation to one another: a new system of differences, which is to say a new taxonomy, was in the process of construction. But there is no single moment of transformation: the vocabulary of the period is marked by attempts at policing the language on the one hand and by constant slippages on the other. While the sharp and unconditional antitheses of Adonis are evidently one option in the 1590s, the indeterminacies of the narrative voice in Shakespeare's poem are another and were probably a more familiar practice in the period. Critics with a strong sense of cultural history, who have nevertheless wanted to identify Adonis as the conscience of the text, have been driven to invoke Neoplatonism, somewhat incongruously, as the moral framework of this racy, salacious Ovidian narrative.[46]

As for Venus herself, she was capable of signifying a whole range of meanings. While the Neoplatonists were anxious to distinguish the heavenly from the earthly Venus, others were content to acknowledge her heterogeneity. Richard Linche's *The Fovntaine of Ancient Fiction,* an early instance of cultural history, derived from Vincenzo Cartari's mid-sixteenth-century Italian book on images of the gods of the ancients, explained to English readers why there were so many classical statues and pictures of the goddess. The reason was that she represented "several natures and conditions," from lechery to holy matrimony:

> According therfore to the opinion of the Poets, Venus was taken to
> be the goddesse of wantonnes & amorous delights, as that she inspired
> into the minds of men, libidinous desires, and lustfull appetites, &

with whose power & assistance they attained the effect of their lose concupiscence: whervpon also they entermed her the mother of loue, because that without a certaine loue and simpathie of affections, those desires are sildome acomplished. And vnto hir they ascribe the care and charge of marriages and holie wedlockes. . . .[47]

Linche does not reveal how anomalous he finds this range of natures and conditions in 1599.

But history was on the side of Adonis. In 1615, more than twenty years after the poem was first printed,[48] Alexander Niccholes cites Adonis, without naming him, as a proper authority on the contrast between love and lust. Niccholes quotes Shakespeare's text anonymously with two minor variations, both well within the range of likely errors in transmission. Love and lust are contraries, Niccholes declares, and in support of this position, he urges, "one thus writeth":

> Loue comforteth like sunne-shine after raine,
> But lusts effect is tempest after sunne.
> Loves golden spring doth euer fresh remaine,
> Lusts winter comes ere summer halfe be done.[49]

In the account Niccholes gives, lust is everything that love is not, so that love is defined by the exclusion of its differentiating opposite. Lust is what does not last, for example, and does not discriminate its objects. It is also impoverished, lacking. Niccholes turns Adonis's "glutton" (l. 803) into a beggar: "In Loue there is no lacke, in Lust there is the greatest penury, for though it be cloyed with too much, it pines for want. . . ." Moreover, lust destroys the domestic enclave that love creates: "the one, most commonly, burnes downe the house that the other would build up."[50] The context of this sequence of antitheses is a treatise giving advice on how to achieve the great blessing of conjugal happiness, *A Discourse, of Marriage and Wiving: and of The greatest Mystery therein contained: How to choose a good Wife from a bad*. The book represents an argument, the title page assures its readers, "Of the dearest vse, but the deepest cunning that man may erre in: which is, to cut by a Thrid [i.e., thread] betweene the greatest Good or euill in the world."

As Niccholes' text indicates, the realignment of love and lust is motivated by the newfound valorization of marriage in the course of the century following the Reformation rejection of the celibate ideal. In this context the radical distinction between love and lust is a critical issue. "Lvst," Niccholes affirms, is "the most potent match-maker in all Marriages under thirty, and the chiefe breaker of all from eighteene to eight[y]. . . ."[51] Lust makes unstable marriages. Love holds the family together; lust endangers it. In consequence, love is now endorsed by the moralists and lust repudiated. The difference between them, and not the irrationality of both, has become the concern of a prescriptive morality.

What philology records, it cannot be too strongly stressed, is not a fall from a merry Middle Ages, when sexual desire was innocent and the body and its pleasures beyond the range of moral judgment. On the contrary, in the earlier epoch lechery was a deadly sin, celibacy the way of perfection, and asceticism the privileged way of life for those capable of sustaining it. Love belonged in romances, which were held to be essentially trivial, mere entertainment. But the celebration of love as the foundation of a lifetime of concord, and the inclusion of desire within the legality of marriage, brought with it an imperative to distinguish between true love, which would lead to conjugal happiness on the one hand and, on the other, appetite, which was the worst possible basis for a stable social institution. True love was sexual, but it was also companionable; lust, by contrast, was precipitate, inconsistent, turbulent, and dangerous.

As markers of a cultural shift, the semantic changes may perhaps be indicated, however sketchily, by comparing two considerations of marriage, widely separated chronologically, both of which address the problems of love and lust. First, in 1411–12, Thomas Hoccleve discusses the question in his *Regement of Princes,* addressed to the Prince of Wales on the eve of his accession to the throne as Henry V. In Hoccleve's account, celibacy is evidently preferable to marriage, but within marriage it is best to struggle against fleshly lusts. A man should take care to choose a wife on the basis of virtue: marrying for lust is bound to lead to disaster.[52] This sounds familiar, but the problems begin, predictably, with the respective meanings of the terms. Hoccleve confesses that he finally gave up waiting for a benefice and took a wife, whom he married for love (l. 1561). His interlocutor, the Beggar who has become his moral guide, is not satisfied with this account; he suspects, rightly as it turns out, that Hoccleve does not know the difference between love and lust, that he sees them as "conuertible" (i.e., interchangeable [l. 1563]). This is a serious error: love, that is, "goode" love (l. 1628), is love of virtue, "loue of the persone" (l. 1633), and it lasts; lust, meanwhile, is sexual desire or pleasure, and though lawful lust is necessary for procreation, lust for lust's sake is against God's commandments. Nowadays, he writes, people use aphrodisiacs, but this is contrary to the will of God.

The Regement of Princes thus holds apart love and lust by identifying as lust everything that has to do with sex. No sooner, however, has the text established this taxonomy than the precarious system of differences it has created with such difficulty collapses in a verse that precisely treats love and lust as "conuertible." Love's heat is suddenly synonymous with lust, and both are sexual:

> Also they that for luste chesen hir make
> Only, as other while it is vsage,
> Wayte wel, that whan fir luste is ouerschake,
> And there-with wole hir loues hete asswage,
> Thanne is to hem an helle, hire marriage.
>
> (ll. 1653–57)[53]

The Beggar, a kind of Adonis *avant la lettre* but invested by the text with a good deal more authority, cannot in the event hold apart the terms he sets out to define as antithetical. There is nothing here about marriage as companionship, no endorsement of nuptial love, no idealization of married pleasure. In the circumstances the only way to differentiate love from lust is to purge it of all sexual reference, and so rigorous a policing of its meaning cannot, it appears, be effectively sustained, since meaning is not at the disposal of the individual speaker.

We have reached a quite different and recognizably modern world, however, when in 1638 Robert Crofts provides a rhapsodic account of the romantic and companionable happiness of married love and family life:

> It is said, there is no pleasure in the world like that of the sweet society of Lovers, in the way of marriage, and of a loving husband and wife. Hee is her head, she commands his heart, he is her Love, her joy, she is his honey, his Doue, his delight.
>
> They may take sweet councell together, assist and comfort one another in all things, their joy is doubled and Redoubled.
>
> By this blessed vnion, the number of Parents, friends, and kindred is increased; It may be an occasion of sweet and lovely Children, who in after times may bee a great felicity and joy to them. . . .
>
> A multitude of felicities, a million of joyfull and blessed effects, spring from true Love.
>
> And indeed this Nuptial Love and society sweetens, all our Actions, discourses, all other pleasures, felicities, and even in all Respects, Encreases true Joy and happinesse.[54]

Crofts sees no reason why married lovers should not have recourse to the arts of love to enhance their pleasure, and he advises husbands to talk to their wives about love and its value or to tell them love stories, both happy and sad. He even includes a selection of sample poems and songs for the purpose. Some people, he continues would think this sort of advice profane:

> But wee may know that it is good and commendable, for such as doe, or intend to liue in that honourable and blessed estate of marriage, to bee possest with conjugall Love, and consequently such honest love discourses, deuices, and pleasures, as encrease the same, are to bee esteemed good and commendable.[55]

On the other hand, Crofts is entirely explicit in his condemnation of lust. He reaffirms the dichotomy between "true," which is to say married, love and those extramarital desires for forbidden objects, which destroy the family and destabilize society: "Let us also (while wee view the excellency of Lawfull and true Loue) beware of unlawfull and Raging Lusts. There is wel nigh as much difference betweene true Love and unlawfull Lusts, as betweene heaven and hell."[56] In Crofts's text the antithesis between love and lust is clear and is beginning to be familiar from a twentieth-century point of view. We could find something of the same taxonomy of desire in any Harlequin romance, where the happy ending depends on the ability of the protagonists to distinguish between true love, on the one hand, and, on the other, an infatuation of the senses, which is no basis for marriage. And yet it is worth noting, first, that Crofts still apparently feels it necessary to invoke an adjective: the repeated phrase in this chapter is "unlawfull lusts."[57] Second, the term is not arbitrary: the text does not base the distinction between love and lust on a dualism of mind and body,[58] but on a duality of lawful and unlawful, married and unmarried: unlawful lusts lead to fornication, adultery, incest, rape, breach of promise. The fully fledged dualism of caring and sensuality in current popular romance is an effect of the Cartesian crystallization of the *cogito,* identity as mind, which was evidently not yet part of Crofts' culture.[59] And third, "love," too, still benefits from a defining adjective: "true love," of course, has survived unchanged into the modern era.

VII

The power and the durability of the cultural change brought about by Shakespeare's Adonis and Niccholes and Crofts, assisted by countless Puritan divines, is evident in the readings of *Venus and Adonis* I have already cited. A substantial proportion of twentieth-century criticism, by endorsing the opposition Adonis formulates and finding in it the thematic truth of the poem, reproduces the taxonomy he helps to cement; such criticism thereby enlists Shakespeare in support of family values, the naturalization of the nuclear family as the only legitimate location of desire. Interpretation takes place within a framework, often unacknowledged, of value judgments about true and false love, "healthy" sexual dispositions, or the proper (which is to say "natural") relations between men and women. True love is identifiable in terms of a set of norms produced in the early modern period, norms now so familiar that they pass for nature. They represent the means by which a culture subjected an anarchic passion to the legality that is marriage, the terms on which unpredictable sexual desire was conscripted as the foundation of a stable social institution. True love is, or ought to be, we are to understand, companionable and based on shared convictions; the rhetoric of lovers is properly transparent, their exchanges honest, not designed to persuade; and genuine love occurs only between equals or near-equals, who treat each other with respect.

Venus, of course, fails on all counts. The love she represents is in these terms palpably unhealthy and contrary to nature. She is altogether too passionate, too persistent, too manipulative, too old. The phrase "Sick-thoughted Venus," virtually a circumlocution for lovesickness, as the Arden editor recognizes, comes in the criticism to justify the diagnosis of a sexual pathology: critics write, for example, that "She is introduced as 'Sick-thoughted' (l. 5), the primary notion of amorous languishment being overlaid with that of sick excess";[60] "in the light of that epithet her desire for the young Adonis can only be taken as unnatural and disorderly."[61] Leonard Barkan's account of the poem finds the love it defines "passionate and excessive,"[62] and Jonathan Bate considers the desire of Venus "perverse," while noting that perversity is also a common element of love. The poem, he proposes, is about transgression as a component of passion; it is thus "a celebration of sexuality even as it is a disturbing exposure of the dark underside of desire."[63]

But what exactly is it that is transgressed in *Venus and Adonis*? Or, what is the "wholesome" arrangement that constitutes the criterion for the critical identification of psychosexual pathology here? Whatever Venus is proposing for Adonis, it is not marriage. In the first place, she is married already. The text does not mention Vulcan, but the invocation of Mars would surely remind most readers of the humiliating story of the adulterous couple caught in her husband's net and exposed to view in the very act of love.[64] And in the second place, it was not yet obvious in the early 1590s that the only proper destiny of lovers was to found a nuclear family. That belief, I have suggested, was still in the process of construction. The condition the poem records is not true love as the basis of marital concord but the tragic passion of the classic love stories, and the narrative bears out the characterization of desire in the goddess' final curse, a definition that applies prophetically for others and retrospectively for her.

The invocation of family values as a framework for making sense of *Venus and Adonis* betrays, it seems to me, both the complexity of cultural history and the polyphony of Shakespeare's text, which draws on Ovid and the poetic and romance traditions as well as on popular morality. If the poem is definitive for the period, it is so to the degree that it brings an emergent taxonomy into conjunction—and conflict—with a residual indeterminacy,[65] an understanding of sexual desire as precisely sensual, irrational, anarchic, dangerous but also, and at the same time, delicate, fragile, and precious.

Family values represent an effort to bring desire into line with Law, in the Lacanian sense of that term, with the taxonomies and the corresponding disciplines inscribed in the symbolic order. The family promises gratification in exchange for submission to the rules: true love is desire that is properly regulated; it is for an appropriate (heterosexual) object; and its story is told in Shakespearean comedy and, in due course, in the nineteenth-century novel. True love obeys the rules of gender and genre, and its moment of closure is marriage, the metonym of a lifetime of happiness.

Venus and Adonis tells a quite different story. It is at the moment when Venus is compelled to realize that gratification is not an option ("All is imaginary she doth prove" [l. 597]) that the text invokes the trompe-l'oeil of the painted grapes. Venus perceives that the fulfillment of her desire is "imaginary" because her entreaties, arguments, threats, and promises fail to arouse any response in Adonis. Passion is not subject to reason or entreaty, to regulation or Law. On the contrary, desire is anarchic, and its cause is not, in the end, the persuasive powers of another person, not even a goddess, but the missing *objet a,* the presence that the ordering mechanisms of the symbolic both promise and withhold. Irrational, irregular, incited by prohibition, and thus quite unable to take "no" for an answer, desire is in every sense of the term an outlaw.

It follows that desire repudiates the rules, the classifications, and the proprieties that historically take up their place in the symbolic order. The queen of love has her own law, the poem affirms (l. 251), but it is a topsy-turvy one that enslaves only the ruler. What the text proposes is that desire rejects the taxonomies of both gender and genre. Love is for a boy who looks like a girl and who is in some sense too young for the difference to matter;

its modes of address are at once absurd and lyrical and tragic. Passion is contrary, contradictory; "love is," the text affirms, "wise in folly, foolish witty" (l. 838).

Venus and Adonis, which participates in the construction of family values, can also be read as indicating the altogether utopian character of a social project that sets out to subject desire to discipline, regulation, legality. Itself a trompe-l'oeil, moving between genres, unclosed, unfurnished with a final signified, the poem sustains the desire of the reader-critic to the degree that it refuses to yield the gratification of a secret meaning, a moral truth concealed behind the folds of its heterogeneous textuality.

NOTES

This essay was written at the Folger Shakespeare Library. It owes a great deal to the stimulus of that environment and to the intellectual generosity of the readers and the staff.

1. *Pliny Natural History,* trans. H. Rackham, Loeb Classical Library, 10 vols. (Cambridge, MA: Harvard UP, 1938–63), Bk. 35, sec. 36.

2. Quotations of *Venus and Adonis* follow the Arden Shakespeare edition of *The Poems,* ed. F.T. Prince (London: Methuen, 1960), 6–12.

3. Jacques Lacan, *The Four Fundamental Concepts of Psycho-analysis,* ed. Jacques-Alain Miller, trans. Alan Sheridan (New York and London: W.W. Norton, 1977), 112.

4. There were sixteen editions by 1640.

5. Leonard Barkan, *The Gods Made Flesh: Metamorphosis and the Pursuit of Paganism* (New Haven, CT, and London: Yale UP, 1986), 19, 27, and passim.

6. Ovid, *Metamorphoses,* trans. Frank Justus Miller, Loeb Classical Library, 2 vols., rev. ed. (Cambridge, MA: Harvard UP, 1984), Bk. 1, ll. 414–15.

7. Ovid, Bk. 1, ll. 450–567.

8. Ovid, Bk. 1, ll. 687–712.

9. T.W. Baldwin, *William Shakespere's Small Latine and Lesse Greeke,* 2 vols. (Urbana: U of Illinois P, 1944), 2:417–55. For an account of Ovid's appeal in the Renaissance, see William Keach, *Elizabethan Erotic Narratives: Irony and Pathos in the Ovidian Poetry of Shakespeare, Marlowe, and Their Contemporaries* (New Brunswick, NJ: Rutgers UP, 1977), 3–35; and Jonathan Bate, *Shakespeare and Ovid* (Oxford: Clarendon Press, 1993), 1–47.

10. Barkan, 80.

11. See Theocritus, "The Festival of Adonis" in *The Idylls of Theocritus and the Eclogues of Virgil,* trans. C.S. Calverley (London: G. Bell and Sons, 1913), 82–91; Bion, "Lament for Adonis" in *The Greek Bucolic Poets,* trans. A.S.F. Gow (Cambridge: Cambridge UP, 1953), 144–47; Plutarch, "Alcibiades" in *Plutarch's Lives,* trans. Bernadotte Perrin, Loeb Classical Library, 11 vols. (London: William Heinemann, 1914–26), 4:1–115, esp. 4:47–49.

12. Ovid, Bk. 10, ll. 519–739.

13. Ovid, Bk. 10, ll. 725–39.

14. Ironically, even the boar, she complains, inadvertently achieves a kind of consummation denied her as a woman:

'Tis true, 'tis true, thus was Adonis slain
He ran upon the boar with his sharp spear,
Who did not whet his teeth at him again,

But by a kiss thought to persuade him there:
And nuzzling in his flank, the loving swine
Sheath'd unaware the tusk in his soft groin.

(ll. 1111–16)

15. For the range of literary classifications, see John Doebler, "The Many Faces of Love: Shakespeare's *Venus and Adonis*," *Shakespeare Studies* 16 (1983): 33–43; and John Klause, "*Venus and Adonis*: Can We Forgive Them?" *Studies in Philology* 85 (1988): 353–77, esp. 353–55. Not everyone, however, has supposed that the poem can be easily classified: New Criticism characteristically celebrates the ambiguity of the text. See, for instance, Kenneth Muir, "*Venus and Adonis*: Comedy or Tragedy?" in *Shakespearean Essays*, Alwin Thaler and Norman Sanders, eds. (Knoxville: U of Tennessee P, 1964), 1–13; Norman Rabkin, "*Venus and Adonis* and the Myth of Love" in *Pacific Coast Studies in Shakespeare*, Waldo F. McNeir and Thelma N. Greenfield, eds. (Eugene: U of Oregon Books, 1966), 20–32.

16. Douglas Bush, *Mythology and the Renaissance Tradition in English Poetry* (Minneapolis: U of Minnesota P, 1932), 139–49, esp. 149. See also C.S. Lewis, *English Literature in the Sixteenth Century Excluding Drama* (Oxford: Clarendon Press, 1954), 498–99.

17. Samuel Taylor Coleridge, *Biographia Literaria*, ed. J. Shawcross, 2 vols. (Oxford: Clarendon Press, 1907), 2:16.

18. Lu Emily Pearson, *Elizabethan Love Conventions* (Berkeley: U of California P. 1933), 285.

19. Heather Dubrow, *Captive Victors: Shakespeare's Narrative Poems and Sonnets* (Ithaca, NY, and London: Cornell UP, 1987), 46. Cf. "Venus lusts after Adonis, but she is also maternally protective of him" (Keach, 77).

20. John Doebler, "The Reluctant Adonis: Titian and Shakespeare," *Shakespeare Quarterly 33* (1982): 480–90, esp. 484. Doebler repeats the earlier judgment of Don Cameron Allen, who proposes that Venus is "a forty-year-old countess with a taste for Chapel Royal altos." Later in the poem Venus comes "to discourse foolishly on love like a fluttery and apprehensive Doll Tearsheet of forty"; see Allen's *Image and Meaning: Metaphoric Traditions in Renaissance Poetry* (Baltimore, MD: Johns Hopkins UP, 1968), 43 and 57.

21. Gordon Williams, "The Coming of Age of Shakespeare's Adonis," *Modern Language Review* 78 (1983): 769–76, esp. 776.

22. Klause, 371 and 364.

23. The most perceptive account I have found of the poem's "tonal shifts" is Nancy Lindheim, "The Shakespearean *Venus and Adonis*," *Shakespeare Quarterly* 37 (1986): 190–203.

24. See the Arden Shakespeare edition of *A Midsummer Night's Dream*, ed. Harold F. Brooks (London: Methuen, 1979).

25. William Baldwin, *A treatise of Morall Phylosophie* . . . (London, 1550), sigs. 18^r and R6^r. I owe this observation to Peter Blayney.

26. William Baldwin, sig. O2^{r-v}.

27. William Baldwin, sig. O2^v.

28. William Baldwin, *A treatyce of moral philosophy* . . . (London, 1564), fols. 185^v and 186^r.

29. William Baldwin, *A treatyce*, fol. 185^{r-v}.

30. Pierre de la Primaudaye, *The French academie*. . . . (London, 1618), 479; see also Pierre de la Primaudaye, *Academie Françoise* (Paris, 1580), fol. 166^r.

31. La Primaudaye, *The French academie*, 480; *Academie Francoise*, fol. 166^v.

32. *Oxford English Dictionary*, sv lust, sb., 1d.

33. Erasmus, *A booke called in latyn Enchiridion militis christiani and in englysshe the manuell of the christen knyght*. . . . (London, 1533), sigs. N1^r, Q5^v, Q6^r,

and R2ᵛ. This English translation of the *Enchiridion* may have been made by William Tyndale; see E.J. Devereaux, *Renaissance English Translations of Erasmus: A Bibliography to 1700* (Toronto: U of Toronto P, 1983), 104.

34. There is one counter-example: the next chapter heading (an epilogue of remedies against incentives to *libido*) is translated as "A shorte recapitulacyon of remedyes agaynst the flame of lust" (sig. R3ᵛ). Here I think the destructive "flame" does some of the work of the other qualifying words or phrases.

35. Erasmus, sigs. Q5ᵛ and Q6ʳ⁻ᵛ.

36. Erasmus, *A Manual for a Christian Soldier* (London, 1687), 184–92.

37. See, for instance, the following modern editions: Erasmus, *Handbook of the Militant Christian*, trans. John P. Dolan (Notre Dame, IN: Fides Publishers, 1962), 147–59; and *The Enchiridion of Erasmus*, ed. and trans. Raymond Himelick (Bloomington: Indiana UP, 1963), 177–84.

38. Cf. Sir Thomas More, *Utopia*, trans. Raphe Robynson, ed. Israel Gollancz (1551; London: Dent, 1898), 102–3.

39. Sir Thomas More, *A Dialogue concernynge heresyes & matters of Religion. . . .* in *The Workes of Sir Thomas More Knyght. . . .* (London, 1557), 103–288, esp. 221.

40. More, *A Dialogue concernynge heresyes*, 222.

41. Erasmus, *A booke called latyn Enchiridion*, sig. Q7ʳ⁻ᵛ.

42. La Primaudaye, *The French academie*, 98–99.

43. Thomas Gainsford, *The Rich Cabinet Furnished with varietie of Excellent discriptions. . . .* (London, 1616), fol. 86ʳ. For the section on "lechery," see fols. 82ᵛ-84ʳ; for "love," see fols. 84ᵛ-87ᵛ.

44. Gainsford, fol. 87ʳ.

45. Gainsford, fol. 84ʳ.

46. See T.W. Baldwin, *On the Literary Genetics of Shakespeare's Poems and Sonnets* (Urbana: U of Illinois P, 1950), 73–93; and Heather Asals, "*Venus and Adonis*: The Education of a Goddess." *Studies in English Literature 1500–1900* 13 (1973): 31–51.

47. Richard Linche, *The Fovntaine of Ancient Fiction. . . .* (London, 1599), sig. Cc2ʳ⁻ᵛ.

48. By this time there had been nine more editions.

49. Alexander Niccholes, *A Discourse, of Marriage and Wiving. . . .* (London, 1615), 31–32.

50. Niccholes, 32.

51. Niccholes, 30.

52. Thomas Hoccleve, *The Regement of Princes* (1405) in *Hoccleve's Works*, ed. Frederick J. Furnivall, Early English Text Society ES 72, 3 vols. (London: Kegan Paul, Trench, Trübner, 1897), Vol. 3, ll. 1555–764.

53. Marrying for lust was still a danger in 1585. In one instance, however, lust is identified as a component of love, but the two are not interchangeable; see "The wanton wyfe, whose love is all for luste. . . . " in Geoffrey Whitney, Ms. Harvard Typ. 14, fol. 48. I owe this reference to Steven W. May.

54. Robert Crofts, *The Lover: or, Nvptiall Love* (London, 1638), sigs. A7ᵛ-A8ʳ.

55. Crofts, sig. C6ᵛ.

56. Crofts, sig. D6ᵛ.

57. Crofts, sigs. D6ᵛ-D8ʳ.

58. There is dualism elsewhere, but "sensual" love is not generally identified in this text as "lust" (Crofts, sigs. B1ᵛ-B2ʳ).

59. See Catherine Belsey, *Desire: Love Stories in Western Culture* (Oxford: Basil Blackwell, 1994), 21–41.

60. Williams, 770. See also Keach, 66.

61. David N. Beauregard, "*Venus and Adonis*: Shakespeare's Representation

of the Passions," *Shakespeare Studies* 8 (1975): 83–98, esp. 94.

62. Barkan, 271.

63. Bate, 48–65, esp. 65.

64. Ovid, Bk. 4, ll. 171–89.

65. For another symptom of this indeterminacy, see Margaret Mikesell's astute account of an unconscious regression to the praise of celibacy within the humanist defense of marriage in Vives' influential conduct book for women ("Marital and Divine Love in Juan Luis Vives' *Instruction of a Christen Woman*" in *Love and Death in the Renaissance,* Kenneth R. Bartlett, Konrad Eisenbichler, and Janice Liedl, eds. [Ottawa: Dovehouse Editions, 1991], 113–34)].

III
VENUS AND ADONIS
IN PRODUCTION

ALMEIDA

VENUS AND LUCRECE

Betty Caplan

Shakespeare knew what he was doing when he penned Venus and Lucrece as poems. After all, if anyone had a nose for drama it was him. Director Bardy Thomas has adapted the poems for the stage, leaving structure and language fairly intact.

In *Venus and Adonis,* three peasant women amuse themselves by teasing an adolescent youth while they rest during the harvest of 1593. They use the story of Venus's seduction of Adonis to get a rise out of him. If you thought there was strength in numbers you were wrong. He turns the tables on them, glorifying pure love and decrying their lust. I must say it does make you sit up and take notice when it's the man who's a sex object for a change, and coming over all weak and vulnerable to boot.

They have a wonderful romp when the women pin him down and get on top, but that's about as far as it goes. No amount of running up or down or panting will make this a play—the form remains obdurately poetic and the language never becomes speech despite thick West Country accents.

The *Rape of Lucrece* has many of the excesses of Victorian melodrama with none of the excitement. The poem is based on the ancient Roman story of the saintly Lucrece who kills herself after Tarquin, her husband's purported friend, has raped her. Chastity tends towards dullness, and never more so than here. "Like a virtuous monument she lies," but monuments ought not to speak (Mozart excepted). This one does, ad nauseam. Speeches and declarations take the place of character or motivation.

Ms. Thomas's new company Art Depot makes its debut with this production, and shows some promise. The actors make a valiant effort, and David Lewis's designs are fetching as is the music composed by Frank Bredley. The moral is to let sleeping poems lie.

Reprinted with permission from *The Guardian,* © January 29, 1988, p. 21.

Venus (played by Katherine Owens, left, and Sarah Rankin, right) mourns the fatally wounded Adonis (played by Nathan Hinton) in the Undermain Theatre production of Venus and Adonis, directed by Ted Davey. Courtesy of the Undermain Theatre of Dallas, Texas.

UNDERMAIN'S *VENUS* SHINES BRIGHTLY

Julie Dam

What would *you* do if you were plagued by a love-crazed goddess with a literal split personality?

I kid thee not.

Rarely (if ever) before dramatized, the Greek myth-turned-Shakespearean love poem *Venus and Adonis* is further transformed by the Undermain Theatre into a fresh, entertaining work of theater. One of three productions co-sponsored by the Shakespeare Festival of Dallas and the Ken Bryant Memorial Fund, *Venus and Adonis* adds welcome variety to the summer's usual Shakespearean offerings.

In depicting the goddess of love's unrequited passion for a beautiful youth, this adaptation addresses the madness of love, a quality that transcends time and space. But this is not merely the same girl-meets-boy, girl-loves-boy, girl-loses-boy plot of the romantic Greek tale. Instead, the speech is poetry but the actions are rough: This *Venus and Adonis* is part epic tragedy, part bawdy comedy and part Obsession commercial. Despite how strange that may sound, it works.

Shakespeare's one sensual Venus is replaced by three well-chosen actresses simultaneously portraying the various aspects of love: Erin Ryan as the deeply feeling Earth Venus; Sara Rankin Weeks as the Water Venus oozing with sexuality; and Katherine Owens as the playful and vibrant Fire Venus. The flurry of action the three women create as they glide, slink and pounce about and generally throw themselves at Adonis aptly depicts the overwhelming emotional roller-coaster ride of Venus' obsessive love.

Nathan Hinton convincingly portrays Adonis as a bewildered, frightened youth fighting off the goddess' unwanted advances—desperately hiding from them; then, failing that, humorously attempting to appease them

Reprinted with permission of *The Dallas Morning News,* July 5, 1991, p. 4C.

Mars/Narrator (Bruce DuBose, left) and Adonis (Nathan Hinton, right) struggle in the Undermain Theatre production of Venus and Adonis, directed by Ted Davey. Courtesy of the Undermain Theatre of Dallas.

by puckering up like a 10-year-old boy forced to kiss his sister. He shows more passion for the boar hunt that ultimately kills him than for any woman. And for good reason: Mr. Hinton's Adonis, smothered with kisses by Venuses everywhere, seems a victim of emotional harassment rather than the rueful jilter of lore.

In adapting the erotic narrative for the stage, director Ted Davey adds a new twist by turning the poem's invisible but clearly interested narrator into Venus' thwarted former lover Mars, the god of war. The only character dressed in contemporary clothes—red shirt, shorts and sneakers—he is the tangible link between the ancient myth and a modern exploration of love. As played by Bruce DuBose, the sarcastic, vengeful Mars also straddles the line between interactive character and omniscient storyteller, allowing the play to flow rather than disrupting it.

Staged in the cavernous, dimly lit basement of the Undermain, *Venus and Adonis* feels half rustic, half ethereal, a mood appropriate to the multifaceted qualities the production applies to love. Light, flowing costumes flutter across huge stone pillars. Words hauntingly chanted in pitch darkness open and close the play. Only when the lights go on at the end is the audience transported back to reality. The Undermain's *Venus and Adonis* has all the mesmerizing power of myth—even the ones it turns upside-down.

STRANGE BEDFELLOWS — VENUS, ADONIS, AND ME

Benjamin Stewart

I was introduced to the performability of Shakespeare's *Venus and Adonis* in, I think it was, 1969 by Professors Krohn and Swilley of the University of St. Thomas in Houston when they decided to "stage" the poem with an actress portraying the goddess, an actor playing the boy and with yours truly as Narrator in a production at the University and at the jazz club Mother Blues downtown for the Houston Shakespeare Society. The next year, when I was living in Los Angeles, I instigated a similar production at the Shakespeare Society of America's Tudor mansion headquarters down the hill in Hollywood from the old Playboy Club. The reason I finally worked the piece up into a one-man show is that however much I talked myself blue in the face trying to convince Shakespeare festival artistic directors that here was an undiscovered "one-act" in the story-theatre vein by the Great Bard, which had never been adequately exposed to public eye and ear, nobody took me up on the venture. In addition, I had always felt the efforts of the actors involved to be less than fully effective in depicting the range of passion and poetry involved and that if I could pull off the stunt of convincingly "suggesting" two characters for whom I was decidedly miscast I could interpret the glories of the poem by my lonesome.

Taking into consideration that there is, in middle age, at least as much of the nubile boy left in me as there was the innocent human lad beneath the carcass of the Elephant Man and that my androgynous nature had provided me with enough of the female touch to portray successfully such characters in the theatre as Mrs. Malaprop, Lady Bracknell, Madame Maniefa, and even, if you really want to stretch the point, one of the witches in Shakespeare's you-know-what, the experiment to see if I could go solo with *Venus and Adonis* merely awaited my memorization of the whole poem so that I could play around with it as well as ascertain what parts to eliminate. The year I was finishing the memorization the great actress Irene Worth presented her self-edited recitation at the Stratford Festival in Canada. I didn't get to see it. I would've been discouraged in continuing if it hadn't been such a top-flight artist who beat me to the punch. But, not being able to see her performance, I still felt I had much to contribute to enacting the work and proceeded to learn and master the text and, while understudying Peter Ustinov in Los Angeles in the fall of 1983, presented my interpretation to the Mark Taper Forum for consideration for the cabaret features at the Itchey Foote, their "third stage." The Taper bought the show and the reviews justified my efforts.

I had the advantage of knowing the work was performable from the two experiences in which I had been joined onstage in the past by an actress and a younger actor. People resolutely forget that the great female characters of Shakespeare were *created* by boy actors: Cleopatra, Juliet, Lady Macbeth, Isabelle, Volumnia, Beatrice, *all* of them. Young boys as close as humans can come to Adonis himself had essayed these women before a demanding Elizabethan public. Once I had memorized the piece and practiced reciting it through very rapidly from beginning to end (which I found ran about sixty-five minutes each time), I decided that cutting a few lines here and there would be tantamount to forgetting my words (a practice with which I am all too familiar, though so were the actor forbears of John Gielgud), and to cut a lot of lines would risk doing surgery on the poetry itself (which is why I did not succumb to the suggested line-cuts of my first producer who wanted me to trim the poem down to the strictly narrative line, which is not the point of the poem at all). I decided to do the poem completely intact. My original performances had no intermission, my succeeding ones had an intermission at the exact spot where the poem itself turns from comedy to tragedy, with a blackout between the words "she" and "whereat" in the line "'The boar!' quoth she, whereat a sudden pale. . . ." All up to then has been romp and comic frustration, everything thereafter will be an almost headlong plunge into despair and darkness. In fact, I came to call Act One "Comedy" and Act Two "Tragedy," as though the separate parts of the show could be represented by the famous masks that symbolize the theatre itself.

I wanted to present to the public an, as it were, unsung masterpiece by Shakespeare that the individual auditors and viewers would probably never read and even if they did would probably, in so doing, miss on the page the delicacies and gemstones of it, as I would have if Mr. Krohn and Mr. Swilley had not provided me with evidence otherwise in the 1960s. (My solo manifestation of the poem is dedicated to them.) I use the Latin quote from Ovid at the beginning as an invocation (and a delightfully tongue-in-cheek one it is: "Let the cheap dazzle the crowd; as for me may Golden Apollo give me deep draughts from the Spring of the Muses"), without translating it for the audience, and go on, equally without comment, to deliver the dedication to the Earl of Southampton. Then the title of the piece and then the uncut (if one wants to be cute, "the uncircumcised") poem itself, virtually "performing" what the reader would see on the page if he or she were perusing it. The text is so descriptive-rich that there is no need for scenery, props or even costume; so I perform on a totally barren stage in dark sweat clothes and black Capezio jazz shoes. The intention is to project a stark, Polish Lab Theatre emptiness into which is poured, rather oracularly, the wealth and sinuosity of Shakespeare's descriptive passionate plea-through-myth with his beloved patron to reproduce his own being in an heir before court intrigue or the vicissitudes of living prevent the endeavor.

In some versions of the myth Venus and Adonis actually do couple and have offspring. That did not serve Shakespeare's purpose. Adonis' dying and Venus' laments make for a moving denouement, but it is excessively difficult to sell a modern audience on the logic of Adonis' refusal of the wiles of such a monumentally sexual goddess. Shakespeare and Adonis make it clear that Adonis refuses because, impossible as it seems, he's afraid of drowning in the superhuman richness she promises. You'd think that in an age of AIDS people would get the message. There are dangers in unbridled passion.

Venus and Adonis is our greatest English poet's version of the story of a famous myth. Its performability lies in telling the story with as much clarity and skill as is at hand. Shakespeare, as usual, does most of the work. The first staging I was in used film and voice-over at the conclusion. My current show uses no extraneous music, sets or props, just the voice, the face, the hands, the text. As I said in the acceptance speech for the first award I received for the show, "Mr. Shakespeare was such a genius of the theatre that, even when he sat down to write his first narrative poem, it turned out to be as eminently actable as any of his great plays."

IV

NEW ESSAYS ON
VENUS AND ADONIS

Shakespeare's Venus and the Venus of Classical Mythology[1]

João Froes

In his book *Elizabethan Erotic Narratives,* William Keach observed that one of the major changes performed by Shakespeare in portraying Venus in *Venus and Adonis* was "to make Venus more aggressively lustful than she is in the *Metamorphoses*" (53). Keach then referred to Ovid's Venus as being "comparatively restrained and decorous in her approaches," and how, in an original manner, Shakespeare had altered the sexual role which would conventionally be ascribed to Venus (i.e., the one who is wooed) into that of a "bold-fac'd suitor" (56, 59). In 1978, S. Clark Hulse accounted for the difference between Shakespeare's and Ovid's Venus by offering Titian's painting of Venus and Adonis, as well as Hero and Leander as the possible source for Shakespeare's portrait of Venus as a "rapist."[2] In 1983, Gordon Williams pointed to the "grotesque" nature of Venus as shown by Shakespeare,[3] and more recently, Tita French Baumlin has explicitly compared the Venus of Ovid's and Shakespeare's poem, emphasizing the aggressiveness of the goddess in Shakespeare as opposed to Ovid's portrait of her.[4] The discrepancy between Shakespeare's passionate Venus and the harmless Venus presented by Ovid was explicitly pointed to by Donald Furber and Anne Callahan. Furber and Callahan demonstrated how Shakespeare's Venus is the "most sexually aggressive woman in modern literature," whereas Ovid depicts her as "eternal love."[5]

The question of Venus's lustful and sex-oriented character as opposed to her "maternal nature"[6] has always been controversial. As early as 1933, Lu Emily Pearson stressed Venus as the representative of "sensual love,"[7] and, in 1980, Michael Stugrin emphasized how Venus represents human passion and animal lust,[8] as did Heather Dubrow in 1987.[9] But, a few years before Dubrow's emphasis on the domineering nature of Venus, several critics concentrated on Venus as a mother figure whose love for Adonis might be seen as offering "complete nourishment and secure protection," as Wayne

Rebhorn and Coppélia Kahn claimed.[10] From these divergent interpretations, another critical trend argued that Venus embodied a combination of love and the lustful desire to enjoy the loved one. According to Nancy Lindheim, Venus' role demonstrates that "love is love even if it incorporates sexual desire" (193). Alternatively, Jonathan Bate recently observed that Venus' coercion of Adonis taints her desire and love for him.[11] In the light of these views of Venus, one might affirm that the personality of Shakespeare's Venus certainly exhibits two aspects: (1) a loving, almost motherly nature, and (2) a lustful passion that makes her wish to possess and enjoy whoever or whatever she feels attracted to.

In showing Venus as someone whose personality is a blend of loving passion and aggressive lust, Shakespeare was being faithful to mythological traditions of Venus, as well as to the Greeks' and Romans' views of the goddess. A review of the mythological traditions about Venus shows that the complex personality of Shakespeare's Venus is much closer to tradition than Ovid's "mild" goddess.

"Venus" was in reality the name given by the Romans to the Greek goddess Aphrodite, and her very name suggests that Shakespeare's lustful goddess is more traditionally appropriate than Ovid's. The goddess's original Greek name is the origin of the English adjectives "aphrodisiacal" and "aphrodisian," relating to sensual love, not to mention the connection between "Venus" and "venereal."[12] Although Venus was said to be the daughter of Zeus and Dione, a strong tradition claimed that she was born when the sexual organs of Uranus (identified with the sun) were cut off by the god Kronos, and, after the organs fell in the sea, the lustful Aphrodite came to life.[13] The East Frieze of the Parthenon contains a figure of Aphrodite with her left arm over the shoulder of Eros,[14] a significant mythological fact. In pre-Biblical times, the primary meaning of the word "eros" was "passionate love which desires the other for itself."[15] Until Plato's time, the Greeks viewed Eros as a sensually joyous and daemonic god,[16] and Eros' presence always indicated lust and sensuality. Clearly, the ancient Greeks already regarded Aphrodite as a sex-oriented deity, but apparently the idea that Aphrodite could be so strongly inclined to the desires of the flesh disturbed Plato, who conceived a theory that there were really two different Aphrodites. According to Plato, the daughter of Uranus was in reality "the goddess of pure love," while the daughter of Dione was "the Aphrodite of the populace" or the "goddess of common love."[17] Plato lifted both Aphrodite and Eros above the level of sensuality, to the point of spiritualizing Eros, changing it into the representation of ecstasy beyond rationality.[18] Although Ovid may not have known about the Platonic concept of Aphrodite and Eros, the Roman poet possibly was a victim of the confusion created by Plato's distinction.

Aphrodite married Hephaestus (or Vulcan), the lame god of Lemnos (*Iliad*, XVIII.368 ff., and *Aeneid*, VIII), but fell in love with Ares (or Mars), the god of war. Aphrodite and Ares were strongly attracted to each other, and their amorous encounters were numerous.[19] Shakespeare alludes to Aphrodite's conquest of Ares in *Venus and Adonis*:

> I have been woo'd, as I entreat thee now,
> Even by the stern and direful god of war,
> Whose sinewy neck in battle ne'er did bow,
> Who conquers where he comes in every jar:
> Yet hath he been my captive and my slave,
> And begg'd for that which thou unask'd shall have.
>
> (ll. 97–102)

[handwritten annotation: — masculine man vs effeminate man ? both beat by Venus.]

Besides seducing Ares, Aphrodite also had a love affair with Anchises, by whom she had Aeneas, the hero of Virgil's epic poem. In fact, in the *Aeneid*, one can see Venus', or Aphrodite's, skill in the art of love, as well as her impulsive nature. In Book I, Venus succeeds in encircling Dido "with love's flame" so that the queen might be "held fast in strong love for Aeneas" (*Aeneid*, I.673–5), a passion that will ultimately destroy Dido. Venus helps Aeneas several times in the *Aeneid*, most notably in Book XII, where Venus cures Aeneas's wound (*Aeneid*, XII.411–19) and thus enables Aeneas to kill Turnus, his adversary. Actually, we see that Venus has only one aim: to ensure that Aeneas become the ruler of Italy, thus propagating through her son a race destined to build a great empire (*Aeneid*, I.229–53). Venus' miraculous cure of Aeneas in Book XII proves that Venus could both exert her motherly care and, simultaneously, actively contribute to make Aeneas the conqueror of the tribes of Italy. In Venus, then, Virgil valorizes the coexistence of motherly devotion and desire for power and glory for her loved one.

In this Virgilian context, Shakespeare's portrait of Venus as an impulsive person who violently pursues her objectives is consistent. Shakespeare's portrait is also faithful to some traditional legends about her in Greek mythology. Aphrodite's almost irrational desire to be praised and loved by men actually caused catastrophic results for entire nations. The women of Lemnos, who had refused to worship her because they learned of her real character, infuriated Aphrodite. She tried hard to win their adoration, and when she perceived she could not, she made them smell so horrible that their husbands abandoned them for Thracian slave girls.[20] A similar incident occurred when Aphrodite punished the goddess Pasiphaë for having despised her cult.[21]

On another occasion, Aphrodite, Athena, and Hera were together on Mount Ida, and began to argue about who the most beautiful among them was. Aphrodite's defense of her own beauty is a reminder of Venus' efforts to convince Adonis of her attractiveness (especially lines 139–44 of *Venus and Adonis*), and, on Mount Ida, the three goddesses presented their argumentation before Paris, the son of Priam, who judged the goddesses' beauty. To make sure she would win, Aphrodite promised Paris the hand of Helen, which made Paris decide for the goddess, and thus the Trojan War began.

Because Venus was the mother of Aeneas, the legendary father of the Roman race, she was hailed as the "mother of Rome," and in 44 B.C. a temple to "mother Venus" was built.[22] At the same time, the Romans regarded Venus as an impulsive goddess whose love and passions were associated with self-indulgence. In his *Roman History,* Dio observes that Julius Caesar had great devotion to Venus, and was eager to persuade everyone that he had received from the goddess a "bloom of youth."[23] Besides wearing a carven image of her in full armor on his ring, Caesar wore a loose girdle as part of his devotion to Venus, a loose girdle being the sign of licentiousness and general laxity of morals.[24] Livy mentions a temple built in 114 B.C. in honor of Venus *Verticordia* (or "the turner of hearts"), and three Roman temples variously honored Venus as mother and bold protector of her loved ones.[25] Moreover, the Romans considered April to be the month of Venus, since it symbolized the joy and excitement brought about by spring (Horace, *Odes,* IV.xi.15–6). The name of Venus was also linked with revelry and gaming; the highest throw of the dice in Roman parties or games was named "Venus-throw" (Horace, *Odes,* II.vii.25–6).

In one of his *Odes,* Horace claims that Venus' delight was "in cruel sport to force beneath her brazen yoke bodies and hearts ill-mated" (I.xxxiii.10–2), an image which recalls Shakespeare's portrait of Venus's attempts to force her union with Adonis, whose restrained personality would certainly be an ill match for Venus herself. Horace's image of Venus' forcing of bodies and hearts "beneath her brazen yoke" is remarkably similar to this description of Venus' embraces and kisses in *Venus and Adonis:*

> Even as an empty eagle, sharp by fast,
> Tires with her beak on feathers, flesh and bone,
> Shaking her wings, devouring all in haste,
> Till either gorge be stuff'd or prey be gone;

Even so she kissed his brow, his cheek, his chin,
And where she ends she doth anew begin.

(ll. 55–60)

In the opening stanzas of *Venus and Adonis,* Shakespeare indicates that the union of the pair would be an ill match. Venus trembles in her passion (l. 27), while Adonis is "frosty in desire" (l. 36); Venus is hot as "coals of glowing fire" (l. 35), and Adonis burns with "bashful shame" (l. 49). Even though Venus sees that Adonis is indifferent to her approaches, she "still entreats" (l. 73), and starts to adopt a different strategy of seduction, beginning on line 95. Instead of physically forcing Adonis, Venus first mentions her previous conquest of Mars (ll. 97–112), and then speaks of her own beauty (ll. 133–50). Venus' words about herself seem to indicate her effort to find a reason for Adonis' refusal of her ("why dost abhor me?") and to reduce the differences she sees between them. Her lips are not as fair as his but they might be united in a kiss (ll. 115–17), and he is "unripe" and yet may "be tasted" (l. 128). Venus then clearly sees that Adonis is not mature enough for love, while she is an experienced lover who had "foil'd" even Mars himself. Still, she persists on her seduction of Adonis even after he confesses that he will never learn about love (l. 409). Finally, after learning of Adonis' intention of hunting the boar, Venus is described as having "assay'd as much as may be proved" (l. 608). Later on, Venus will hope that Adonis is alive after the hunt, trying to extenuate her suspicion (ll. 1009–10). To the very end of *Venus and Adonis,* Venus appears as a persistent goddess who even tries to overlook the obvious obstacles preventing the realization of her wishes. Horace's definition of Venus as the goddess who delighted in forcing the union of ill-mated couples found an even more radical expression in *Venus and Adonis.* In Shakespeare, the ill match involves the goddess herself, and she will be the ultimate victim of her "cruel sport," as she fails to seduce Adonis and is thus defeated in the game of love in which she had always been victorious with her "brazen yoke."

Lastly, commenting on the riot by silversmiths of Ephesus caused by Saint Paul's preaching, since it was taking away the customers of their "miniature silver shrines of Artemis,"[26] Father Alfred McBride observes that besides being the home of the great temple of Artemis, Ephesus also had a temple of Aphrodite, or Venus, where orgies and male prostitution were practiced, supposedly at the goddess's own request.[27] In relation to Shakespeare's faithfulness to traditions about Venus, this fact is significant if we remember that *Comedy of Errors* is set in Ephesus, a land inhabited by wizards, and where sexual allegiances are unclear and threatened.

Considering, then, the historical and mythological evidence regarding Venus, the goddess cannot be said to represent love in the sense of *agape,* as the Greeks understand it. *Agape,* which can be rendered in Latin as *caritas,* is the feeling of those who "show love without expecting it to be returned, lend where there is little hope of payment, give without reserve or limit."[28] In *Venus and Adonis,* Venus expects and demands that Adonis love her with the same intensity with which she loves him. Venus is willing to give herself entirely to Adonis, but she requires him to pay a price for her self-giving: the surrender of his whole self to her. Like Aeneas, Adonis becomes the object of Venus' undivided attention, but Venus also requires Adonis to let her use his body as an object of sexual pleasure. Venus may indeed have motherly inclinations toward Adonis, but such affection also has incestuous implications. This curious mixture of the maternal and sexual in Venus was clear to the Romans and to Shakespeare, who knew Horace and Ovid, and was possibly familiar with accounts of Venus by Roman historians such as Livy and Dio. Shakespeare presented a mother-figure with impulsive sexual instincts in the same sense that the Venus *Genetrix* of the Romans was also the Venus who had devotees wearing loose girdles. In *Venus and Adonis,* Shakespeare once more showed he could not only write brilliant poetry, but also write it in full accordance with tradition, whether it be of history or mythology.

NOTES

1. With filial love, I dedicate this essay to the honor of our *true* Mother, the Blessed Virgin Mary.

2. S. Clark Hulse, "Shakespeare's Myth of Venus and Adonis," *Publications of the Modern Language Association* 93 (1978): 95.

3. Gordon Williams, "The Coming of Age of Shakespeare's Adonis," *Modern Language Review* 78 (1983): 770.

4. Tita French Baumlin, "The Birth of the Bard: *Venus and Adonis* and Poetic Apotheosis," *Papers on Language and Literature* 26 (1990): 192.

5. Donald Furber and Anne Callahan, *Erotic Love in Literature: From Medieval Legend to Romantic Illusion* (Troy, NY: Whitston, 1982), 61.

6. Wayne A. Rebhorn, "Mother Venus: Temptation in Shakespeare's *Venus and Adonis,*" *Shakespeare Studies* 11 (1978): 1.

7. Lu Emily Pearson, *Elizabethan Love Conventions* (Berkeley: U of California P, 1933), 285.

8. Michael Stugrin, "'But I must also feel it as a man': Pathos and Knowledge in Shakespearean Tragedy," *Iowa State Journal of Research* 54 (1980): 476.

9. Heather Dubrow, *Captive Victors: Shakespeare's Narrative Poems and Sonnets* (Ithaca: Cornell UP, 1987), 27–31.

10. Wayne A. Rebhorn, "Mother Venus: Temptation in Shakespeare's *Venus and Adonis,*" *Shakespeare Studies* 11 (1978): 1–16; Coppélia Kahn, *Man's Estate: Masculine Identity in Shakespeare* (Berkeley: U of California P, 1981), chap. 2.

11. Jonathan Bate, *Shakespeare and Ovid* (Oxford: Clarendon Press, 1993), 64.

12. See *Oxford English Dictionary,* second edition, I, 548.

13. Pierre Grimal, *The Dictionary of Classical Mythology,* trans. A.R. Maxwell-Hyslop (Oxford: Basil Blackwell, 1987), 46.

14. *The Carrey Drawings of the Parthenon Sculptures,* ed. Theodore Bowie and Diether Thimme (Bloomington and London: Indiana UP, 1971), p. 70.

15. *Theological Dictionary of the New Testament,* ed. Gerhard Kittel (Grand Rapids, MI: William B. Eerdmans, 1964), I, 35.

16. *Theological Dictionary of the New Testament,* I, 35.

17. Pierre Grimal, *The Dictionary of Classical Mythology,* 46.

18. See *Phaedrus,* 237 ff., and 242 ff.

19. Pierre Grimal, *The Dictionary of Classical Mythology,* 46.

20. Pierre Grimal, *The Dictionary of Classical Mythology,* 46.

21. Pierre Grimal, *The Dictionary of Classical Mythology,* 348.

22. See note 25.

23. Dio, *Roman History,* trans. Earnest Cary (Loeb Classical Library), XLIII.3.

24. See Dio, *Roman History,* XLIII.4–5.

25. They are: Venus *Erycina,* built 181 B.C. on the Via Salaria near the Porta Colina; Venus *Obsequens,* built 295 B.C. near the east end of the Circus Maximus; Venus *Genetrix* (Mother Venus), in existence in 44 B.C. See *Livy* (Loeb Classical Library), VIII, 350–1, 512–3, and XIV, 145. See also Livy, *Julius Obsequens,* 37.

26. See Acts of the Apostles, XIX.23–40.

27. Father Alfred McBride, *The Gospel of the Holy Spirit* (Huntington, IN: Our Sunday Visitor, 1994). See specifically Father McBride's discussion of Acts of the Apostles, XIX.

28. *Theological Dictionary of the New Testament,* I, 46.

Venus as Praeceptor

The *Ars Amatoria* in *Venus and Adonis*

M.L. Stapleton

Ego sum praecaptor amoris.

(*Ars Amatoria* [*AA*] 1.17)

Tell me, love's master, shall we meet tomorrow?

(*Venus and Adonis* [*VA*] l. 585)[1]

Scholars since Malone's time have agreed that Ovid informs *Venus and Adonis* in some fashion. Shakespeare usefully complicates the story he found in Book 10 of the *Metamorphoses* by conflating it with the Hermaphroditus-Salmacis episode in Book 4 and the tale of Narcissus in Book 3. The doomed and not-unwilling youth from antiquity becomes recalcitrant and sick of self-love in the ornate Elizabethan epyllion, roughly wooed by a desperate *dea amoris*. A minor controversy (rooted in the question of Shakespeare's facility in Latin) still exists over whether Ovid's hexameters or Arthur Golding's fourteeners provided the means of transmission.[2] Whether in Latin or in the English translations that were published with great frequency throughout the Renaissance,[3] Shakespeare had access to most of the Ovidian corpus, a poetical body that he cannibalized, reconstituted, and tranfused into his own works. Besides the *Metamorphoses*, the *Amores*, *Ars Amatoria*, and *Remedia Amoris* occasionally show themselves in the plays and poems.

I will propose that Shakespeare uses the *Ars Amatoria* as intertext in *Venus and Adonis* along with Ovid's protean epic.[4] This notorious guide to love—praised, castigated, and imitated so frequently in the West between 1100 and 1700—features as its speaker the comic praeceptor, or master, of love, a man who dispenses (bad) advice to men and women about seduction. Shakespeare adapts some of the imagery and commonplaces of the *Ars* to his poem and appropriates the figure of the praeceptor for his conception of his sick-thoughted Venus. She dutifully follows some of his precepts in her furiously unsuccessful attempts upon Adonis' virtue. Venus even subverts some of the *dicta* of Ovid's amatory pedant. Oddly, such subversion proves more disastrous for her than following the advice.

The praeceptor-as-paradigm may explain the qualities in Venus that some contemporary critics find disagreeable. S. Clark Hulse suggests that she "seems to become a sweaty, muscular rapist";[5] Gordon Williams writes that Venus "appears too grotesque to command . . . the reader's wholehearted sympathy";[6] Tita French Baumlin compares Shakespeare's incarnation to Ovid's version of the goddess in the *Metamorphoses* and finds the former "gracelessly verbose, largely a grotesque, all-too-humanly ineffectual character."[7] In short, Shakespeare's garrulous Venus is a sexual aggressor. Yet this is precisely the behavior that Ovid's narrator recommends for successful seduction, even the verbosity.

One of Baumlin's pronouncements on the poem is useful for my purposes. "Shakespeare's Venus, far from being the artful Ovidian goddess of love, proves to be merely a querulous pedant in the arts of poetic seduction."[8] This last clause is an excellent description of the praeceptor, and represents at least one way that medieval and Renaissance writers looked at this character. Ovid himself hints broadly in the *Ars* that his master of love is a comic oaf whose contradictory advice is quite inadequate for its intended purpose.[9] So if Shakespeare sought to create a travesty (as well as a refashioning) of a myth, he needed only to look into a different text by the very author who had initially provided him with the mythical material.

Is Shakespeare attempting to "outdo his poetic forefather, to 'out-Ovid' Ovid"[10] in some way? Perhaps. Yet parodic competition can be a form of tribute. If Jonathan Bate's assertion about *Venus and Adonis* is correct, that it "shows that a sexual relationship based on coercion is doomed,"[11] Shakespeare could have used no better classical intertext than the *Ars Amatoria* as precedent to establish such a theme and to explore its possibilities. His imitation of Ovid is what we might, along with Thomas Greene, label "dialectical," a practice prescribed by Renaissance theorists such as Petrarch, Erasmus, Ricci, and Ascham.[12]

I

Shakespeare scatters manifold allusions to the *Ars* as a text and genre in *Venus and Adonis*. His aggressive protagonist adopts the guise of a teacher; much of what she says to the youth she hopes to seduce is in lecture form. Actually, one of Shakespeare's manifold ironies is that the goddess who literally embodies venereal desire behaves in such a way as to preclude it, physically and verbally. As Heather Dubrow explains of Venus: "deceitful rhetoricians are their own principal victims, hoist with their own linguistic petards."[13] The goddess finishes one particularly tedious and ineffectual set of persuasions with:

> O learn to love, the lesson is but plain,
> And once made perfect, never lost again.
> (*VA* ll. 407–08)

Here Shakespeare roughly paraphrases the opening lines of the *Ars,* in which the praeceptor makes the first of several specious claims for his authority:

> Siquis in hoc artem populo non nouit amandi,
> Me legat, & lecto carmine, doctus amet.
> (1.1–2)

> [If someone does not understand the art of loving, let him read me, and having read my poem, he will love learnedly.]

Shakespeare distills the essence of Ovid's opening message. Venus assures Adonis that love is a skill that can be learned, and easily at that. Although she does not use the first person in her injunction, the first person is implied; indeed, the Goddess of Love is in her very presence an authority, or would seem to be. But Shakespeare's Venus is hardly the ethereal being who glides above the ground and wraps her son in a mist in the *Aeneid* (1.402–62). Nor is she the goddess whom the praeceptor uses as imprimatur in the *Ars Amatoria,* replete with myrtle (3.43–56). Like the master of love, Shakespeare's Venus is a bit pedantic, somewhat less assured of her efficacy than she would admit. In the manner of her paradigm in the *Ars,* her "lesson" proves to be anything but "plain," and is easily lost.

Like many a student, Adonis does not enjoy lessons that confuse him, and is even less fond of floods of unsolicited information. He feels intellectually, textually, and sexually harrassed: "Your treatise makes me like you worse and worse" (*VA* l. 774). In "treatise," a common term for the genre to which the *Ars* belongs, Shakespeare keeps the vestiges of his Ovidian metaphor current. Modern editors uniformly hypercorrect the First Quarto punctuation, "Your treatise makes me like you, worse & worse," and thereby obliterate a pun. If we read "like" as a verb, Adonis explains that his tormentor's didacticism heightens his distaste for her. It is also possible to gloss "like" as a preposition. The hero feels an undesirable affinity by proximity; Venus' presence debases him. It is a dreadful, though not unexpected, insult.

Besides "lesson" and "treatise," Shakespeare leaves other small clues to his intertext. When Venus asks her blushing boy, "Tell me, love's master, shall we meet tomorrow?" (l. 585), the epithet in the vocative anglicizes the Ovidian phrase in which the master of love asserts his authoritative identity to the *iuuenes Romae:* "ego sum praeceptor [sic] amoris" [I am the master of love] (*AA* 1.17). Venus, who has dominated her charge physically and verbally from the first line of the poem, carefully reverses gender roles to their traditional positions with her question. Presumably, she wishes to deceive her quarry into thinking that she, not he, is overmastered.

But Venus does not fool Adonis, nor should she fool us. She, not he, is "love's master." Her torrent of talk "reflects her desire to impose her presence."[14] And when Adonis is finally able to stem the verbal maelstrom, his replies seem to be not only refutations of Venus, but of the *Ars* Ovid:

> I hate not love but your device in love,
> That lends imbracements unto every stranger.
>   (*VA* ll. 789–90)

In some ways, "device" also points at the *Ars,* since deceit and craft are hallmarks of this text that were well known in the Renaissance. "Fallite fallentes" [Deceive the deceivers] (*AA* 1.647), counsels the master of love, which the first printed translation of the *Ars* in England, *The Flores of Ovide De Arte Amandi* (1513), renders "Begyle the begylers" (A3v), a text that Shakespeare could well have seen. The promiscuity that Adonis decries is another commonplace in the *Ars:* "cunctas / Posse capi" [all can be ensnared] (*AA* 1.269–70):

> Love is all truth, lust full of forged lies.
> More I could tell, but more I dare not say,
> The text is old, the orator too green,
> Therefore in sadness now I will away,
> My face is full of shame, my heart of teen,
> Mine ears that to your wanton talk attended,
> Do burn themselves, for having so offended.
>   (*VA* ll. 804–10)

To Venus' "treatise," Adonis offers his own "text" in refutation. He knows that Venus is love's master. Although he says it makes him like her worse and worse, his anxiety is that he is "like her, worse & worse." Or worse. However, as repulsive as he finds the goddess' Ovidian blandishments to be, one must not assume that Shakespeare's character represents his creator's disavowal of the *Ars Amatoria*. Adonis's recalcitrance is just as "unnatural" a reversal of gender roles as Venus' aggression: what woman's son will sourly leave her till she hath prevailed?

II

The praeceptor, full of wise sentences illustrated by metaphor, often compares his ideal male lover to a predatory animal, such as an eagle. In turn, women are prey, rabbits who run for their lives, the wingspan above inexorably shadowing their flight. It is worth emphasizing that Ovid's notion of gender is fixed, and that his animal kingdom is hierarchical. The hawk, something less than Jove's bird, the eagle, is hateful for his excessive aggression: "Odimus accipitrem: quia viuit semper in armis" [I hate the hawk because she lives only to kill] (2.147). So, when Shakespeare applies the figure of the *female* eagle to Venus,

> Even as an empty eagle sharp by fast
> Tires with her beak on feathers, flesh, and bone,
>
> (*VA* ll. 55–56)

he transfers Ovid's opprobrium for the hawk to her in order to underscore what he may have perceived as the "unnatural dealing" of a woman, goddess or no, who acts as aggressor. Venus' sexuality, despite all of her blandishments, is violent. Five hundred lines later, it is, to quote Williams and Baumlin, "grotesque":

> And having felt the sweetness of the spoil,
> With blindfold fury she begins to forage;
> Her face doth reek and smoke, her blood doth boil,
> And careless lust stirs up a desperate courage,
> Planting oblivion, beating reason back,
> Forgetting shame's pure blush and honor's wrack.
>
> (ll. 553–58)

Venus is "careless" and "desperate," without reason, shameless, a despoiler of honor. Adonis' ears do not burn without warrant (ll. 809–10). As John Velz explains, Venus "is reminiscent of Apollo and other Ovidian virgin-violators."[15] Here Ovid is reprocessed and reconfigured almost completely; Shakespeare swallows him.

This kind of authorial cannibalism metamorphoses yet again when

Shakespeare transfers the *avis* figure to Venus' prey:

> Look how a bird lies tangled in a net,
> So fastened in her arms Adonis lies.
>
> (*VA* ll. 67–68)

Three Ovidian commonplaces may have been braided together: the hunter who is skilled with his nets; "Scit bene venator, ceruis vbi retia tendat" (*AA* 1.45); the fowler who knows where the birds are; "Aucupibus noti frutices" (1.47); a lover who, like a bird, struggles in the toils of his captivity; "Dum caedat in laqueos, captus quoque nuper amator" (3.591). The classical and Renaissance texts are ensnared by each other, almost indistinguishable whenever Venus opens her mouth. Shakespeare makes no explicit comment on his master, but by absorbing, reanimating, and refashioning Ovid, he implicitly acknowledges a debt.

III

One of Shakespeare's more subtle tributes to the master of love is to make his protagonist embody some of Ovid's precepts. Venus lusts continuously: "She red and hot as coals of glowing fire" (*VA* l. 35). Such observations would seem to reverse the dictum that women are more constant and conceal their desires better: "Vir male dissimulat: tectius illa cupit" [Men hide their desires poorly; women are more clever] (*AA* 1.276), the "illa" serving metonymically as "femina." We may also be reminded of Orsino's comment to Viola-Cesario, which would seem to support Ovid's observation:

> boy, howeuer we do praise ourselues,
> Our fancies are more giddie and vnfirme,
> More longing, wauering, sooner lost and worne,
> Then womens are.   (*Twelfth Night* 2.4.31–34)[16]

However, Shakespeare and Ovid are just as changeable and as malleable as Orsino. The praeceptor also assures us: "Parcior in nobis, nec tam furiosa libido est" [We men are not so savage as women in their lust] (*AA* 1.281). So Venus, who burns and glows for Adonis, is the figurative embodiment of Ovid's contradictory observation after all.

At times, the *magister* offers advice that would be highly distasteful to women from Christine de Pizan in the fourteenth century to the present. "Vim licet appellent: grata est vis illa puellis" [Using force is permissible, and women welcome it] (*AA* 1.675). Or, similarly: "Quis sapiens blandis non misceat oscula verbis? / Illa licet non det: non data sume tamen" [What wise man does not mingle kisses with flattering words? Since it is not permissible for her to give, take what is ungiven] (1.665–66). In Thomas Heywood's translation of the *Ars, Loues Schoole* (c. 1600–13), he amplifies the couplet into a commentary:

> Who but a foole that cannot iudge of blisses,
> But when he speakes will with his words mixe kisses?
> Say she be coy, and will giue none at all,
> Take them vngiuen, perhaps at first shee'll brawle,
> Striue and resist her all the wayes she can,
> And say withall away you naughtie man.
> Yet will she fight like one would lose the field,
> And striuing gladly be constrain'd to yeeld.
>
> (B6ᵛ–B7ʳ [1. 868–75])

The "Vim licet appellent" argument is encoded carefully within. Shakespeare's Venus does not *offer* such precepts. Again, in the reversal of gender roles, she *enacts* them. Her wooing takes the form of the Ovidian self-fulfilling prophecy: "If thou wilt chide, thy lips shall never open" (*VA* l. 48). And she would certainly welcome the force she offers:

> Backward she pushed him as she would be thrust,
> And governed him in strength, though not in lust.
>
> (ll. 41–42)

As her *magister* counsels, she seizes the kisses that her victim does not offer:

> Even so she kissed his brow, his cheek, his chin,
> And where she ends, she doth anew begin.
> Forced to content, but never to obey,
> Panting he lies, and breatheth in her face.
>
> (ll. 59–62)

Adonis does not gladly constrain to yield: "away you naughtie [wo]man," his behavior implies. At this point, one might be tempted to say that Shakespeare demonstrates the invalidity of the Ovidian method. At the same time, Venus' understanding of this method does not take into account Ovid's advice for temperance: "cogere noli" (*AA* 1.481). Or, as Heywood translates: "Enforce her not" (B3ʳ [1.614]). Shakespeare learned a great deal from Ovid besides mythology: the use of narrative, characters, voices, and personae. He has no interest in summoning Ovid to the sessions of his sweet (un)silent thought in order to find him guilty of creating characters who give bad advice. Venus, perhaps, misreads.

IV

Not only does Venus embody some of Ovid's metaphorical commonplaces about women; at times, she seems to have read the *Ars Amatoria,* and appears to be following its advice. The praeceptor urges his pupils to choose an object for love and to move aggressively in pursuit of her: "Principio, quod amare velis, reperire labora" [First, strive to gain whom you wish to love] (*AA* 1.35). So Venus:

> Sick-thoughted Venus makes amain unto him,
> And like a bold faced suitor 'gins to woo him.
>
> (*VA* ll. 5–6)

Ovid's narrator waits thirty-five lines to establish this principle; Venus goes to it in the first sestet of the poem without much ado. Similarly, the *Ars* recommends that one be pitiable in order to lime the twigs for the unsuspecting: "Curaque, & in magno qui fit amore, dolor" [Whoever would love should show grief and care] (*AA* 1.737). Shakespeare's Venus begs Adonis incessantly, so much so that "impatience chokes her pleading tongue" (*VA* l. 217). However, Adonis meets her attempts to induce pity with complete contempt and repulses her forwardness defiantly.

The *Ars* suggests that tears can mollify the flintiest breast: "lacrymae prosunt" (*AA* 1.661); earlier, Ovid had used Ariadne as an example to work toward this generalization: "Clamabat, flebat simul" (*AA* l. 535). Whether sincere or not, Venus cries constantly in Shakespeare's poem: "And now she weeps, and now she fain would speak / And now her sobs do her intendments break" (*VA* ll. 221–22). These intendments, like all else, accomplishing nothing, and appear in the form of flattery:

> Thrice fairer than myself (thus she began),
> The field's chief flower, sweet above compare,
> Stain to all nymphs, more lovely than a man,
> More white and red than doves or roses are
>
> (*VA* ll. 7–10)

After all, Ovid's narrator suggests that blandishments can be the best way to steal the soul of another: "Blanditijs animum furtim deprehendere nunc sit" (*AA* 1.621). Why shouldn't flattery work on Adonis? For that matter, why shouldn't promises work? The praeceptor thinks them foolproof: "Nec timide promitte" [Don't be afraid to make promises] (*AA* l. 633). However, upon the pledge that "one sweet kiss shall pay this comptless debt" (*VA* l. 84), Adonis "winks and turns his lips another way" (l. 90) after raising his chin as a tease (l. 85). So love as a premeditated and calculating activity has no dominion, something that Ovid knew, as well.

Venus, in a greater testament to her maker's learning and ingenuity than her own,[17] uses a number of arguments from precedent taken directly from the *Ars:*

> Make use of time, let not advantage slip,
> Beauty within itself should not be wasted,
> Fair flowers that are not gathered in their prime
> Rot and consume themselves in little time.
>
> (*VA* ll. 129–32)

This is the shopworn *carpe diem* convention, almost always used for seduction in the seventeenth-century lyric poetry that would follow Shakespeare (who in turn gives it a different spin in his sonnets to his young man). Although its progenitor, Horace, does not use it in this sense (*Odes* 1.11.8), Ovid usually does. In *Ars* 2, he encodes the convention in his advice to young men: "Forma bonum fragile est" [Beauty is fleeting] (113–20). Predictably, he uses the same convention in his advice to women to make them easier for these same young men to seduce: "Venturae memores iam nunc estore senectae" [Remember even now the old age that will come to you] (3.59–100).

The praeceptor advises lovers to persist and be obdurate: "Perfer, & obdura" (*AA* 2.178). Surely Venus obeys both imperatives implicitly:

> Look how she entreats, and prettily entreats,
> For to a pretty ear she tunes her tale.
> Still is he sullen, still he lowers and frets
> 'Twixt crimson shame and anger ashy pale.
>
> (*VA* ll. 73–76)

However, obstreperousness has its pratfalls; she embarrasses and enrages Adonis. Ovid's narrator would have us persist, but he reminds us that in order to be loved, one should be lovable: "vt ameris, amabilis esto" (*AA*

2.107). He also suggests that if art is hidden (subtle), it is useful (one will get what one wants): "Si latet ars, prodest" (2.313). Three hundred lines later, the praeceptor graphically illustrates the truth of this dictum with Venus herself, who covers the essence of her biological femaleness with her hand: "Ipsa Venus pubem, quoties velamina ponit, / Protegitur laeua semireducta manu" [Even Venus herself, as often as she disrobes, covers her sex with her left hand when she bends down] (2.613–14). Shakespeare's Venus makes herself unlovable and she uses no art at all. And what her hands are covering (or not covering) is left for us to discover. Although she follows many of the more brazenly "amoral" precepts of the *Ars* and fails, her tendency to misapply some of them makes her fail more decisively. To paraphrase Touchstone in *As You Like It,* Venus is certainly a lover who runs into strange capers (of her own making). Although she is intended to be immortal, her love is mortal in its folly.

Even if "grotesque" is inaccurate as description of Venus, Shakespeare certainly intends for her to be comic. As she straddles Adonis, unwittingly crushing the life out of him in an (attempted) erotic embrace, her "Nay do not struggle, for thou shalt not rise" (*VA* l. 710) ensures that no part of him will rise, even that part that she is trying so desperately to make rise. This pun emblematizes the comedy of fallacious sexual pedagogy that Shakespeare found in the *Ars Amatoria* and so profitably transfused into *Venus and Adonis.*

The end of the poem also points to Ovid's comic treatise. Instead of the expected lamentation at Adonis' death, Venus delivers a valedictory address in which she defines love and decrees what its nature will be, fully in keeping with the power that she represents: "It shall be fickle, false, and full of fraud" (*VA* l. 1141); "most deceiving when it seems most just" (l. 1156). Shakespeare's new myth does not represent a travesty of the old, nor does it affirm that love-by-coercion is doomed. Instead, it accounts for the cynical view of love that the *Ars* promulgates. Venus' decree that love be fickle and false coincides exactly with the views of the praeceptor on *amor.* This should not surprise us, since the *Ars* informs Shakespeare's conception of her throughout the poem. In a masterstroke of anachronism, he makes his goddess enunciate his master's precepts in a time before *magister* or *praecepta* could have possibly existed. So Shakespeare's Venus wills herself into existence. She decrees that love is a cynical business, an idea that requires an Ovid to enunciate it, and in turn requires a Shakespeare to refashion it—in the form of a poetic goddess who will be left "upon her back, deeply distressed" (l. 814), and therefore moved to decree that love be fickle, false, and full of fraud.

1. My text of the *Ars* is a reprint of the edition published by Aldus Manutius (1516–17) that Thomas Vautrollier was given an exclusive patent to print in England in 1574: *Publii Ouidii Nasonis Heroidum epistolae, Amorum libri iii, De arte amandi libri iii, De remedio amoris lib. ii, Omnia ex acuratiss*, ed. A. Naugerius et al. (London: T. Vautrollerius, 1583). 203–68. Its line numbers and spelling differ very slightly from modern editions (i.e., *praecaptor* rather than *praeceptor*). It is almost certainly Shakespeare's *Ars*. Citations from *Venus and Adonis* are from *The Complete Works of Shakespeare*, 4th ed., ed. David Bevington (New York: HarperCollins, 1994).

2. Muriel C. Bradbrook argues that *Venus* was "designed not to answer" Robert Greene's scurrilous charges in a *Groats-Worth of Witte* that Shakespeare's classical learning was nonexistent, "but to obliterate the impression he had tried to make." See "Beasts and Gods: Greene's *Groats-Worth of Witte* and the Social Purpose of *Venus and Adonis*," *Shakespeare Survey* 15 (1962): 68. Hyder E. Rollins discusses Malone's conjectures on Shakespeare's source material and reprints passages from Golding and others. See *A New Variorum Edition of Shakespeare: The Poems* (Philadelphia: Lippincott, 1938), 393. Geoffrey Bullough cites Arthur Golding's 1567 translation, *The XV. Bookes of P Ouidius Naso, Entytuled Metamorphosis* as the source for the poem. See *Narrative and Dramatic Sources of Shakespeare*, 7 vols. (New York: Columbia UP, 1957–73) 1:161–78. T.W. Baldwin thinks that Shakespeare relies much less on Golding than on Ovid's Latin. See *William Shakspere's Small Latine and Lesse Greeke*, 2 vols. (Urbana: U of Illinois P, 1950) 2:417–55. Jonathan Bate takes the opposite position from Baldwin; it is the thesis of his book, *Shakespeare and Ovid* (Oxford: Clarendon P, 1993). S. Clark Hulse suggests that *Hero and Leander* and Titian's painting of Venus and Adonis may have figured in Shakespeare's alteration of his predecessor. See "Shakespeare's Myth of Venus and Adonis," *PMLA* 93 (1978): 95; reprinted in this volume. Gordon Williams dismisses both notions without dismissing Hulse. See "The Coming of Age in Shakespeare's Adonis," *Modern Language Review* 78 (1983): 769–70.

3. There were at least sixteen separate verse translations of different parts of the Ovidian corpus between 1513 and 1640, most of them reaching multiple editions. For a listing of these, see Alfred W. Pollard and G.R. Redgrave, *A Short-Title Catalogue of Books Printed in England, Scotland, & Ireland & of English Books Printed Abroad*, 2nd. ed., 3 vols. (Oxford: Oxford UP, 1976) 2:201–202.

4. Very little has been written on the general connection. R.K. Root implies that Shakespeare, in Venus' boast to Adonis concerning her conquest of Mars (*VA* 97–114), depends on *Ars* 2.561–92, where the notion of conquest is stressed. Baldwin makes the parallel explicit in *On the Literary Genetics of Shakespeare's Poems and Sonnets* (Urbana: U of Illinois P, 1950), 15. Ovid's account of the relationship in *Metamorphoses* 4.169–89 merely relates the discovery of the lovers. Bate (50 n. 4) suggests that Venus' argument concerning the palfrey (*VA* 385–96) "borrows" from *Ars* 1.277–80, a point that he seems to have "borrowed" from T.W. Baldwin. Baldwin says, "It looks as if Shakspere had read *The Art of Love*, and found there not only art, but also technique for the steed of Adonis to contrast with his master and to demonstrate Ovid's doctrine at length. The parallel is exact and probable, but I see nothing to make it absolutely certain that Shakspere is using Ovid directly" (*Literary Genetics* 26).

Shakespeare had no Arthur Golding to help him with Ovid's Latin. Except for *The Flores of Ovide De Arte Amandi with Theyr Englysshe afore Them* (London: Wynkin de Worde, 1513), a bilingual primer for schoolboys and their masters, there is no English translation of the *Ars* printed in England before 1600. Thomas Heywood's *Loues Schoole: Publii Ouidii Nasonis De Arte Amandi: Or, The Art of Loue*, probably pirated by the bookseller Henry Austin and printed surreptitiously across the Channel in Holland like Christopher Marlowe's version of the *Amores, All Ovid's Elegies*, could have been published at any time between 1600 and 1613. Since it exemplifies the way that Shakespeare's contemporaries read Ovid's poem, I will use it occasionally as translation. I am currently compiling a critical old-spelling edition of *Loues Schoole* for publication; signature numbers are those of B.M. 1068. g. 20 (3) / STC 18935.5, and line numbers in square brackets are my own.

5. "Shakespeare's Myth," 95.

6. "Coming of Age," 770.

7. "The Birth of the Bard: *Venus and Adonis* and Poetic Apotheosis," *Papers on Language and Literature* 26 (1990): 192.

8. Idem, 202.

9. For instance: "vestri peccata magistri / Effugite" (*AA* 2.173–74): "Avoid your master's mistakes." The *magister* refers to the past, but Ovid, fond of keeping an ironic distance from his amatory personae, could certainly mean the present, as well. John M. Fyler stresses the "unreliability" of Ovid's narrator, and argues that Chaucer completely understood and carefully imitated this technique: "the teacher of this *ars* is a pedantic fool; we err greatly if we identify him with Ovid or take his self-characterization seriously." See *Chaucer and Ovid* (New Haven: Yale UP, 1979), 11. Furthermore: "The comic result [of following such advice] appears in the *Amores*, which can be considered a presentation of the diploma-carrying lover in action" (13). I explore Ovid's personae and their legacy to the West in *Harmful Eloquence: Ovid's "Amores" from Antiquity to Shakespeare* (Ann Arbor: U of Michigan P, 1996).

Our own general deafness to the nuances of ancient languages, indeed, our very awe at those who possess a facility in them superior to our own, should not deceive us into thinking that authors such as Chaucer and Shakespeare possessed a similar deafness. They were capable of seeing the praeceptor as a dolt.

The "other way" that medieval and early modern readers are alleged to have interpreted Ovid's narrator: an infallible authority on love, to be taken seriously at all times. This reading strategy even has a name: "Ovid misunderstood," somewhat wrongly attributed to C.S. Lewis, from which he attempted to defend himself in *The Allegory of Love* (Oxford: Oxford UP, 1936), 7–8, 43 n.

10. Baumlin, 207.

11. *Shakespeare and Ovid*, 64.

12. For Greene's term, see *The Light in Troy: Imitation and Discovery in Renaissance Poetry* (New Haven: Yale UP, 1982), 45–46. Even a perfunctory analysis of Shakespeare's use of his predecessors underscores the inadequacy of a word such as "source," which implies a fixed locus of emanation, and hence is not descriptive of his practice (always polyglot, multiplex). Furthermore, what poststructuralists claim is a new way to look at texts is surely an ancient idea in both theory and practice. Julia Kristeva's preference for "transposition" over "intertextuality" or "source" as a term has its roots in Renaissance thinking: "If one grants that every signifying practice is a field of transpositions of various signifying systems (an intertextuality), one then understands that its 'place' of enunciation and its denoted 'object' are never single, complete, and identical to themselves, but always plural, shattered, capable of being tabulated." See *Revolution in Poetic Language*, trans. Margaret Walker (New York: Columbia UP, 1984), 60. Greene (54–103) and George W. Pigman ("Versions of Imitation in the Renaissance," *Renaissance Quarterly* 33 [1980]: 1–32) demonstrate conclusively that sixteenth-century theorists such as Erasmus and Ricci identify and advocate a similar polyvocality in poetic composition (minus the deconstructive semiotics). Or, to invoke Bate again: "the creative imitator interprets his source narrative partly by means of other narratives that lie both outside and inside, around and within [the text]" (51).

13. *Captive Victors: Shakespeare's Narrative Poems and Sonnets* (Ithaca: Cornell UP, 1987), 22.

14. Idem, 28.

15. "The Ovidian Soliloquy in Shakespeare," *Shakespeare Studies* 18 (1986): 3.

16. All references to the plays follow the Helge Kökeritz facsimile edition of

the First Folio, *Mr. William Shakespeares Comedies, Histories, & Tragedies* (London, 1623; New Haven: Yale UP, 1954).

17. Ovid's arguments from precedent are so numerous as to defy cataloguing, but some of them are particularly devilish. As the praeceptor praises his own era as being more civilized, he looks wistfully to the past as a model that his own era foolishly ignores. The emotional complexity of Ovid's rhetoric is exemplified in the passage on the theater and the rape of the Sabine women that Romulus orders (*AA* 1.89–134). After the masterful (and surprisingly sympathetic) description of the frightened young women, Ovid concludes with the words of one lust-crazed soldier to his prey:

> Atque ita, quid teneros lacrymis corrumpis ocellos?
> Quod matri pater est, hoc tibi, dixit, ero.
> > (*AA* 1.129–30)

Heywood's colloquial yet precise translation suggests that he bestowed some care upon the passage:

> why weepest thou, sweet, what ailst my dear?
> Dry vp those drops, these clouds of sorrow cleare.
> Ile be to thee, if thou thy griefe wilt smother,
> Such as thy father was vnto thy mother.
> > (A3ᵛ [1.121–24])

Venus uses the same male-oriented argument:

> O had thy mother borne so hard a mind,
> She had not brought forth thee, but died unkind.
> > (*VA* ll. 203–04)

Shakespeare uses this again in the words of one of his more villainous seducers, Bertram, as he seeks the virtue of the maid Diana:

> you are cold and sterne,
> And now you should be as your mother was
> When your sweet selfe was got.
> > (*All's Well That Ends Well* 4.2.9–11)

WRIOTHESLEY'S RESISTANCE

WARDSHIP PRACTICES AND OVIDIAN NARRATIVES IN SHAKESPEARE'S *VENUS AND ADONIS*

Patrick M. Murphy

The real subject is not primarily sexual lewdness at all, but "social lewdness" mythically expressed in sexual terms.[1]

I

In 1592 or 1593 Shakespeare dedicated *Venus and Adonis* to Henry Wriothesley, the third Earl of Southampton, who was a minor under the guardianship of William Cecil. At the time the nineteen-year-old Southampton was negotiating the personal, economic, and intergenerational complexities of the wardship system, a feudal practice revived by the Tudors as a fiscal device and used by Cecil to his considerable financial and political advantage. Under feudal law wardship meant that "the King enjoyed rights over the lands and the disposal in marriage of any of his tenants in chief who inherited his estates while still a minor."[2] Henry VII and Henry VIII found in the residual feudal practice of wardship a method for turning land and marriage arrangements into money for the crown. The Court of Wards gradually evolved into the crown's mechanism for selling wardships and for arbitrating disputes about rights over land, marriage arrangements, and custody. During Elizabeth's reign William Cecil (who held the offices of Secretary of State, Lord Treasurer, and Master of Wards) improved upon the process as a way of educating the young and manipulating political and familial alliances.[3]

After the death of his father in 1581, Henry Wriothesley's wardship was sold to Lord Howard of Effingham, the Lord Chamberlain, and at some point the rights over Wriothesley's personal custody and marriage were transferred to Burghley while Howard remained in charge of Southampton's lands. When he was eight years old, Wriothesley was apparently brought to live and to learn at Cecil House. For sometime Burghley desired to marry Southampton to his granddaughter and ward, Elizabeth Vere, but Southampton delayed until he reached legal maturity. On November 19, 1594, Father Garnet, the Superior of the English Jesuits, wrote that: "The young Erle of Southampton refusing the Lady Veere payeth 5000[li] of present payment."[4] Father Garnet's letter, as Akrigg notices, was dated about six weeks after Southampton turned twenty-one, and in January of 1595 Elizabeth Vere married the Earl of Derby. Southampton's separation from Cecil's household and guardianship came at a considerable cost. He not only had to pay the crown the customary fee for the transfer of his lands back into his own possession, but he also had to pay Burghley a fine for refusing his choice of a bride. In light of these circumstances, the question is: Why would Shakespeare find in Ovid's narrative of Venus and Adonis appropriate materials for a person in Southampton's situation?[5]

Shakespeare dedicated *Venus and Adonis* to Southampton after Burghley's intended arrangement was public, before Southampton's final refusal was secure, and shortly after one of Burghley's clerks, John Clapham, dedicated the poem *Narcissus* to Southampton.[6] The first evidence of Burghley's intentions is found in a letter written to Burghley by Thomas Stanhope on July 15, 1590—about four years before Southampton could legally assume control over the properties he inherited from his father. Stanhope, writing that he was not involved in arrangements to have his daughter marry Southampton, describes a conversation he had with Southampton's mother to assure Burghley of her honesty in the matter concerning Elizabeth Vere. In his letter Stanhope says that Lady Southampton would "in good faith do her best in the cause, but sayth she I do not fynd a disposition in my sonne to be tyed as yett, what wilbe hereafter time shall trye, and no want shalbe found on my behalfe."[7] Between 1590 and late 1594 we can only assume that some rather complex social, economic, and personal negotiations between Southampton, his family, and Burghley must have occurred. In a letter from Viscount Montagu, who was Southampton's maternal grandfather, to Burghley, written after their meeting at Oatlands, Montagu tells of the advice he and his daughter gave to Southampton: "First my daughter affirms upon her faith and honor that she is not acquaynted *with any alteration* of her sonnes mynd *from* this your grandchild. And wee have layd abrode unto hym *both the comodityes and hindrances* likely to grow unto him by chanuge."[8] Biographers have often thought that Montagu and his daughter sided with Burghley against (the narcissistic or sexually timid) Southampton.[9] When read closely, however, their comments are ambiguous. According to Montagu's statement, we cannot tell (nor perhaps could Burghley) what plan Southampton had not altered: the arranged marriage to Elizabeth Vere or its refusal. Removed by a (not unexpected) formality of tone, their statements appear to assist Southampton in delaying his decision, while avoiding direct confrontation with Burghley.

The law did not leave wards completely unprotected or without options when their guardians or others acted against their interests.[10] The statute of Merton, one relevant law in this matter, allowed for delay: "If an heir, of what age soever he be, will not marry at the request of his lord, he shall not be compelled thereunto; but when he cometh to full age he shall give to his lord, and pay him as much as any would have given him for the marriage."[11] Southampton's delay may not have been the result of some personal, sexual disposition but rather a deliberate legal strategy. Furthermore, under certain circumstances wards could possibly avoid the fine and refuse the marriage arrangement by claiming "disparagement." Edward Coke lists many different kinds of disparagement including: first, defects of the mind, involving a lunatic or an idiot; second, defects of the blood, involving persons of lower social station, aliens, or bastards; and third, defects of the body, including missing limbs or other deformities.[12] Hurstfield finds only a little evidence for "direct action to prevent disparagement, including that of Shakespeare's Bertram," and admits that there is no evidence of "lawsuits for disparagement."[13] It appears that, when the possibility of disparagement arose, matters were settled out of court, or the ward, as in Wriothesley's case, paid a fine. Southampton's refusal may have caused some personal strain in the relationship he had with Burghley, but there appears to be nothing fundamentally revolutionary, rebellious, or subversive in his choice. Although the fine appears to be somewhat excessive,[14] the law had clearly provided for this contingency, and Southampton was within his rights to deny Burghley's wishes. Eventually, in 1598, Southampton married Elizabeth Vernon, Essex's cousin and one of Queen Elizabeth's maids of honor, after she became pregnant.[15]

Montagu, Mary Wriothesley, and Southampton, however, probably knew that Edward de Vere participated in (and apparently, at times, believed) rumors that Elizabeth Vere was not his daughter. When we foreground the details surrounding these rumors about the purported illegitimacy of Elizabeth Vere, about wardship practices (including the possibility of disparagement), and about Wriothesley's own situation, Shakespeare's *Venus and Adonis*, often understood as early modern erotica or as a debate between pleasure and virtue, may also function as a form of advice literature, counseling about the kinds of human and cultural problems that inform Burghley's insistence upon the marriage to his granddaughter and Southampton's delay and resistance to the arrangement. Typically, Shakespeare's erotic epyllion is discussed in terms of Elizabethan love poetry, or in terms of Shakespeare's development as a playwright and poet during the brief time when the theaters were closed because of plague. But the interpretive turns made in the criticism have overlooked the possibility that Shakespeare's poem, as a social practice, addresses the politics of wardship, an institution of considerable force and complexity situated at the crossroads between personal and social and political life. Through this "first heir" of his invention, Shakespeare, while establishing himself as a poet, may have provided Southampton with a disguised critique of social pressures and economic practices which enabled him to avoid complicity with intolerable prescriptions, on one hand, and a destructive revenge against the loss of human (ontological) distinctions, on the other.

II

The relations between Shakespeare's poem and Southampton's refusal to marry Elizabeth Vere are difficult to trace without falling into the problem of localization or of topical reading. While exploring new possibilities for topical approaches, Leah Marcus has noticed that "local reading tends to be associated with antiquarianism and the valorization of origins, with an older mode of historicism that deciphered texts in order to discover and fix the meaning of Shakespeare."[16] Topical reading has traditionally sought to find the key to unlock the historical identity of persons disguised through the distortions of type and caricature. Building upon the work of Raymond Williams and Fredric Jameson, Marcus has shown how Shakespeare's texts are related to social processes but *not necessarily* in the manner desired by topical readers who think a reading achieves closure by deciphering the way the work *reflects* specific historical circumstances and persons. For Marcus, however, topical or "local" reading *mediates* social processes by studying (through a provisional positivism) how ideology is dispersed "prismatically" through correspondences and homologies.[17] For Williams, Jameson, and Marcus, poems are social processes that interact with other, often discontinuous, social processes. "We have to have enough confidence in our historical data to be able to perceive homologies and differences between the texts we are working with and other social formations," Marcus writes; "we have to get our texts to coalesce into identifiable patterns long enough to allow us to sort out their idiosyncratic ways of creating meaning."[18]

One mechanism for mapping the interactions or coalescence among discontinuous social processes, as Jameson demonstrates, is the semiotic or semantic square (or rectangle) developed by Greimas. Nancy Armstrong explains how to read the diagram of the semiotic square in an efficient and clear way: "Once any unit of meaning (S1) is conceived, we automatically conceive of the absence of that meaning (–S1), as well as an opposing system of meaning (S2) that correspondingly implies its own absence (–S2)."[19] Greimas designed three models for processes concerning *sexual relations*: a cultural (or social) model (C), an economic model (E), and a model for personal or individual values (P). And he observed that meaning occurs when different semiotic processes interact within an "epistemy" or hierarchy of semiotic systems determined by a particular culture.[20] For instance, in a specific marriage in a given society the *social or cultural model* of sexual relations and the *economic model* of sexual relations interact with each other and with the *model of individual values*. The meaning of a specific practice results from the interactions among these homologous (but perhaps conflicting) systems and rules, and at times one system might predominate. As in Southampton's situation, personal values may win out over cultural prescriptions and economic profit, or economic concerns may overrule personal and cultural demands.

S1: unit of meaning

    C1: prescribed sexual relations: culture
    P1: desired sexual relations (marriage)
    E1: profitable relations (trade)

S2: opposing system of meaning

    C2: prohibited sexual relations: nature
    P2: feared sexual relations (incest)
    E2: economic loss or harm (theft)

–S2: absence of opposing meaning

    –C2: non-prohibited sexual relations: non-nature (art)
    –P2: non-feared sexual relations (male adultery)
    –E2: non-harmful economic relations (gift as non-prohibited "theft")

–S1: absence of unit of meaning

    –C1: non-prescribed sexual relations: non-culture (wild beasts)
    –P1: non-desired sexual relations (female adultery)
    –E1: non-profitable sexual relations (gift as non-profitable "trade")

These semiotic models make it possible to examine connections among discontinuous materials related to Wriothesley's refusal to marry Elizabeth Vere: Shakespeare's source materials in Book X of Ovid's *Metamorphoses,* Shakespeare's poem, and some biographical anecdotes and documents related to Southampton and Elizabeth Vere.

In a manner that delicately alludes to an inheritance left to a minor who needs maternal comfort and protection to compensate for the loss of a father, Venus speaks her final words to the anemone after she plucks and embraces it:

> Here was *thy father's bed,* here in my breast;
> Thou art the *next of blood,* and 'tis thy *right.*
> Lo in this hollow cradle take thy rest,
> My throbbing heart shall rock thee day and night:
> There shall not be one minute in an hour
> Wherein I will not kiss my sweet love's flower.[21]

By using the images of nursing and cradling, Venus describes her incestuous desires for the son of Adonis in terms of guardianship: that is, she cares for a minor heir. The anemone inherits Venus (as lover, mother, and custodian) by right of blood. Curiously enough, Shakespeare introduces this variation. Ovid and Golding do not treat the anemone as the child of Adonis with rights of inheritance. In Shakespeare's poem Venus imagines herself as both the guardian of the child and the property the ward will inherit even before reaching maturity. Yet, when alive, Adonis never fully possessed Venus, no matter how much she overwhelmed him or tried to refigure herself as an enclosed park or pleasant land: "'Fondling,' she saith, 'since I have hemm'd thee here / Within the circuit of this ivory pale, / I'll be a park, and thou shalt be my deer'" ; "'Graze on my lips, and if those hills be dry, / Stray lower, where the pleasant fountains lie.'"[22] Apart from its primary sense as "a foolish person," the word *fondling* was also a variant for *foundling,* "a deserted infant whose parents are unknown, a child whom there is no one to claim."[23] With this word Venus implies that Adonis' motive for revenge may be feelings of abandonment (by Myrrha) that may be cured by Venus' pleasures.

Shakespeare concealed two matters about the teller and the tale of his Ovidian source that concern prescribed and prohibited social acts. Nevertheless, these details continue to function in Shakespeare's poem, forming crucial connections between his use of Ovidian materials and Southampton's personal, economic, and intergenerational situation. *First,* by choosing to retell only the tale of Venus and Adonis from among many linked tales, Shakespeare (perhaps inadvertently) concealed that the story of Adonis' origins contains a complicated incest narrative extending over several generations. Myrrha conceives Adonis through an incestuous union with her father Cinyras who descends from Paphos, the son (or daughter) of Pygmalion, and his metamorphosed ivory statue. Furthermore, Shakespeare excludes the materials that explain why the "sick-thoughted" goddess pursues the blushing youth. Nor does Shakespeare tell us that Adonis seeks to "avenge his mother's passion."[24] As we will see later, homologies exist between Ovid's stories and topical anecdotes about passionate mothers who subvert the rules of patriarchy: both Mary Wriothesley (Southampton's mother) and Anne Cecil Vere (Elizabeth Vere's mother) were accused by their husbands of committing non-prescribed or prohibited sexual acts. The second Earl of Southampton separated his son from his mother and unsuccessfully tried to separate his daughter from her as well; Edward de Vere withdrew from his wife and child who went to live with William Cecil.

Second, Shakespeare concealed the function of his narrator by not naming him as Ovid names Orpheus, a figure traditionally associated with the simultaneous emergence of poetry and civil order. In both ancient and early modern contexts Orpheus is the semantic function that distinguishes between socially *permissible* and socially *unacceptable* practices. In the *Ars Poetica* Horace wrote: "When primitive men roamed the forests, / Orpheus, the sacred interpreter of heavenly will, / Turned them away from killing and living like beasts / And hence is said to have tamed wild lions and tigers."[25] Relying upon Horace, Puttenham discussed Orpheus in his chapter on "How Poets were the first priests, the first prophets, the first Legislators and politicians in the world," and he speculates:

> The profession and use of Poesie is most ancient from the beginning, and not as many erroneously suppose, *after,* but *before* any civil society was among men. For it is written, that Poesie was the original cause and occasion of their first assemblies, when before the people remained in the woods and mountains, vagarant and dispersed like the wild beasts, lawless and naked, or very ill-clad, and of all good and necessary provision for harbour or sustenance utterly unfurnished: so as they little differed for their manner of life, from the very brute beasts of the field.[26]

Ovid qualifies this Horatian understanding of Orpheus by making him into a figure who prescribes pederasty *and* resists sexual relations with passionate women *because* he either keeps his vow to Eurydice or punishes himself for inadvertently breaking his promise to her.[27] According to Ovid, Orpheus governs his life by principle and (self-inaugurated) law. His songs are about what happens when ontological distinctions are lost between the savage and the tame, nature and culture, permissible and impermissible acts.

"It is accepted, in accordance with Lévi-Strauss's description,"

Greimas writes, "that human societies divide their semantic universes into two dimensions, culture and nature. The first is defined by the contents they assume and with which they invest themselves [prescriptions], the second by those they reject [prohibitions]."[28] As the materials from Horace, Ovid, and Puttenham suggest, *Orpheus* functions as a substantive term for this semantic distinction or "actantial" predication. Similarly, Shakespeare's narrator stages a debate (complicated by chiasmus) between Venus and Adonis about different orders of prescription and prohibition, acceptable and unacceptable acts. But the narrator himself, as Coleridge astutely noticed, remains aloof from the debate he sketches:

> It is throughout as if a superior spirit more intuitive, more intimately conscious, even than the characters themselves, not only of every outward look and act, but of the flux and reflux of the mind in all its subtlest thoughts and feelings, were placing the whole before our view; himself meanwhile unparticipating in the passions, and actuated only by that pleasurable excitement, which had resulted from the energetic fervor of his own spirit in so vividly exhibiting, what it had so accurately and profoundly contemplated.[29]

Shakespeare's erotic writing, for Coleridge, as a writing of dissipation and diversion, avoids the offensive sensuality of the "animal impulse" while it preserves the contemplation of such passion by a detached, intuitive spirit. For Coleridge, art acts as a censor and filter; in Hegelian terms, it is the negation of the negation [from S2 and –S1 to –S2 and S1]. When Shakespeare borrows the story of Venus and Adonis but elides the name of the narrator, the figure of Orpheus is put under erasure (or forgotten) only to return when Coleridge finds the abstract attributes for poetic genius in a Shakespeare, who has displaced Orpheus and Ovid, as author.

We can use Coleridge's description of Shakespeare's (or the narrator's) qualities to map the *personal values* concerning sexual relations [P] on to a semiotic square. Based upon the idea that "individuals are defined, in a way analogous to society, by the assumption of contents in which they invest and that constitute their personalities, and by the denegation of other contents,"[30] Greimas builds this semiotic model around the one he developed for *the social or cultural model* of sexual relations [C]. At times a person's values agree and at other times disagree with the prescribed and the prohibited terms of the culture. When everything is working in a cooperative direction, there will be correspondence between socially prescribed actions [C1] and personally desired objects [P1], as well as agreement about socially unacceptable actions [C2] and personally feared or repulsive objects [P2]. The semiotic map in the diagram takes shape around Coleridge's (Orphic) description of the narrator: between a "superior spirit" detached from the world and "the passions," which are seen but not felt as such [P1<—>P2].

Culture / Prescriptions (C1) desired sexual relations		Nature / Prohibitions (C2) feared sexual relations
Promises (boys)	<——— Orpheus ———>	Passion / Circonians
Spirit	<——— (Coleridge) ———>	Passion
Passion (incest)	<——— Venus ———>	Boar hunt
Revenge & boar hunt	<——— Adonis ———>	Venus (incest)

Non-nature / Non-prohibited (–C2) non-feared sexual relations art / non-passion	Non-culture / Non-prescribed (–C1) non-desired sexual relations non-culture / boar, wild beasts

Shakespeare complicates and problematizes the correspondences between the *cultural* and *personal* models of sexual relations by combining contrary and contradictory elements within Venus and Adonis. Appealing to Adonis through her narrative about the seduction of Mars, on the one hand, and the example of the breeding jennet, on the other, Venus misses the mark and is unable to overcome Adonis' resistance. Adonis is neither a god nor a beast; he must answer to another order of ontological distinctions, to another order of acceptable and unacceptable acts: "Love surfeits not, lust like a glutton dies; / Love is all truth, lust full of forged lies."[31] His error, vengeance, leads to his own annihilation, and he is changed, like his mother, into the realm of vegetative life. Driven by an incestuous passion, the immortal Venus prescribes erotic pleasures for a mortal Adonis who (motivated by a destructive desire to disgrace love and avenge his mother's transgressive passion) prescribes a disciplined restraint, on one hand, and violent domination of wildness, on the other. "I hate not love," Adonis tells her, "but your device in love / That lends embracements unto every stranger. / You do it for increase: O strange excuse, / When reason is the bawd to lust's abuse!"[32] Venus *is* the incestuous desire that Adonis fears and desires to avenge. Adonis desires what Venus prohibits: to hunt and defeat the boar. The tale of

Atalanta and Hippomenes provides a clue to the narrative function of the boar, one of those savage beasts that "do not turn their backs in flight."[33] Venus' direct appeal at the end of her story is: "do you, for my sake, dear boy, avoid [the boar], lest your manly courage be the ruin of us both."[34] But Adonis pursues the ruin of the incestuous passion that is the shared feature (or seme) of both Venus and Myrrha: "My love to love is love but to disgrace it."[35] Venus gives Adonis a prohibition which conforms to the prescription that determines his character, and a simple binary logic takes over: instead of avoiding the boar, Adonis has even more reason to pursue it.

The boar is a highly overdetermined agent for a complicated sequence of functions. The boar and Adonis share a semic unity—vengeance against Venus. Yet, Venus and the boar may also share a semic function if we think that lust and aggression are different manifestations of the same drive or instinct. Shakespeare's poem invites this identification when Venus compares herself to the boar: "Had I been tooth'd like him, I must confess, / With kissing him I should have kill'd him first."[36] However, the *function* of Orpheus represents the (perhaps impossible) hope that by distinguishing between acceptable and unacceptable acts, lust and aggression may be separated—or at least tamed, altered, or changed by art. The boar represents the wildness of a world where no ontological distinctions are made or recognized: "Being ireful, on the lion he will venture. / The thorny brambles and embracing bushes, / As fearful of him, part; through whom he rushes."[37] And Adonis' desire to kill the boar *appears* to be a way of conquering this savage force and of establishing his manhood. Unlike the hunter Adonis wishes to be, Orpheus tames wild and savage elements through song rather than through slaughter. By killing Adonis, the boar negates the object of Venus' incestuous passion (Atalanta and Hippomenes are avenged), but that vengeance is overcome and conquered in turn when Venus plucks the anemone, which will again escape her grasp as it withers. The boar, therefore, in denying Venus satisfaction, appears to enforce the prohibition against incest [and would appear to function therefore on the axis C1<—> C2]. However, since the boar's murder of Adonis also negates the voice of prescription against lust, the boar more accurately occupies the place of non-culture: the place on the semiotic square of the metamorphosed Atalanta and Hippomenes as well as of the Cerastae (the horned women changed into savage bulls) [−C1]. From this perspective the boar is a regressive signifier, returning us to a time and a place, as Puttenham would say, "before" the emergence of poetry and civil order.

Interpretations of Shakespeare's poem often side with Venus (understood as the affirmation of sensuous pleasure) or Adonis (disciplined virtue).

However, Shakespeare represents a different problem in the poem—even though both Venus and Adonis use rhetorical strategies to convince each other that pleasure and virtue are their respective motives. By making his poem the site of a debate between contradictory prescriptions about acceptable and unacceptable acts, Shakespeare's narrator demonstrates the structural similarities between intolerable prescriptions that reduce culture (or acceptable acts) to degenerative practices, on one hand, and a self-destructive vengeance that tries to insist upon culture by using "non-cultural" or savage methods, on the other. Wriothesley seems to have faced this problem when confronting his options concerning the marriage to Elizabeth Vere, and by reconstructing the details of that situation, which shares homologies with Shakespeare's poem, we can better understand his choice to pay the £5,000 fine.

III

The abuse of wards did not go unnoticed by sixteenth-century preachers and writers. Hugh Latimer criticized the neglected education of wards in his "Sermon of the Plow," and Thomas Smith, indicting the whole practice, wrote in De Republica Anglorum: "Many men do esteem this wardship by knights-service very unreasonable and unjust, and contrary to nature, that a freeman and gentleman should be bought and sold like an horse or an ox."[38] Smith's simile drives home the point that economic forces have metamorphic (often degenerative) consequences. Trade in wardships profited guardians and the crown while it also sometimes symbolically transgressed cultural prescriptions and personal values about sexual relations. The legal option to claim disparagement reveals that concerns over financial or political power sometimes conflicted with the wards' needs to preserve their social standing and the noble lineage of their families.[39] The infrequency of its use in the legal record, however, demonstrates that when questions of disparagement arose, they were probably handled with discretion.

"The heiress Elizabeth Trussell," Lawrence Stone writes, "was bought from Henry VII by George Earl of Kent for £266 and left by will in marriage to his younger son Henry. But she was seized by force by the eldest son, presumably out of spite towards his stepbrother, and returned to Henry VII, who then resold her for £1,333 to John Earl of Oxford, who married her."[40] Elizabeth Trussell was Edward de Vere's grandmother. And Stone leaves little doubt that the second purchase and marriage of Elizabeth Trussell by John of Oxford (the fifteenth Earl) was a kind of metaphorical and economic incest. In other words, Edward de Vere (once a ward of Burghley and the husband of Anne Cecil) was the descendant of a patriarch who deployed and transgressed (at least metaphorically) the rules of the wardship system, by occupying the place of both guardian and husband. John of Oxford is *like* Pygmalion. Just as Pygmalion purchased the metamorphosed statue through his creative efforts at sculpting the ivory, Elizabeth Trussell was purchased by Oxford's effort: he is both guardian/father and husband, exchanging the item of his own purchase with himself. Southampton and Shakespeare may have known about the bas relief of Elizabeth Trussell and John of Oxford that marks their grave in the chancel of the parish church of Castle Hedingham.[41] In some literal sense the generations that followed may have thought of their ancestors as semblances in stone, and the living generations, their warmed and embodied repetition. Stymied by an unresponsive Adonis, Venus uses images which reverse this metamorphosis from flesh to stone, while alluding to Pygmalion's fetish for his ivory carving and Myrrha's metamorphosis. She insults Adonis, describing him as a "Statue contenting but the eye alone, / Thing like a man, but of no woman bred!"[42]

Several documents indicate that Oxford either started rumors about Elizabeth Vere's illegitimacy or that he believed rumors by someone else. After Oxford refused to live with his wife and child upon returning from the Continent in April 1576, Burghley concluded that Oxford's first suspicions occurred earlier that month, (about seven months after the child's birth): "No unkindness known on his [Oxford's] part at his departure. She [Ann] made him privy that she thought she was with child, whereof he said he was glad. When he heard she was delivered he gave me thanks by his letters for advertising thereof."[43] Yet, on January 3, 1576, Burghley had already written a confusing note that Oxford "confessed to my Lord Howard that he lay not with his wife but at Hampton Court, and that then the child could not be his, because the child was born in July which was not the space of twelve months."[44] The pregnancy, which began sometime in late September or October 1574, was confirmed at Court on March 7, 1575, by Richard Masters, a physician for both Ann Vere and the Queen. Masters' letter has the air of a cover story. He writes about Anne's sad response to the news of her pregnancy ("she kept it secret four or five days") and quotes her as saying she doubts if Oxford will "pass upon me and it or not" Masters tells the Queen that Anne worried her "long sickness of body" might give way to a "sorrow of mind": "At this Her Majesty showed great compassion as your Lordship shall hear hereafter. And repeated my Lord of Oxford's answer to me, which he made openly in the presence chamber of Her Majesty, viz., that if she were with child it was not his."[45] Clearly Oxford had made some rather scandalous remarks about his wife's pregnancy before he left England on January 7, 1575. Burghley wrote to Oxford about the events reported by Masters and encouraged him to return to England. On March 17, 1575, Oxford wrote of his happiness at the news that the pregnancy was confirmed ("I thank God therefore, with your Lordship, that it hath pleased Him to make me a father, where your Lordship is a grandfather"), but his letter is troubled by a curious ambiguity of phrasing that may politely suggest his doubts about paternity: "for now it hath pleased God to give me a son of my own *(as I hope it is)* methinks I have the better occasion to travel, sith whatsoever becometh of me I leave behind me one to supply my duty and service, either to my Prince or else my country."[46] Oxford never *unequivocally* claimed that he was Elizabeth's father. After her birth, Oxford thanked Burghley for the "good news of *my wife's delivery,*" but made no mention of the child.[47] Upon his return from the continent, Oxford withdrew from his wife, his daughter, and Cecil, agreeing that Anne should live in her father's house, "for there, as your daughter, or her mother's, the more than my wife, you may take comfort of her, and I, rid of the cumber thereby, shall remain well eased of many griefs."[48] Accusing his wife of an unspecified misdeed, Oxford removed himself from Anne and Elizabeth for about six years before they were formally reconciled in 1582. Later they had a son who died in infancy and two daughters. Burghley eventually became the guardian for all three of Anne's girls after their mother's death in 1588. The cumulative force of these details refocuses our understanding of Wriothesley's situation: the young woman he refused to marry, Burghley's granddaughter, was rumored (by her own legal father) to be illegitimate. [Elizabeth Vere is a contradiction: neither C1<—> –C1; nor C2<—> –C2].)

Clearly in Anne's life Burghley experienced some of the bleak personal consequences of the wardship system he officially supervised and perfected, and he felt his own integrity questioned by Oxford's accusations. That is, Burghley is one site where personal, cultural, official, and economic prescriptions come into conflict. Before Anne's marriage to Oxford, William Cecil had planned for Anne to wed Philip Sidney. However, shortly after Cecil was appointed Lord Treasurer, Edward de Vere asked to marry her, and a pattern similar to the abduction of Elizabeth Trussell develops in which a gift is negated by a purchase. Cecil apparently felt he could not refuse Oxford because of the status of de Vere's family. Writing on August 15, 1571, to Rutland about the marriage, Cecil said in a tone of guarded ambiguity: "I never meant to seek it nor hoped of it. And yet reason moved me to think well of my Lord, and to acknowledge myself greatly beholden to him, as indeed I do."[49] Oxford and Anne Cecil were married on December 15, 1571. In 1586 Burghley wrote Walsingham: "No enemy I have can envy me this match, for thereby neither honour nor land nor goods shall come to their children, for whom . . . I am only at charge even with sundry families in sundry places for their sustenance." In the same letter Burghley confided: "I was so vexed yesternight very late by some grievous sight of my poor daughter's affliction who her husband had in the afternoon so troubled *with words of reproach of me* to her . . . as she spent all the evening in dolour and weeping."[50] Burghley had been Oxford's guardian, and Oxford had some financial difficulty while traveling in Europe that caused both men some strain; there were at times political differences between them as well (including the problems with Norfolk). In a letter to Queen Elizabeth, Burghley wrote: "and in the cause betwixt my Lord of Oxford and her, whether it be *for respect of misliking in me* or misdeeming of hers, whereof I cannot yet know the certainty, I do avow in the presence of God and of his angels whom I do call as ministers of his ire, if in this I do utter any untruth."[51]

Although it is beyond proof, it is not beyond speculation that Oxford may have accused, implied, or suspected Anne and her father, William Cecil, of an incestuous liaison that resulted in the birth of Elizabeth. As unlikely as this scenario is, the threat of an accusation of incest could be a powerful weapon. On April 27, 1576, Oxford reserved an unnamed, disruptive power for himself. Writing to Burghley about "some mislikes" pertaining to his wife, Oxford said: "What they are—because some are not to be spoken of or written upon as imperfections—I will not deal withal. Some that otherwise discontented me I will not blaze or publish until it please me."[52] Perhaps Oxford decided to mention his possible suspicions to someone else, for in Montagu's letter, written to Burghley on September 19, 1590, after the Oatlands meeting, Southampton's grandfather describes Elizabeth Vere first as Burghley's "grandchild" and then as his "child."[53] There is on the surface nothing improper about this: Elizabeth was Burghley's granddaughter and ward. If Montagu is, however, tactfully suggesting that Southampton's refusal is motivated by disparagement, the message would not be lost on the Master of the Wards.

Given these details, the picture changes. Southampton did not have to pay the £5,000 fine. He had two other options: either to marry Elizabeth Vere or to claim disparagement. Wriothesley could have objected to Burghley's granddaughter on the grounds that she was rumored, by her own father, to be illegitimate. This (self-) destructive strategy, however, would be an affront to Burghley, beyond proof and acceptable persuasion, and politically very dangerous, as well as personally offensive to feelings of mutual concern likely shared between the ward, his guardian, and perhaps Elizabeth herself.[54] Instead of pursuing the legal strategy of disparagement, Southampton paid the fine. He may also have paid Shakespeare for his poem.[55] Perhaps this is the advice Shakespeare gives to Southampton: showing him how to avoid complicity with intolerable prescriptions (represented by Venus) and with a destructive vengeance (represented by Adonis). Shakespeare's poem may also defend Southampton by redescribing what some, like Clapham, may have thought was narcissism in terms of a restrained and principled Orphic virtue.

Acts of promiscuity, infidelity, adultery, sodomy, and incest were (semiotically speaking) the predictable ways to subvert the cultural, personal, and economic prescriptions that maintained the patriarchy and its apparent civilities. Accusations of these prohibited or non-prescribed behaviors could also be used to contain subversive persons or to coerce or check powerful ones. The second Earl of Southampton's accusations of adultery against Mary Wriothesley are also well-documented, since she wrote a long letter to her father, Montagu, which is her defense and counter-accusation. In the letter Mary Wriothesley complains that her husband used Thomas Dymock, who she blames as "the begynner & contynnuer of this dissention betwene us," as an intermediary and obstacle between them.[56] That is, Mary Wriothesley appears to have answered her husband's slanderous charges by deploying the full force of ideologically prohibited sexuality [–C1 <—> C2; –E2 <—> E2]. Her letter to Montagu implies that her husband's affections for Dymock were homoerotic, feelings which some see confirmed by the arrangements in the Earl's will for this serving-man.[57] These implications deploy against the second Earl of Southampton the troubled early modern discourses about sodomy, specifically involving masters and their servants.[58] Mary Wriothesley also used her son, Southampton, to carry a copy of her letter to her husband. In the postscript to her father she writes: "That your Lordship shall be witnes of my desir to wyn my Lord by all such meanes as resteth in me, I have sent yowe what I sent to him by my litle boye. butt his harte was to greate to bestowe the readinge of it cominge from me."[59] This image of Southampton as the messenger between his mother and father can be seen from several of the perspectives delimited by the semiotic square. For instance, in standing between the mother and the father, destined by (or sent by) the mother, Southampton marks the divide between the prohibitive father who determines or reinforces the acceptable (permissible relations) of culture and the subversive mother who engages in (semiotically speaking) the unacceptable, the harmful, and unprofitable sexual relations of adultery, a non-prescribed action which the son will repeat in his future affair with Elizabeth Vernon, the mother of his future child, conceived out of wedlock.[60]

A topical reading of Venus and Adonis can, therefore, resist one-to-one correspondence between fictional and historical agents. Each person and character can only be understood as a combination of semic functions, which alters depending upon one's perspective. For example, as the consequence of (potentially alleged) incest, Elizabeth Vere may occupy the place of Adonis. From Southampton's perspective, she might also function like the boar (a non-prescriptive sexuality). Elizabeth's family's name is associated with the boar both etymologically *(verres)* and through figures on the de Vere coat of arms. From Burghley's point of view, however, she occupies the place of prescription, a legitimate (grand-) daughter and a profitable match. Raised in Cecil's household, Wriothesley and Elizabeth Vere may have thought of each other as brother and sister. The prescription of the economic system of wardship would then be incompatible with the social and personal models for sexual relations, structured, as they often are, around the incest taboo.[61] The permutations among these systems are certainly too elaborate to be spelled out. The point is that homologous systems combine and interact and through that intersection they expose the conjunctive and disjunctive logic that shapes a given ideological matrix. When read as a real social practice, *Venus and Adonis* may critique the degenerative uses of wardship by gesturing to topical homologies among the families of Southampton, Oxford, and Burghley and the source materials in Book X of Ovid's *Metamorphoses*. By deploying the shared (yet discontinuous) semiotics of sexual relations in cultural, personal, and economic contexts, Shakespeare may enact through the instructive pleasure of words what some ancient and early modern writers thought was the purpose of poetry: to bring a rude and savage people to civil and orderly life.[62]

NOTES

1. Kenneth Burke, *A Rhetoric of Motives* (Berkeley and Los Angeles: U of California P, 1969), 208.

2. Lawrence Stone, *The Crisis of the Aristocracy 1558–1641* (Oxford: Clarendon P, 1965), 600.

3. For Southampton, consult: Charlotte Carmichael Stopes, *The Life of Henry, Third Earl of Southampton* (Cambridge: Cambridge UP, 1922); G.P.V. Akrigg, *Shakespeare and the Earl of Southampton* (Cambridge: Harvard UP, 1968); A.L. Rowse, *Shakespeare's Southampton: Patron of Virginia* (New York: Harper and Row, 1965). For wardship, consult: H.E. Bell, *An Introduction to the History and Records of the Court of Wards and Liveries* (Cambridge: Cambridge UP, 1953) and Joel Hurstfield, *The Queen's Wards: Wardship and Marriage Under Elizabeth I,* 2nd ed. (London: Frank Cass, 1973). For William Cecil: B.W. Beckingsale, *Burghley: Tudor Statesman 1520–1598* (London: Macmillan and New York: St. Martin's P, 1967); Conyers Read, *Lord Burghley and Queen Elizabeth* (New York: Alfred A. Knopf, 1960); Mary Thomas Crane, *Framing Authority: Sayings, Self, and Society in Sixteenth-Century England* (Princeton: Princeton UP, 1993), 116–135.

4. Akrigg, 39; Stopes, 85–86.

5. For a recent reading about Shakespeare's use of Ovidian materials which sees the Myrrha narrative as a pre-text for *Venus and Adonis,* see Jonathan Bate,

Shakespeare and Ovid (Oxford: Clarendon P, 1993), 48–65.

6. Hurstfield briefly speculates on Clapham's role as intermediary in the granting of wards, a position which was open to bribery and gifts (67, 193–94). Clapham's work is available; see Charles Martindale and Colin Burrow, "Clapham's *Narcissus*: A Pre-Text for Shakespeare's *Venus and Adonis?* (Text, Translation, and Commentary)," *English Literary Renaissance* 22 (1992): 147–175.

7. Stopes, 36.

8. Stopes, 37, emphasis added.

9. Akrigg, 32; Stopes, 37.

10. Bell, 112–132.

11. Akrigg, 39; Hurstfield, 142.

12. Hurstfield, 139–140.

13. Hurstfield, 141.

14. Akrigg speculates that the excessive nature of the fine may also be linked to Southampton's participation in the flight of the Danvers brothers after the murder of Henry Long (46). Hurstfield says that the law allowed a fine to reach double the value of the marriage arrangement; therefore, the fine might not be so excessive (142).

15. Akrigg, 70–71.

16. Leah Marcus, *Puzzling Shakespeare: Local Reading and Its Discontents,* (Berkeley: U of California P, 1988), 33.

17. Marcus 218. For a discussion of types and homologies, see Raymond Williams, *Marxism and Literature* (Oxford: Oxford UP, 1977), 101–107. For mediation, see Fredric Jameson, *The Political Unconscious: Narrative as a Socially Symbolic Act* (Ithaca: Cornell UP, 1981), 39–44.

18. Marcus, 214.

19. Nancy Armstrong is quoted by Ron Schleifer in his introduction to A.-J. Greimas, *Structural Semantics: An Attempt at a Method,* introduction by Ronald Schleifer, translated by Daniele McDowell, Ronald Schleifer, and Alan Velie (Lincoln and London: U of Nebraska P, 1966), xxxiii.

20. A.-J. Greimas, "The Interaction of Semiotic Constraints," collected in *On Meaning: Selected Writings in Semiotic Theory,* foreword by Fredric Jameson (Minneapolis: U of Minnesota P, 1987), 48–62.

21. All quotations of the poem are taken from F.T. Prince, *The Poems: The Arden Edition of the Works of William Shakespeare* (London and Cambridge, Massachusetts: Methuen, 1960) emphasis added, 1183–1188.

22. *Ven.,* 229–231, 233–234.

23. *Oxford English Dictionary.*

24. Ovid, *Metamorphoses,* trans. Frank Justus Miller, 2nd ed. 2 vols. (Cambridge: Harvard UP, 1966) Book X, 524. I have cited the line numbers.

25. Horace, "The Art of Poetry," *Satires and Epistles of Horace,* trans. Smith Palmer Bovie (Chicago: U of Chicago P, 1959), 287.

26. George Puttenham, *The Arte of English Poesie,* eds., Gladys Doidge Willcock and Alice Walker, 1936 (Cambridge: Cambridge UP, 1970) emphasis added, 6.

27. *Metamorphoses* Book X, 79–82.

28. Greimas, "Interaction," 53.

29. Samuel Taylor Coleridge, *Biographia Literaria or Biographical Sketches of My Literary Life and Opinions,* eds., James Engell and W. Jackson Bate (Princeton: Princeton UP, 1984) Vol. 2, 21.

30. Greimas, "Interaction," 55.

31. *Ven.,* 803–804.

32. *Ven.,* 789–792.

33. *Metamorphoses* Book X, 706.

34. *Metamorphoses* Book X, 707.

35. *Ven.,* 412.

36. *Ven.,* 1117–1118.

37. *Ven.*, 628–630.

38. Sir Thomas Smith, *De Republica Anglorum,* 1583, A Scolar Press Facsimile (Menston, England: Scolar Press Limited, 1970), 98.

39. Hurstfield, 141.

40. Stone, 600.

41. B.M. Ward, *The Seventeenth Earl of Oxford* (London:John Murray, 1928), 6–7.

42. *Ven.* 213–214.

43. Read, 134.

44. Ward, 115.

45. Ward, 114–115.

46. Ward, 102, emphasis added.

47. Ward, 108, emphasis added.

48. Read, 135.

49. Read, 127.

50. Read, 138, emphasis added.

51. Read, 136, emphasis added.

52. Ward, 121.

53. Stopes, 37–38.

54. As far as I know, we have no record of Elizabeth Vere's feelings on these matters; Stopes confirms this (34), but future work could perhaps still prove otherwise.

55. The anecdote, originating with Nicholas Rowe, about Southampton's gift of £1,000 to Shakespeare is highly debated among the biographers including Akrigg (220), S. Schoenbaum, *William Shakespeare: A Compact Documentary Life* (Oxford: Oxford UP, 1977), 178–179, and recently Russell Fraser, *Young Shakespeare* (New York: Columbia UP, 1988), 176.

56. Akrigg, 13; Stopes, 523.

57. Rowse, 36–42.

58. Alan Bray, "Homosexuality and the Signs of Male Friendship in Elizabethan England," *History Workshop Journal* 29 (1990):1–19; Jonathan Goldberg, *Sodometries: Renaissance Texts, Modern Sexualities* (Stanford: Stanford UP, 1992).

59. Akrigg, 14.

60. The proper names throughout this story are amusing and suggestive of the way transgressions are repetitions. The adulterer is Donesame and the accused go-between Dymock. The woman Wriothesley marries is Elizabeth Ver-*non,* a name that suggests, in this marriage to the cousin of Essex, the negation of Burghley's arrangement. Much more work also remains to be done on the subversive nature of Mary Wriothesley's letters.

61. Akrigg finds strong parallels between Bertram and Southampton (254–256). For a reading of *All's Well* that thinks of Bertram's resistance to Helena in terms of the incest taboo, see Richard P. Wheeler, *Shakespeare's Development and the Problem Comedies: Turn and Counter-Turn* (Berkeley: U of California P, 1981), 34–45.

62. I would like to thank Philip Kolin for superb editorial advice and my colleagues and friends for their assistance with this project, especially Ed O'Shea, Ed Keen, Robert Moore, Leigh Wilson, Don Masterson, Shelly Ekhtiar, Inez Alfors, John Duvall, Jack Schoppman, and Christopher Felker.

"Lo, in This Hollow Cradle Take Thy Rest"

Sexual Conflict and Resolution in *Venus and Adonis*

Robert P. Merrix

I

Recent scholarly articles on Shakespeare's *Venus and Adonis* more and more focus on the complexity of the poem, a complexity that exposes earlier allegorical interpretations as naive or reductive. The simple allegorical interpretations have given way to more profound iconographic or mythographic analyses of the poem.[1] When allegory yields to myth or symbolism, ambivalence inevitably results. The simple one-dimensional relationship between the human attribute and its allegorical vehicle is replaced with what one scholar calls "a mystery, a complexity, even a self-contradiction."[2] Norman Rabkin also speaks of the poem as expressing the "self-contradiction implicit in a central human activity."[3] J.D. Jahn emphasizes the "sophisticated moral conception" that is similar to the complexity "underlying the great tragedies."[4] And S. Clark Hulse notes that "the debate between Venus and Adonis is never resolved"; the paradoxes of love (life and death, bliss and agony) "teeter out of sight on the even feet of oxymoron."[5]

There is, however, a residual tendency to assign allegorical categories to the main characters or to assess their conflict in neoplatonic terms, thus maintaining the traditional dualism that has provided the basis for so many interpretations of the poem. Robin Bowers and Heather Asals exemplify such allegorical treatments of the poem.[6] For Bowers, Shakespeare had a "definite" moral aim in mind in writing the poem. Venus is the "Goddess of Lust" and Adonis (apparently) the embodiment of male virtue. Bowers attempts to solve the problem of the boar, the *bête noire* of the allegorists, by calling it the "wrathful effects of lust" that "represent the fatal pains which follow the feeble pleasures of Venus." Bowers' interpretation hinges on his assertion that the sexual kiss (ll. 549–64) is actually coitus (9). Thus, by succumbing to Venus' lust Adonis is weakened and "consequently unable to succeed in the hunt of the 'savage Boare.'" Bowers sounds like the macho football coach warning his boys to avoid sexual contact with women before the big game. Bowers also ignores lines 595–600, which specifically state that though Venus is "in the very lists of love, / Her champion mounted for the hot encounter. . . . He will not manage her, although he mount her."[7] "Manage" (French *manege*) means literally to put a horse through its paces, thus reflecting Adonis' failure to do what his horse did.

Asals offers an interesting variation on the standard neoplatonic pattern by having Venus herself transcend her own initial earthly nature—Venus Vulgaris—to her divine one. She "purges from herself the nature of the boar" (i.e., Lust) and "by the end of the poem . . . finds also the better angel, the Heavenly Venus within her soul" (48–49). Interestingly, such dualistic approaches mandate a heaven-earth dichotomy and lead both scholars to interpret Venus' mounting "through the empty skies" as a return to "heaven," rather than to Paphos, her very earthly home.[8]

There are, then, two sharply different critical approaches to *Venus and Adonis*. The first is clearly allegorical and exclusive, in which critics assign specific moral attributes to Venus and Adonis or to their "surrogates"—the boar, the horses, the eagle, and the rabbit. The other approach, which Bowers denigrates as the "ambivalent school," is really symbolic and mythic, thus inclusive. It emphasizes the diversity and complexity of the main characters. For the allegorists, Venus is *Love*—either Venus Genetrix or Venus Vulgaris—and Adonis is *Beauty* or *Virtue*. For the symbolists, Venus is *love,* sometimes sensual,[9] sometimes maternal,[10] and Adonis is *beauty* or *virtue,* embodied, as different commentators have suggested, in an innocent adolescent boy,[11] a prig,[12] or a young nobleman and courtier.[13] Hulse reflects this inclusive approach succinctly in his summation of Venus:

> We have, in effect, not one but three Venuses—comic, sensual and violent—all embodying earthly love but differently depicted to reveal different aspects. Venus is the empty eagle, the randy jennet, the tender snail, the anguished doe and the timid hare. (98)

Both of these critical approaches tend to focus on the theme of love and beauty or the moral relationship between Venus and Adonis with little or no regard to the dramatic structure and social context of the poem within which the relationship unfolds. Dramatic structure and social context are critical to any analysis. The dialectic created by the conflicts among the main characters or their surrogates, and the bifurcated structure, revealing two radically different settings and tones for those conflicts, require a closer structural analysis of Shakespeare's poem than heretofore attempted.[14] Rather than trying to identify the allegorical absolutes or interpret the moral meanings, it may be more fruitful to analyze the sexual conflicts structurally embodied in the poem. Does Venus tempt Adonis for moral reasons—either to destroy him through lust or to preserve him by urging him to propagate his beauty? Or does she attempt to impose on him sexual or psychological norms antithetical to his own? Does Adonis reject Venus for those same moral reasons, or for other, more fundamental, ones? An analysis of the *sexual* content of the carefully patterned debate between Venus and Adonis and the psychologically and physically diverse settings in the poem will yield more personal and human reasons for their behavior, something that allegory and myth do not allow.

It is certainly true that we cannot escape some kind of allegorical or mythic meaning in the metamorphosis of Adonis at the end of the poem; but we need not imbue the entire work with one or the other critical approach. As Leonard Barkan has pointed out, Renaissance writers often employed myth and allegory to suit their own purposes without regard to the carefully structured relationship between the vehicle and its attribute.[15] Certainly numerous critics see Venus and Adonis as anything but mythological absolutes. Moreover both allegorical and mythical approaches invite and often require a purely moral or ritual interpretation of the poem. The conflict between Venus and Adonis is not moral or ritual; it is social and sexual and concerns conflicting lifestyles, one domestic, fruitful, and secure, and the other exotic, sterile, and dangerous.

These two lifestyles are reflected in Venus and the boar. Venus represents both a social and biological imperative whereby humanity domesticates and increases itself. The boar embodies all that operates against such a culture and offers instead a deadly transcendence from biological necessity. The ensuing conflict between Venus and the boar-loving Adonis adumbrates the eternal struggle of humanity to reject the ecstatic temptation of absolute freedom that leads only to narcissism and the annihilation of culture. The force represented by the boar, which historically has drawn Western man from domestic security into alien worlds, is embodied in the early tales of Actaeon, the mythic representation of the hunting frenzy. As several scholars have noted, the hunt exerts a magnetic attraction over certain men.[16] An excellent example of this transcendent quest appears in Giordano Bruno's version of Actaeon in *Gl'Eroici Furen*. Actaeon's ecstasy leads to this apotheosis as decribed by Bruno:

> In that divine and universal chase he comes to apprehend that it is
> himself who necessarily remains captured, absorbed and united.

Therefore, from the vulgar, civil and ordinary man he was, he becomes free as the deer, and an inhabitant of the wilderness; he lives like a god under the protection of the woods . . . where he contemplates the sources of the great rivers . . . and converses most freely with the divinity, to which so many men have aspired.[17]

As often noted, Venus may indeed represent lust, simple procreation, sexual maternalism, or even the *femme fatale*. She may be both comic and tragic. Indeed, as Hulse suggests, she is a composite of all these roles. In order to function successfully in each role each one or, rather, the action implied by each one, must be reciprocated. Otherwise there is no moral nexus by which to judge the dynamics of a moral relationship: lust needs an object upon which to act, procreation requires two mates, the maternal female needs the willing child. Adonis' failure to reciprocate any of these sexual modes distorts all of them. Venus, the embodiment of all, runs the gamut from voluptuous mother to lusty temptress to frustrated lover to abandoned woman. Because of Adonis' failure to reciprocate these personifications, each is intensified to the point of grotesqueness. As Venus notes in her analogy: "An oven that is stop'd, or river stay'd / Burneth more hotly, swelleth with more rage" (ll. 331–32). Venus' initial sexual desire, perhaps comic, but certainly not repellant, eventually becomes ugly and frightful as reflected by the bizarre images associated with her—the "amazon," the eagle, and vulture. Whatever sexual roles Venus embodies, all require a reciprocal experience, an involvement, which is diametrically opposite to what Adonis desires. He therefore rejects the goddess for an entirely different composite—the boar.

For Shakespeare, sexual reciprocity is the sine qua non in human relationships. It is most clearly demonstrated, of course, in the "procreation" sonnets (1–17) where the poet urges the young man to "Make thee another self, for love of me, / That beauty still may live in thine and thee" (10.13–14). He accuses the young man of making a "waste in niggarding" (1.12) and "having traffic with thyself alone" (4.9); he warns him that "nothing 'gainst Time's scythe can make defence / Save breed to brave him when he takes thee hence." (12.13–14) But the theme of sexual reciprocity runs through many of the plays as well, especially the comedies. Only in *Love's Labor's Lost* does "Jack hath not Gill"; and even there the consummation will occur at a twelvemonth's end when the men are purged from their sins of "faults and perjury" (5.2.870–75).[18] In *All's Well That Ends Well*, Bertram, who, like Adonis, refuses sexual consummation, is tricked into it by Helena. In *As You Like It*, Touchstone reinforces the biological mandate when he tells Jaques: "As the ox hath his bow, sir, the horse his curb, and the falcon her bells, so wedlock would be nibbling" (3.3.79–82). Indeed, *As You Like It* provides an excellent example of two different kinds of love—the first realistic and sexual and the second "romantic" and transcendental. Touchstone's "rhyme" to Rosalind bluntly depicts the former: "Wint'red garments must be lin'd, / So must slender Rosalind / He that sweetest rose will find / Must find love's prick and Rosalind" (3.2.105–12). Fruitless transcendental love is represented by Silvius, who pines and weeps for the uncaring Phebe. Her rejection of his overtures leads him to inane protestations of love ("O Phebe, Phebe, Phebe!"), which ultimately earn him the contempt of Rosalind. She, of course, successfully embodies the romantic-realistic nexus in her relationship with Orlando.

Each of the composites in the poem—Venus and the boar—is associated with its own setting, imagery, narrative or dramatic style, and psychological imperative. The poem itself is broken into two major sections, the first 810 lines containing the sexual conflict between Venus and Adonis; and the second section of 383 lines involving Venus' search for Adonis. Venus meets Adonis at early morning in a static, pastoral setting replete with images of sensuality and a "primrose bank" upon which such sensual desire may be fulfilled. The poem here is both narrative and dramatic, the dramatic part revealing a sexual conflict between Venus and the boy. Adonis is urged to forgo his hunting trip and be "hemm'd . . . within the circle of [Venus'] ivory pale"; in short, to become ensconced in a societal structure that promises security, comfort, and physical pleasures. He refuses to accept this composite and leaves. In part two of the poem, he hunts the boar, the counter composite, in an alien environment, and is quickly killed. With the transformation of Adonis into the anemone at the end of the poem the two composites are united, forming a sexual resolution, a synthesis in which the major attributes of each are embodied in the other.[19] After plucking the flower, Venus places it in her bosom:

> Lo, in this hollow cradle take thy rest;
> My throbbing heart shall rock thee day and night:
> There shall not be one minute in an hour
> Wherein I will not kiss my sweet love's flower.
>
> (ll. 1185–88)

II

Like Ovid in *The Metamorphoses*,[20] Shakespeare does not create setting graphically. There are few specific references to scenery—the "primrose bank" with its "forceless flowers," the "copse" from which the jennet comes, the twining "bushes" and, of course, the "anemone" being the most vivid. Setting is created by allegorical episodes, such as the horses, allusions to classical figures such as Mars and Diana, and rhetorical descriptions of animals' actions or features—all of which inform the amorphous or vague terrain into psychological equivalents. Setting thus is essentially presentational, as in Shakespeare's drama, its physical or psychological manifestations emerging from actions being narrated or features being described at any given moment in the poem. Most obvious, for example, is the episode of the horses in which the setting reflects the violent sexual foreplay: Adonis' palfrey "wounds" the "bearing earth with his hard hoof" and the earth itself, described as a "hollow womb," becomes a synecdochic extension of equine sexual fruition (ll. 265–70).

Another device Shakespeare uses—again borrowed from Ovid—to create setting is time: both day and night are personified, the former by a classical equivalent—"Titan"—and the latter by epithets ("black-fac'd"; "merciless and pitchy"). Both also are associated with their symbolic birds— the larks for morning and the "shrieking" owl for night. Just as Ovid presented tales of intense sexuality during midday, "the panic hour of noon" (Segal 4), so Shakespeare presents the "sweating" couple being watched by Titan "in the midday heat," who "With burning eye did hotly overlook them" (ll. 127–178).

In the first section of the poem, various formal elements—narration, rhetorical description, dialogue—combine to reveal a world filled with fecundity, security, and domesticity in which Venus, as the major procreative and domestic force in the world, attempts to fulfill her nature. First of all, images of security or domestic taming echo throughout the first part of the poem, from the moment Venus first plucks Adonis from his horse until he leaves her. At various times Venus fastens Adonis in her arms "like a bird tangled in a net" (l. 67); she lies atop him; "her arms infold him like a band" (l. 225); she entwines her arms about him; she "hems" him in; she "prisons" his hand in "a jail of snow" (l. 362); and finally, she falls to the earth with him, "their lips together glued" (l. 546). Even the analogies reinforce the domestic imagery. Adonis is "Like a wild bird being tam'd with too much handling, / Or as the fleet-foot roe that's tir'd with chasing, / Or like the froward infant still'd with dandling" (ll. 560–562). The animals referred to in part one are associated with the benign setting. When Adonis announces that he intends to hunt the boar, Venus urges him to "uncouple at the timorous flying hare, / Or at the fox which lives by subtlety, / Or at the roe which no encounter dares" (ll. 674–76). So frightened is she of his hunting the boar that she launches into two long rhetorical descriptions of the boar and hare for contrast. The boar is a creature so fearful that even the "thorny brambles and embracing bushes . . . part" (ll. 629–30) to let him through.

Diametrically opposite and thus safe is the hare, which, unlike the boar, is torn and scratched by the "envious brier." The famous hare digression serves as the concluding face to the many-faceted icon of Venus. Though the hare, emblematic of Venus, represents fecundity and benign domesticity, it is preceded by voracious and ugly predation imagery. Earlier in part one, an epic simile ties Venus to "an empty eagle" that tears "with her beak on feathers, flesh and bone" (ll. 55–56). In the long sexual kiss (ll. 538–576) she feeds "glutton-like" on Adonis' lips, her "vulture thought" so powerful "That she will draw his lips' rich treasure dry." The hare digression also serves a second purpose. It foreshadows Venus' own pursuit of Adonis in part two and delineates the hostile environment. Like the hare in part one, Venus is encumbered by the envious brier (ll. 872–73).

Like the hare who listens fearfully for his foes and who grieves at "loud alarums" (l. 700), Venus similarly listens for the sounds of the chase. The "timorous yelping of the hounds" immediately "Appals her senses and her spirit confounds" (ll. 881–82) and she stands finally "in a trembling ecstasy" (l. 895).

These rhetorical and narrative techniques together form the composite role of Venus. She reflects the fecundity and the stultification of domestic love, but also the vulnerability of that love when it is subjected to a counterexperience more attractive to someone like Adonis.

Venus also utilizes six separate *carpe diem* motifs from society or nature in her efforts to entice Adonis to sexual union. She starts with her general physical attributes: "my eyes are grey, and bright, and quick in turning. . . . My flesh is soft and plump, my marrow burning" (ll. 140–142); she then moves to her social charms: "Bid me discourse, I will enchant thine ear, / Or like a fairy trip upon the green" (ll. 145–146). She calls attention to the secluded and sexually conducive setting: "Witness this primrose bank whereon I lie" (l. 151). She employs the traditional utilitarian argument both from society and from nature: "Torches are made to light, jewels to wear. . . . Seeds spring from seeds and beauty breedeth beauty; / Thou was begot; to get it is thy duty" (ll. 163–168). When these arguments fail, she turns to invective, calling his manhood into question: "Fie lifeless picture, cold and senseless stone. . . . Thou art no man, though of a man's complexion, / For men will kiss even by their own direction" (ll. 211–216). Finally she returns full circle with the famous sexual description of her body in traditional topographical terms, in which her breasts are "pleasant fountains" leading to "sweet bottom-grass, and high delightful plain / Round rising hillocks, brakes obscure and rough" (ll. 229–240).[21]

Adonis rejects these enticements, releases himself from Venus' "twin-ing arms" and hastens to his horse. But at this point Shakespeare presents another image of procreation and reciprocity: the horses. The wooing action between the animals, of course, parallels that of Venus and Adonis, al-though in reverse. The jennet, like Adonis, "puts on outward strangeness, seems unkind" a pose that renders the courser a "melancholy malcontent." He "vails his tail . . . like a falling plume," until in his rage and sexual frus-tration he "stamps and bites the poor flies in his fume" (l. 316). The pas-sage echoes Venus' own similar frustration: "Red cheeks and fiery eyes blaze forth her wrong. . . . And now she weeps and now she fain would speak, / And now her sobs do her intendments break" (ll. 219–222). The contrast between sexual fulfillment and sexual frustration is strikingly exemplified when the jennet "perceiving how [the courser] is enrag'd / Grew kinder [so that] his fury was assuag'd" (ll. 318–319). In short, the horses, a part of the world of nature, as are Venus and Adonis in the pastoral setting, mate as they should. Reciprocity thus cools the sexual rage and prevents the gro-tesqueness that sexual frustration leads to. Venus points this out to the sul-len Adonis:

> Thy palfrey, as he should,
> Welcomes the warm approach of sweet desire:
> Affection is the coal that must be cool'd;
> Else, suffer'd it will set the heart on fire.
>
> (ll. 385–388)

Her inducements for him to imitate his horse, however, fail, and lead to Adonis' first speech, appropriately one that delineates his militant yearnings and his revulsion of domesticity:

> "I know not love," quoth he, "nor will not know it,
> Unless it be a boar, and then I chase it;
> . . . .
> My love to love is love but to disgrace it;
>   For I have heard it is a life in death,
>   That laughs, and weeps, and all but with a breath."
>
> (ll. 409–416)

With his reference to love as "life in death" Adonis firmly rejects the do-mestic composite embodied in Venus. "Life in death" involves social and sexual responsibility and, eventually, for the young courtier, domestic "drudgery"—what Edgar in *King Lear* terms the "dull, stale, tired marriage bed." Adonis embraces, then, not the dulling *life in death* [22] but, in the boar, its opposite, the exhilarating and dangerous *death in life*—the eternal human desire to transcend all physical and social limits, the compulsion to "immerse oneself into the destructive element"; "to pluck bright honor from the pale-fac'd moon, / Or dive into the bottom of the deep." He seeks, in short, the Romantic quest with its concomitant metaphysical aspirations. In desire he is a youthful Tamburlaine, "always moving as the restless spheres." Unfortunately, in execution, he resembles Don Quixote's Sancho Panza.

That Adonis understands the role Venus attempts to impose on him is evident in his differentiation between love and lust:

> I hate not love but your device in love,
> That lends embracements unto every stranger.
> You do it for increase: O Strange excuse,
> When reason is the bawd to lust's abuse.
>
> (ll. 789–792)

Adonis correctly sees that the "device in love" that leads to "increase" carries with it domestic obligations antithetical to his own desires.[23] His conclusion follows the earlier sexual kiss. In that kiss, Adonis' reluctance creates in Venus the distorted image of sexual frustration earlier alluded to. In short, Adonis' refusal to reciprocate the various social and sexual roles embodied in Venus—procreator, mistress, aggressive lover, temptress—leads to the grotesque images of unfulfilled sexuality.[24] Venus' attempts in part one to fulfill her domestic function fail. From this moment on she takes on another series of roles in keeping with the new setting and narrative focus—abandoned lover (or wife), anxious mother searching for her child, or romantic heroine venturing into the unknown in search for her knight. As such Venus is related to Ovid's Oenone (as illustrated in T. H.'s *Oenone and Paris*), Virgil's Dido, Ishtar/Astarte in *Gilgamesh,* and other romantic heroines.

III

Just as various formal elements make up the domestic world of part one, such elements also inform the diametrically opposite world of part two. Adonis, having spent the morning, noon, and afternoon with Venus, "Leaves Love in darkness," such "a merciless and pitchy night" (l. 821) that Venus is confounded and loses her way. In part two she enters a sinister, demonic world similar to that portrayed by Northrop Frye in the *Anatomy of Criticism.*[25] In

Frye's world a "demonic erotic relation becomes a fierce destructive passion." But the sexuality is sterile and grotesque. The animals (Frye's "animal world") are "monsters or beasts of prey" and the landscape (Frye's "vegetable world") is sinister and dangerous. It is the savage jungle of Kurtz, the Dark Tower of Childe Roland, the appropriate setting for the transcendent Faustian.

Venus searches for the doomed Adonis in this cold and alien setting. Leaving the comforting primrose bank, she struggles through unknown lands where "bushes . . . catch her about the neck" or "twine about her thigh"(ll. 871–873). Images of "adders," "blunt boar, rough bear, or lion proud" replace the benign animals in part one. The hounds, vigorous and eager like their master in part one, are now wounded, licking "venom'd sores and howling." The hostile environment adds to Venus' psychological state of mind as she stands "in a trembling ecstasy." She spies the boar "bepainted all with red, / Like milk and blood being mingled both together" (ll. 901-903).[26] Eventually she finds Adonis, his death verifying her earlier vision and justifying her warning to him. In leaving the static primrose bank, Adonis enters the deadly world of the hunt—the world of militant chivalry. In engaging the boar, the composite of all that is antithetical to Venus, he has achieved his *death in life* at last.[27] Ironically this death is also sexual. Both Ovid and Golding make clear that the death follows an erotic coupling. Ovid says the boar sank his tusks into the "groin" *(sub inguine)* of Adonis. And in Golding's translation the boar strikes Adonis in the "codds."[28] The loving swine," says Venus, "But by a kiss thought to persuade him there / And nuzzling in his flank . . . Sheath'd unaware the tusk in his soft groin" (ll. 1114–1116).

But what does the boar in *Venus and Adonis* represent?[29] Must we view it in purely allegorical or mythic terms? As has often been noted, the boar itself is associated with the initiation of the young squire into manhood. Even more important, as Marcelle Thiébaux in his seminal article[30] shows, the boar became related in late medieval times with militant activity as dangerous and exhilarating as warfare:

> Eventually, the boar as adversary becomes the object of a hunt. It is noteworthy that in romances, as in certain of the *chansons de geste,* the battles characteristic of heroic literature become increasingly replaced by, or interspersed with, hunting expeditions of a rigorous sort. Hunting itself not only ranked as a courtly accomplishment, but was also regarded by medieval theorists as a substitute for the more strenuous diversion of war, and a means by which the knight might exercise arms between campaigns. (284)

Significant also for Thiébaux is the "epic magnitude in which boars loom . . . as adversaries, even as the destroyers, directly or indirectly, of heroes." Moreover, like Adonis, "those heroes . . . are lured into danger or to their deaths once they have followed boars into the territories of their enemies." In short, the boar's role is that of "a conductor into the fateful or the unknown" (290).

It is this last role that the boar plays initially in *Venus and Adonis.* And the subsequent hunt reflects those irrational adventurous experiences that some men yearn for, a compulsion that binds them in a quest for the unknown, the search for apocalypse. The quest is chaste, exotic, an anti-life force that is set against the fruitful, domestic life by which humanity survives. In his *Love in the Western World,*[31] Denis de Rougemont characterizes this type of sterile quest as an "alien factor . . . having the power to make instinct turn away from its natural goal and to transfer desire into limitless aspiration, into something . . . which does not serve, and indeed operates against, biological ends" (62).

These two forces vying for Adonis, one domestic and procreative, and the other militant and chaste, are embodied mythically in Venus and Diana and in the two animals usually associated with them, the fecund rabbit for Venus and the boar for Diana. But sexually the two forces are reflected in the activities associated with the hearth and the hunt. In part one of *Venus and Adonis,* Venus catalogues the anti-life forces related to "modest Dian": they are "fruitless chastity, / Love-lacking vestals, and self-loving nuns, / That on the earth would breed a scarcity / And barren dearth of daughters and of sons" (ll. 751–754). When Adonis chooses to hunt the boar, then, he chooses chastity over fruitfulness, danger and death over security and long life, the mysterious over the known.[32]

IV

Following the death of Adonis and thus his failure to reciprocate the sexual love offered by Venus, the goddess makes her famous prophecy of future love. Love will be "waited on with jealousy. . . . It shall be fickle, false and full of fraud / Bud and be blasted in a breathing while." Most importantly, love shall be "the cause of war and dire events, / And set dissention twixt the son and sire" (ll. 1136–1160). Venus' prophecy is not, as some have suggested, a curse or a "law" placed on humanity by her.[33] It is simply a description of the human condition following the rise of romantic love—the love delineated by de Rougemont—which thrives on jealousy, suffering, and separation, a love that refuses reciprocity and indeed denies reciprocal relationships altogether. The new world is a postlapsarian madhouse where disunity and chaos rule. The failure to achieve sexual resolution—to propagate the race—leads to death, however glorious that death may be. If there is any truth emerging from the conflicts in *Venus and Adonis,* it is surely that humanity cannot escape its sexual nature except through constant flight into the unknown. It seems similarly true that some men cannot be satisfied with the "dull, stale, tired marriage bed" and will risk the apocalypse, that *death in life,* in order to escape. From Gottfried's *Tristan* to Byron's *Manfred* to Melville's *Moby Dick,* Faustian man, as young and pathetic as Adonis, or as old and sad as Don Quixote, has attempted to escape from what Ishmael termed the "attainable felicity" of the "wife, the bed, the table, the saddle, the fire-side." Is there, then, no reprieve for such a world of disharmony and chaos? Is there no mean to the extremes of dull domesticity and deadly exoticism?

Whatever respite comes must certainly involve the metamorphosis of Adonis, which occurs immediately after Venus' prophecy. It is here that we must include an allegorical dimension in the poem. This metamorphosis of Adonis reflects other Ovidian transformations of those who similarly rejected sexual overtures: Daphne into a tree, Picus into a bird, and Narcissus into a flower. But the transformation of Adonis into the anemone— emblematic both of fragile early love and resurrection—operates more positively. It softens Venus' harsh prophecy and provides an alternative to the earlier two choices. Just as the militant chastity of the medieval warrior was gradually transformed into more courtly and societal rituals, so the hunt itself turns from the composite exemplified by the boar and towards that exemplified by Venus. In short, the wooing ritual replaces the hunt. Such activity is now both possible and desirable, for Venus herself has undergone a change. This transformation, ignored by many critics, is interpreted by others primarily in spiritual and aesthetic terms. Asals, as earlier noted, presents a modified neoplatonic reading, as does Doebler. For them, Venus' transformation is epistemological. Doebler's Venus, moving towards knowledge, can be "mere lust in one persona and heavenly beauty in another" (34). S. Clark Hulse grounds his analysis of the "shifting character of Venus" in myth. Venus is a "sweaty muscular rapist," then a "philosopher," and finally a "grieving lover," reflecting the force of myth to overcome "seeming contradictions and improbalities" (95–96). For Tita French Baumlin, Venus' change is a "poetic apotheosis" and reflects Shakespeare's own aesthetic growth:

> Venus' apotheosis from shallow rhetorician into elegiac poet mirrors
> the 'apotheosis' of the new poet himself, who must break the rules

of poetic form and violently unmake his [Ovidian] model to create his own mature expression of his aesthetic principles.[34]

A. C. Hamilton is really the only critic to evaluate Venus' change in more earthy terms:

> The bawdy, even comic, account of Venus' actions which we see through the witty and dispassionate eye of the poet gives place to a plaintive, even tragic, lament.[35]

Finally, a recent and provocative feminist essay by Nona Fienberg emphasizes Venus' "mutability and diversity" and her ability to change roles and positions in contrast to Adonis' patriarchal fixity and absoluteness: "Venus' flexibility and ability to neogotiate [value] suggest a liberating reevaluation of the patriarchal world she both plays in and subverts."[36]

For me, however, the major transformation is social and psychological and occurs when Venus leaves the primrose bank. From the moment she steps into the horrific world of the boar she becomes vulnerable, and is softened and humanized by the alien environment over which she has no control. Since Adonis' transformation occurs in this alien world, the flower retains elements from that world. By plucking the flower and placing it in her bosom, Venus brings the two worlds together. One could of course see the union in traditional mythic terms: the flower (Adonis) symbolizing the spirit of annual vegetation. However, one can also see the transformation in more simple social terms. In an important article on Empedocles in Rome, James Arieti speaks of the socialization of the mythic union of Mars and Venus as a cultural strategy for creating and maintaining the "tension of opposites" which kept Rome strong and vital.[37] That tension implies a dynamic political alternative, a mingling of the attributes of both Venus and Mars. While not an Hegelian paradigm, a similar *sexual* synthesis emerges from the transformation of Adonis. As Renaissance verse narratives like Abraham Fraunce's *The Countess of Pembrokes Yvy Church;* Marlowe's *Hero and Leander;* Thomas Edwards' two poems *Cephalus and Procris* and *Narcissus;* T. H.'s *Oenone and Paris;* and Robert Toften's *Alba,* with his "melancholy lover," all illustrate, the Renaissance attitudes about love reflect a union of these two worlds, the sexual and the "romantic." The static and stultifying sexual world of Venus is made more endurable by elevating it into the realm of physical danger and the unknown. Sexual love is now imbued with either the spirit of the chase (as in *Hero and Leander*) or with romantic suffering and separation *(Cephalus and Procris),* which, as de Rougemont notes, seem such a vital part of human love. Similarly, the chaste, dynamic world of adventure is drawn closer to the world of humanity: the quest for the boar is transformed to the quest for the mistress, from the inevitable physical death to the "little death," the sexual release so often depicted by Shakespeare, Donne, and others. In Shakespeare's mature comedies, especially, one can experience these degrees of love. As noted before, the two major extremes—domestic, sexual love and idealistic transcendental love—are humorously depicted in *As You Like It* by, respectively, Touchstone and Audrey and Phebe and Silvius. More seriously, in *All's Well That Ends Well,* the Adonis-like Bertram flees the aggressive Helena, preferring the Tuscan wars to the domestic bedding of the maid. No better parody on the Romantic Imperative exists than Parolles' subsequent apostrophe to it:

> To th' wars, my boy, to the wars!
> He wears his honor in a box unseen,
> That hugs his kicky-wicky here at home,
> Spending his manly marrow in her arms,
> Which should sustain the proud and high curvet
> Of Mars' fiery steed.
>
> (II.iii.279–283)

The chaotic romantic love with its jealousy and hate that Venus speaks of is, of course, most clearly exemplified in *Romeo and Juliet* and *Othello,* where the romantic nexus leads to just those woes listed in Venus' catalogue. But such tragedy cannot be attributed solely to the love itself. When love fails in Shakespeare, it fails because the synthesis of solid realism and transcendent romanticism is not permitted to occur. When the love succeeds, as with Rosalind and Orlando, a dynamic and fruitful future is presaged. In *A Midsummer Night's Dream* (c. 1595), written shortly after *Venus and Adonis,* Shakespeare plays with various combinations of love in four distinct subplots. Theseus, in his comments to Hippolyta, exemplifies the realistic, matter-of-fact course of love: "I wooed thee with my sword. . . . But I will wed thee in another key." The young lovers reflect the highly-charged emotional component of love —the "romantic"—which needs to be redirected into more fruitful wooing by both Oberon's and Theseus' interventions. Oberon, especially in his treatment of Titania, demonstrates a prideful narcissistic love. The rude mechanicals in the hilarious scatalogical and sexual version of *Pyramus and Thisby* are early versions of Touchstone, and proffer the necessary parodic jab in the ribs to remind us that love is both serious and comic, spiritual and sexual, logical and silly. But the lesson emerging from the plays is that love is not love when it is not reciprocated.

Venus and Adonis certainly lends itself to allegorical and mythic analyses. But the sexual conflict and its eventual resolution—suggested by the structure and the rhetorical techniques—must be considered. While I certainly would not argue that the poem has topical parallels to Shakespeare's own flight from Stratford and married love to London and its teeming excitement, I think *Venus and Adonis* exemplifies his understanding of the tension between society's strong need to procreate and fulfill its duty to nature, and its equally strong desire to escape from the bonds of that procreativeness into the exciting and mysterious world of the unknown, a romantic haven far from the burdens of husbandry. These counterimperatives can never be reconciled; but by imbuing each with the best elements of the other, a workable alternative may emerge that allows us to survive, and, more importantly, to create artistic works that reflect our struggle with and eventual acceptance of the imperatives. For me, the alternative to those two worlds emerges clearly from the sexual conflict in the poem. The synthesis of the domestic and the exotic reflects the reality of human relationships, and is as valid today as in Shakespeare's time.

NOTES

1. See Wayne A. Rebhorn for an excellent summary of the changing critical attitudes in analyses of the poem. He suggests that major critical change began during the 1960s when Venus "received more sympathetic treatment and was identified as Venus Genetrix." "Mother Venus: Temptation in Shakespeare's *Venus and Adonis,*" *Shakespeare Studies* 11 (1978): 1–19.

2. Leonard Barkan, "Diana and Actaeon: The Myth as Synthesis," *English Literary Renaissance* 10 (Autumn, 1981): 317-359.

3. *Shakespeare and the Common Understanding* (New York: Free Press, 1967), 159.

4. "The Lamb of Lust: The Role of Adonis in Shakespeare's *Venus and Adonis,*" *Shakespeare Studies* 6 (1970): 11–25.

5. "Shakespeare's Myth of Venus and Adonis," *PMLA* 93 (Jan 1978): 95–105.

6. A. Robin Bowers, "'Hard Armours' and 'Delicate Amours' in Shakespeare's *Venus and Adonis,*" *Shakespeare Quarterly* 12 (1979): 1–23; Heather Asals, "*Venus and Adonis*: The Education of a Goddess," *Studies in English Literature* 13 (1973): 31–51.

7. I use the edition by Edward Hubler, *Shakespeare's Songs and Poems* (New York: McGraw-Hill, 1959) for both the sonnets and the poem.

8. Eugene Cantelupe takes issue with the neoplatonic approach. He insists that Shakespeare is parodying the pattern. The neoplatonic conventions, "love, beauty, procreation and the spirit" are "unrealistic and absurd." The pursuit of such love leads to "propelling and repugnant lust." See "An Iconographical Interpretation of *Venus and Adonis,* Shakespeare's Ovidian Comedy," *Shakespeare Quarterly* 14 (1963): 141.

9. Rabkin, "*Venus and Adonis* and the Myth of Love," *Pacific Coast Studies in Shakespeare,* eds. Waldo McNeir and Thelma Greenfield (Eugene, Oregon: U of Oregon P, 1966), 20–32.

10. Rebhorn, 1.

11. Cantelupe, 141–42.

12. Kenneth Muir, "*Venus and Adonis*: Comedy or Tragedy?" in *Shakespearean Essays*, eds. Alwin Thaler and Norman Sanders (Knoxville: U of Tennessee P, 1964), 1–13.

13. W.R. Streitberger, "Ideal Conduct in *Venus and Adonis*," *Shakespeare Quarterly* 26 (Summer, 1975): 285–91.

14. David N. Beauregard interprets the two halves in terms of Renaissance faculty psychology. The first illustrates the concupiscent part of the sensitive soul and the second represents the irascible part with Venus now a "pathetic figure." "*Venus and Adonis*: Shakespeare's Representation of the Passions," *Shakespeare Studies* 8 (1975): 83–98; Donald Watson further develops this concupiscent/irascible dichotomy: "The Contrarieties of Venus and Adonis," *Studies in Philology* 75 (1978): 32–63.

15. Barkan asserts, "The mythographers add moralistic alternatives: the norms of economic behavior, the norms of social and political behavior, and finally the recapitulation of the Christian story" (330). See also D.W. Robertson, Jr., *A Preface to Chaucer: Studies in Medieval Perspectives* (Princeton: Princeton UP, 1973), 299; and Graham Hough, *A Preface to the Faerie Queene* (New York: Norton, 1963), 100–37. Speaking of religious allegorical techniques, Robertson warns that "spiritual exegetes do not systematically make use of every detail in the texts before them." Hough asserts that pure allegory ("naive allegory") seldom occurs in the great allegorical works, especially *The Faerie Queen*: "I cannot agree with Frye, or Spenser himself for that matter, that *The Fairie Queene* as a whole is continuous allegory" (108).

16. See Marcelle Thiébaux, *The Stag of Love: The Chase in Medieval Literature* (Ithaca: Cornell Univ. Press, 1974); Robert P. Merrix, "The 'Beste Noire': The Medieval Role of the Boar in *Venus and Adonis*," *The Upstart Crow* 11 (1991): 117–30; and Barkan, 339–44.

17. Quoted from Barkan, 344.

18. All references to the plays are from *The Riverside Shakespeare*, ed. G. Blakemore Evans (Boston: Houghton Mifflin, 1974).

19. William Sheidley sees a kind of synthesis in the poem. The "sexual gluttony of Venus" and the "unnatural frigidity of Adonis" must be joined "into a creative union on the human level." In the poem, "Shakespeare distills a . . . sane and joyful spirit by raising his reader to a viewpoint from which love is revealed not to present (as it seems to Adonis) a dreary choice between lust and chastity, but to offer a welcome alternative in the 'warme effects' of charity to the self-defeating paralysis of pride" ("'Unless It Be a Boar': Love and Wisdom in Shakespeare's *Venus and Adonis*," *Modern Language Quarterly* 35 [March 1974]: 3–15). Norman Rabkin, on the other hand, denies a synthesis: "In this romance of the self-denying Adonis whose definition of love leads him to the search for a purity attainable only in death, and of the earth-bound Venus whose love never reaches beyond apotheosized animality, Shakespeare reflects the hopelessly opposed elements of love as he found it in Renaissance neoplatonism" ("*Venus and Adonis* and the Myth of Love," 32).

20. Charles Paul Segal, *Landscape in Ovid's Metamorphoses: A Study of the Transformation of a Literary Symbol* (Wiesbaden: Franz Steiner Verlag GMBH, 1969), 5–7.

21. Topographical or geographical sexual imagery became a quite popular topos in Renaissance poetry. Sidney in "What Tongue Can Her Perfections Tell"; Donne in "Love's Progress"; Carew in "A Rapture"; Spenser (the undressing of Serena: VI, viii, 41–43); Nashe in the notorious *The Choice of Valentines*; and others all vividly describe the various parts of female anatomy. Most descriptions are analogical: breasts are "pommels," "rising apples," or the "Sestos and Abydos" marking the "Hellespont" of the mistress' chest (Donne); bellies are "Cupid's Hill," "a vale of Lillies" or "the mound of Venus," and so on. Donne's heroic sailor travels to his mistress' "fair Atlantic navel" and thence to the "forest [pubic hair] where many shipwrack and no further get." For a more thorough treatment of this technique see Robert P.

Merrix, "'The Vale of Lillies and the Bower of Bliss': Soft-Core Pornography in Elizabethan Poetry," *Journal of Popular Culture* 19 (Spring 1986): 3–16; and David O. Frantz, "'Leud Priapians' and Renaissance Pornography," *Studies in English Literature* 12 (1972): 157–72.

22. It is not clear whether Shakespeare was familiar with Aphrodite's classical epithet: the "Death-in-Life Goddess." See Robert Graves, *The Greek Myths* (New York: George Braziller, 1959), 71. If so, either Adonis confuses the epithets or the poet is being even more ironic in reversing the syntax.

23. Robert P. Miller asserts that Venus seeks Adonis only for physical love. Venus abuses the "purpose" of her body (procreation), desiring Adonis only for pleasure. "Venus, Adonis and the Horses," *English Literary History* 26 (1952): 249–64; W.R. Streitberger has a similarly harsh view of Venus: "Venus presents the temptations—not merely to lust, but to neglect of duty—to succumb to the easy pleasures and endeavors of life, and exhibits in her actions the results of giving in to those temptations" (286).

24. Both S. Clark Hulse ("Shakespeare's Myth of *Venus and Adonis*") and Jonathan Hart view Venus as rapacious. For Hulse she is a "sweaty muscular rapist" (95) and Hart asserts that "*Venus and Adonis* begins with a goddess' attempted rape of a 'mortal' boy" (37). However, J.D. Jahn ("The Lamb of Lust") denies that Adonis is a rape victim: "Adonis' brusque disdain of Venus throughout the early scenes, his childishness and physical vanity, ought to dissuade readers from the belief that he is somehow a sacrificial lamb of a lustful goddess" (13). See Jonathan Hart, "'Till Forging Nature Be Comdemned for Treason': Representational Strife in *Venus and Adonis*," *Cahiers élisabethains* 36 (Oct 1989): 37–47.

25. Northrop Frye, *Anatomy of Criticism* (Princeton: Princeton UP, 1973), 147–50.

26. Hereward T. Price examines the red and white imagery in great detail. The colors are always in conflict until Adonis dies, at which time "the red and white are reconciled" ("The Function of Imagery in *Venus and Adonis*," *Papers of the Michigan Academy of Science, Arts and Letters* 31 (1945): 275–97). Red and white imagery was often associated with sexual violation in relation to the boar, especially to the tusks which often are covered with "foam" (semen) and blood. In Grottfried's *Tristan*, Marjodoc, steward to King Mark, dreams of a boar "foaming at the mouth. . . . Arriving at Mark's chamber [where Isolde lies] he . . . tossed the king's appointed bed in all directions, and fouled the royal linen with his foam." Shortly after, Tristan (the boar in Marjodoc's dream), bloodies the bed clothes, after a vein in his arm breaks open (*Gottfried Von Strassburg: Tristan*, trans. A.T. Hatto [New York: Penguin Books, 1978] 219–42.)

27. Rabkin ("*Venus and Adonis* and the Myth of Love") notes that "Adonis rejects the animal in himself only to be destroyed by the insentient beast he seeks" (32).

28. Ovid, *The Metamorphoses,* trans. Frank Justus Miller, vol. 2, bk. 10 (Harvard: Cambridge Univ Press, 1984), ll. 713–16; *Shakespeare's Ovid: Arthur Golding's Translation of the Metamorphoses*, ed. W.H.D. Rouse (New York: W.W. Norton, 1961): "The Boare . . . on *Adonis* did pursew, / Who trembling and retyring back too place of refuge drew, / And hyding in his codds his tusks as farre as he could thrust / He layd him all along for dead upon the yellow dust" (ll. 836–40).

29. Like Venus, the boar runs the gamut of meanings. On the one hand it represents lust (Miller, 294), the evil effects of lust (Bowers, 9), a surrogate of a lustful Venus (Price, 290–94) or something bent on the destruction of beauty (J.C. Maxwell, ed., *The Poems* (Boston: Cambridge UP, 1969), xiv). On the other hand, the boar is associated with strength and virility (Hatto, 41). Another time it is a "worthy adversary" (Don Cameron Allen, "On *Venus and Adonis*," in *Elizabethan and Jacobean Studies* (Oxford: Clarendon Press, 1959, 100–11).

30. Marcelle Thiébaux, "The Mouth of the Boar as a Symbol in Medieval Literature," *Romance Philology* 22 (1968): 281–99.

31. Denis de Rougemont, *Love in the Western World* (Greenwich: Fawcett, 1969).

32. Barry Pegg grimly comments: "Any attempt of man's spirit to find salvation or transcendence by denying his physical nature is bound to fail. . . . There is no optimistic sense of participation in an energetic life-style, for Venus is stupid and the boar depraved and cruel." See "Generation and Corruption in Shakespeare's *Venus and Adonis*," *Michigan Academician* 8 (Summer 1975): 105–15.

33. For example, see Jahn: "The law [Venus] lays down perpetuates coquetry and insures the frustration of future lovers" (23).

34. Tita French Baumlin, "The Birth of the Bard: *Venus and Adonis* and Poetic Apothesis," *Papers on Language and Literature* 26 (Spring 1990): 191-211.

35. A.C. Hamilton, "*Venus and Adonis*." *Studies in English Literature* 1 (1961): 1–15.

36. Nona Fienberg, "Thematics of Value in *Venus and Adonis*," *Criticism: A Quarterly for Literature and the Arts* 31 (Winter 1989): 21–32.

37. James Arieti, "Empedocles in Rome: Rape and the Roman Ethos," *CLIO* 10 (1980): 5–17.

Shakespeare's *Venus and Adonis*

A Lacanian Tragicomedy of Desire

James Schiffer

I

Why? She's neither fish nor flesh. A man knows not where to have her.
(Henry IV, Part I, 3.3.128–29)[1]

The subject of Shakespeare's *Venus and Adonis* is desire, its comedy and anguish, desire in all its multifaceted, paradoxical forms: "high desire" (l. 277), "sweet desire" (l. 386), "deep desire" (l. 389), "quick desire" (l. 547), but perhaps most of all "hot desire" (l. 1074), that "coal that must be cooled" (l. 387). Of the twelve uses of the word "desire" in the poem, seven come at the end of lines; of these seven, six rhyme with "fire." Venus' burning passion for Adonis powers the action. The lusty, "sick-thoughted" goddess "pants" and "sweats"; "Her face doth reek and smoke, her blood doth boil" (l. 555). Her heart is in danger of smoldering like "an oven that is stopped" (l. 331). "Enraged" with passion, "desire doth lend her force / Courageously to pluck [Adonis] from his horse" (ll. 29–30). At the end of the poem, discovering Adonis slain, the goddess laments:

> Mine eyes are turned to fire, my heart to lead.
> Heavy heart's lead, melt at mine eyes' red fire!
> So shall I die by drops of hot desire.
> (ll. 1072–74)

As important as fire's quality of searing heat is to Shakespeare's depiction of unfulfilled passion, a second quality of fire (and of desire), its constantly changing form, best describes the style of *Venus and Adonis*: fast and glowing, unpredictable, restlessly shifting throughout the work in diction, imagery, tone, mood, and distance from the protagonists. The poem's many stylistic modulations result, of course, in complex shifts and slippages in meaning, genre, and effects.

For much of its critical history, this complexity has not been appreciated. Faced with the poem's combination of so many disparate elements (Ovidian, neoplatonic, epyllionic, comic, tragic, erotic, moral, allegorical, satiric, elegiac, etc.), several scholars have tended to dismiss the work as a flawed product of Shakespeare's apprenticeship. Thus, Don Cameron Allen declares that the poem is "clearly the result of a young and unfinished artist" (101), while C.S. Lewis complains that *Venus and Adonis* fails to be successfully one thing or the other, either coherently didactic or engagingly erotic (see also Watkins 710; Smith 89; and Bush 139). According to Lewis, Shakespeare's Venus is a "very ill-conceived temptress. She is made so much larger than her victim that she can throw his horse's reins over one arm and tuck him under the other, and knows her art so badly that she threatens, almost in her first words, to 'smother him with kisses.' Certain horrible interviews with voluminous female relatives inevitably recur to mind" (498). Others have held a higher opinion of the poem but have tried to defend it by reducing its complexity, Rufus Putney by arguing the poem's comedy while ignoring its pathos, James Lake by stressing tragedy while overlooking deflating ironies after Adonis is slain. A number of recent critics, beginning with A.C. Hamilton and Kenneth Muir, have been both sensitive to and appreciative of the poem's many sudden shifts in tone and feeling. Muir finds that *Venus and Adonis* is neither "an argument against lust" nor a "straightforward eulogy of sexual love. Almost everything in the poem appears to be ambivalent" (9). This ambivalence, Muir later concludes, "is caused by the poet's own acceptance of conflicting feelings about love" (12). Muir's reading has been reinforced by a number of later critics, among them Norman Rabkin, William Keach, and Heather Dubrow.[2] In fact, Clark Hulse, who presents an iconographic reading in many ways compatible with Muir's, has used the phrase "the new orthodoxy of an ambivalent *Venus and Adonis*" to characterize the seeming consensus among critics over the past three decades (147).[3] Yet this new orthodoxy of ambivalence has left many questions about the poem unanswered. As John Doebler observes, "The problem of redeeming the poem from defectiveness by the discovery of a single 'theme' or 'unified impression,' however complex or 'ambivalent,' has been the unsolved problem of this century" (37; see also Klause 353–56).

Since the subject of *Venus and Adonis* is desire, since many of its meanings are ambiguous, and since its effect is to create a deep ambivalence in its readers, it is surprising that the poem has not received more attention from psychoanalytical critics, though there have been a few studies of this kind, the most notable by Peter Dow Webster, Alan Baer Rothenberg, Coppélia Kahn, and Wayne A. Rebhorn.[4] Webster uses the Jungian archetype of the Universal Mother to describe Venus and to make psychobiographical inferences about Shakespeare. In his opinion, Venus represents Shakespeare's "poetic version of his own infantile fantasy of his own mother" (298). Adonis' preference of the boar over Venus, according to Webster, is Adonis' "projection of his defense against a carefully concealed inner oralism" (303). Rothenberg's Freudian analysis discovers that "through Shakespeare's imagery the attempted seduction of Adonis by Venus is revealed to be substructured by a preoedipal conflict between an overactive, too-loving mother and her resistant nursing infant. . . . The imagery of seduction becomes the fantasy of an oral rape of a passive infant's mouth by the breast or mouth of his aggressive mother (or nurse), with results that are ultimately fatal to the infant" (3). Kahn draws on post-Freudian ego psychologists Margaret Mahler, Edith Jacobson, Erik Erikson, D.W. Winnicott, and others in her study of male psychosexual development, *Man's Estate: Masculine Identity in Shakespeare*. For her, the main conflict of the poem is "between eros and death fought within the narcissistic self" (22). Adonis' narcissism, Kahn maintains, is "a masculine defense against the fear of women—women perceived as an engulfing maternal presence by a youth not fully separated from that presence" (23). The threat that Venus poses is also the emphasis of Rebhorn, who unlike Kahn, sees Adonis' rejection of Venus not as a sign of stunted or retrograde development but as an understandable reaction to the ravenous, smothering quality of Venus' maternal love; the work "derives its comedy and pathos," he argues, "from playing with a deep-seated male fear of emasculation through infantilization at the hands of a woman" (8).

To my knowledge, no one has yet published a Lacanian reading of *Venus and Adonis,* though with the proliferation of Lacanian Shakespeareans these days, one can never be sure (not that any two Lacanian readings could be the same for long!).* In any case, there are several compelling reasons for viewing *Venus and Adonis* through the lens of Lacanian theory. First of all, like the poem, much of Lacan's work is devoted to the phenomenology of desire, its etiology, its dialectical structure, its significance, and its effects. For Lacan (and here, he could have cited Venus' pursuit of Adonis as an illustration), desire's "paradoxical, deviant, erratic, eccentric, even scandalous character" distinguishes it from need, on the one hand, and from demand (ultimately the demand for love) on the other ("Signification" 286). Desire, he writes, "is neither the appetite for satisfaction, nor the demand for love, but the difference that results from the subtraction of the first from the second, the phenomenon of their splitting *(Spaltung)*" ("Signification" 287). A related idea follows from this definition, one that has important relevance to Shakespeare's poem: the structural impossibility of desire's satisfaction. Desire, according to Lacanian interpreter Valerie Traub, can never be fulfilled because desire is always "substitutive, founded on a lack, and hence, always the desire of an other" (7). In Lacanian psychoanalysis, she explains:

> the individual is constituted simultaneously as a subject, a gender, and sexuality through the entrance into the symbolic order of language. With the insertion of the third term, the phallus, into the imaginary preoedipal relation of mother and child, the child loses its fantasized symbiosis with the mother, falling into a pre-existing order of culture that through its endlessly substitutive chain of signification, enforces an always-divided subjectivity or 'lack-in-being.' The signifier for this lack-in-being is the phallus: first, because, by breaking the imaginary dyad, it inaugurates all subsequent desire as substitutive; and, second, because all subjects, male and female, are psychically castrated, learning the meaning of separation and difference through their alienation into language. (53)

Lacan's notion that desire is governed by castration, "whether in the normal or abnormal" ("Subversion" 323), has intriguing application to *Venus and Adonis*, especially to Adonis' death by a wound to the groin. It is the threat of castration, explains Catherine Belsey, that initially "impels [the subject] to submit to the imperatives of the cultural order and renounce incest" (52). The phallus, meanwhile, is multivalent in its status as a signifier. It designates "as a whole the effects of the signified" (Lacan, "Signification" 285) and embodies "*jouissance* in the dialectic of desire" (Lacan, "Subversion" 319). It is at once "a signifier of the *fiction* of unmediated presence and integrated identity" and "the metaphor for a fragmented and precarious subjectivity" (Traub 54). It represents both the castrating agency of the symbolic order, the *Nom-du-Pere*, and "the unnameable object of desire, the desire of the Other, and it represents (stands in place of) the *objet a*, the lost object in the real" (Belsey 63).

II

Backward she pushed him, as she would be thrust . . .
                                                        (*Venus and Adonis*, l. 41)

In light of Lacan's notion of the phallus, one notices right away the unusual circumstance, unique in the Shakespearean canon, of the absence of a psychosexually mature, heterosexual male, human or divine, through the entire work (mature, heterosexual male animals are another matter, as we see in the examples of the stallion and the boar). Mars and Titan are alluded to, but as a way of emphasizing what is absent from the present scene, the erect penis of heterosexual male desire (Sheidley 10). Certainly this is the rhetorical context, Adonis' lack of response to her seduction, in which Venus conjures her affair with Mars:

> I have been wooed, as I entreat thee now,
> Even by the stern and direful god of war,
> Whose sinewy neck in battle ne'er did bow,
> Who conquers where he comes in every jar;
>   Yet hath he been my captive and my slave,
>   And begged for that which thou unasked shalt have.
>
> (ll. 97–102)

Never mind that her boast of enslaving Mars and "Leading him prisoner in a red-rose chain" (l. 110) has the unintended effect of threatening emasculation; this is not the way to win Adonis or allay his fears. She intends her account of her affair with Mars to offer Adonis a model of "normal" male response to her beauty, just as later she appeals to Adonis (again with unintended ironies) to learn from the example of his stallion:

> Thy palfrey, as he should,
> Welcomes the warm approach of sweet desire.
> . . . .
> Who sees his true love in her naked bed,
> Teaching the sheets a whiter hue than white,
> But when his glutton eye so full hath fed,
> His other agents aim at like delight?
>   Who is so faint that dares not be so bold
>   To touch the fire, the weather being cold?
>
> Let me excuse thy courser, gentle boy;
> And learn of him, I heartily beseech thee,
> To take advantage on presented joy.
> Though I were dumb, yet his proceedings teach thee.
>
> (ll. 385–86; 397–406)[5]

This absence of a character embodying the masculine heterosexual response, a situation that Lacan would no doubt recognize as signifying the absence of the phallus, is responsible for many of the poem's most interesting effects and meanings. The phenomenon is similar, yet opposite to the marginalization, absence, disappearance, or destruction of the feminine in several Shakespearean history plays and tragedies. Since Shakespeare wrote his plays for an all-male, mostly adult cast, it is not surprising that each of his dramatic works features adult male characters. Despite the important presence of men in every Shakespearean play, there are scenes in several (and in certain sonnets) that recall in one way or another the dramatic situation in *Venus and Adonis*. Some scenes, for example, emphasize the impossibility of desire's satisfaction because of an inappropriate object of desire; this is the implied situation in Sonnet 20, as well as with Phebe in love with the disguised Rosalind in *As You Like It*, or the proud Countess Olivia in love with the disguised Viola in *Twelfth Night*. Other scenes in the plays remind us of *Venus and Adonis* because they depict "sexual initiatives by women" (Duncan-Jones 499). Cousins to the aggressive Venus can be found in Nell the kitchen wench in pursuit of Dromio of Syracuse in *The Comedy of Errors*, Helena in pursuit of Demetrius in *A Midsummer Night's Dream*, and that very different Helena who substitutes herself into Bertram's bed in *All's Well That Ends Well*. Cleopatra's exchange with the eunuch Mardian after Antony has departed for Rome illustrates the comic potential of a situation from which the phallus is absent, in this case, has just departed:

> *Mardian.* What's Your Highness' pleasure?
> *Cleopatra.* Not now to hear thee sing. I take no pleasure
> In aught an eunuch has. 'Tis well for thee
> That, being unseminared, thy freer thoughts
> May not fly forth of Egypt. Hast thou affections?
> *Mardian.* Yes, gracious madam.
> *Cleopatra.* Indeed?
> *Mardian.* Not in deed, madam, for I can do nothing
> But what indeed is honest to be done.
> Yet have I fierce affections, and think
> What Venus did with Mars.
> *Cleopatra.* O Charmian
> Where think'st thou he is now? Stands he or sits he?
> Or does he walk? Or is he on his horse?
> O happy horse, to bear the weight of Antony!
> (*Antony and Cleopatra*, 1.5.9–22)

The absence of the phallus in *Venus and Adonis* makes possible the comedy and the erotics of gender and sex role reversals, reversals that are anticipated in the antitheses and chiasmic inversion (l. 4) of the first stanza:

> Even as the sun with purple-colored face
> Had ta'en his last leave of the weeping morn,
> Rose-cheeked Adonis hied him to the chase.
> Hunting he loved, but love he laughed to scorn.
> > Sick-thoughted Venus makes amain unto him,
> > And like a bold-faced suitor 'gins to woo him.
>
> > (ll. 1–6)

In the vacuum of the absent male, Venus takes charge, becomes the "bold fac'd suitor," while "rose-cheeked Adonis," "more lovely than a man," (l. 9) assumes the role of coy, disdainful maiden.[6] The situation, states Donald G. Watson, dramatizes the "inadequacies of the Petrarchan treatment of amorous experience. . . . The reversal of the roles of Petrarchan *Frauendienst* in the aggressive female-passive male pattern mocks current fashion: coming at the height of the vogue in sonnets, this must have been thought marvelously witty in itself" (45–46). In changing roles, Venus does not escape the dialectic of desire; she simply occupies a different position within it. Instead of being the object of desire, self-sufficient and unmoved, she becomes the one who desires. Paradoxically, in assuming the conventionally active male role, Venus relinquishes her usual power in love to the passive, unresponsive Adonis. Not just gender but sex roles are turned topsy-turvy, a phenomenon signaled by the inverted mirroring of the letters "V" and "A," letters suggestive of the female and male genitalia. Not only does Venus push Adonis as she would be thrust, but many of the images suggest attempted phallic entry, either by breast or by the mouth as a beak (Rothenberg):

> Even as an empty eagle, sharp by fast,
> Tires with her beak on feathers, flesh, and bone,
> Shaking her wings, devouring all in haste,
> Till either gorge be stuffed or prey be gone,
> > Even so she kissed his brow, his cheek, his chin,
> > And where she ends she doth anew begin.
>
> > (ll. 55–60)

Even Venus' loquaciousness has phallic implications. She speaks 537 of the poem's 1,194 lines (Dubrow 27). She pours her rhetorical spirits into Adonis' ear, hoping to screw his courage to the sticking place. But though Venus might wish to be the phallus, she cannot ultimately succeed, no more than Adonis can. All she can do is wish: "Would thou wert as I am, and I a man" (l. 369).

The comedy of the absent phallus reaches its anticlimactic pinnacle when Venus pulls the unwilling Adonis on top of her after he says he intends to "hunt the boar with certain of his friends" (l. 588):

> She sinketh down, still hanging by his neck;
> He on her belly falls, she on her back.
>
> Now is she in the very lists of love,
> Her champion mounted for the hot encounter.
> All is imaginary she doth prove.
> He will not manage her, although he mount her,
>   That worse than Tantalus' is her annoy,
>   To clip Elysium and to lack her joy.
>   (ll. 593–600)

As Robert Sheidley explains, "The poem functions as a problem in subtraction. The equation that nicely balances for the horses, when drawn up for Venus and Adonis, obviously lacks one crucial factor which, if present, would allow Venus' hopes and those of the sympathetic reader to be fulfilled: that is, simply, an erect phallus, which Adonis will not and Venus cannot provide" (9–10). Our erotic response to this moment is no doubt a deeply personal matter, determined by our individual sexual preferences and attitudes to sex, as Heather Dubrow observes (62). Heterosexual males may fantasize "being seduced by the goddess of beauty" (Bevington 1561) and wish to provide the missing phallus.[7] In effect, they find themselves in the position of Titan, who:

> . . . tirèd in the midday heat,
> With burning eye did hotly overlook them,
>   Wishing Adonis had his team to guide,
>   So he were like him, and by Venus' side.
>   (ll. 177–180)

Rather than desire Venus, heterosexual women might well identify with Venus and share her passion for the "tender boy." So, in fact, might homosexual males. Though the degree to which this moment seems comic will probably vary from reader to reader as much as individual erotic responses do, there is something about the image of Tantalus—and even more about the image of an inert Adonis atop a volcanic Venus—that goes beyond comedy and titillation, that goes more deeply, to the very heart of desire, which is always absent, always, it seems, just out of reach, just around the corner, just on the other side of the glass. It is a short jump indeed from Venus' anguish of unfulfilled desire to our own.

Why Adonis does not respond to Venus is one of the unresolvable puzzles of the poem, not because Adonis fails to provide reasons, but because, Iago-like, he provides too many. The overdetermination of Adonis' motives makes it difficult to settle on a single cause: physiological, rational, moral, or unconscious, or a combination of some or all of the above. In Ovid's *Metamorphoses* revenge for his mother's horrible fate (incest with her father and transformation into a tree) apparently motivates Adonis,

> . . . and by and by a man,
> And every day more beawtifull than other he becam.
> That in the end Dame *Venus* fell in love with him: wherby
> He did revenge the outrage of his mothers villanye.
> (Golding trans., X.602–05),

though it is unclear how he exacts his revenge in Ovid since Adonis does not spurn Venus' advances. True, he fails to listen to Venus' advice about the boar, but surely this error hurts him at least as much as it hurts Venus. There is, perhaps, a hint of revenge in the phrase "love he laughed to scorn" (l. 4) and in Adonis' boast that his "love to love is but to disgrace it" (l. 412), but this thread is not consistently emphasized throughout the poem. Katherine Duncan-Jones notes "Shakespeare's emphasis on Adonis's youth, which appears possibly even pre-pubertal" (489). That he is still physiologically immature is Adonis' first line of defense:

> Who wears a garment shapeless and unfinished?
> Who plucks the bud before one leaf put forth?
> If springing things be any jot diminished,
> They wither in their prime, prove nothing worth.
> > The colt that's backed and burdened being young
> > Loseth his pride and never waxeth strong.
> > (ll. 415–20)

Measure my strangeness with my unripe years.
Before I know myself, seek not to know me.

> No fisher but the ungrown fry forbears.
>> The mellow plum doth fall; the green sticks fast,
>> Or being early plucked is sour to taste.
>>> (ll. 524–28)

Venus' resolve to taste Adonis even though "The tender spring upon [his] tempting lip / Shows [him] unripe" (ll. 127–28) also supports the idea that Adonis is not yet physically ready for a sexual encounter.

Elsewhere Adonis seems not so much incapable of love as hostile to it for fairly rational—that is, practical—reasons. Thus he calls love "a life in death / That laughs and weeps, and all but with a breath," (ll. 413–14) and declares that his "heart longs not to groan, / But soundly sleeps, while now it sleeps alone" (ll. 785–86). Finally, he resorts to the moral argument, based upon the distinction between love and lust:

> I hate not love, but your device in love,
> That lends embracements unto every stranger,
>> You do it for increase. O strange excuse,
>> When reason is the bawd to lust's abuse!

> Call it not love, for Love to heaven is fled,
> Since sweating Lust on earth usurped his name . . .
>> (ll. 789–94)

The problem, as Kenneth Muir points out, is that this moral argument, coming as late as it does, strikes us as an afterthought rather than a deeply held conviction (7). Then, there are the unconscious motives, or at least motives Adonis never states. Under this category comes the explanation that Adonis fails to respond because he is locked in a narcissistic desire to "grow unto himself" (l. 1180), either as a normal stage in the process of maturation or as an abnormal case of arrested development. The latter seems to be Coppélia Kahn's position: the narcissist's "primary need," she argues, "is to defend against sexual involvement in order to protect the fragile inner self. This defense is ironically self-destructive" (32–33). Jonathan Bate offers a different unconscious motive for Adonis' resistance, the fear of incest. After observing that Venus behaves as both a lover and a mother to Adonis, he argues that "such juxtapositions of sexuality and parenting suggest that Adonis is forced to re-enact, with generational roles reversed, his mother's incestuous affair" (84). Or is Adonis' motive neither narcissism nor fear of incest, but rather a quite understandable reaction to the role reversals brought on by Venus's hot pursuit? Perhaps he simply wishes to avoid sacrificing his "adult, male autonomy" (Rebhorn 9). Perhaps he chooses to be the active rather than the passive party, the hunter rather than the hunted, as a way of preserving—or even attaining—his emerging sense of manhood.

From Venus' point of view the reasons for Adonis' rejection are less important than the fact of his refusal. As with Adonis, Shakespeare does away with Ovid's explanation of Venus's motive—that she is accidentally grazed by one of Cupid's arrows; only then did the "beawty of the lad / [Inflaam] hir" (Golding trans., X.611). In Shakespeare's poem we join the action *in medias res* with Venus already "inflaamd." What Shakespeare stresses is that for Venus this is a first-time experience, the experience of the pain of mortal desire. Her love for Adonis is thus an incarnation and a submission (possibly involuntary) to her own law:

> Poor queen of love, in thy own law forlorn,
> To love a cheek that smiles at thee in scorn!
>
> (ll. 251–252)

Her law, like Lacan's, dictates that desire can never truly be satisfied, because desire is always for absence, for lack, for what is not there. The parallel has been made between Adonis and Ovid's Narcissus, but a closer comparison exists between Venus and Narcissus. A disappointed male lover prays that Narcissus "may once feele fierce *Cupids* fire / As I doe now, and yet not joy the things he doth desire" (Golding trans., III.505–06). Surely this is Venus's fate: "She's Love, she loves, and yet she is not loved" (l. 610). If Adonis were like Mars, or like his stallion, if he actually had an erect phallus and desired Venus, one doubts that he would appeal to the goddess. She is attracted to his feminine, childish qualities, to his sulking refusal, to his very inability to respond.

III

It's a question of the phallus, and that's why he will never be able to strike it, until the moment when he has made the complete sacrifice—without wanting to, moreover—of all narcissistic attachments, i.e., when he is mortally wounded and knows it.

> —Lacan, "Desire and the Interpretation of Desire in *Hamlet*" (51)

We come now to the boar, that "beste noire" for critics, the "most puzzling object in the poem and the most controversial" (Merrix 117). Several critics, including Don Cameron Allen and Kenneth Muir, agree that the boar represents death, which seems reasonable enough. But death for what? In Ovid, Adonis dies after apparently consummating his relationship with Venus; therefore, in *The Metamorphoses* his death could be construed as a punishment for lust. Since Shakespeare's Adonis does not give in to Venus, however, his punishment is more often viewed as a punishment for turning away from sexuality and love (Muir 5–7; Sheidley 5; Kahn 42). For Gordon Williams, however, Adonis' death is not a punishment, but "a consummation devoutly to be wished" (770), while Hereward T. Price believes it represents "the destruction of something exquisite by what is outrageously vile" (277). In his view the boar stands for "the complete irrationality of evil" (277). Several interpreters have associated the boar with Venus, or with Adonis' projection of Venus' lust, an identification she herself invites when she imagines the boar's assault as a kind of "homosexual rape" (Barber and Wheeler 147):

> If he did see his face, why then I know
> He thought to kiss him, and hath killed him so.

> 'Tis true, 'tis true! Thus was Adonis slain:
> He ran upon the boar with his sharp spear,
> Who did not whet his teeth at him again,
> But by a kiss thought to persuade him there;
> And, nuzzling in his flank, the loving swine
> Sheathed unaware the tusk in his soft groin.

> Had I been toothed like him, I must confess,
> With kissing him I should have killed him first.
> (*Venus and Adonis*, ll. 1109–1118)

While this speech seems to reveal Venus' affinity with the boar, it actually shows only her affinity with the boar's desire. As A.T. Hatto correctly observes, the boar "is a symbol of overmastering virility" (354). It is Venus' masculine rival, perhaps, but not her double. Venus, to her regret, is not "toothed like him"; consequently, the "boar establishes a kind of contact such as Venus never had" (Asals 46). Peter Dow Webster also sees the boar as distinctively masculine, a version of the castrating "archetypal primal father" (300). Finally, concluding this line of phallic inquiry, William E. Sheidley contends that the boar is "the locus of [Adonis'] missing phallic impulse," the return in objective form of what Adonis has repressed (10).

Instead of yielding to Venus as he should, Sheidley argues, Adonis "perversely pursues to its end a policy of self-castration" (11).

One can easily imagine Lacan delighting in the multiplicity of meanings here, the almost endless substitutions of symbol and metaphor, the almost endless play of signifier and signified. Of these rival theories about the boar, few, he would observe, are mutually exclusive. Like Webster and Alan Baer Rothenberg, he would recognize in Venus' mixture of maternal and erotic passion a clue to the preoedipal configuration of the poem. Lacan would also probably see Adonis' wound to his groin as a castration, perhaps as a punishment for threatened incest ("Signification" 282).[8] But for Lacan, the physical castration is only a metaphor for psychic castration, the result of the advent of signification, the subject's initiation into the symbolic order of language. Lacan would agree with Webster that the boar symbolizes the castrating father, though in Lacanian terms, the boar would more properly be termed the *Nom-du-Pere,* the Name-of-the-Father, representative of the symbolic order, the Other (as locus of signification), the Law. At the same time, as Sheidley points out, the boar stands for Adonis' missing phallic impulse. In Lacanian terms, the boar represents the return of the repressed phallus, signifying both the agency of castration (the *Nom-du-Pere*) and the illusion of potency and completeness which Adonis has lost:

> This is our starting point: through his relationship to the signifier, the subject is deprived of something of himself, of his very life, which has assumed the value of that which binds him to the signifier. The phallus is our term for the signifier of his alienation in signification. When the subject is deprived of this signifier, a particular object becomes for him the object of desire. (Lacan, "Desire" 28)

The object for Venus, the impossible object of desire, is Adonis; for Adonis, that object is the boar. In this "profoundly enigmatic" process, Lacan writes, "[s]omething becomes an object of desire when it takes the place of what by its very nature remains concealed from the subject: that self-sacrifice, that pound of flesh which is mortgaged *[engagé]* in his relationship to the signifier" ("Desire" 28).

Adonis' death represents his escape from the dialectic of desire. The only end of desire is death—or retreat. For Venus, her earlier inability to seduce the boy becomes the permanent impossibility of satisfaction. The prophecy she utters is interesting for a variety of reasons. First, as many have observed, her predictions are as much about the past as about the future; they describe what has just happened to her as much as they forecast the fate of love on earth. For this reason, it is possible to construe the prophecy as a mean-spirited curse on mortal love (if she cannot have her love, then no one will):

> Since thou art dead, lo, here I prophesy:
> Sorrow on love hereafter shall attend.
> It shall be waited on with jealousy,
> Find sweet beginning but unsavory end,
> > Ne'er settled equally, but high or low,
> > That all love's pleasure shall not match his woe.
> > > (ll. 1135–40)

> It shall be cause of war and dire events
> And set dissention twixt the son and sire,
> Subject and servile to all discontents,
> As dry combustious matter is to fire.
> > Sith in his prime Death doth my love destroy,
> > They that love best their loves shall not enjoy.
> > > (ll. 1159–64)

The words "Since" (l. 1135) and "Sith" (l. 1163) certainly suggest a causal relationship. Even more than the spirit of revenge, however, the speech expresses sad resignation, a submission to her own law, which is greater than she, beyond either her control or comprehension (which is why the speech seems more a sad prediction than a vengeful curse). It is in this spirit of resignation that she withdraws at the end of the poem from the realm of mortal desire:

> Thus, weary of the world, away she hies
> And yokes her silver doves, by whose swift aid
> Their mistress mounted through the empty skies
> In her light chariot quickly is conveyed,
> > Holding their course to Paphos, where their queen
> > Means to immure herself and not be seen.
> > > (ll. 1189–94)

Venus' prophecy-curse also reminds us of the relationship throughout the poem between language and desire. Desire makes Venus voluble—as we have seen, her speeches dominate the poem. It is through language, through rhetorical virtuosity, that she pleads her case to Adonis. Language also provides an outlet for her frustrated yearnings; as the narrator says, "Free vent of words love's fire doth assuage" (l. 334). Most important of all, language substitutes for the object of desire, who is himself merely the *petite objet a*, the lost object in the real. Yet words are a poor consolation for the loss of Adonis, even for an Adonis she never possessed. Like Caliban, Venus might well say, "You taught me language, and my profit on 't / Is I know how to curse" (*The Tempest,* 1.2.366–67). The very conditions that make language necessary make desire's fulfillment impossible.

Like the boar, the purple flower "checkered with white" that rises from Adonis' blood is rich in multivalent meanings. In Ovid, Venus causes the metamorphosis (Golding trans., X.847–863), but not in Shakespeare's poem: Venus merely discovers it on the ground. Although she later addresses the flower as the offspring of her love with Adonis, at first she compares the flower with Adonis himself, suggesting that he has been metamorphosed (of course, in the Shakespearean economy of desire, procreation is a kind of metamorphic perpetuation of the self):

> She bows her head, the new-sprung flower to smell,
> Comparing it to her Adonis' breath,
> And says within her bosom it shall dwell,
> Since he himself is reft from her by death.
>> She crops the stalk, and in the breach appears
>> Green drooping sap, which she compares to tears.
>> (*Venus and Adonis,* ll. 1171–76)

The moment is rich in ironies. First of all, as Coppélia Kahn points out, "as a flower, [Adonis] can 'grow unto himself' as he wanted to in life, and Venus can possess him totally and forever as she could not before" (44–45). The irony of her plucking the flower has not been lost on earlier scholars either. This is a fulfillment of Adonis' earlier question, "Who plucks the bud before one leaf put forth?" (l. 416), as well as "a reenactment of her plucking Adonis off his horse" (Asals 49). In Hereward T. Price's opinion, "Adonis was twice butchered, once in blindness by the boar, and the second time in equal blindness but no less effectively by Venus. I know of no irony in literature so savage as this" (295). In Oedipal terms, the plucking is a second castration. The child must navigate the Scylla and Charybdis of the emasculating mother and the castrating father. Poor Adonis shipwrecks twice. The phallus thus has yet another incarnation in the flower, and this is true in the Lacanian sense of the term as well as the Freudian. The flower, itself a substitution, stands for the process of substitution and signification that is language, necessary as a means of representing what is absent or lost.

The flower's difference from Adonis is the gap between signifier and signified, the gap in which we all must live. Its significance is the reality of absence, of insufficiency, of alienation in language. The flower in this phallic sense (Lacan's sense of the term) is, finally, the poem *Venus and Adonis* itself, forged in the dialectic of desire, its petals of meaning spread upon the winds of endless metaphor and metonymy, endless difference and *différance*, endless deferral of the phallocentric "right reading" (which is the reader's desire), a poem that "laughs and weeps, and all but with a breath."[9]

NOTES

*Just a few months after completing this essay, I read with great interest Catherine Belsey's "Love as Tromp-l'oeil: Taxonomies of Desire in *Venus and Adonis* in the Fall 1995 (46:3) issue of *Shakespeare Quarterly*. Belsey's essay is reprinted in this volume.

1. All citations from Shakespeare are to *The Complete Works of Shakespeare*, 4th ed., ed. David Bevington.

2. Rabkin states that "in portraying the genesis of love," the poem explains love's "tragicomic complementarity in the fallen world in which we live" (151); Keach argues that "Shakespeare's handling of the mythological material is . . . deeply, at times even confusingly, ambivalent" (53) and that the poem's "seriousness—its insight into the turbulence and frustration of sexual love—is inseparable from its comedy and its entertaining eroticism" (60); Dubrow calls *Venus and Adonis* a "problem epyllion" (78). See also Rebhorn, Watson, Lindheim, and Fienberg.

3. In a footnote, Hulse cites A. Robin Bowers and David Beauregard as two recent critics who disagree with the "new orthodoxy of an ambivalent *Venus and Adonis*" (147–48).

4. Many studies of *Venus and Adonis*—most in fact—are *psychological* (as opposed to psychoanalytical) in their attempt to interpret the motivations of the two main characters. The studies I refer to (except perhaps for Rebhorn's), however, are grounded in the specific ideas of modern or contemporary psychoanalytical theorists.

5. See Robert P. Miller for a view of the horses as representative of the lower appetite ungoverned by reason.

6. See J.D. Jahn for an analysis of Adonis' coyness; in general, I think Jahn overstates the case for Adonis' *deliberate* coquetry and tends to blame the victim rather than the sexual aggressor. However, I agree with Jahn's emphasis on the way Adonis' passivity "engenders" Venus' passion (14).

7. The original audience—the Earl of Southampton and his circle of friends—was presumably mostly male, though not necessarily heterosexual; see Smith (88) and Duncan-Jones (485–86).

8. Lacan might observe as well that the boar's disruption of the mother-son relationship has its parallel in the murderous intrusion of Macbeth's henchmen into the scene between Lady Macduff and her son in *Macbeth* (4.2) and in the startling return of the Ghost in the closet scene of *Hamlet* (3.4). The Zeffirelli film version of *Hamlet* does a superb job of capturing Hamlet's guilty terror when the Ghost reappears (at the very moment that Hamlet kisses Gertrude on the mouth).

9. The image of a poem as a flower was a commonplace of Elizabethan poetry. See, for example, George Gascoigne's *A Hundred Sundry Flowers* (1573).

WORKS CITED

Allen, Don Cameron. "On *Venus and Adonis*." *Elizabethan and Jacobean*

Studies Presented to Frank Percy Wilson. Oxford: Clarendon, 1959. 100–111.

Asals, Heather. "*Venus and Adonis:* The Education of a Goddess." *Studies in English Literature* 13 (1973): 31–51.

Barber, C.L., and Richard P. Wheeler. *The Whole Journey: Shakespeare's Power of Development.* Berkeley: U of California P, 1986.

Bate, Jonathan. "Sexual Perversity in *Venus and Adonis.*" *Yearbook of English Studies* 23 (1993): 80–92.

Beauregard, David N. "*Venus and Adonis:* Shakespeare's Representation of the Passions." *Shakespeare Studies* 8 (1975): 83–98.

Belsey, Catherine. *Desire: Love Stories in Western Culture.* Oxford: Blackwell, 1994.

Bevington, David. "Introduction to *Venus and Adonis.*" *The Complete Works of Shakespeare.* 4th ed. New York: HarperCollins, 1992. 1560–61.

Bowers, A. Robin. "'Hard Armours' and 'Delicate Amours' in Shakespeare's *Venus and Adonis.*" *Shakespeare Studies* 12 (1979): 1–23.

Bush, Douglas. *Mythology and the Renaissance Tradition.* 1932; New York: Pageant, 1957.

Doebler, John. "The Many Faces of Love: Shakespeare's *Venus and Adonis.*" *Shakespeare Studies* 16 (1983): 33–43.

Dubrow, Heather. *Captive Victors: Shakespeare's Narrative Poems and Sonnets.* Ithaca: Cornell UP, 1987.

Duncan-Jones, Katherine. "Much Ado with Red and White: The Earliest Readers of Shakespeare's *Venus and Adonis.*" *Review of English Studies* 44 (1993): 479–501.

Fienberg, Nona. "Thematics of Value in *Venus and Adonis.*" *Criticism* 31 (1989): 21–32.

Hamilton, A.C. "*Venus and Adonis.*" *Studies in English Literature* 1 (1961): 1–15.

Hatto, A.T. "*Venus and Adonis*—and the Boar." *Modern Language Review* 41 (1946): 353–61.

Hulse, S. Clark. *Metamorphic Verse: The Elizabethan Minor Epic.* Princeton: Princeton UP, 1981.

Jahn, J.D. "The Lamb of Lust: The Role of Adonis in Shakespeare's *Venus and Adonis.*" *Shakespeare Studies* 6 (1970): 11–25.

Kahn, Coppélia. *Man's Estate: Masculine Identity in Shakespeare.* Berkeley: U of California P, 1981.

Keach, William. *Elizabethan Erotic Narratives: Irony and Pathos in the Ovidian Poetry of Shakespeare, Marlowe, and Their Contemporaries.* New Brunswick: Rutgers UP, 1977.

Klause, John. "*Venus and Adonis:* Can We Forgive Them?" *Studies in Philology* 85 (1988): 353–77.

Lacan, Jacques. "Desire and the Interpretation of Desire in *Hamlet.*" Ed. Jacques-Alain Miller. Trans. James Hulbert. *Literature and Psychoanalysis.* Ed. Shoshana Felman. Baltimore: Johns Hopkins UP, 1982. 11–52.

———. "The Signification of the Phallus." *Écrits.* Trans. Alan Sheridan. 1966. New York: Norton, 1977. 281–91.

———. "The Subversion of the Subject and the Dialectic of Desire in the Freudian Unconscious." *Écrits.* Trans. Alan Sheridan. 1966. New York: Norton, 1977. 292–325.

Lake, James H. "Shakespeare's Venus: An Experiment in Tragedy." *Shakespeare Quarterly* 25 (1974): 351–55.

Lewis, C.S. *English Literature in the Sixteenth Century.* Oxford: Clarendon, 1954.

Lindheim, Nancy. "The Shakespearean *Venus and Adonis.*" *Shakespeare Quarterly* 37 (1986): 190–203.

Merrix, Robert P. "The 'Beste Noire': The Medieval Role of the Boar in *Venus and Adonis*." *Upstart Crow* 11 (1991): 117–30.

Miller, Robert P. "Venus, Adonis, and the Horses." *English Literary History* 19 (1952): 250–64.

Muir, Kenneth. "*Venus and Adonis:* Comedy or Tragedy?" *Shakespearean Essays.* Eds. Alwin Thayer and Norman Sanders. Knoxville: U Tennessee P, 1964. 1–13.

Ovid. *Shakespeare's Ovid Being Arthur Golding's Translation of the Metamorphoses.* Ed. W.H.D. Rouse. London: Centaur, 1961.

Price, Hereward T. "The Function of Imagery in *Venus and Adonis*." *Papers of the Michigan Academy of Science, Arts, and Letters* 31 (1945): 275–297.

Putney, Rufus. "Venus *Agonistes*." *University of Colorado Studies* 4 (1953): 52–66.

Rabkin, Norman. *Shakespeare and the Common Understanding.* New York: Free Press, 1967.

Rebhorn, Wayne A. "Temptation in Shakespeare's *Venus and Adonis*." *Shakespeare Studies* 11 (1978): 1–19.

Rothenberg, Alan Baer. "The Oral Rape Fantasy and the Rejection of the Mother in the Imagery of Shakespeare's *Venus and Adonis*." *Psychoanalytic Quarterly* 40 (1971): 447–68.

Shakespeare, William. *The Complete Works of Shakespeare.* 4th ed. Ed. David Bevington. New York: HarperCollins, 1992.

Sheidley, William E. "'Unless It Be a Boar': Love and Wisdom in Shakespeare's *Venus and Adonis*." *Modern Language Quarterly* 35 (1974): 3–15.

Smith, Hallett. *Elizabethan Poetry.* 1952; Ann Arbor, Michigan: Ann Arbor Paperback, 1968.

Traub, Valerie. *Desire and Anxiety: Circulations of Sexuality in Shakespearean Drama.* London: Routledge, 1992.

Watkins, W.B.C. "Shakespeare's Banquet of Sense." *Southern Review* 7 (1942): 710.

Watson, Donald G. "The Contrarieties of *Venus and Adonis*." *Studies in Philology* 75 (1978): 32–63.

Webster, Peter Dow. "A Critical Fantasy or Fugue." *American Imago* 6 (1949): 297–309.

Williams, Gordon. "The Coming of Age of Shakespeare's Adonis." *Modern Language Review* 78 (1983): 769–76.

Zeffirelli, Franco, dir. *Hamlet.* Los Angeles: Warner, 1990.

"PINING THEIR MAWS"

FEMALE READERS AND THE EROTIC ONTOLOGY
OF THE TEXT IN SHAKESPEARE'S *VENUS AND ADONIS*

Richard Halpern

The prefatory material to Shakespeare's *Venus and Adonis* is a study in disingenuousness and misdirection, beginning with the epigraph from Ovid's *Amores*: "Vilia miretur vulgus: mihi flavus Apollo / Pocula Castalia plena ministret aqua."[1] ("Let cheap things dazzle the crowd; may Apollo serve me cups filled with water from the Castalian spring"). In what is at once a change of genre and a change of vocation, these lines apparently signal Shakespeare's conversion from popular playwright to classicizing poet.[2] (In Sonnet 111 he would similarly disparage his playwrighting as "public means which public manners breeds.") But of course his abandonment of the stage was hardly voluntary; he turned to writing Ovidian verse in 1593 not because he heard a higher calling but because the theaters had been closed on account of the plague.[3] Moreover, *Venus and Adonis* bears more than a little resemblance to the plays that Shakespeare seems to be rejecting. The poem divides rather neatly into comic and tragic halves, and the former of these explores issues central to Shakespeare's early romantic comedies. By depicting the sexual fascination exerted by a beautiful and androgynous young man, Shakespeare draws on the appeal that the boy-actors added to his crossdressing plays. Indeed, Venus' frustration at the sight of a physically compelling but sexually unforthcoming youth foreshadows Olivia's plight when confronted with the disguised Viola in *Twelfth Night*. Despite the Apollonian pretensions of its epigraph, *Venus and Adonis* is neither nobler nor purer than Shakespeare's "cheap" plays.

The suggestion that Shakespeare wanted to abandon a popular literary form for a more elite one is reinforced by the poem's dedication to the Earl of Southampton. Having deserted the crowd, Shakespeare apparently tries to accommodate the cultural tastes of the aristocracy. Yet if *Venus and Adonis* was meant to perplex and annoy the vulgar, it failed miserably. The poem was, in fact, immensely popular, going through sixteen editions by

1640.[4] If the Earl of Southampton read it, so, according to contemporary accounts, did tapsters and courtesans.[5]

Shakespeare misidentifies not only the class composition of his audience but also its gender. The dedication to Southampton suggests an ideal or intended reader who is not only aristocratic but male. Recent critics of English Ovidian verse have had relatively little to say about the composition of its readership, but there seems to be a general if sometimes unstated assumption that such verse was written for, and read by, men. And there is good reason to think so. The humor of *Venus and Adonis*, like that of much Ovidian verse, is intensely and often viciously misogynist. Moreover, the English tradition of Ovidian poetry was fostered in the universities and the Inns of Court,[6] exclusively male bastions that cultivated a homosocial style.[7]

While plausible, however, the hypothesis of a predominantly male readership is contradicted by most of the early references to *Venus and Adonis*. Contemporaries tended to depict Shakespeare's poem as the reading matter of courtesans, lascivious nuns, adulterous housewives, or libidinous young girls.[8] In Thomas Middleton's *A Mad World My Masters* (1608), the jealous Harebrain confiscates his wife's copies of *Venus and Adonis* and *Hero and Leander*, declaring: "O, two luscious marrow-bone pies for a young married wife!" Conversely, in Thomas Heywood's *The Fair Maid of the Exchange* (1607), Bowdler tries to seduce Mall Berry by reading passages aloud from *Venus and Adonis*.[9] Young women were often imagined as hiding copies of the poem about their persons or rooms, and imbibing loose morals or illicit sexual pleasures from it. The most vivid portrait of the poem and its readers comes from John Davies' *Paper's Complaint* (1610–11):

> Another (ah Lord helpe) mee vilifies
> With Art of Love, and how to subtilize,
> Making lewd *Venus*, with eternall Lines,
> To tye *Adonis* to her loves designes:
> Fine wit is shew'n therein: but finer twere
> If not attired in such bawdy Geare.
> But be it as it will: the coyest Dames
> In private read it for their Closet-games:
> For, sooth to say, the Lines so draw them on,
> To the venerian speculation,
> That will they, nill they (if of flesh they bee)
> They will think of it, sith *loose* Thought is free.
>
> (ll. 47–58)[10]

Davies himself, like the women he imagines, is rather coy here, for the very vagueness of his language prompts "venerian speculations" in the reader. What exactly are "closet games," and what is the "it" about which female readers find themselves compelled to think (the poem? the sexual act?)? By implicating *Venus and Adonis* in an autoerotic, possibly masturbatory scene, Davies may tell us more about the way men fantasized female readers than he does about the fantasies of those readers; yet his lines reflect widely expressed anxieties about the effects of *Venus and Adonis* on women.

The reactions of Davies and other contemporary moralists and playwrights underscore the ironies of Shakespeare's epigraph from Ovid. While *Venus and Adonis* announces itself as an Apollonian exercise as pure as the Castalian spring, it is in fact a piece of soft-core pornography. While it distinguishes itself from "cheap" drama, moralists feared it would provoke the same kinds of lascivious desires and acts as did stage comedies. And while it poses as an offering to a male, aristocratic readership, it actually appealed to a broadly popular and (to judge by contemporary accounts) a largely if not predominantly female audience. As I shall argue, however, the ironies of the poem's reception are by no means accidental. *Venus and Adonis* is largely "about" the paradoxical status of Ovidian verse, which is at once a high literary form and a source of pornographic thrills. It is also intensely self-conscious about the effect of such verse on female readers.

John Davies' lines on *Venus and Adonis* open the way to a reading of the poem by suggesting parallels between female readers and Shakespeare's Venus. Just as Venus is captured or overcome by Adonis' beauty, so the female readers of Shakespeare's text are depicted as the victims of a somewhat involuntary eros generated by the poem itself: the poem's lines "*draw* them on / To the venerian speculation," so that "will they nill they . . . they will think of it." Moreover, the phrase "venerian speculation" indirectly compares the readers' imaginations and Venus' more literal "speculation" or act of looking at Adonis. Shakespeare's Venus is, in fact, a prisoner in the realm of speculation or vision. Overcome by Adonis' charms but frustrated by his lack of sexual response, she can do nothing more than gaze at him. "Be bold to play," she urges, "our sport is not in sight" (l. 124). Later, she invokes one of a series of interlocked Ovidian allusions by comparing Adonis in all but name to Pygmalion's statue:

> Fie, liveless picture, cold and senseless stone,
> Well-painted idol, image dull and dead,
> Statue contenting but the eye alone,

Thing like a man, but of no woman bred!
(ll. 211–214)

Adonis is, according to Ovid, the great-grandson of Pygmalion and the transformed statue. Venus' phrase "of no woman bred" may thus refer not only
to Adonis' birth from the myrrh tree but to his more distant descent from a
piece of female sculpture.

In John Marston's poem "The Metamorphosis of Pygmalion's Image,"
Pygmalion actually attempts to make love to his statue; he kisses it, rubs
its breasts, and lies against it: "Yet viewing, touching, kissing (common
favour,) / Could never satiate his loves ardencie."[11] This scene depicts the
power of the artwork as its capacity to frustrate the viewer—to provoke,
yet not fulfil, an erotic desire. Here the viewing subject is male, and when
Pygmalion berates his uncooperative beloved as "relentless stone," it is clear
that she simply materializes the spiritual qualities of the traditional
Petrarchan mistress. Shakespeare's innovation with respect to the Pygmalion
myth—as in *Venus and Adonis* generally—is to explore the "comic"
possibilites of reversing this situation. Hence he places Venus in Pygmalion's
place, lusting hopelessly after an unresponsive image—a situation which is
highly ironic, since it was Venus who granted Pygmalion's prayers by transforming the statue into a real woman. Here she proves unable to effect a
similar change, and the failure of her erotic power is thus matched by the
failure of her metamorphic power. Ironically, the first half of Shakespeare's
Ovidian poem depends on the denial of a wished-for "metamorphosis."

The interest of John Davies' analogy, with which I began, is that it is
subject to reversal: that is to say, Venus' sexual frustration at the hands of
an arousing but unresponsive artwork allegorizes the plight of the female
reader of Shakespeare's erotic text. As a mildly pornographic poem, *Venus
and Adonis* is meant to generate some kind of sexual thrill or tension. But
since it is, in the end, only a book, the female reader, like Shakespeare's Venus, must content herself with "venerian speculation" alone. The theological gap that separates Venus from the merely mortal Adonis stands in for
the ontological gap between the female reader and the empty imaginations
generated by the poem.

The misogynist humor of *Venus and Adonis* centers on Shakespeare's
debasing and slightly grotesque portrayal of female sexual desire. The resentment of every male sonneteer who ever wooed a lady in vain doubtless
found satisfaction in the spectacle of Venus, the very embodiment of female
sexual power, grovelling helplessly before a beautiful, androgynous man. But
Shakespeare considerably deepens this troubling strain by extending it alle-

gorically to his female readers. *Venus and Adonis*, in other words, is not only a poem about female sexual frustration; it is meant to produce such frustration. Just as Adonis' beauty arouses Venus but refuses to satisfy her, so Shakespeare's poem aims to arouse and frustrate the female reader. If Shakespeare was himself no Adonis, his art produced a similar though somewhat mediated effect.

This somewhat peculiar allegory of reading becomes unmistakably evident in the three stanzas that occupy the numerical center of the poem. Adonis has announced his intention to hunt the boar, whereupon Venus, overcome with both sexual frustration and fear for his life, faints, pulling Adonis on top of her as she falls:

> "The boar!" quoth she, whereat a sudden pale,
> Like lawn being spread upon the blushing rose,
> Usurps her cheek; she trembles at his tale,
> And on his neck her yoking arms she throws.
> > She sinketh down, still hanging by his neck,
> > He on her belly falls, she on her back.
>
> Now is she in the very lists of love,
> Her champion mounted for the hot encounter;
> All is imaginary she doth prove,
> He will not manage her, although he mount her,
> > That worse than Tantalus' is her annoy,
> > To clip Elysium and to lack her joy.
>
> Even so poor birds, deceiv'd with painted grapes,
> Do surfeit by the eye and pine the maw;
> Even so she languisheth in her mishaps,
> As those poor birds that helpless berries saw.
> > The warm effects which she in him finds missing
> > She seeks to kindle with continual kissing.
>
> But all in vain, good queen, it will not be!
> > (ll. 589–607)

Commentators on Shakespeare's poem have scrupulously avoided this tasteless passage. Venus' sexual pratfall, her vain attempts to coax Adonis into an erection by kissing him, and the crude sexual innuendo behind the figure of the useless grapes, are both socially offensive and erotically unappealing. Nevertheless, these lines offer a rather complex statement on the relation between eros and art, and manage in some sense to move through, if not quite beyond, their own misogyny.

At least three classical references, all of them more or less implicit, organize this passage: the Ovidian myths of Pygmalion and Narcissus, and Pliny's story of the competition between the painters Zeuxis and Parrhasios. All three, moreover, pertain to Shakespeare's extended allegory of the female reader of the erotic text. Pygmalion returns in the general problem of the appealing and unresponsive image, but in reversing the genders of Ovid's tale Shakespeare anatomically specifies the failure of the artwork: it lacks the phallus. The female reader who is somehow aroused by Shakespeare's poem will find herself in Venus' position, missing the member which, this poem assumes, provides the only possible satisfaction for female sexual desire.[12] I think it is safe to assume two things here. First, while Shakespeare meant his poem to be mildly titillating, he could not possibly belive that it would produce the kind of desperately intense desire experienced by Venus. Second, he surely knew that in the unlikely event that any female reader of the poem found it seriously arousing, she possessed the means to satisfy her own needs, and did not require the magical incarnation of an imaginary phallus. Nevertheless, the strategic absence of Adonis' erection locates the ontological lack structuring the literary artwork, and particularly the erotic artwork. The point is that literary imagination, without some sort of physical intervention, lacks the means to satisfy erotic desire.

This moral is reinforced by the allusion to Pliny's famous story of the Greek artist Zeuxis, whose painted grapes were so realistic that they fooled birds into trying to eat them. Zeuxis, who thinks he has thus won his competition with the painter Parrhasios, nevertheless finds that he has lost when he tries to part the veil covering Parrhasios' painting and discovers that the veil *is* the painting. The point of this little parable is missed, I think, if it is read as suggesting that the power of art rests solely in mimesis or illusion. For Pliny's tale suggests that the power of mimesis depends in turn on its ability to *frustrate* the viewer, to arouse a desire which it then does not fulfill. The force of art lies not its capacity to grant some kind of aesthetic satisfaction, but precisely in its capacity to deny satisfaction and thus assert its mastery over the viewer.

The tale of Zeuxis and Parrhasios offers a stunning riposte to a Platonic ontology of art. For Plato, the mimetic work of art is a mere simulacrum, an empty shadow of the real. The painting of a grape is an ontological nullity in comparison with a real grape, just as the shadows on the wall of the cave are nothing in comparison with the real objects that cast them. Pliny's tale also contains a moment that manifests the merely simulacral status of the image. But now to reveal the image's emptiness is precisely to confirm its power. Zeuxis' temporary victory occurs when his grapes prove unable to feed the birds; and Parrhasios' ultimate victory comes when he subjects Zeuxis in his turn to the emptiness of the image. Indeed, a kind of metamorphic inversion occurs between viewer and object, for the unsatisfied hunger of the birds indicates *their own emptiness* in relation to the image, which is complete unto itself. In the paradoxical ontology of the artwork, it is the real birds who are hollow and the painted grapes that are full.

In Shakespeare's poem, of course, it is not birds but women who "surfeit by the eye [but] pine the maw." Caught in the toils of the erotic text, the female reader is presumed to be afflicted with need, mastered by the mimetic power of a poem that renders her unsatisfied, empty. Earlier, the text seemed ontologically hollow in relation to the reader because it lacked the phallus. Now the text is full and the reader is empty. It is not the text but the reader—particularly the female reader—who represents the void of castration.

This ontological reversal is represented within the poem by the fact that Adonis, a mere mortal, triumphs over the divinity of Venus. I say "triumphs" because, paradoxically, in this episode of sexual failure or uninterest it is Venus, not Adonis, who appears more ridiculous. Adonis' presumed incapacity is balanced by his emotional self-containment, while Venus is made risible by the intensity of her unsatisfied need. Like the birds in Pliny, she is left absurdly pecking at a painted grape. Venus' "pining maw" has become the poem's primary signifier of lack.[13]

I remarked earlier that this episode provides an allegory of reading, but it is more accurate to say that its allegory concerns textual consumption. After all, the birds in Pliny do not "read" the grapes, they try to eat them. Earlier in the poem, Venus is likewise depicted as trying to "consume" Adonis sexually:

> Even as an empty eagle, sharp by fast,
> Tires with her beak on feathers, flesh, and bone,
> Shaking her wings, devouring all in haste,
> Till either gorge be stuff'd, or prey be gone;
> Even so she kiss'd his brow, his cheek, his chin,
> And where she ends, she doth anew begin.
>
> (ll. 55–60)

Venus as eagle is a frighteningly powerful magnification of Pliny's delicate birds. Her frenzied efforts at sexual consumption make her precisely into an image of the consumer of a pornographic text. Such a consumer does not "read" in the academic sense, insofar as this activity suggests some attention to the literary or figurative status of the text. Rather, pornography requires, at least at some level, a naive submission to the representational claims of the work. *Venus and Adonis* is, as I shall argue later, intensely aware of the mimetic claims of pornography. If Pliny's bird is to represent the frustrated consumer of the text, the text itself must aspire to the condition of a perfectly painted grape, a pure mimetic surface without textual depth.

While the passage I have have been interpreting is ostensibly organized by Pliny's tale of Zeuxis, it is also more subtly permeated by another, Ovidian, tale: that of Narcissus. Various commentators have noted the importance of Narcissus to Shakespeare's poem, but they invariably identify Adonis as the poem's Narcissus-figure. In so doing they are following Venus' lead, for she herself berates Adonis by comparing him to the self-absorbed youth:

> Is thine own heart to thine own face affected?
> Can thy right hand seize love upon thy left?
> Then woo thyself, be of thyself rejected;
> Steal thine own freedom, and complain on theft.
> Narcissus so himself himself forsook,
> And died to kiss his shadow in the brook.
>
> (ll. 157–162)

One of the ironies of the passage I have been addressing is that Venus, not Adonis, now occupies the narcissistic position. For it is she who attempts to kiss a shadow or empty image in the reluctant Adonis. Like Narcissus, who wastes away while peering at his reflection, Venus "surfeits by the eye and pines the maw."

In one sense, Narcissus just rounds out the cast of mythological characters who unsucccessfully attempt to embrace an image. In his *De Pictura*, Leon Battista Alberti employs the myth of Narcissus to depict art's attempt to grasp the world of alluring surfaces: "Consequently, I used to tell my friends that the inventor of painting, according to the poets, was Narcissus, who was turned into a flower; for, as painting is the flower of all the arts, so the tale of Narcissus fits our purposes perfectly. What is painting but the art of embracing by means of art the surface of the pool? (*Quid est enim aliud pingere quam arte superficiem illam fontis amplecti?*)"[14] Like

Pygmalion, who makes love to a statue, or the birds in Pliny who peck at the painted grapes, Narcissus falls prey to the power of the image and mistakes it for the real. He thus represents once more the ontological and sexual dilemmas of Shakespeare's imagined female reader.[15] Yet Narcissus diverts the problem of frustration into new directions. In the story of Pygmalion, the spectator's desire eventually wins out over the coldness of the image when the statue is metamorphosed, with Venus' aid, into a real woman. But the tale of Narcissus reverses this plot, for here the image remains intransigently empty, and it is the viewer himself who is therefore transformed by his own desire. In Golding's translation of Ovid (1567), Narcissus perfectly reverses the Pygmalion story by becoming like a piece of sculpture: "Astraughted like an Ymage made of Marble stone he lyes, / There gazing on his shadowe still with fixed staring eyes."[16] Narcissus' tale differs from that of Zeuxis' birds as well, for after his initial mistake, Narcissus comes to understand that what he loves is his own reflection. But he is no less captured for having recognized the emptiness of the image, and he continues to adore it until he dies and is metamorphosed into a flower. Pliny's birds, one assumes, eventually abandon the painted grapes once they come to learn that they cannot be eaten. The birds, that is, are temporarily fooled by an illusion. But the desire of Narcissus survives even this moment of disillusionment and remains impossibly attached to its object. If Pliny's birds are captured by some ontological misrecognition, Narcissus' desire absorbs into itself the ontological discrepancy between spectator and image.

This difference between human and animal desire occupies Jacques Lacan at the opening of his famous essay on the mirror stage, where he contrasts the responses of a monkey and a human child when confronted with their images in a mirror: "This act, far from exhausting itself, as in the case of the monkey, once the image has been mastered and found empty, immediately rebounds in the case of the child in a series of gestures in which he experiences in play the relation between the movements assumed in the image and the reflected environment, and between this virtual complex and the reality it duplicates—the child's own body, and the persons and things, around him."[17] In this moment, which constitutes the birth of the imaginary, the child moves through the emptiness of the image, thereby incorporating the simulacrum as such into the structure of its desire. The power of the image no longer resides exclusively in its capacity to "dupe" the spectator, to make a monkey of him or her.

It is in this Lacanian and anachronistic sense that one must read the word "imaginary" in Shakespeare's line: "All is imaginary she doth prove." Like Pliny's birds, Venus is duped into hoping for real sustenance from a mere image. But unlike the birds, she does not abandon the image once it is ascertained to be empty. Her impossible love for Adonis survives even this decisive proof that she can expect nothing from him in the way of sexual satisfaction. Here we discover the difference between an erotic ontology and a philosophical one. Desire sustains the reality of its object even when that object has proven disappointing or frustrating.

If Venus' continued attachment to Adonis, beyond any hope of sexual consummation, signifies a kind of enslavement and hence a continued degradation, the tone of her representation nevertheless undergoes a change. After this episode she takes on an increasing grandeur, becoming less a comically failed suitor than a tragically failed protector. Just as the unresponsiveness of his reflected image provokes a metamorphosis in Narcissus as spectator, so Adonis' unresponsiveness causes a change in Venus. It is as if these stanzas, occupying the very center of the poem, were the mirroring pool in which the two halves engage in a chiastic and transformative reflection.

The erotic ontology of the text, which sustains it beyond the exhaustion of its sexual use-value, also transforms Venus' role as symbol of the female reader. For the frustration of sexual need has enabled the emergence of a desire which accords more harmoniously with the nature of the poetic object. The failure to receive physical satisfaction from the text passes over into a state in which the text is desired *as* a simulacrum. In effect, then, this episode registers the birth of the aesthetic from the sexual. And none too soon, for from this point on the poem offers nothing in the way of erotic pleasure or titillation. As the poem metamorphoses from a comically erotic to a tragic mode, so Venus as representative of the female reader evolves from the frustrated consumer of a pornographic text to the subject of an (aesthetic) desire which incorporates the death or emptiness of its object. I am not claiming that this movement in any way mitigates the misogyny of *Venus and Adonis*. It may even be said to deepen it. The best that can be said here is that Venus transcends her own degradation. Like Narcissus' image, she is not depleted by being emptied out.

NOTES

1. Ovid, *Amores*, I.xv.35–36. All quotations of Shakespeare's works are from *The Riverside Shakespeare*, ed. G. Blakemore Evans, Harry Levin et al. (Boston: Houghton Mifflin, 1974).

2. In *Amores* I.xv, Ovid gives thanks for the privacy and leisure needed for lyric poetry. Early in that poem he thanks Envy for not "prostituting my voice in the ungrateful forum" ("me / Ingrato vocem prostituisse foro") (5–6), thus clarifying what he later means by the "vilia" that please the crowd. Ovid, *Les Amours*, ed. and trans. Henri Bornecque (Paris: Société d' Edition des Belles Lettres, 1968). This reference to

public oratory makes it even likelier that Shakespeare takes "vilia" to refer to public theater.

3. See, e.g., Leeds Barroll, *Politics, Plague, and Shakespeare's Theater: The Stuart Years* (Ithaca: Cornell UP, 1991), 17.

4. Heather Dubrow, *Captive Victors: Shakespeare's Narrative Poems and Sonnets* (Ithaca: Cornell UP, 1987), 15.

5. In George Peele's *Merry and Conceited Jests,* Shakespeare's poem is read by "a tapster . . . much given to poetry." *Dramatic and Poetical Works of Robert Greene and George Peele,* ed. Alexander Dyce (London: Routledge, [n.d.]), 619. *Venus and Adonis* is listed as part of the courtesan's library in Thomas Cranley, *The Converted Courtezan* (1639) sig. E4ᵛ.

6. William Keach, *Elizabethan Erotic Narratives: Irony and Pathos in the Ovidian Poetry of Shakespeare, Marlowe, and their Contemporaries* (New Brunswick: Rutgers UP, 1977), 31–33.

7. See Arthur F. Marotti, *John Donne, Coterie Poet* (Madison: University of Wisconsin Press, 1986), 25–37: "The Inns of Court as a Socioliterary Milieu."

8. See the references to *Venus and Adonis* in volume one of *The Shakespere Allusion-Book: A Collection of Allusions to Shakespere From 1591 to 1700,* 2 vols. (London: Oxford University Press, 1932).

9. *Shakespere Allusion-Book,* 1: 189, 177.

10. *The Complete Works of John Davies of Hereford,* ed. Alexander B. Grosart, 2 vols. (New York: AMS, 1967).

11. John Marston, "The Metamorphosis of Pigmalions Image," *Elizabethan Minor Epics,* ed. Elizabeth Story Donno (New York: Columbia UP, 1963), stanza 20.

12. The image of the phallic text appears in Richard Brathwait's *The English Gentlewoman* (1631), which warns women against reading Shakespeare's poem: "*Venus* and *Adonis* are unfitting Consorts for a Ladies bosome. Remove them timely from you, if they ever had entertainment by you, lest, like the *Snake* in the fable, they annoy you" (139; quoted in *The Shakespere Allusion-Book,* 354). In Brathwait's imagination, Shakespeare's Ovidian poem undergoes something very like a metamorphosis. Brathwait's image of the snake at the bosom recalls Shakespeare's Cleopatra and her phallic "joy o' the worm." (Cleopatra, it should be recalled, fashions herself after Venus in Shakespeare's play.) Paradoxically, then, Brathwait's warning constitutes a virtual wish-fulfillment for Venus, since the text becomes the living phallus that she longs for. The danger of the poem is precisely its capacity to produce pleasure.

An interesting inversion of this problem occurs in Sonnet 20, which compares Shakespeare's "master-mistress" to the painting of a woman: "A woman's face with Nature's own hand painted / Hast thou. . . ." (1–2). Here, however, it is the presence, rather than the absence, of a penis which inhibits sexual consummation:

> And for a woman wert thou first created,
> Till Nature as she wrought thee fell a-doting,
> And by addition me of thee defeated,
> By adding one thing to my purpose nothing.
> > But since she prick'd thee out for women's pleasure,
> > Mine be thy love, and thy love's use their treasure.
> > > (9–14)

The image of Nature as an artist or sculptor who "fell a-doting" over her creation recalls Venus' position as female Pygmalion.

13. The association of Venus and castration is made explicit by sonnet IX of *The Passionate Pilgrim:*

> Fair was the morn when the fair queen of love,
>
> . . . .

Paler for sorrow than her milk-white dove,
For Adon's sake, a youngster proud and wild,
Her stand she takes upon a steep-up hill.
Anon Adonis comes with horns and hounds;
She, silly queen, with more than love's good will,
Forbade the boy he should not pass those grounds.
"Once," quoth she, "did I see a sweet fair youth
Here in these brakes deep-wounded with a boar,
Deep in the thigh, a spectacle of ruth!
See in my thigh," quoth she, "here was the sore."
    She showed hers, he saw more wounds than one,
    And blushing fled, and left her all alone.

14. Leon Battista Alberti, *On Painting and On Sculpture,* trans. and ed. Cecil Grayson (London: Phaidon, 1972), II.26. Leonardo da Vinci probably has Narcissus' pool in mind, although he does not directly mention it, in the section of his *Treatise on Painting* entitled "How the mirror is master of painters": "The painting is intangible insofar as that which seems round and detached cannot be surrounded [*circondare*] with the hands, and the same is true of a mirror" (Leonardo da Vinci, *Treatise on Painting,* trans. A. Philip McMahon, 2 vols. [Princeton: Princeton UP, 1956], 1:160).

15. The ontological dilemmas of the reader are suggested by Shakespeare's apostrophe to Venus at the end of the above-quoted passage: "But all in vain. Good Queen, it will not be!" (l. 607). It is no accident that the pretense of direct address to a fictional character occurs just at the end of a passage depicting the non-responsiveness of the work of art. Here, I think, Shakespeare imitates Ovid's apostrophe to Narcissus in *Metamorphoses* III.432–436, which in turn anticipates Narcissus' vain address to his own image in lines 477–479. Ovid, *Metamorphoses,* trans. Frank Justus Miller, 2 vols. (Cambridge: Harvard University Press, 1921).

Shakespeare has in effect "split" the attributes of Narcissus between his two protagonists. Adonis embodies the problem of self-love while Venus represents desire for the image.

16. *Shakespeare's Ovid, Being Arthur Golding's Translation of the Metamorphoses,* ed. W.H.D. Rouse (Carbondale: Southern Illinois UP, 1961), III.523–524.

17. Jacques Lacan, *Écrits: A Selection,* trans. Alan Sheridan (New York: W.W. Norton, 1977), 1.

PICTURING VENUS AND ADONIS

SHAKESPEARE AND THE ARTISTS

Georgianna Ziegler

"The present narrative only includes the disappointment of an eager female, and the death of an unsusceptible boy. . . . It is not indeed very clear whether Shakspeare meant on this occasion, with Le Brun, to recommend continence as a virtue, or to try his hand with Aretine on a licentious canvas. If our poet had any moral design in view, he has been unfortunate in his conduct of it."[1] This comment by the editor George Steevens at the end of the eighteenth century, with the passage that follows by Edmund Malone, represents briefly the ambiguous attitude toward Shakespeare's *Venus and Adonis*. Malone delivers his measured rebuttal to the effect that this youthful piece of Shakespeare's is written in response to the Ovidian myth, with no particular moral view in mind, and is not "so void of poetical merit as it has been represented" (in Shakespeare 1790, 71–72). Such a conflicted response—licentious, amoral, moral—applies as well to viewers as to readers of the myth. Is Titian's famous painting of Venus attempting to detain Adonis licentious because it shows the heated desire of a naked woman for a young man; is it amoral because Titian painted it as an experiment in showing the back of a nude;[2] or is it moral because it shows Adonis' obvious distaste for the seduction? Much depends on the mind of the beholder/reader. What *is* clear is that the illustrative tradition for Shakespeare's Ovidian poem reflects its progressive cultural contexts.

Something needs to be said first briefly about the painterly tradition of the story of Venus and Adonis. Shakespeareans and art historians alike have been intrigued by the fact that both Shakespeare and Titian change Ovid's version of the story by making Adonis "a reluctant lover."[3] Erwin Panofsky, the noted art historian, went so far as to suggest that Titian's painting, or rather prints made from it, may have influenced Shakespeare. The painting was originally commissioned by Philip II of Spain and delivered to England when he was living there in 1554 as husband to Mary Tudor. It "was widely accessible in sixteenth-century prints by Giulio Sanuto (dated 1559) and Martino Rota (died 1583)."[4] Titian scholar Charles Wethey has more recently dismissed this idea, inclining instead to see Shakespeare's sources as mainly literary (Wethey, III, 188–189). From the Shakespearean side, John Doebler accepts the notion that the poet may have seen one of the popular engravings based on Titian, but feels that "Titian is . . . consistent with Ovid in a way that Shakespeare is not. He retains the emphasis upon the conflict as vocational rather than erotic." In other words, in the painting, Adonis is merely anxious to get back to his hunting, while in the poem, he is disturbed by the sexual advances of Venus.[5]

"Both Venus with Mars and Venus with Adonis became favorite subjects of Renaissance and baroque artists and were rendered many times, including by Botticelli, Veronese, Marcantonio, and Rubens."[6] The three episodes most frequently represented from the story of Venus and Adonis were "the courtship of Venus and Adonis, Venus Lamenting the Death of Adonis (the least often represented), and the Departure of Adonis."[7] Otherwise known as "The Leave-Taking of Venus," suggested in paintings by a depiction of her waiting chariot, this theme was changed by Titian into what is more correctly called "The Flight of Adonis" (see Panofsky 152).

Turning to the editions of Shakespeare's poems, we can say in general that the eighteenth century uses one or two plates for *Venus and Adonis,* while beginning in the mid-nineteenth century, the poem tends to be illustrated throughout, and with the twentieth century, we arrive at the era of the special, private press edition. The eighteenth-century illustrations seem to draw most directly on the tradition of Venus and Adonis paintings described above and circulated during the seventeenth century in engravings. They owe little or nothing to the sixteenth-century woodcuts illustrating the story in Ovid's *Metamorphoses.* These mostly show the "Courtship" episode, with the two lovers together beneath a tree, usually Adonis with his head in the lap of Venus, as in the Lyon 1557 edition with woodcuts by the famous illustrator, Bernard Salomon (similarly the Frankfurt edition, 1582; and the Paris edition, 1587), with a variation in the version by Pieter van der Borcht (Antwerp, 1591) showing Venus in the lap of Adonis in the foreground, and in the distance, chasing a tiny Adonis as he attempts to hunt the deer. Interestingly, the later twentieth-century editions owe more to this early woodcut tradition.

Venus and Adonis was first published in a "modern" edition in 1710 by Curll, along with the other poems and with critical remarks by Charles Gildon, as the seventh volume to Rowe's *Works of Mr. William Shakespear,* 1709.[8] The engraved frontispiece to the internal title page for *Venus and*

Adonis depicts the lament of Venus over the dead Adonis. He lies beneath a tree in his hunting garb, his spear and horn by his side, while she stands leaning over him, her arms outstretched in grief, cloak flying behind her. In a nice touch, down in the corner, Adonis' dog bays his private sorrow, but two cupids play above him and Venus' swan-drawn chariot hovers in the clouds, waiting to carry her away. The depiction of the chariot probably comes from the Titian tradition, where his Venus detaining Adonis often shows a tiny chariot drawn by doves in the upper corner. Shakespeare also refers to doves:

> away she hies,
> And yokes her silver Doves, by whose swift Aid,
> Their Mistress mounted, thro' the empty Skies
> In her light Chariot quickly is conveyed.

but in Ovid the chariot is swan-drawn, and it is this detail that the artist chooses to show.

In 1725, George Sewell issued a spurious volume 7 to Pope's edition, containing Shakespeare's poems; in fact, it is a reissue of volume 10 to Rowe's edition (Vickers, II, 419). This volume was issued again in 1728 as volume 10 of *The Works,* printed for Knapton, Darby, et al. The frontispiece to the half-title of *Venus and Adonis* is engraved by Michiel Van Der Gucht, a Flemish artist born in 1660 who made a career engraving for the London booksellers.[9] A rather thin Venus, naked except for drapery over her lower body, sits beneath a tree to the right and attempts to detain Adonis. Dressed in classical armor and carrying a large spear in his right hand, Adonis tries to stride away from her. A cupid holds one of his dogs, another tries to stop him, and a third flies over the couple's head. The design is not attributed to any artist, but it is a pale reflection of a tradition of painted variations on Titian, where the body of Venus is reversed (right side instead of left) such as those by Veronese, Delignon, Zelotti, and others.

Bell's 1774 edition of Shakespeare's *Poems* contains an engraving that represents yet a third theme: Venus plucking Adonis from his horse. Without the quotation from the poem that accompanies the fine engraving, however ("desire doth lend her force / courageously to pluck him from his Horse"), we would be hard-pressed to recognize this as the exact theme. Venus stands to the left in classical garb, a strap over her breast holding her billowing cloak. She has one arm around the shoulders of Adonis, who stands looking (kindly) at her, one hand on his horse's bridle, the other holding his spear. They seem to be engaged in friendly conversation rather than in a lusty struggle, but perhaps this "cleaned-up" version was thought more suitable to Bell's family audience. He himself had great qualms about publishing Shakespeare's poems as "many of his subjects are trifling, his versification mostly laboured and quibbling, with too great a degree of licentiousness." Nevertheless, "the desire of gratifying the admirers of our Author with an entire addition [sic] of his works, has induced us to suffer some passages to remain, which we are ourselves as far from approving, as the most scrupulous of our Readers" (Introduction 36).

Cooke's 1797 edition of Shakespeare's *Poetical Works,* "embellished with superb engravings," was also obviously made for the popular market, like his inexpensive *Cheap and Elegant Pocket Library of Select Poets* and *Select British Classics.* It is a small volume, easily held in the hand, and includes two exquisite engravings by C. Warren and J. Neagle, based on paintings by Thomas Kirk, who was one of Cooke's chief illustrators.[10] Each picture is presented in a rondel within an elaborate frame whose decorative elements signify aspects of the story. Atop the first frame rest an empty quiver, several arrows, a bow, and a hunting horn, representing Adonis' passion for the hunt. The picture shows Venus in a wooded landscape, blond hair flowing and her bare right leg extended from her chiton, putting her arms around the waist of Adonis to detain him. He stands to her left, leaning on the spear in his right hand, his knee bent as though to go, his hunting dog looking hopefully up at him. The quotation beneath the picture reads: "Thou hadst gone quoth she Sweet Boy ere this, / But that thou told'st me thou would'st hunt the boar, / O! be advised thou knowest not what it is / With javelins point a churlish swine to gore."

The frame of the second picture, which shows the Death of Adonis, has at the top a boar's tusked head and the tip of a spear, representing his manner of death, and a scythe and cut flowers, representing the passage of life and the anemone, flower of Adonis. In the picture, Venus kneels beneath a tree, her left hand holding Adonis' left hand to her bare breast, her right hand at her head in mourning over his body. The quotation reads: "Death of Adonis. This solemn sympathy poor Venus noteth. / Over one shoulder doth she hang her head: / Dumbly the passions, frantickly she doteth: / She thinks he could not die, he is not dead." The style of these pictures is similar to the literary designs by Angelica Kauffman and other artists of the period used to decorate ceilings, furniture, and chinaware.[11]

The 1804 *Poems by William Shakespeare . . . In two volumes,* printed by C. Chapple and with the text from the Bell edition, returns to the theme of Venus plucking Adonis off his horse. W.M. Craig is the artist and Mackenzie the engraver. Their rendering of the theme is a little more convincing than that in the Bell edition. Here Venus stands behind Adonis with

SHAKESPEAR'S POEMS.

DEATH OF ADONIS.
This solemn sympathy poor Venus noteth,
Over one shoulder doth she hang her head;
Dumbly the passions, frantickly she doteth;
She thinks he could not die, he is not dead.
Vide page 70 line 1057.

Painted by T. Kirk.   Printed for C. Cooke, March 14. 1797.   Engraved by J. Neagle.

William Shakespeare, The Poetical Works . . . Cooke's edition. Embellished with superb engravings. *London; for C. Cooke, 1797. Engravings by C. Warren and J. Neagle based on paintings by Thomas Kirt. By permission of the Folger Shakespeare Library.*

Shakespeare's *Love Poems . . . with Beautiful Engravings,* published by James Cundee, uses the same illustration.

Some of the most delicate and beautifully conceived engravings from this period are the three plates to *The Poems,* published by J.F. Dove (London, 1830). The engravings by C. Rolls are based on paintings by Henry Corbould, most of whose career was spent making drawings on commission from collections of ancient marbles, including those of the British Museum.[12] He was also a noted book illustrator, and one can see the classical influence inherent in his designs for these poems. His Venus stands gracefully like a Greek statue as she gestures to Adonis to dismount his horse.

A.J. Valpy's edition of *The Plays and Poems* (London, 1832–34) includes a line engraving by Starling based on a painting by Giovanni Francesco Romanelli (1610–1662) showing Venus reclining seductively beneath a canopy with Cupid at her shoulder, while in the distance, Adonis walks by with his hunting dog. This version presents a different iconographic moment than those usually depicted, and the outline form replicates a popular mode begun with Flaxman's drawings for Homer then taken up by the German, Retzsch, whose designs for Shakespeare were quite the rage in England as well.

Knight's edition of *The Poems* (London, 1841) begins a different trend in illustrating *Venus and Adonis.* Each poem has an engraved half-title and then is illustrated throughout with small engraved vignettes by William Harvey, in the pen-and-ink sketch style he used for Knight's edition of the plays (1838). These are a Victorian Venus and Adonis, fully dressed in pseudo-classic style, but appropriately restrained from any display of sensuality. The first vignette shows Venus peering demurely from behind a rock as Adonis rides proudly by on his horse, and the closest they ever come to interacting is the vignette where Adonis finds Venus apparently fainting under a tree. He has a hand placed chastely on her shoulder and looks more terrified than anything else, while she lies as gracefully as any swooning Victorian maiden. Several other scenes focus on the horse, the deer, or the killing of the boar. These same illustrations are used, with their 1841 title page, in Knight's re-issue of his Pictorial Shakespeare in 1846. Several of them—the engraved half-title, the portrait of the Earl of Southampton, and the vignette of the deer—are used again in William J. Rolfe's edition of *Shakespeare's Poems* (New York, 1890), but in this version, Venus and Adonis have disappeared completely from the illustrations!

Hyder Rollins notes the taste for deluxe editions of *Venus and Adonis* and Shakespeare's other poems in the twentieth century. He guesses, I think correctly, that "some of these were designed to revive interest in the poem because of its eroticism" (*Variorum* 475), but they are also products

William Shakespeare. The Poems . . . London: J.F. Dove, 1830. Engravings by C. Rolls based on paintings by Henry Corbould. By permission of the Folger Shakespeare Library.

engraved half-title, the portrait of the Earl of Southampton, and the vignette of the deer—are used again in William J. Rolfe's edition of *Shakespeare's Poems* (New York, 1890), but in this version, Venus and Adonis have disappeared completely from the illustrations!

Hyder Rollins notes the taste for deluxe editions of *Venus and Adonis* and Shakespeare's other poems in the twentieth century. He guesses, I think correctly, that "some of these were designed to revive interest in the poem because of its eroticism" (*Variorum* 475), but they are also products

He wrings her nose, he strikes her on the cheeks,
He bends her fingers, holds her pulses hard ;
He chafes her lips, a thousand ways he seeks
To mend the hurt that his unkindness marr'd ;
  He kisses her ; and she, by her good will,
  Will never rise so he will kiss her still.

  ᵃ *Flaws* is here used in the sense of violent blasts.
  16

The night of sorrow now is turn'd to day :
Her two blue windows ᵃ faintly she upheaveth,

  ᵃ The windows are doubtless the eyelids, but the epithet
  blue is somewhat startling. We must remember that
  Shakspere has described violets as
      " Sweeter than the lids of Juno's eyes."
  The propriety of this epithet is fully noticed by us in Cymbeline, Act II., Scene II.

William Shakespeare. *The Poems* . . . London: C, Knight & Co., 1841. Design by William
Harvey. By permission of the Folger Shakespeare Library.

of the growing interest in fine hand-press books. Not all are illustrated; some
are printed in exquisite typeface, sometimes with decorative capitals, on
Japanese or other fine paper, and may be bound in vellum or gold-stamped
leather. The trend actually begins in 1893 with one of the most beautiful
private press editions of Shakespeare's *Poems* ever made, printed by William Morris at the Kelmscott Press. Morris allows the text, in lush dark ink
on cream vellum pages, to stand for itself. The only decoration appears in
the form of Morris' signature medieval-style borders on the first page of each
poem, and in the running title of each poem in red on the upper margin of
every page. The silky softness of the sheepskin vellum under a reader's fingers contributes to the sensual pleasure of this beautiful book.

The 1899 Essex House Press *Poems* limited edition of 450 copies is
obviously influenced by Morris' work. The volume is about the same size
with a plain vellum binding, but the text is printed in dark ink on heavy
rag paper instead of on vellum. Similar rubrication for the running titles also

TO THE RIGHT HONORABLE
HENRIE WRIOTHESLEY, EARLE
OF SOUTHAMPTON, AND BARON
OF TITCHFIELD.

RIGHT Honourable, I know not
how I shall offend in dedicating
my vnpolisht lines to your Lord,
ship, nor how the worlde will cen,
sure mee for choosing so strong a
proppe to support so weake a bur,
then, onelye if your Honour seeme but pleased, I
account myselfe highly praised, and vowe to take
advantage of all idle houres, till I have honoured
you with some graver labour. But if the first heire
of my invention proove deformed, I shall be sorie it
had so noble a god-father: and never after care so
barren a land, for feare it yeeld me still so bad a
harvest. I leave it to your Honourable survey, &
your Honor to your heart's content, which I wish
may alwaies answere your owne wish, and the
world's hopefull expectation.

Your Honor's in all dutie,

William Shakespeare.

VENVS AND ADONIS.

EVEN AS THE
SVNNE WITH PVR,
PLE-COL,
OVRD FACE,
HAD TANE
HIS LAST
LEAVE OF
THE WEEP,
INGMORNE,
ROSE-CHEEKT ADONIS HIED
HIM TO THE CHACE,
HVNTING HE LOV'D, BVT
LOVE HE LAVGHT TO SCORNE:
SICK-THOVGHTED VENVS
MAKES AMAINE VNTO HIM,
AND LIKE A BOLD FAC'D
SVTER GINNES TO WOO HIM.

THRISE FAIRER THEN MY
SELFE, (THVS SHE BEGAN)
THE FIELDS CHIEFE FLOWER,
SWEET ABOVE ALL NIMPHS,
MORE LOVELY THEN A MAN,
MORE WHITE, AND RED,
THEN DOVES, OR ROSES ARE:

William Shakespeare. The Poems . . . London: [William Morris] The Kelmscott Press, 1893. By permission of the Folger Shakespeare Library.

occurs, but in this edition, each stanza or sonnet begins with a fancifully decorative capital. Less luxurious but following in a similar style is T.J. Cobden-Sanderson's *Venus and Adonis* from the Dove Press in 1912. Here the Dedication to the Earl of Southampton and the colophon page are printed in red, as well as the initial letter "e". Two hundred copies were printed on paper and fifteen on vellum. Also influenced by Morris, I think, is Byam Shaw's work for the Chiswick Shakespeare (1899–1902). He does richly decorative black and white woodcut full-page designs, the one for *Venus and Adonis* showing Venus grieving, her hair flowing sensually behind her naked body, as she is carried off in her chariot by hundreds of doves. The iconography echoes the Botticelli Venus rising from the sea, but the style and interpretation are emphatically of Shaw's period. Two hundred copies were printed on Japanese vellum paper and bound in white cloth with vellum spine, the front board and spine stamped with Shaw's elaborate gold design.

As their first publication in 1930, Harrison of Paris brought out an edition of *Venus and Adonis* designed by Monroe Wheeler.[13] A limited number of copies were printed on China paper or Japanese vellum, and 440 on Arches vellum. As with the Essex House and Cobden-Sanderson editions, there are no illustrations. Each page has a simple design of blue bars at the top with the page number in blue at the foot, and the endpapers are done in silver. An interesting aspect of this edition is what it tells us about the reception of Shakespeare's poem at the time. Obviously designed to sell the volume, the silver label on the black slipcase says:

> Among Shakespeare's poems *Venus and Adonis* is perhaps the most generously pleasure-giving. It is simpler than the Sonnets . . . more realistic, more touching. And amid its mingling of voluptuousness and Elizabethan wit, there is a brilliant analysis of a most modern and most important psychological problem—the inability to love—which no modern writer seems to have had the courage to attempt.

Here we are at the end of the "flapper" era, when modern views on sex and the study of psychology are "in." Wilde's *Salomé* with Beardsley's sensuous drawings was published in 1893, Joyce's *Ulysses* in 1922; the early twentieth century saw "a radical alteration in the very conception of female sexuality, an alteration that began with the proselytizings of Free Love advocates like Victoria Woodhull and Emma Goldman and was further implemented by the obviously influential works of the sexologists Edward Carpenter and Havelock Ellis and, . . . by the writings of Sigmund Freud." [14]

In this social and bibliographic context, the limited edition of

Shakespeare's *Amatory Poems* put out by the Bennett Libraries of New York in 1928 seems relatively tame. Though bound in gold-stamped red leather with a provocative title, and printed in Baskerville type, the book reverts to the older kind of illustration we saw in the eighteenth century. For *Venus and Adonis* there is an engraving of Rubens' painting showing Venus stepping out of her swan-drawn chariot and holding Adonis by the neck. More interesting as reflective of the newer sexual freedom are the original illustrations created by such artists as Ben Kutcher, Rockwell Kent, and J. Yunge-Bateman.

Kutcher's *Venus and Adonis* was published by the Dial Press in New York in 1930. The twelve illustrations and the text itself are printed in shades of mauve that presumably were meant to enhance the sensual appeal. The illustrations look almost like set designs, with large forest trees silhouetted against each other dwarfing the figures of Venus and Adonis beneath. Only four focus on the stylized naked figures themselves: the frontispiece showing Adonis on his horse; Venus with a large Mars behind her; Adonis running naked through the woods; and Venus naked in a landscape, her back to us. In 1934, Leo Hart of Rochester, New York, printed an edition with Rockwell Kent's illustrations in brown-line. Kent was a prolific book illustrator, but here, he relies not on full-page illustrations, but on vignettes as did Knight's edition in the 1840s. Kent's interpretation of the scenes is thoroughly modern, however, and openly sensuous. His lovers fondle each other and lie unashamedly on top of each other, and in one simple but brilliant design, illustrating the line "I'll be a park, and thou shalt be my deer," a brown deer runs through a landscape that only on closer observation is shown to be composed of the torso, breasts, and arm of a naked woman.

The sixteen full-page illustrations by J. Yunge-Bateman for the Winchester Publications edition of *Venus and Adonis* (London, 1948) are printed in black rather than brown ink. These pictures are, I think, less successful than Rockwell Kent's because they rely more on fussy detail than on subtle, pure design. The bodies loom large in these drawings, but at times, as though the artist were photographing with a zoom lens for television, he focuses in on the heads. Some of the pictures suggest a dream quality to the story, as the one illustrating the line, "And at his look she flatly falleth down," which shows a large head of Adonis backed by lightning in the sky, looming over a sleeping Venus. These fully-illustrated editions of the text, however, do not replace the simpler richer luxury editions from the William Morris/Essex House tradition.

In 1960 the Golden Cockerel Press published *The Poems & Sonnets*, edited by Gwyn Jones. The designer, Christopher Sandford, chose Caslon's

'Fondling,' she saith, 'since I have hemm'd thee here
Within the circuit of this ivory pale,
I'll be a park, and thou shalt be my deer;
Feed where thou wilt, on mountain or in dale:
     Graze on my lips, and if those hills be dry,
     Stray lower, where the pleasant fountains lie.

'Within this limit is relief enough,
Sweet bottom-grass and high delightful plain,
Round rising hillocks, brakes obscure and rough,
To shelter thee from tempest and from rain:
     Then be my deer, since I am such a park;
     No dog shall rouse thee, though a thousand bark.'

[23]

William Shakespeare. Venus and Adonis with Illustrations by Rockwell Kent. *Rochester, NY: The Printing House of Leo Hart, 1934. By permission of the Folger Shakespeare Library. Courtesy of Mrs. Horace Hart.*

Old Face type on handmade, deckle-edged paper, limited to 470 numbered copies. Again the press relies on the richness of the type on the page, rather than illustration or decoration, to create an aesthetic experience for the reader. Only the titles of each poem are framed in floral woodcut borders, and the initial capital of each is rubricated.

The 1975 edition of *Venus and Adonis* by Andrew Hoyem at the Arion Press in San Francisco is printed in Bauer Bodoni type, a flowing script style, ornamented with rose pink capitals for each stanza. The flowing design is carried through on the double title page and on several other full-page minimal line illustrations of male and female torsos designed from foundry ornaments and printed in the same rose ink. Again, the total effect created by the choice of color, curved line, and flowing script is sensual.

Finally, we come to the beautifully executed 1984 edition by the Pyracantha Press in Tempe, Arizona. The making of this book was sponsored by the Arizona State University Centennial Commission, where both the editor, John Doebler, and the lithographer, Leonard Lehrer, are on the faculty. In the preface they write: "Shakespeare . . . was deeply concerned about seeing this poem in print and printed well. The standard of the printer's craft revealed in the surviving copy [of Shakespeare's 1593 edition] is very high for the time and place in which the poem appeared. . . ." Later in a closing note, they set out their plan more specifically:

> this edition of *Venus and Adonis* is intended to reflect something of the first edition of 1593 without being a facsimile: . . . its typeface is Monotype Bembo, the one available metal type most like the original; the 100% rag handmade paper was created to be typical in color, content, and texture of many late 16th century papers . . . ; the typographic ornaments were drawn in the style of the times with elements pertinent to this poem.

The reader thus experiences something of the look and feel of a sixteenth-century book, but within a decidedly modern design, and the marriage is a happy one. Lehrer includes two full-page lithographs, a frontispiece showing Adonis and Venus as classical Greek statues facing each other, and an end-piece design of a landscape. For the text itself, he uses a classical fruit and flower design in pale mauve giving the effect of a bar of printer's ornament at the top of each page. As early as 1817, Coleridge, one of the first admirers of the poem, noticed its "never broken chain of imagery, always vivid and because unbroken, often minute; by the highest effort of the picturesque in words . . . than was ever realized by any other poet."[15] The presentation of Shakespeare's poem substantially without illustration, as in this Pyracantha and similar editions, allows the reader to savor the luxurious physical setting of the text, while freeing the language to evoke its own lush images.

Books such as these provide an answer to those who ask if the book as we know it will disappear in our computer age. If we merely want to read a text, or to consult it, then a computer screen is fine. But if we want to engage in a personal exchange with Shakespeare and other artists, both printers and draughtsmen, in order to experience something of the creative process itself renewed through the eyes of every era, then we will always need to hold such books in our hands, to feel the grain of their paper or the smoothness of their vellum, savor the shape of their type, and delight in their design.

NOTES

1. *The Plays and Poems of William Shakspeare*, vol. 10 (London: H. Baldwin, etc., 1790), 70.

This study of the illustrations of *Venus and Adonis* does not pretend to be exhaustive, but it tries to give a good survey over the published history of the poem, based on the collections of the Folger Shakespeare Library and the Library of Congress.

2. See Harold E. Wethey, *The Paintings of Titian*, III, "The Mythological and Historical Paintings" (London: Phaidon, 1975), 59. Titian wrote to Philip II, who had commissioned the painting: "Because the *Danaë* which I have already sent to your Majesty was visible entirely in the front part, I have wanted in this other *poesia* to vary and to show the opposite part [of the body] so that it will make the room in which they are to hang more pleasing to see."

3. Rensselaer W. Lee notes that as early as 1584, Raphael Borghini took "Titian seriously to task for a misreading of Ovid and others in a painting of Venus and Adonis. Thus the painter, no matter what his source, must quote literally both chapter and verse." *Ut Pictura Poesis: The Humanistic Theory of Painting* (New York: W.W. Norton, 1967), 44.

4. Erwin Panofsky, *Problems in Titian: Mostly Iconographic* (NY: New York U P, 1969), 153.

5. John Doebler, "The Reluctant Adonis: Titian and Shakespeare," *Shakespeare Quarterly,* 33 (1982): 486 ff.

Other critics have taken slightly different approaches to the relation between Titian and Shakespeare. Eugene B. Cantelupe in "An Iconographical Interpretation of *Venus and Adonis,* Shakespeare's Ovidian Comedy," *Shakespeare Quarterly,* 14 (1963): 141–151, sees the Italian artists as painting "paragons of physical beauty" in "pastoral settings, reminiscent of the Golden Age," while Shakespeare creates an "outrageously comic" couple "in the English countryside" (141). William Keach in *Elizabethan Erotic Narratives: Irony and Pathos in the Ovidian Poetry of Shakespeare, Marlowe, and Their Contemporaries* (Sussex: Harvester Press, 1977) takes issue with a couple of Panofsky's points but decides, based on "the striking correspondences between Titian's painting and the pivotal stanza of Shakespeare's narrative, that Shakespeare's handling of the myth was quite possibly influenced by Titian's *Venus and Adonis* or by a sixteenth-century print after it" (56). Clark Hulse in *Metamorphic Verse: The Elizabethan Minor Epic* (Princeton: Princeton UP, 1981) decides that "as a source for Shakespeare, Titian is at best highly equivocal," but he goes on to show how Shakespeare nevertheless works within "a highly sophisticated tradition of allegorical poetry and painting" (146–147).

Elizabeth Truax in "Venus, Lucrece, and Bess of Hardwick: Portraits to Please," contemplates the reception of Shakespeare's two love poems by the Countess of Shrewsbury and her ladies, within the context of depictions of Venus, Lucrece, Diana, and Acteon in the furnishings of Hardwick Hall (in Cecile Williamson Cary and Henry S. Limouze, eds., *Shakespeare and the Arts* [Washington, DC: UP of America, 1982], 35–56.)

For earlier mentions of *Venus and Adonis* with Renaissance painting, see Taine, Brandes, and Wyndham as excerpted in William Shakespeare, *The Poems, A New Variorum Edition* by Hyder E. Rollins (Philadelphia: Lippincott, 1938), 486, 499, 502.

6. H. Diane Russell and Bernadine Barnes, *Eva/Ave: Woman in Renaissance and Baroque Prints* (Washington: National Gallery of Art, 1990), 131.

7. Eric J. Sluijter, "Depiction of Mythological Themes," in Albert Blankert, Beatrijs Brenninkmeyer-de Rooij, et al., *Gods, Saints & Heroes: Dutch Painting in the Age of Rembrandt* (Washington: National Gallery of Art, 1980), 60.

8. Though Shakespeare's poem was popular during his own lifetime, going through "at least ten editions" before 1616, by 1700 it "had fallen into considerable disrepute and neglect, and had become completely subordinated to the plays. During the eighteenth century it is editions, rather than allusions and references, that keep [it] from sinking out of sight." See Hyder Rollins, "The Vogue of *Venus and Adonis* and *Lucrece*," in *Variorum*, 447, 458. Before the volume attached to Rowe's edition of the Plays, *Venus and Adonis* had been published in 1707 in the fourth volume of *Poems on Affairs of State* (*Variorum*, 458).

9. For brief biographies of him and his sons see George C. Williamson, rev. *Bryan's Dictionary of Painters and Engravers,* vol. 5 (London: G. Bell, 1927), 243.

10. For more information on Kirk and on the popular editions of Bell and Cooke, see Richard Altick, *Paintings from Books: Art and Literature in Britain, 1760–1900* (Columbus: Ohio State UP, 1985), 38–39. *Venus and Adonis* also appears as a separate, pink-paper-bound volume in the "Select Poets" series with the same illustration for one shilling; a good bargain.

11. See Malise Forbes Adam and Mary Mauchline, "Kauffman's Decorative Work" in Wendy Wassyng Roworth, ed. *Angelica Kauffman: A Continental Artist in Georgian England* (London: Reaktion Books, 1992), 113 ff.

12. *Bryan's Dictionary,* I, 328.

13. It is beyond the scope of this paper to survey the illustrative tradition in foreign-language editions of *Venus and Adonis.* Suffice it to say that there are some very fine ones. Two of these were published in Paris in 1921. The first, a prose translation by Paul Vulliaud, contains a full-page and a number of smaller lithographs by André Hofer. The black and white line drawings are styled after Dürer with modernized nude figures. The other, a prose translation by Émile Godefroy, published by Léon Pichon, is illustrated with heavy-line woodcuts by Roger Grillon.

14. Sandra M. Gilbert and Susan Gubar, *No Man's Land: The Place of the Woman Writer in the Twentieth Century,* vol. 1, *The War of the Words* (New Haven: Yale UP, 1988), 34.

15. As quoted in *Variorum,* 477.

V
A Chronological Bibliography

A CHRONOLOGICAL BIBLIOGRAPHY OF SCHOLARSHIP AND COMMENTARY ON *VENUS AND ADONIS*, INCLUDING EDITIONS AND REVIEWS OF PERFORMANCES

Philip C. Kolin

The following chronologically arranged bibliography includes scholarship on and editions and reviews of productions of *Venus and Adonis*. Although it reflects the year-by-year work that has been done on the poem, this bibliography is in no way intended as exhaustive. Professor Robert P. Merrix is currently preparing a much more detailed (and annotated) bibliography on the poem as part of the Garland Shakespeare Bibliography Series. In the following bibliography, information about reprints and revised editions can be found immediately after the work's initial publication date.

1774
Shakespeare, William. *Poems.* . . . London: J. Bell & C. Etherington, 1774. Also issued as Vol. 9 of the 1774 ed. of the *Works.*

1790
Malone, Edmond. *Plays and Poems.* Vol. 10. London, 1790; rpt. New York: AMS, 1970.

1797
Shakespeare, William. *The Poetical Works.* . . . *Cooke's edition.* . . . *embellished with superb engravings.* London: for C. Cooke, 1797.

1804
Shakespeare, William. *Poems* . . . *with illustrative remarks.* . . . *with engravings.* . . . London: for C. Chapple, 1804. 2 vols.

1808
Shakespeare, William. *Love Poems.* . . . *with beautiful engravings.* . . . London: for James Cundee, 1808. 2 vols.

1817
Coleridge, Samuel Taylor. *Biographia Literaria.* 2 vols. London: Kirk and Merein, 1817. 2:13–22.

Hazlitt, William. *The Round Table. Characters of Shakespear's Plays*. London, 1817; rpt. New York: Dent, 1960.

1818

Coleridge, Samuel Taylor. "The Lectures and Notes of 1818: Shakespere as a Poet Generally." *Lectures and Notes on Shakespere and Other English Poets*. Ed. T. Ashe. London: George Bell, 1897. 218–23.

1823

Y.J. "Shakspeare's Poems." *New Monthly Magazine* (May 1823): 470–73, 476.

1830

Shakespeare, William. *The Poems.* . . . London: Printed and published by J.F. Dove, 1830.

1832–34

Shakespeare, William. *The Plays and Poems* . . . Edited by A.J. Valpy. . . . London: A.J. Valpy, 1832–34. Vol. 15.

1839

Hallam, Henry. *Introduction to the Literature of Europe in the 15th, 16th, and 17th Centuries*. London: Ward, Lock, 1839. 194.

1841

Shakespeare, William. *Poems.* . . . London: C. Knight & Co., 1841. The same illustrations appear in vol. 1 of *The Standard Edition of the Pictorial Shakspere;* ed. Charles Knight. London: Charles Knight & Co., 1846.

1847

Reardon, J.P. "Shakespeare's *Venus and Adonis* and Lodge's 'Scilla's Metamorphosis.'" *The Shakespeare Society's Papers* 3 (1847): 143–46.

1849

Gervinus, G.G. *Shakespeare Commentaries*. 1849. Trans. F. E. Burnett. London, 1863.

1850

Hart, John S. "Shakespeare's Minor Poems." *Sartain's Union Magazine* 6 (Feb. 1850): 129–32.

1857

Reed, Henry. *Lectures on the British Poets I*. Philadelphia: Parry & McMillan, 1857. 174.

1862

Fullom, S.W. *History of William Shakespeare, Player and Poet*. London: Saunders, Otley, 1862. 252.

1866

Sievers, E.W. *William Shakspeare. Sein leben und dichten.* Gotha: R. Besser 1866. 166–79.

1869

Whipple, E.P. *Literature in the Age of Elizabeth.* Boston: n. p., 1869. 60.

1870

Green, Henry. *Shakespeare and the Emblem Writers.* London: Trübner, 1870.

1873

"Chaucer and Shakespeare." *Quarterly Review* (Jan. 1873): 251.

1875

Dowden, Edward. *Shakspere: A Critical Study of His Mind and Art.* London: Henry S. King, 1875. 49–51.

Swinburne, Algernon Charles. "Essay on the Poetical and Dramatic Works of George Chapman." *The Works of George Chapman: Poems and Minor Translations.* London: Chatto and Windus, 1875. ix–lxxi.

1878

Winsor, Justin. "Shakespeare's Poems. A Bibliography of the Earlier Editions." *Harvard University Library Bulletin* 1 (1878–1879).

1879

Baynes, T.S. "What Shakespeare Learnt at School." *Fraser's Magazine* 20 (Nov. 1879, Jan., May 1880); rpt. in *Shakespeare Studies.* London: Longmans, 1894.

Stapfer, Paul. *Shakespeare et l'Antiquité.* Paris, 1879. 115–119, 121.

Swinburne, A.C. A *Study of Shakespeare.* London, 1879.

1883

Tompkins, F. *Adaptations of Shakespeare's* Venus and Adonis. New York: n. p., 1883.

1884

Isaac, Hermann. "Die Sonett-Period in Shakespeare's Leben." *Jahrbuch der Deutsche Shakespeare-Gesellschaft* 19 (1884): 184–86.

1885

Symons, Arthur. *Shakspere's* Venus and Adonis . . . A *Fac-simile* . . . *by William Griggs* . . . *With an Introduction by Arthur Symons.* London, 1885.

1889

Duplesses, Georges. *Essai bibliographique sur les différentes editons des oeuvres d'Ovide ornees de planches publiées au XVe et XVIe siecles.* Paris, 1889.

Wilde, Oscar. *The Portrait of Mr W. H.* London, 1889; expanded, rev. ed. *The Riddle of Shakespeare's Sonnets: The Text of the Sonnets with Interpretive Essays by Edward Hubler [and others] and Including the Full Text of Oscar Wilde's* The Portrait of Mr W. H. New York: Basic Books, 1962. 165–256.

1890

Dürnhöfer, Max. *"Shakespeare's* Venus und Adonis *im Verhältnis zu Ovids Metamorphosen und Constables Schäfergesang."* Ph.D. diss., Halle, 1890.

Shakespeare, William. *Poems.* . . . Ed. William J. Rolfe. With Engravings. New York: Harper, 1890.

1893

Shakespeare, William. *The Poems* . . . *Printed after the original copies.* . . . London: Kelmscott Press, 1893.

1896

Boas, F.S. *Shakespere and His Predecessors.* New York, 1896.

Saeger, H.W. *Natural History in Shakespeare's Time: Being Extracts Illustrative of the Subject as He Knew It.* London: E. Stock, 1896.

1898

Wyndham, George. *The Poems of Shakespeare. Edited with an Introduction and Notes by George Wyndham.* London: Methuen, 1898. xxix–xciii.

1899

Shakespeare, William. *The Poems* . . . *Including the Lyrics, Songs, and Snatches Found in His Dramas.* London: Edward Arnold. Printed at the Essex House Press, under the care of C.R. Ashbee, December 1899.

1899

Barohm, Ernst. *Shakespeare's* Venus and Adonis. Halle: Jahrebericht des Koniglichen Siftsgym, 1899.

Shakespeare, William. *The Chiswick Shakespeare.* . . . *with an Introduction and Notes by John Dennis and Illustrations by Byam Shaw.* London: George Bell & Sons, 1899–1902.

1900

Morgan, James Appleton. Venus and Adonis: *A Study in the Warwickshire Dialect.* New York: The Shakespeare Press, 1900; rev. ed. New York: AMS 1971.

1901

Bagehot, Walter. *Shakespeare the Man.* New York: McClure, Phillips, 1901.

1902

Eichoff, Theodor. *Shakespeares Forderung einer absoluten Moral. Eine Erläuterung seiner Gedichte* Venus und Adonis *und* Die Schäandung der Lukretia. Halle: S. Niemeyer, 1902.

1903

Root, R.K. "Classical Mythology in Shakespeare." *Yale Studies in English* 19. New York, 1903.

1904

Creighton, Charles. *Shakespeare's Story of His Life.* London, 1904.

1905

Carter, Thomas. *Shakespeare and the Holy Scripture.* London, 1905.

Creizenach, W. "Shakespeare and Ovid." *Jahrbuch der Deutsche Shakespeare-Gesellschaft* 41 (1905): 211.

Lee, Sidney, ed. "Introduction." *Shakespeare's* Venus and Adonis: *Being a Reproduction in Facsimile of the First Edition, 1593.* Oxford: Clarendon, 1905. 1–75.

1907

Raleigh, Walter. *Shakespeare.* New York: Macmillan, 1907. 63–93.

Wolff, Max. *Shakespeare der Dichter und Sein Werk.* Munich, 1907.

1908

Greenwood, G.G. *The Shakespeare Problem Revisited.* London: John Lane the Bodely Head, 1908. 31 passim; rpt. Westport, CT: Greenwood, 1970.

Furnivall, F.J., and John Munro. *Shakespear: Life and Work.* London, 1908.

1909

Harris, Frank. *The Man Shakespeare and His Tragic Life-Story.* New York: Mitchell Kennerly, 1909. 127 passim.

Munro, John. ed. *The Shakespeare Allusion-Book: A Collection of Allusions to Shakespeare From 1591 to 1700.* New York, 1909; reissued London: Oxford UP, 1932.

Robertson, John M. "Shakespeare's Culture-Evolution." *Montaigne and Shakespeare: And Other Essays on Cognate Questions.* London: Adam and Charles Black, 1909. 139–60.

Swinburne, Algernon Charles. *Shakespere.* London: Oxford UP, 1909.

1910

Courthope, W.J. *A History of English Poetry.* New York, 1910.

Saintsbury, George. "Shakespeare's Poems." *Cambridge History of English Literature* 5: 250–63. New York, 1910.

1911

Gollancz, Israel. "Preface, Glossary, Etc." *Shakespeare's* Venus and Adonis. London: Dent, 1911. v–xvi; 100–07.

Przychocki, G. "Accessus Ovidiani." *Dissertations of the Polish Academy of Sciences.* Series 3. Krakow, 1911. 65–126.

1912

Shakespeare, William. *Venus and Adonis.* London: The Doves Press, 1912; Printed by T.J. Cobden-Sanderson.

1913

Brown, Carleton. *Introduction to* Venus and Adonis, The Rape of Lucrece *and Other Poems.* New York, 1913. x–xii.

Faral, Edmond. *Recherches sur les sources latines des contes et romans courtois du moyen age.* Paris, 1913.

Schevill, R. "Ovid and the Renascence in Spain." *University of California Publications in Modern Philology* 4 (1913): 1–268.

1914

Schoell, Frank L. "Les Mythologistes Italiens de la Renaissance et la Poésie Elisabéthaine." *Revue de Littérature. Comparée* 4 (1914): 5–25.

1915

Rick, Leo. *Ovids Metamorphosen in der englischen Renaissance.* Münster: I.W., 1915.

1921

Parsons, J. Denham. "Gravestones and Inscriptions, or The Suppressed Evidence of the Elizabethan Satirists, Marston and Hall, Concerning the Author of *Venus and Adonis.*" Stratford-upon-Avon, 1921.

1922

Frazer, Sir J.G. *The Golden Bough.* New York: Macmillan, 1922; abridged ed. New York, 1948. 6, 8, 9.

Joyce, James. *Ulysses.* Paris, 1922; rev. ed. New York: Random House, 1961.

Stopes, C.C. *The Life of Henry, Third Earl of Southampton, Shakespeare's Patron.* Cambridge: Cambridge UP, 1922.

1923

Hartog, W.G. *The Kiss in English Poetry.* London: A.M. Philpot, 1923.

1924

Hibbard, L. *Medieval Romance in England.* New York, 1924.

1925

Rand, E.K. *Ovid and His Influence.* Boston: Marshall Jones, 1925; rpt. New York: Cooper Square, 1963. 134–35.

1926

Butler, Samuel. *The Note-Books of Samuel Butler.* Vol. 20. *The Works of Samuel Butler.* London, 1926; rpt. New York: AMS Press, 1968.

1927

Bush, Douglas. "Notes on Shakespeare's Classical Mythology." *Philological Quarterly* 6 (1927): 291–302.

1928

Shakespeare, William. *Will Shakespeare His Amatory Poems . . . Elaborated with frontispiece portrait and four engravings from classic originals.* New York: The Bennett Libraries, 1928.

Spurgeon, Caroline. *Shakespeare: A Descriptive Study.* Oxford, 1928. 42–43; rpt. 1966.

1929

Bailey, John. *Shakespeare.* London and New York: Longmans Green 1929.

Crosse, G. "A Shakespeare Allusion." *Times Literary Supplement* (Aug. 1, 1929): 608.

Spencer, Hazelton. "Shakespeare's Use of Golding in *Venus and Adonis.*" *Modern Language Notes* 44 (Nov. 1929): 435–7.

1930

Chambers, Sir E.K. *William Shakespeare: A Study of Facts and Problems.* 2 vols. Oxford: Clarendon P, 1930. I: 61, 543; II: 193–95 passim.

Coon, R.H. "The Vogue of Ovid Since the Renaissance." *Classical Journal* 25 (1930): 277–90.

Forrest, H.T.S. *The Original* Venus and Adonis. London: Lane, 1930.

Fripp, Edgar I. "Shakespeare's Use of Ovid's *Metamorphoses.*" *Shakespeare Studies, Biographical and Literary.* Oxford: Oxford UP, 1930. 98–128.

Raysor, T.M. *Coleridge's Shakespearean Criticism.* London, 1930.

Shakespeare, William. *Venus and Adonis.* Paris: Harrison, 1930. Designed by Monroe Wheeler; printed by Ducros & Colas.

Shakespeare, William. *Venus and Adonis.* . . . *Illustrated by Ben Kutcher.* New York: Lincoln Macveagh-The Dial Press; Toronto: Longmans Green, 1930.

1931

Shakespeare, William. *Venus and Adonis. With wood engravings by Horace Walter Bray.* Harrow Weald, England: Raven, 1931.

1932

Bush, Douglas. *Mythology and the Renaissance Tradition in English Poetry.* Minneapolis: U of Minnesota P, 1932; rev. ed. New York: Norton, 1963. 137–48.

1933

Pearson, Lu Emily. *Elizabethan Love Conventions.* Berkeley: U of California P, 1933. 283–85.

1934

Lucas, Wilfried Irving. *"Die epischen Dichtungen Shakespeares in Deutschland."* Ph.D. diss., Philippsburg, 1934.

Newberry, John Strong. "Beauty and the Boar." *The Rainbow Bridge: A Study of Paganism.* Boston and New York: Houghton Mifflin, 1934. 209–26.

Rylands, George. "Shakespeare the Poet." *A Companion to Shakespeare Studies.* Ed. Harley Granville-Barker and G.B. Harrison. Cambridge: Cambridge UP, 1934. 103–109 passim.

Shakespeare, William. *Venus and Adonis with illustrations by Rockwell Kent.* Rochester, NY: The Printing House of Leo Hart, 1934; rpt. 1956.

1935

Craig, Hardin. *The Enchanted Glass.* Oxford: Blackwell, 1935.

Spurgeon, Caroline F.I. *Shakespeare's Imagery and What It Tells Us.* Cambridge: Cambridge UP, 1935.

1936

Ridley, M.R. *William Shakespeare, A Commentary.* London: J.M. Dent, 1936. 11–12.

1937

Fairchild, A.H.R. *Shakespeare and the Art of Design.* Columbia: U of Missouri P, 1937. 137–39.

1938

Fripp, Edgar I. "*Venus and Adonis.*" *Shakespeare Man and Artist.* 2 vols. Oxford: Oxford UP, 1938. 2: 331–44.

Rollins, Hyder Edward, ed. *A New Variorum Edition of Shakespeare: The Poems.* Philadelphia: J.B. Lippincott, 1938. 476–523.

1939

Alexander, Peter. *Shakespeare's Life and Art.* London: Nisbet, 1939.

Hotson, Leslie. "An Elizabethan Madman: Publication of *Venus and Adonis.*" *The [London] Times* (Apr. 21, 1939): 19.

Knight, G. Wilson. *The Burning Oracle: Studies in the Poetry of Action.* Oxford: Oxford UP, 1939. 30–31, 47.

Peeters, Félix. *Les "Fastes" d'Ovide: Histoire du Texte.* Bruxelles: G. van Campenhout, 1939.

1940

Loane, G.G. "Notes on Shakespeare's Poems: New Variorum Edition." *Notes and Queries* 178 (1940): 188–89.

1941

Putney, Rufus. "*Venus and Adonis:* Amour with Humor." *Philological Quarterly* 20 (Oct. 1941): 533–48.

1942

Watkins, W.B.C. "Shakespeare's Banquet of Sense." *Southern Review* 7 (1942): 706–34.

1943

T. H. *Oenone and Paris. Reprinted from the Unique Copy in the Folger Shakespeare Library, with an Introduction and Notes by Joseph Quincy Adams.* Washington, DC: Folger Shakespeare Library, 1943.

1945

Price, Hereward T. "Function of Imagery in *Venus and Adonis.*" *Papers of the Michigan Academy of Science, Arts, and Letters* 31 (1945): 275–97.

1946

Hatto, A.T. "*Venus and Adonis*—And the Boar." *Modern Language Review* 41 (Oct. 1946): 353–61.

Schaus, Hermann. "The Relationship of *Comus* to *Hero and Leander* and *Venus and*

Adonis." *Texas Studies in English* 25 (1945–1946): 129–41.

Shakespeare, William. *Venus and Adonis. Introduction, Translation, and Notes by Maraiano de Vedia y Mitre.* Buenos Aires: Academia Argentina de Letras, 1946. 1–103.

1947

Boas, Fredrick S. *Ovid and the Elizabethans.* London: The English Association, 1947.

Tuve, Rosemond. *Elizabethan and Metaphysical Imagery.* Chicago: U of Chicago P, 1947.

1948

Hardin, Craig. *An Interpretation of Shakespeare.* New York: Dryden, 1948. 3 passim.

Jackson, William A. "The Lamport Hall—Brittwell Court Books." *Joseph Quincy Adams Memorial Studies.* Ed. James G. McManaway, Giles E. Dawson, and Edwin E. Willoughby. Washington, DC: Folger Shakespeare Library, 1948. 587–99.

Shakespeare, William. *Venus and Adonis. Designed and Drawn by Peter Rudland.* London: W.H. Allen, 1948.

———. *Venus and Adonis . . . Illustrated by J. Yunge-Bateman.* London: Winchester Publications, 1948.

1949

Chute, Marchette. *Shakespeare of London.* New York: E.P. Dutton, 1949. 110–20 passim.

A. D. "Weever, Ovid and Shakespeare." *Notes and Queries* 194 (1949): 524–25.

Halliday, F.E. *Shakespeare and His Critics.* London: Duckworth, 1949.

Highet, Gilbert. *The Classical Tradition: Greek and Roman Influences on Western Literature.* New York: Oxford UP, 1949. 203–205, 415, 618.

Hotson, Leslie. *Shakspeare's Sonnets Dated, and Other Essays.* London: Rupert Hart-Davis, 1949; Toronto: Clarke, Irwin, 1949. 141–46.

Webster, Peter Dow. "A Critical Fantasy or Fugue." *American Imago* 6 (1949): 297–309.

1950

Baldwin, T.W. "The Literary Genetics of *Venus and Adonis.*" *On the Literary Genetics of Shakespeare's Poems and Sonnets.* Urbana: U of Illinois P, 1950. 1–93.

Burke, Kenneth. "Socioangogic Interpretation of *Venus and Adonis.*" *A Rhetoric of Motives.* New York: Prentice-Hall, 1950. 212–21.

Krklec, Gustav. *Venegra i Adonis.* Zagreb: Drzavo Izdavacko Poduzece Hrvatske, 1950.

Tillyard, E.M.W. The *Elizabethan World Picture.* London: Chatto and Windus, 1950.

Watkins, W.B.C. "Shakespeare's Banquet of Sense." *Shakespeare and Spenser.* Princeton: Princeton UP, 1950. 3–24; rpt. in *Elizabethan Poetry: Modern Essays in Criticism.* Ed. Paul Alpers. Oxford, 1967. 251–73; rpt. Washington, DC: University Press of America, 1982.

Zocca, Louis R. *Elizabethan Narrative Poetry.* New Brunswick: Rutgers UP, 1950. 248–61.

1951

Bradbrook, M.C. "The Ovidian Romance." *Shakespeare and Renaissance Poetry: A Study of His Earlier Work in Relation to the Poetry of the Time.* London: Chatto and Windus, 1951. 51–74.

1952

Bartlett, Phyllis. "Ovid's 'Banquet of Sense'?" *Notes and Queries* 197 (1952): 46–47.

Hubler, Edward. *The Sense of Shakespeare's Sonnets.* Princeton: Princeton UP, 1952. 5, 22, 50, 70.

Lewis, C.S. "*Hero and Leander.*" *Proceedings of the British Academy 1952.* London: Oxford UP, 1952. 23–37.

Miller, Robert P. "Venus, Adonis and the Horses." *ELH: Journal of English Literary History* 19 (Dec. 1952): 249–64.

Shakespeare, William. Venus and Adonis: *With Marlowe's* Hero and Leander. Ed. Gabriel Baldini. Parma: Ugo Grande Editore, 1952.

Smith, Hallett. "Ovidian Poetry: The Growth and Adaptations of Forms." *Elizabethan Poetry: A Study in Conventions, Meaning, and Expression.* Cambridge: Harvard UP, 1952; rpt. U of Michigan P, 1968. 64–130.

Thomson, J.A.K. *Shakespeare and the Classics.* London: Allen & Unwin, 1952. 41–42.

Titherley, A.W. *Shakespeare's Identity: William Stanley, 6th Earl of Derby.* Winchester, U.K.: Warren & Son, 1952. 86, 158, 235 passim.

1953

Hankins, John Erskine. *Shakespeare's Derived Imagery.* Lawrence: U of Kansas P, 1953. 232–35.

Putney, Rufus. "Venus *Agonistes.*" *University of Colorado Studies. Series in Language and Literature,* No. 4 (1953): 52–66.

Van Doren, Mark. *Shakespeare.* New York: Holt, 1939; rpt. New York: Doubleday Anchor, 1953.

Whitaker, Vergil K. *Shakespeare's Use of Learning.* San Marino: Huntington Library, 1953. 117–20 passim.

1954

Lewis, C.S. *English Literature in the Sixteenth Century, Excluding Drama.* Oxford: Oxford UP, 1954. 486–89.

Miller, Robert P. "The Double Hunt of Love: A Study of Shakespeare's *Venus and Adonis* as a Christian Mythological Narrative." *DAI* 14 (1954): 2338. Princeton U.

Partridge, A.C. "Shakespeare's Orthography in V*enus and Adonis* and Some Early Quartos." *Shakespeare Survey* 7 (1954): 35–47.

Thayer, Calvin G. "Ben Jonson, Markham, and Shakespeare." *Notes and Queries* NS 1 (1954): 469–70.

1956

Cross, K. Gustav. "'Balm' in Donne and Shakespeare: Ironic Intention in *The Extasie.*" *Modern Language Notes* 71 (Nov. 1956): 480–82.

1957

Bullough, Geoffrey. *"Venus and Adonis."* *Narrative and Dramatic Sources of Shakespeare, Vol. I, Early Comedies, Poems, "Romeo and Juliet."* London: Routledge and Kegan Paul, 1957. 161–78.

Dickey, Franklin M. *"Not Wisely but Too Well": Shakespeare's Love Tragedies.* San Marino, CA: Huntington Library, 1957. 46–62.

1958

Jackson, Robert Sumner. "Narrative and Imagery in Shakespeare's *Venus and Ado-*

nis." Papers of the Michigan Academy of Science, Arts, and Letters 43 (1958): 315–20.

Miller, Paul "The Elizabethan Minor Epic." *Studies in Philology* 55 (1958): 31–38.

1959

Allen, Don Cameron. "On *Venus and Adonis*." *Elizabethan and Jacobean Studies Presented to Frank Percy Wilson*. Oxford: Clarendon, 1959. 100–11.

Miller, Robert P. "The Myth of Mars's Hot Minion in *Venus and Adonis*." *ELH: Journal of English Literary History* 26 (Dec. 1959): 470–81.

1960

Brown, Ivor. *Shakespeare in His Time*. Edinburgh: Thomas Nelson and Sons, 1960. 50 passim.

Prince, F.T. "Introduction." *The Arden Edition of the Works of William Shakespeare: The Poems*. 3rd. ed. London: Methuen, 1960. xi–xxxiii.

Shakespeare, William. *The Poems & Sonnets . . . edited by Gwyn Jones*. London: The Golden Cockerel Press, 1960.

1961

Craig, Hardin, ed. *The Complete Works of Shakespeare*. Glenview, IL: Scott, Foresman, 1961. 425–26; 439.

Hamilton, A.C. "*Venus and Adonis*." *Studies in English Literature, 1500–1900* 1 (Winter 1961): 1–15.

Palmatier, M.A. "A Suggested New Source in Ovid's *Metamorphoses* for Shakespeare's *Venus and Adonis*." *Huntington Library Quarterly* 24 (1961): 163–69.

1962

Bonjour, Adrien. "From Shakespeare's Venus to Cleopatra's Cupids." *Shakespeare Survey* 15 (1962): 73–80.

Bowers, R.H. "Anagnorisis, or the Shock of Recognition, in Shakespeare's *Venus and Adonis*." *Renaissance Papers 1962* (1962): 3–8.

Bradbrook, Muriel C. "Beasts and Gods: Greene's *Groats-Worth of Witte* and the Social Purpose of *Venus and Adonis*." *Shakespeare Survey* 15 (1962): 62–72.

Fiedler, Leslie A. "Some Contexts of Shakespeare's Sonnets." *The Riddles of Shakespeare's Sonnets*. New York: Basic Books, 1962. 67–73.

Lever, J.W. "Twentieth-Century Studies in Shakespeare's Songs, Sonnets, and Poems." *Shakespeare Survey* 15 (1962): 19–22.

———. "Venus and the Second Chance." *Shakespeare Survey* 15 (1962): 81–88.

Panofsky, Erwin. *Studies in Iconology*. New York: Harper, 1962. 129–230.

1963

Cantelupe, Eugene B. "An Iconographical Interpretation of *Venus and Adonis*, Shakespeare's Ovidian Comedy." *Shakespeare Quarterly* 14 (Spring 1963): 141–51.

Cutts, John P. "*Venus and Adonis* in an Early Seventeenth-Century Song-Book." *Notes and Queries* 10 (Aug. 1963): 302–3.

Donno, Elizabeth Story. *Elizabethan Minor Epic*. New York: Columbia UP, 1963. 6.

Marder, Louis. *His Exits and Entrances: The Story of Shakespeare's Reputation*. Philadelphia: Lippincott, 1963. 86–88 passim.

1964

Bemrose, J.M. "A Critical Examination of the Borrowings from *Venus and Adonis* and *Lucrece* in Samuel Nicholson's *Acolastus.*" *Shakespeare Quarterly* 15 (Winter 1964): 89–96.

Burgess, Anthony. *Nothing Like the Sun: A Story of Shakespeare's Love-life.* New York: Norton, 1964.

Butler, Christopher and Alastair Fowler. "Time-Beguiling Sport: Number Symbolism in Shakespeare's *Venus and Adonis.*" *Shakespeare 1554–1964: A Collection of Modern Essays by Various Hands.* Ed. Edward A. Bloom. Providence: Brown UP, 1964. 124–33.

Castrop, Helmut. *"Shakespeares Verserzählungen. Eine Untersuchung der ovidischen Epik im elisabethanischen England."* Ph.D. diss., Marburg, 1964.

Gerritsen, Johan. "*Venus* Preserved: Some Notes on Frances Wolfrestan." *English Studies: A Journal of English Letters and Philology* 45 (1964): 271–4.

Griffin, Robert J. "'These Contraries Such Unity Do Hold': Patterned Imagery in Shakespeare's Narrative Poems." *Studies in English Literature, 1500–1900* 4 (Winter 1964): 43–55.

Muir, Kenneth. "*Venus and Adonis:* Comedy or Tragedy?" *Shakespearean Essays. Tennessee Studies in Literature* 2. Ed. Alwin Thaler and Norman Sanders. Knoxville: U of Tennessee P, 1964. 1–13.

Shakespeare, William. *Shakespeare's Poems: Venus and Adonis, Lucrece, The Passionate Pilgrim, The Phoenix and the Turtle, The Sonnets, A Lover's Complaint. Fascsimile of the Earliest Editions.* New Haven: Yale UP for the Elizabethan Club, 1964.

1965

Halliday, F.E. *Shakespeare in His Age.* South Brunswick, NJ: Thomas Yoseloff, 1965. 152 passim.

Leech, Clifford. "Venus and Her Nun: Portraits of Women in Love by Shakespeare and Marlowe." *Studies in English Literature, 1500–1900* 5 (Spring 1965): 247–68.

Rowse, A.L. *Shakespeare's Southampton: Patron of Virginia.* New York: Harper, 1965. 79–81; 94–96.

Whidden, Mary Bess. "Love's Fool: Shakespeare's Venus and the English Petrarchans." *DAI* 26 (1965): 1030. U of Texas at Austin.

1966

Maxwell, J.C. "Introduction." *The Poems. By William Shakespeare.* Cambridge: Cambridge UP, 1966.

Palmer, Paulina. "Thomas Carew: An Allusion to *Venus and Adonis.*" *Notes and Queries* 13 (July 1966): 255–56.

Rabkin, Norman. "*Venus and Adonis* and the Myth of Love." *Pacific Coast Studies in Shakespeare.* Ed. Waldo F. McNeir and Thelma N. Greenfield. Eugene: U of Oregon P, 1966. 20–32; rpt. in *Shakespeare and the Common Understanding.* New York, Free Press, 1967. 150–64.

Tyson, Mary Hanna. "Marlowe, Shakespeare, and the Ovidian Narrative Tradition." *DAI* 27 (1966): 752A-3A. U of California-Berkeley.

1967

Evans, Maurice. *English Poetry in the Sixteenth Century.* New York: Norton, 1967. 86.

Hamilton, A.C. *The Early Shakespeare.* San Marino, CA: Huntington, 1967.

Maxwell, J.C. "'Black Chaos': Shakespeare and Muretus." *Notes and Queries* 14 (1967): 138–39.

Muir, Kenneth. *Introduction to Elizabethan Literature*. New York: Random House, 1967. 98, 167.

1968

Akrigg, G.P.V. *Shakespeare and the Earl of Southampton*. Cambridge, MA: Harvard UP, 1968. 33–34, 195–98.

Allen, Michael J.B. "The Chase: The Development of a Renaissance Theme." *Comparative Literature* 20 (Fall 1968): 301–12.

Arens, J.C. "Shakespeare's *Venus and Adonis* (1–810): A Dutch Translation Printed in 1621." *Noophilologus* 52 (Oct. 1968): 421–30.

Klose, Dietrich. "Shakespeare and Ovid." *Shakespeare Jahrbuch* [Heidelberg] (1968): 72–93.

Thornton, Weldon. *Allusions in* Ulysses. Chapel Hill: U of North Carolina P, 1968. 191 passim.

William Shakespeare's Venus and Adonis: *1593: A Scolar Press Facsimile Edition*. Menston, England: Scolar, 1968.

Winny, James. *The Master-Mistress: A Study of Shakespeare's Sonnets*. NY: Barnes & Noble, 1968. 136 passim.

1969

Berry, J. Wilkes. "Loss of Adonis and Light in *Venus and Adonis*." *Discourse* 12 (Winter 1969): 72–76.

Brown, Huntington. "*Venus and Adonis:* The Action, the Narrator, and the Critics." *Michigan Academician* 2 (Fall 1969): 73–87.

Burke, Kenneth. *A Rhetoric of Motives*. Berkeley, CA: U of California P, 1969.

Panofsky, Erwin. "Titian and Ovid." *Problems in Titian: Mostly Iconographic*. New York: New York UP, 1969.

Wilbur, Richard, ed. "The Narrative Poems." *The Pelican Shakespeare*. Ed. Alfred Harbage. Baltimore: Penquin, 1969. 1401–1405.

1970

Asimov, Isaac. *"Venus and Adonis." Asimov's Guide to Shakespeare. Vol. 1: The Greek, Roman, and Italian Plays*. Illustrated by Rafael Palacios. New York: Avenel, 1970. 3–15.

Burgess, Anthony. *Shakespeare*. New York: Knopf, 1970.

Donno, Elizabeth Story. "The Epyllion." *English Poetry and Prose, 1540–1674*. Ed. Christopher Ricks. London: Barrie and Jenkins, 1970. 82–100.

Jahn, J. D. "The Lamb of Lust: The Role of Adonis in Shakespeare's *Venus and Adonis*." *Shakespeare Studies* 6 (1970): 11–25.

Keach, William C. "Artifice, Eroticism, and Irony in the Elizabethan Epyllion." *DAI* 31 (1970): 2922–A. Yale U.

Kostic, Veselin. *"Venera i Adoni* i tradicija ovidijevskih poema u engleskoj renesansi." *Filoloski pregled* 1–2 (1970): 63–78.

Popescu, Nicolae. "Venus si Adonis." *Luceafarul* 13 (Oct. 7, 1970): 42.

1971

Harrison, Thomas P. "Shakespeare's Glowworms." *Shakespeare Quarterly* 22 (1971): 395–96.

Lever, J.W. "Shakespeare's Narrative Poems." *A New Companion to Shakespeare Studies*. Ed. Kenneth Muir and S. Schoenbaum. Cambridge: Cambridge UP, 1971. 116–124.

Partridge, A.C. "Non-Dramatic Poetry: Marlowe and Shakespeare." *The Language*

of *Renaissance Poetry: Spenser, Shakespeare, Donne, Milton*. London: Andre
Deutsch, 1971. 102–40.

Rothenberg, Alan Baer. "The Oral Rape Fantasy and the Rejection of the Mother in
the Imagery of Shakespeare's *Venus and Adonis*." *Psychoanalytic Quarterly*
40 (1971): 447–68.

Smith, Gordon Ross. "Mannerist Frivolity in Shakespeare's *Venus and Adonis*." *University of Hartford Studies in Literature* 3 (1971): 1–11.

1972

Boyar, Billy T. "Keats's 'Isabella': Shakespeare's *Venus and Adonis* and the Venus-Adonis Myth." *Keats and Shelley Journal* 21–22 (1972–73): 160–69.

Donaldson, Ian. "Adonis and His Horse." *Notes and Queries* 19 (April 1972): 123–25.

Empson, William. "Introduction." *Poems*. New York: Signet, 1972.

Fredin, Lowell Edward. "The Variant Muse. A Study of *Hero and Leander* and the
Elizabethan Love Lyric." *DAI* 32 (1972): 5180A-5181A. Ohio U.

Goldman, Michael. *Shakespeare and the Energies of Drama*. Princeton: Princeton UP,
1972. 10–11, 12–19.

Jahn, Jerald Duane. "The Elizabethan Epyllion: Its Art and Narrative Conventions."
DAI 33 (1972): 2331–A. Indiana U.

Johnson, Paula. *Form and Transformation in Music and Poetry of the English Renaissance*. New Haven: Yale UP, 1972. 143–52.

1973

Asals, Heather. "*Venus and Adonis:* The Education of a Goddess." *Studies in English
Literature, 1500–1900* 13 (Winter 1973): 31–51.

Adams, Percy. G. "The Historical Importance of Assonance to Poets." *PMLA* 88 (Jan.
1973): 8–18.

Bromley, Laura A. "1. Continuity in Milton's Sonnets. 2. Attitudes Toward Love in
Venus and Adonis 3. The Victorian 'Good Woman' and the Fiction of Charlotte Bronte." *DAI* 34 (1973):3336A. Rutgers U.

Hobday, C.H. "Shakespeare's Venus and Adonis Sonnets." *Shakespeare Survey* 26
(1973): 103–09.

Muir, Kenneth. *Shakespeare the Professional and Related Studies*. London: Heinemann,
1973. 185–86.

Nosworthy, J.M. "The Sonnets and Other Poems." *Shakespeare: Select Bibliographical Guides*. Ed. Stanley Wells. London: Oxford UP, 1973. 44–53.

Ramsey, Allen. "*Venus and Adonis* as a Type of Ovidian Narrative Poetry." *DAI* 33
(1973): 6322A-23A. Tulane U.

Rowse, A.L. *Shakespeare the Man*. London: Macmillan, 1973; rev. ed. 1988.

Watson, Donald Gwynn. "Transformation of Ovid: The Mythological Narrative Poem
in Elizabethan England." *DAI* 33 (1973): 3679A-3680A. U of Virginia.

1974

Adkins, Betty J. "A Critical Analysis of the Erotic Mythological Narrative Poem, 1589–
1598." *DAI* 35 (1974): 2211A. Miami U.

Bauer, Robert J. "Rhetoric and Picture in *Venus and Adonis*." *Explorations in Renaissance Culture* 1 (1974): 41–56.

Gent, Lucy. "*Venus and Adonis:* The Triumph of Rhetoric." *Modern Language Review* 69 (Oct. 1974): 721–29.

Lake, James H. "Shakespeare's Venus: An Experiment in Tragedy." *Shakespeare Quarterly* 25 (Summer 1974): 351–55.

Sheidley, William E. "'Unless It Be a Boar': Love and Wisdom in Shakespeare's *Venus* and Adonis." *Modern Language Quarterly* 35 (March 1974): 3–15.

Smith, Hallett. "Introduction to *Venus and Adonis*." *The Riverside Shakespeare*. Ed. G. Blakemore Evans. Boston: Houghton Mifflin, 1974. 1703–04.

1975

Barnes, R.G., ed. Venus and Adonis *by William Shakespeare together with Sources for the Poem in Ovid's* Metamorphoses *Translated by Arthur Golding*. San Francisco: Arion, 1975.

Beauregard, David N. "*Venus and Adonis:* Shakespeare's Representation of the Passions." *Shakespeare Studies* 8 (1975): 83–98.

Hulse, S. Clark. "Myth and Narrative in Elizabethan Poetry." *DAI* 35 (1975): 5408A. Claremont Graduate School.

Pegg, Barry. "Generation and Corruption in Shakespeare's *Venus and Adonis*." *Michigan Academician* 8 (Summer 1975): 105–15.

Salter, Nancy Kay Clark. "Masks and Roles: A Study of Women in Shakespeare's Drama." *DAI* 36 (1975): 1535A. U of Connecticut.

Streitberger, W.R. "Ideal Conduct in *Venus and Adonis*." *Shakespeare Quarterly* 26 (Summer 1975): 285–91.

1976

Hulse, S. Clarke. "Elizabethan Minor Epic: Toward a Definition of a Genre." *Studies in Philology* 73 (July 1976): 302–19.

Kahn, Coppélia. "Self and Eros in *Venus and Adonis*." *Centennial Review* 4 (1976): 351–71; revised as chapt. 2 in Kahn's *Man's Estate: Masculine Identity in Shakespeare*. Berkeley: U of California P, 1981.

Lanham, Richard A. "The Ovidian Shakespeare: *Venus and Adonis* and *Lucrece*." *The Motives of Eloquence: Literary Rhetoric in the Renaissance*. New Haven: Yale UP, 1976. 82–94.

Marder, Louis. "Shakespeare in America until 1776." *Shakespeare Newsletter* 26 (Feb. 1976): 2, 8.

Partridge, A.C. *A Substantive Grammar of Shakespeare's Nondramatic Texts*. Charlottesville: U of Virginia P for the Bibliographical Society of America, 1976.

Ramsey, Allen. "Pastoral as Structure in Shakespeare's *Venus and Adonis*." *Publications of the Arkansas Philological Association* 2 (1976): 37–42.

Shakespeare, William. *Venuse a Adonis*. Trans. Kamie Bednár; illustrator Ota Janecek. Praha: Lyra Pragenis, 1976.

Wright, Ellen Faber. "Rhetoricke to Deceive: The Elizabethan Epyilla." *DAI* 36 (1976): 7449A-50A. Indiana U.

1977

Daigle, Lennet Joseph. "*Venus and Adonis:* Genre and Meaning." *DAI* 38 (1977): 275–76A. U of South Carolina.

Harwood, Ellen Aprill. "*Venus and Adonis:* Shakespeare's Critique of Spenser." *The Journal of the Rutgers University Library* 39 (June 1977): 44–60.

Keach, William C. "*Venus and Adonis*." *Elizabethan Erotic Narratives: Irony and Pathos in the Ovidian Poetry of Shakespeare, Marlowe, and Their Contemporaries*. New Brunswick, NJ: Rutgers UP, 1977. 52–84.

Meyer, Russell J. "Tudor Laughter: A Preliminary Study for a Theory of Humor." *DAI* (1977): 6504–05A. U of Minnesota.

Rudat, Wolfgang E.H. "Pope's 'Summer.'" *Explicator* 35 (Spring 1977): 9–11.

Schoenbaum, S. *Shakespeare: A Compact Documentary Life*. New York: Oxford UP, 1977. 176–77; rev. ed. 1987.

1978

Bledsoe, Audrey S. "Shakespeare's *Venus and Adonis:* A Myth of Failed Love." *South Atlantic Bulletin* 43 (May 1978): 89.

Blumenfeld, Harold. "Hugo Weisgall's 66th Birthday and the *New Gardens of Adonis.*" *Perspectives of New Music* 16 (1978): 156–66.

Gira, C.R. "Shakespeare's Venus—Figures and Renaissance Tradition." *Studies in Iconography* 4 (1978): 95–114.

Hulse, S. Clark. "Shakespeare's Myth of Venus and Adonis." *PMLA* 93 (Jan. 1978): 95–105.

Nakhjavani, Bahiyyih. "The Voyeur in Epyllia of the 1590's: 'Rage of Lust by Gazing Qualified.'" *DAI* 39 (1978): 298A.

Rebhorn, Wayne A. "Mother Venus: Temptation in Shakespeare's *Venus and Adonis.*" *Shakespeare Studies* 11 (1978): 1–19.

Spiegelman, Willard. "Another Shakespearean Echo in Keats." *American Notes & Queries* 17 (1978): 3–4.

Watson, Donald G. "The Contrarieties of *Venus and Adonis.*" *Studies in Philology* 75 (Jan. 1978): 32–63.

1979

Bowers, A. Robin. "'Hard Armours' and 'Delicate Amours' in Shakespeare's *Venus and Adonis.*" *Shakespeare Studies* 12 (1979): 1–23.

Grudin, Robert. *Mighty Opposites: Shakespeare and Renaissance Contrariety.* Berkeley: U of California P, 1979. 171, 207.

Jahn, Jerald D. "Chapman's *Enargia* and the Popular Perspective on *Ovids Banquet of Sence.*" *Tennessee Studies in Literature* 23 (1979): 15–30.

Pegg, Barry Malcolm. "Optimistic and Pessimistic Attitudes to Generation and Corruption in Selected Literary and Scientific Texts, 1599–1660." *DAI* 37 (1979): 6508A-09A. U of Wisconsin.

Phelps, Wayne H. "The Leakes of St. Dunstan's in the West: A Family of Seventeenth-Century Stationers." *Publications of the Bibliographic Society of America* 73 (1979): 86–89.

Rothenberg, Alan B. "The 'Speaking Breast': A Theory of Shakespearean Creativity." *Psychocultural Review* 3 (1979): 239–56.

1980

Bensimon, Marc. "*Venus and Adonis* de Shakespeare: Metamorphoses d'une metamorphose; Actes du Colloque Internat. de Valenciennes, 1979." *La Metamorphose dans la poésie baroque francaise et anglaise: Variations et resurgences.* Ed. Gisèle Mathieu-Castellani. Tubingen: G. Narr, 1980.

Daigle, Lennet J. "*Venus and Adonis:* Some Traditional Contexts." *Shakespeare Studies* 13 (1980): 31–46.

De Armas, Frederick A. "Italian Canvases in Lope de Vega's Comedias: The Case of *Venus and Adonis.*" *Critica Hispanica* 2 (1980): 135–42.

Greenblatt, Stephen. *Renaissance Self-Fashioning from More to Shakespeare.* Chicago: U of Chicago P, 1980. 227–28

Harrison, G.B. *Shakespeare at Work, 1592–1603.* Westport, CT: Greenwood, 1980. 39 passim.

Yoch, James J. "The Eye of Venus: Shakespeare's Erotic Landscape." *Studies in English Literature, 1500–1900* 20 (Winter 1980): 59–71.

1981

Bowers, A. Robin. "'Faire-fall the wit': Narrative Irony and Crux in Shakespeare's

Venus and Adonis." *Papers on Language and Literature* 17 (Spring 1981): 198–203.

Cyr, Gordon C. "The Latest Shakespearean Mare's Nest: Southampton's 'Secretary.'" *Shakespeare Newsletter* 31 (Feb. 1981): 4

Gent, Lucy. *Picture and Poetry, 1560–1620. Relations between Literature and the Visual Arts in the English Renaissance.* Lemington Spa, Warwickshire: Hall, 1981.

Hulse, S. Clark. *Metamorphic Verse: The Elizabethan Minor Epic.* Princeton: Princeton UP, 1981. 142–76.

Jum'ah, Badi' Mohammed. "Qasidat Finus wa Adunis li-William Shakisbir" [The Poem of *Venus and Adonis* by William Shakespeare]. *Usturat Finus wa Adonis* [The Myth of Venus and Adonis]. Beirut: Dar al-budhah al-Arabiyyah lil-Tib'ah wa al-Nashr, 1981. 63–113.

Shecktor, Nina. "La Interpretación del mito en el Adonis y Venus de Lope." *Lope de Vega y los orígenes del teatro espanol.* Ed. Manuel Criado de Val. Madrid, 1981. 361–364.

Tuzet, Hèléne. "Essai pour dégager les constantes et la fonction d'un mythe: Adonis." *Mythes, Images, Représentations.* Paris: Didier, 1981. 51–59.

Vessey, D.W. Thompson. "Venery and Sophistication: Shakespeare's *Venus and Adonis* and Marlowe's *Hero and Leander.*" *The Bard* 3 (1981): 74–91.

Wilson, Katherine M. *Shakespeare's Sugared Sonnets.* London: Routledge, 1981. 357–63.

1982

Chand, Sunil. "'A Tale Told.' Shakespeare's Exploration of the Narrative Mode in *Venus and Adonis, Othello,* and the Falstaff Plays." *DAI* 43 (Sept. 1982): 806–A. Kent State U.

Doebler, John. "The Reluctant Adonis: Titian and Shakespeare." *Shakespeare Quarterly* 33 (Winter 1982): 480–90.

Furber, Donald, and Anne Callahan. *Erotic Love in Literature: From Medieval Legend to Romantic Illusion.* Troy, NY: Whiston, 1982. 61–65.

Jucan, Marius. "Univers si imagine baroca: *Venus si Adonis.*" *Shakespeare Studies* [Cluj-Napoca] (1982).

Mulvihill, James D. "Jonson's *Poetaster* and the Ovidian Debate." *Studies in English Literature, 1500–1900* 22 (Spring 1982): 239–55.

Rowan, Nicole. "Gezelles 'De slekke' en Shakespeares *Venus and Adonis:* Een 'Missing Link.'" *Spiegel der Letteren* 24, 3–4 (1982): 232–334.

Sherbo, Arthur. "A Neglected Critic of Shakespeare's Poetry." *Shakespeare Quarterly* 33 (Spring 1982): 102–05.

Truax, Elizabeth. "Venus, Lucrece, and Bess of Hardwick: Portraits to Please." *Shakespeare and the Arts: A Collection of Essays from the Ohio Shakespeare Conference, 1981.* Ed. Cecile Williamson Cary and Henry S. Limouze. Washington, DC: University Press of America, 1982. 35–56.

1983

Doebler, John. "The Many Faces of Love: Shakespeare's *Venus and Adonis.*" *Shakespeare Studies* 16 (1983): 33–43.

Dundas, Judith. "Shakespeare's Imagery: Emblem and the Imitation of Nature." *Shakespeare Studies* 16 (1983): 45–56.

Fang, Ping. "Viewing Young Shakespeare from *Venus and Adonis.*" *Foreign Literature Studies* 21 (Sept. 1983): 29–36.

Gallagher, Noel. "Worth's Recitation Captivating But Too Brief." (*London, Ontario*) *Free Paper Press,* July 13, 1983.

Goodwin, Carol. "Irene Worth Brings a Love Poem to Life." *Kitchener Waterloo* (Ontario) *Record*, July 13, 1983.

Kuhl, E.P. *Shakespeare: Soul of the Age.* Iowa City, Iowa: Belting Publications, 1983. 44–96.

Montrose, Louis. "'Shaping Fantasies': Figurations of Gender and Power in Elizabethan Culture." *Representations* 1 (Spring 1983): 61–94.

Uhlmann, Dale C. "Red and White Imagery in *Venus and Adonis*." *Selected Papers from the West Virginia Shakespeare and Renaissance Association* 8 (Spring 1983): 15–20.

Weston, Lynda. "Intimate Third Stage Matches Intimate Letters." *Stratford* (Ontario) *Beacon Herald* , July 11, 1983.

Williams, Gordon. "The Coming of Age of Shakespeare's Adonis." *Modern Language Review* 78 (Oct. 1983): 769–76.

1984

Besnard-Coursodon, Micheline. "Monsieur Venus, Madame Adonis: Sex et Discours." *Littérature* 54 (1984): 121–27.

Doebler, John, ed. *Venus and Adonis.* Tempe, AZ: Pyracantha, 1984.

Ghrenassia, Patrick. Rev. of Luis Menasé's *Venus and Adonis. Cahiers élisabethains: Études sur la Pre-Renaissance et la Renaissance anglaises* 26 (Oct. 1984): 131–32.

Haskins, Anne. "Theater." *L.A. Weekly,* Jan. 24, 1984.

Hitchcock, Laura. *"Venus and Adonis." Hollywood Reporter*, Jan. 24, 1984.

Kishimoto, Yoshitaka. "Venus to Adonis ni okeru chowa." *Shakespeare no shiki.* Tokyo: Shinzaki, 1984. 375–83.

McEvoy, S.S. "Ferme les yeux!" *Semantikos* 8, 1 (1984): 1–13.

Miura, Itsue, "A Reading of *Venus and Adonis*." *Kiyo* [Shitennoji Kokusai Bukko Univ.] 15 (1983): 113–19.

Ozeki, Emi. "The Poetic Madness and the Love's Madness—On the Horse Imagery in *Venus and Adonis, Henry V* and *Sonnets* L-LI." *Colloquia* [Keio Univ.], 4 (1983): 33–55.

Poole, Richard. *Venus and Adonis.* Notts, England: Brynmill, Ltd., 1984 [a pamphlet that is an offprint of an article in *The Gadfly Literary Supplement*].

Smith, M.W.A. "Stylometry: The Authorship of *A Lover's Complaint*—Was It Chapman?" *Computers and the Humanities* 18 (1984): 23–37.

Warfield, Polly. "Benjamin Stewart Reprises *Venus and Adonis* at LAAT." *Drama-Logue* (Jan.-Feb. 1984): 1, 6.

Weinstock, Hortst, ed. *Die englische Literatur in Text und Darstellung. Jahrhundert* 2. Stuttgart: Reclam, 1984.

1985

Horne, R.C. "Two Unrecorded Contemporary References to Shakespeare." *Notes and Queries* 31 (June 1984): 218–20.

Pequigney, Joseph. *Such Is My Love: A Study of Shakespeare's Sonnets.* Chicago: U of Chicago P, 1985.

1986

Barkan, Leonard. *The Gods Made Flesh: Metamorphosis and the Pursuit of Paganism.* New Haven: Yale UP, 1986.

Buxton, John. "Shakespeare's *Venus and Adonis* and Sidney." *Sir Philip Sidney: 1586 and the Creation of a Legend.* Ed. Dominic Baker-Smith, Jan Van Dorsten, and Arthur F. Kinney. Leiden: E.J. Brill, 1986. 104–110.

Le Doeuff, Michèle. *Venus et Adonis Suivi de genèse d'une catastrophe.* Paris: Alidades, 1986.

Lindheim, Nancy. "The Shakespearean *Venus and Adonis.*" *Shakespeare Quarterly* 37 (Summer 1986): 190–203.

1987

Calvert, Hugh. *Shakespeare's Sonnets and Problems of Autobiography.* Devon, UK: Merlin Books, 1987. 53–57 passim.

Dubrow, Heather. "'Upon Misprision Growing': *Venus and Adonis.*" *Captive Victors: Shakespeare's Narrative Poems and Sonnets.* Ithaca: Cornell UP, 1987. 21–79.

Dundas, Judith. "Wat the Hare, or Shakespearean Decorum." *Shakespeare Studies* 19 (1987): 1–15.

1988

Bevington, David, ed. *The Poems.* Toronto: Bantam, 1988.

Caplan, Betty. "Almeida: *Venus* and *Lucrece.*" *The Guardian,* Jan. 29, 1988: 21.

Cherchi, Paolo. "Molte Veneri e pochi Adoni (con un inedito attribuibile a G.B. Strozzi)." *Esperienze Letterarie: Rivista Trimestrale di Critica e Cultura* 13 (1988): 15–38.

Doebler, John. "Venus and Adonis: Shakespeare's Horses." *Images of Shakespeare: Proceedings of the Third Congress of the International Shakespeare Association, 1986.* Newark: U of Delaware P, 1988. 64–72.

Duncan-Jones, Katherine. "*Venus* and *Lucrece.*" *Times Literary Supplement,* May 11, 1988: 136.

Dworkin, Norine. "Actor Flushes Out Shakespeare's Poetry with a Touch from Beckett." *Orange County* (California) *Register,* July 5, 1988: 1, 6.

Hilley, James. "Off the Rails." *The Listener,* Feb. 4, 1988.

Klause, John. "*Venus and Adonis:* Can We Forgive Them?" *Studies in Philology* 85 (Summer 1988): 353–77.

Koehler, Robert. "*Venus and Adonis* Takes Stage at the Gem." *Los Angeles Times* (Orange County edition), July 7, 1988.

Martindale, Charles, ed. *Ovid Renewed: Ovidian Influences on Literature and Art from the Middle Ages to the Twentieth Century.* Cambridge: Cambridge UP, 1988.

O'Connor, Thomas. "Theatrical Dessert Is upon Us in the Form of *Venus and Adonis.*" *Orange County* (California) *Register,* July 11, 1988: 1, 5.

Wardle, Irving. "Adonis Reduced to Pastoral Gang-bang." *London Times,* Jan. 28, 1988: 20G.

1989

Bate, Jonathan. *Shakespeare and the English Romantic Imagination.* Oxford: Clarendon, 1989. 135–36.

Evans, Maurice, ed. "Introduction: *Venus and Adonis.*" *William Shakespeare: The Narrative Poems.* Baltimore: Penguin, 1989. 4–24.

Farrell, Kirby. *Play, Death, and Heroism in Shakespeare.* Chapel Hill: U of North Carolina P, 1989. 117–30.

Fienberg, Nona. "Thematics of Value in *Venus and Adonis.*" *Criticism* 31 (Winter 1989): 21–32.

Hart, Jonathan. "'Till forging nature be condemned of treason': Representational Strife in *Venus and Adonis.*" *Cahiers élisabethains: Études sur la Pre-Renaissance et la Renaissance anglaises* 36 (Oct. 1989): 37–47.

Jehmlich, Reimer. "'O learn to love, the lesson is but plain': Fachiliches und

Didaktisches zu Shakespeares Liebessprache." In *Sweet William und der Siegener Geist. Festschrift für Ruth Freifrau Von Ledebur.* Fachbereich 3: *Sprach und Literatur,* 1989. 35–51.

Murphy, Patrick Martin. "The Perplexity of Desire: Representation and Poetic Thinking in Shakespeare's *Venus and Adonis* and *Love's Labor's Lost.*" *DAI* 50 (1989): 2066A. U of Illinois.

1990

Baumlin, Tita French. "The Birth of the Bard: *Venus and Adonis* and Poetic Apotheosis." *Papers on Language and Literature* 26 (Spring 1990): 191–211.

Bokenham, T.D. "The Ancient Mural at the White Hart, St. Albans." *Baconiana* 72 (1990): 88–89.

Boyce, Charles. *Shakespeare A to Z.* New York: Roundtable Press, 1990. 687–89.

Kelliher, Hilton. "Unrecorded Extracts from Shakespeare, Sidney, and Dyer." *English Manuscript Studies, 1100–1700* 2 (1990): 163–87.

Materna, Linda S. "El episodio *Venus-Adonis* en Noche de guerra en el Museo del Prado de Rafael Alberti: Intertextualidad lingüística, pictorica e ideológica." *Anales de la Literatura Española Contemporánea* 15, 1–3 (1990): 83–95.

1991

Anderson, Porter. Rev. of *Venus and Adonis,* dir. Ted Davey. Undermain Theatre, Dallas, TX. *Dallas Times Herald,* July 7, 1991: G1, G6.

Barroll, J. Leeds. *Politics, Plague, and Shakespeare's Theater: The Stuart Years.* Ithaca: Cornell UP, 1991. 17–18.

Dam, Julie. "Undermain's *Venus* Shines Brightly." *The Dallas Morning News,* July 5, 1991: 4C.

Erikson, Peter. *Rewriting Shakespeare: Rewriting Ourselves.* Berkeley, CA: U of California P, 1991.

Franson, J. Karl. "Numbers in Shakespeare's Dedications to *Venus and Adonis* and *The Rape of Lucrece.*" *Notes and Queries* 38 (March 1991): 51–54.

Maras, Mate. "Venus and Adonis." Croation trans. *Republika* (Zagreb), 9–10 (1991): 171–202.

Merrix, Robert P. "The 'Beste Noir': The Medieval Role of the Boar in *Venus and Adonis.*" *The Upstart Crow* 11 (1991): 117–30.

Roberts, Byron. "Saving the Bard's Bacon." *Sunday Telegraph* [London], March 31, 1991.

Roberts, Jeanne Addison. *The Shakespearean Wild: Geography, Genus, and Gender.* Lincoln: U of Nebraska P, 1991. 34–35 passim.

Sato, Saburo. "*Venus and Adonis* in Shimazaki Toson's Literary Evolution." *Comparative Literature Studies* 28 (1991): 283–95.

Smith, Bruce R. *Homosexual Desire in Shakespeare's England: A Cultural Poetics.* Chicago: U of Chicago P, 1991. 134–36 passim.

Thomas, Troy. "Interart Analogy: Practice and Theory in Comparing the Arts." *Journal of Aesthetic Education* 25 (1991): 17–36.

1992

Bevington, David. *Venus and Adonis. The Complete Works of Shakespeare.* 4th ed. New York: HarperCollins, 1992.

Coveney, Michael. Rev. of Citizens 3 *Venus and Adonis. Observer* [London], Oct. 18, 1992.

Desmet, Christy. *Reading Shakespeare's Characters: Rhetoric, Ethics, and Identity.* Amherst: U of Massachusetts P, 1992. 137–44; 162–63.

Hernandez-Araico, Surana. "*Venus y Adonis* en Calderón y Sor Juana: La primera opera Americana." Campbell-Ysla, Coord. *Relaciones literarias entre España y America en los siglos XVI y XVII.* Ciudad Juárez: U Autonoma de Ciudad Juarez, 1992. 137–51.

Hughes, Ted. *Shakespeare and the Goddess of Complete Being.* New York: Farrar, 1992.

Kingston, Jeremy. "Bird and Bard Have Timely Messages." *London Times,* Oct. 12, 1992: 33.

Martindale, Charles, and Colin Burrow. "Clapham's Narcissus: A Pre-Text for Shakespeare's *Venus and Adonis.*" *English Literary Renaissance* 22 (Spring 1992): 147–76.

Roe, John, ed. "Introduction." *The Poems: Venus and Adonis, The Rape of Lucrece, The Phoenix and the Turtle, The Passionate Pilgrim, A Lover's Complaint.* Cambridge: Cambridge UP, 1992. 3–21.

1993

Bate, Jonathan. *Shakespeare and Ovid.* Oxford: Clarendon, 1993. 48–67.

———. "Sexual Perversity in *Venus and Adonis.*" *Yearbook of English Studies* 23 (1993): 80–92.

Duncan-Jones, Katherine. "Much Ado with Red and White: The Earliest Readers of Shakespeare's *Venus and Adonis.*" *Review of English Studies* 44 (Nov. 1993): 479–501.

Elliot, Philip L. "'The Violet and the Star.'" *English Language Notes* 30 (March 1993): 41–43.

Green, Martin. *Wriothesley's Roses in Shakespeare's Sonnets, Poems, and Plays.* Baltimore: Clevedon Books, 1993.

Humes, James C. *Citizen Shakespeare: A Social and Political Portrait.* Westport, CT: Praeger, 1993. 52–53 passim.

McEvoy, Sebastian T. "De l'usure à chasteté: La Métaphore requalifiante." *Shakespeare et l'argent.* Ed. M.T. Jones-Davies. Paris: Belles Lettres, 1993. 39–55.

Smith, Jeffrey C. Rev. of *The Gardens of Adonis. Opera Canada* 34 (Spring 1993): 25.

Sorelius, Gunnar. *Shakespeare's Early Comedies: Myth, Metamorphosis, Mannerism.* Uppsala: Uppsala UP, 1993. 95–117.

1994

Cousins, A.D. "Venus Reconsidered: The Goddess of Love in *Venus and Adonis.*" *Studia Neophilologica* 66 (1974): 197–207.

Feitelberg, Doreen. "The Theme of Love and Wooing and the Consequences of Seduction in Shakespeare's Poems *Venus and Adonis* and *The Rape of Lucrece.*" *Shakespeare in Southern Africa* 7 (1994): 51–60.

Greenfield, Sayre. "Allegorical Impulses and Critical Ends: Shakespeare's and Spenser's *Venus and Adonis.*" *Criticism* 36 (Fall 1994): 475–98.

Matus, Irvin Leigh. *Shakespeare, IN FACT* [sic]. New York: Continuum, 1994. 55.

Phillips, Graham, and Martin Keatman. *The Shakespeare Conspiracy.* London: Century, 1994. 4, 15, 25, passim.

Pancheva, Eugenia. *Poemi. William Shekspir. Kristofer Marlow.* Ed. Alexander Shurbanov. Sofia: Obsidian, 1994. Bulgarian translation of *Venus and Adonis* and *Hero and Leander.*

Roe, John. "Italian Platonism and the Poetry of Sidney, Shakespeare, Chapman, and Donne." In *Platonism and the English Imagination.* Eds. Anna Baldwin and Sarah Hutton. Cambridge: Cambridge UP, 1994. 100–116.

Stanivukovic, Goran R. "Shakespeare, Dunstan Gale, and Golding." *Notes & Queries* 41 (1994): 35–37.

Wells, Stanley. *Shakespeare: A Dramatic Life*. London: Sinclair-Stevenson, 1994. 116–20.

Whalen, Richard F. *Shakespeare—Who Was He?* Westport, CT: Praeger, 1994. 95–96; 98–99.

Wortis, Joseph, M.D. "*Venus and Adonis*: An Early Account of Sexual Harassment." *Biological Psychiatry* 35 (March 1994): 293–4.

Yank, Baoyu. "Yiqu ai' Yu 'Mei' de songge—shilun shashibiya shushishi. *Weinasi yu Aduni*" [A Song in Praise of Love and Beauty—A Tentative Study of *Venus and Adonis*]. *Waiguo Wenxue Yanjiu [Foreign Literature Studies]* 4 (1994): 50–52.

1995

Adams, David. Rev. of Actor's Touring Company with the Hairy Mary's Production of *Venus and Adonis*, dir. Nick Philippou. *Guardian*, April 5, 1995.

Bassett, Kate. Rev. of Actor's Touring Company with the Hairy Mary's Production of *Venus and Adonis*, dir. Nick Philippou. *Times* [London], Feb. 20, 1995.

Belsey, Catherine. "Love as Trompe-l'oeil: Taxonomies of Desire in *Venus and Adonis*." *Shakespeare Quarterly* 46 (Fall 1995): 257–76.

Blythe, David-Everett. "Shakespeare's *Venus and Adonis*." *The Explicator* 53 (Winter 1995): 68–70.

Bray, Alan. *Homosexuality in Renaissance England*. New York: Columbia UP, 1995.

Christopher, James. Rev. of Actor's Touring Company with The Hairy Mary's Production of *Venus and Adonis*, dir. Nick Philippou. *Time Out* [London], April 5, 1995.

Donald, Colin. Rev. of Actor's Touring Company with The Hairy Mary's Production of *Venus and Adonis*, dir. Nick Philippou. *The Scotsman*, April 7, 1995.

Gil, Eric. *Shakespeare for Lovers*. New York: Citadel Press, 1995. Rpt. of *All the Love Poems of Shakespeare*. 1963.

Herman, Jan. "Charisma Carries *Venus*." *Los Angeles Times*, June 19, 1995: F4.

———. "Heavenly Embodiment of Shakespeare's *Venus*." *Los Angeles Times*, June 19, 1995: F3, F11.

———. "People Need to Hear a Poem Being Emoted. Q/A with Benjamin Stewart." *Los Angeles Times*, "Orange County Calendar," June 16, 1995: F1, F27.

Hodgins, Paul. "All the Poem's a Stage for Stewart." *Orange County Register*, "Show," June 16, 1995: 68.

———. "Venus' Wiles, Adonis Resists and Audience Delights." *Orange County Register*, "Stage," June 19, 1995.

Kiernan, Pauline. "Death by Rhetorical Trope: Poetry Metamorphosed in *Venus and Adonis* and the Sonnets." *Review of English Studies* 46 (1995): 475–501.

Massey, Paul. Rev. of Actor's Touring Company with The Hairy Mary's Production of *Venus and Adonis*, dir. Nick Philippou. *Herald* [Glasgow] March 3, 1995.

Mortimer, Anthony. "Shakespeare and the Italian Tradition of *Venus and Adonis*." *Colloquium Helveticum* 22 (1995): 93–116.

Myer, Michael Grosvenor. Rev. of Actor's Touring Company with The Hairy Mary's Production of *Venus and Adonis*, dir. Nick Philippou. *Plays and Players* 49 (1995): 32.

Roberts, Sasha. "Reading the Shakespearean Text in Early Modern England." *Critical Survey* 7 (1995): 299–306.

Smith, Neil. Rev. of Actor's Touring Company with The Hairy Mary's Production of *Venus and Adonis*, dir. Nick Philippou. *What's On* [London], April 15, 1995

1996

Benkert-Rasmussen, Lysbeth E. "Class, Gender, and the Formation of the Epistemic Positions of Renaissance Narrative Versifiers." *DAI* 56 (1995–96): 939A.

Ellis, James R. "Architectonics of the Self: Negotiating Male Subjectivity in Elizabethan Narrative Poetry." *DAI* 56 (1995–96): 3973A.

Faherty, Teresa J. "Shakespeare's Poetics of Ravishment." *DAI* 56 (1995–96): 3592A.

Kiernan, Pauline. *Shakespeare's Theory of Drama.* Cambridge: Cambridge UP, 1996

1997

Froes, João. "Shakespeare's Venus and the Venus of Classical Mythology." *Venus and Adonis: Critical Essays.* Ed. Philip C. Kolin. New York: Garland, 1997. 301–07.

Halpern, Richard. "'Pining Their Maws': Female Readers and the Erotic Ontology of the Text in Shakespeare's *Venus and Adonis.*" *Venus and Adonis: Critical Essays.* Ed. Philip C. Kolin. New York: Garland, 1997. 377–87.

Kolin, Philip C. "Venus and/or Adonis Among the Critics." *Venus and Adonis: Critical Essays.* Ed. Philip C. Kolin. New York: Garland, 1997. 3–65.

Merrix, Robert P. "'Lo, in This Hollow Cradle Take thy Rest': Sexual Conflict and Resolution in *Venus and Adonis.*" *Venus and Adonis: Critical Essays.* Ed. Philip C. Kolin. New York: Garland, 1997. 341–58.

Murphy, Patrick M. "Wriothesley's Resistance: Wardship Practices and Ovidian Narratives in Shakespeare's *Venus and Adonis.*" *Venus and Adonis: Critical Essays.* Ed. Philip C. Kolin. New York: Garland, 1997. 323–40.

Schiffer, James. "Shakespeare's *Venus and Adonis*: A Lacanian Tragicomedy of Desire." *Venus and Adonis: Critical Essays.* Ed. Philip C. Kolin. New York: Garland, 1997. 359–376.

Stapleton, M.L. "Venus as *Praeceptor: The Ars Amatoria* in *Venus and Adonis.*" *Venus and Adonis: Critical Essays.* Ed. Philip C. Kolin. New York: Garland, 1997. 309–21.

Stewart, Benjamin. "Strange Bedfellows—Venus, Adonis, and Me." *Venus and Adonis: Critical Essays.* Ed. Philip C. Kolin. New York: Garland, 1997. 295–97.

Ziegler, Georgianna. "Picturing Venus and Adonis: Shakespeare and the Artists." *Venus and Adonis: Critical Essays.* Ed. Philip C. Kolin. New York: Garland, 1997. 389–403.